CW01338724

YACHT INTERIORS

daab

Introduction 4

Achille Salvagni | Canados 86	8
Andrew Winch Design Group, German Frers | Unfurled	18
Birgit Schnaase, Bill Dixon | Phoenix	24
Carlo Galeazzi, Stefano Righini | Leonardo 98	34
Couedel Hugon Design, German Frers | Only Now	40
Craig Loomes Design Group, Paolo Sampa | Sampitres	50
Dick Young Designs | Gimlä	60
Egg and Dart Design Corporation | Baron 102 Ocean of Love	70
Foster & Partner, German Frers, Wally | Dark Shadow	80
Francesca Leone, Cantieri di Pisa | Unica	88
Fulvio de Simoni | Pershing 50	96
Fulvio de Simoni | Pershing 62	106
Fulvio de Simoni | Pershing 76	114
Fulvio de Simoni | Pershing 88	122
Fulvio de Simoni | Pershing 115	132
Guy Couach | Guy Couach 3600	140
Lazzarini Pickering Architetti, Farr Yacht Design, Wally | Dangerous But Fun	152
Lazzarini Pickering Architetti | Kaitos 76	162
Lazzarini Pickering Architetti | Sai Ram	170
Lazzarini Pickering Architetti, Luca Brenta & Co | Wally B	180
Luca Dini | Velvet 35	190
Nuvolari Lenard Naval Design | Sarnico 50	204
Officina Italiana Design | Opera 85	212

Officina Italiana Design	Rivale	220
Officina Italiana Design	Splendida	228
Omega Architects	Sweet Doll	236
Philippe Briand	Grand Bleu Vintage	246
Philippe Starck, Devoogt Naval Architects	Wedge Too	258
Studio Victory Design	72 Dolphin	266
Vismara Yacht Design	Mistress	274
Wally, Farr Yacht Design	Wallyño	282
Wally, German Frers	Magic Carpet Squared	292
Wally, German Frers	Y3K	302
Wally, Lazzarini & Pickering Architetti, Intermarine	Wallypower	314
Wally, SERENA ANIBALDI, German Frers	WY 88.2 Tiketitoo	324
Zuccon International Project Studio	Ferretti 460	334
Zuccon International Project Studio	Ferretti 500	342
Zuccon International Project Studio	Ferretti 530	348
Zuccon International Project Studio	Ferretti 550	354
Zuccon International Project Studio	Ferretti 590	362
Zuccon International Project Studio	Ferretti 620	368
Zuccon International Project Studio	Ferretti 731	376
Zuccon International Project Studio	Ferretti 761	384
Zuccon International Project Studio	Ferretti 830	390
Index	396
Imprint	400

During the last 10 years there has been a significant leap forward in the development of yacht designing. A decisive factor here was the introduction of the computer in the production process, which has greatly shortened the design phase and allowed more freedom when simulating and visualizing models. As a result, new boat forms, as well as more aerodynamic sails, have emerged, which could be carefully designed and built. These new forms were also made possible through the use of new materials, like aluminium and carbon fibre, which are very light weight and extremely strong. These innovative materials have also been employed in interior designing. The dinner table of the yacht Wallypower, for instance, is made of carbon fibre. The table can be lowered into the floor on demand, which allows for a flexible spatial organization. This example shows that modern boat designs put a premium on an optimal use of interior space. Besides improvements in the structure of yachts and innovative interior design solutions, furniture is also used as a way to accomplish this. On the yacht Wally B, for example, the furniture modules in the lounge can be combined to create individual chairs, an armchair or a chaise longue. The creation of modern yacht interiors reflects current design trends. There is, for instance, a clear trend towards plain and minimalist interiors. Here the designer renounces unnecessary decorative elements and employs pale colours, like white, grey and beige, which make interiors seem larger. In addition to Asian décor elements, there are also very colourful interior designs, which are appealing for their playfulness, among other reasons. Taking their place onboard today's swimming dwellings, next to furniture and other products of modern interior design, are flat-screen TVs and stereo equipment from famous-name companies like Bang & Olufsen. These, however, have to be adapted to the special conditions onboard. Besides having the latest entertainment systems, today's modern yacht also has the latest in GPS navigation technology. These satellite controlled navigation systems increase ship safety and assist in route planning. Modern yachts, then, do not take a back seat to living quarters on land when it comes to comfort and design, and it is not surprising that, besides famous yacht designers, creative personalities like Norman Foster or Philipp Starck have discovered a love for designing yachts interiors.

In den letzten 10 Jahren hat es einen bedeutenden Entwicklungssprung beim Yacht Design gegeben. Ein entscheidender Faktor hierfür war die Einführung des Computers im Produktionsprozess. Der Einsatz des Rechners hat zum einen die Entwurfszeit enorm beschleunigt und zum anderen ermöglichte er eine größere Freiheit beim Simulieren und Visualisieren der Modelle. So entstanden neue Bootsformen und aerodynamischere Segelschnitte, die sorgfältiger geplant und konstruiert werden konnten. Möglich wurden diese Formen auch durch die Anwendung neuer Materialien, wie zum Beispiel Aluminium und Karbonfaser. Diese Materialien verfügen über ein sehr geringes Gewicht und sind zugleich extrem widerstandsfähig. Auch beim Innendesign wurden diese innovativen Rohstoffe verwendet. So wurde beispielsweise bei der Yacht Wallypower der Esstisch aus Karbonfaser gefertigt. Er lässt sich bei Bedarf im Boden versenken und ermöglicht so eine flexible Raumaufteilung. Dieses Beispiel zeigt, dass heutzutage sehr viel Wert auf eine optimierte Raumausnutzung gelegt wird. Neben Verbesserungen in der Struktur der Yachten und innovativeren Gestaltungsmöglichkeiten der Raumaufteilung wird diese Optimierung auch durch das Mobiliar erreicht. So können zum Beispiel in der Yacht Wally B Sitzgruppen als Sofa, Sessel oder auch Liege kombiniert werden. Bei der Gestaltung des Innenraumes spiegeln sich die aktuellen Designtrends wider. Es zeigt sich ein klarer Trend hin zu schlichten und minimalen Interiors. Die Designer verzichten auf unnötige Dekorationselemente und verwenden helle Farben, wie weiß, grau und beige, die die Räume optisch vergrößern. Darüber hinaus gibt es neben asiatischen Dekorelementen auch sehr farbenrohe Einrichtungsvarianten, die unter anderem durch ihre Verspieltheit überzeugen. Bei Mobiliar und anderen Produkten des aktuellen Innendesign finden sich in den heutigen schwimmenden Unterkünften auch Flachbildschirme und edles Hi-Fi Equipment von renommierten Unternehmen wie beispielsweise Bang & Olufsen wieder. Diese werden allerdings den speziellen Bedingungen an Bord angepasst . Neben neuester Unterhaltungselektronik verfügen moderne Yachten natürlich auch über modernste GPS-Navigationstechnik. Diese satellitengelenkten Steuerungssysteme erhöhen die Sicherheit der Schiffe und helfen bei der Routenplanung. Moderne Yachten stehen in Komfort und Design einem immobilen Wohnraum in nichts nach und so ist es auch nicht erstaunlich, dass neben renommierten Yachtdesignern, auch kreative Köpfe wie Norman Foster oder Philipp Starck, Lust am Gestalten der Yachten gefunden haben.

Au cours des dix dernières années, le design de yacht a connu un essor extraordinaire. L'introduction de l'informatique dans le processus de production en est un facteur décisif. En effet, grâce à l'ordinateur, la conception est plus rapide, l'ampleur des possibilités de visualisation et de simulation des modèles est considérable. Cela permet de concevoir et de construire, de manière plus précise et minutieuse, de nouvelles formes de bateaux et des voiles plus aérodynamiques. De telles réalisations sont aussi dues à l'emploi de nouveaux matériaux à la fois ultra légers et résistants comme l'aluminium et la fibre de carbone, utilisés également dans le design d'intérieur, à l'instar de la table réalisée en fibre de carbone pour le Yacht. Wallypower. Escamotable, elle disparaît dans le sol, permettant ainsi de moduler l'espace : exemple qui souligne l'importance actuelle de l'optimalisation de l'espace. A côté des progrès structurels des yachts et des conceptions innovatrices dans la distribution de l'espace, le mobilier contribue aussi à l'optimiser. Dans le Yacht Wally B, par exemple, les meubles de salon sont modulables en divan, fauteuils ou chaise longue, au gré des besoins. L'agencement de la cabine reflète les dernières tendances du design. Les intérieurs sobres et minimalistes sont très en vogue actuellement. Les designers renoncent à une décoration surchargée, au profit de couleurs claires, comme le blanc, le gris et le beige qui, sur le plan visuel, agrandissent les pièces. Aux décors d'inspiration asiatique, s'ajoute un engouement pour les agencements hauts en couleurs vives et gaies. La panoplie de meubles et d'autres objets de design d'intérieur, décorant ces salons flottants, est complétée aujourd'hui par les écrans plats et tout l'équipement Hi-Fi haut de gamme aux noms prestigieux, comme Bang & Olufsen. Toutefois, ces appareils doivent être adaptés aux exigences de l'environnement nautique. A côté d'un équipement électronique de pointe, les yachts modernes sont équipés de la meilleure technique de navigation avec GPS. Ces systèmes de commande par satellite permettent une plus grande sûreté de navigation et de précision dans l'établissement des itinéraires. Sur le plan du confort et du design, les yachts modernes n'ont rien à envier aux maisons sur la terre ferme. En effet, à côté des plus grands noms de designers nautiques, de plus en plus de créateurs prestigieux, comme Norman Foster ou Philipp Starck, se passionnent pour l'aménagement des Yachts.

El diseño de yates ha experimentado una gran evolución en los últimos diez años. Un factor decisivo ha sido, sin duda, la informatización del proceso de producción. Por una parte, el uso del ordenador agiliza la concepción y el diseño, por otra, ofrece un gran abanico de posibilidades a la hora de visualizar los modelos y hacer simulaciones. De esta manera, ha sido posible proyectar barcos de formas innovadoras y veleros de diseño aerodinámico, cuidadosamente planeados y construidos. La evolución de las líneas ha sido posible gracias a nuevos materiales ligeros y extremadamente resistentes, como el aluminio y la fibra de carbón. Incluso el diseño de los interiores se ha beneficiado de estos avances; el yate Wallypower dispone de una mesa de comedor abatible de fibra de carbón que permite una distribución del espacio muy flexible, un ejemplo que ilustra la importancia que se concede hoy en día al aprovechamiento óptimo del espacio.El proceso de mejora en la estructura de los yates y en las posibilidades decorativas de la distribución de los espacios culmina en el mobiliario; así, el yate Wally B ofrece el confort que se obtiene al combinar un sofá, sillones y hamacas. En la decoración de los interiores se reflejan las tendencias del diseño actual con una incuestionable preferencia por las líneas claras y sencillas del minimalismo. Destaca, sobre todo, la renuncia a elementos ornamentales superfluos y el uso de colores claros, como el blanco, el gris y el beige, que confieren amplitud a los espacios. Junto a influencias decorativas orientales, se aprecian variantes estilísticas de sobrio cromatismo que convencen y seducen por su carácter caprichoso. Pero en estas residencias flotantes también se instalan modernos aparatos, como equipos de alta fidelidad y pantallas planas de prestigiosas marcas (Bang & Olufsen, por ejemplo), que, normalmente, hay que adaptar a las condiciones específicas de a bordo. Además de los últimos productos de la electrónica del entretenimiento, en un barco no puede faltar la tecnología de navegación por satélite GPS, que incrementa la seguridad y simplifica la planificación de las rutas. Tampoco se renuncia al confort y a los espacios de líneas modernas. Por eso, no sorprende que, además de diseñadores náuticos de renombre, también personalidades de la talla creativa de Norman Foster o Philipp Starck hayan querido medir su talento en el diseño de yates.

Negli ultimi dieci anni abbiamo assistito a notevoli progressi nel campo della progettazione di yacht. L'introduzione dei computer nel processo di produzione è stato sicuramente uno dei fattori decisivi di questo salto in avanti. L'utilizzo della informatica ha enormemente accelerato la fase di progettazione e ha consentito una maggiore libertà nella simulazione e nella visualizzazione dei modelli. Grazie a questi fattori sono nate barche dalle forme totalmente nuove, con vele aerodinamiche, progettate e costruite con enorme attenzione. L'impiego di nuovi materiali come l'alluminio e la fibra di carbonio è stato determinante nella creazione di nuove forme per le imbarcazioni; possiedono un peso molto limitato ma sono allo stesso tempo estremamente resistenti. Anche nel design dell'interno sono state utilizzate materie prime innovative. Un esempio: nello yacht Wallypower il tavolo da pranzo è in fibra di carbonio e può essere inserito nel pavimento per consentire una suddivisione flessibile dello spazio. Questo esempio dimostra come oggi si dedichi molta attenzione all'organizzazione razionale degli ambienti. L'ottimizzazione non riguarda soltanto la struttura dello yacht e le innovative possibilità di suddivisione dello spazio, ma anche la scelta dell'arredamento. Nello yacht Wally B, per esempio, si possono combinare elementi per creare un sofà, una poltrona o un lettino. L'arredamento è fortemente influenzato dalle attuali tendenze del design; si evidenzia una predilezione per interni sobri e minimalisti. I progettisti rinunciano a elementi decorativi superflui e utilizzano colori chiari come il bianco, il grigio e il beige, che aumentano la sensazione di spazio. In alternativa, accanto alle decorazioni in stile asiatico è possibile optare per varianti molto colorate, di carattere vivace. In mezzo ai mobili e agli altri elementi che compongono l'arredamento delle barche troviamo anche schermi al plasma e impianti stereo, selezionati attentamente per adattarsi alle condizioni di bordo. Gli yacht di ultima generazione dispongono anche della tecnologia GPS per la navigazione. I nuovi sistemi di comando seguiti dal satellite garantiscono una maggiore sicurezza delle navi e rappresentano un valido aiuto nella scelta della rotta. Gli yacht moderni non rinunciano al comfort e al design e accanto a rinomati designer di yacht, anche menti creative come Norman Foster o Philipp Starck si occupano della progettazione di bordo.

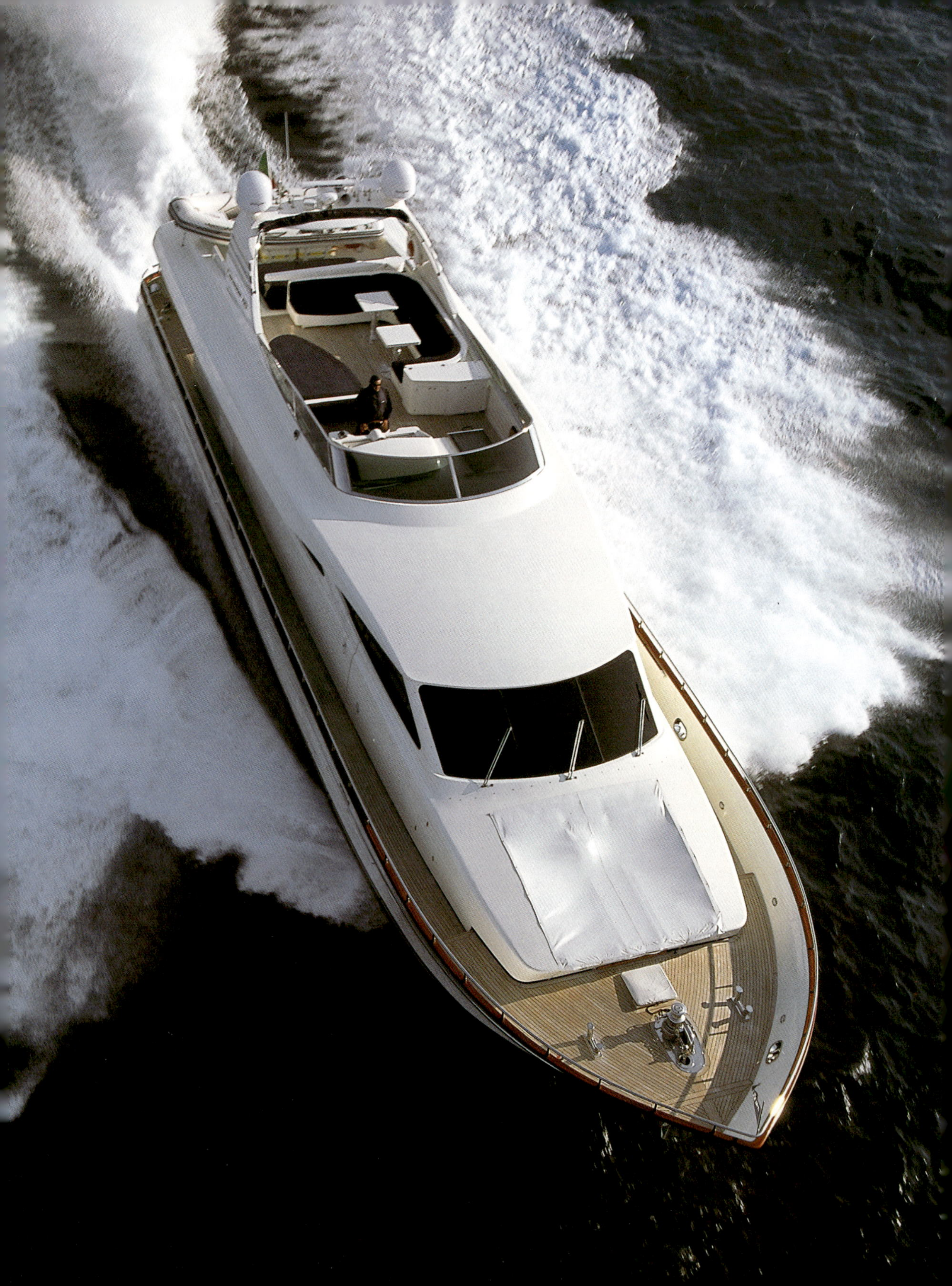

ACHILLE SALVAGNI
CANADOS 86 | 2003
Canados Group

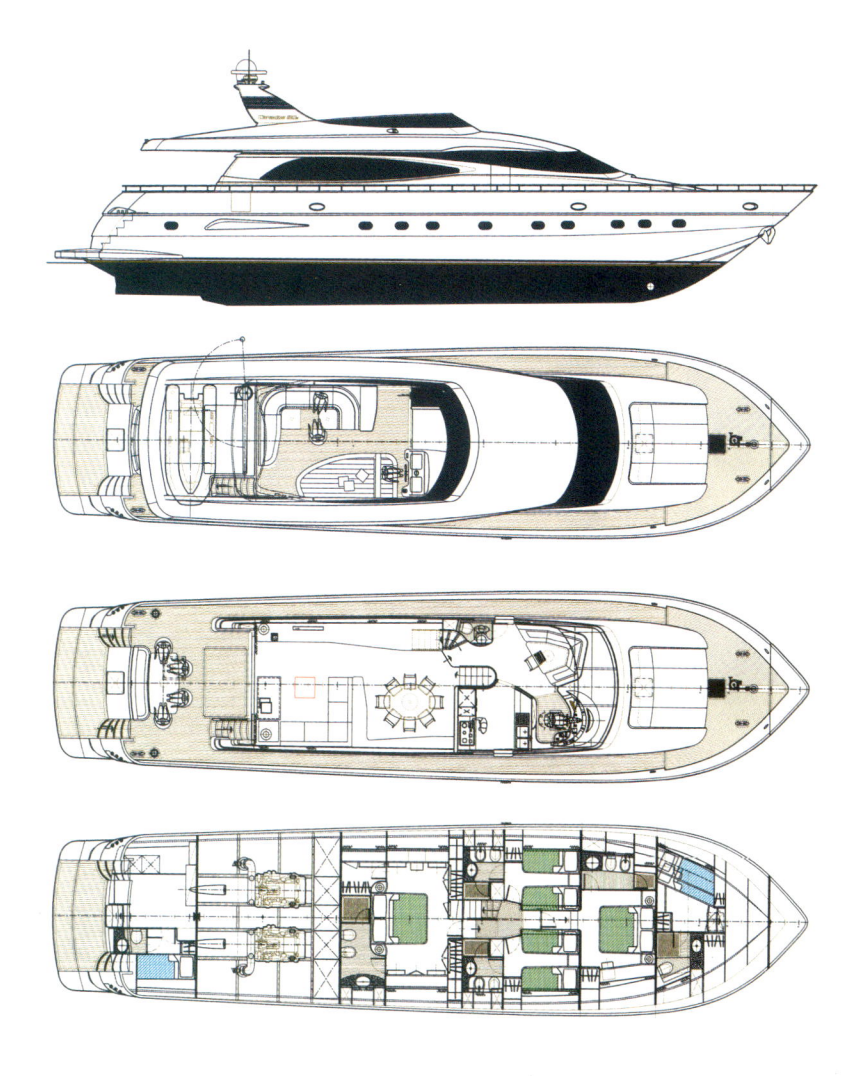

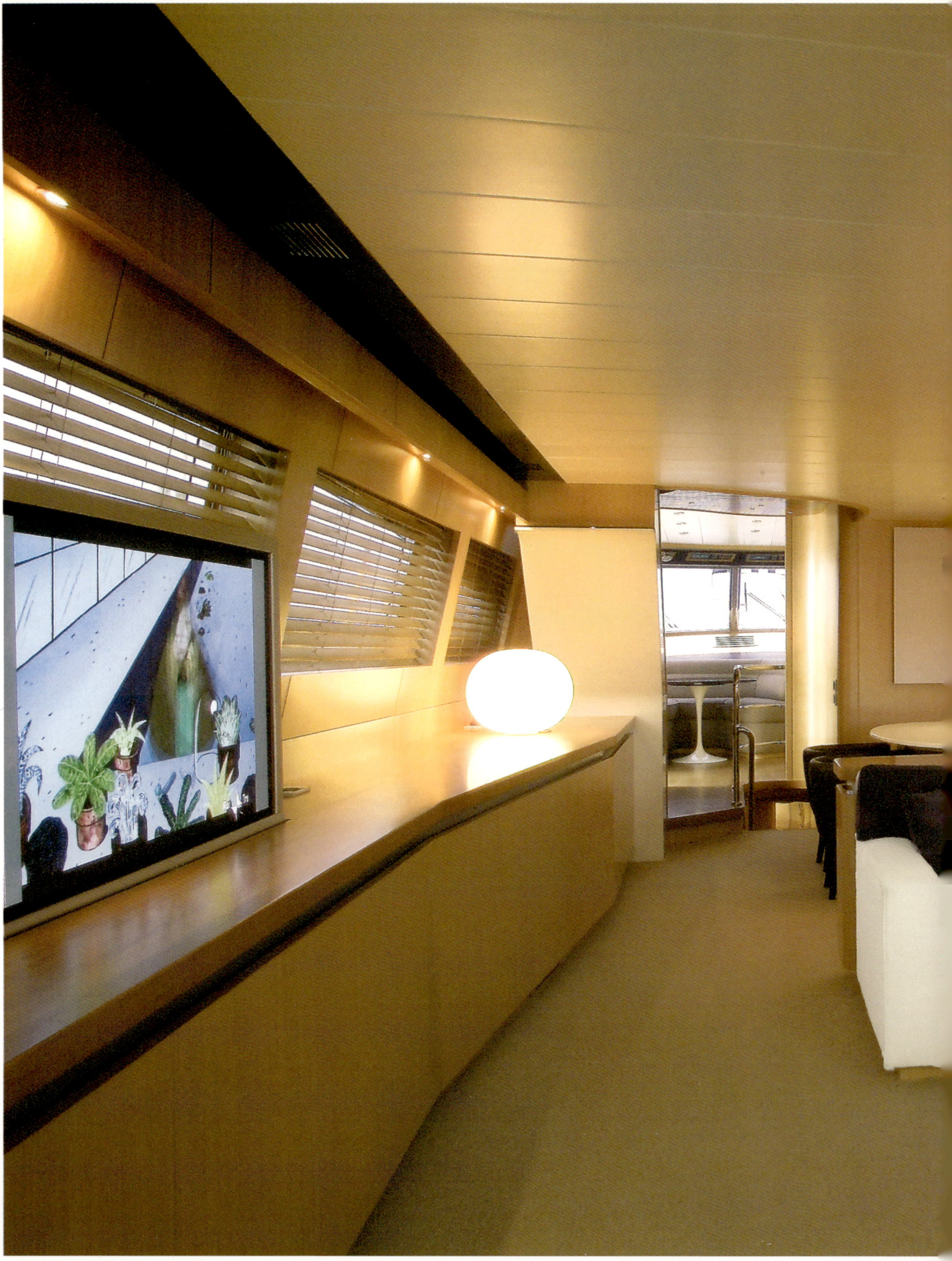

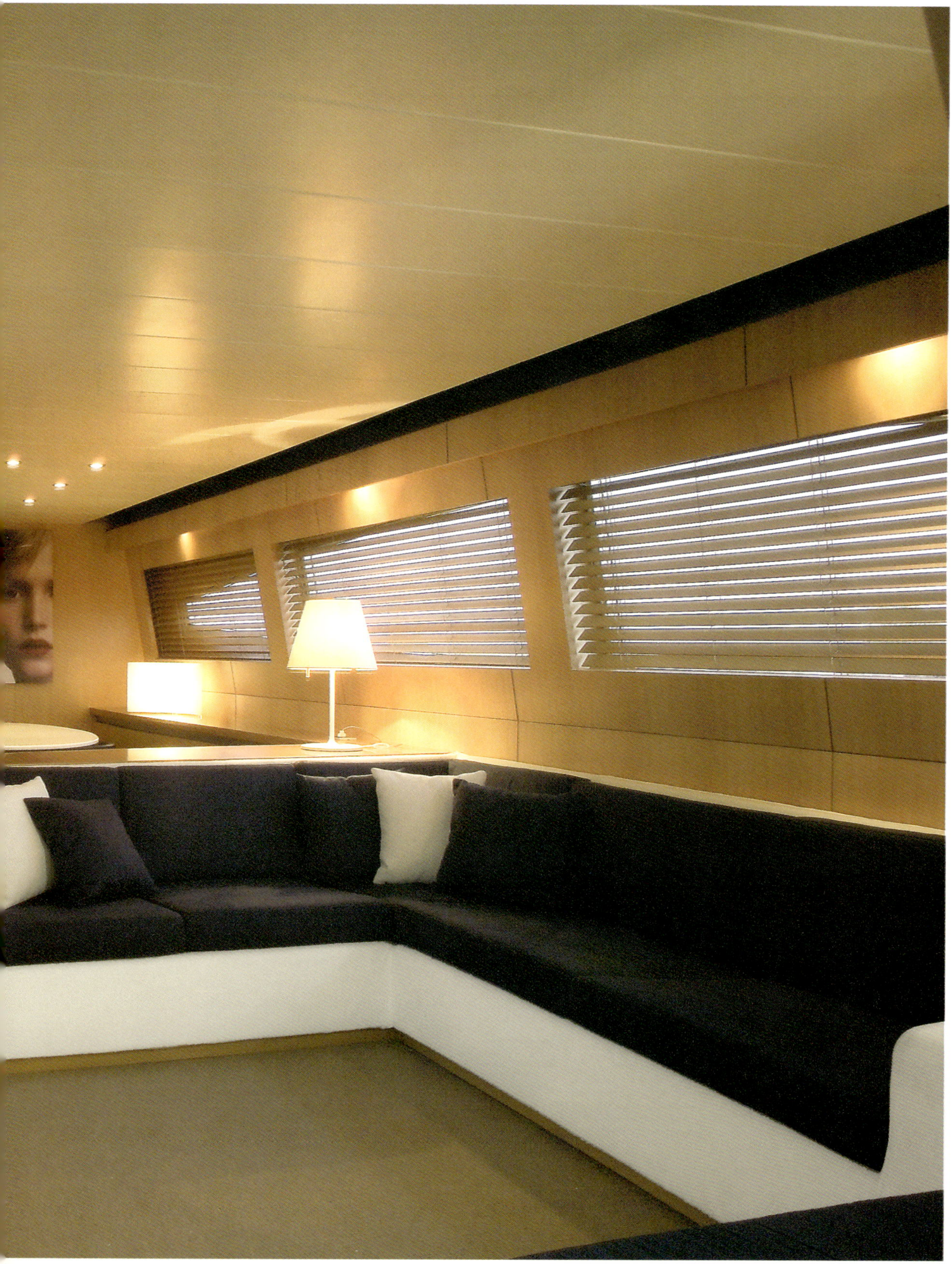

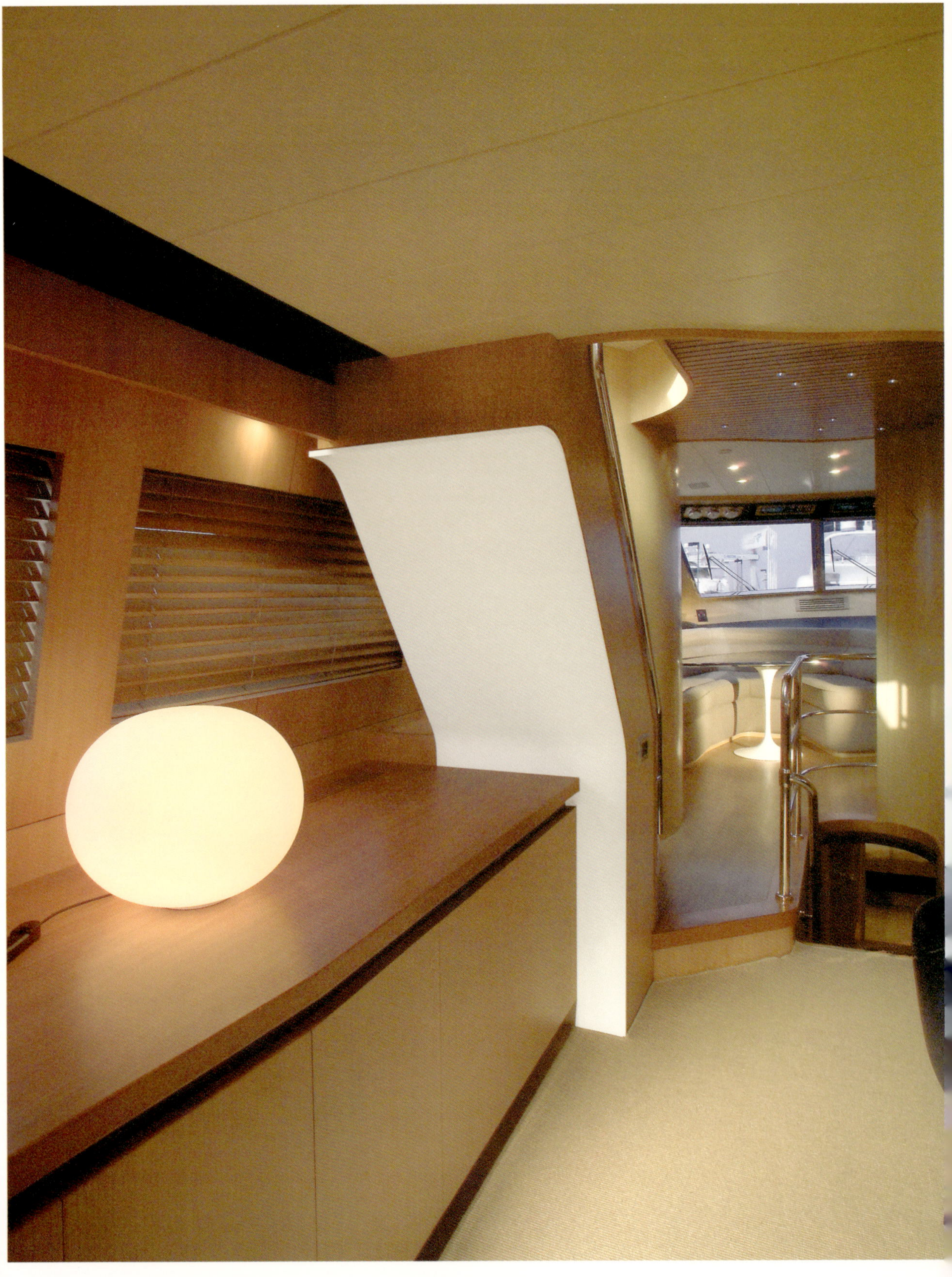

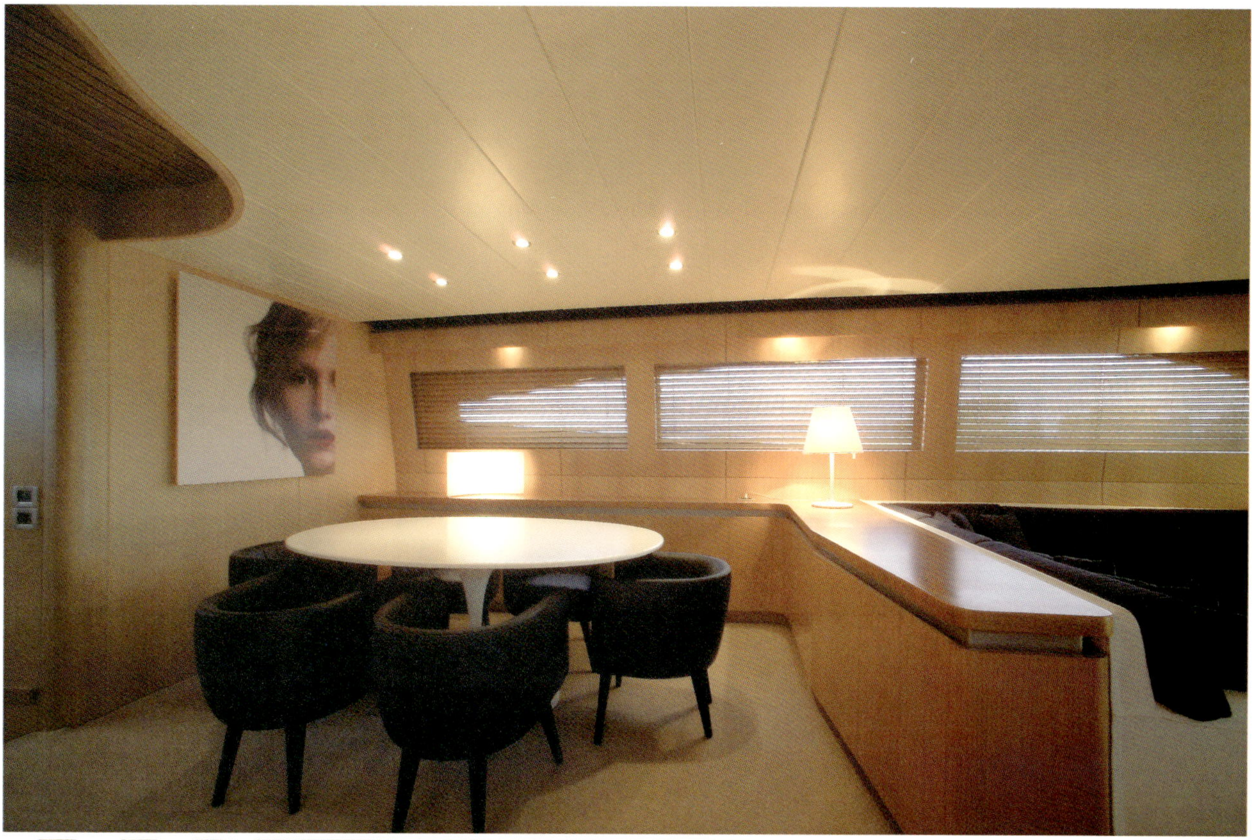
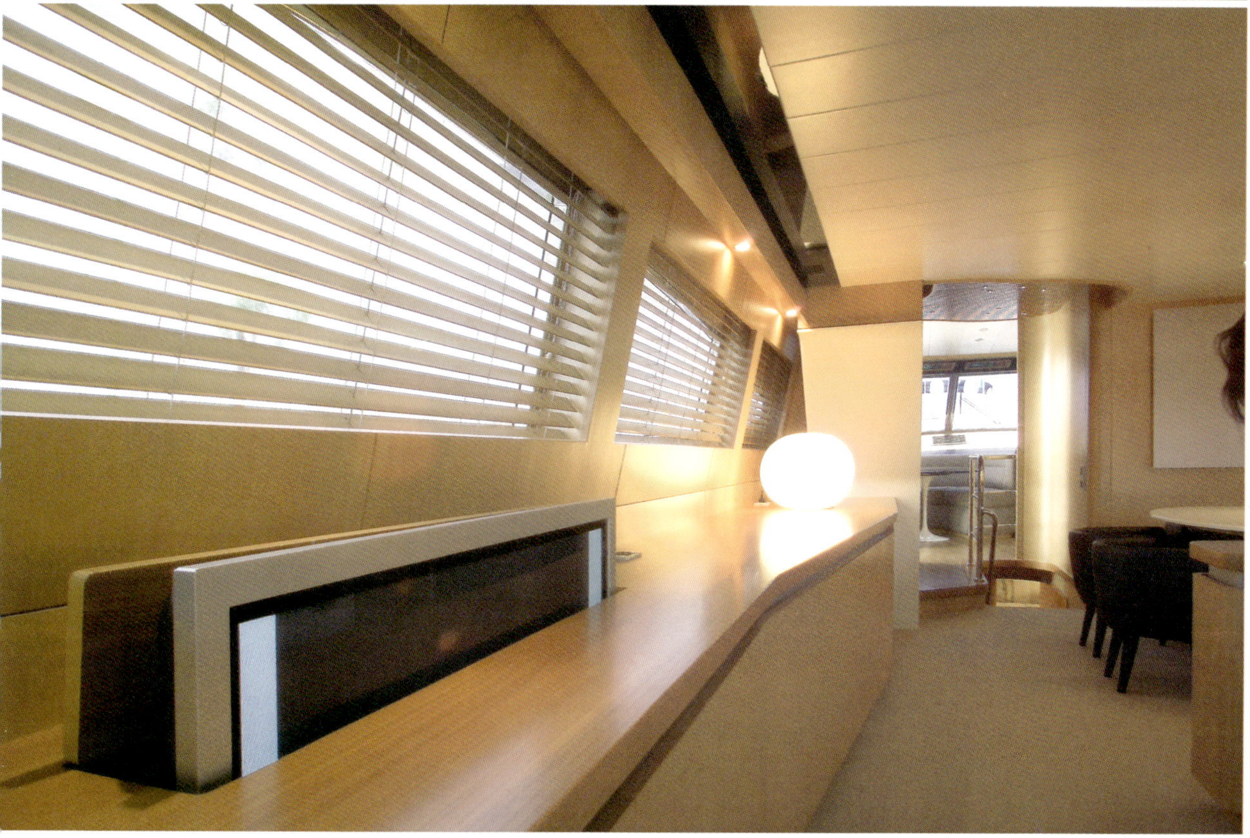

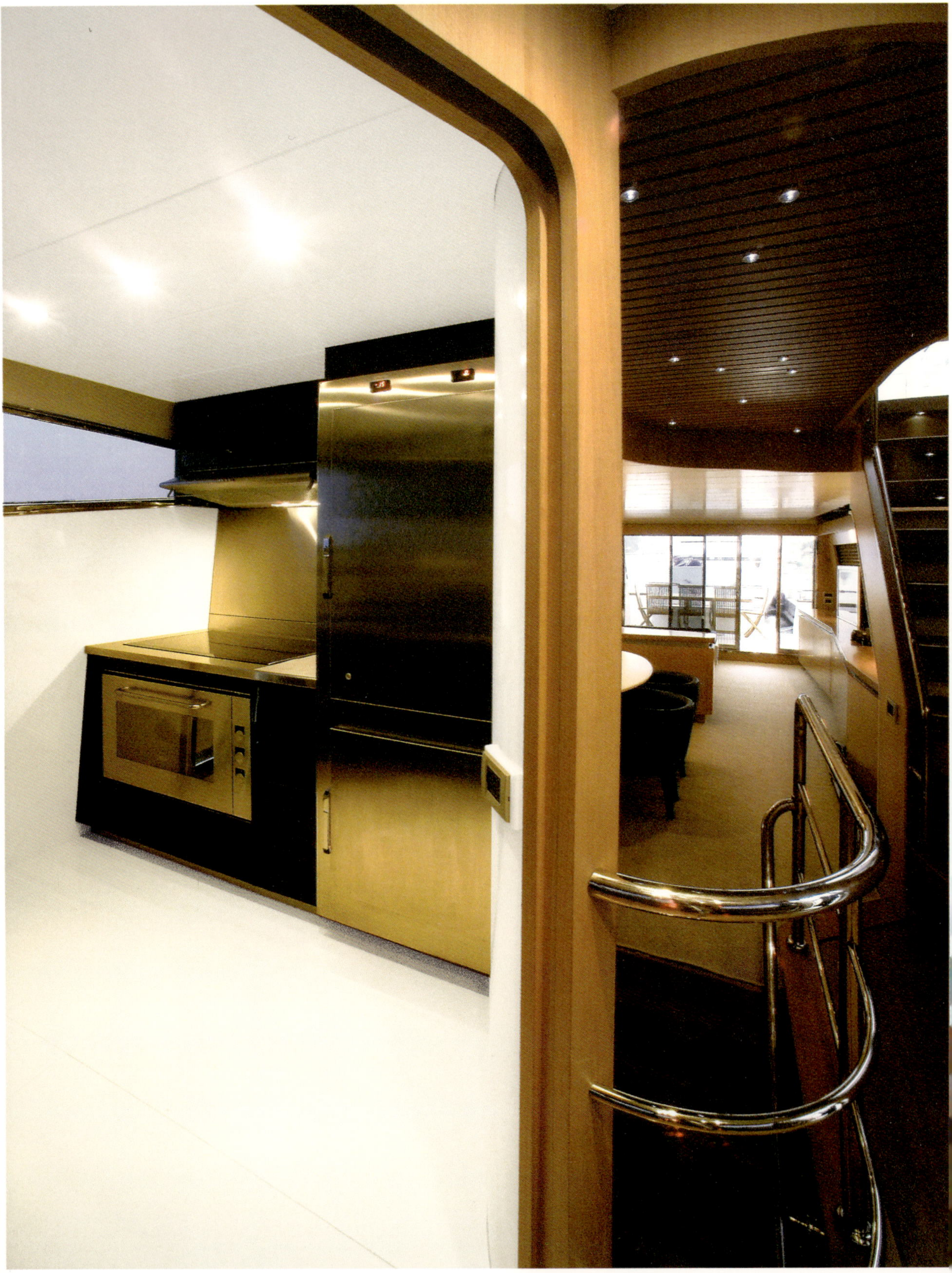

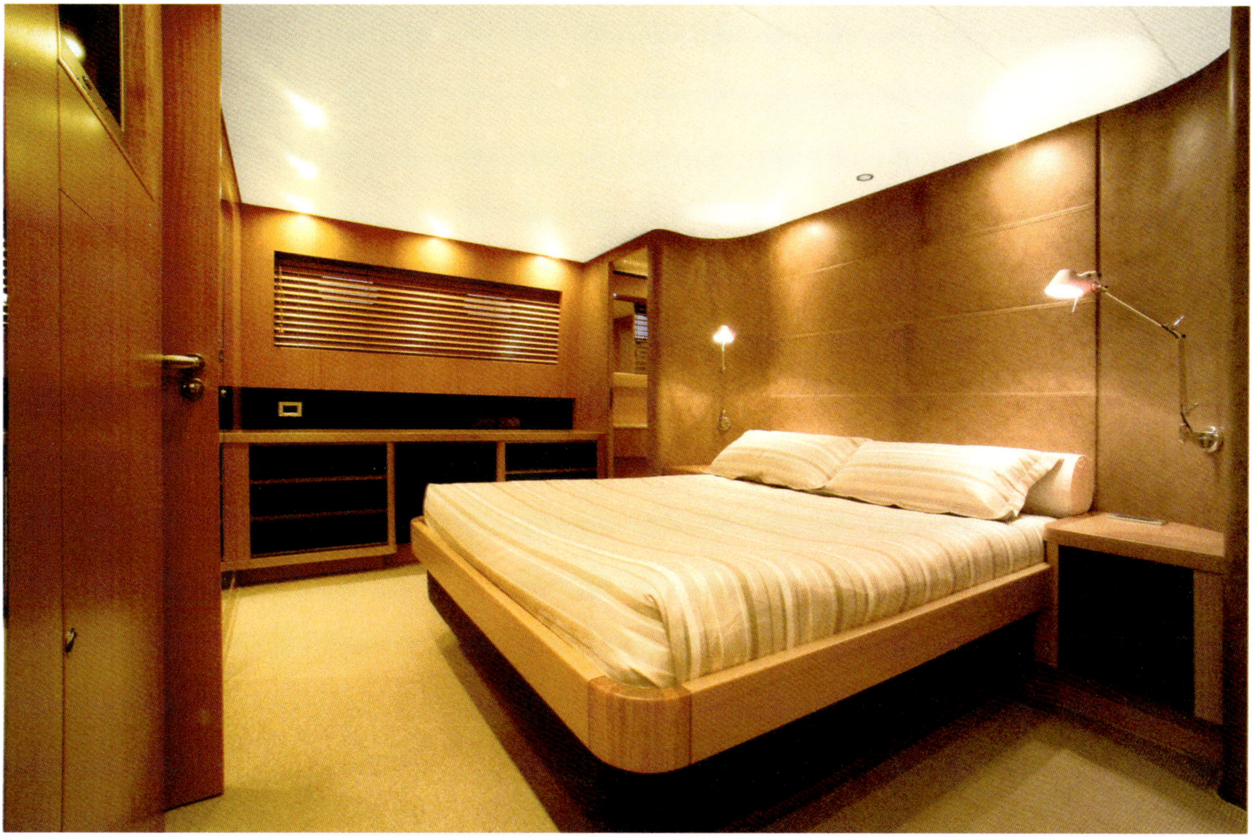

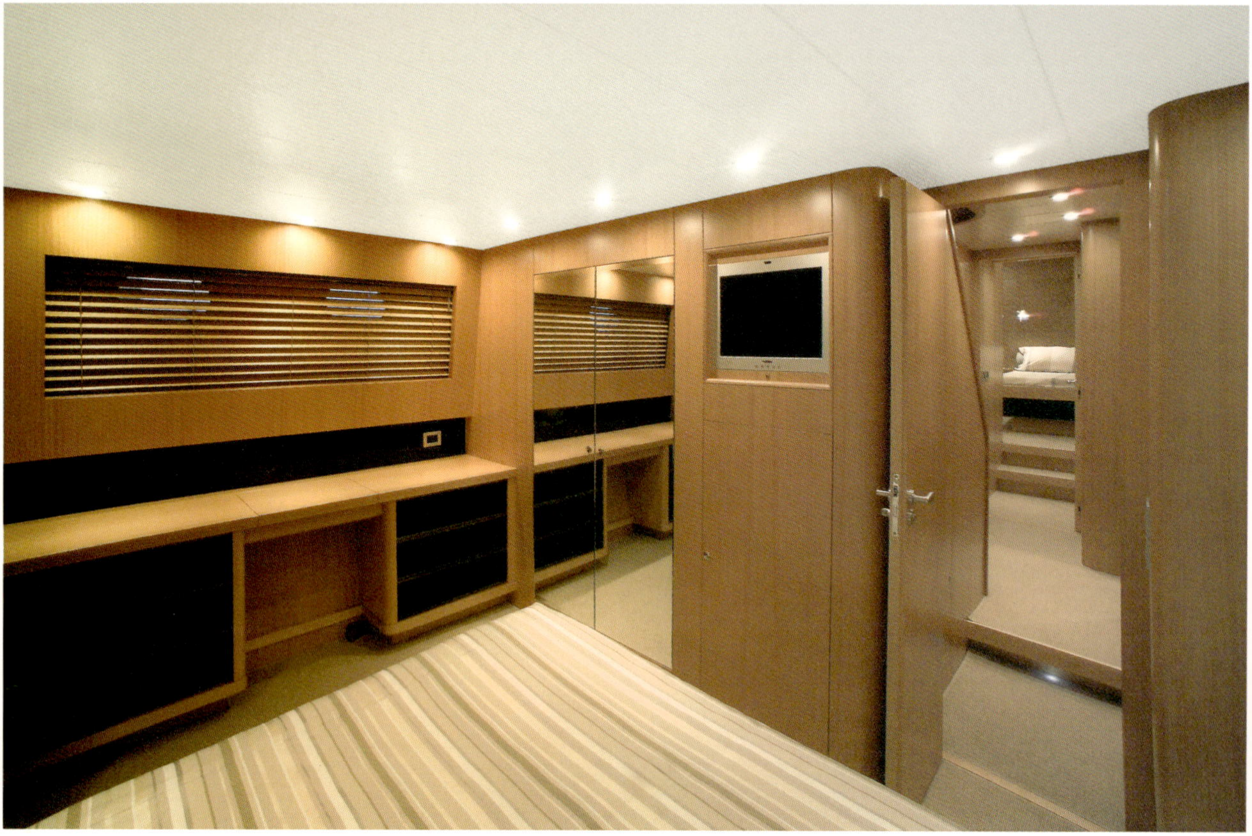

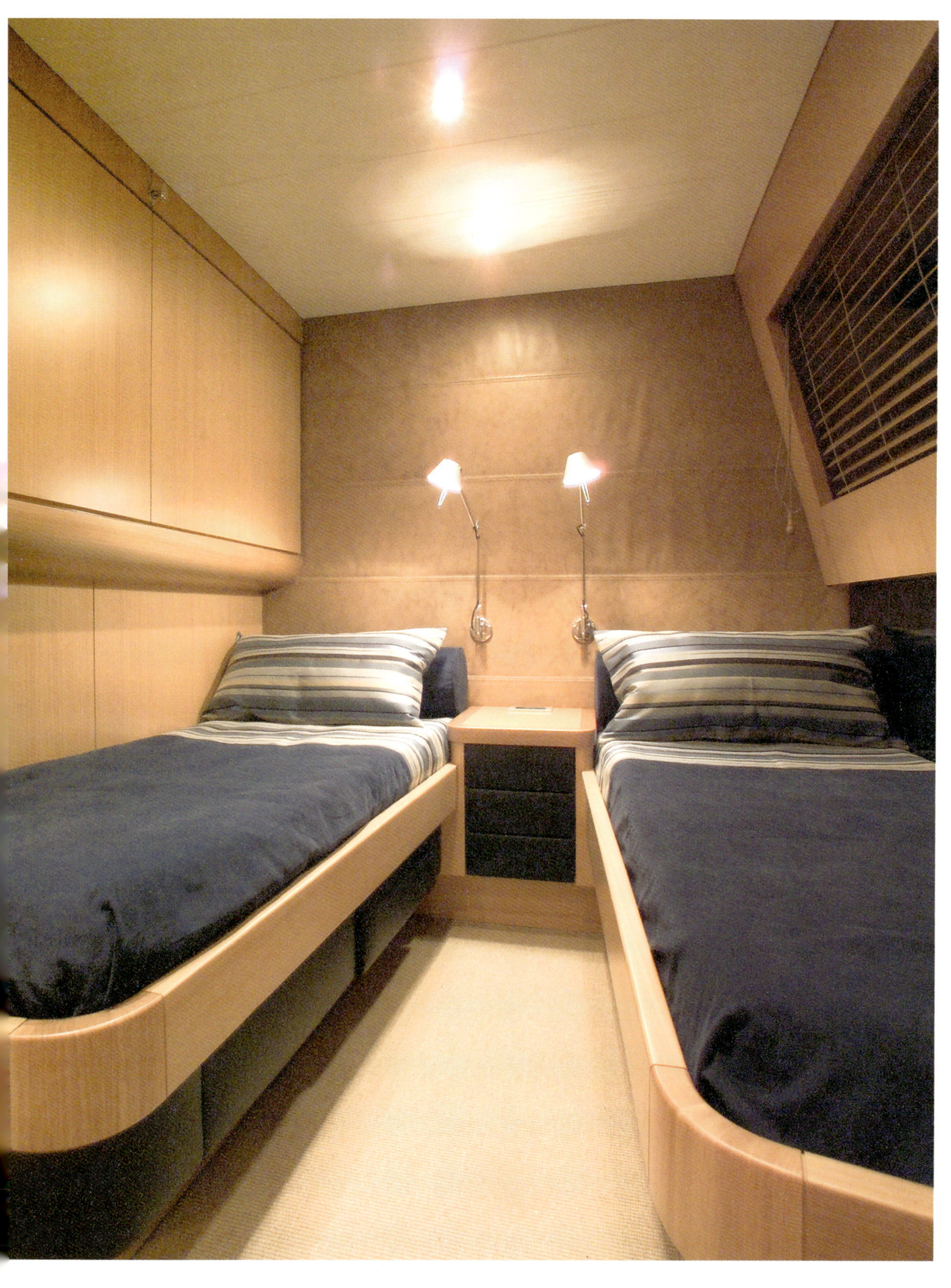

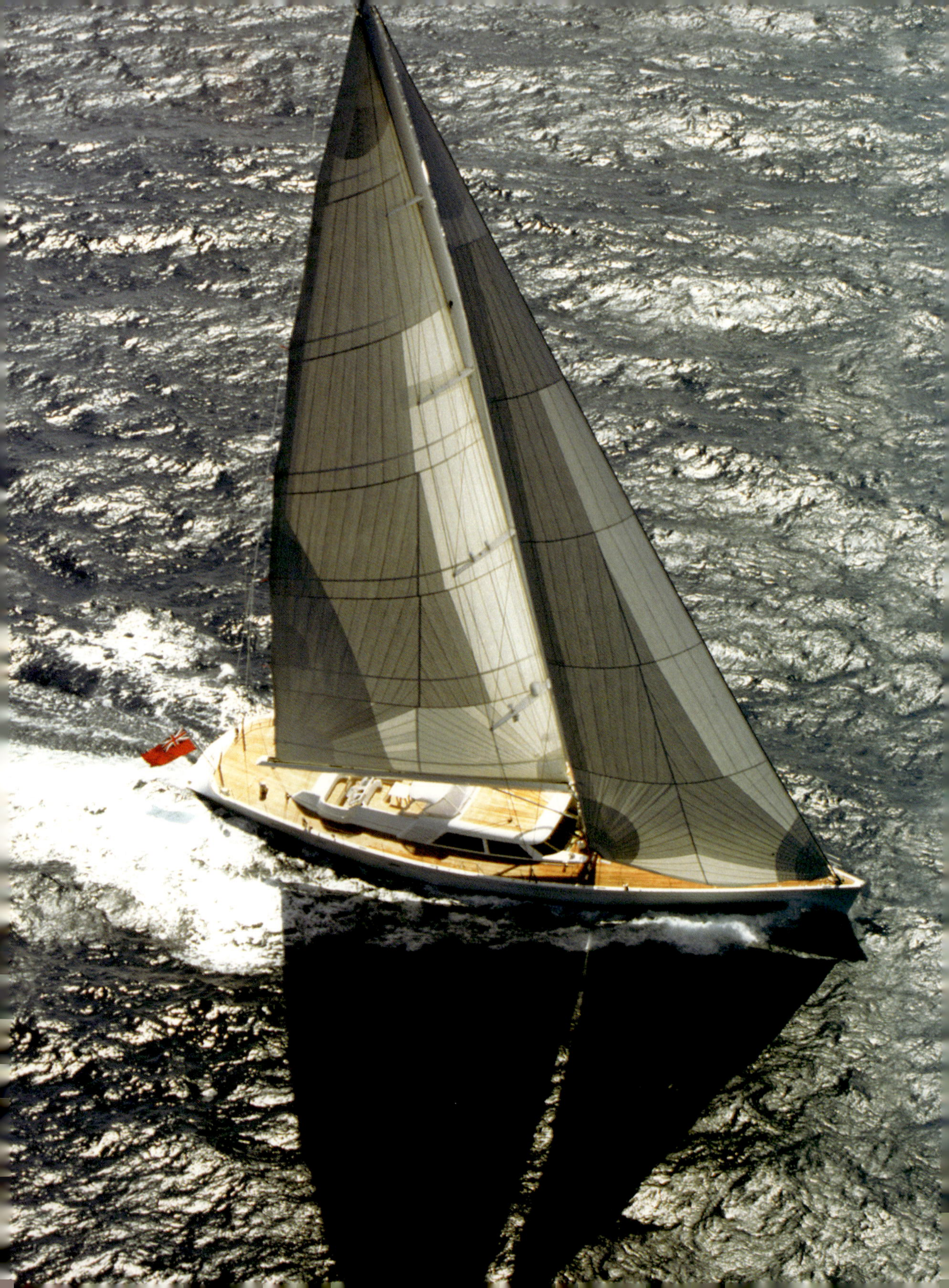

ANDREW WINCH DESIGN GROUP, GERMAN FRERS
UNFURLED | 2000
Royal Huisman Shipyard

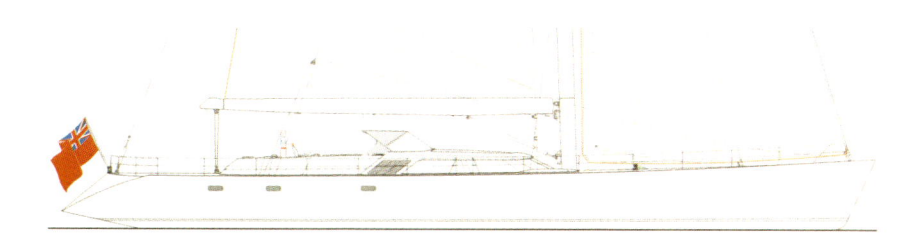

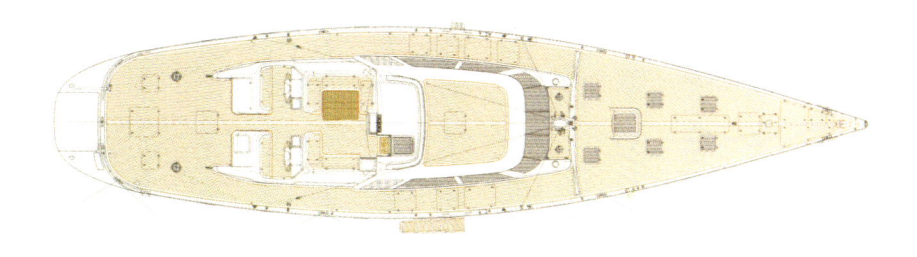

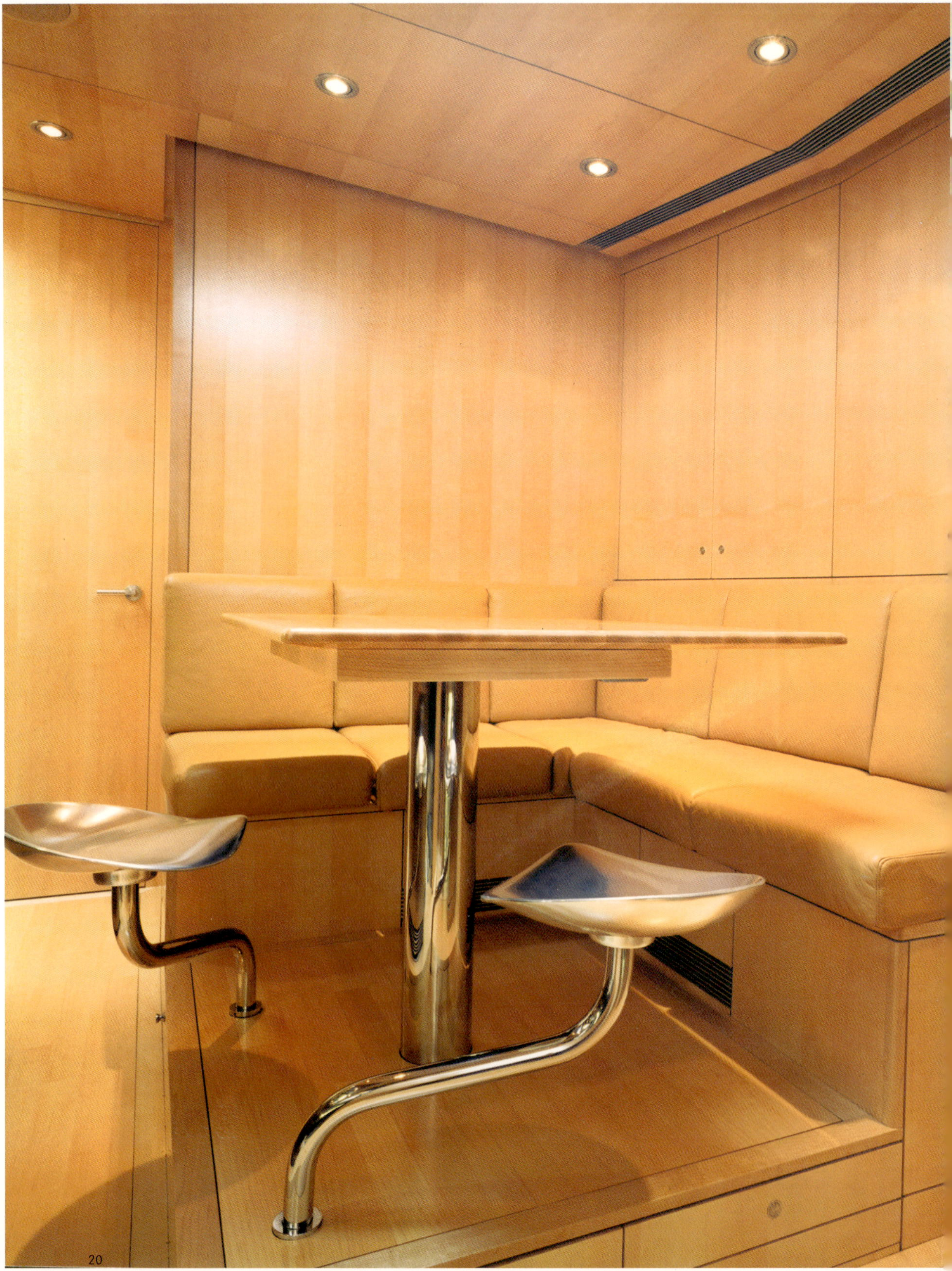

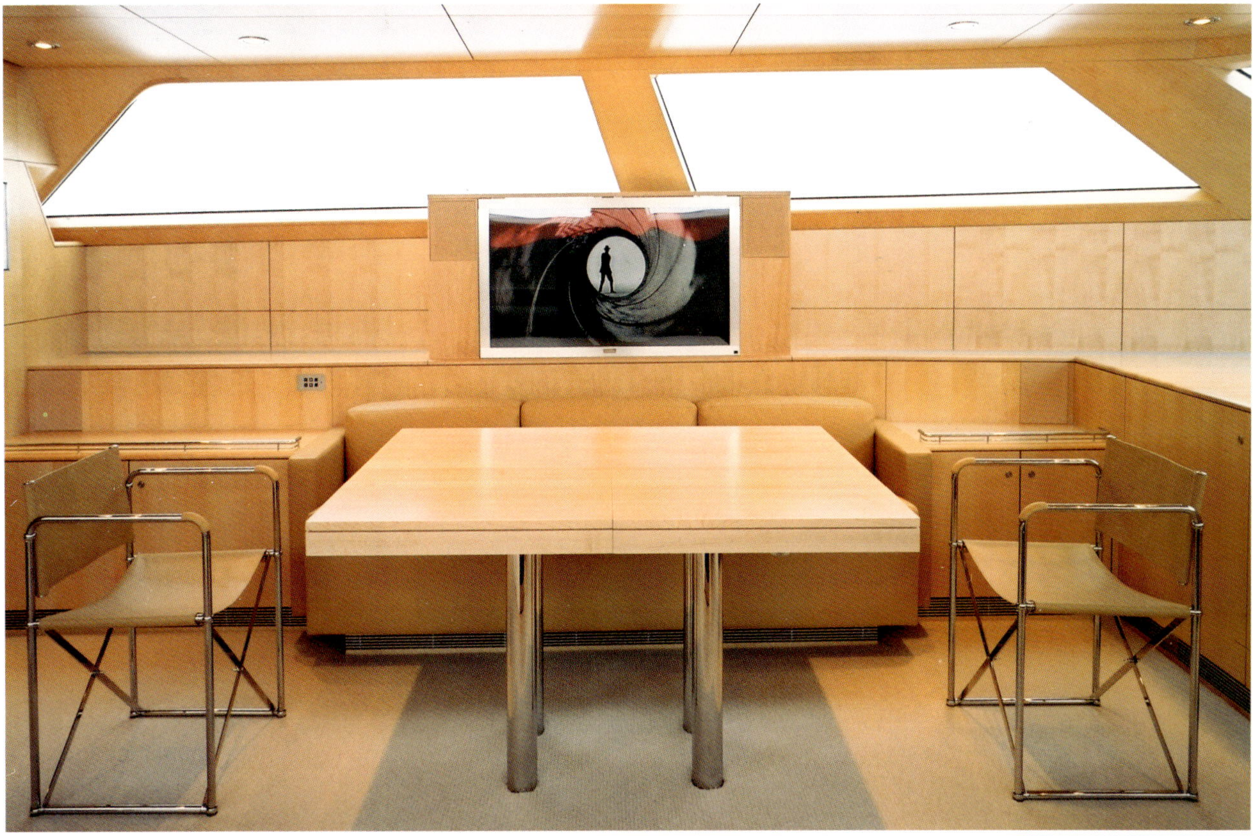

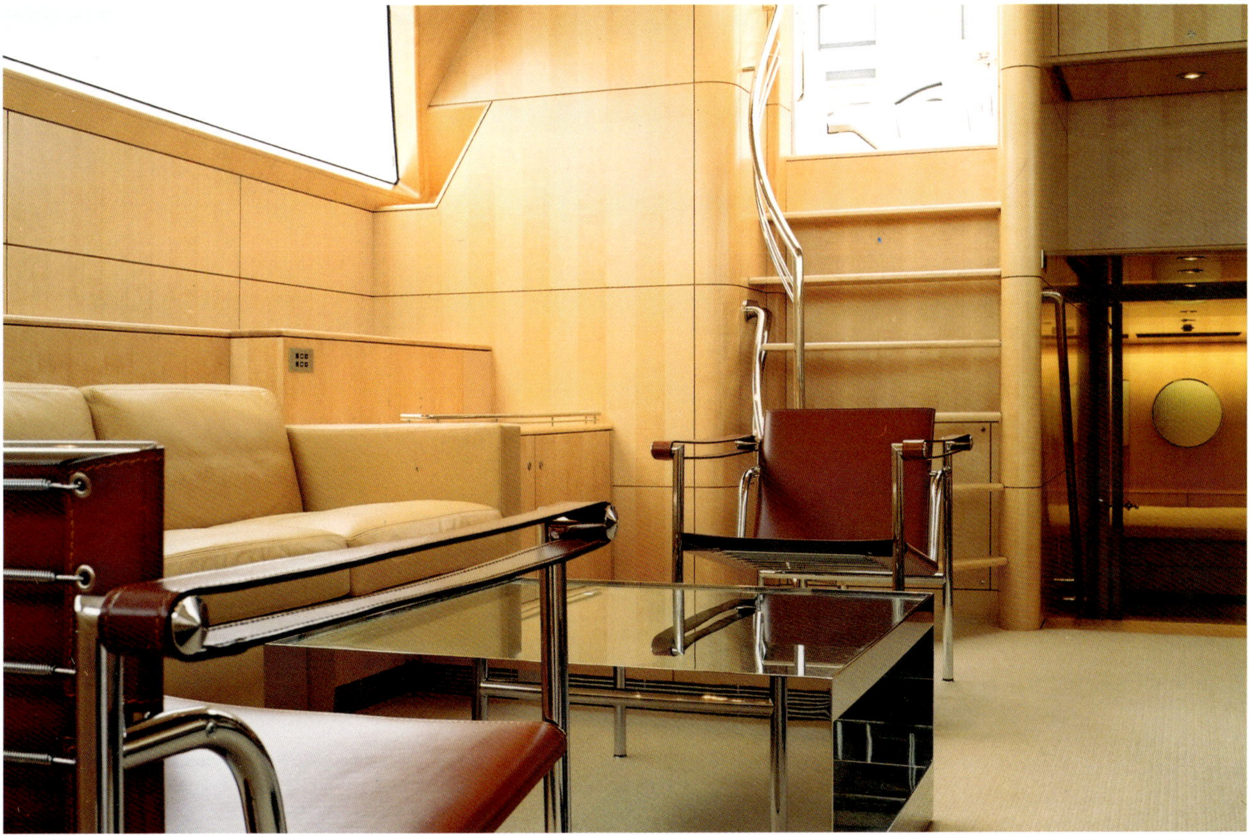

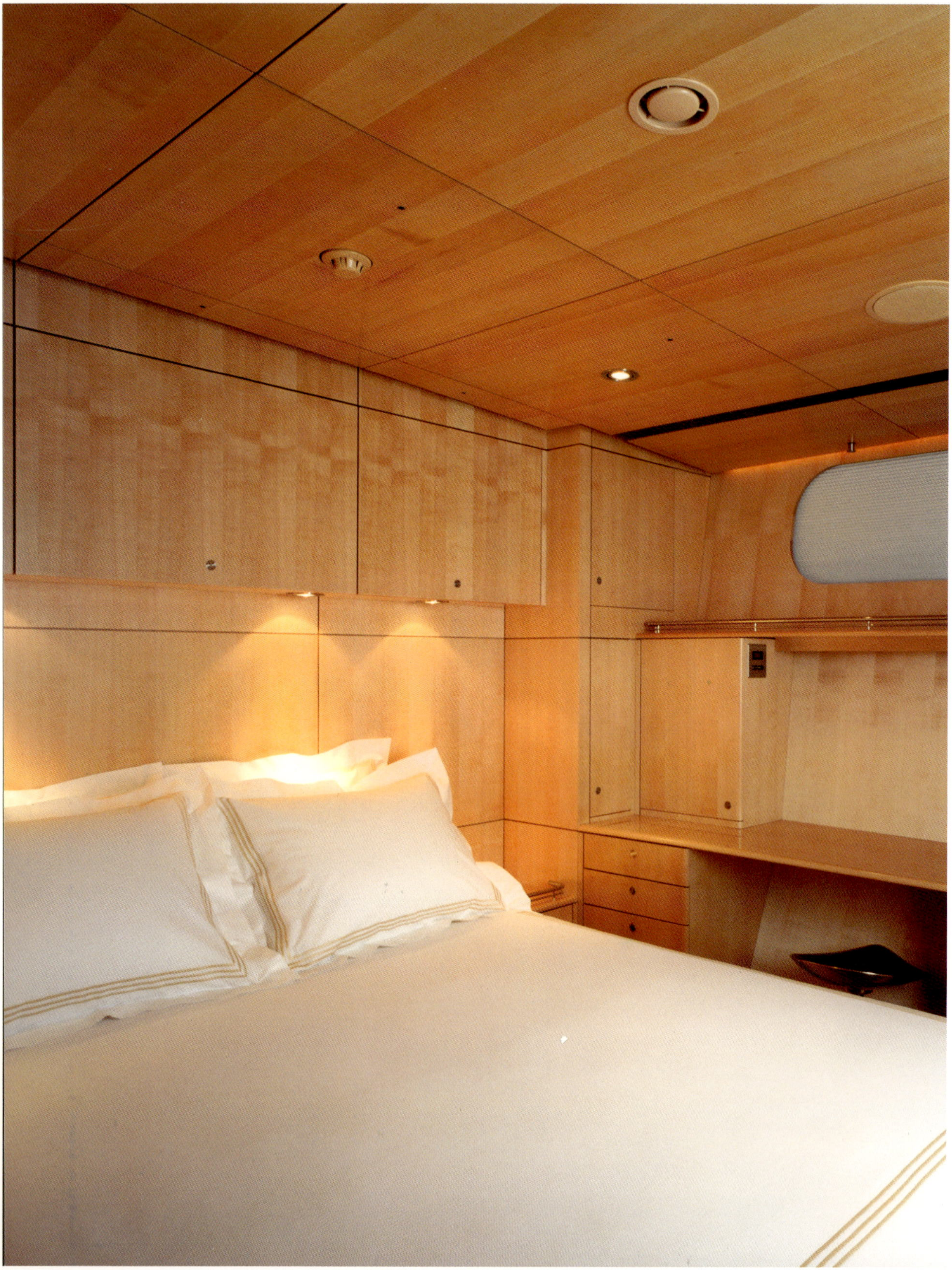

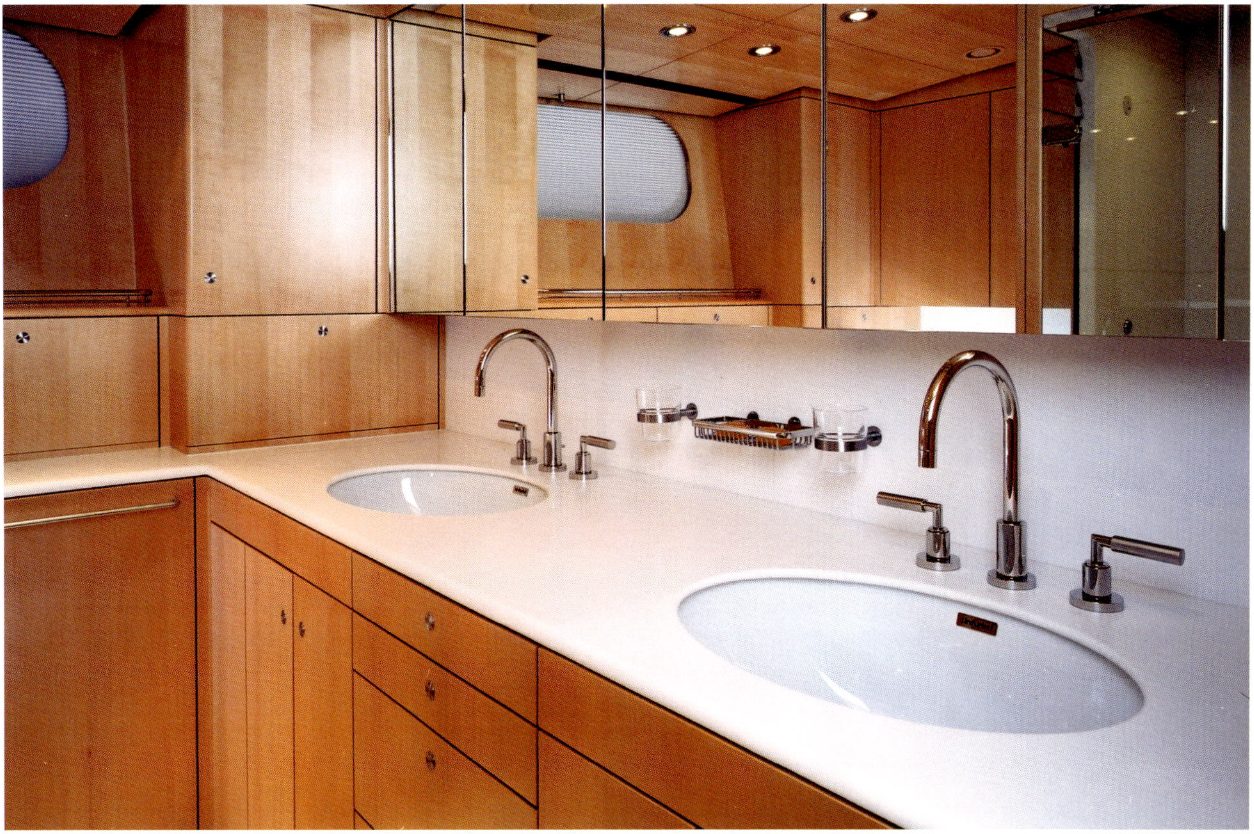

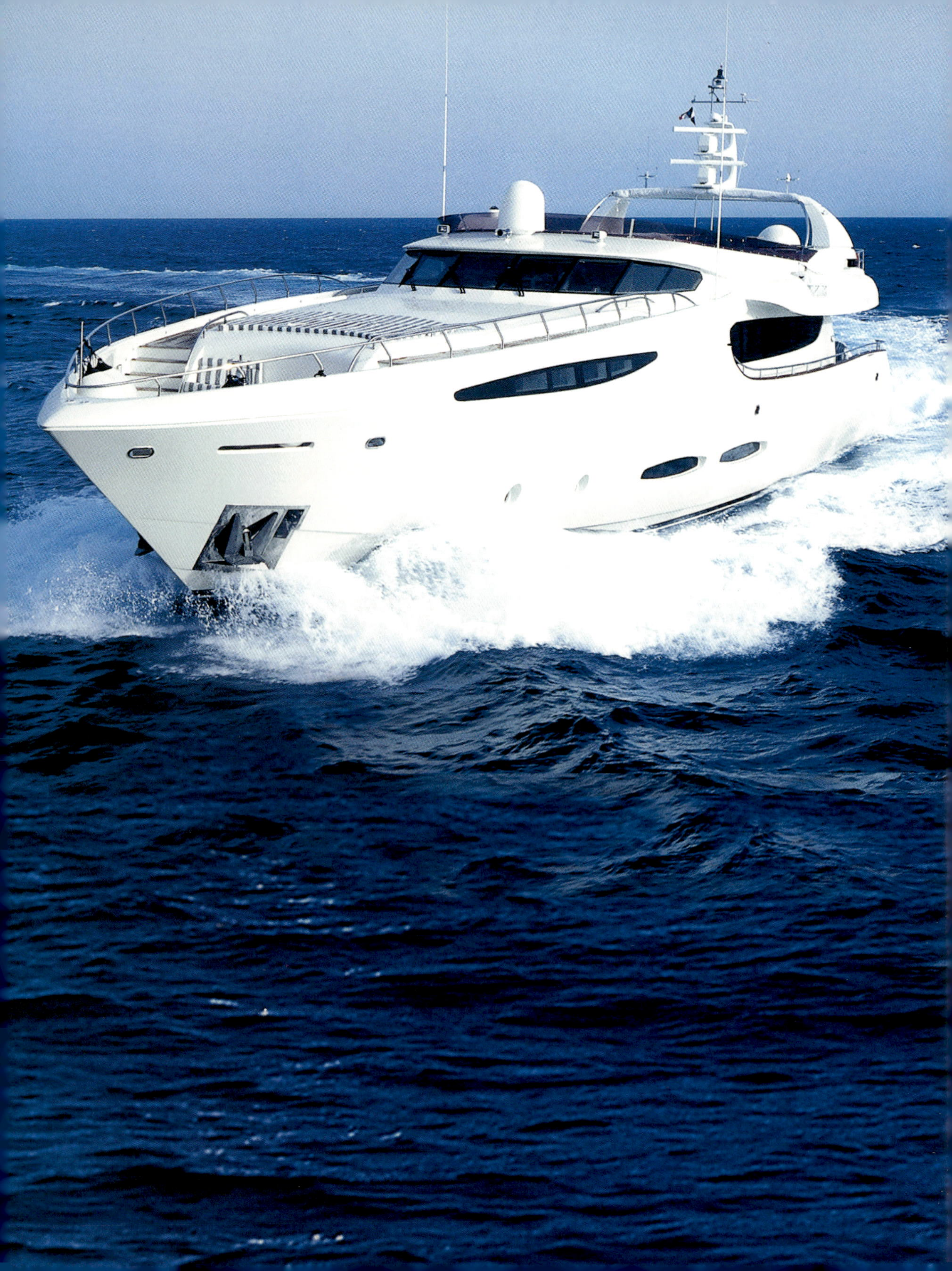

BIRGIT SCHNAASE, BILL DIXON
PHOENIX | 2004
Leight Notika
Sea Independences SL

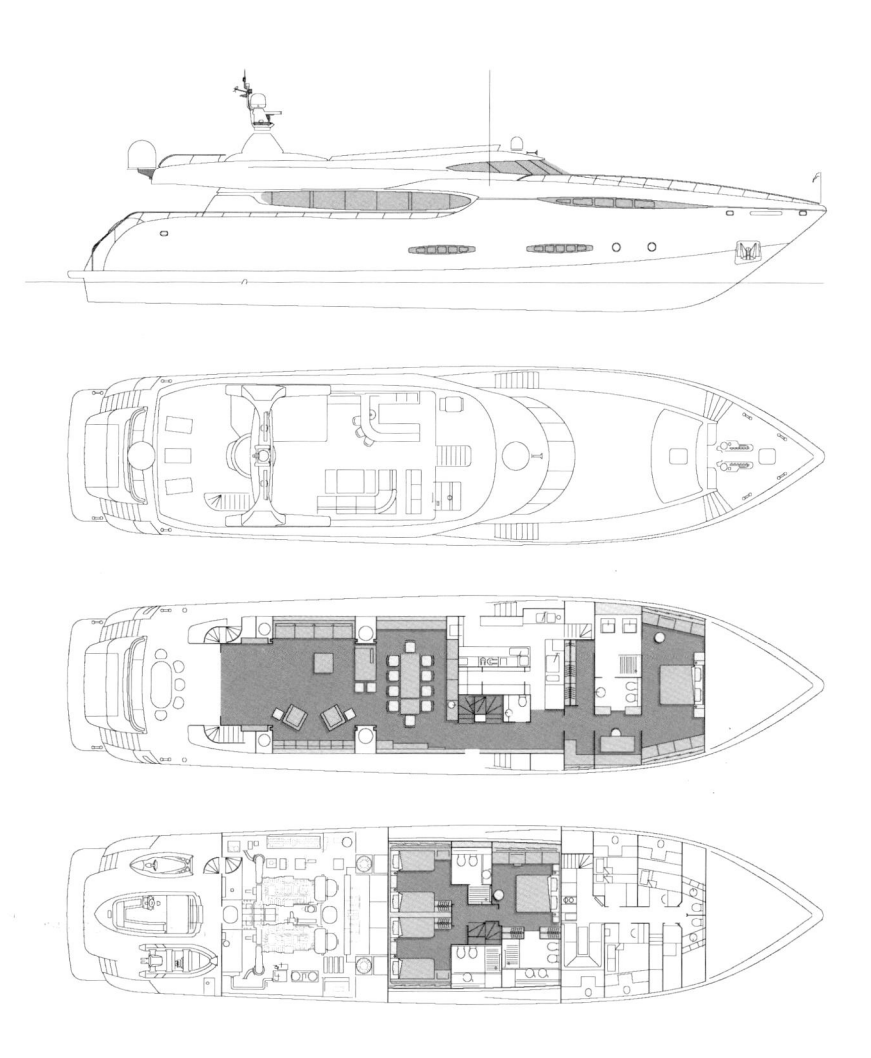

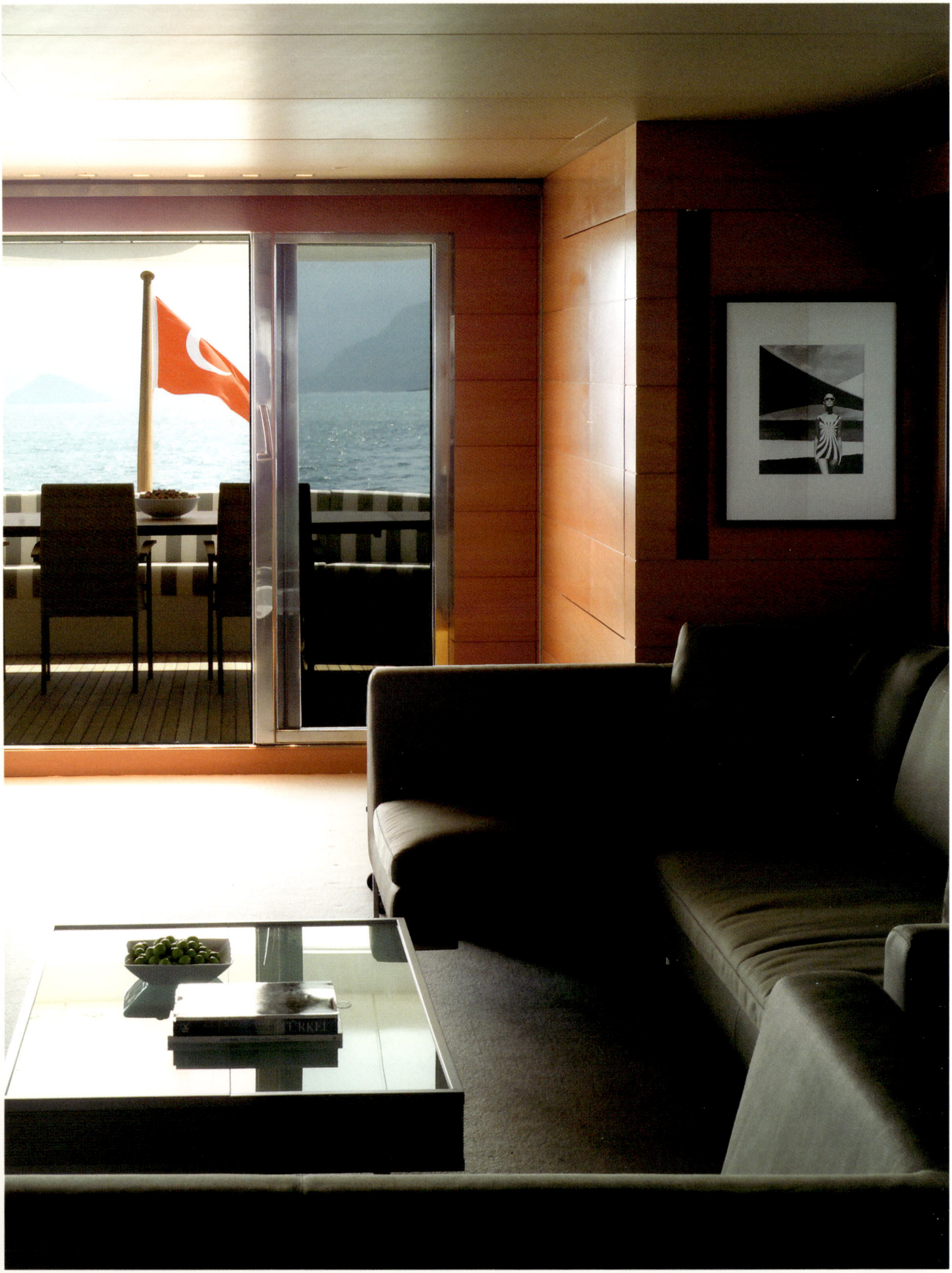

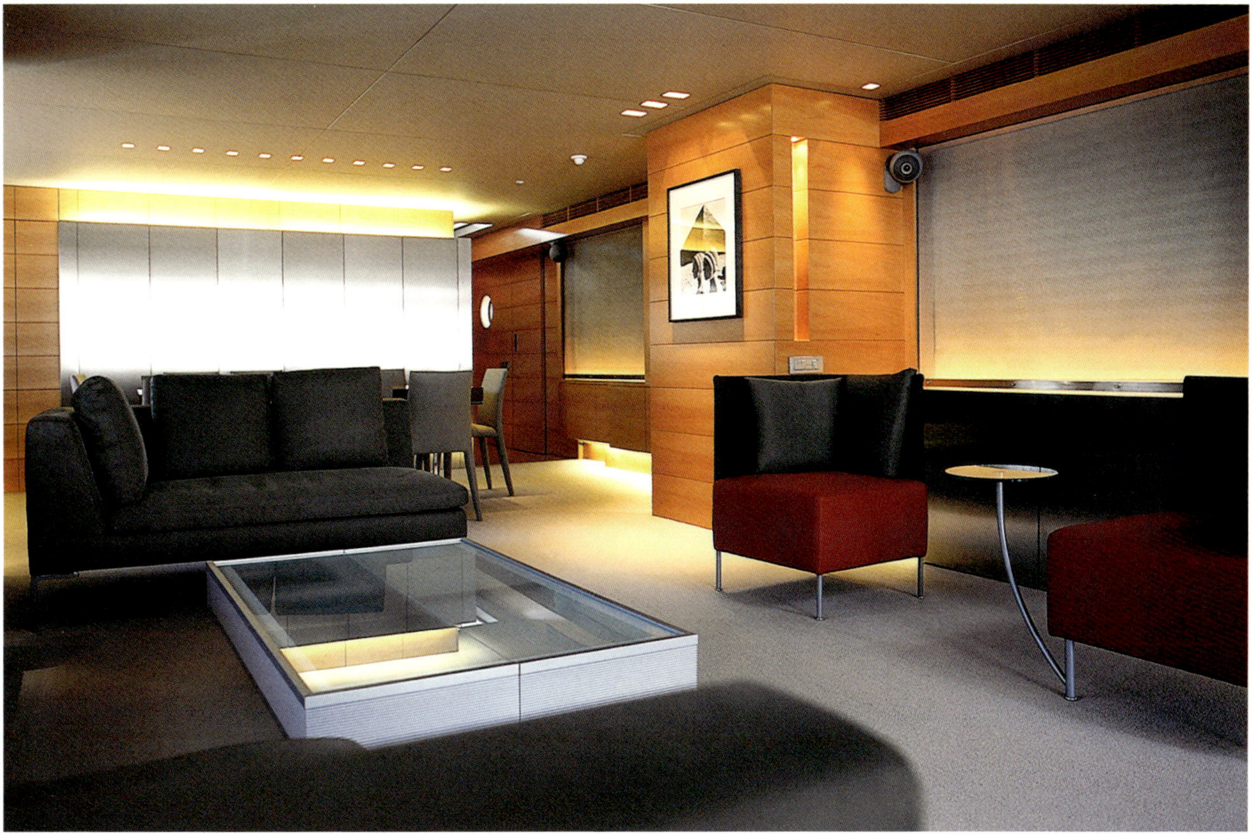

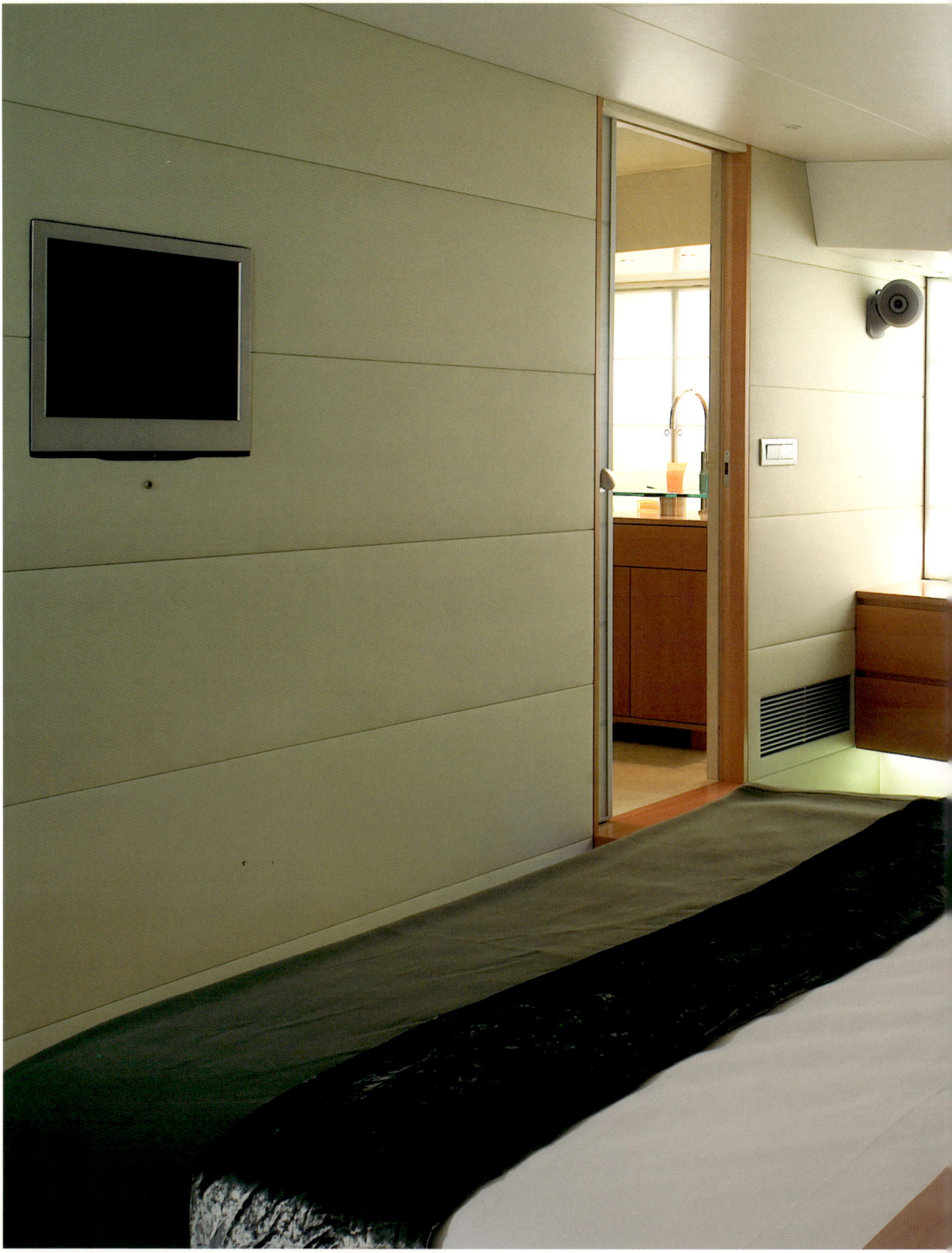

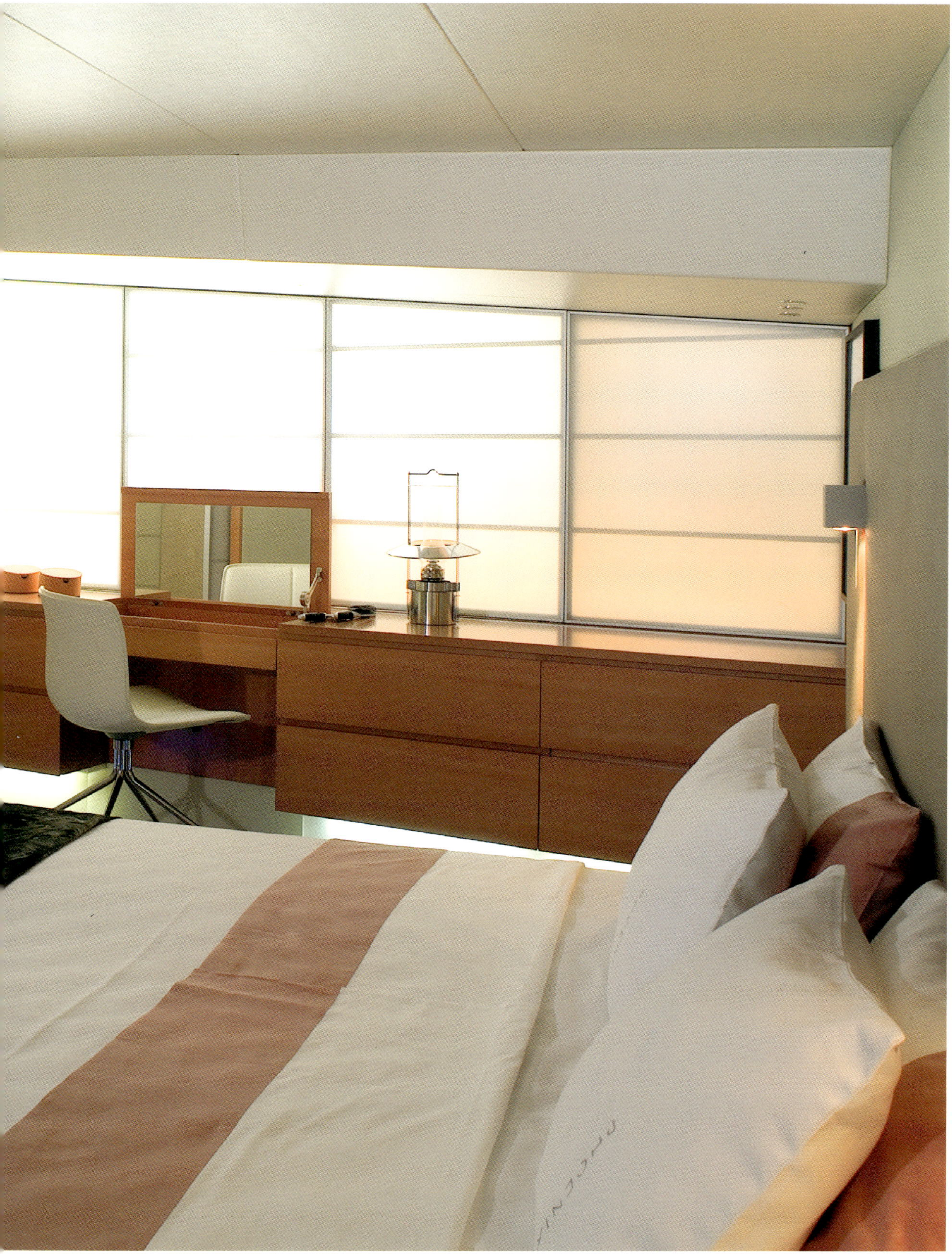
PHOENIX

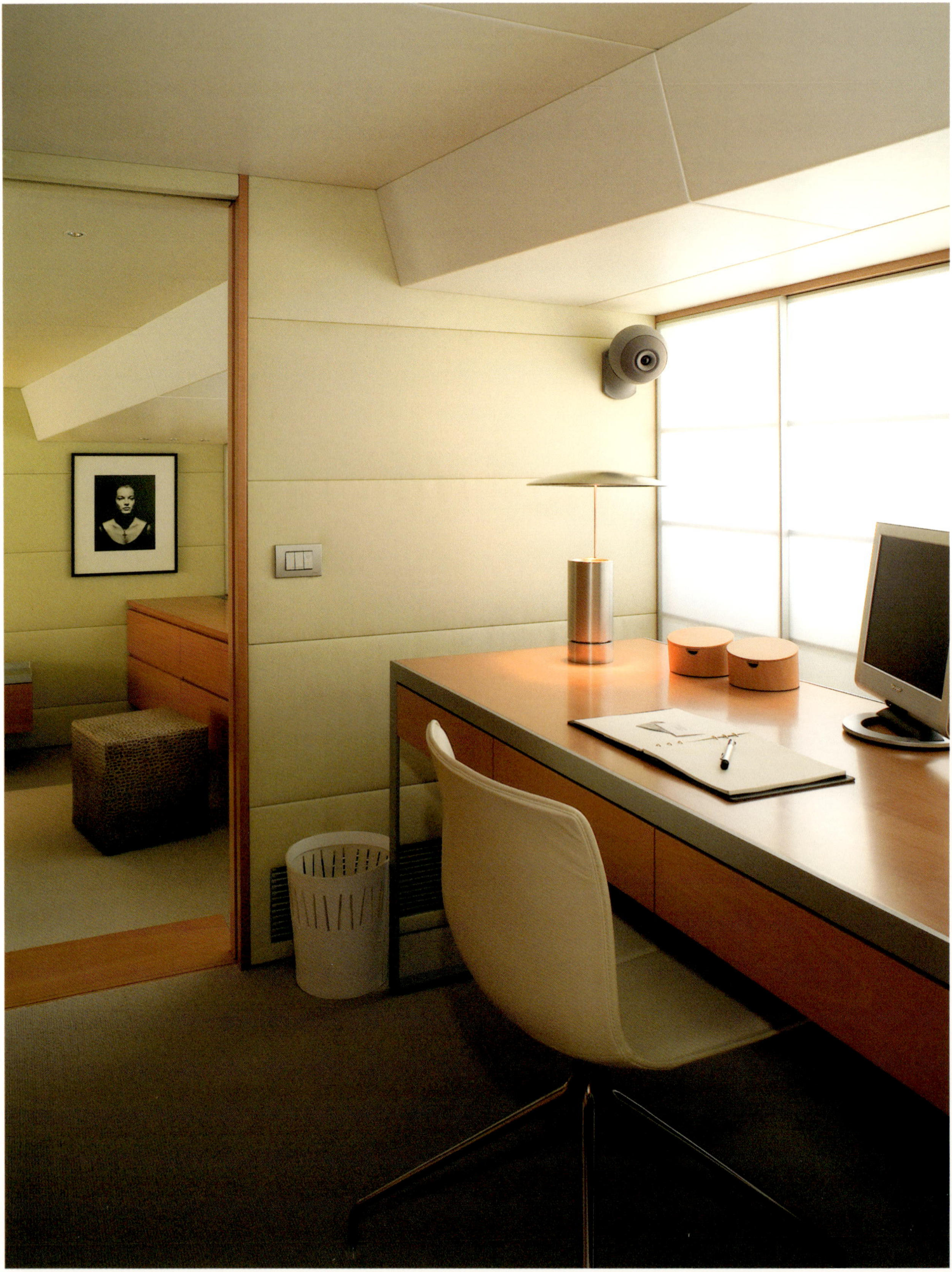

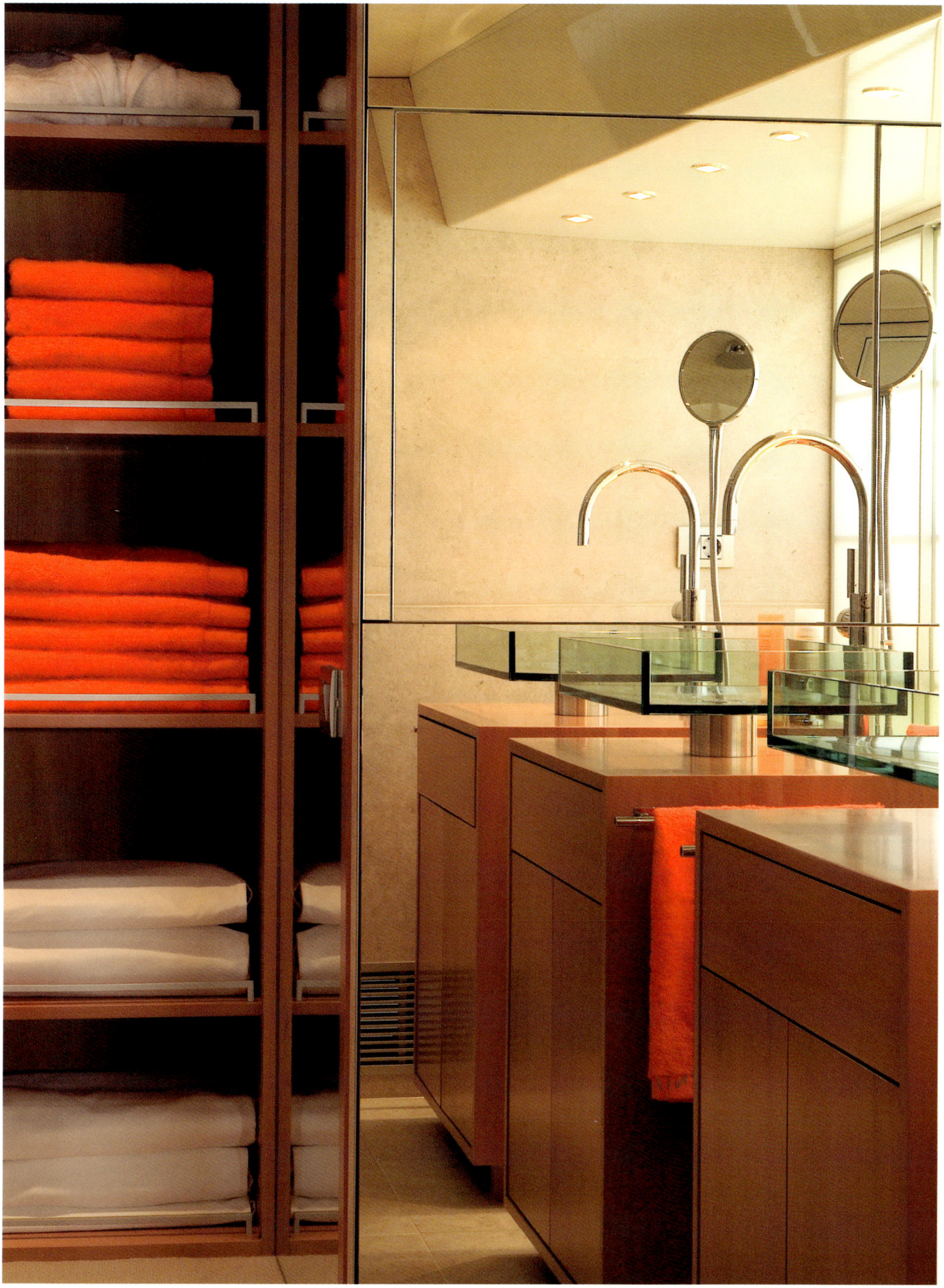

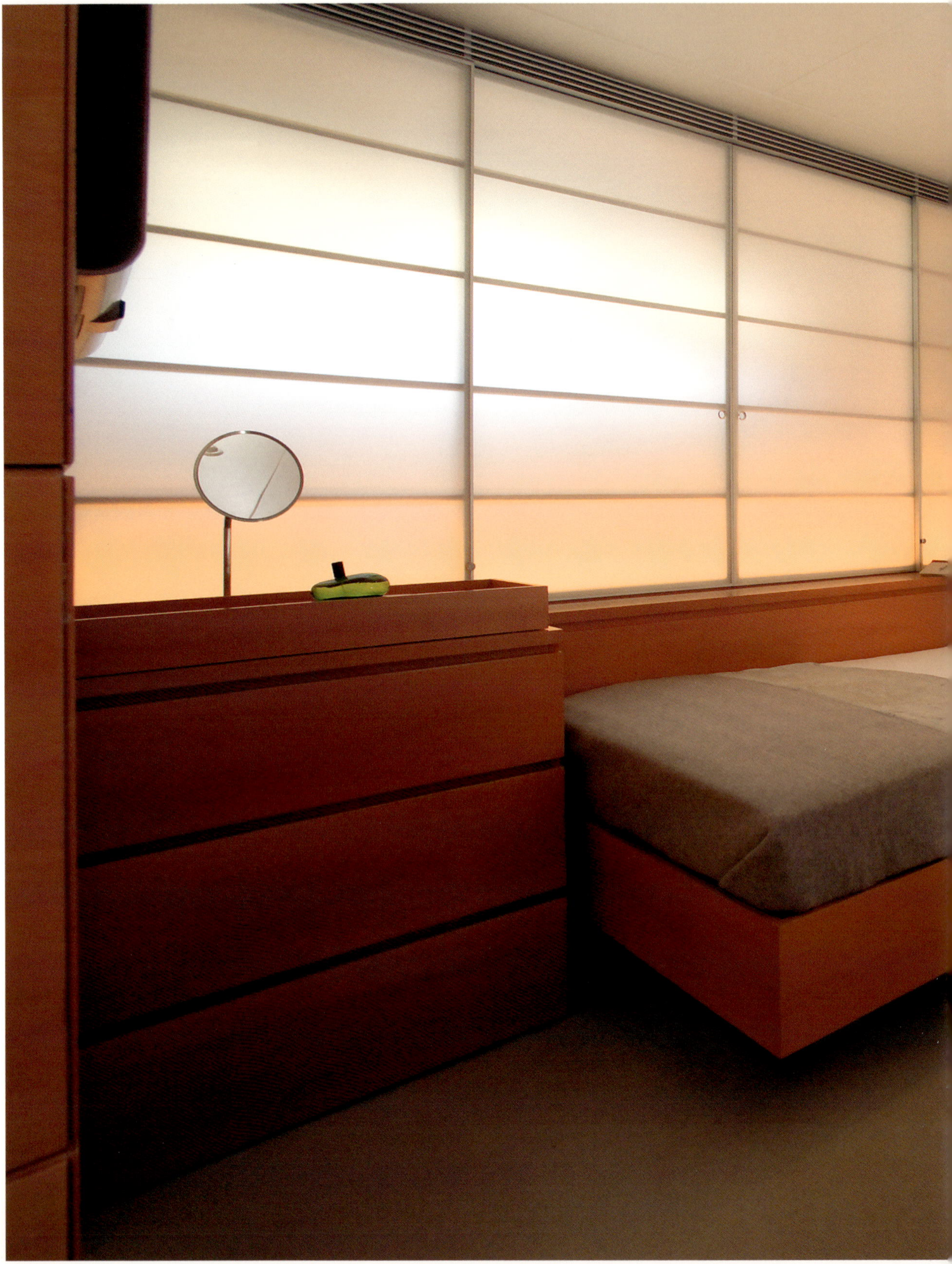

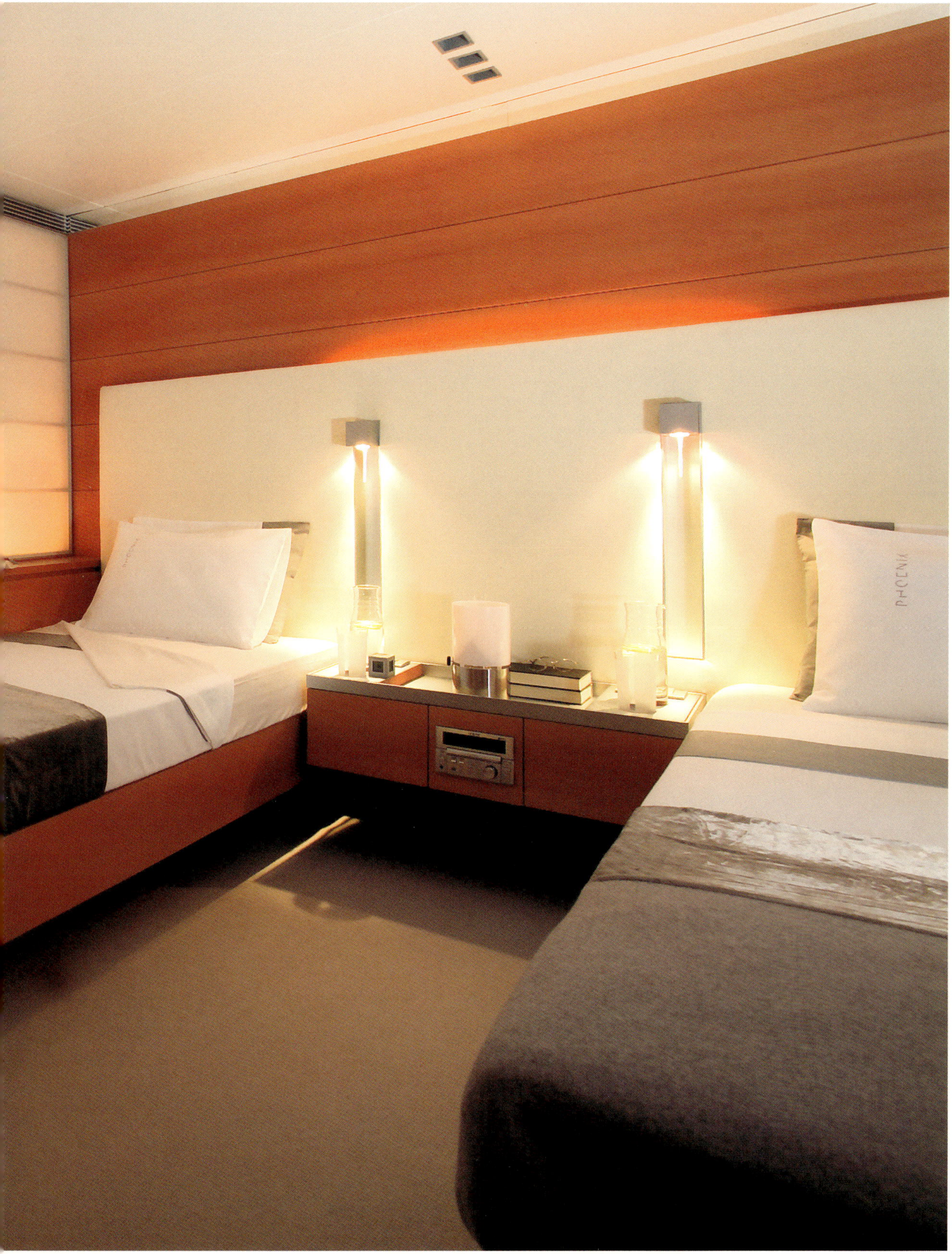

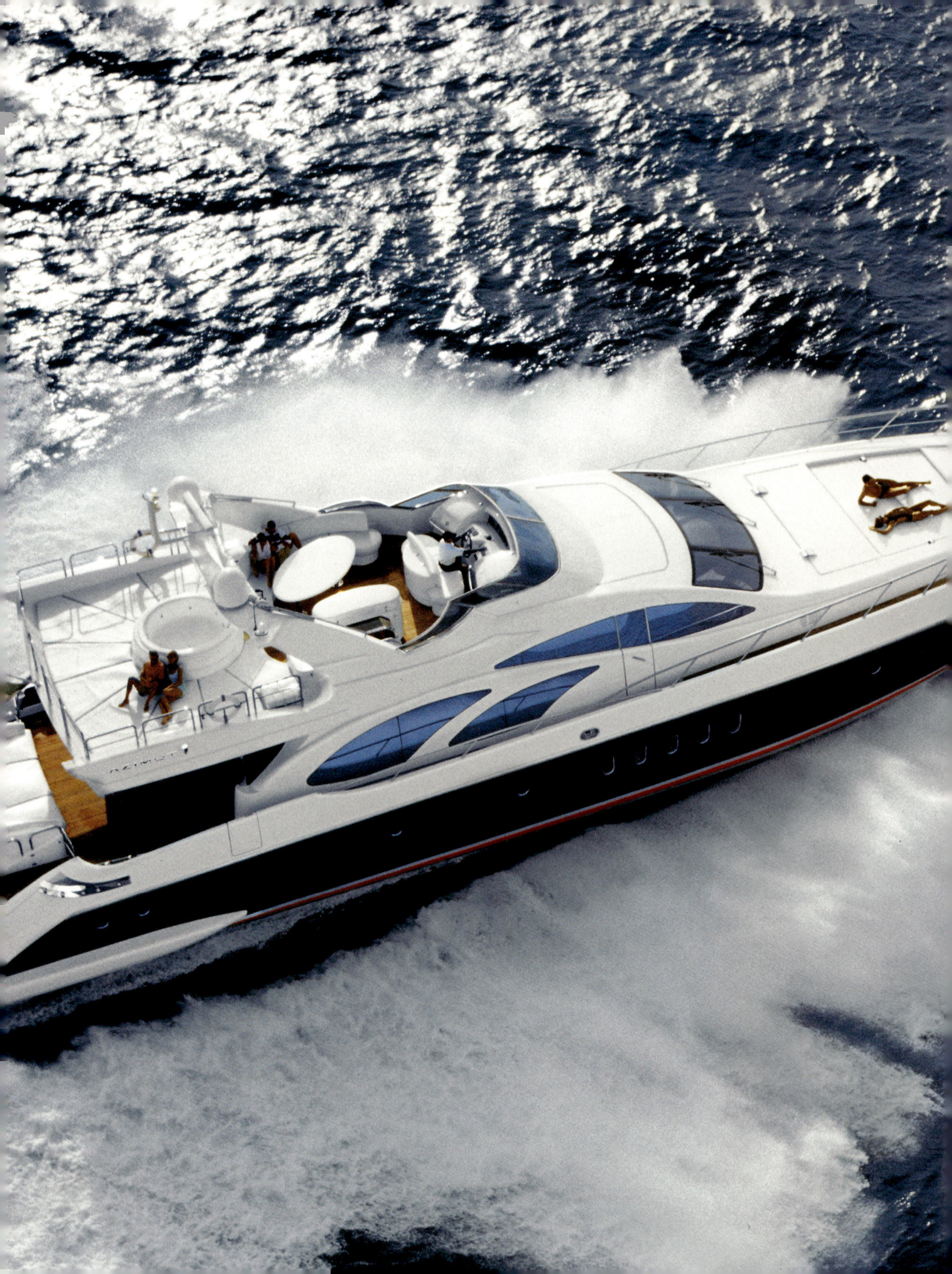

CARLO GALEAZZI, STEFANO RIGHINI
LEONARDO 98 | 2003
Azimut Yachts

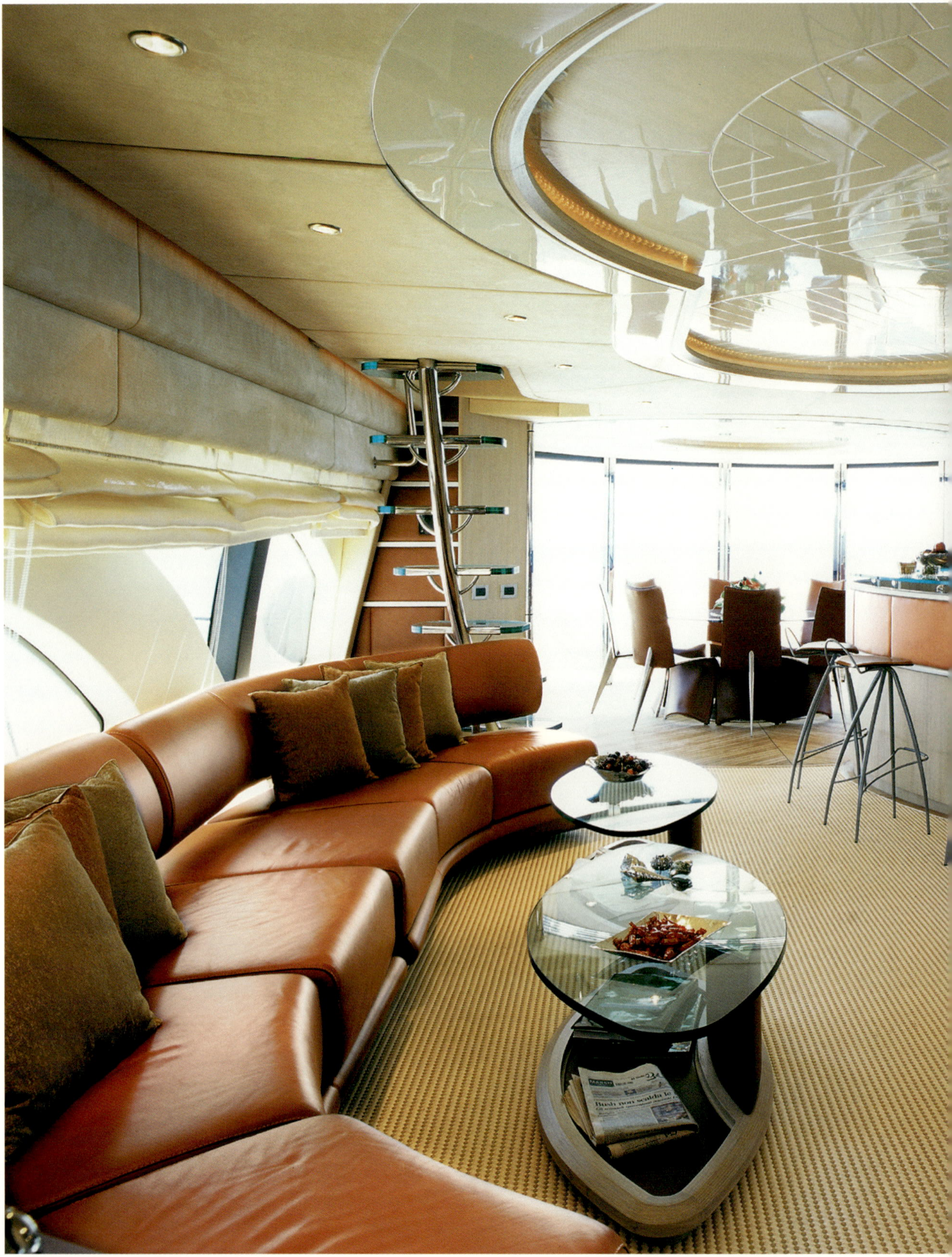

37

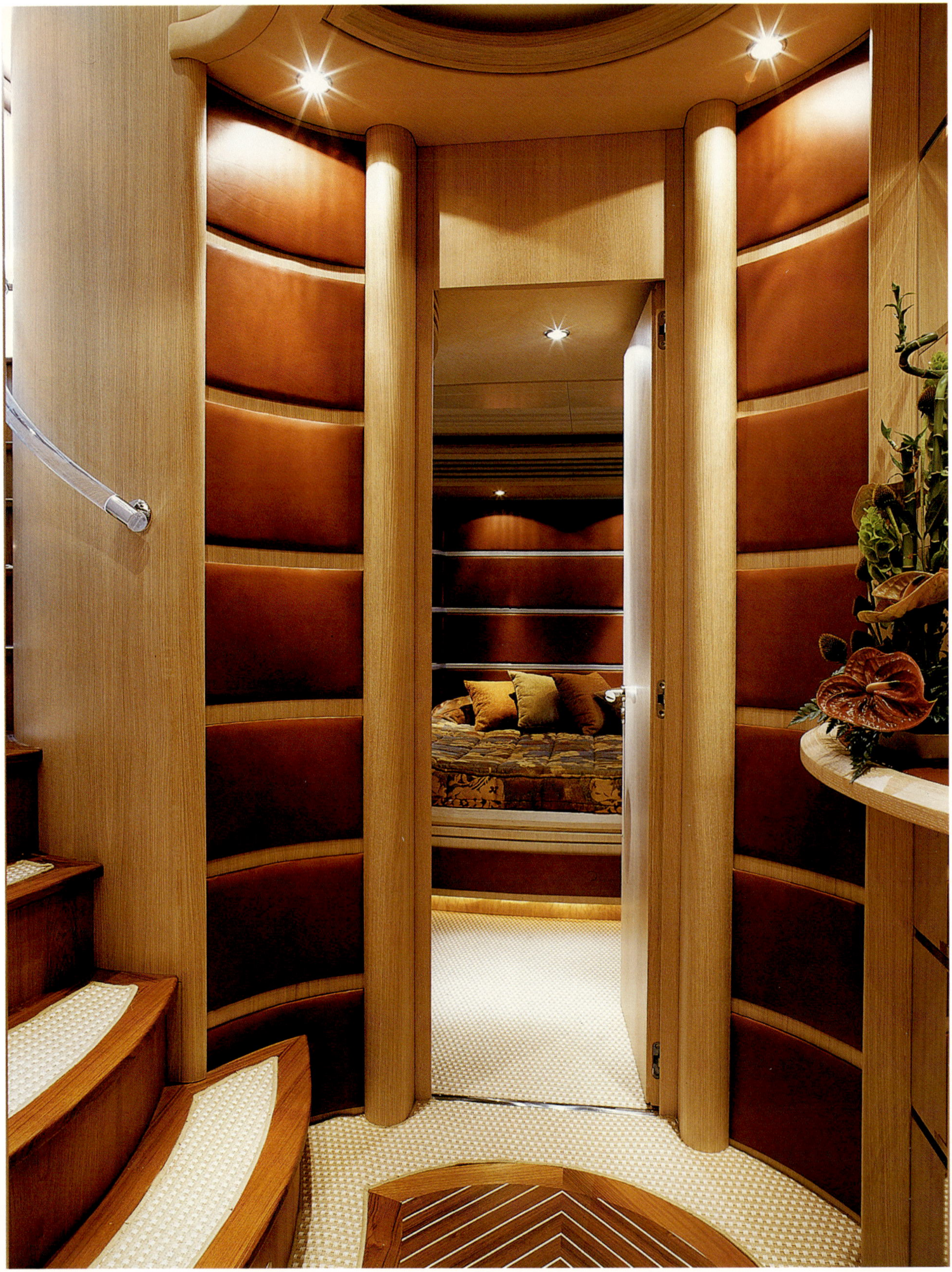

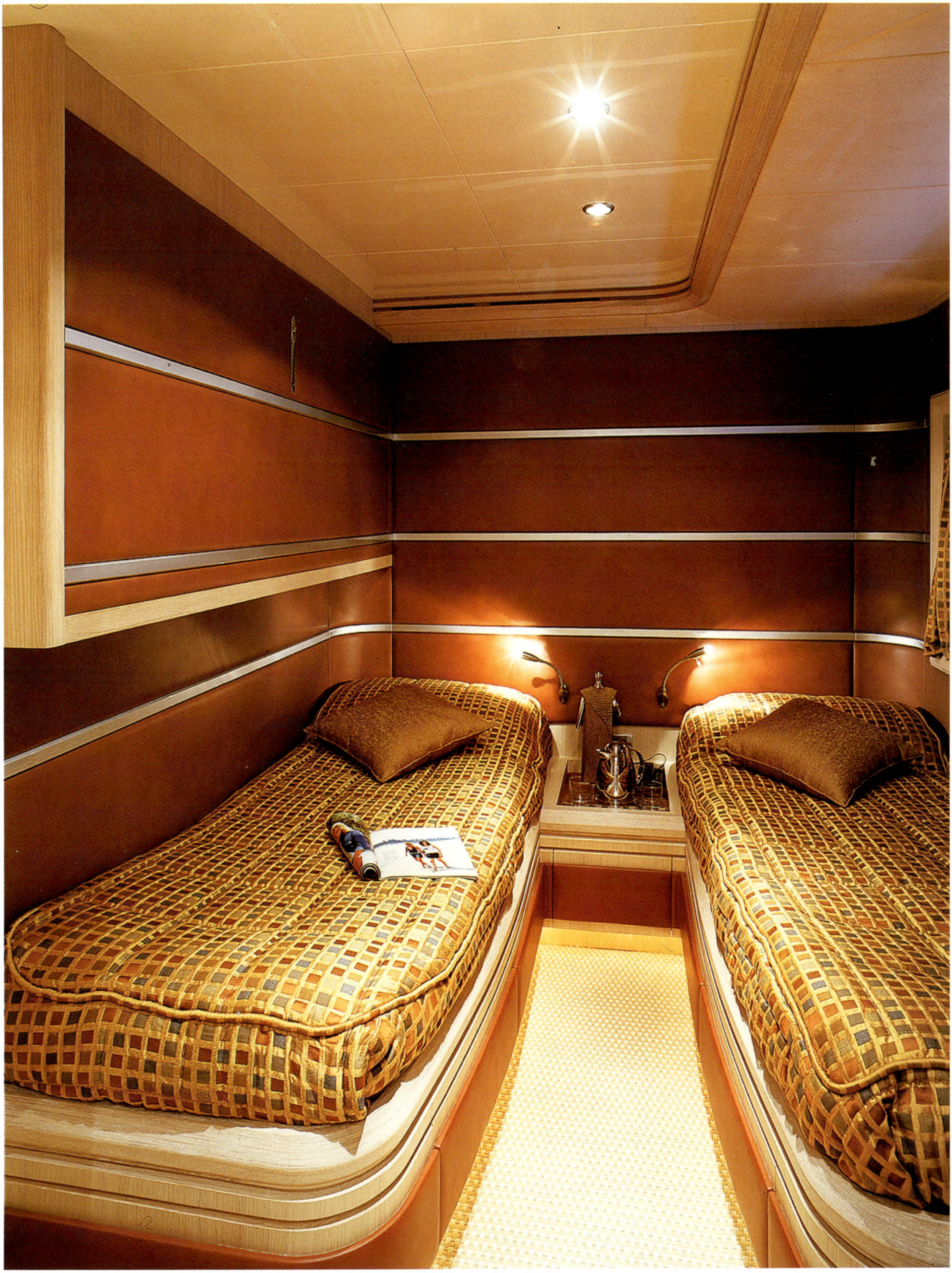

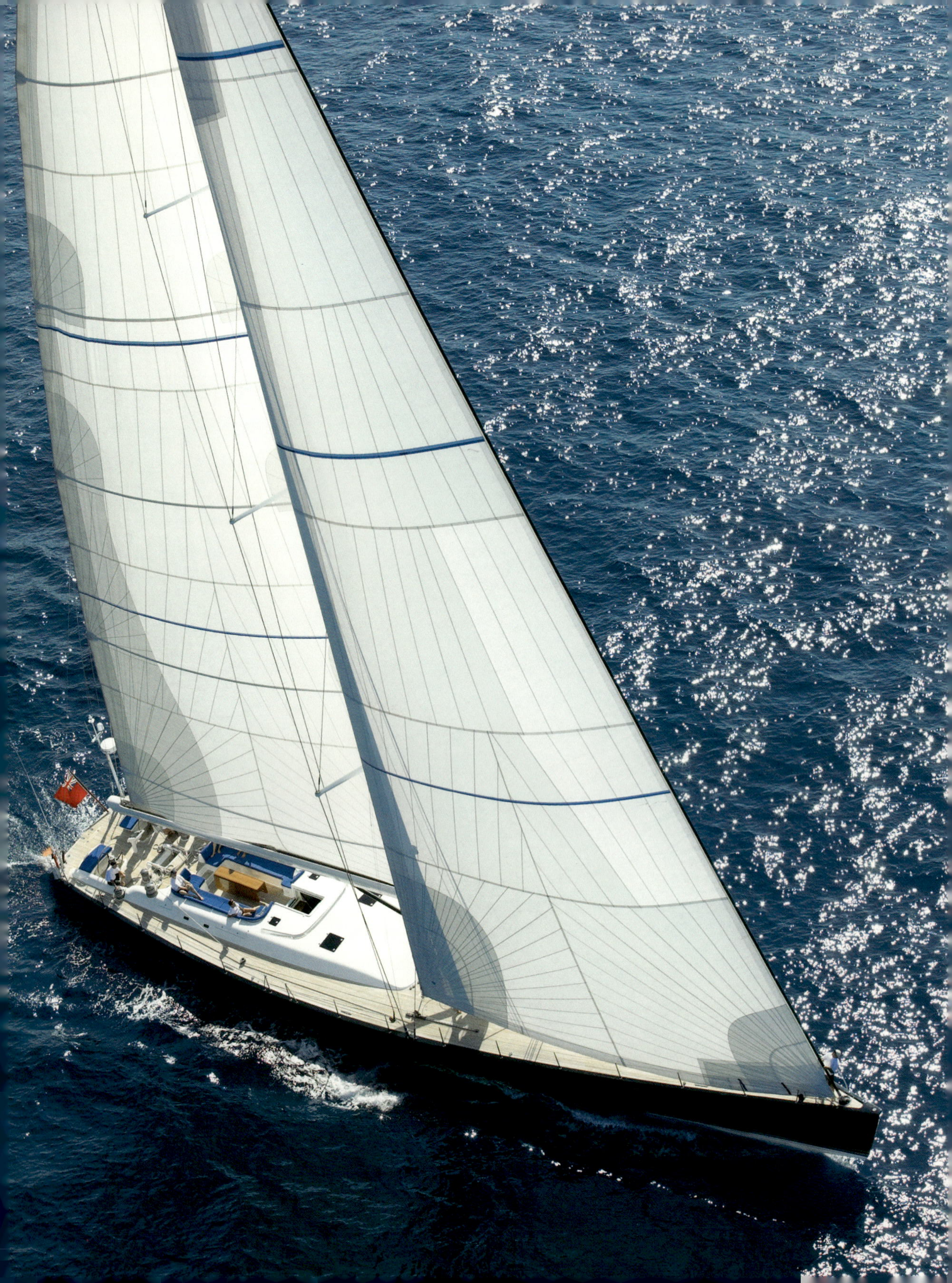

COUEDEL HUGON DESIGN, GERMAN FRERS
ONLY NOW | 2004
CNB

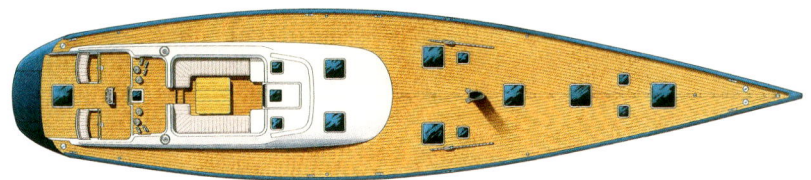

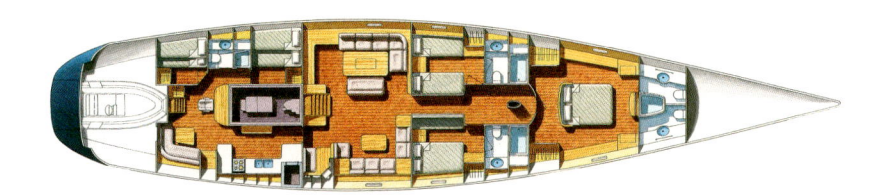

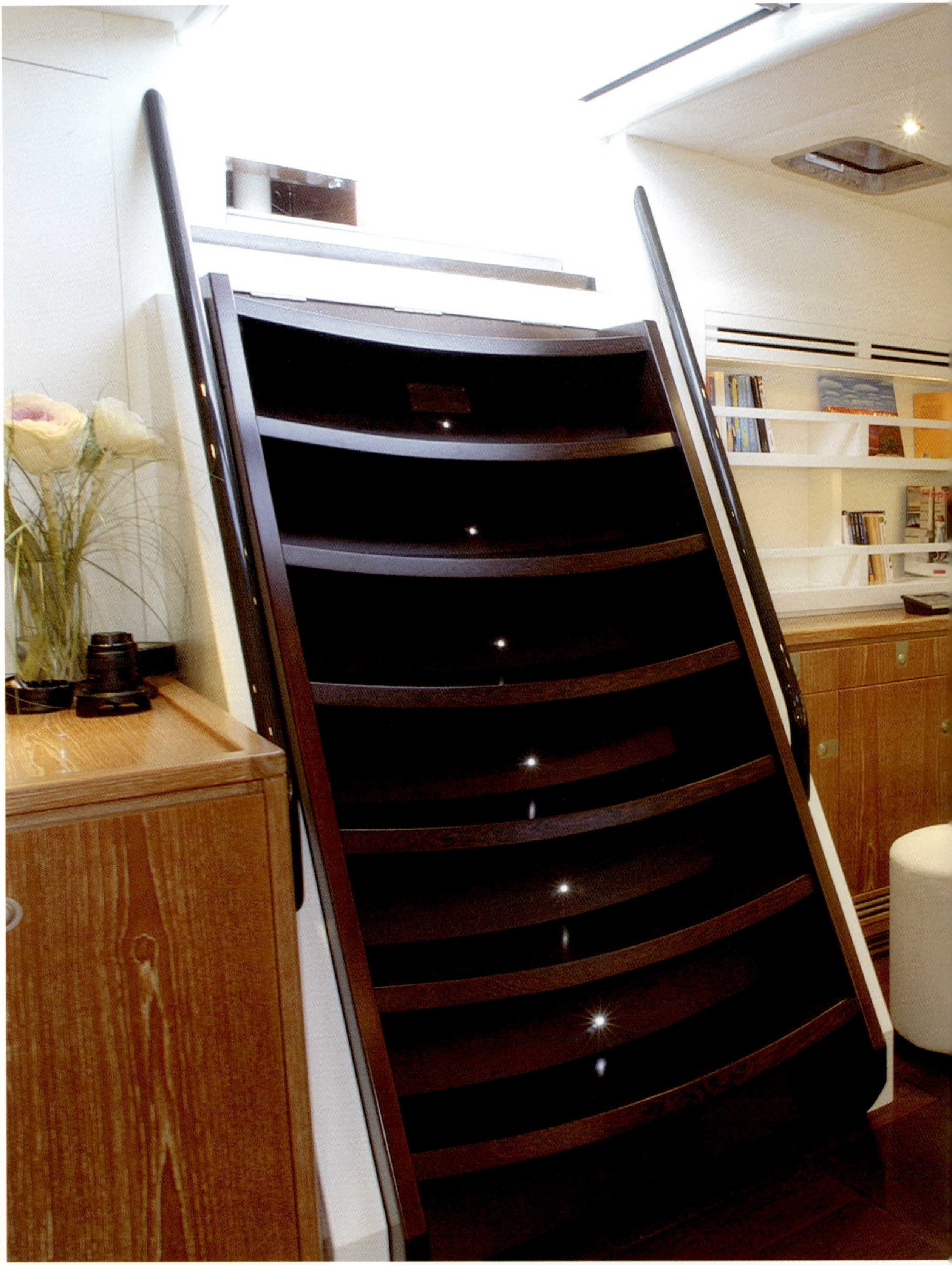

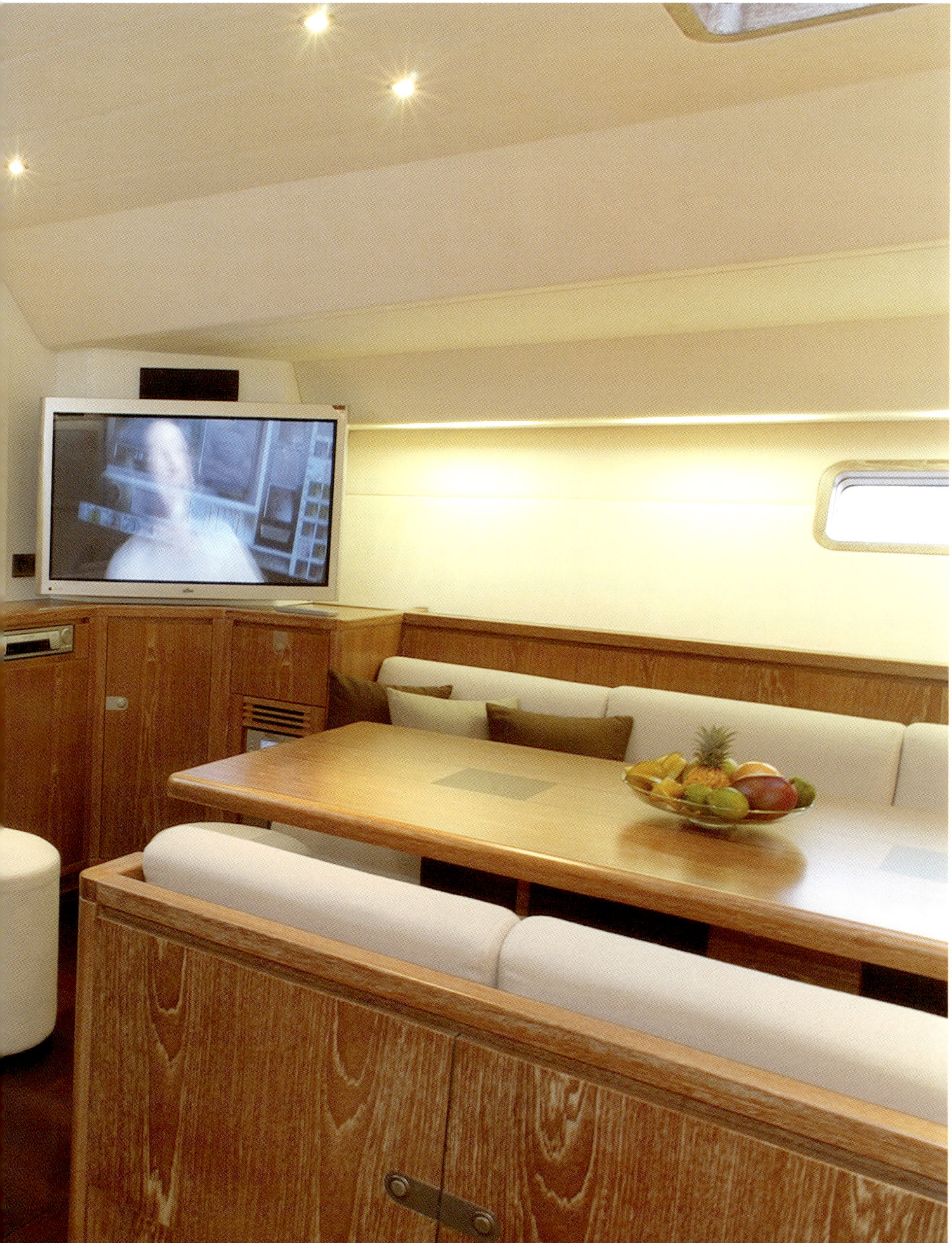

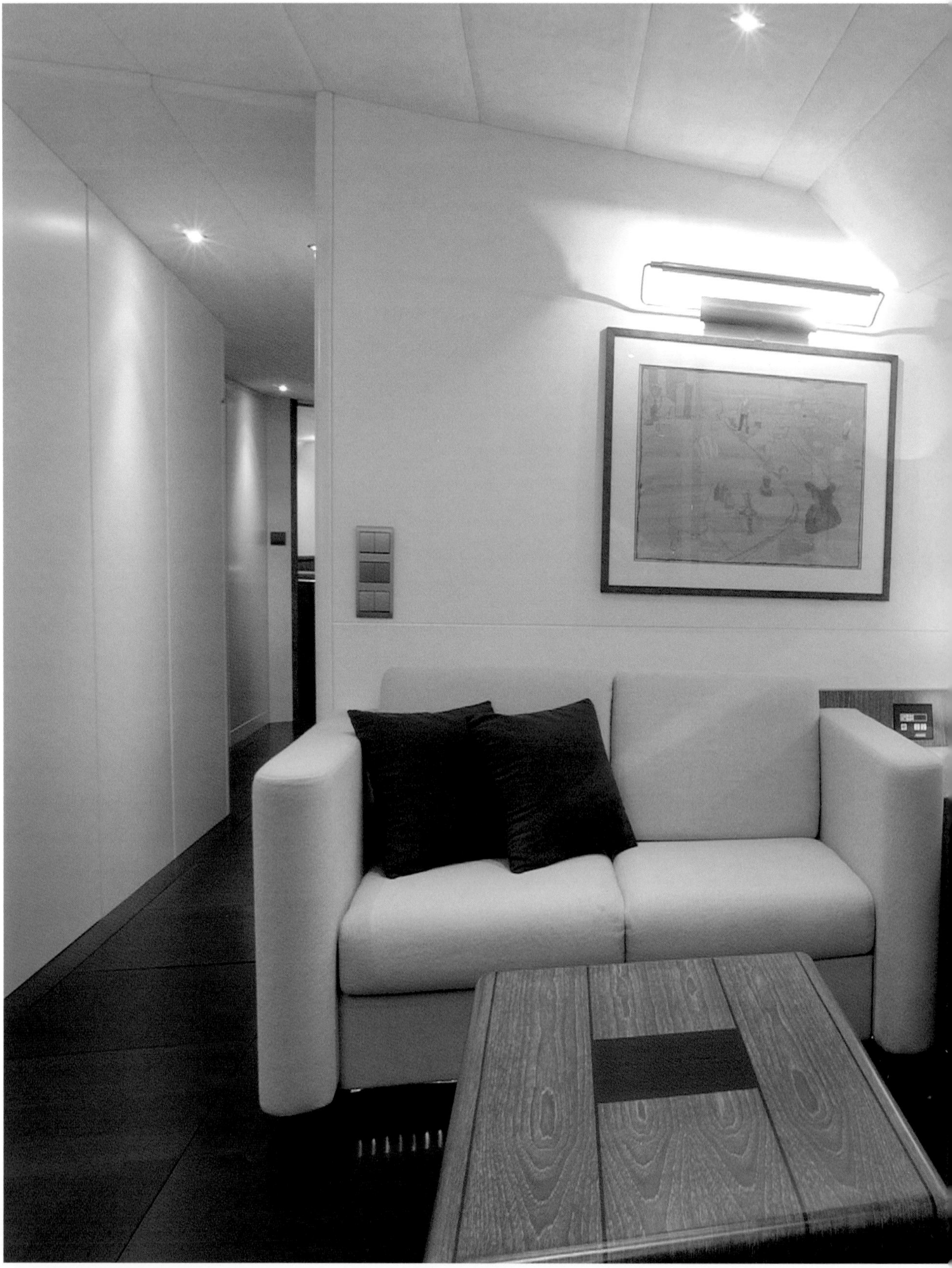

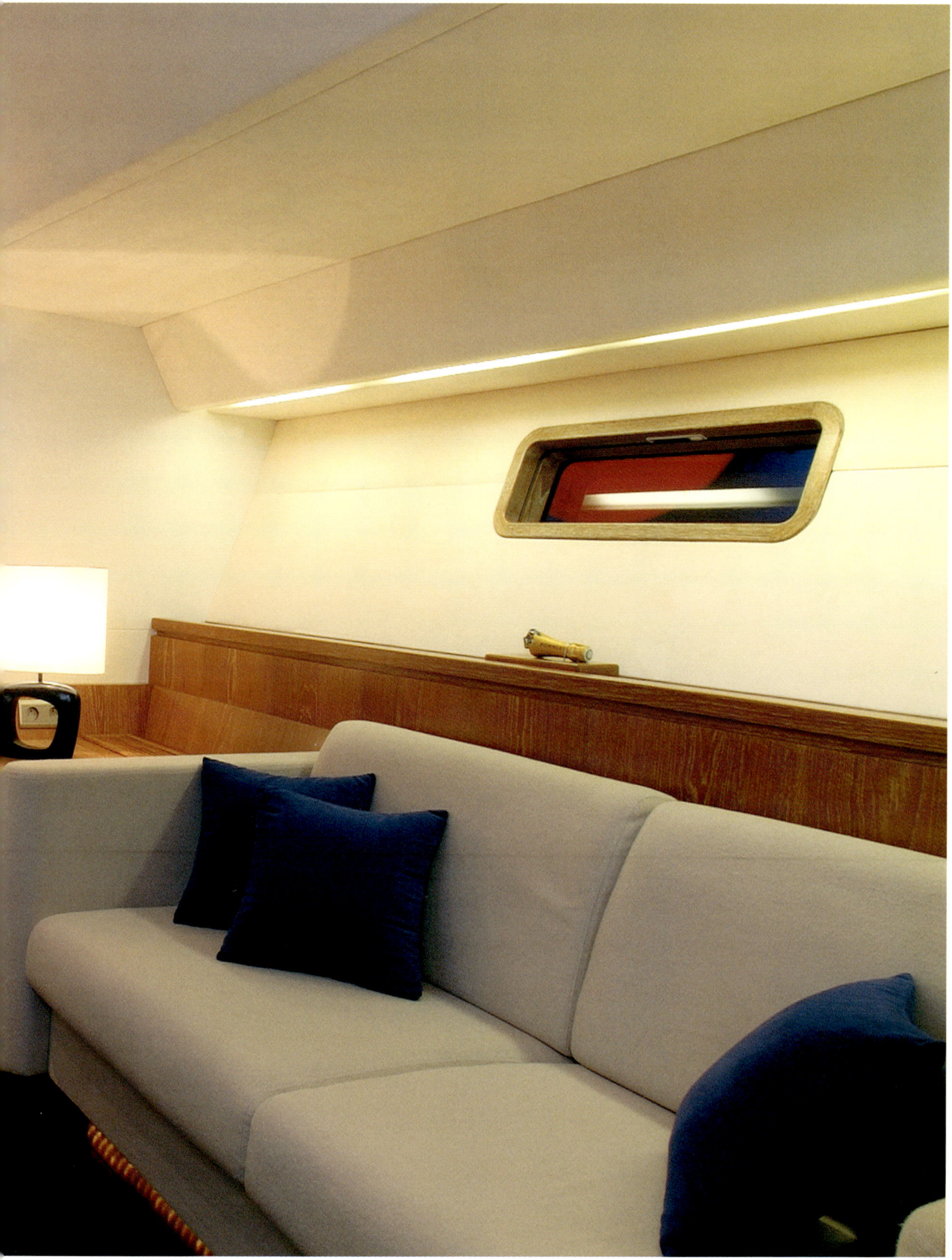

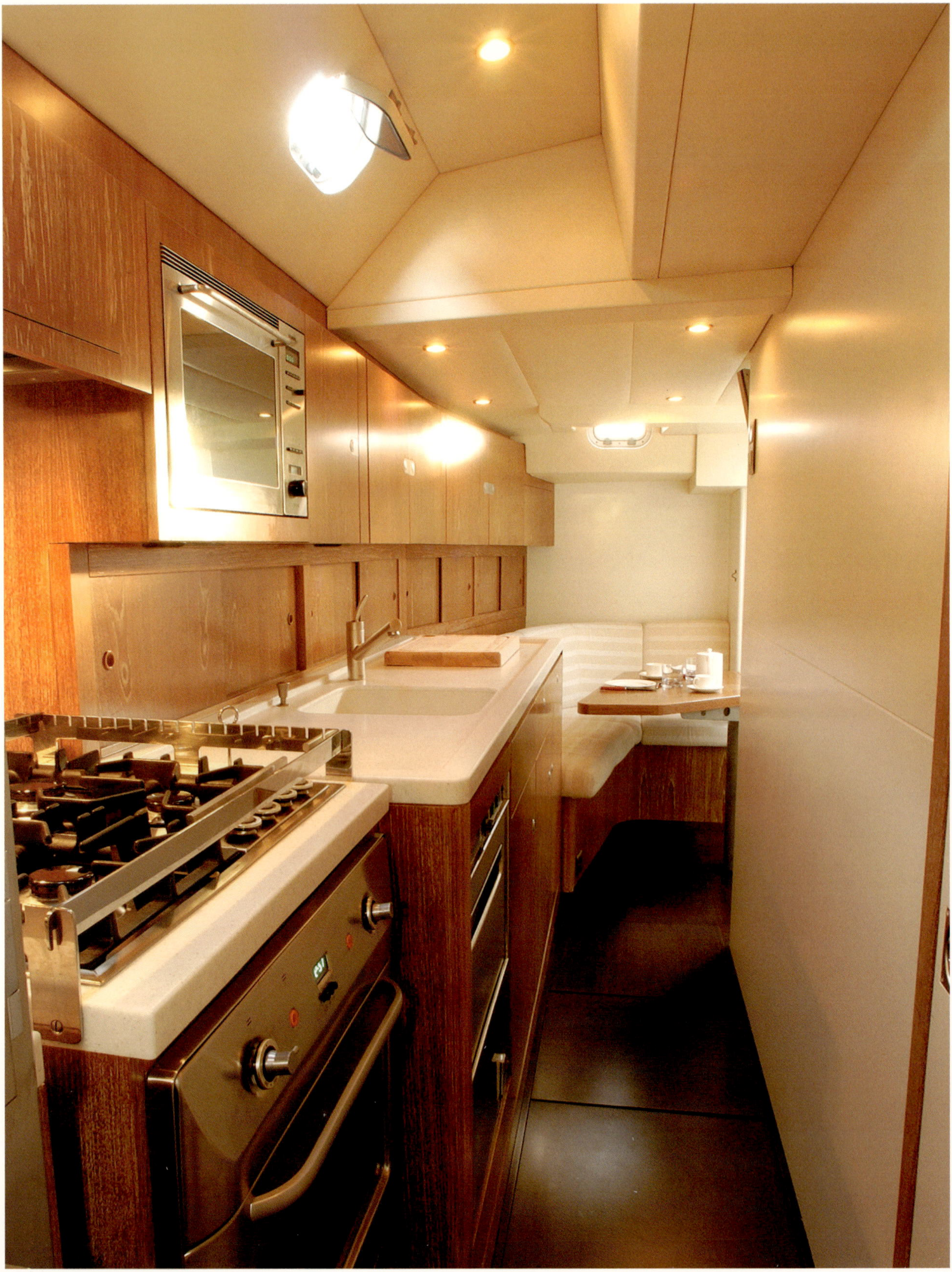

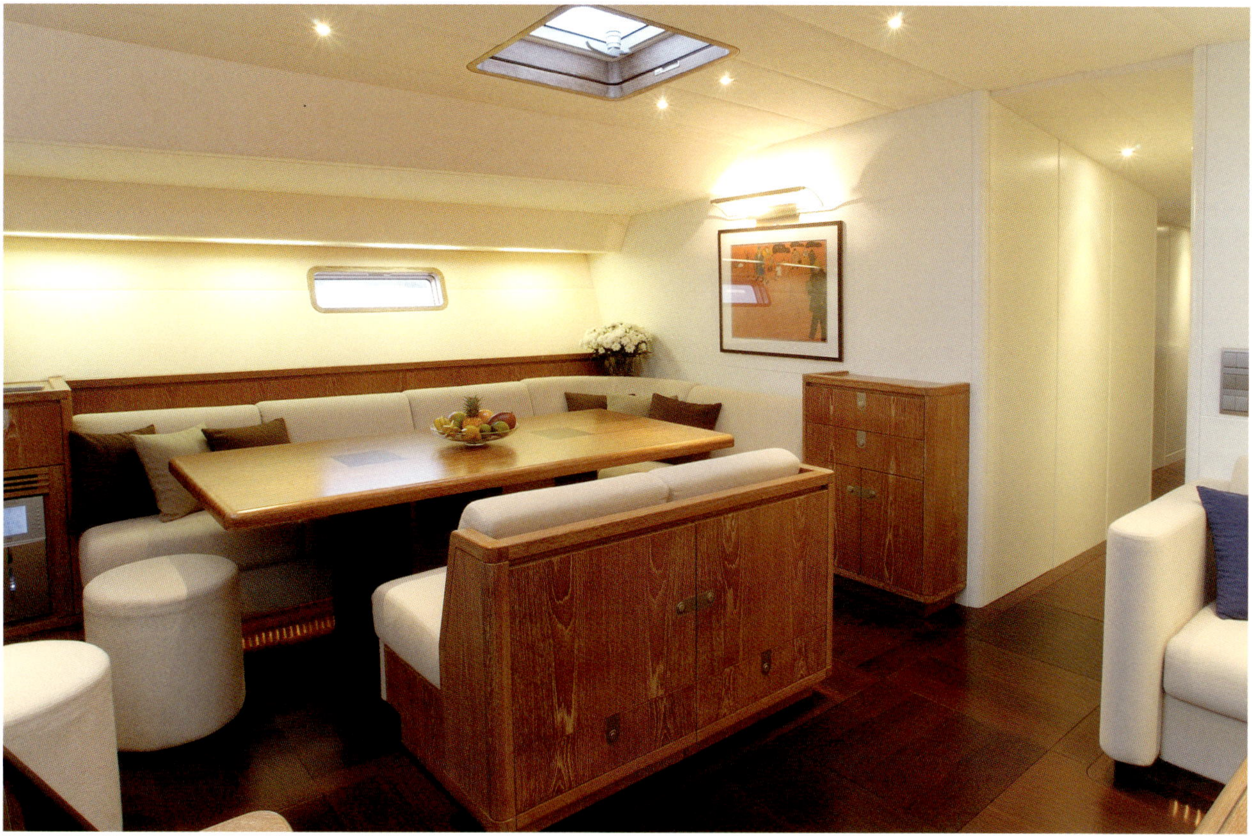

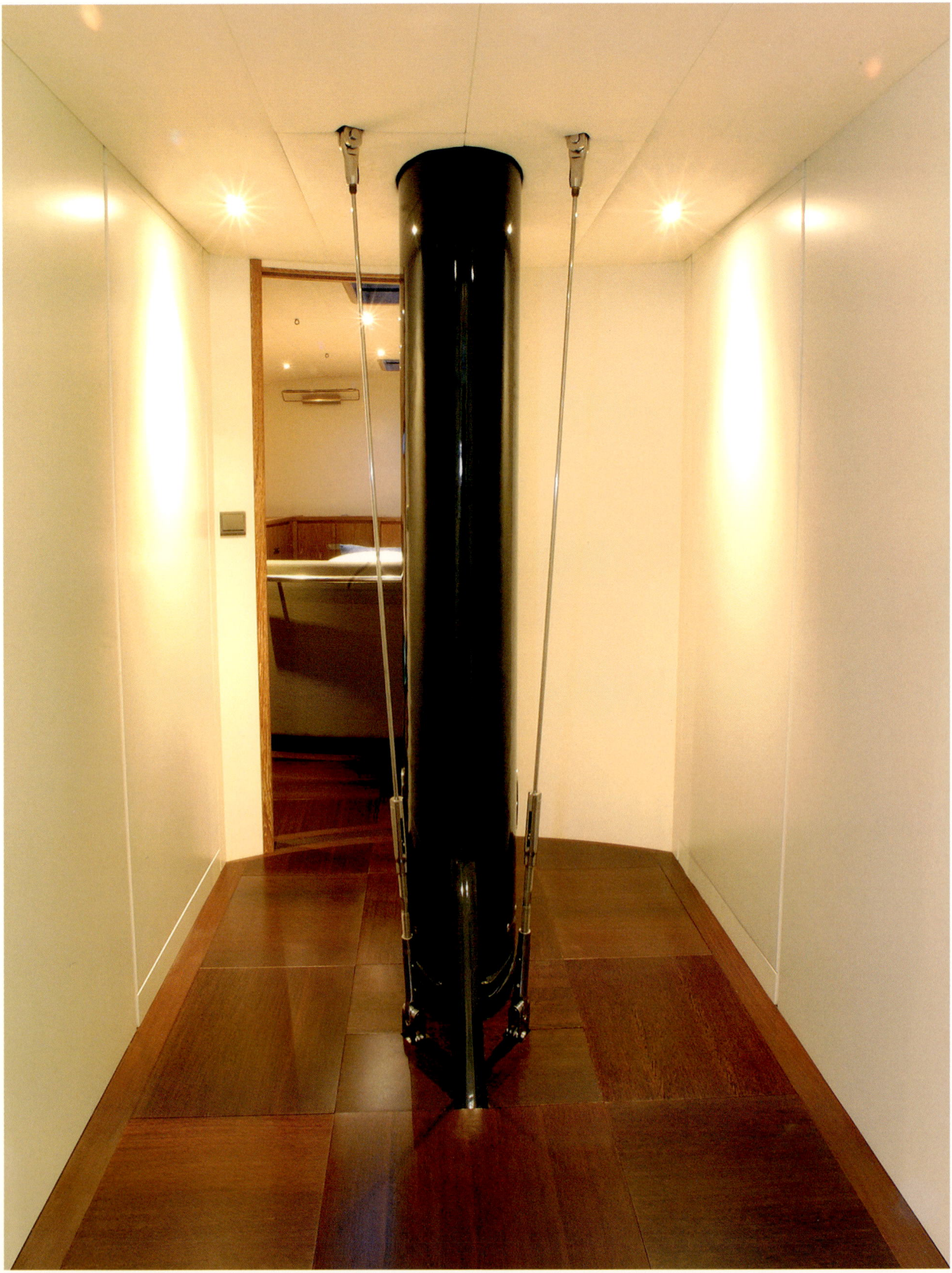

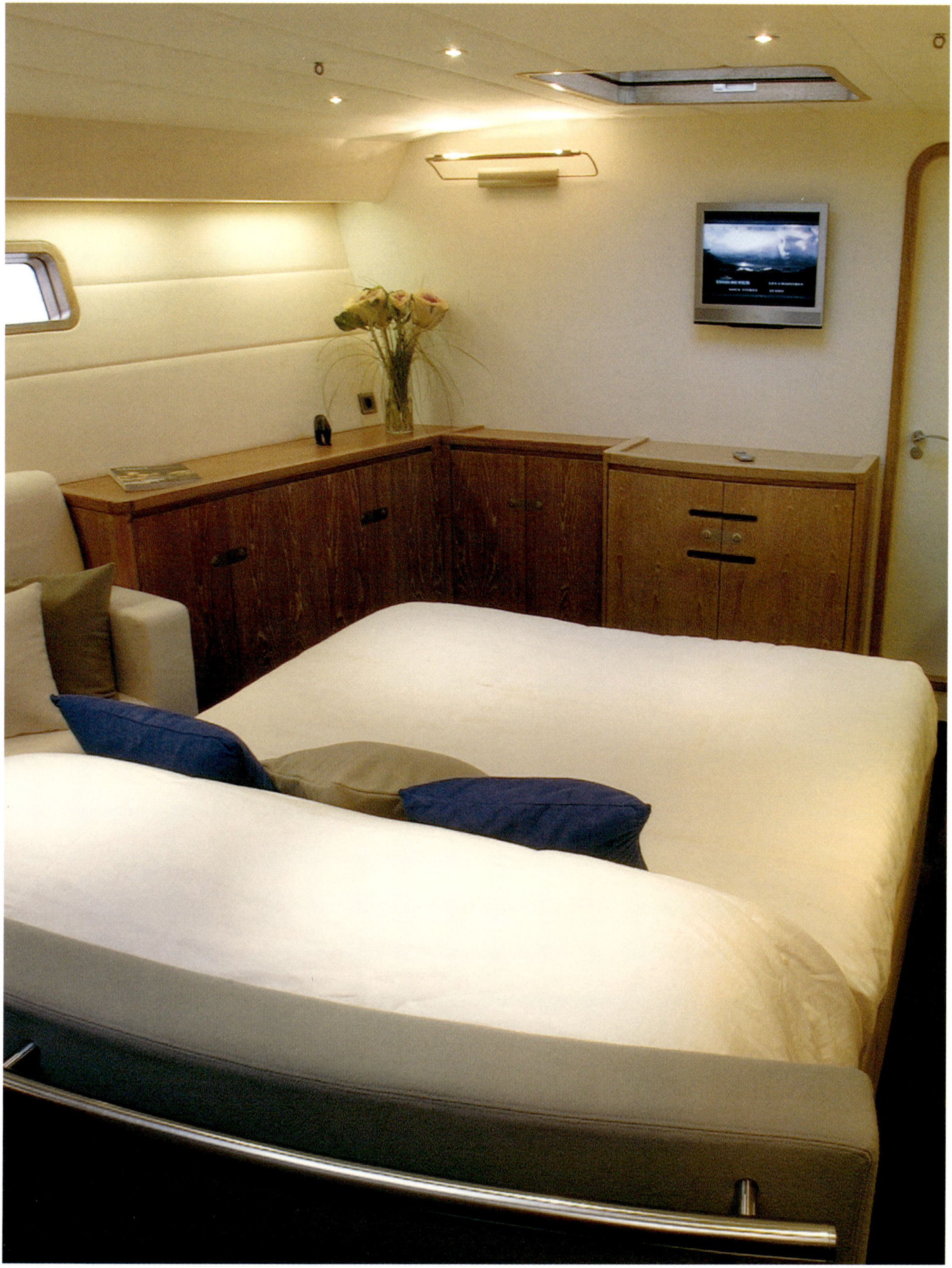

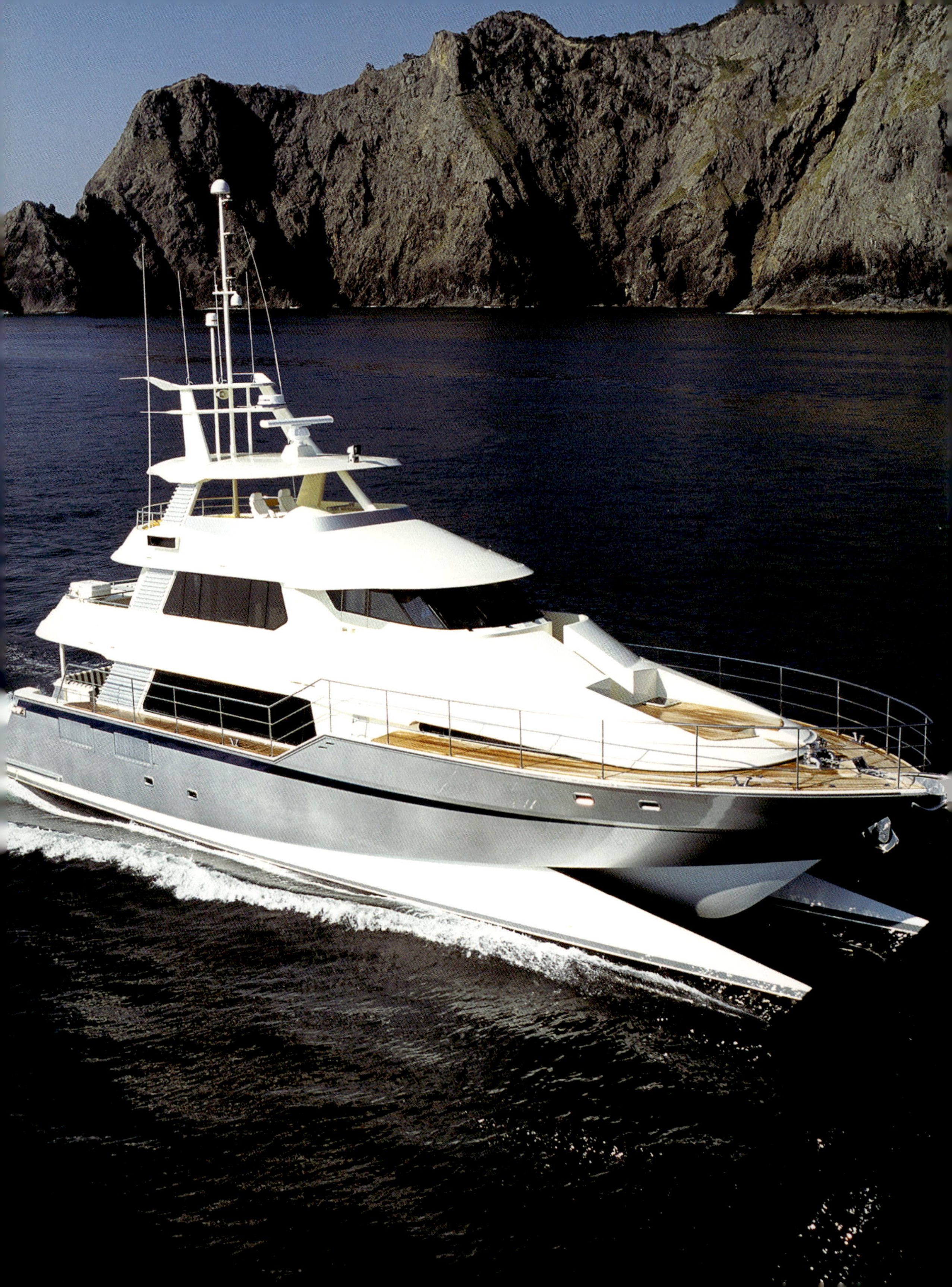

CRAIG LOOMES DESIGN GROUP, PAOLO SAMPA
SAMPITRES | 2002
Vaudrey Miller Yachts
Craig Loomes Design Group Limited

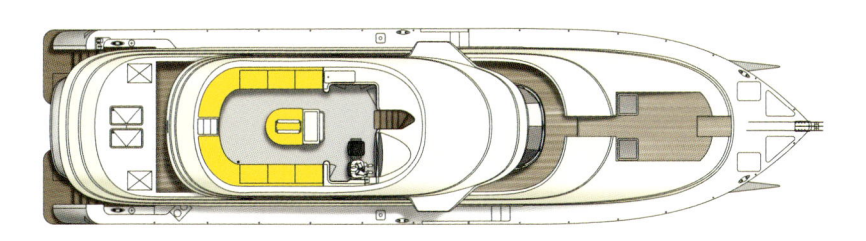

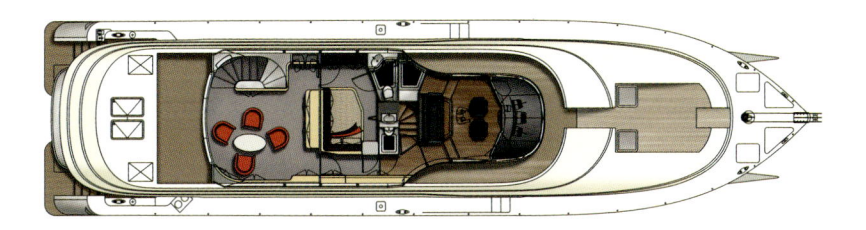

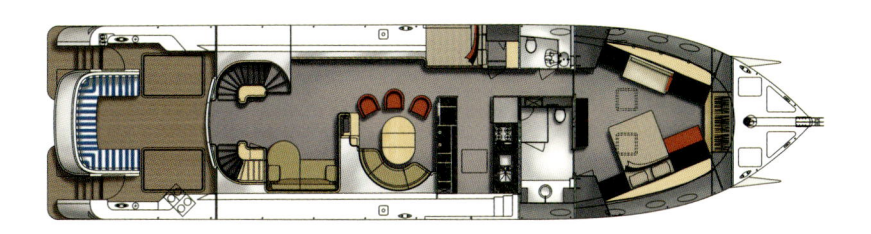

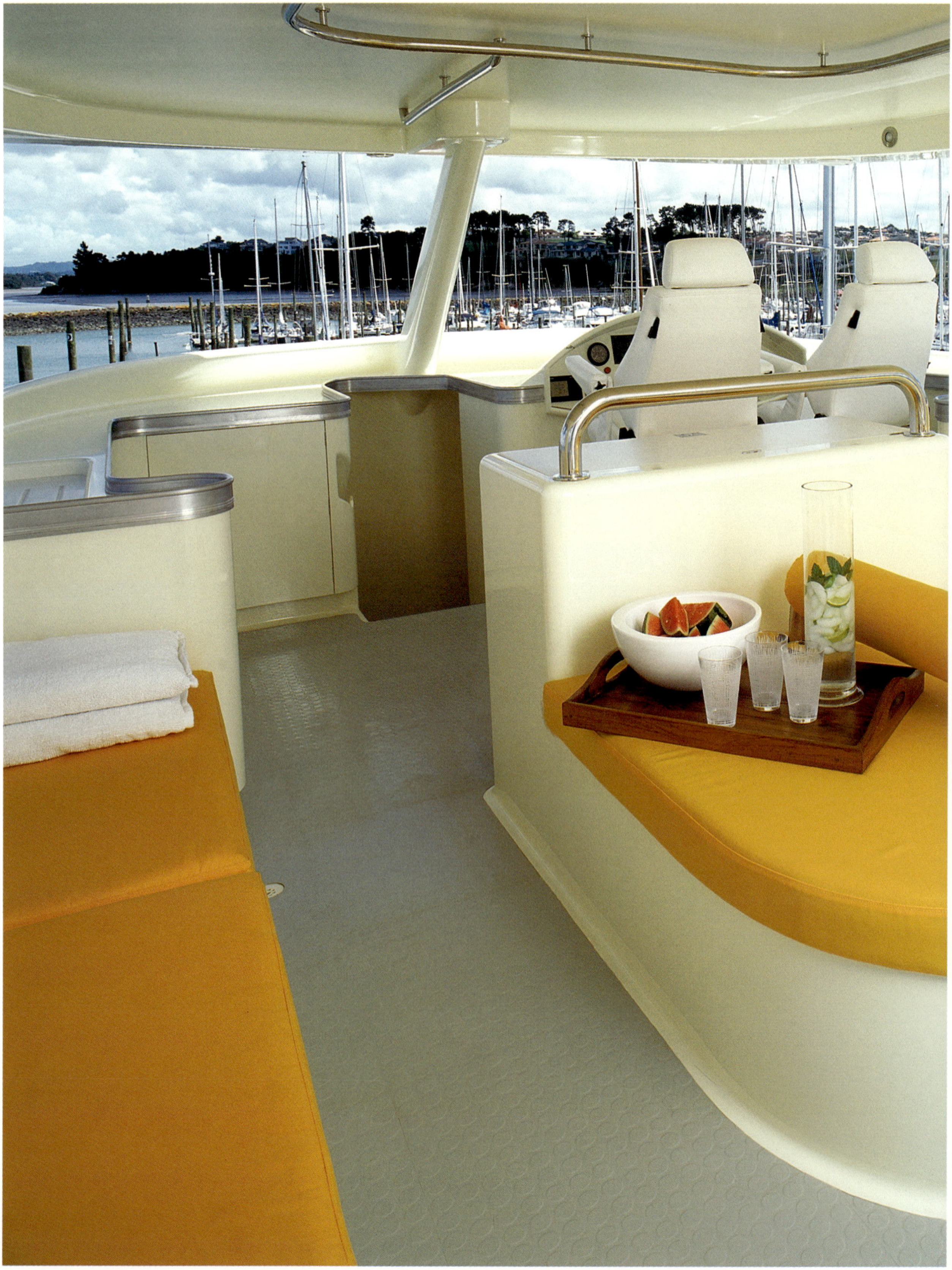

53

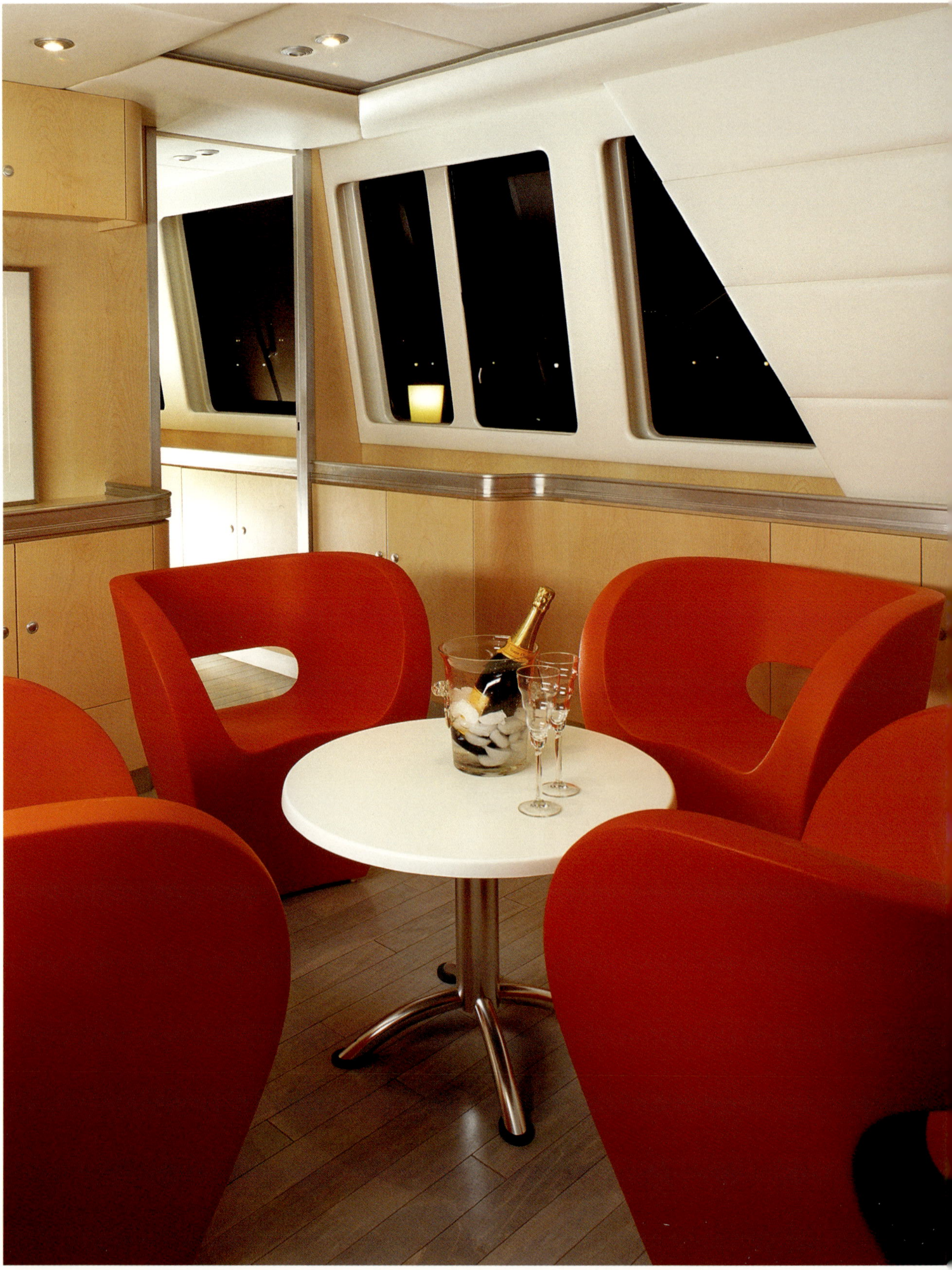

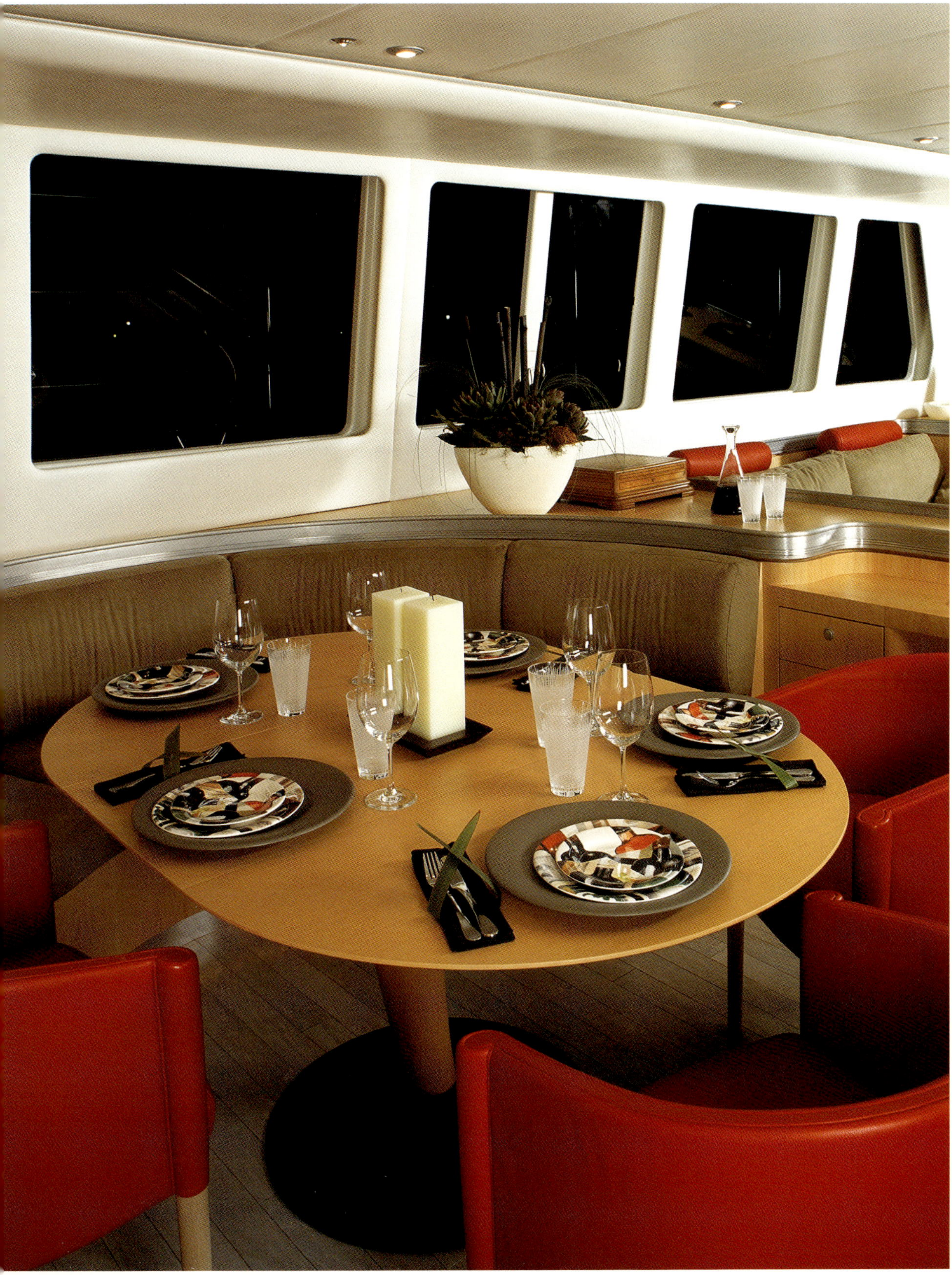

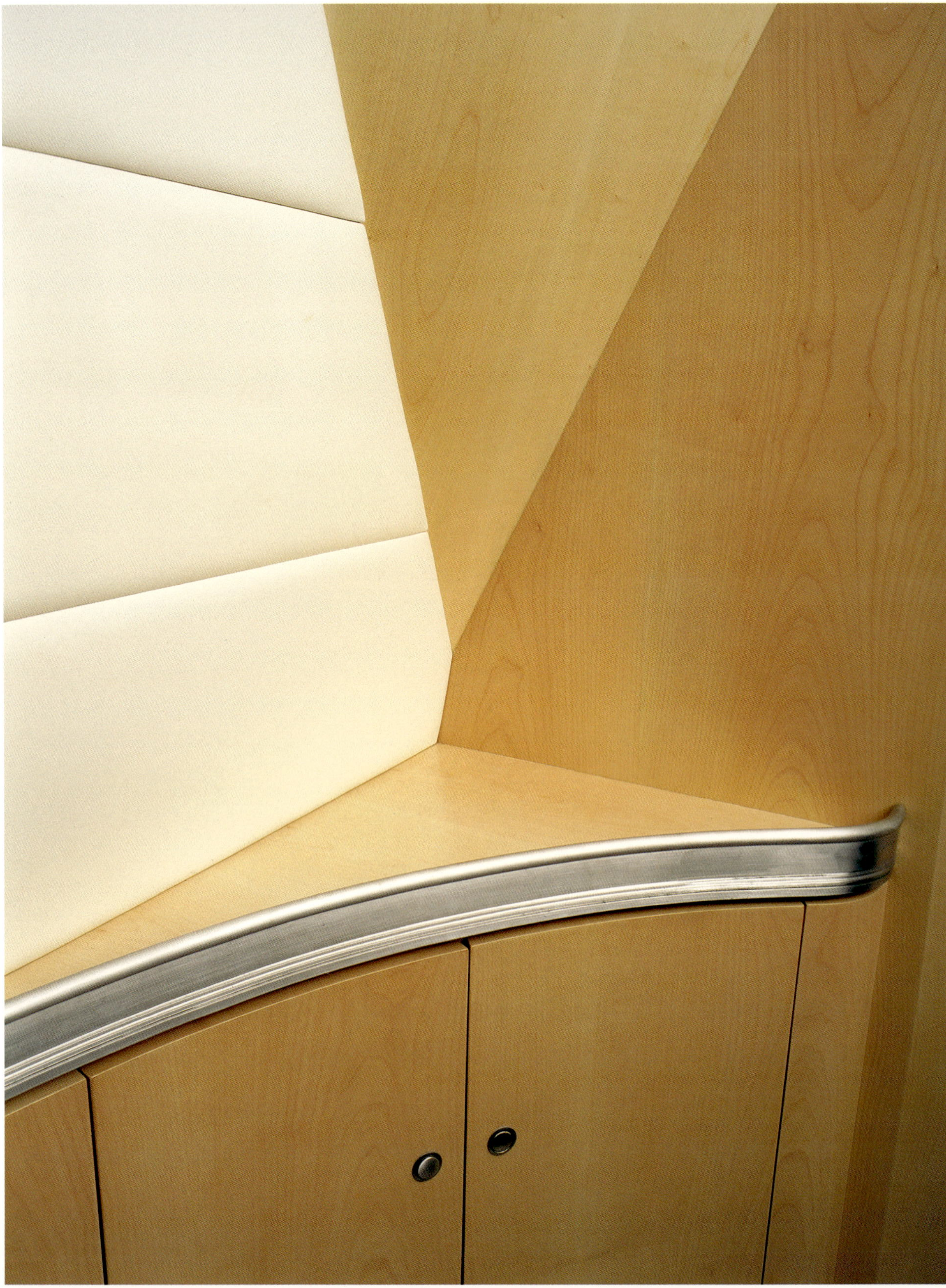

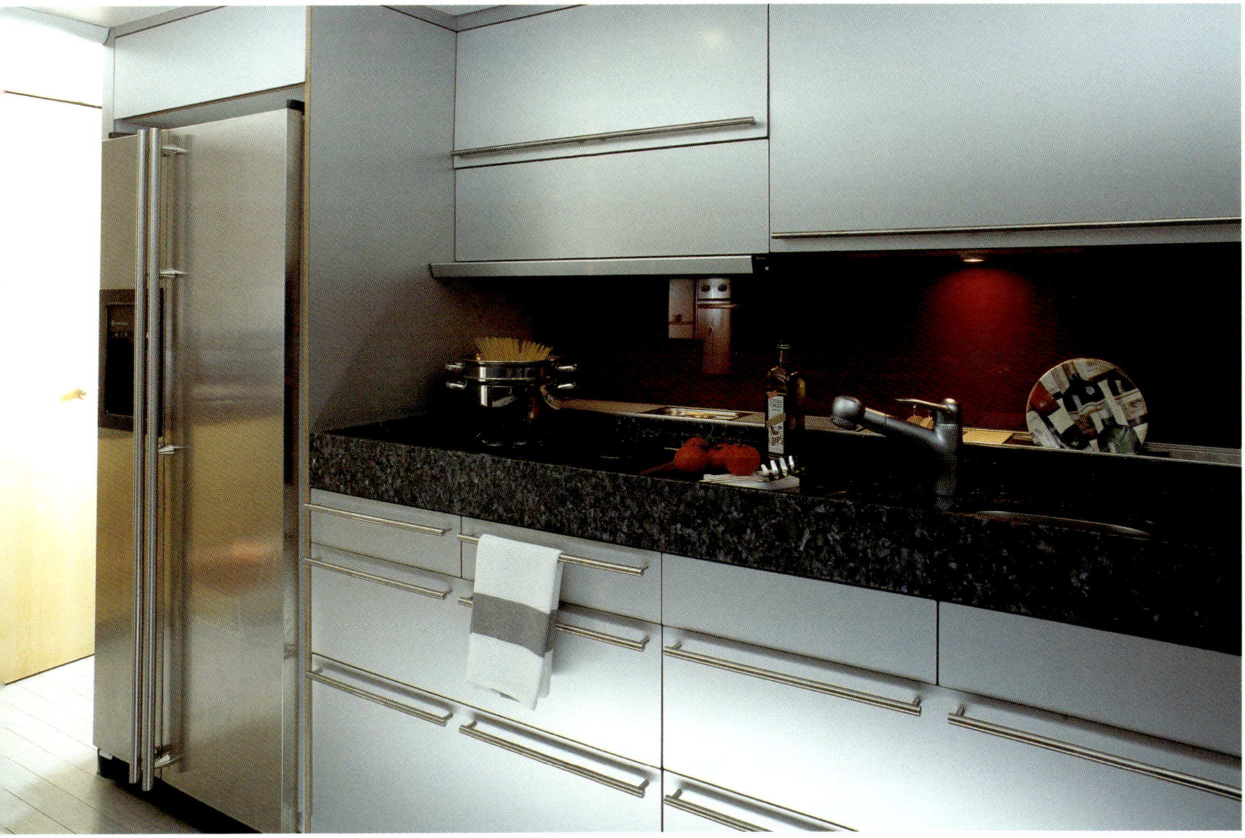

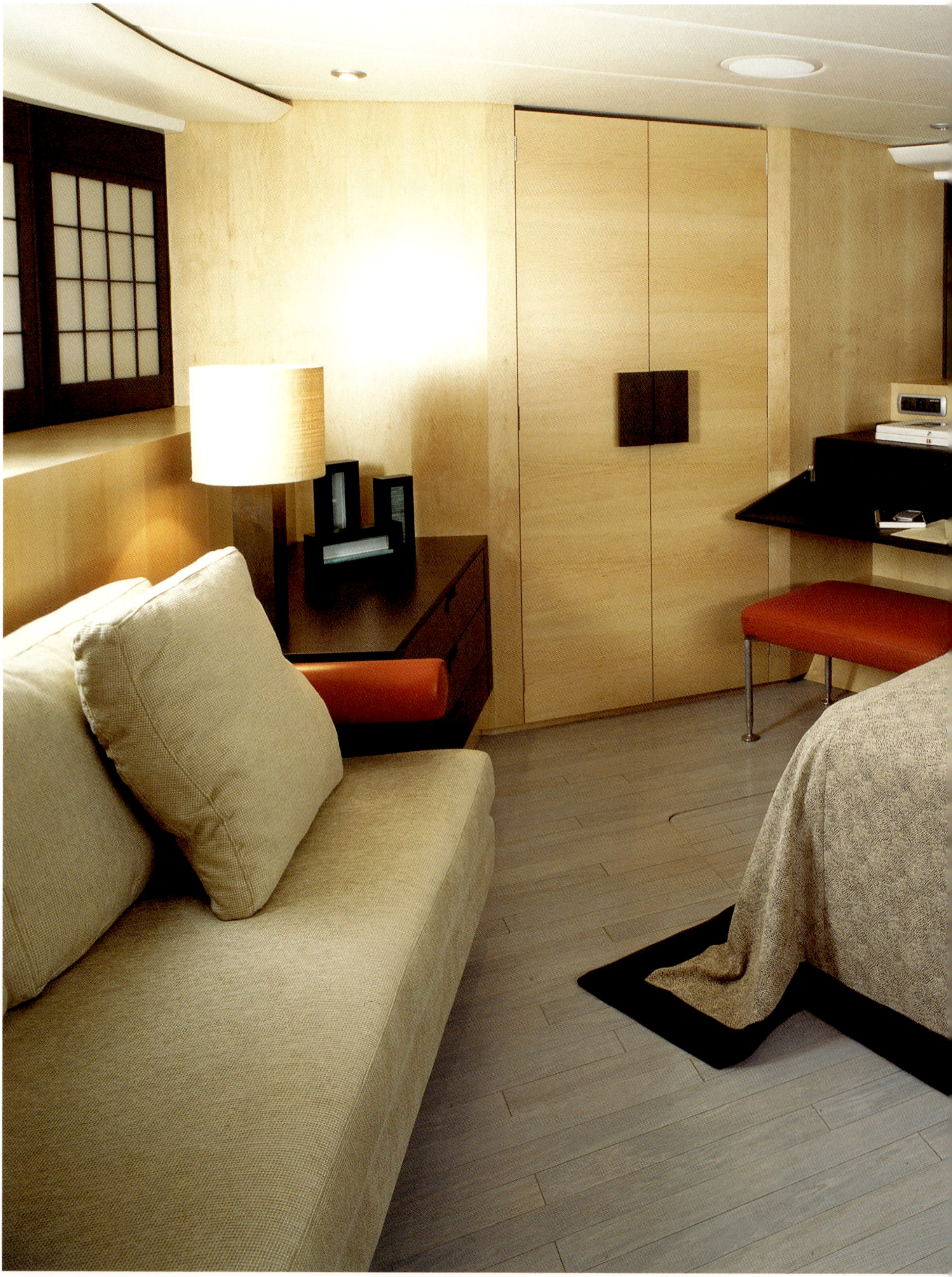

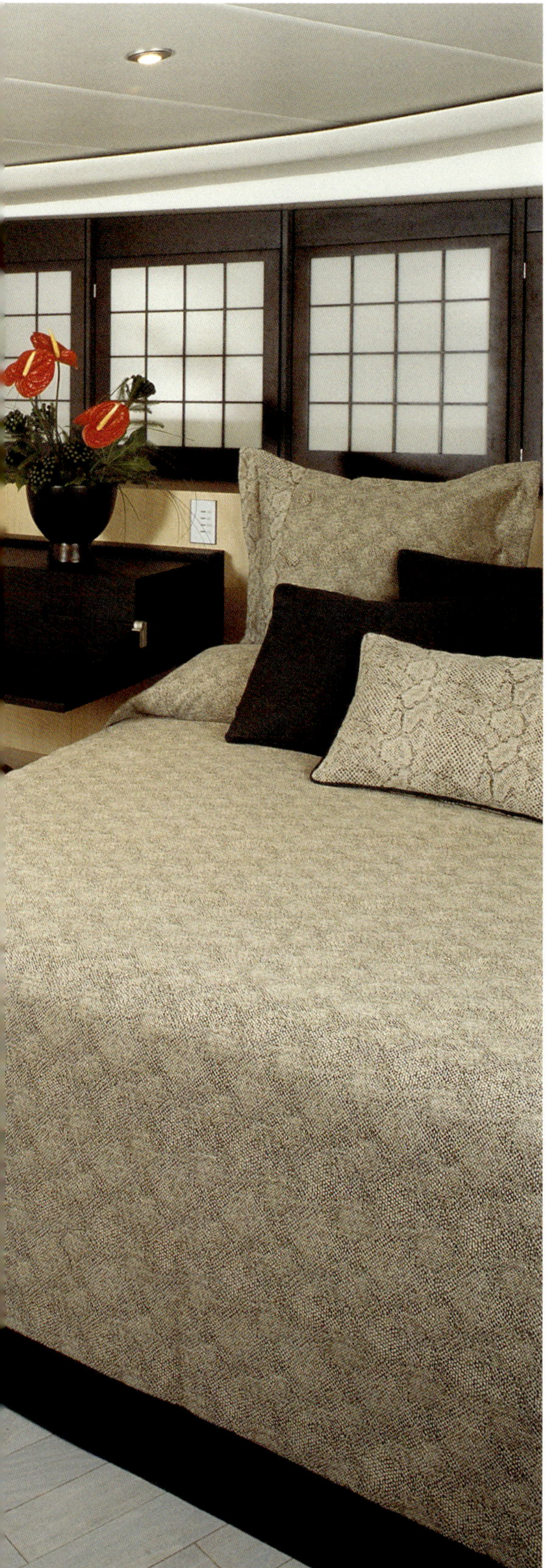

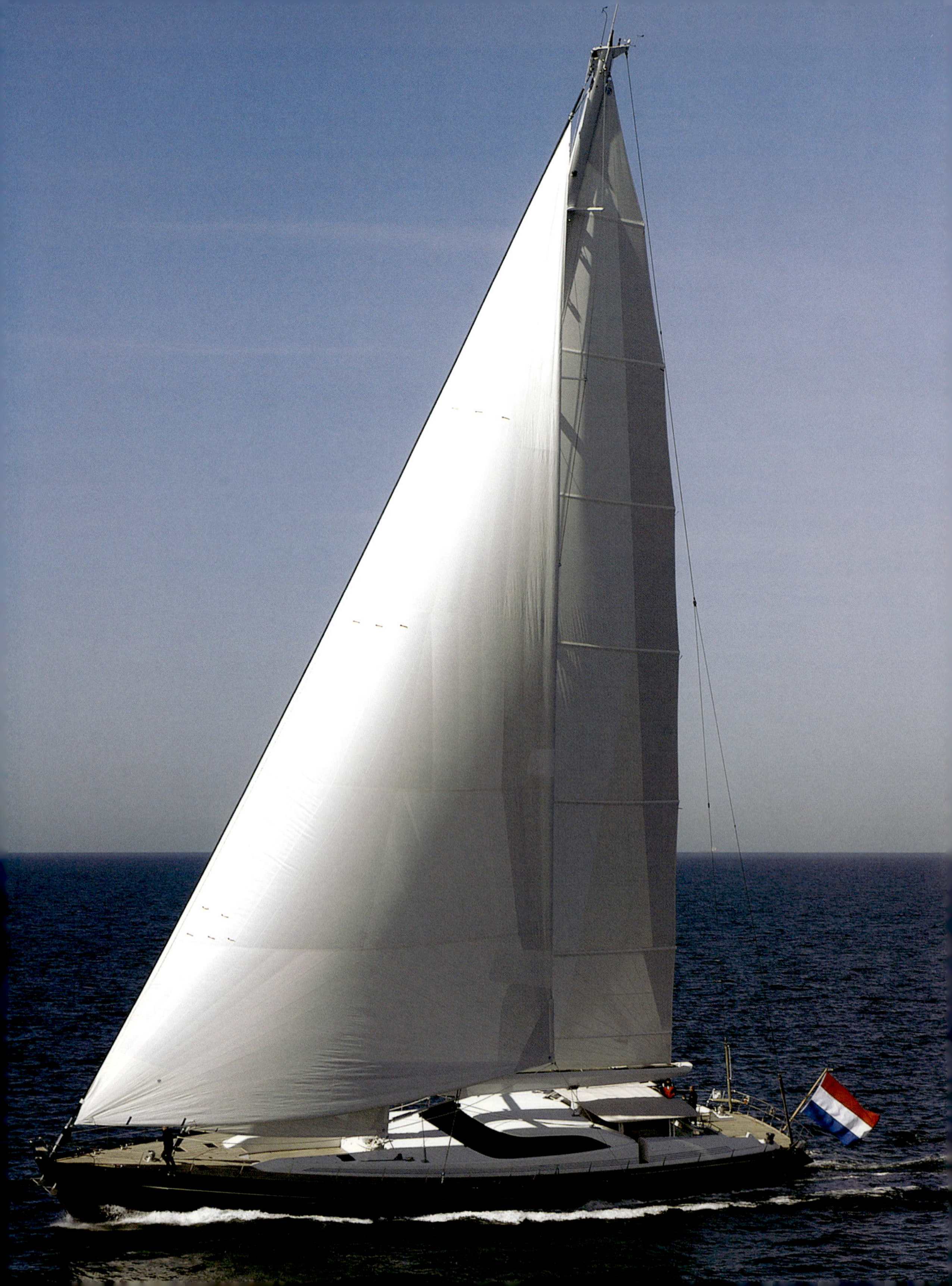

DICK YOUNG DESIGNS
GIMLÄ | 2004
Vitters Shipyard

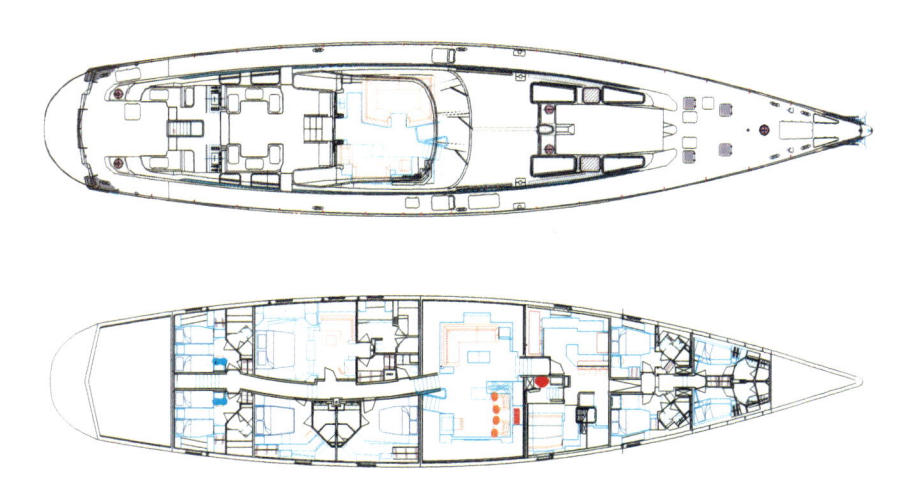

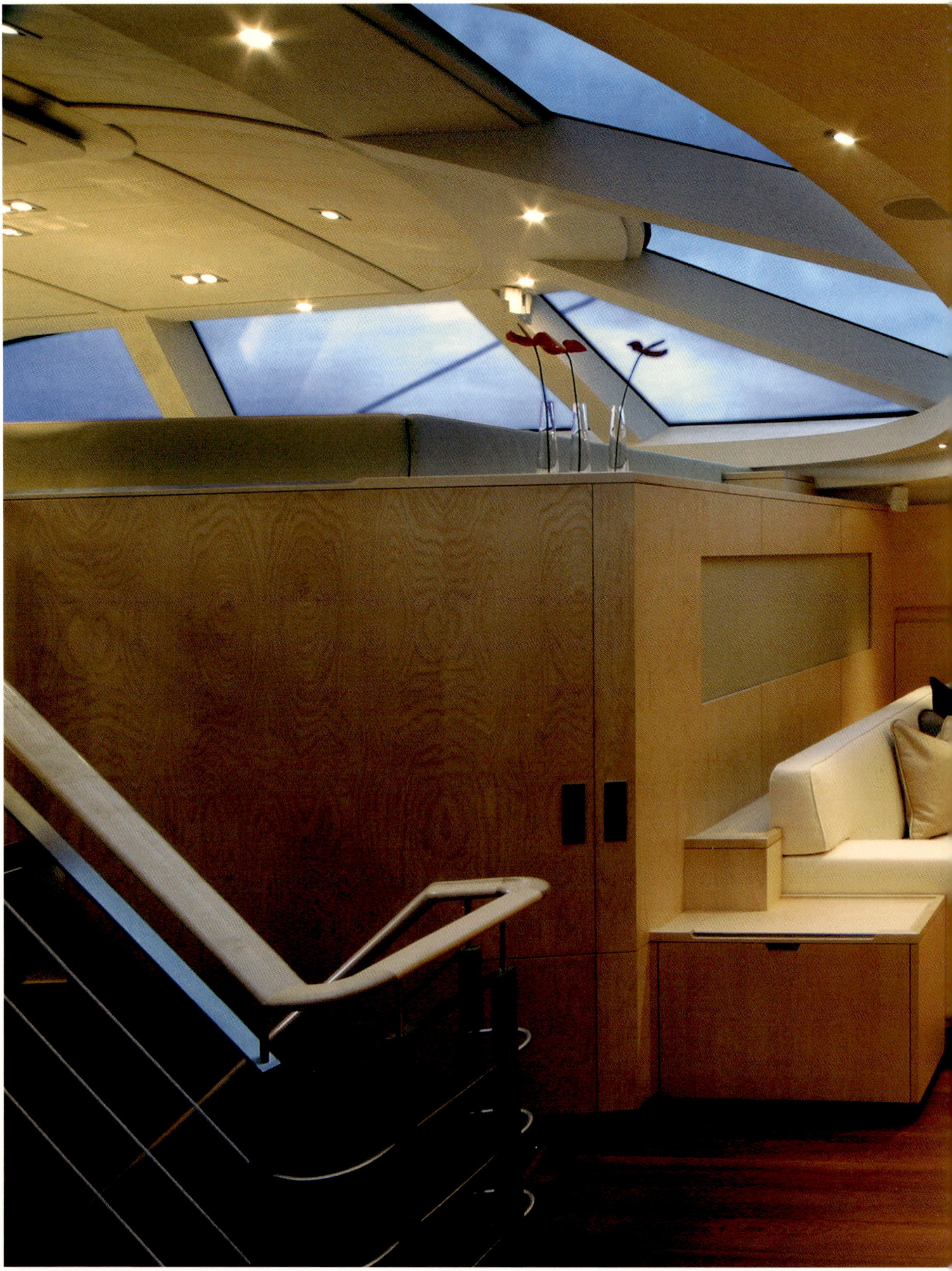

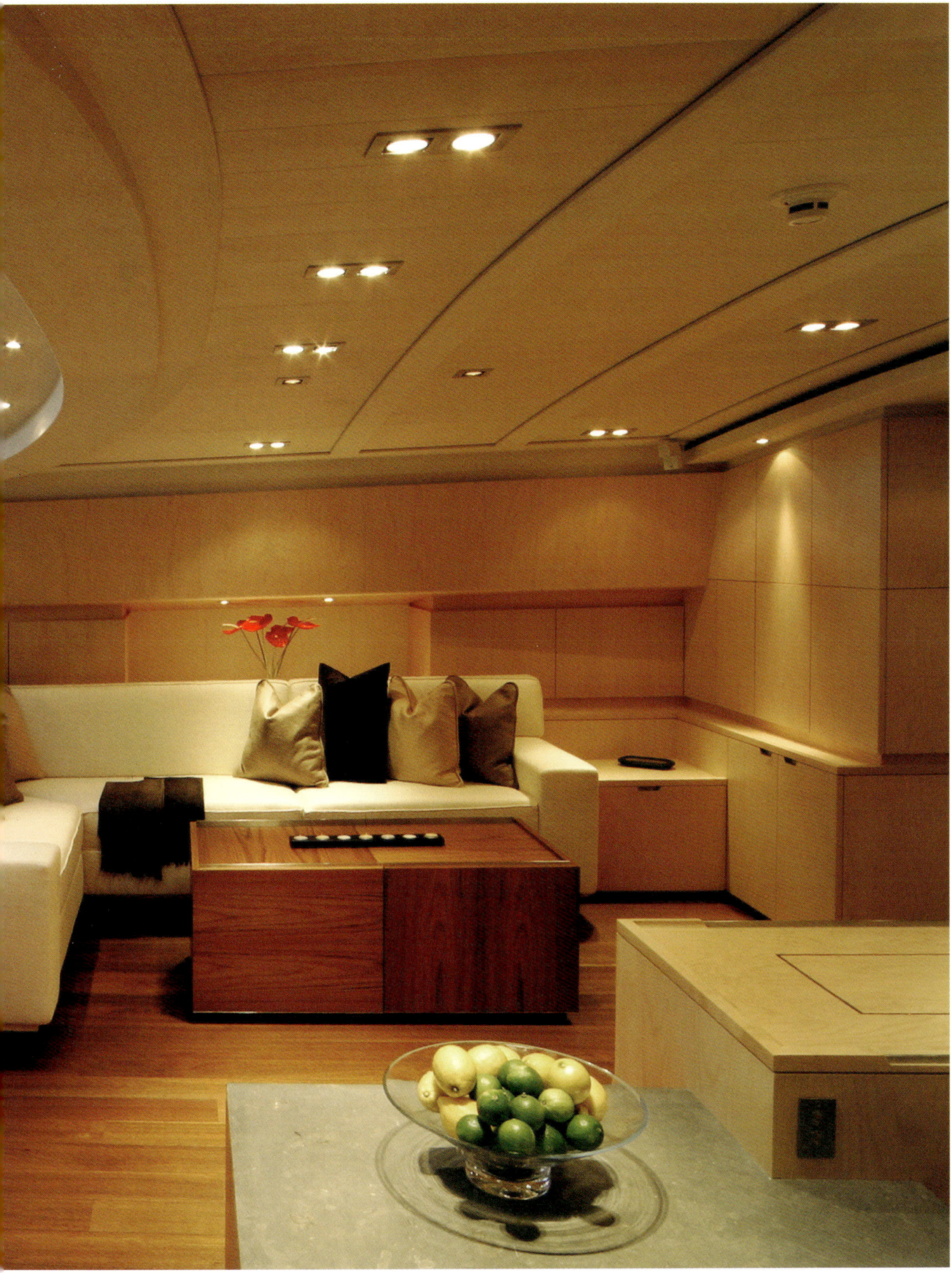

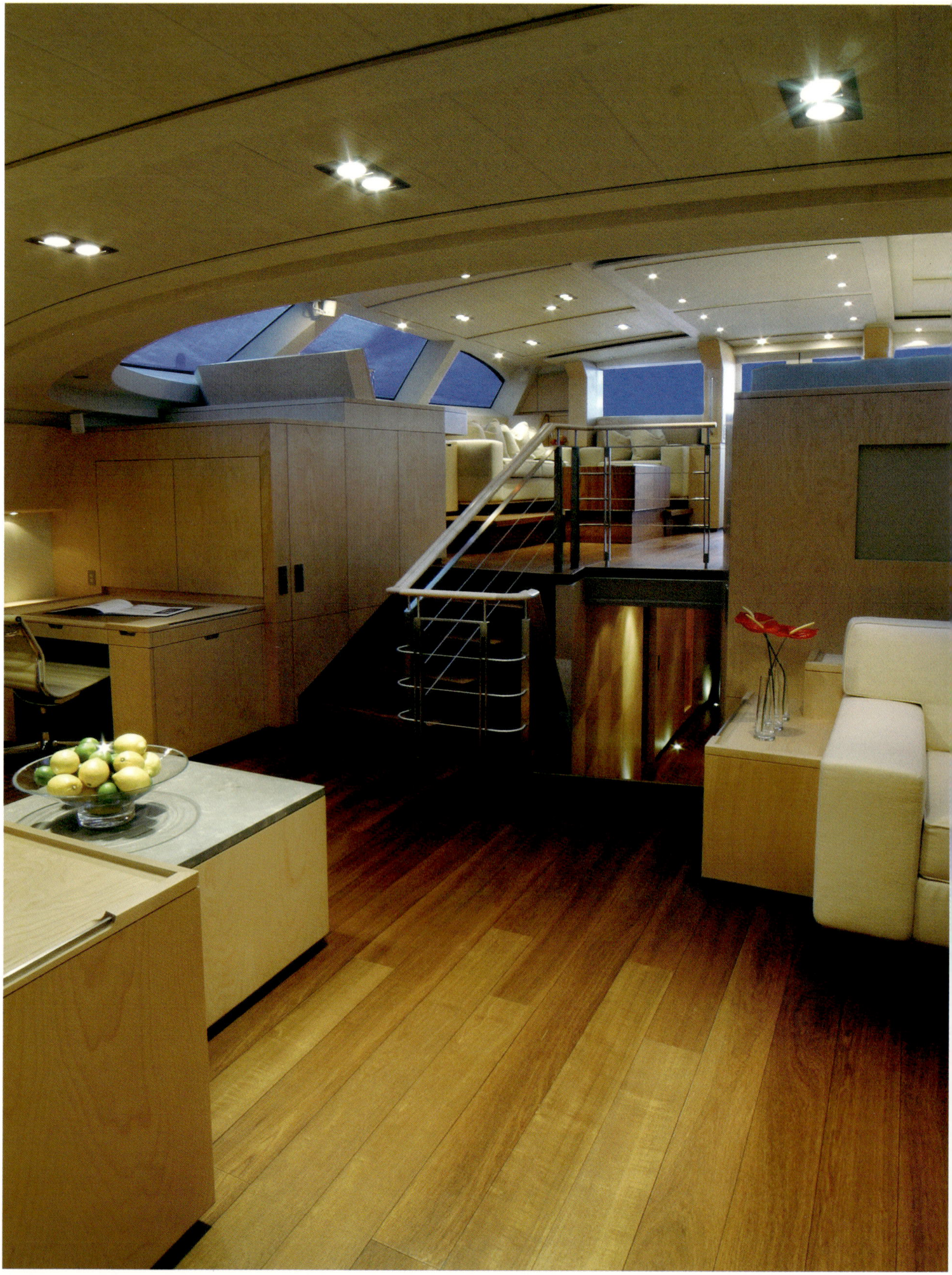

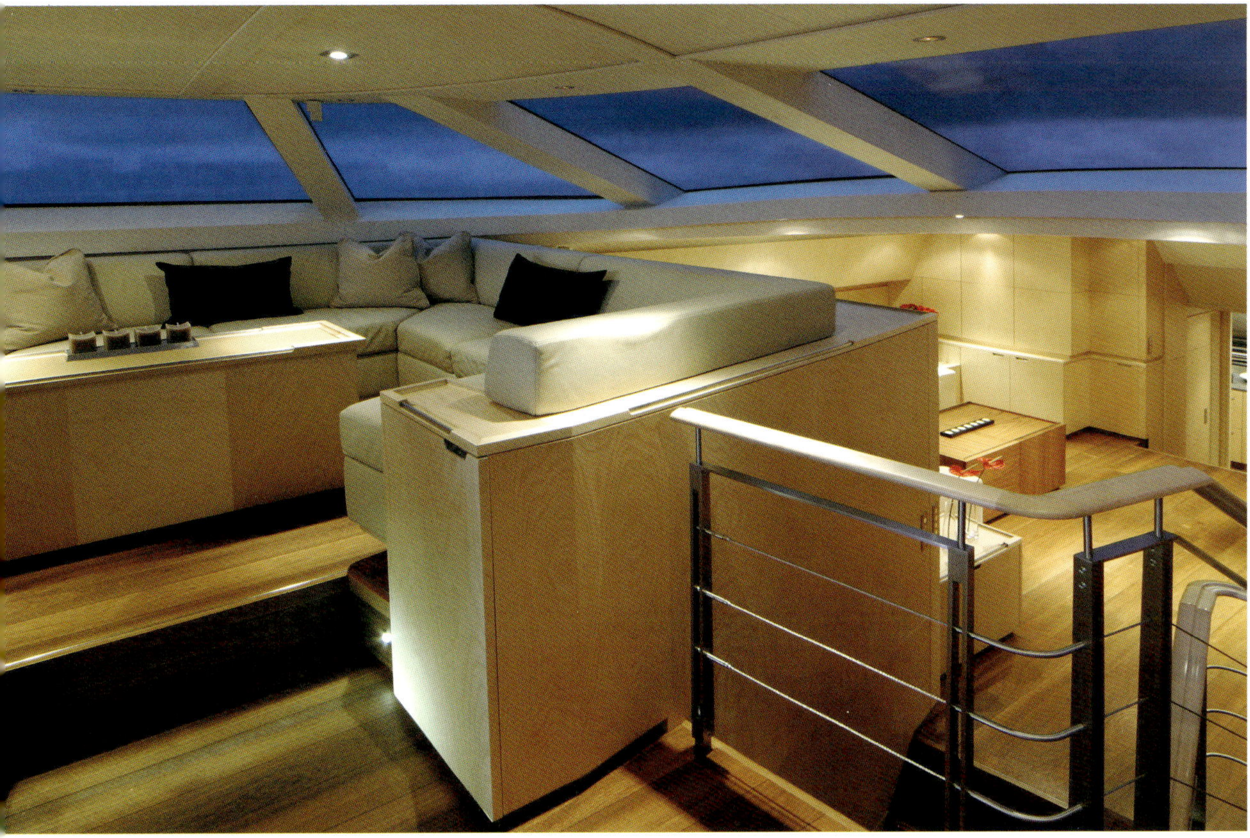

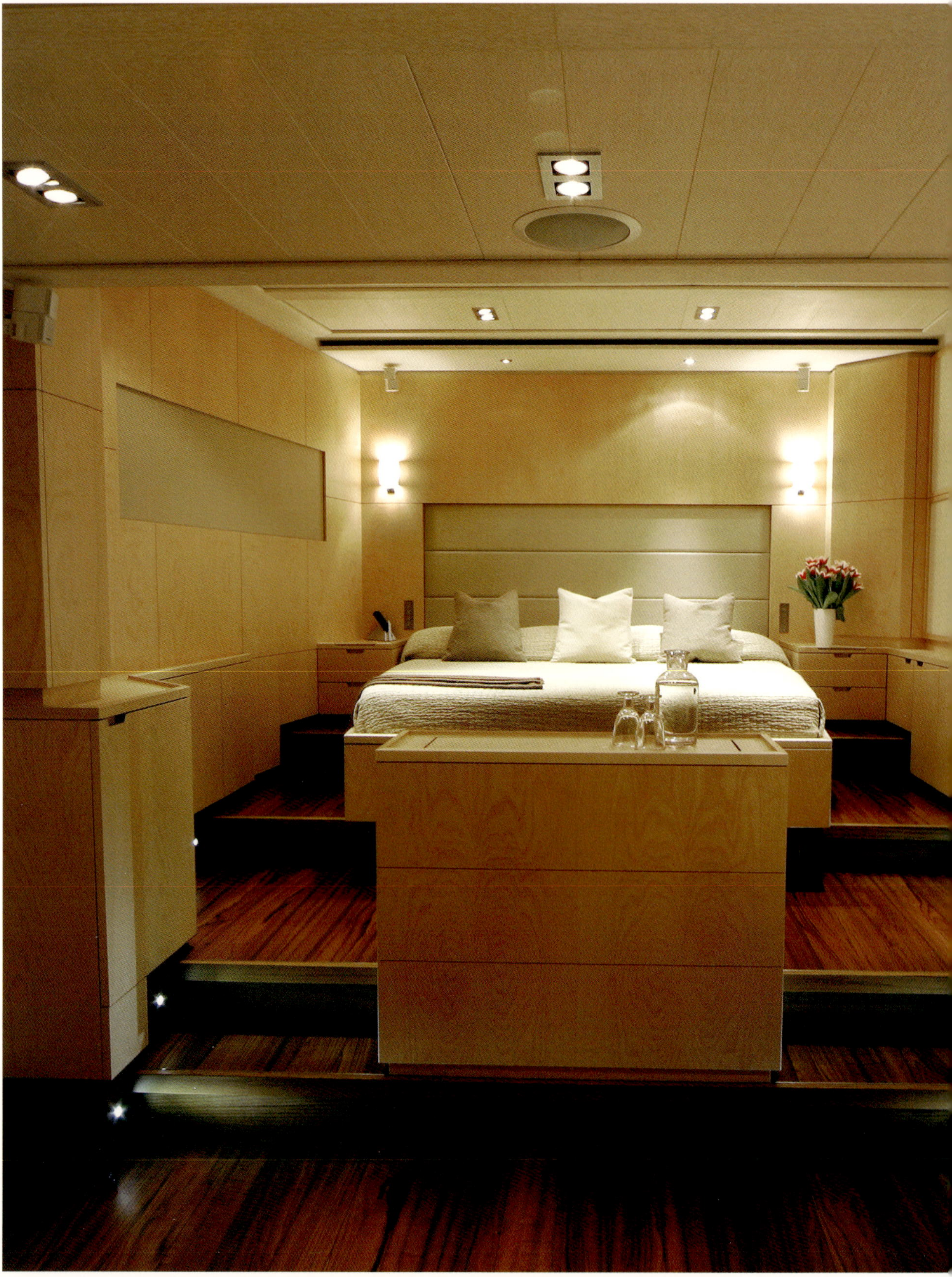

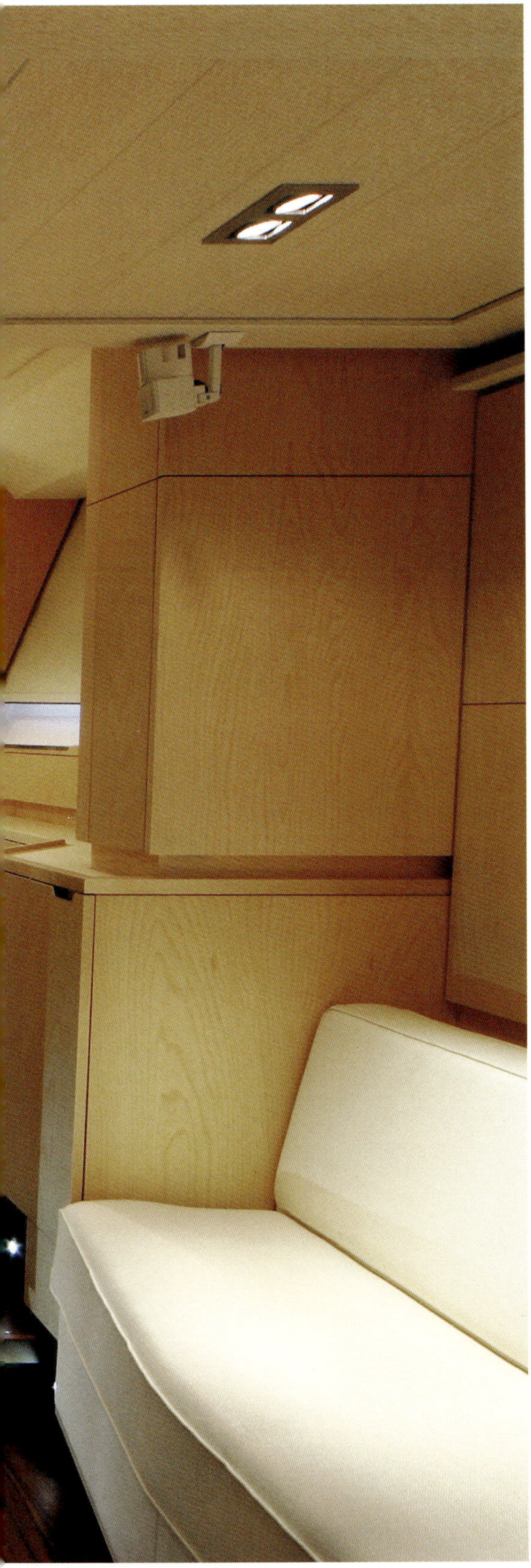

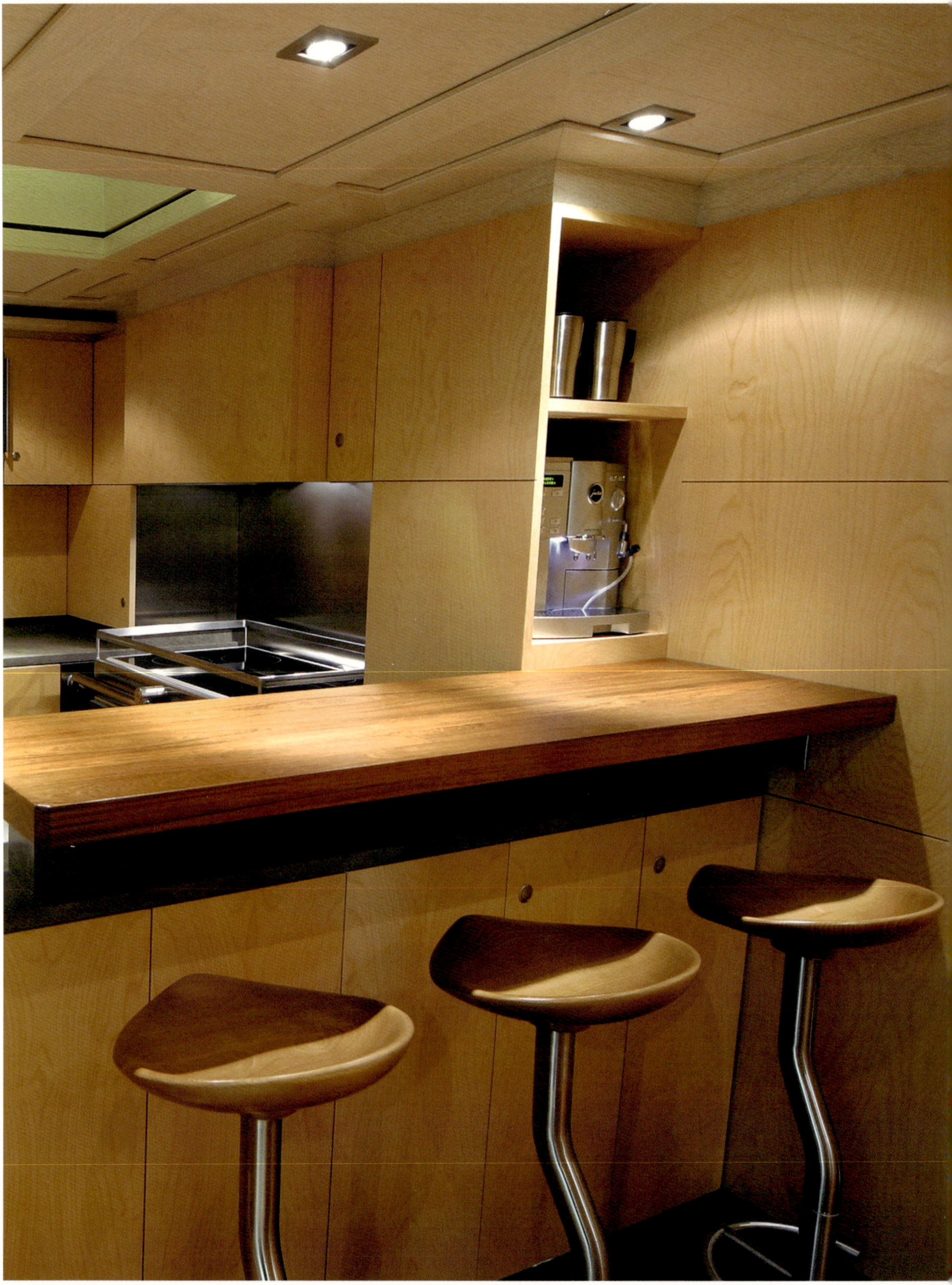

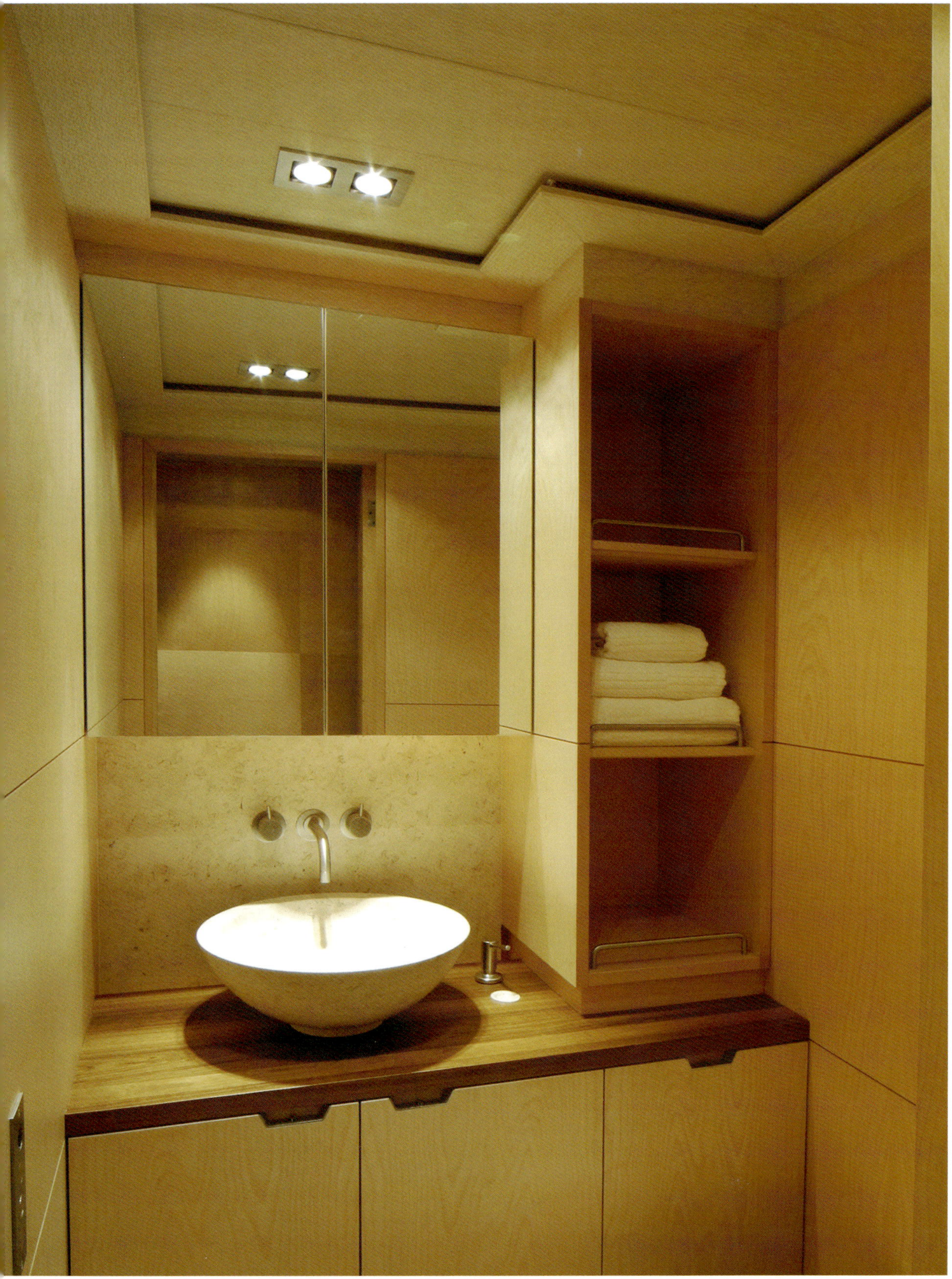

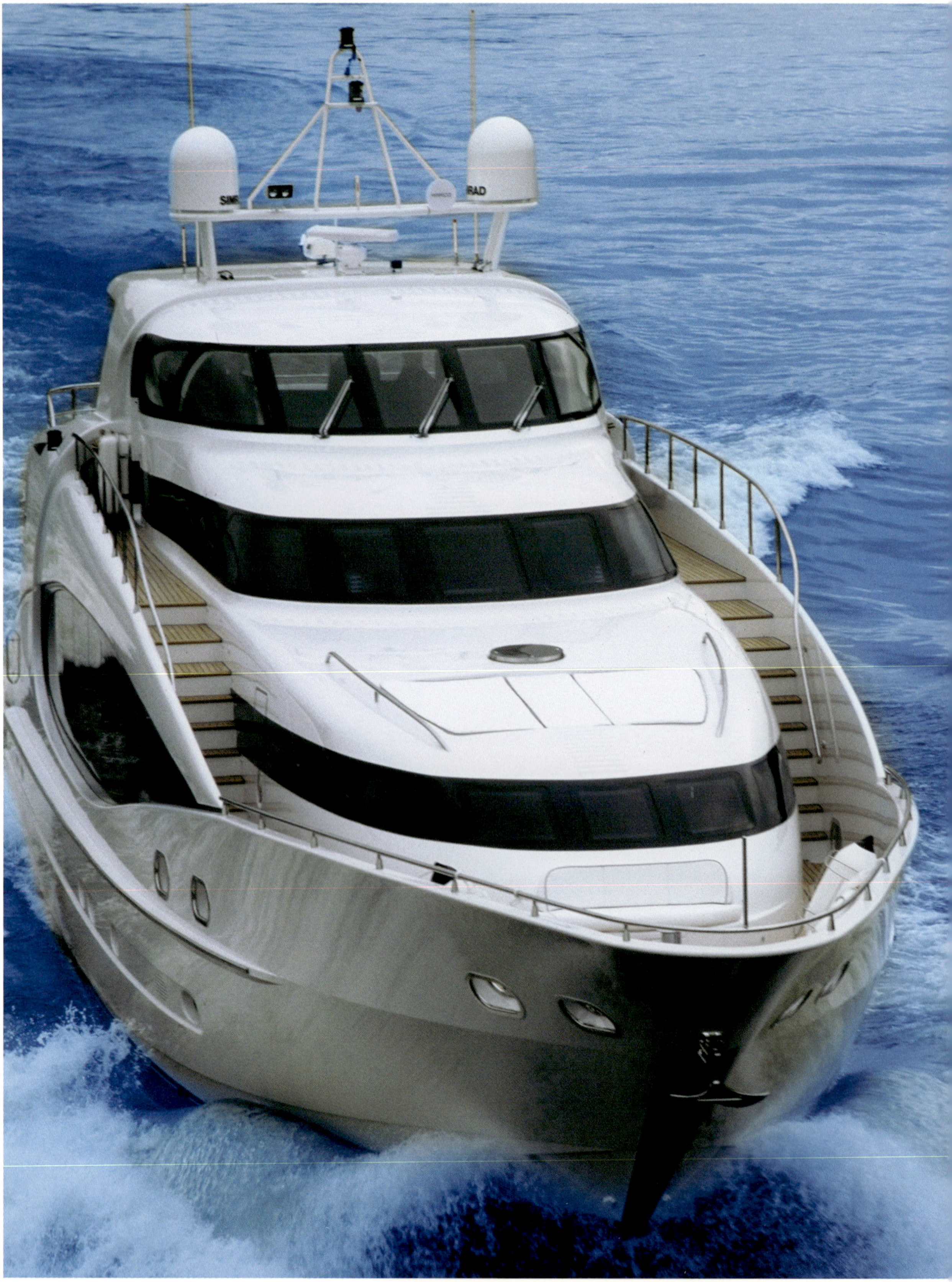

EGG AND DART DESIGN CORPORATION
BARON 102 OCEAN OF LOVE | 2004
KaiserWerft
Egg and Dart Design Corporation

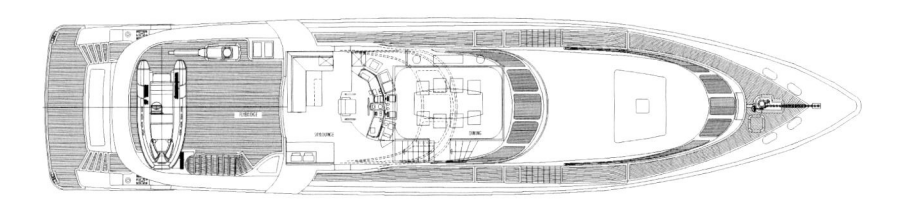

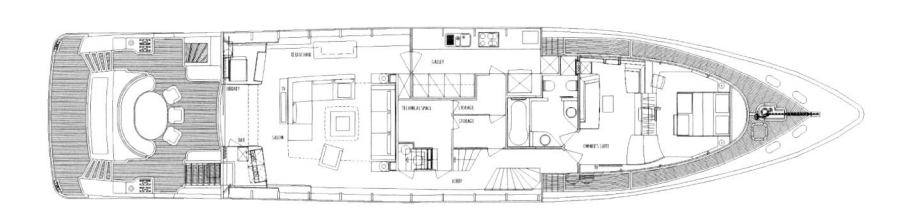

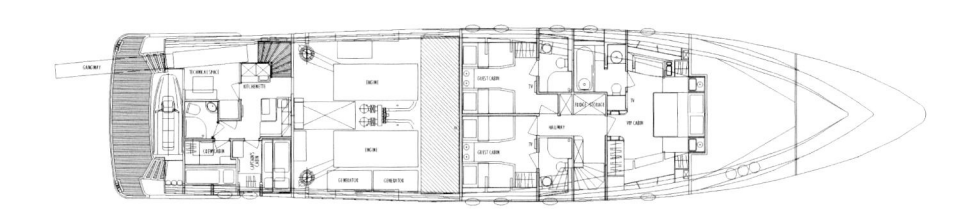

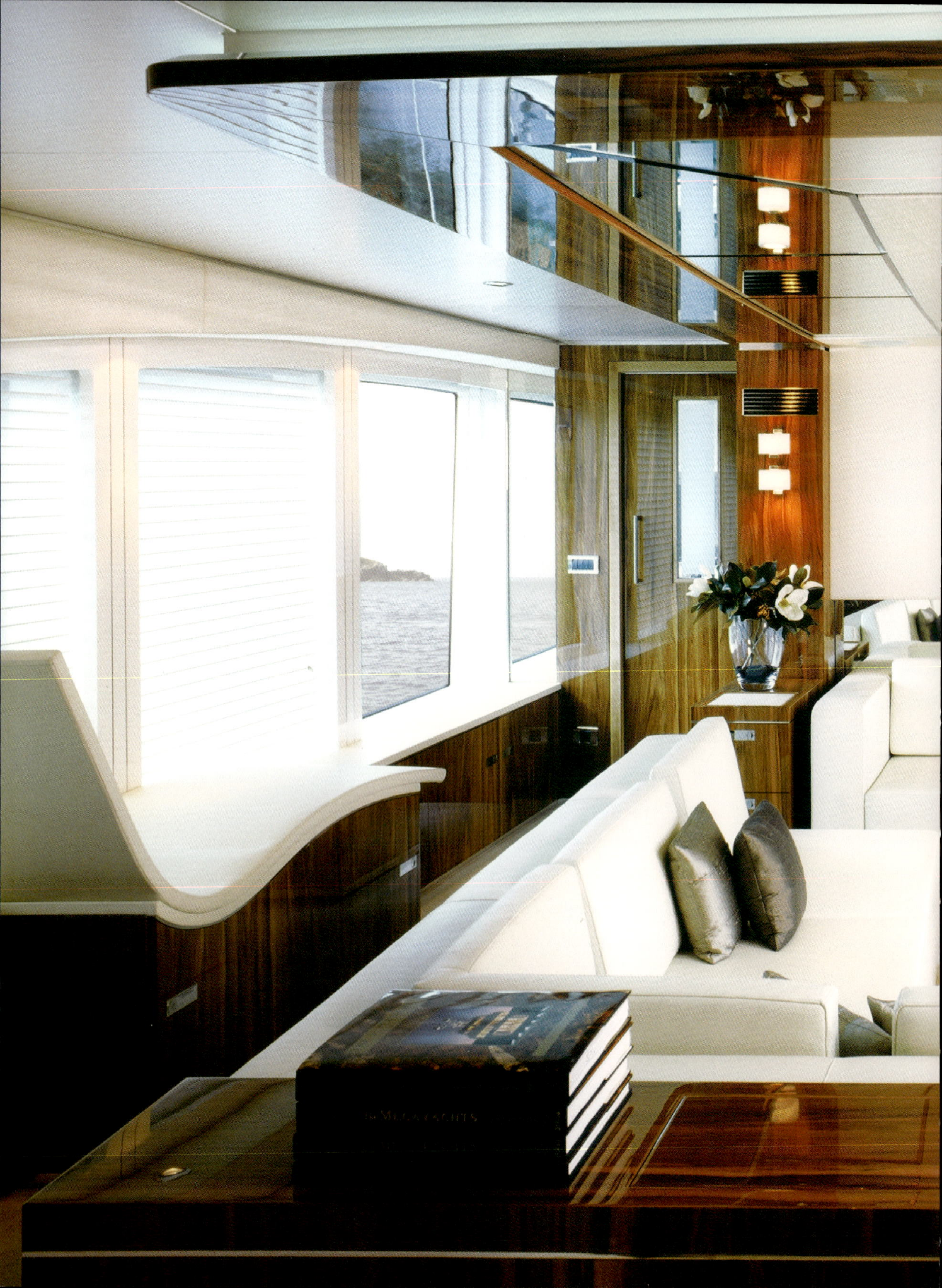

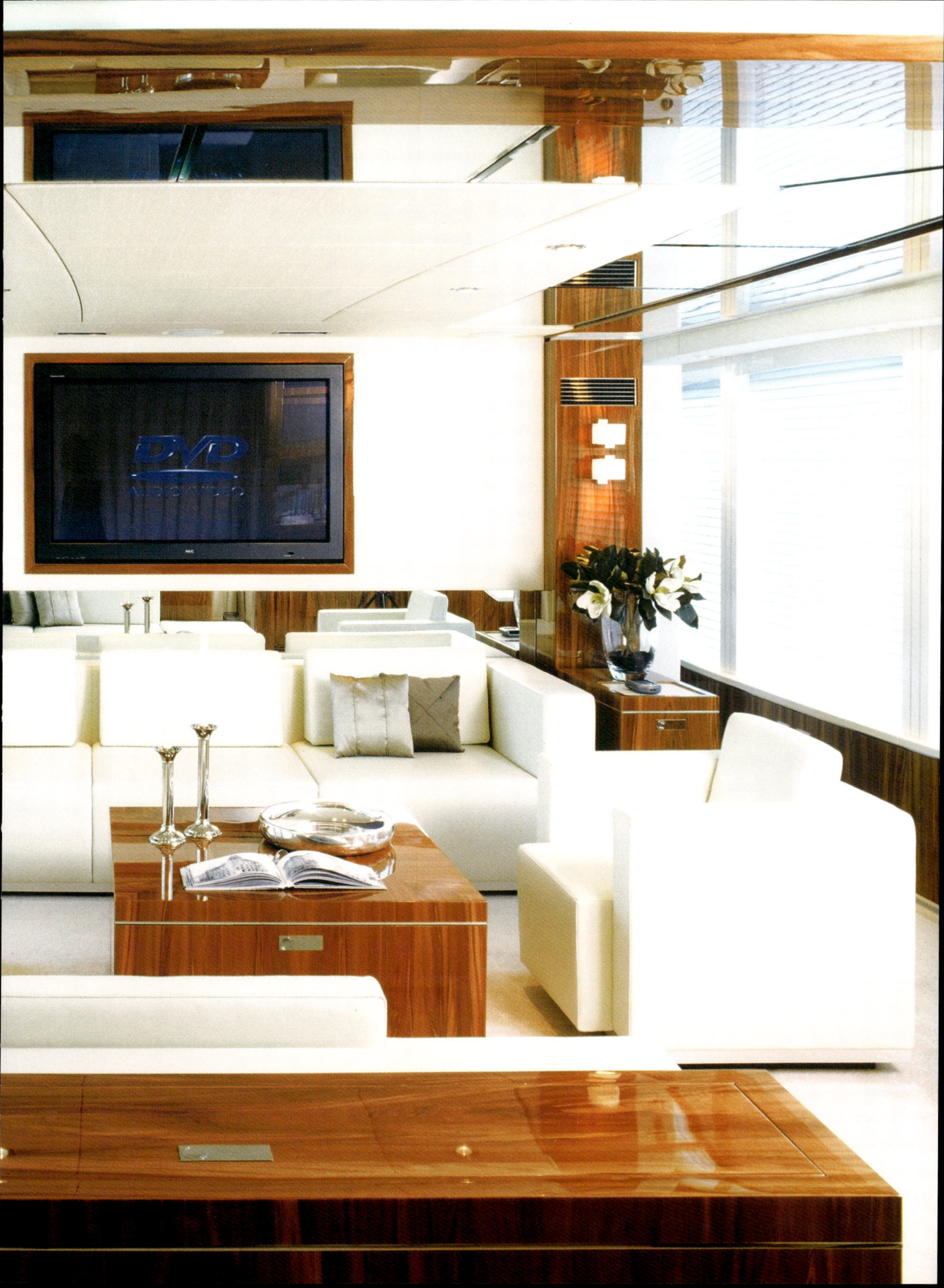
DVD

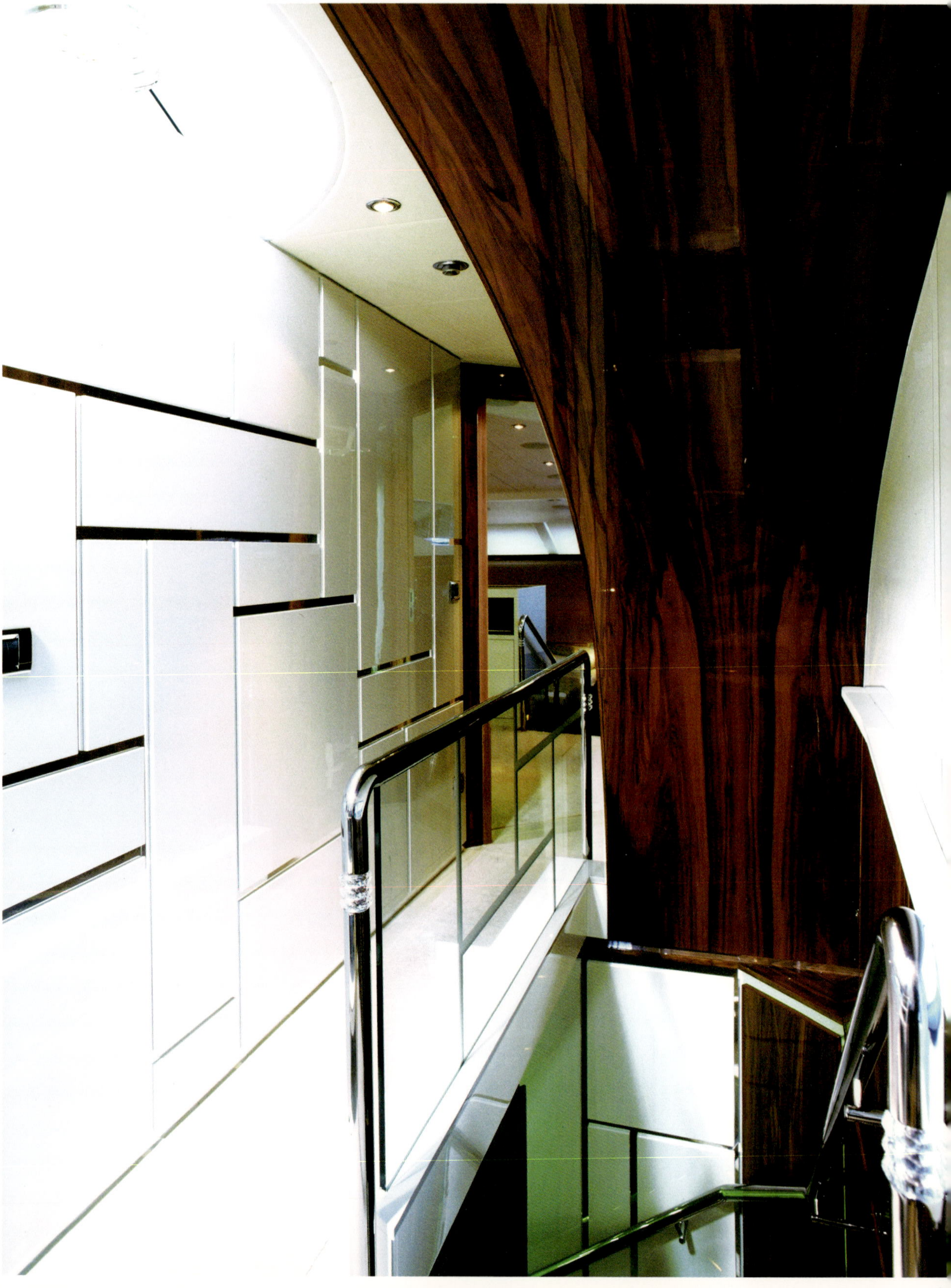

75

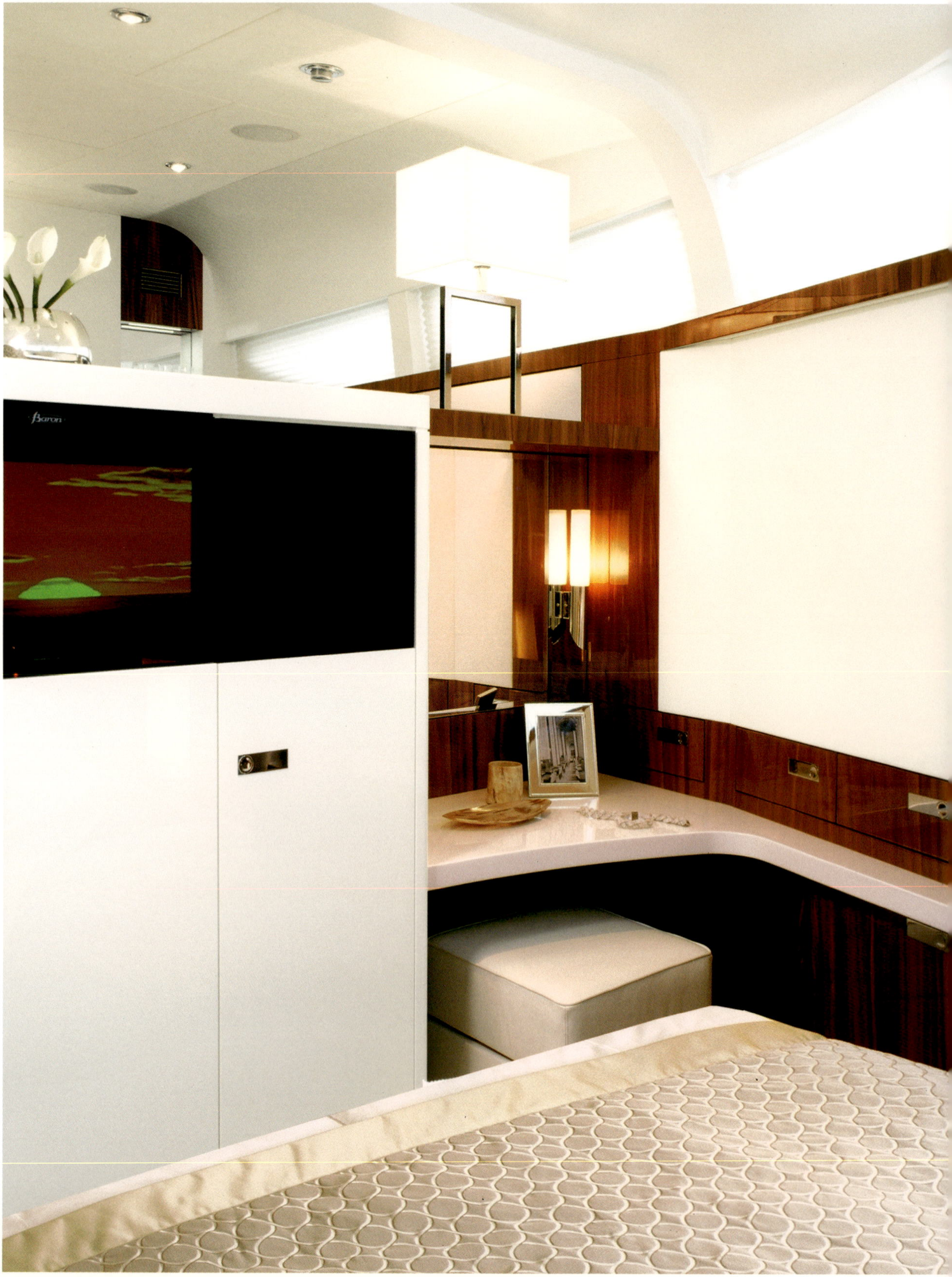
Baron

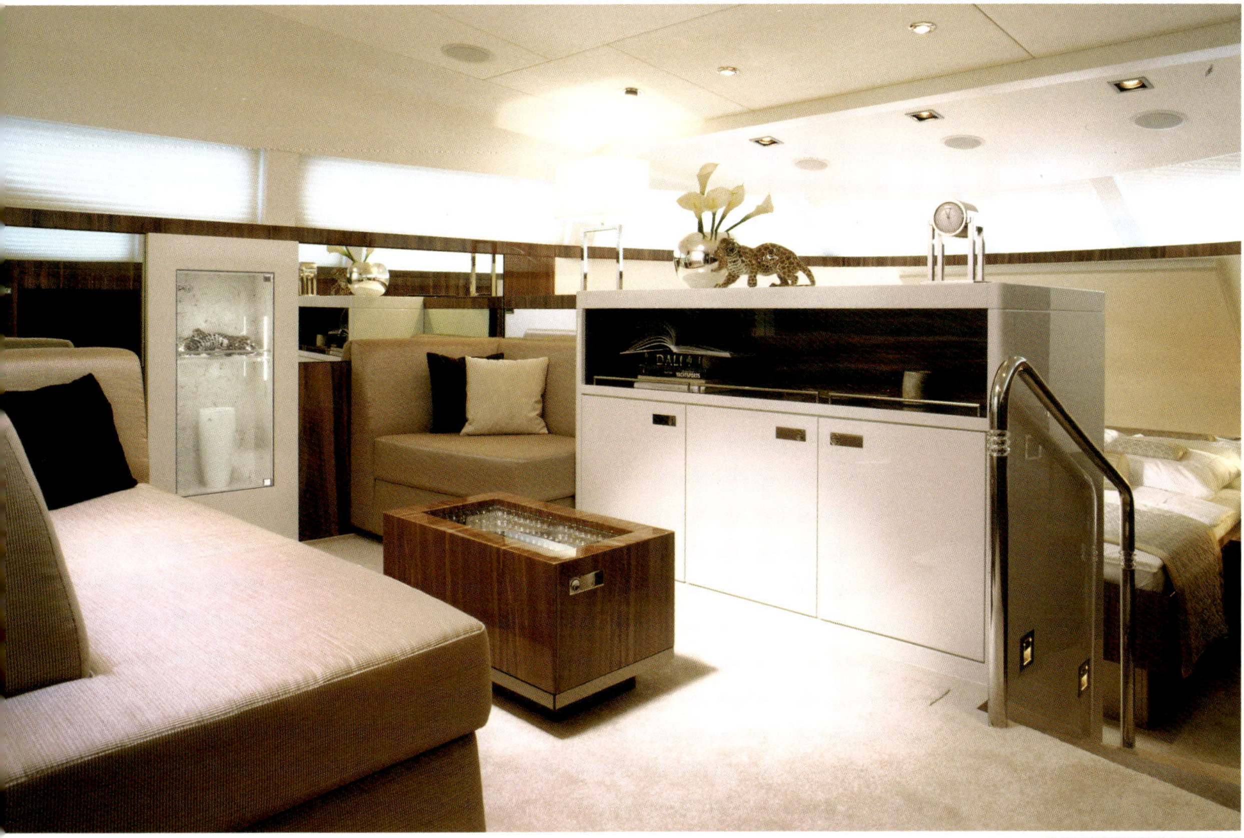

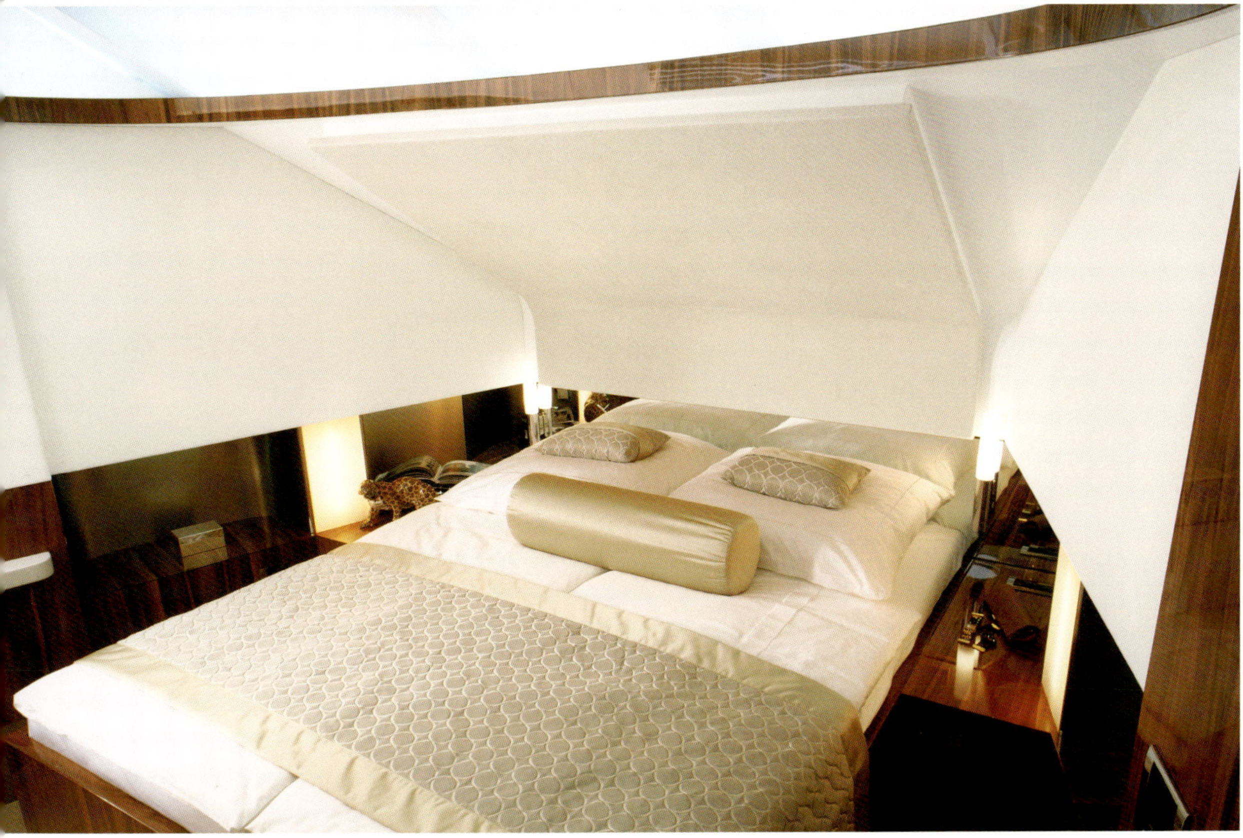

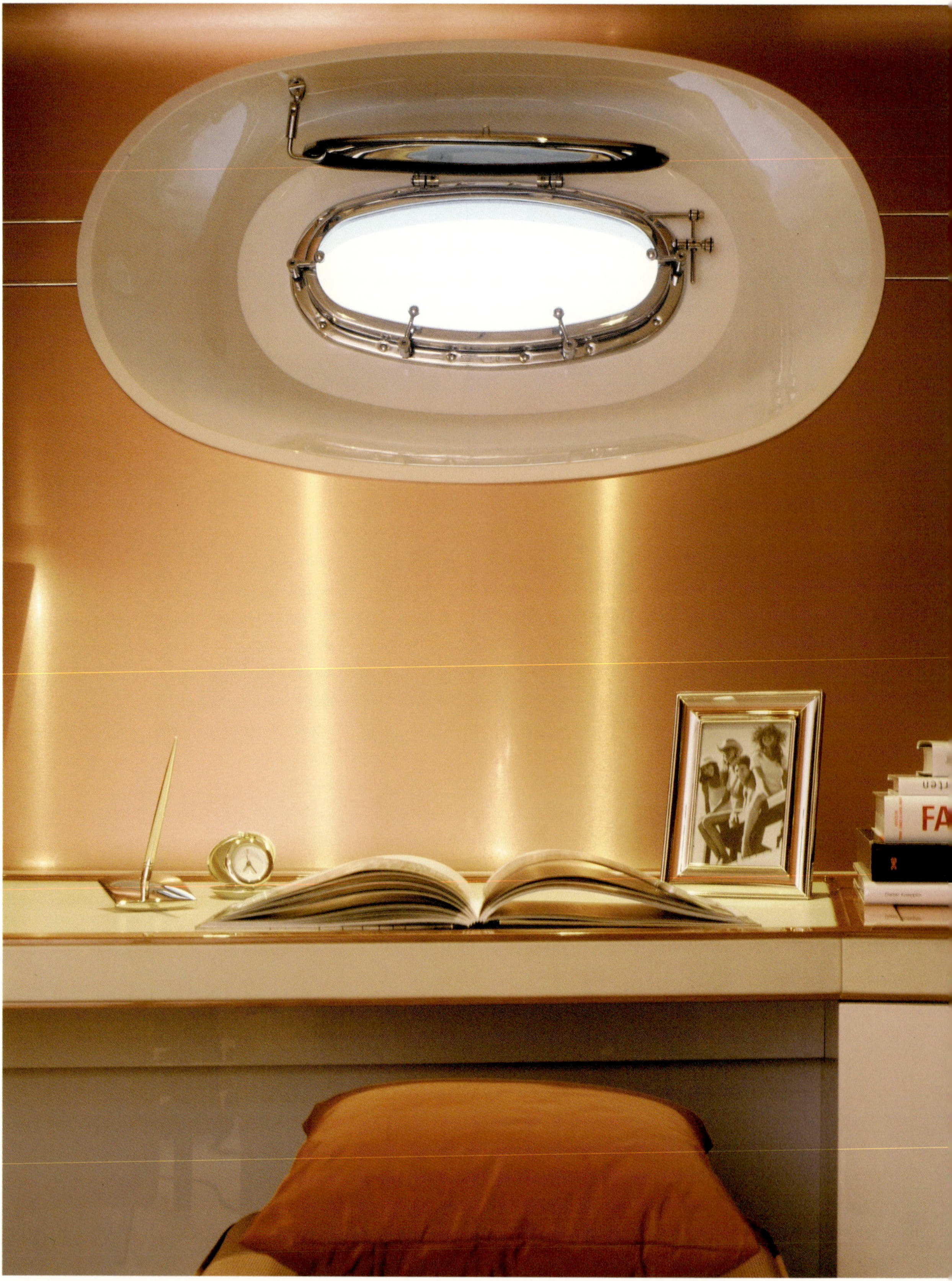

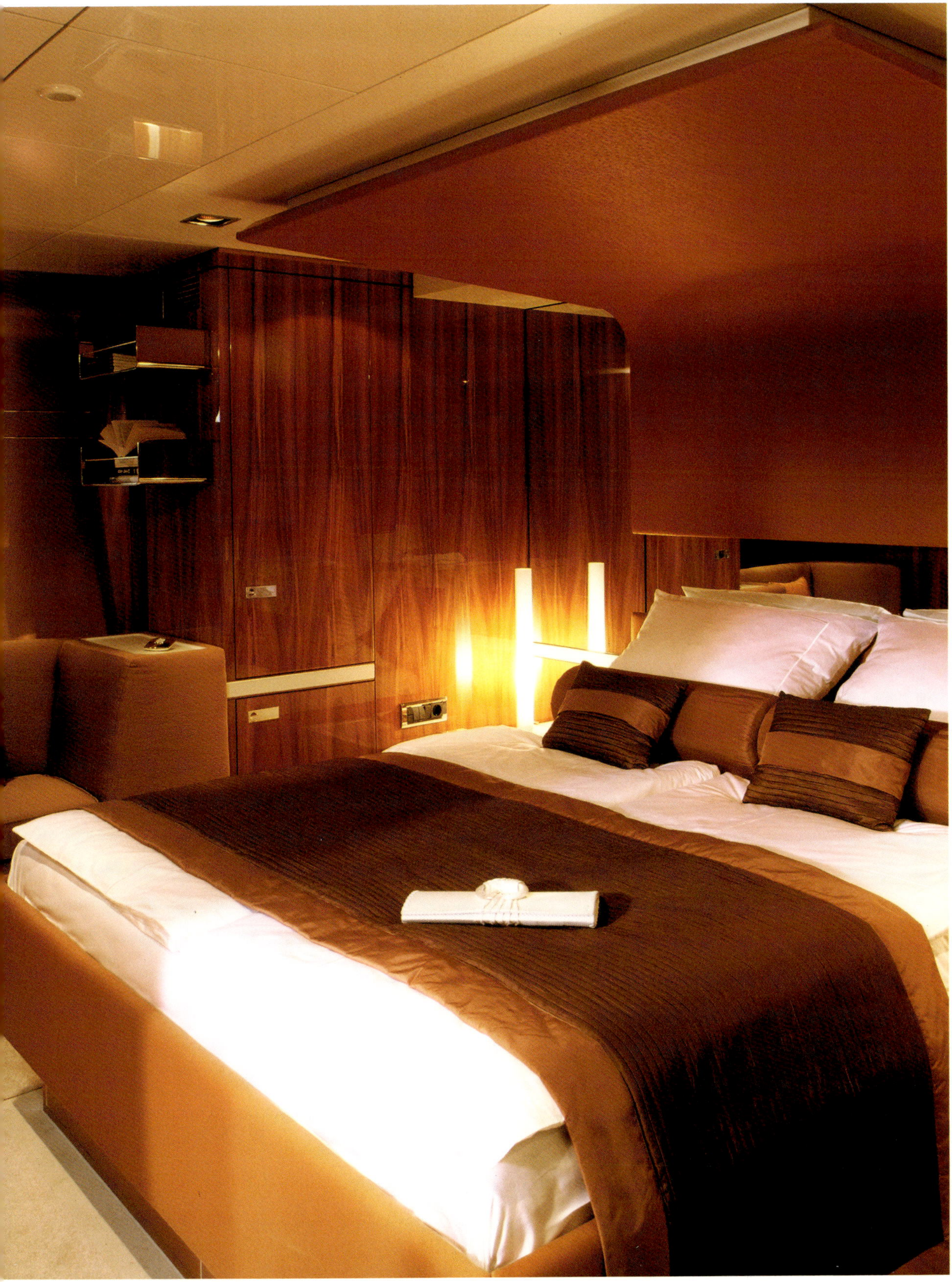

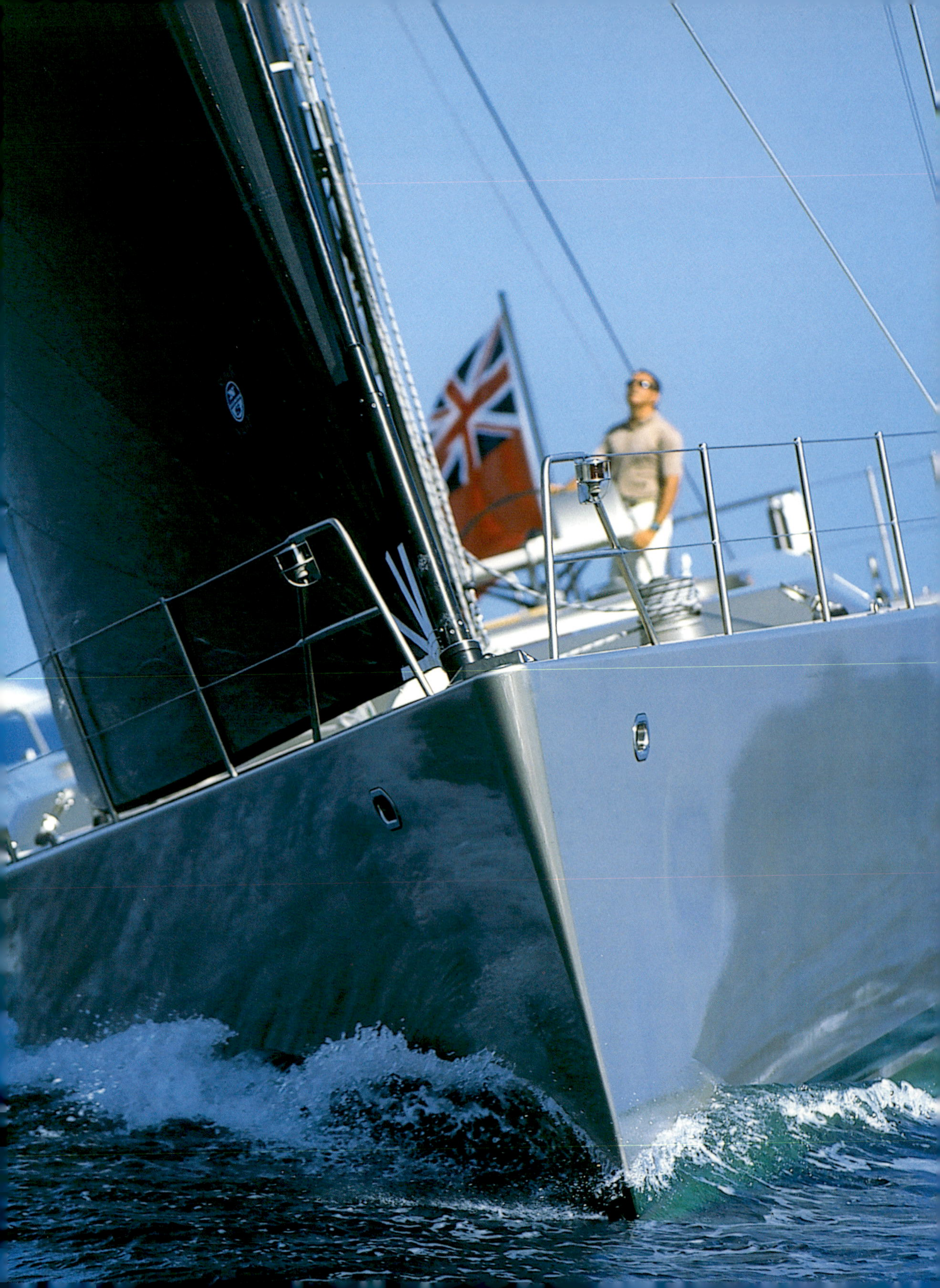

FOSTER & PARTNER, GERMAN FRERS, WALLY
DARK SHADOW | 2002
Wally

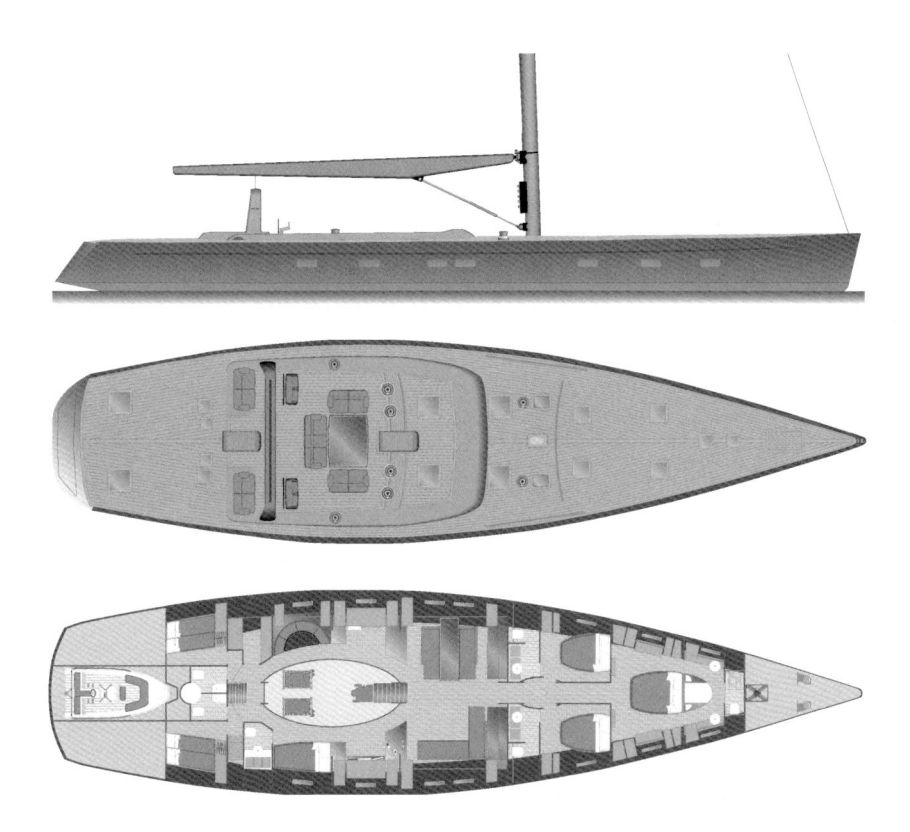

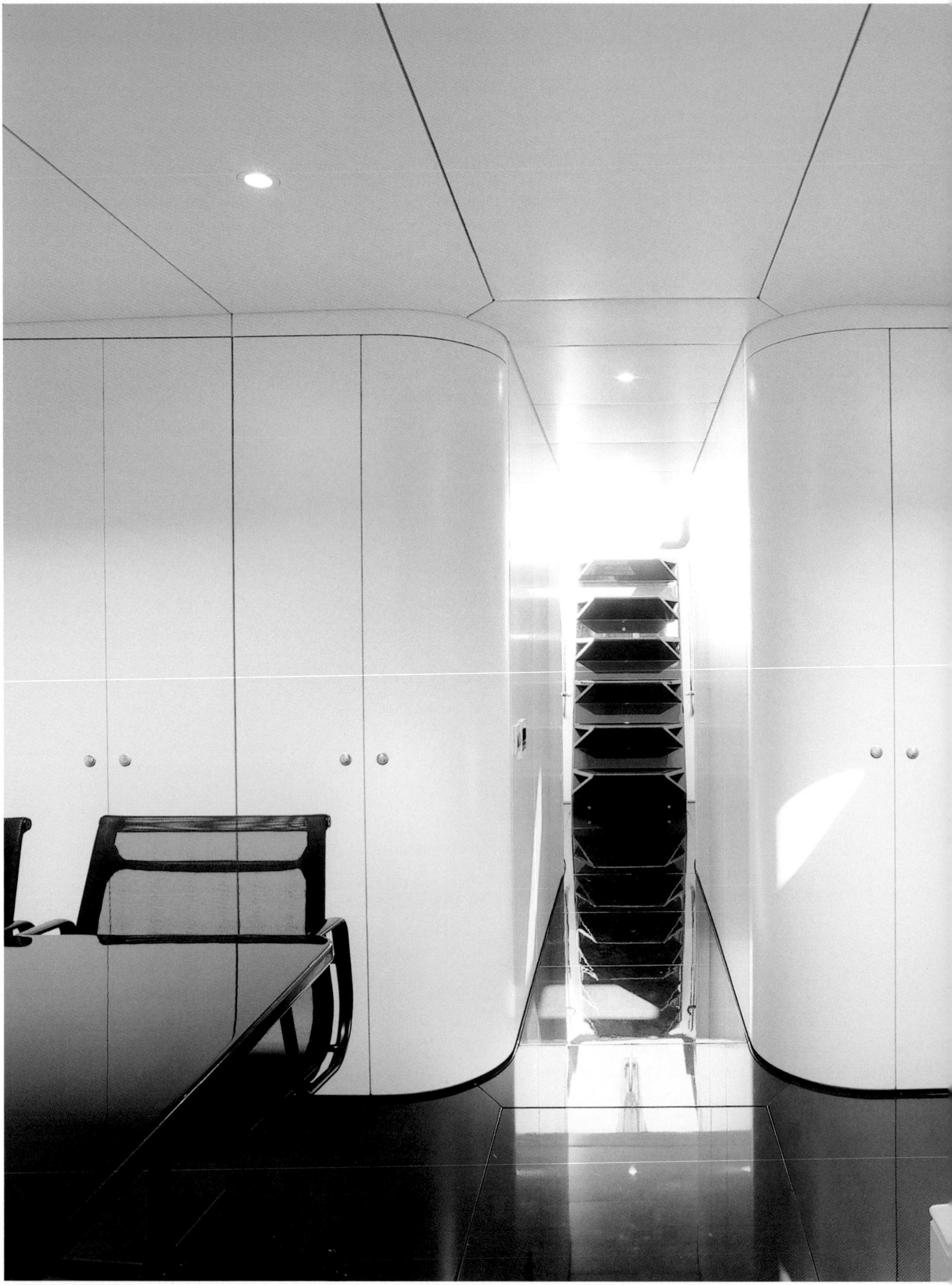

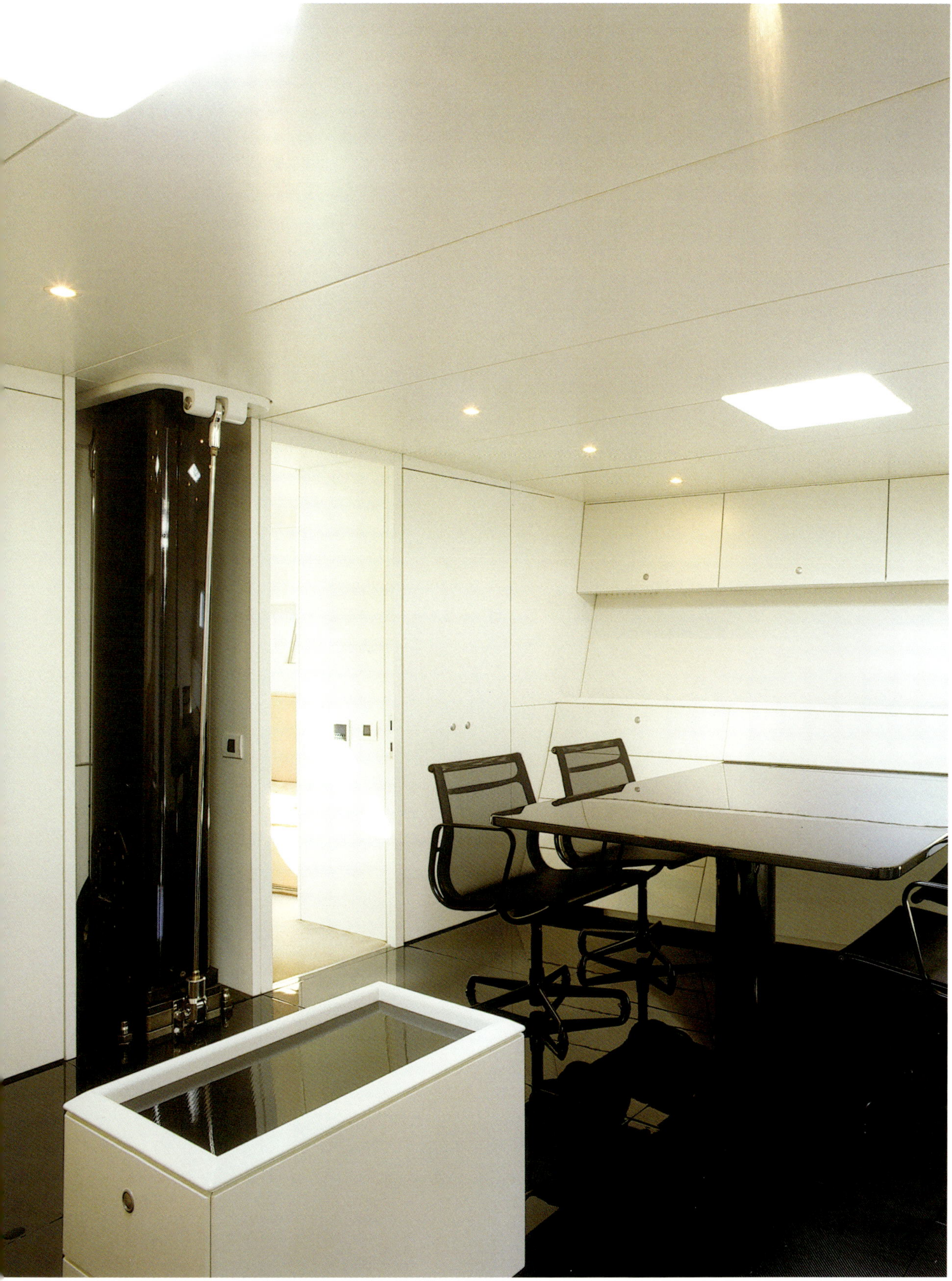

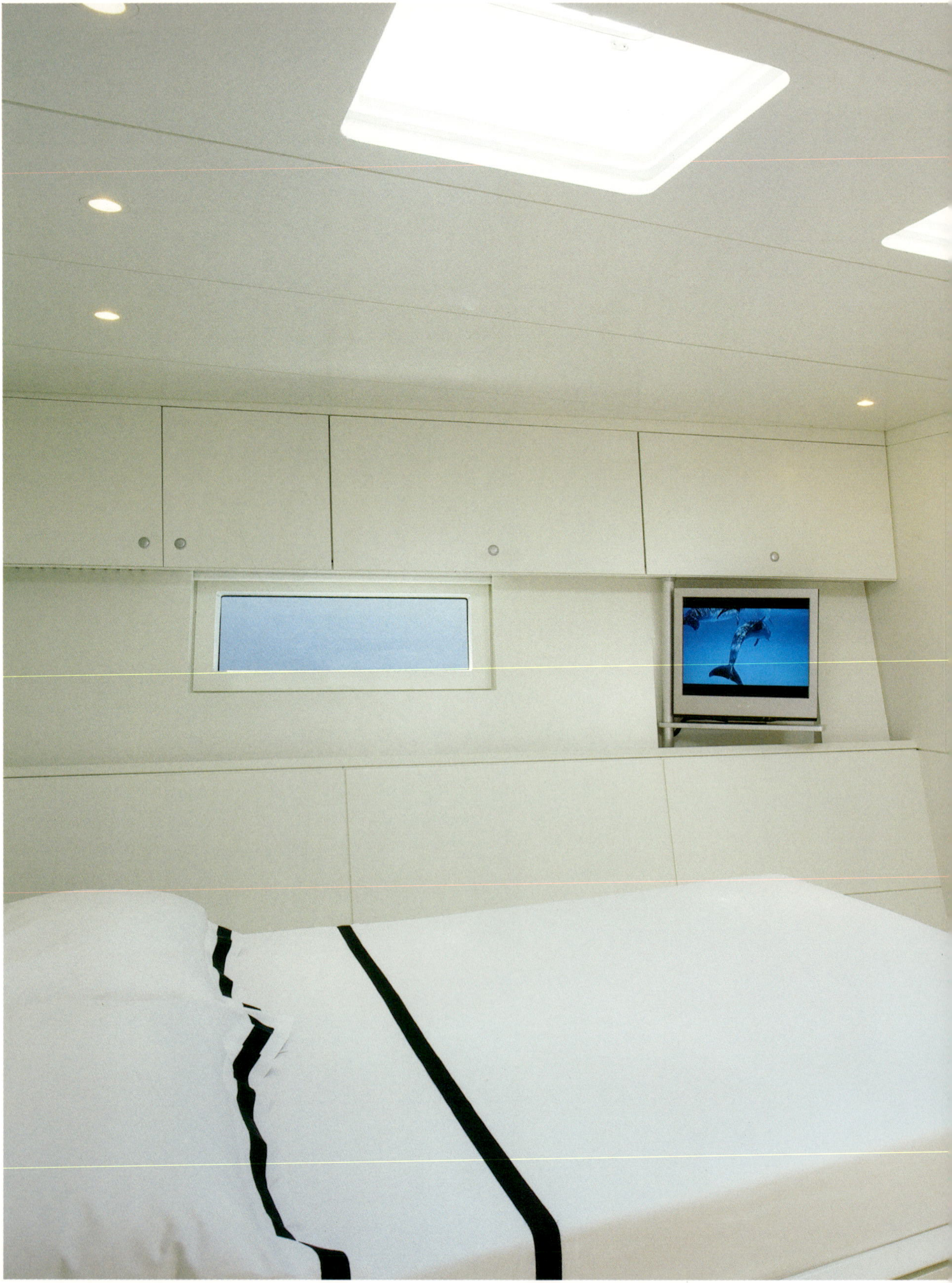

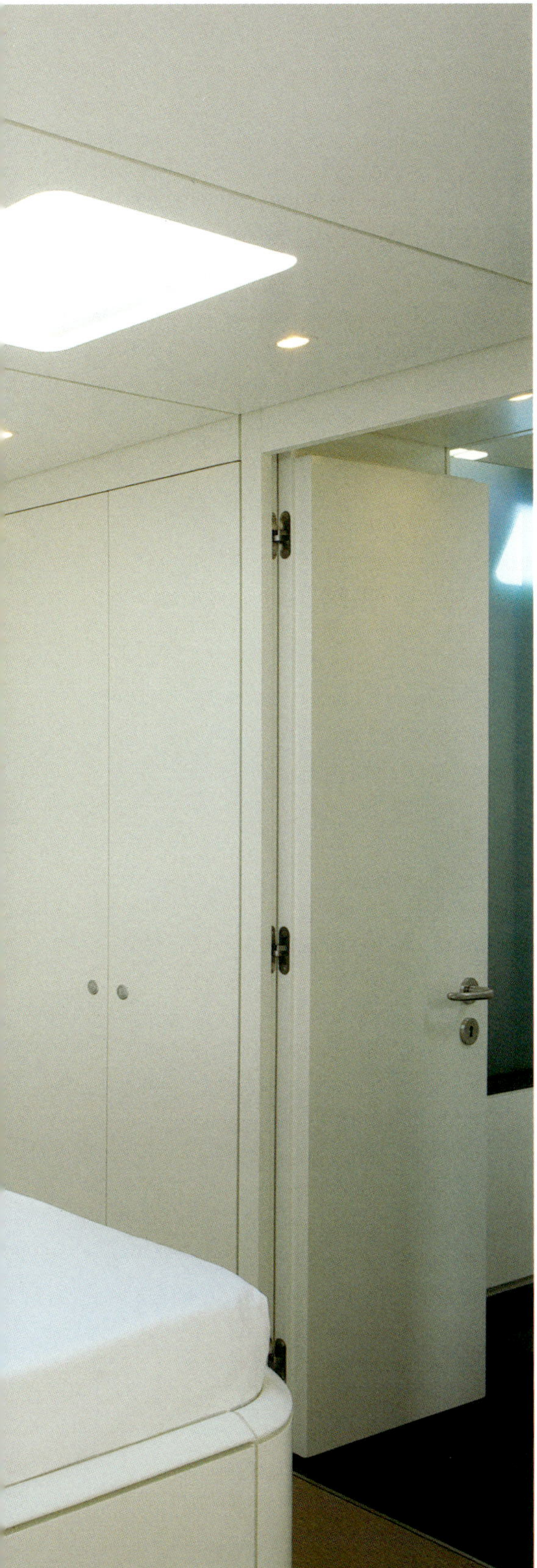

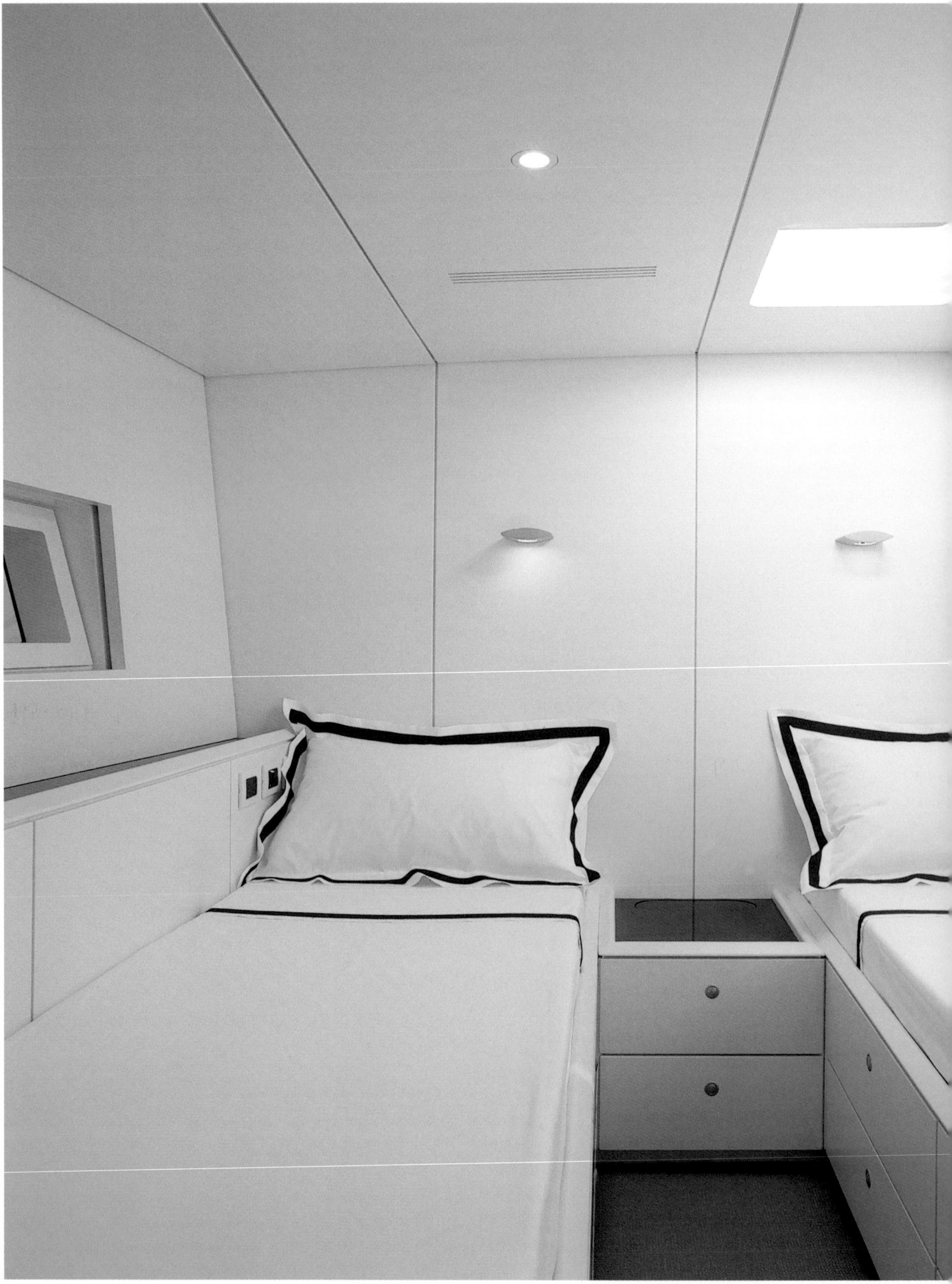

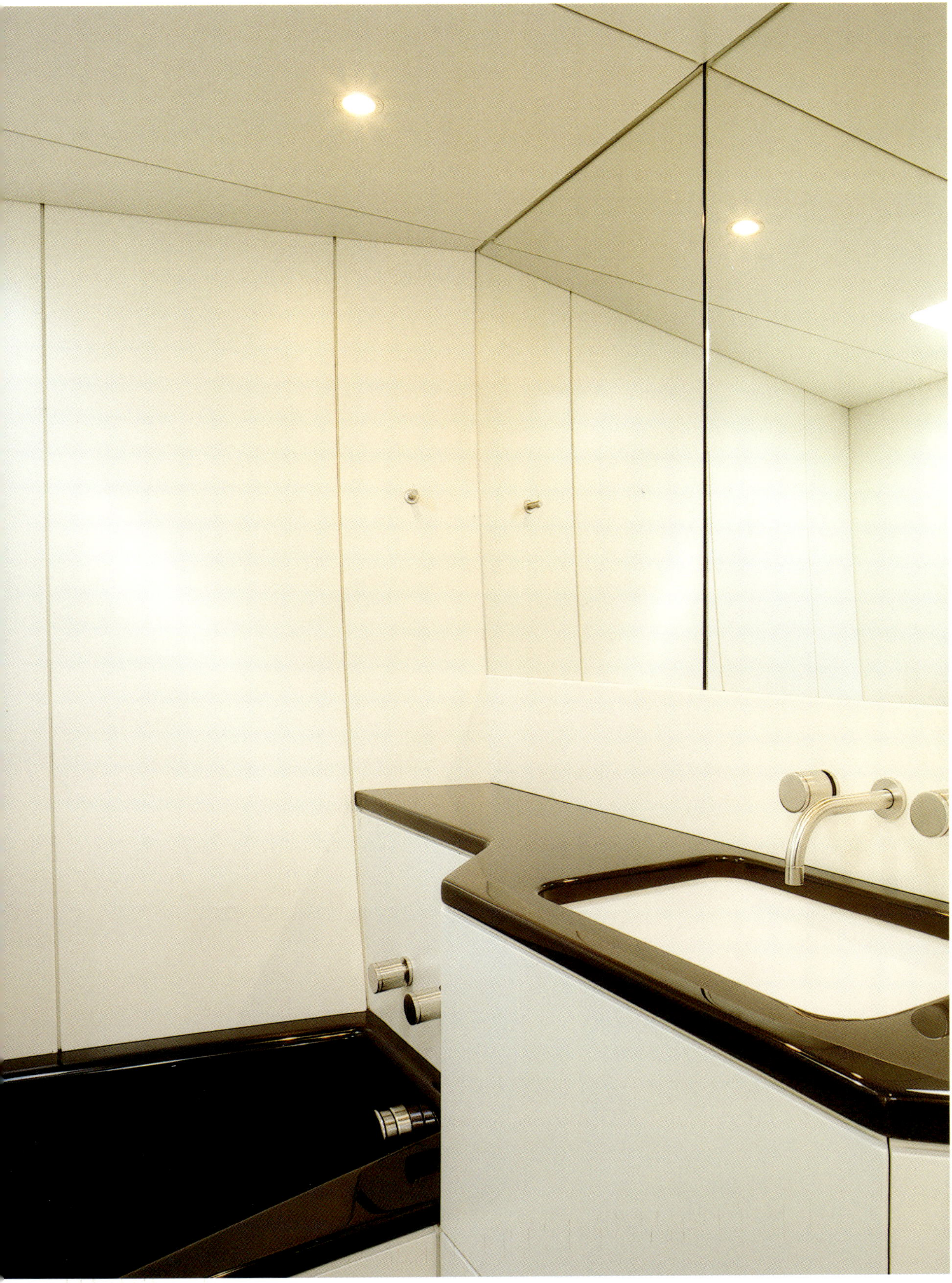

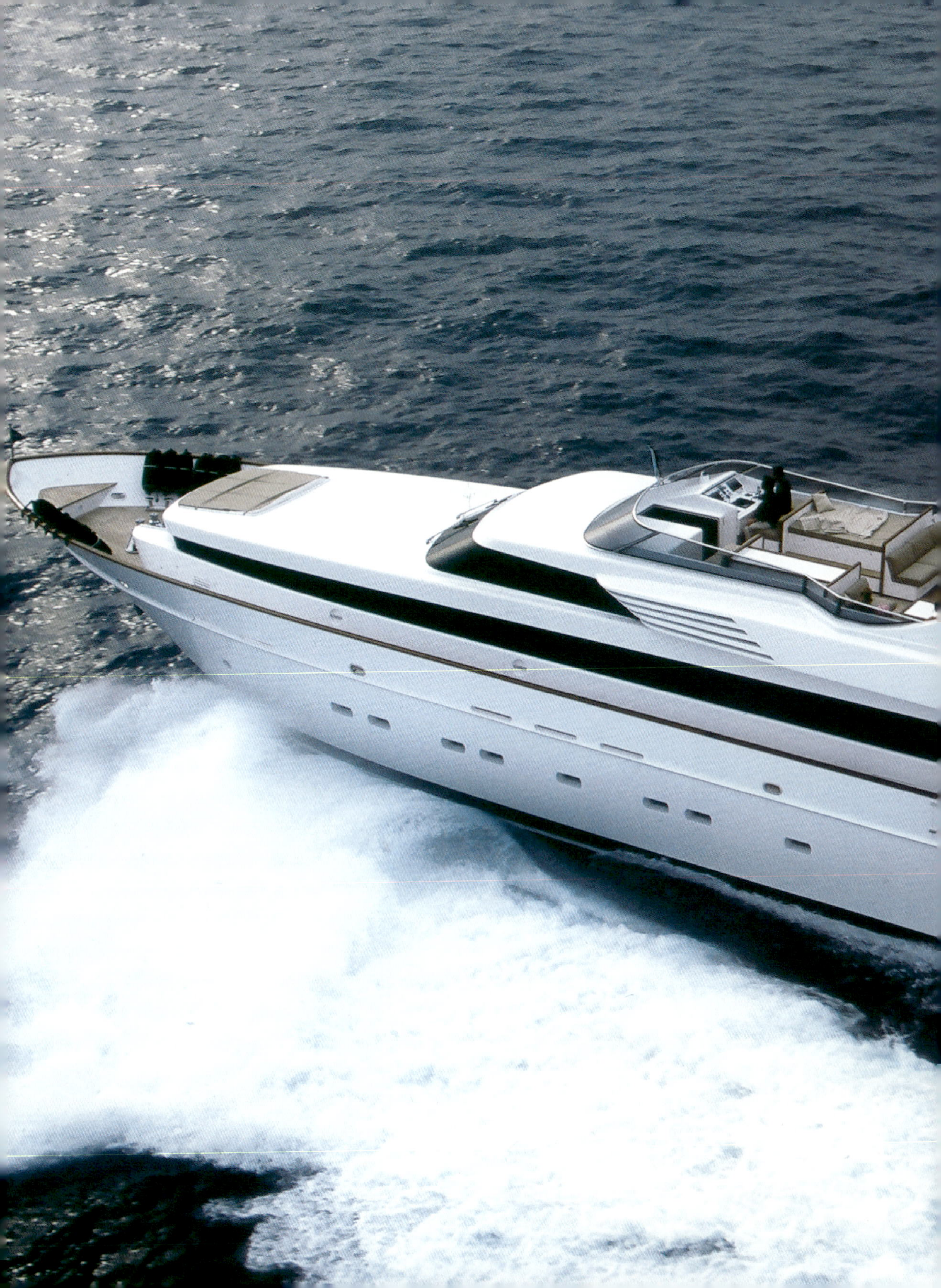

FRANCESCA LEONE, CANTIERI DI PISA
UNICA | 2003
Cantieri di Pisa

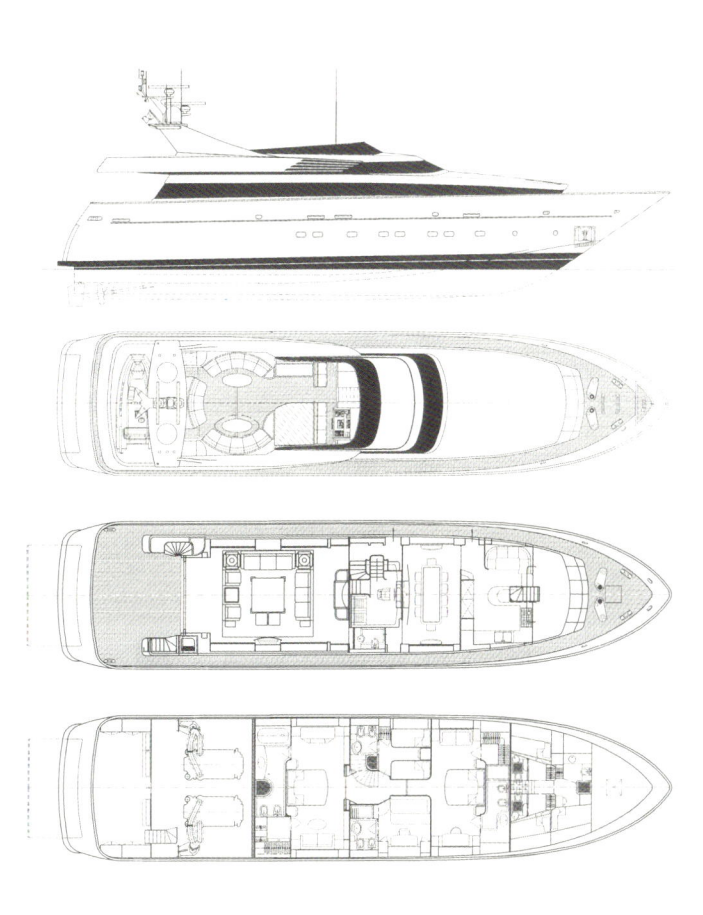

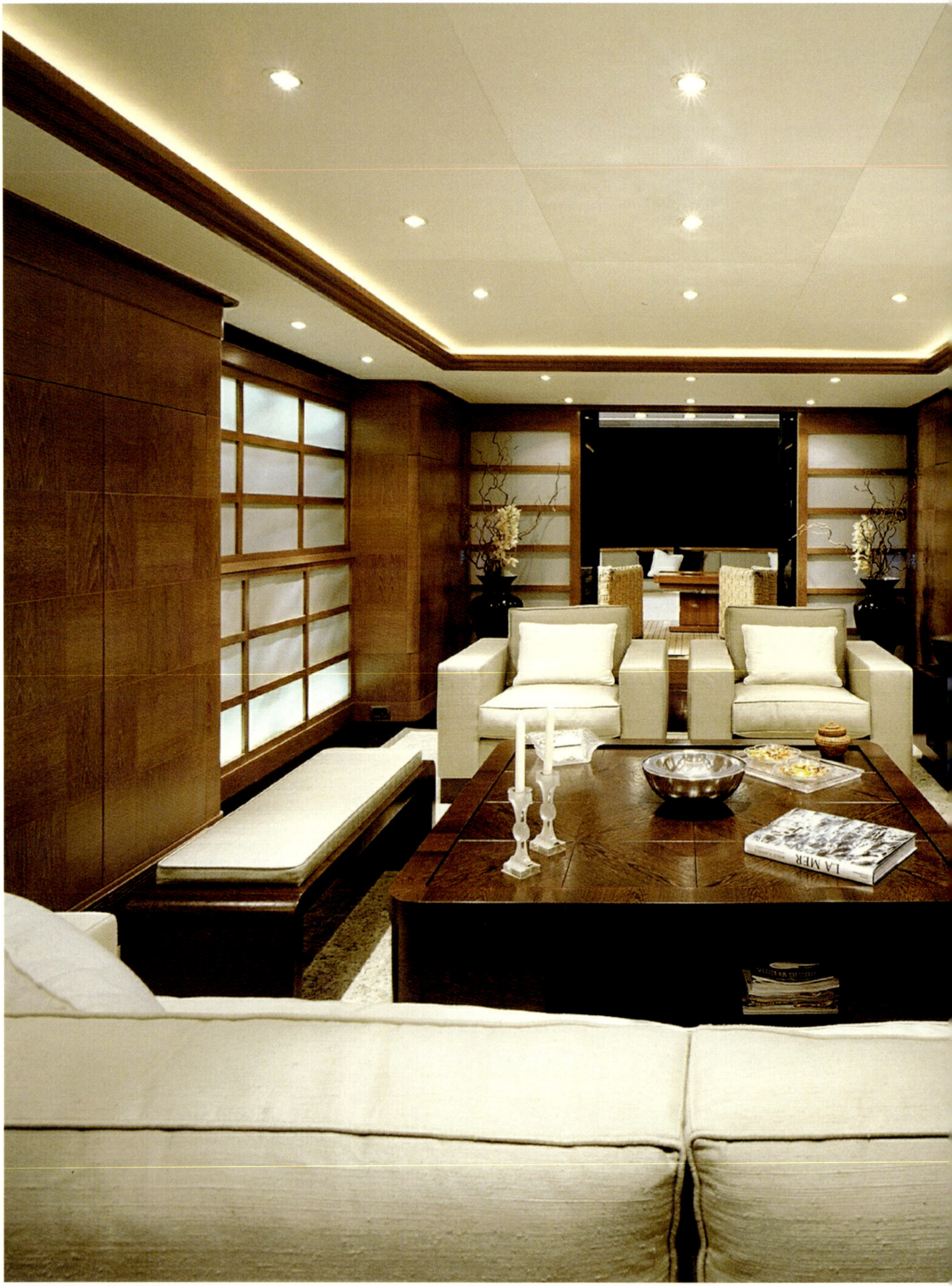
LA MER

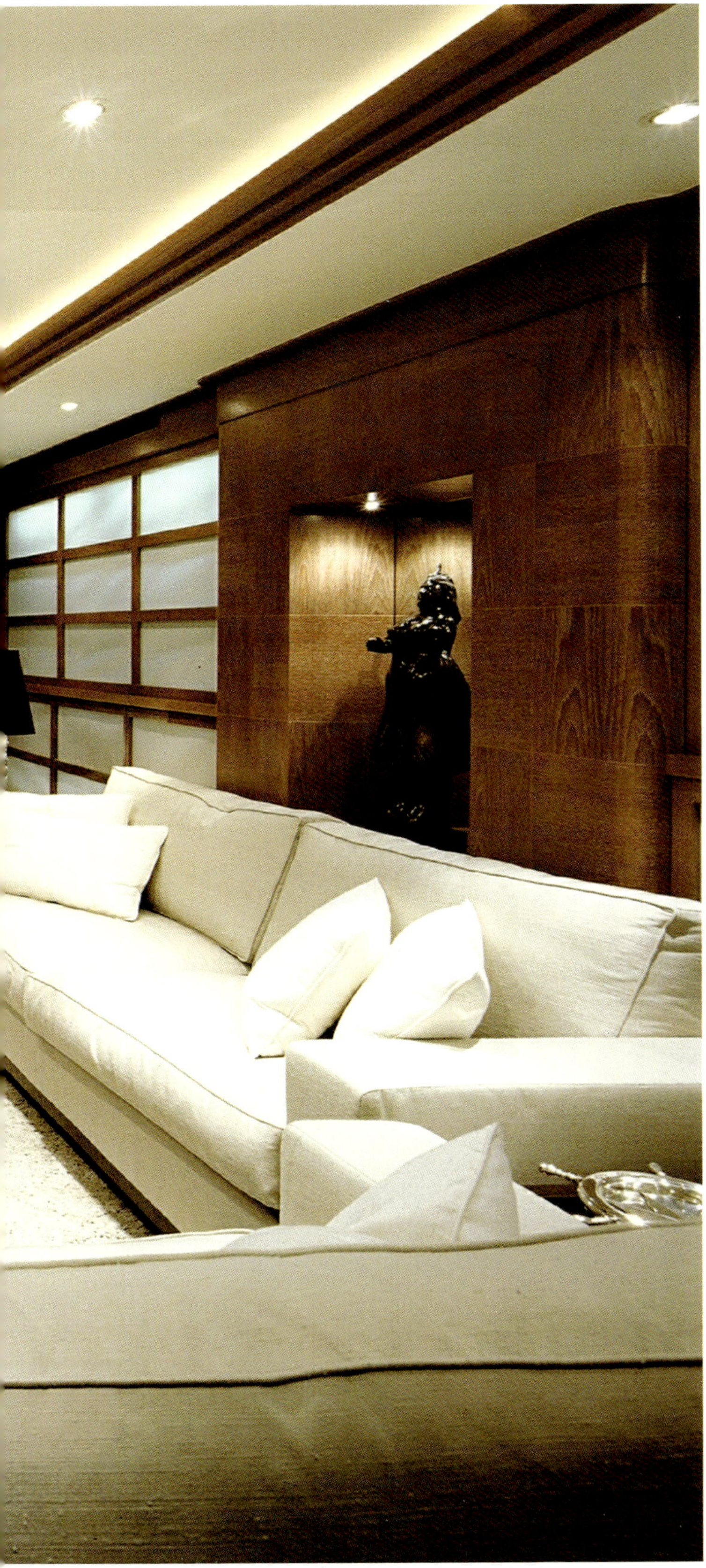

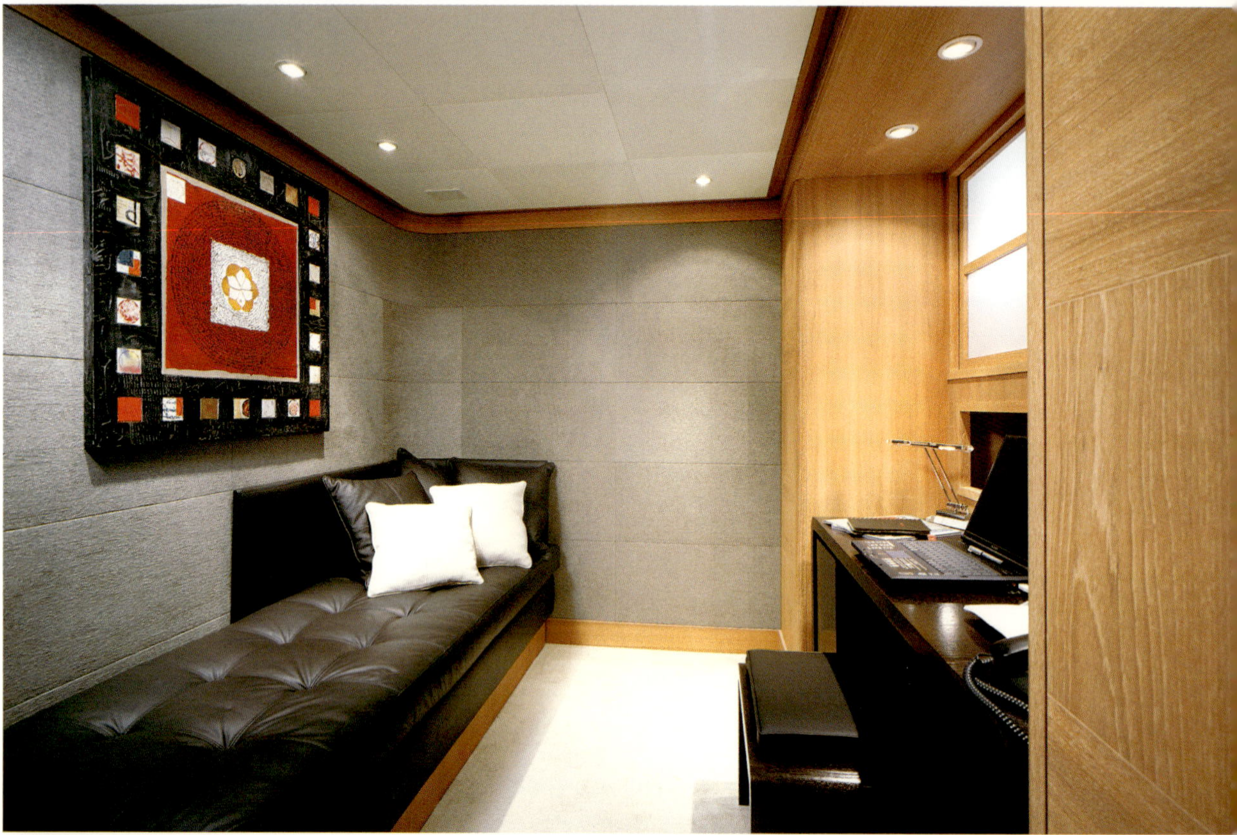

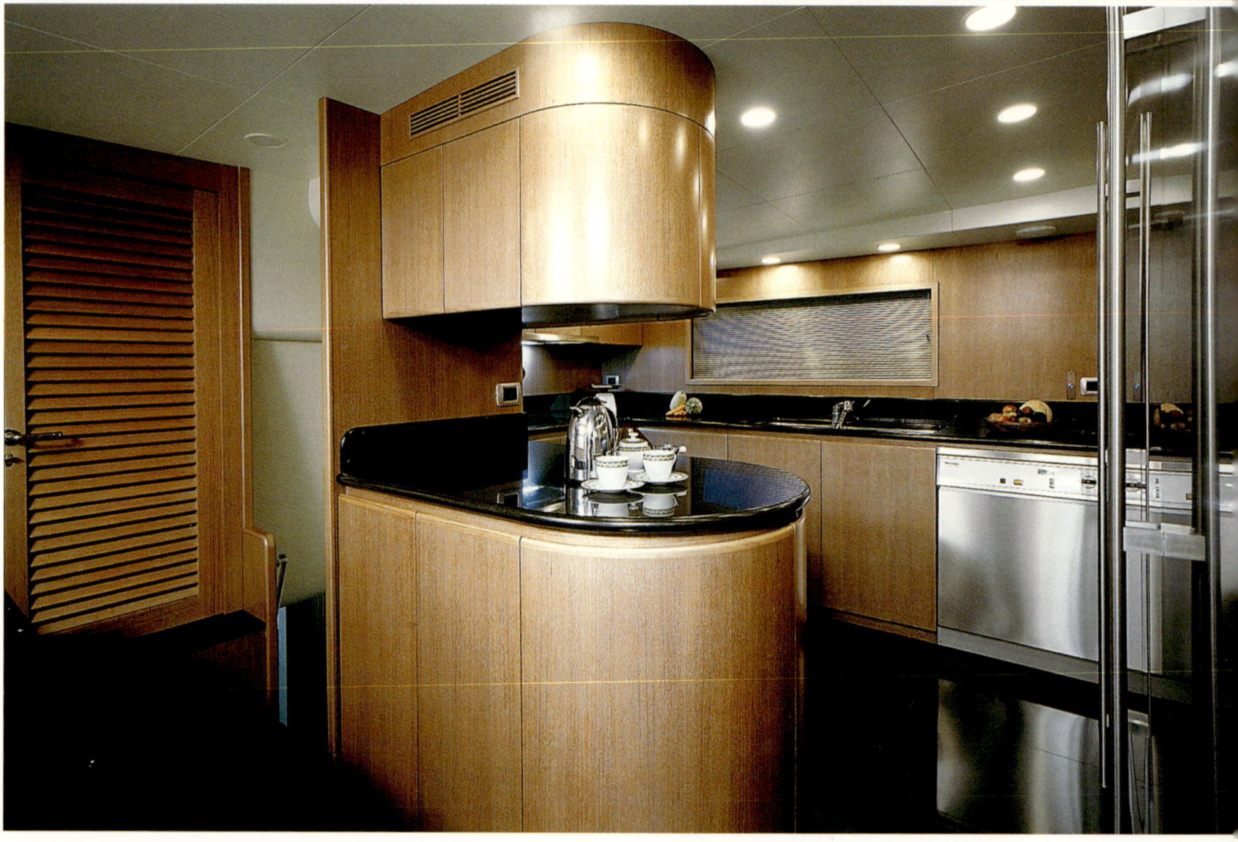

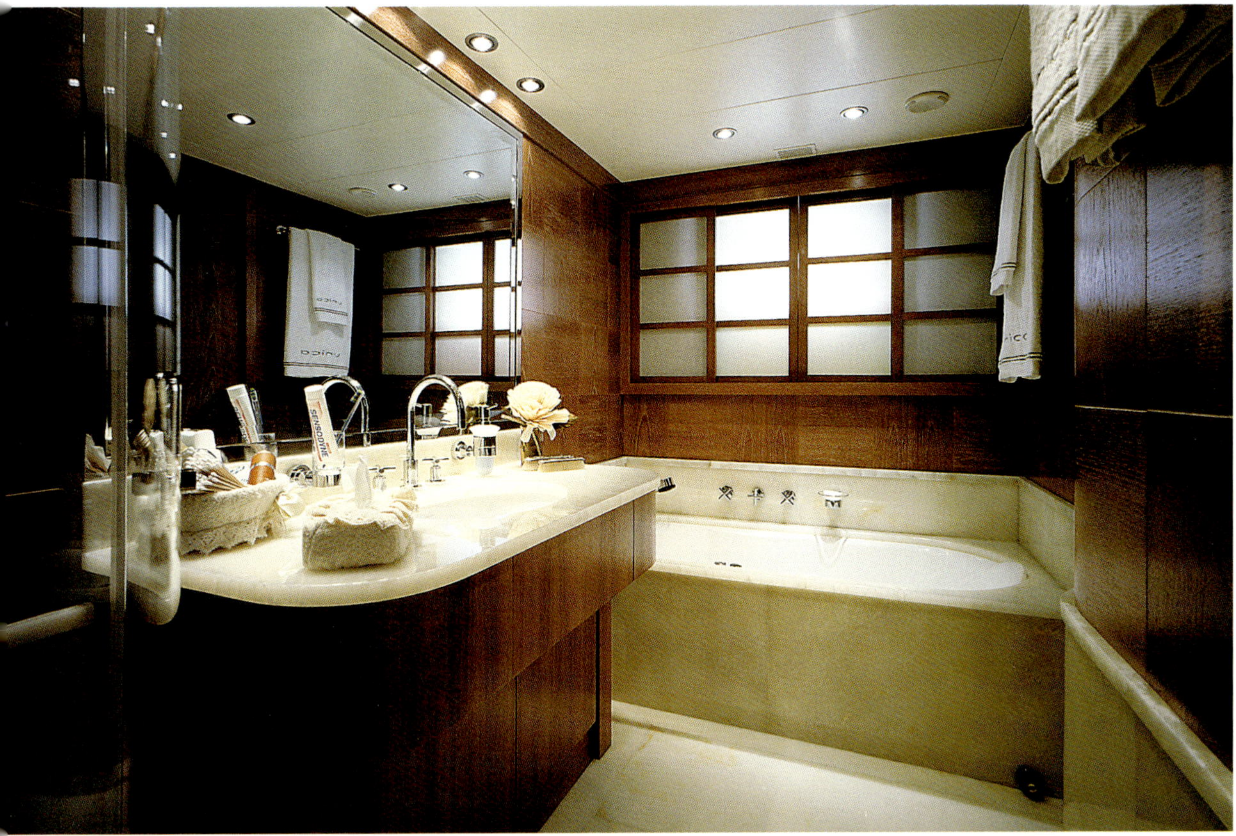
SENSODYNE

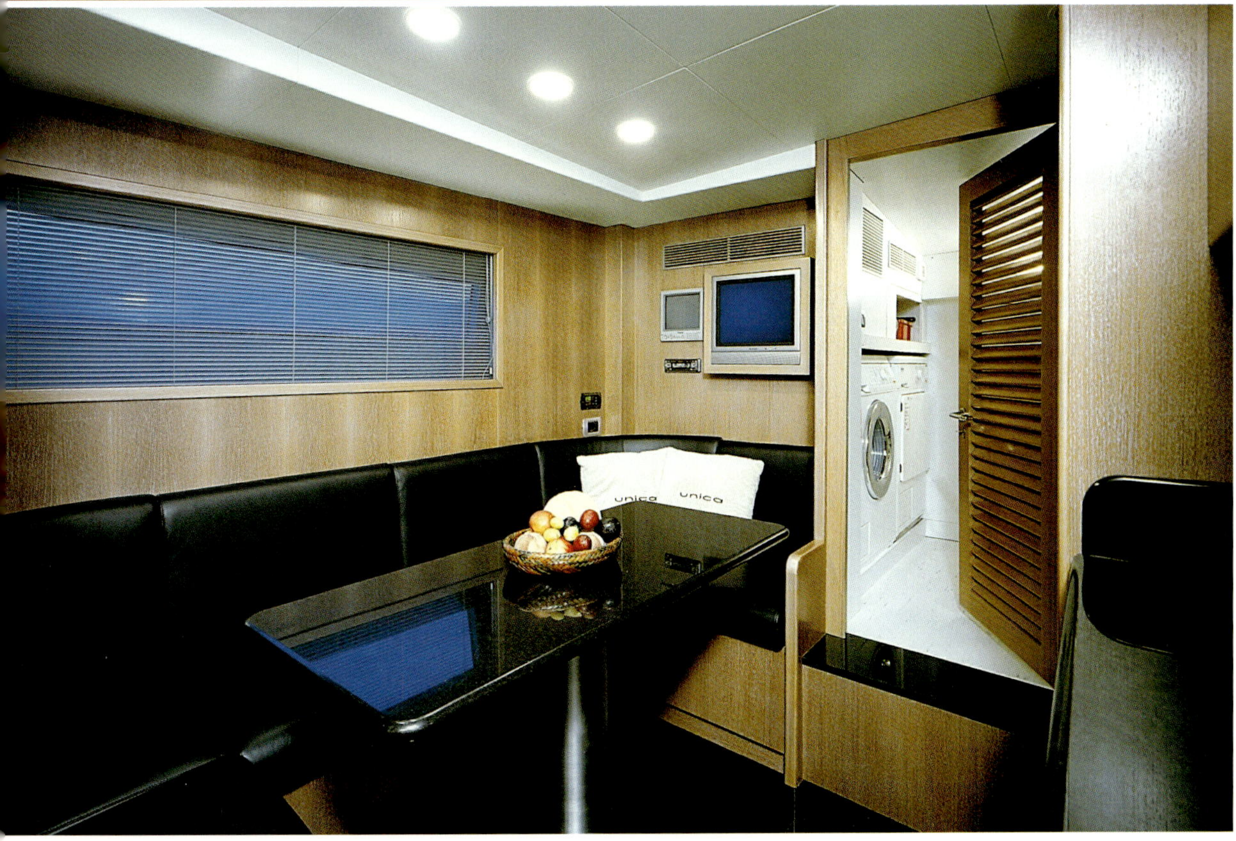
unica
unica

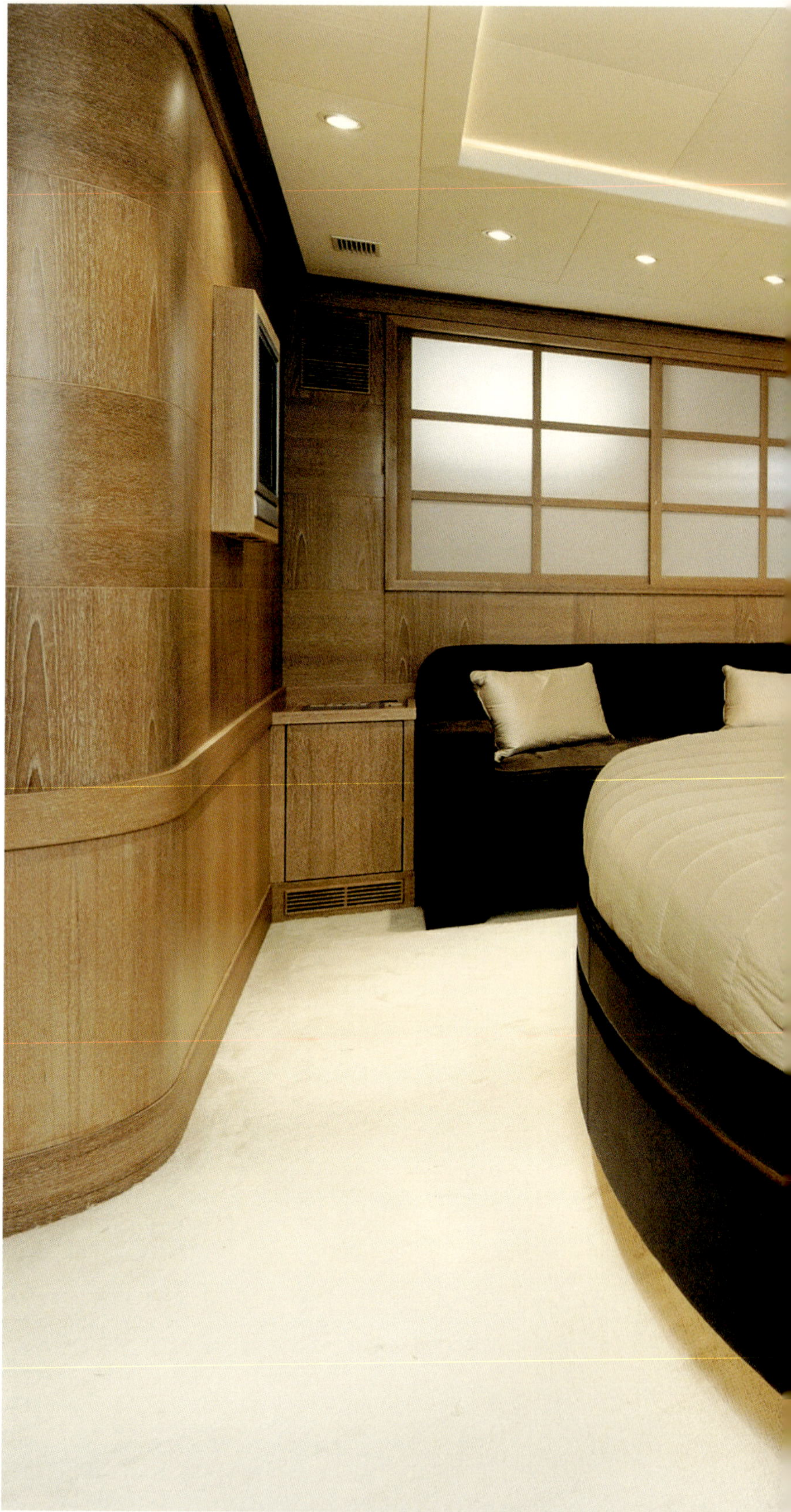

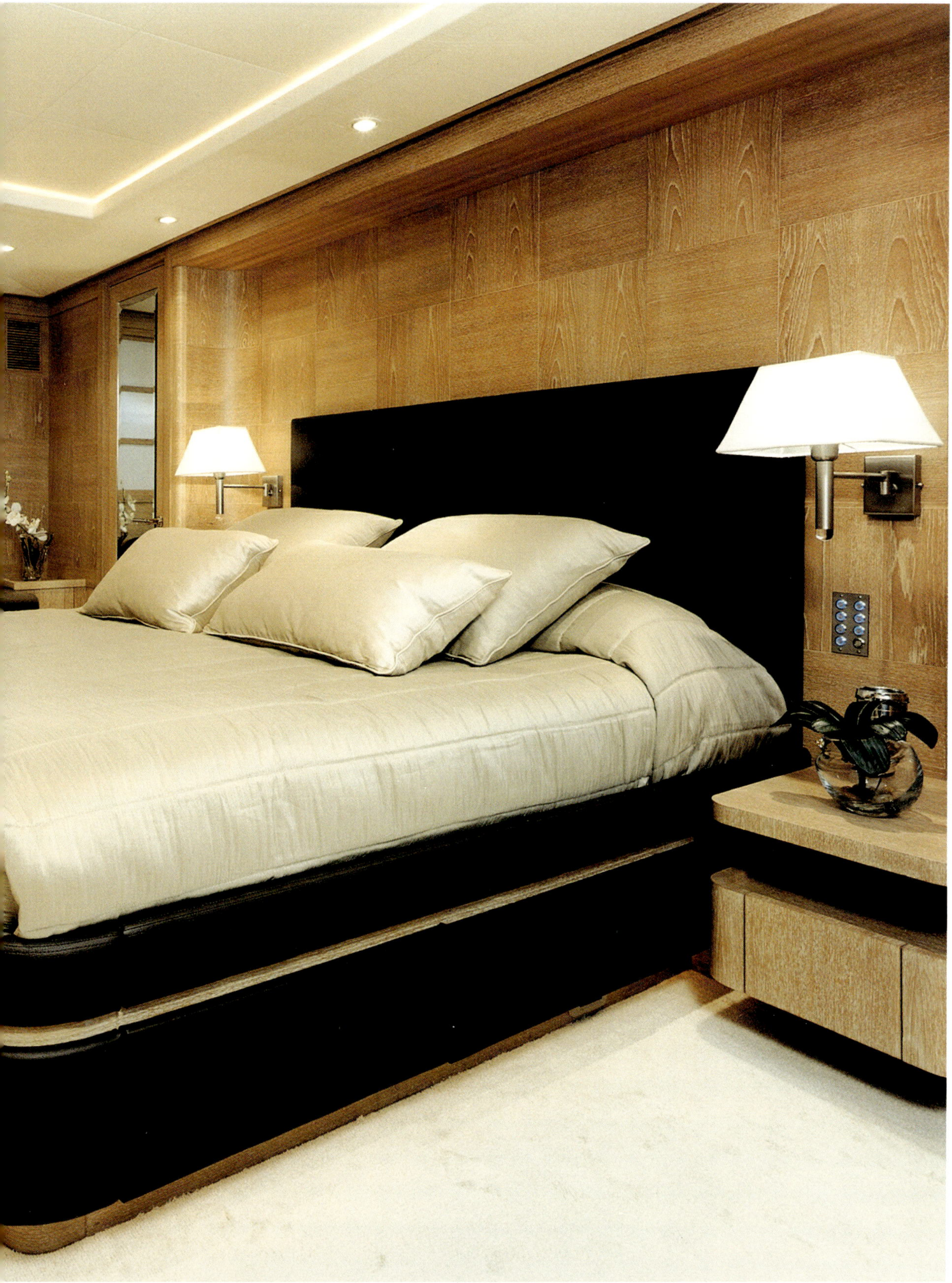

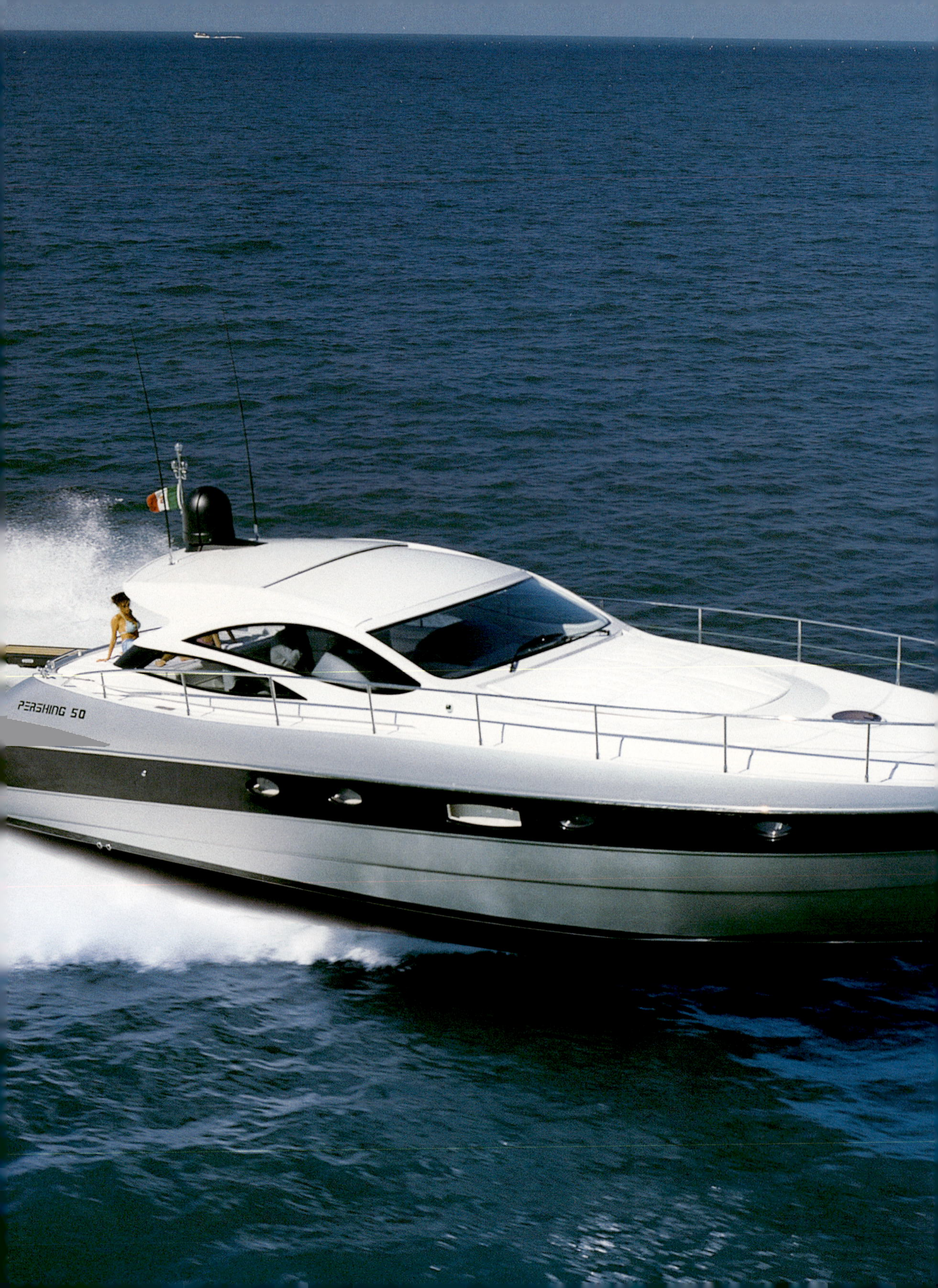
PERSHING 50

FULVIO DE SIMONI
PERSHING 50 | 2004
Pershing

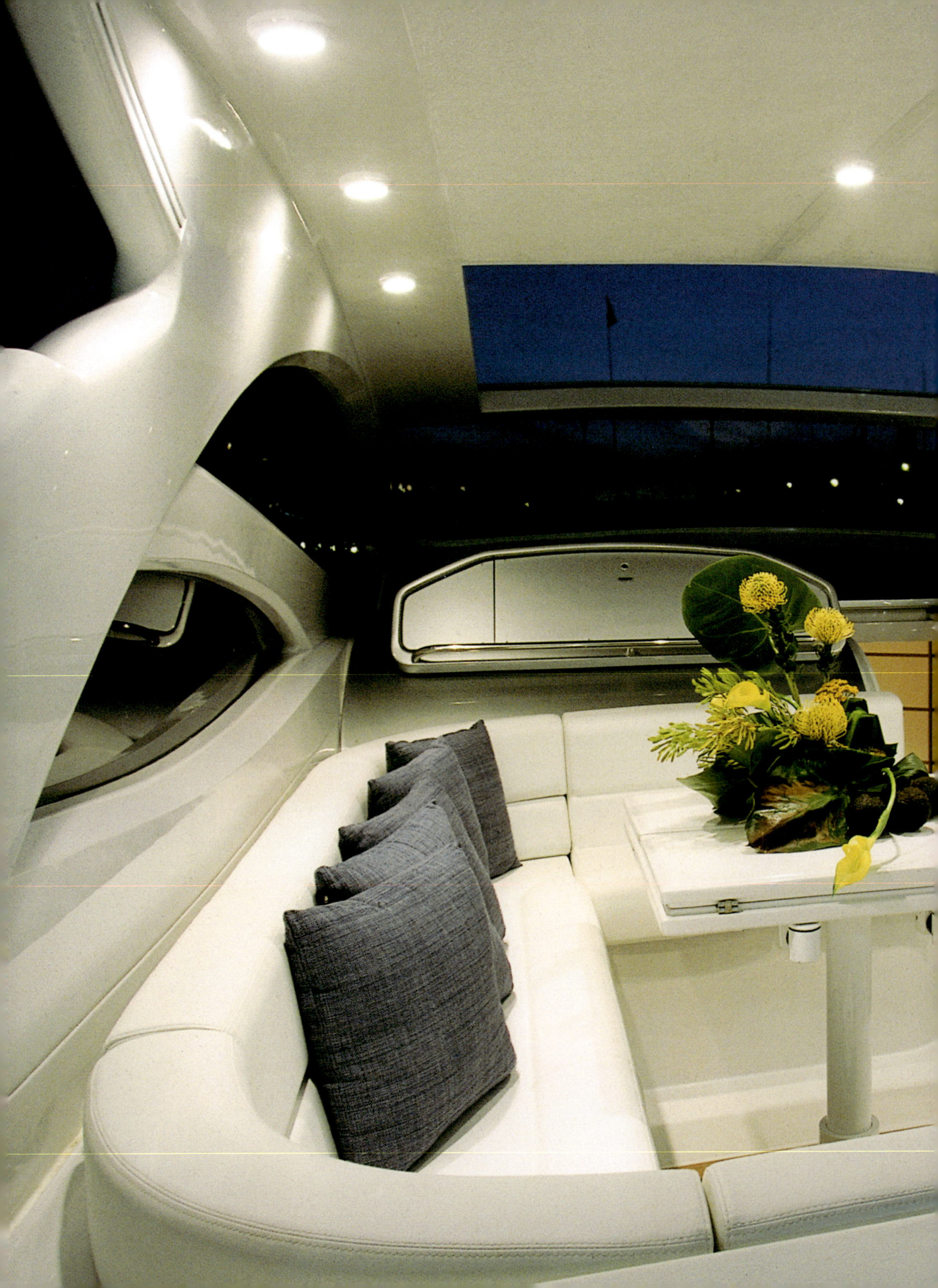

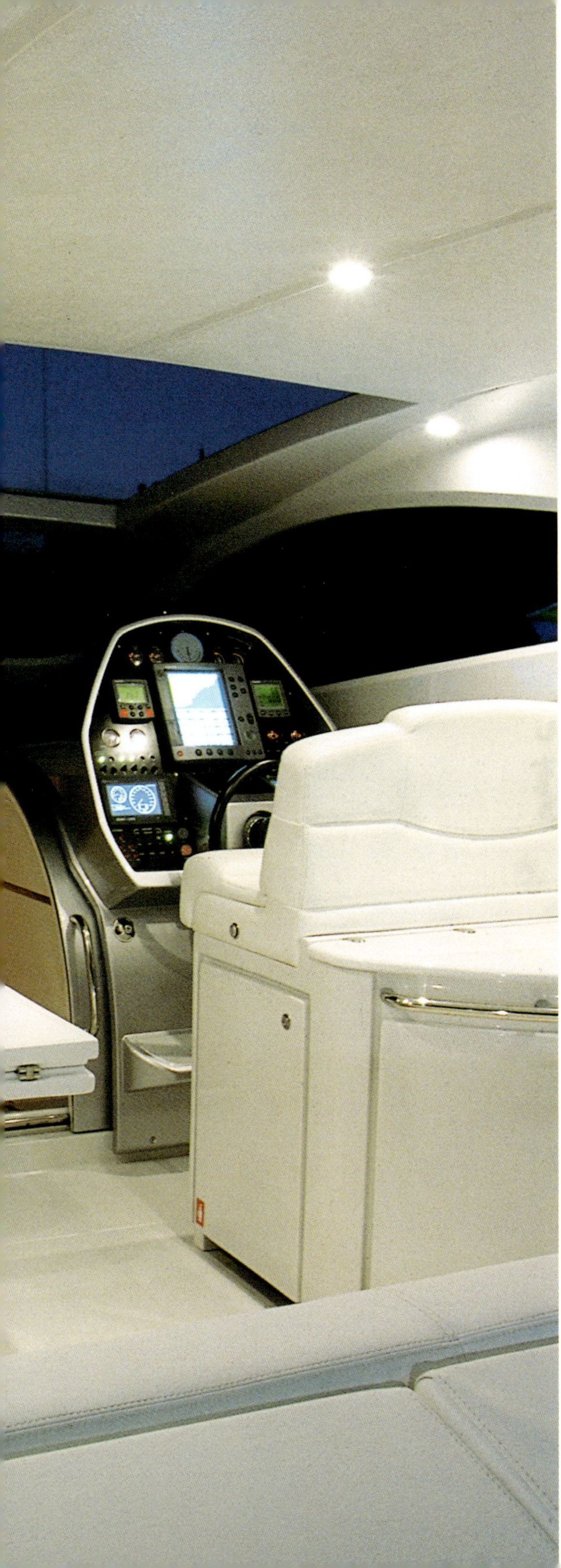

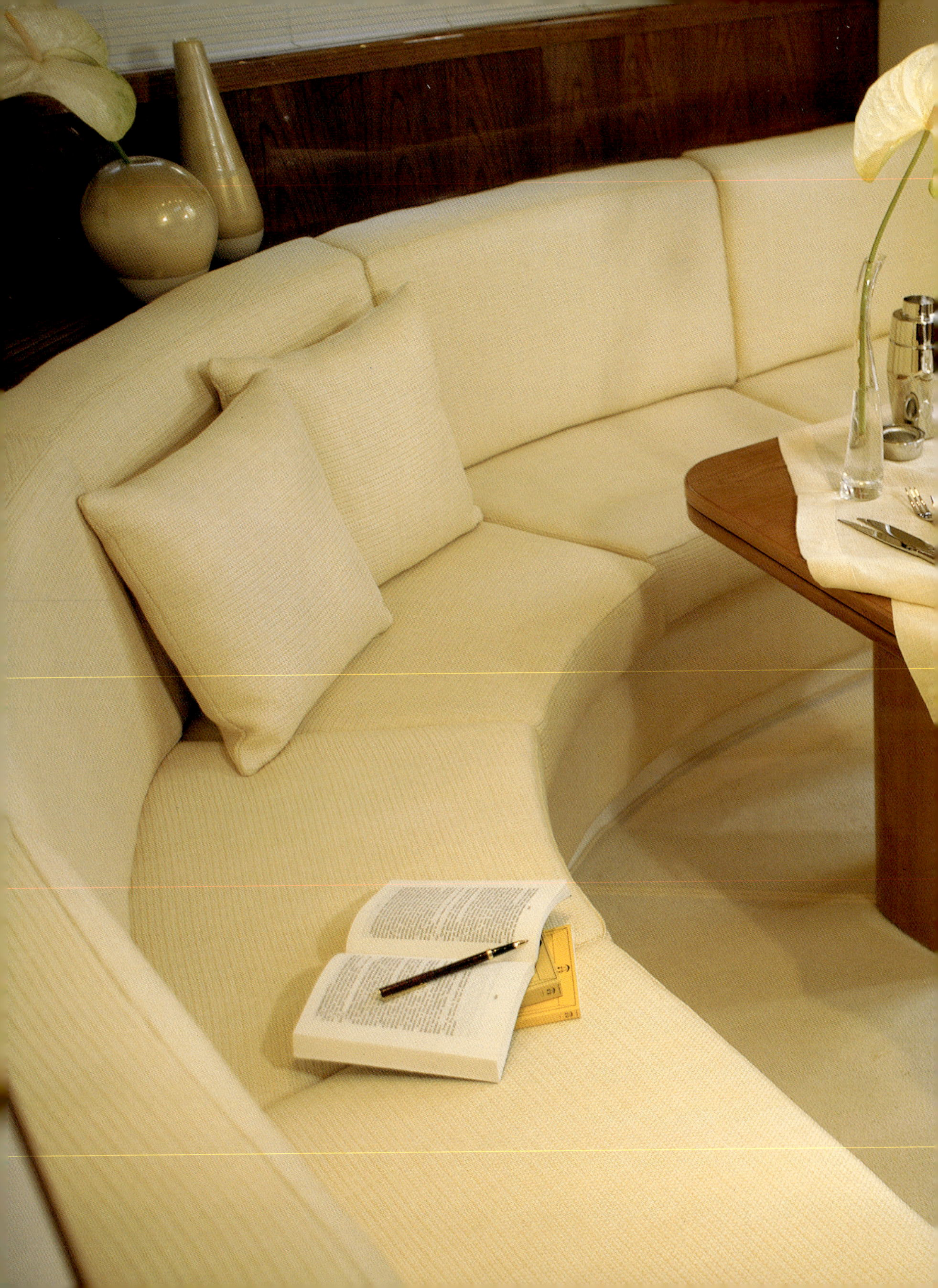

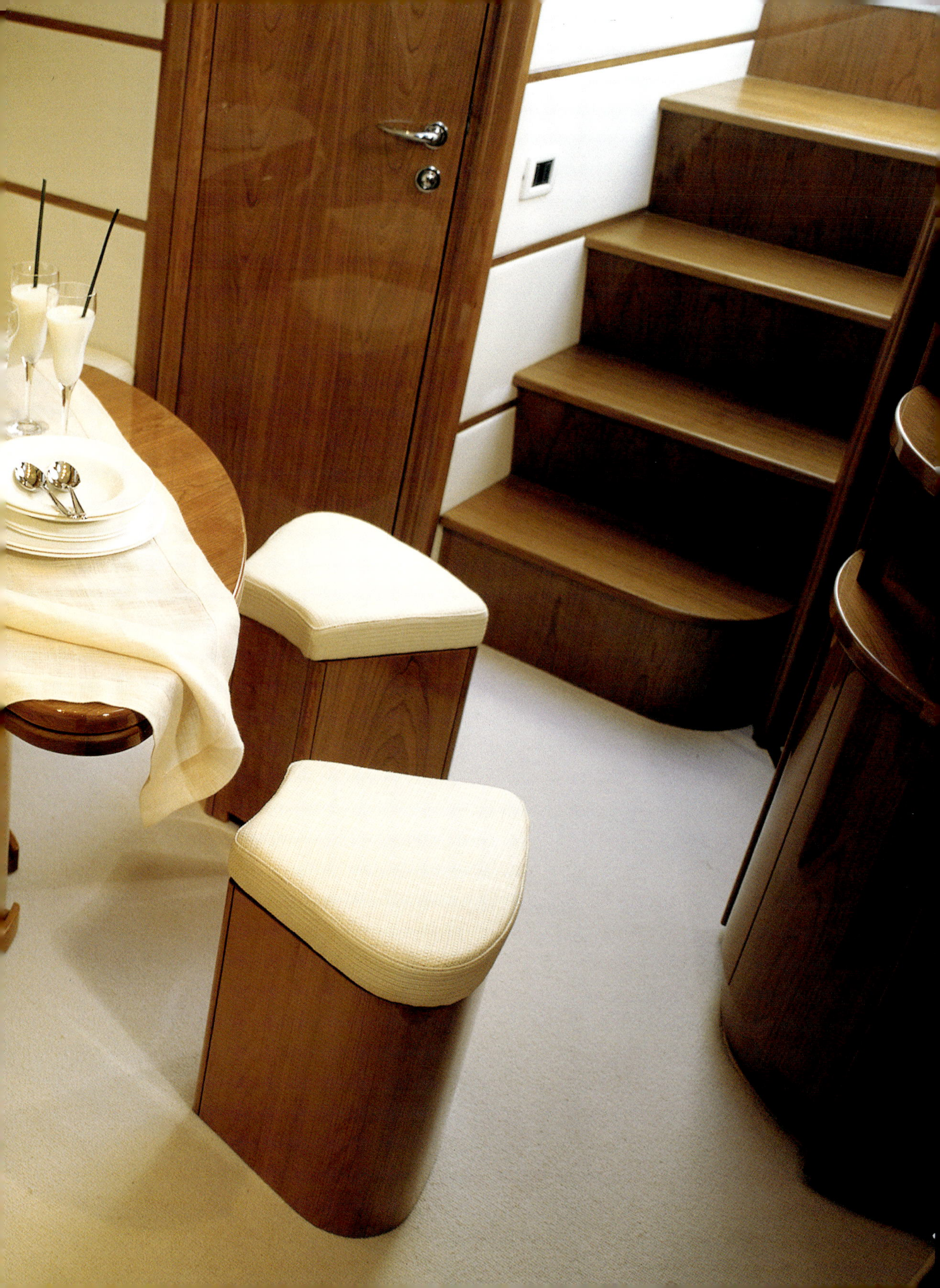

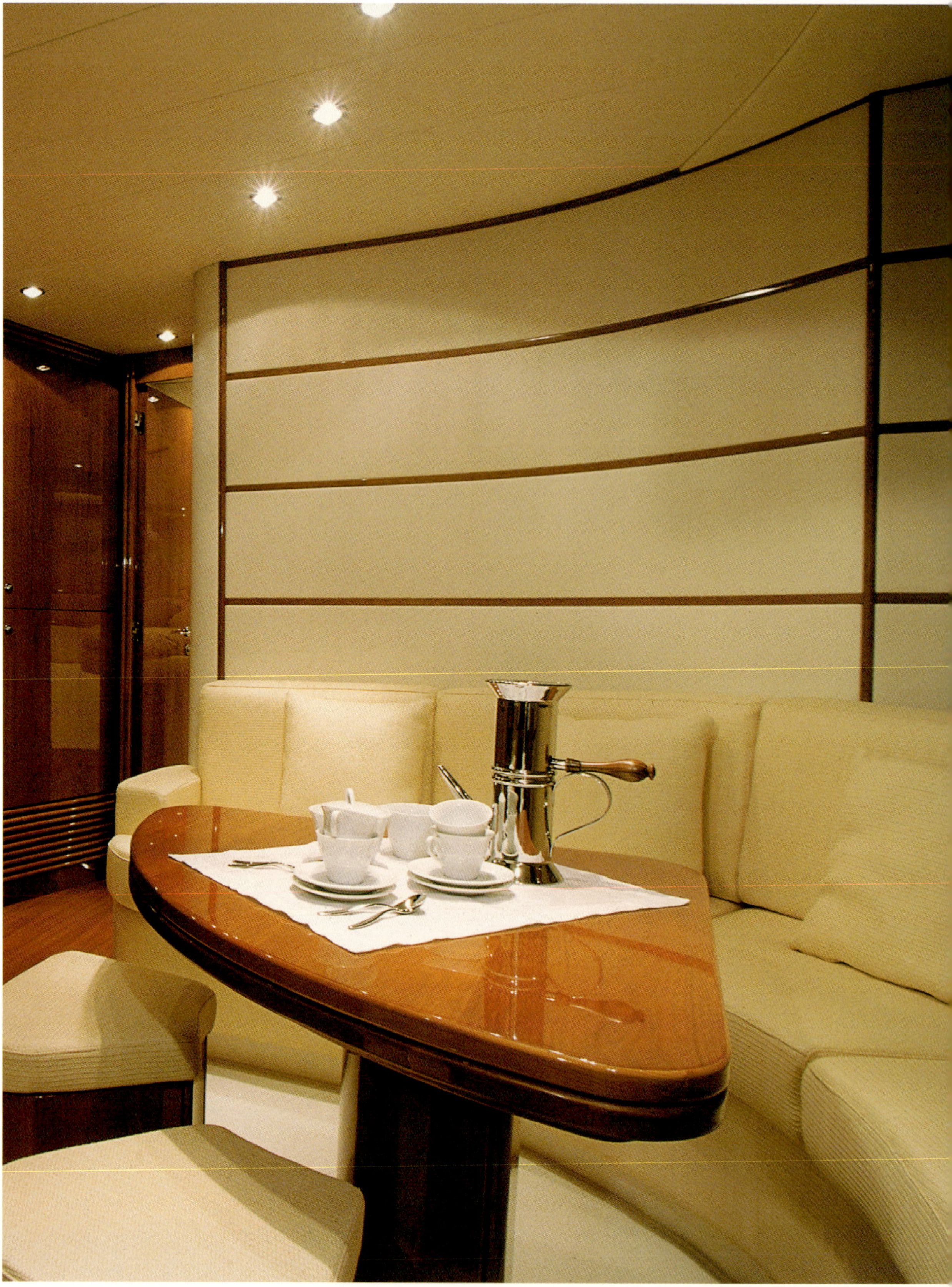

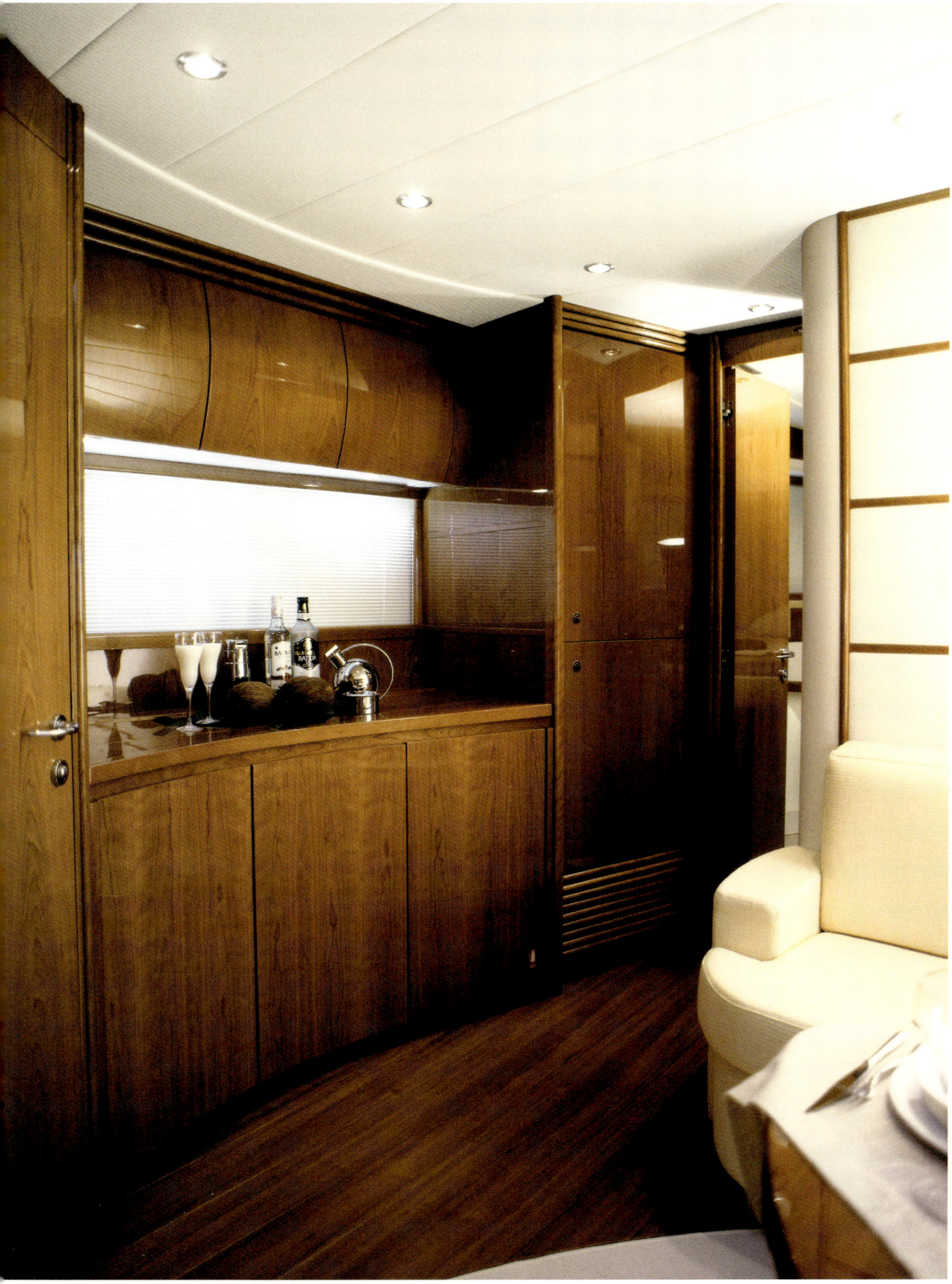

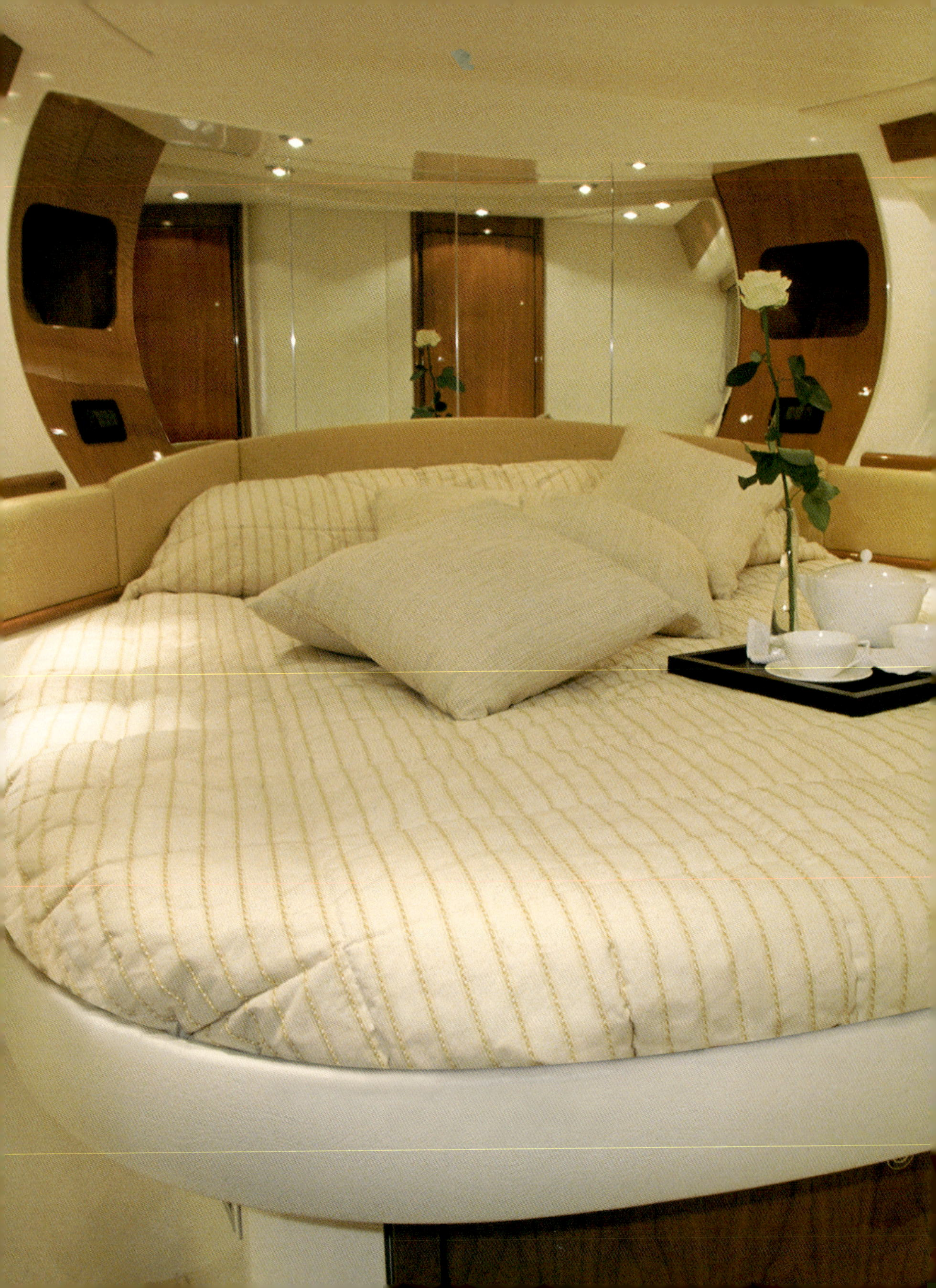

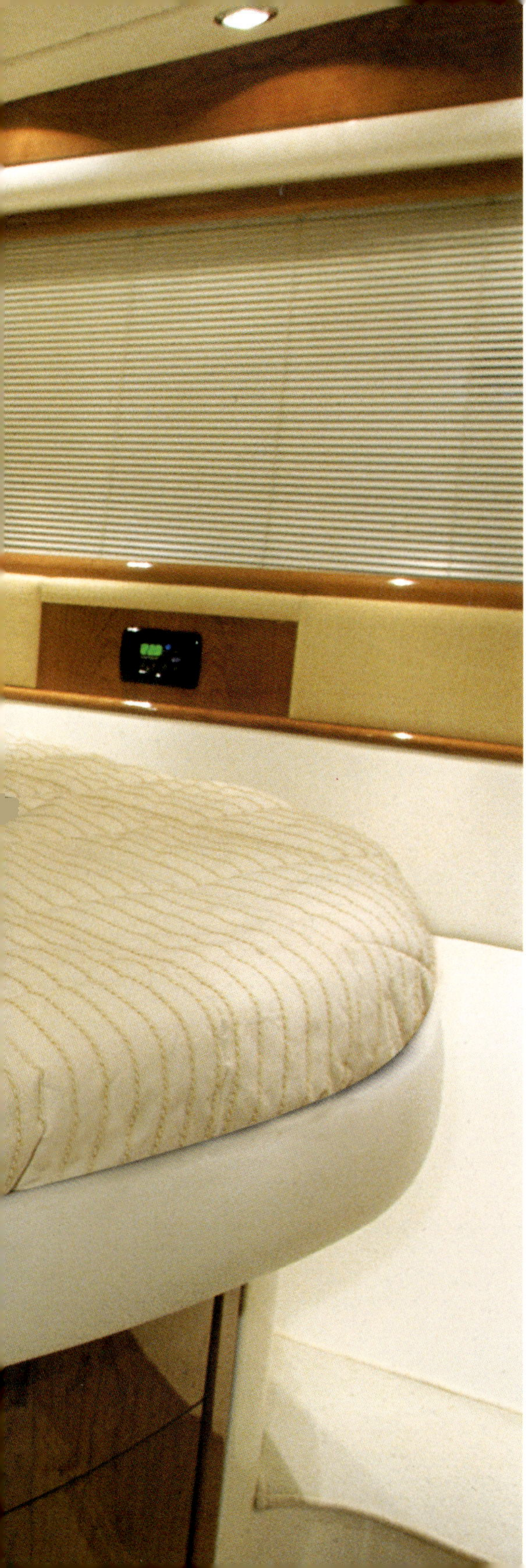

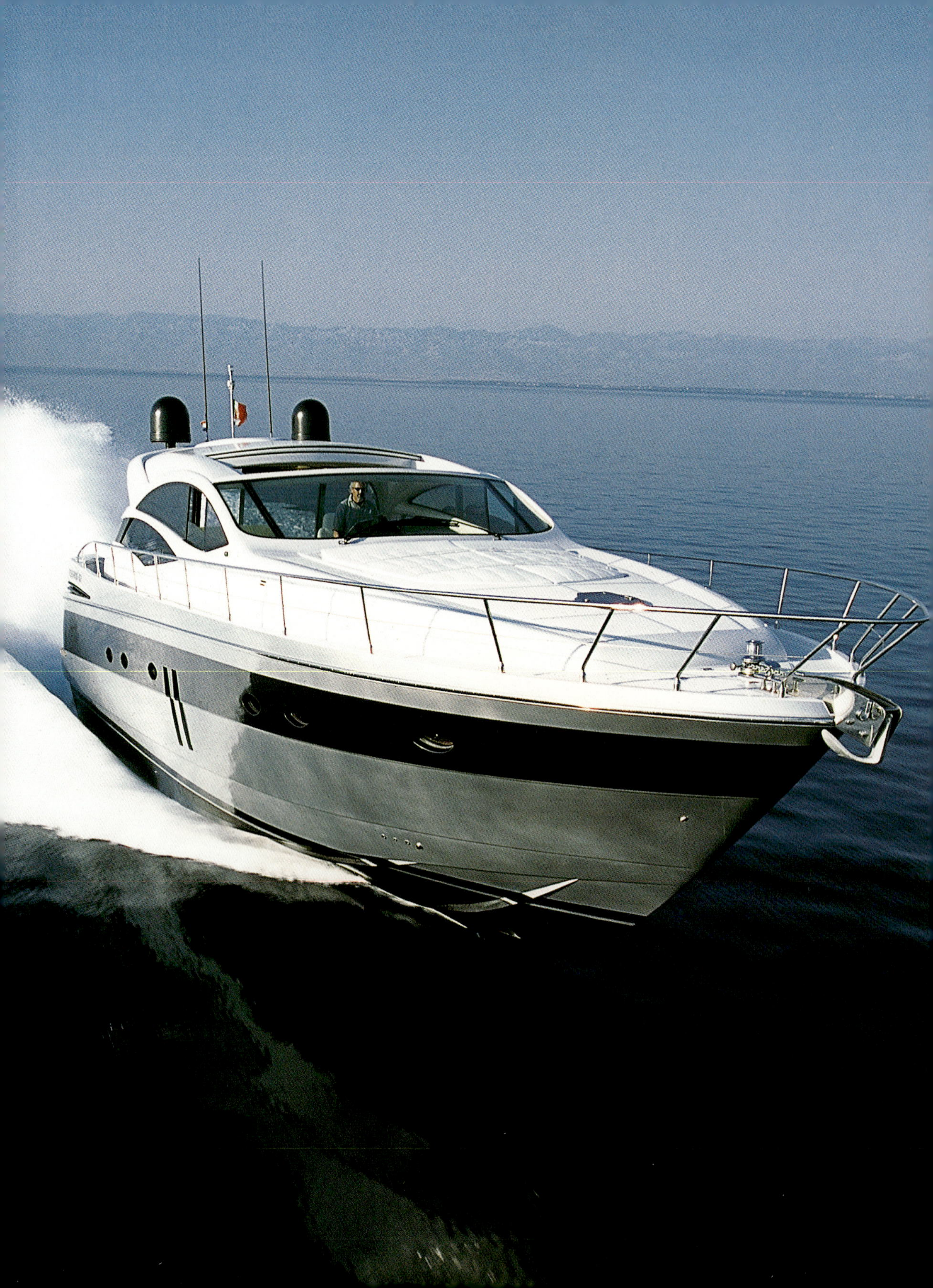

FULVIO DE SIMONI
PERSHING 62 | 2005
Pershing

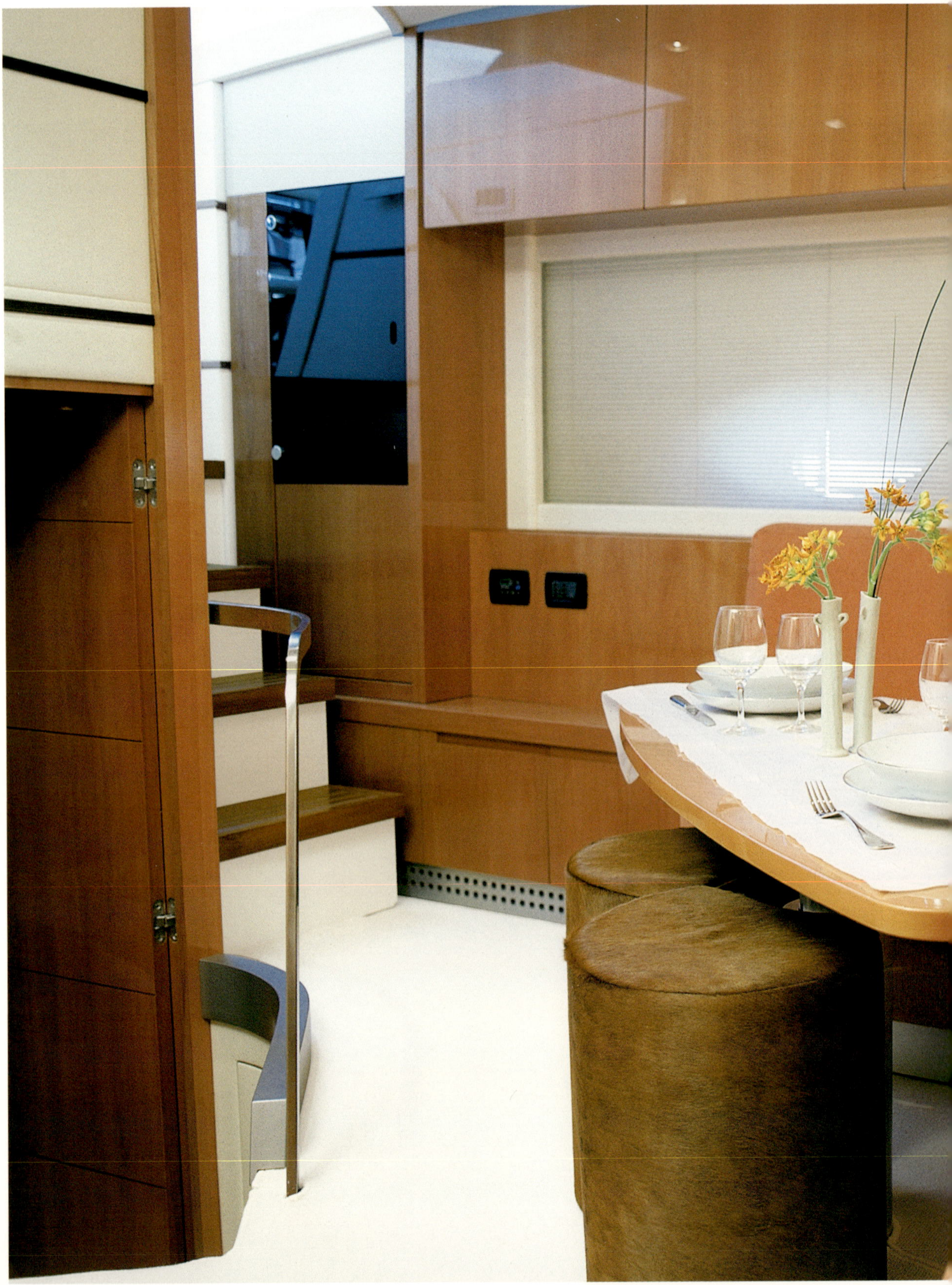

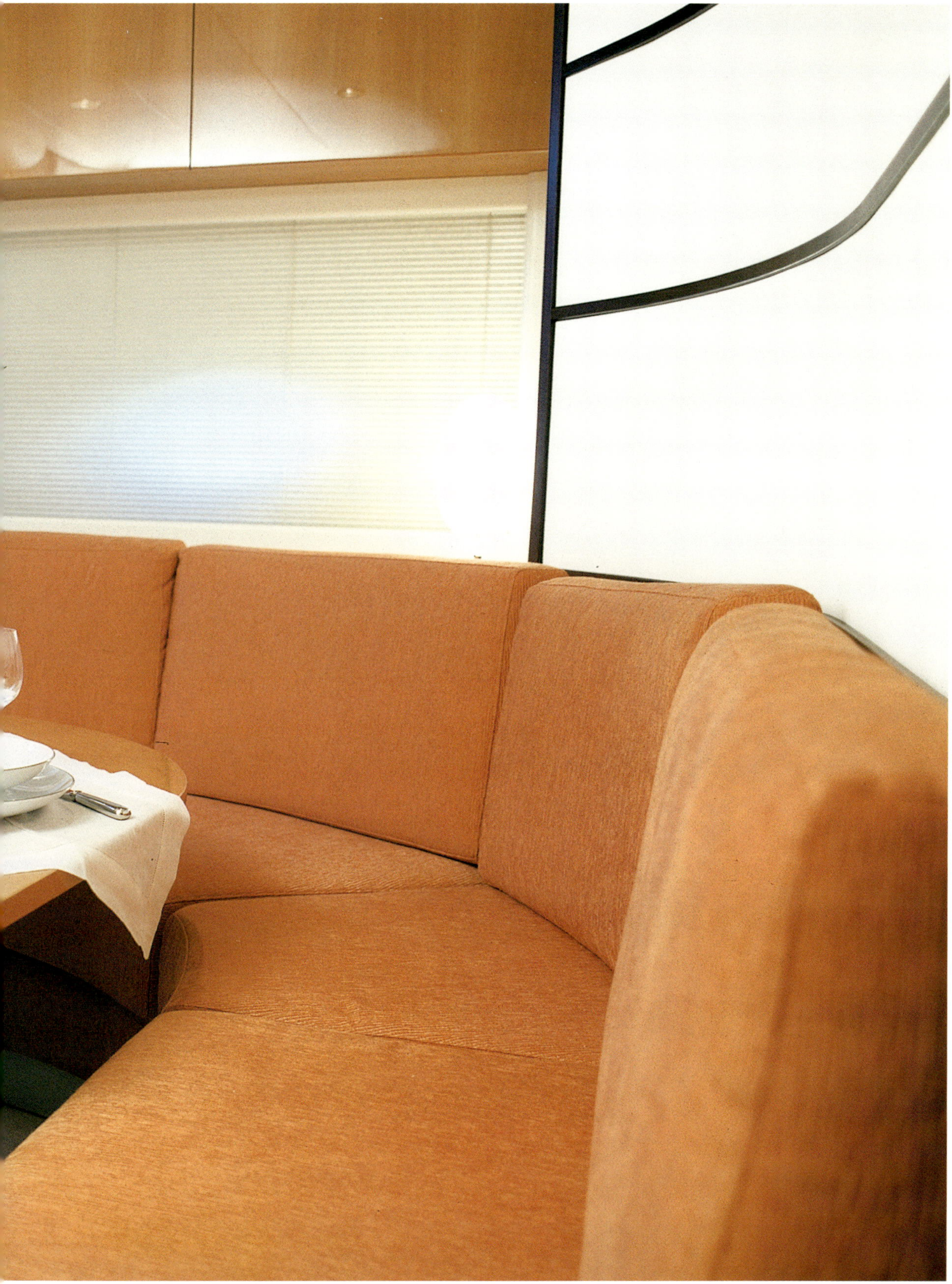

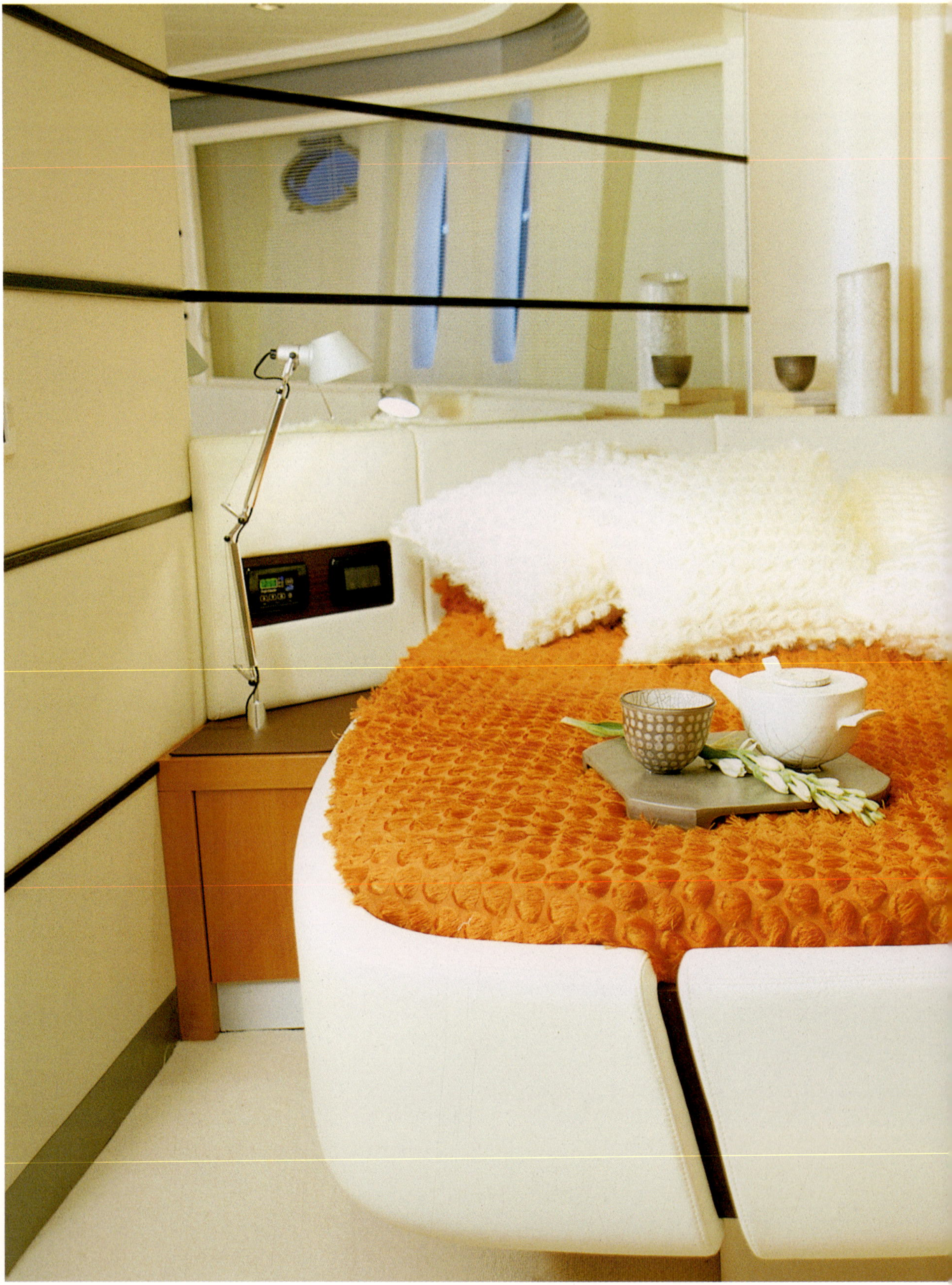

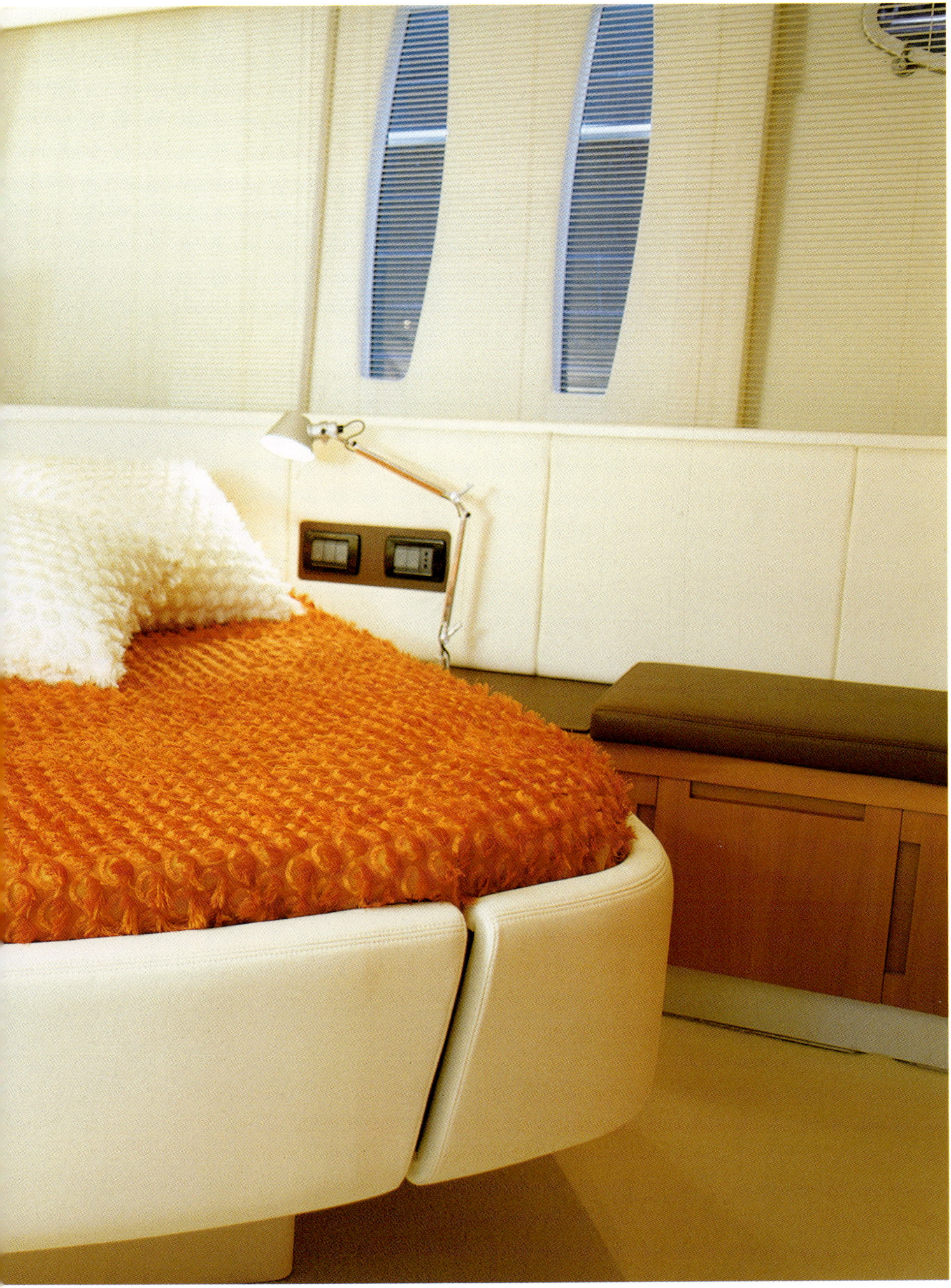

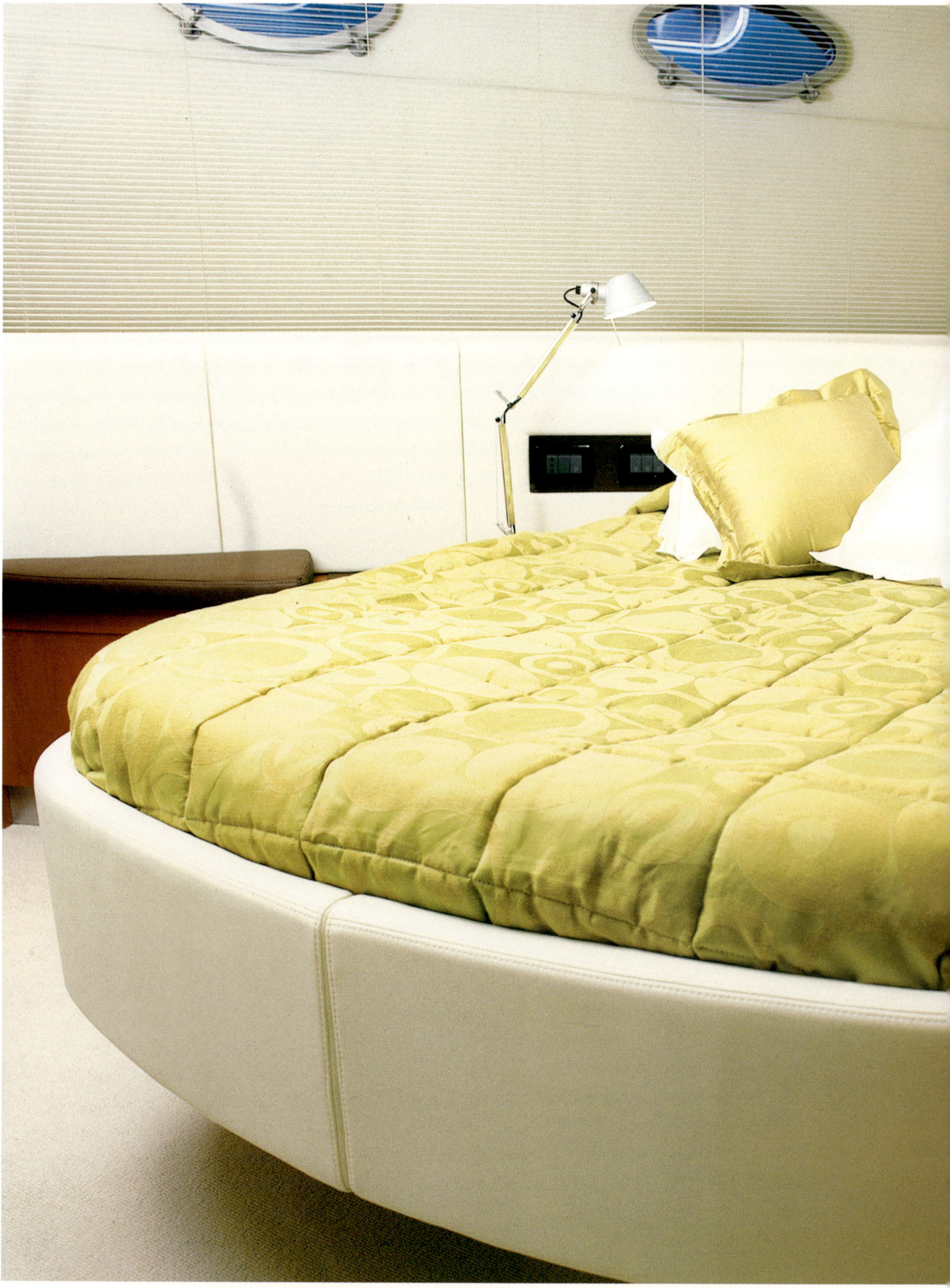

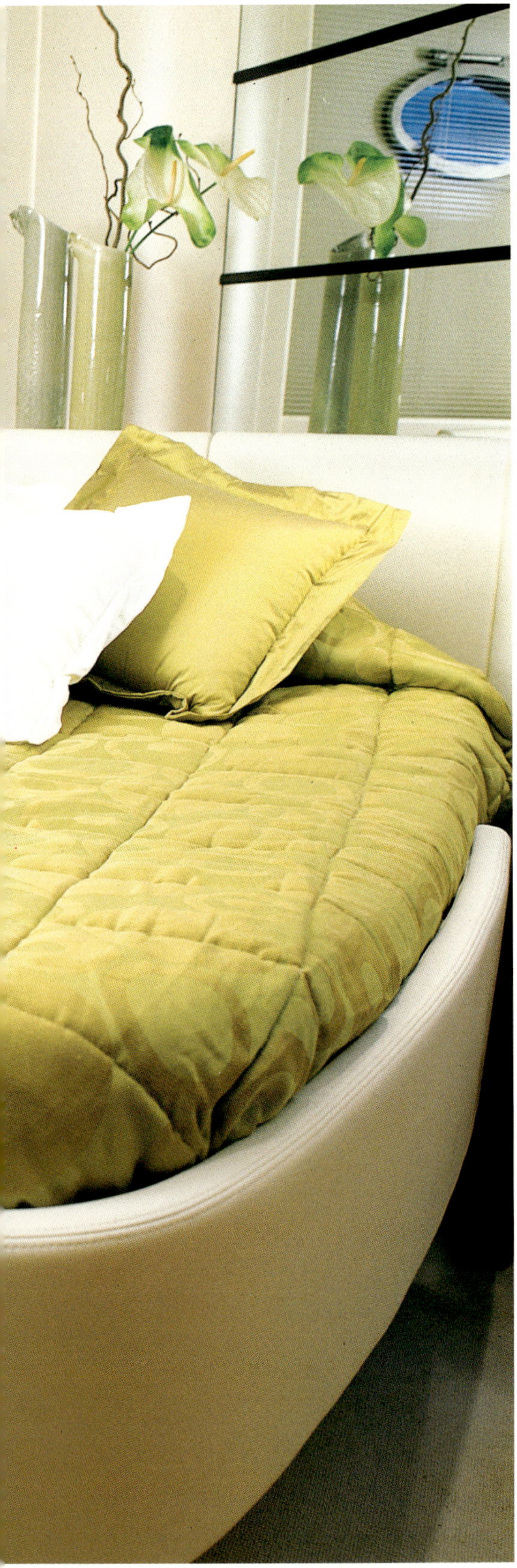

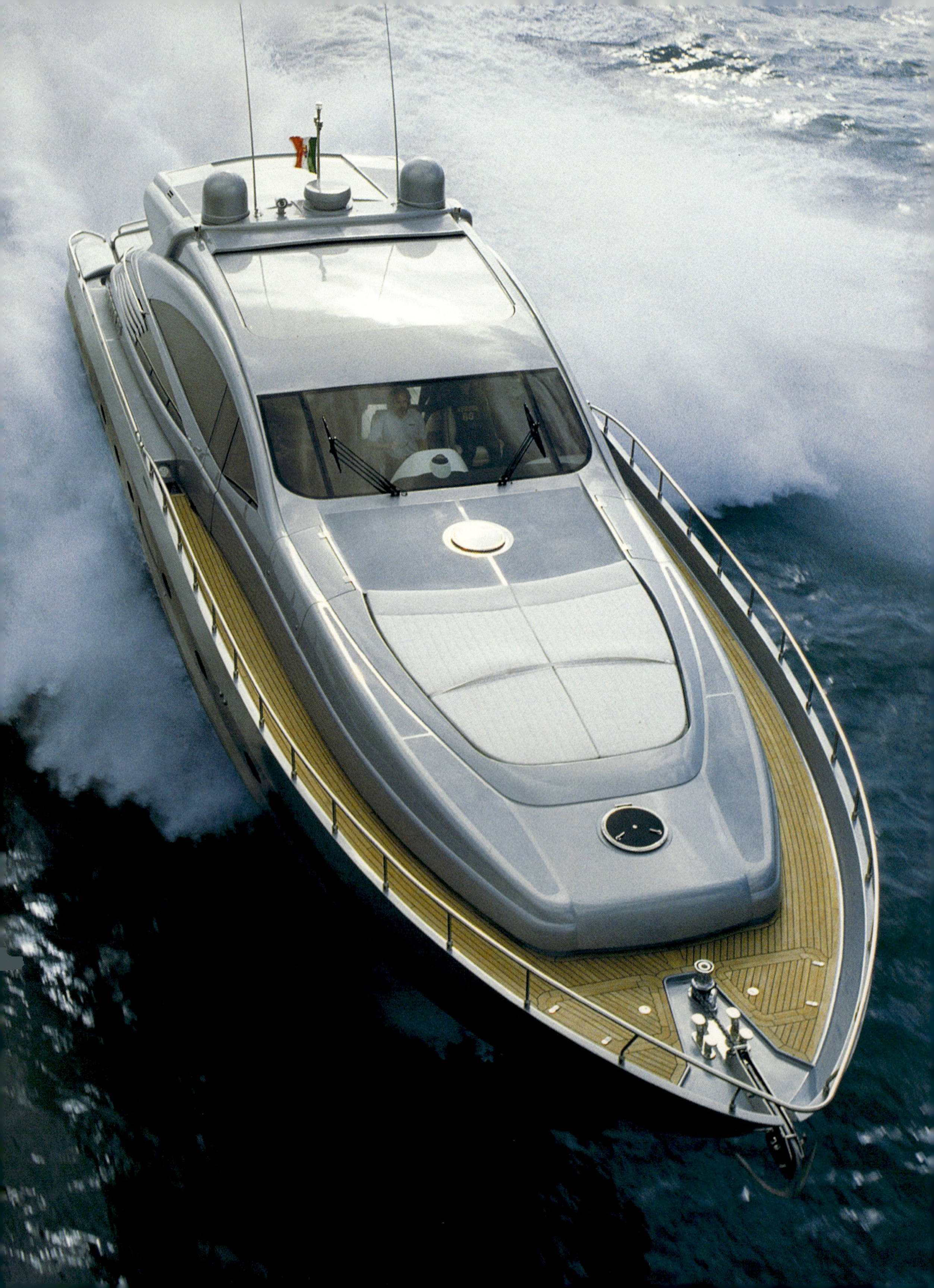

FULVIO DE SIMONI
PERSHING 76 | 2003
Pershing

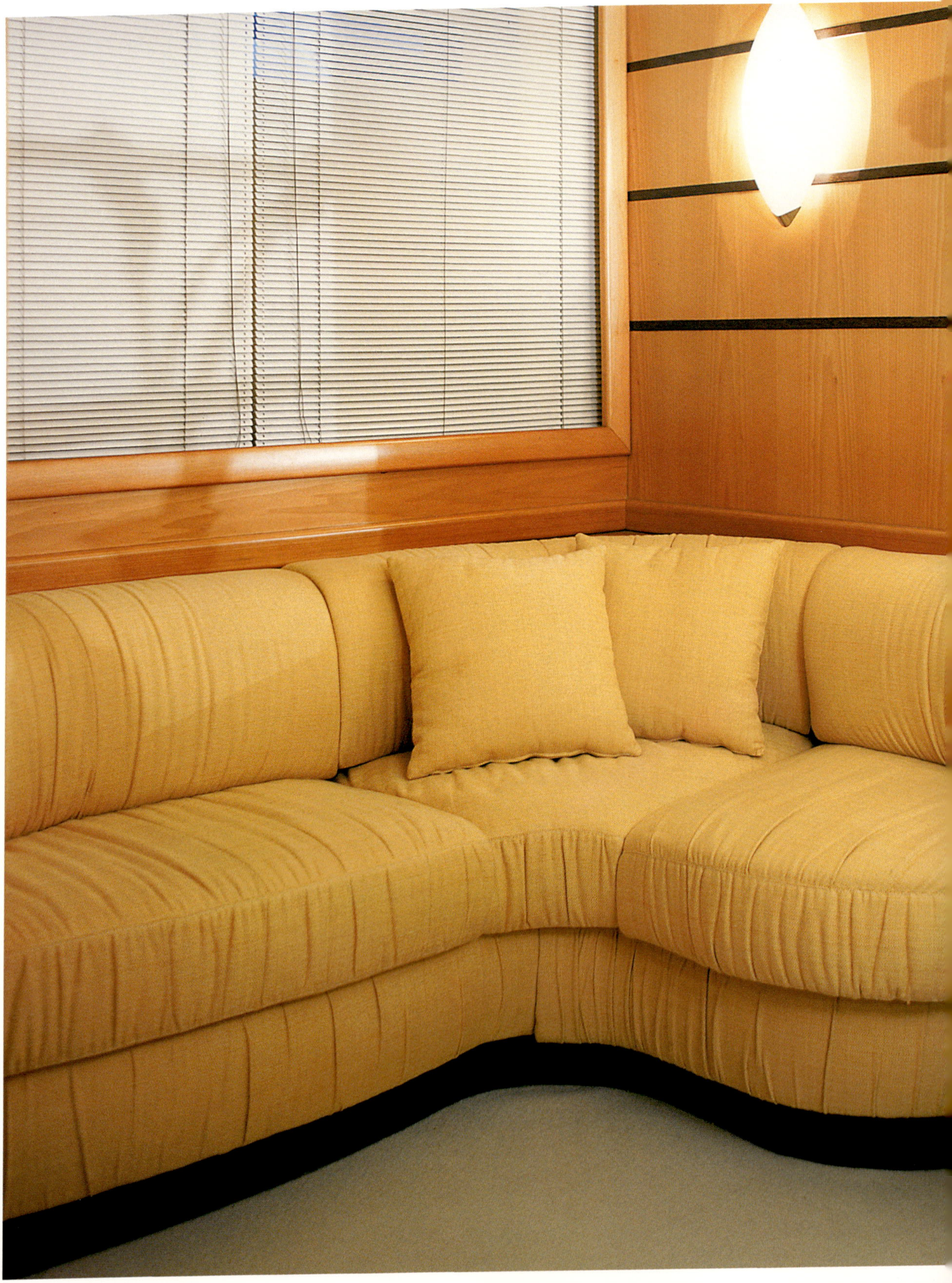

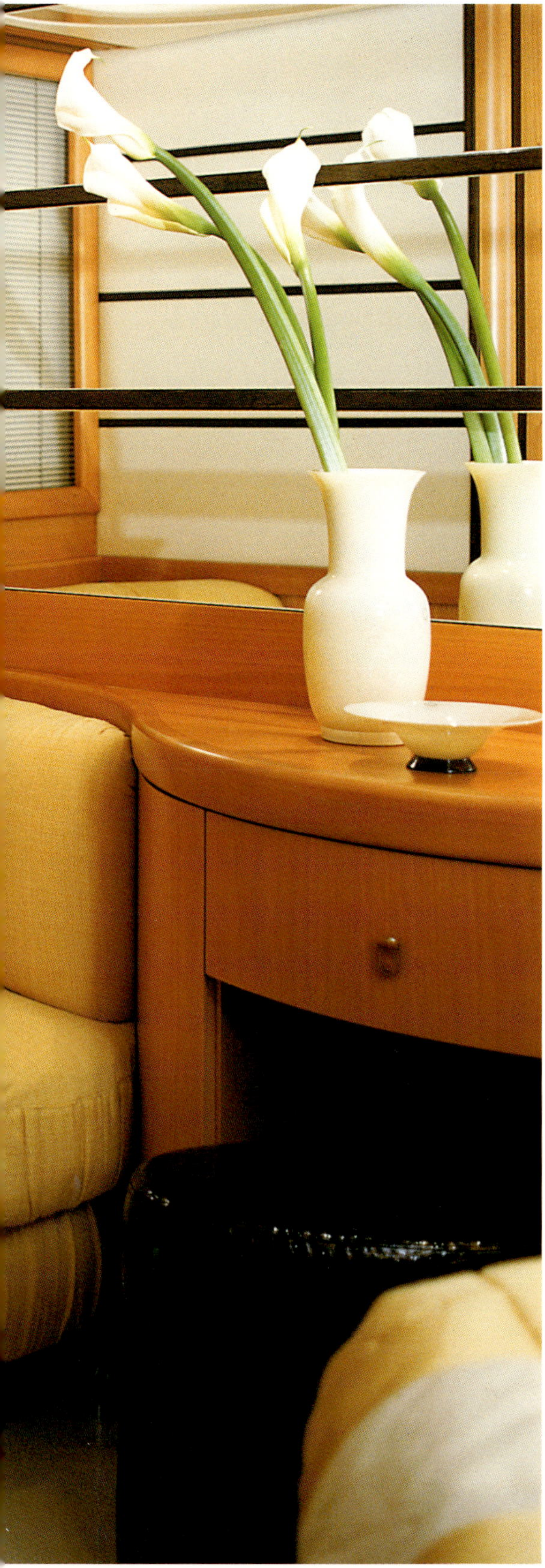

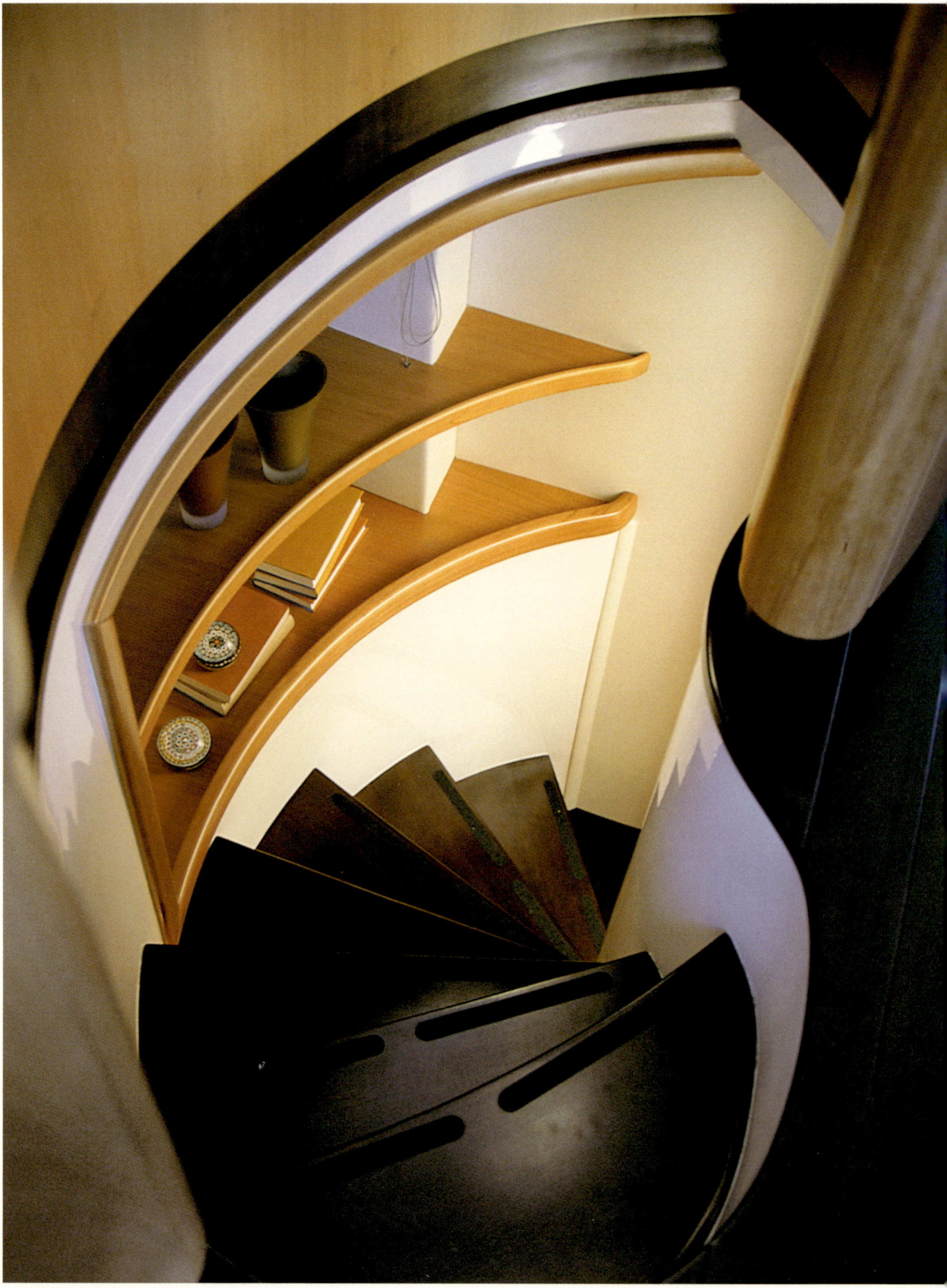

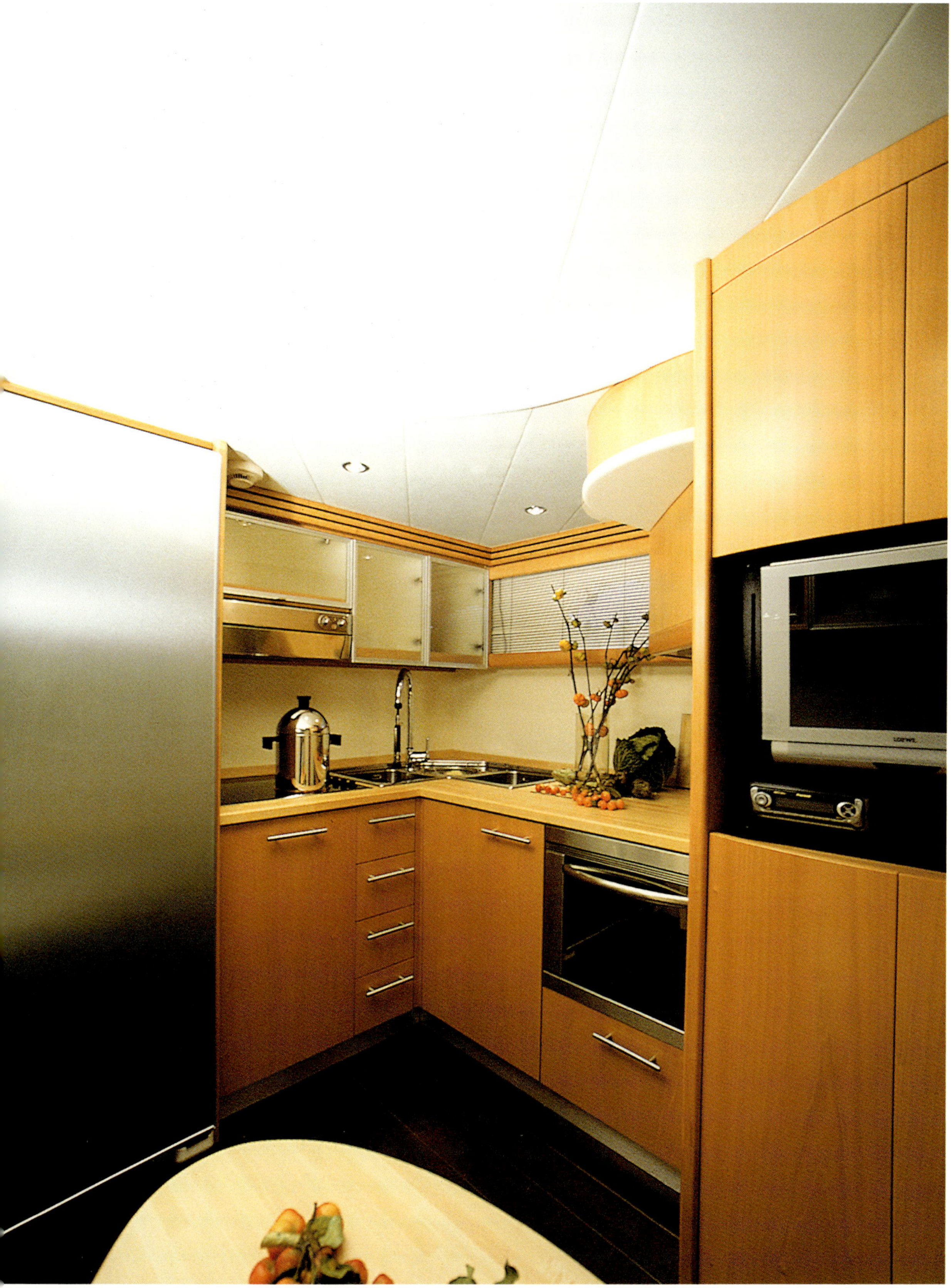

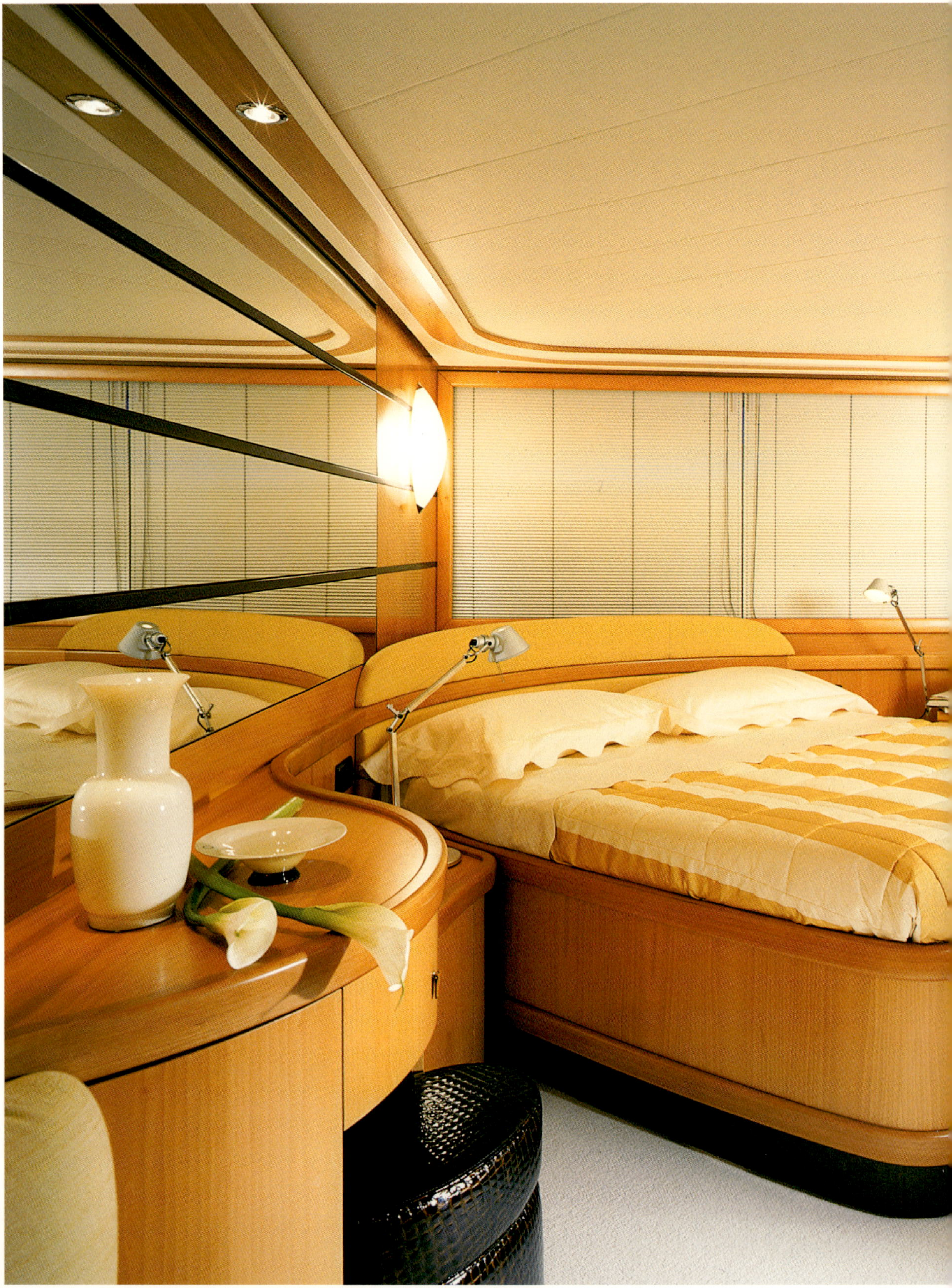

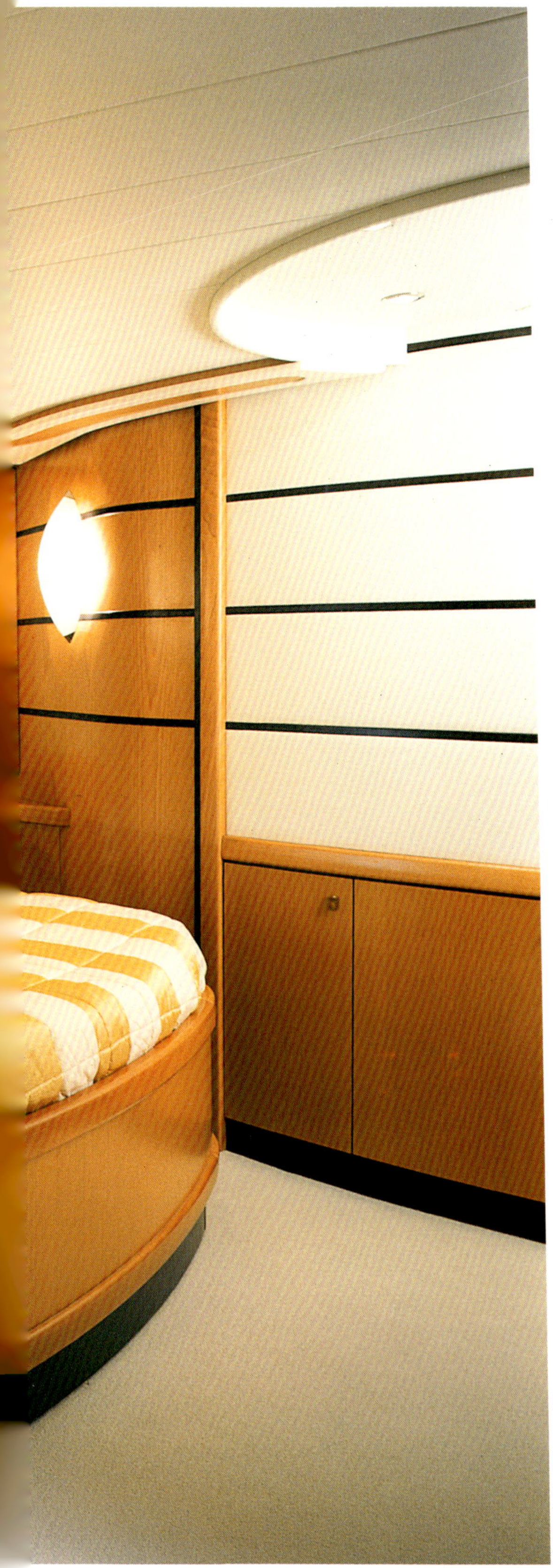

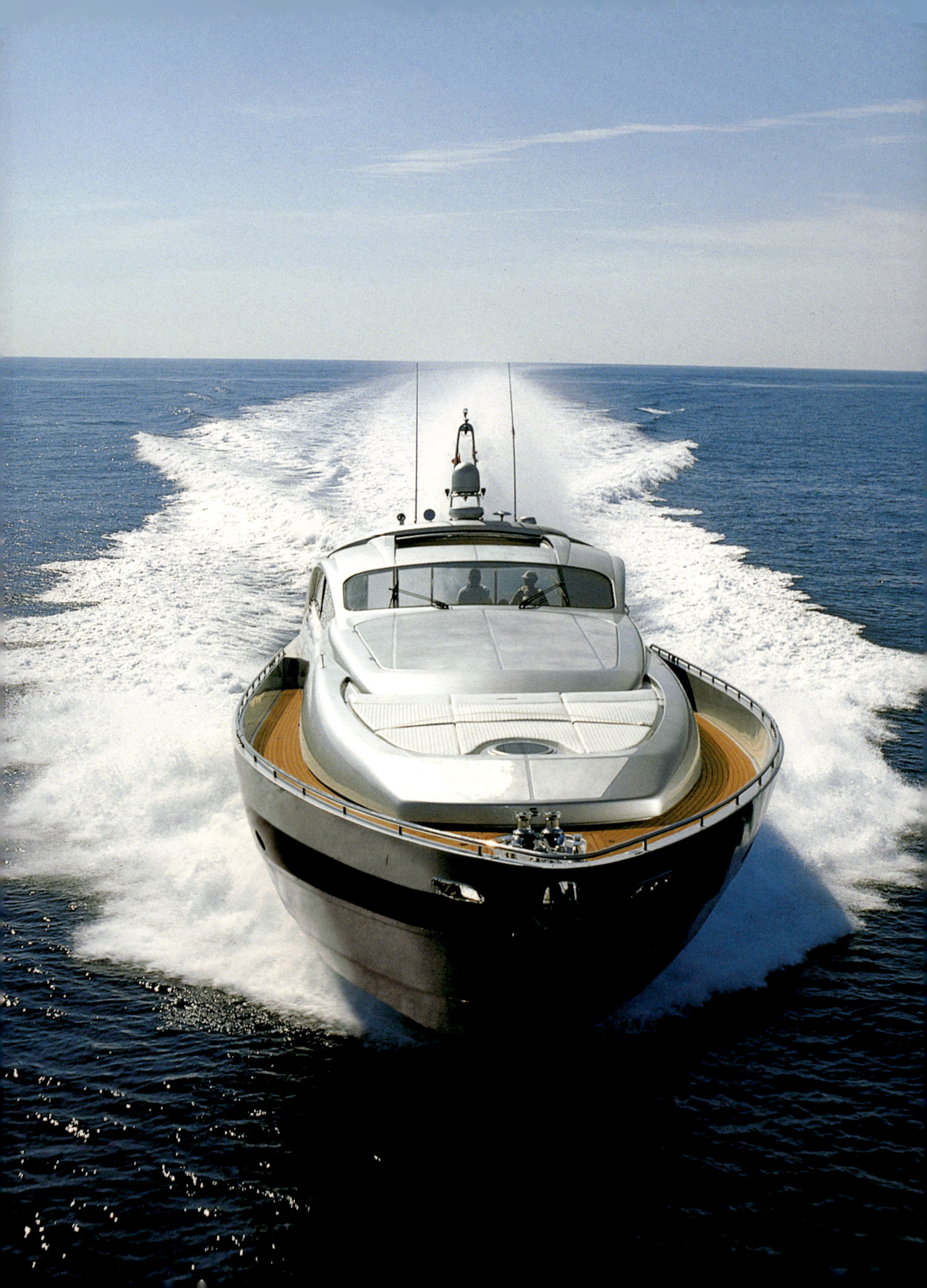

FULVIO DE SIMONI
PERSHING 88 | 2001
Pershing

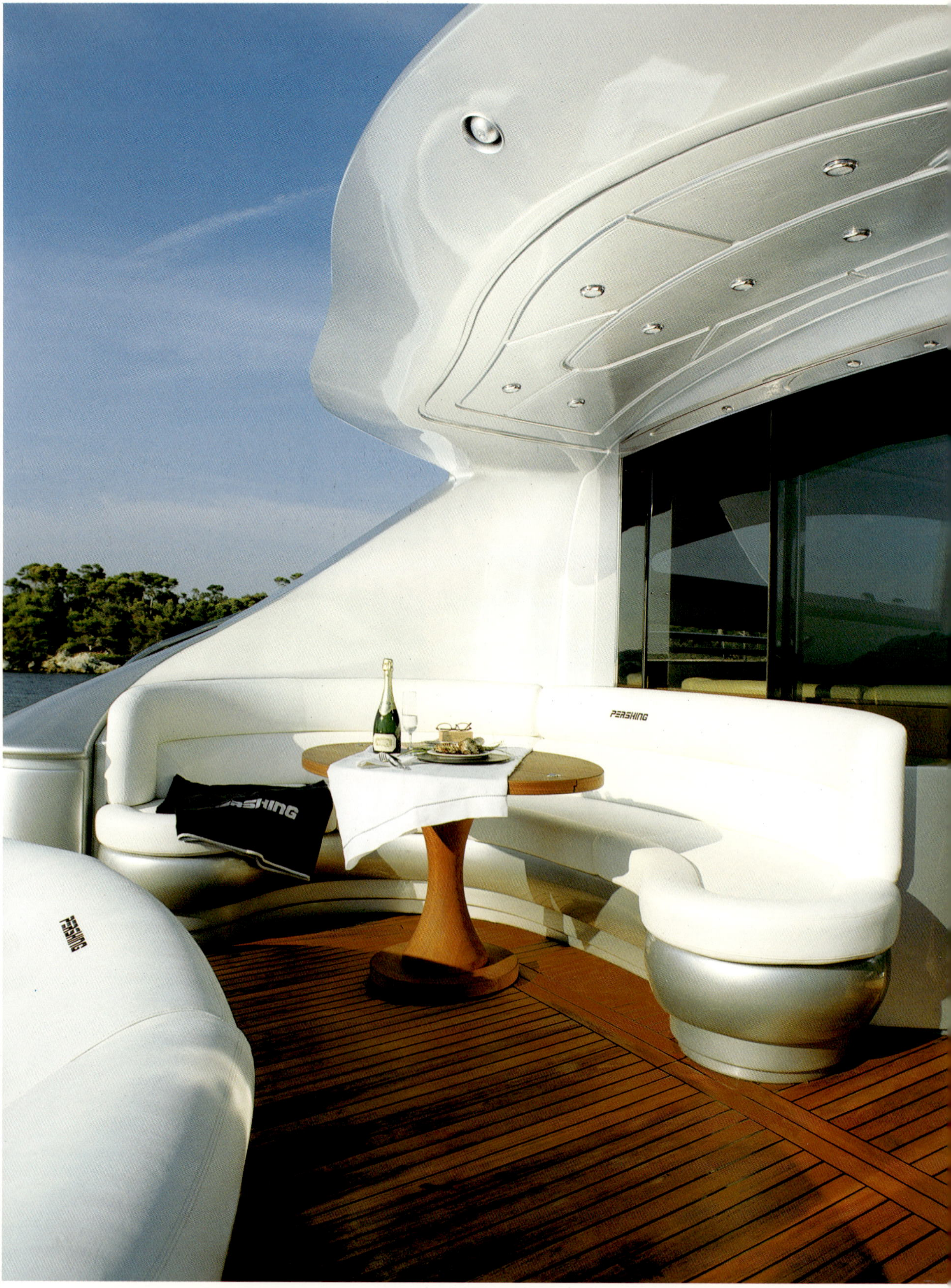
PERSHING
PERSHING

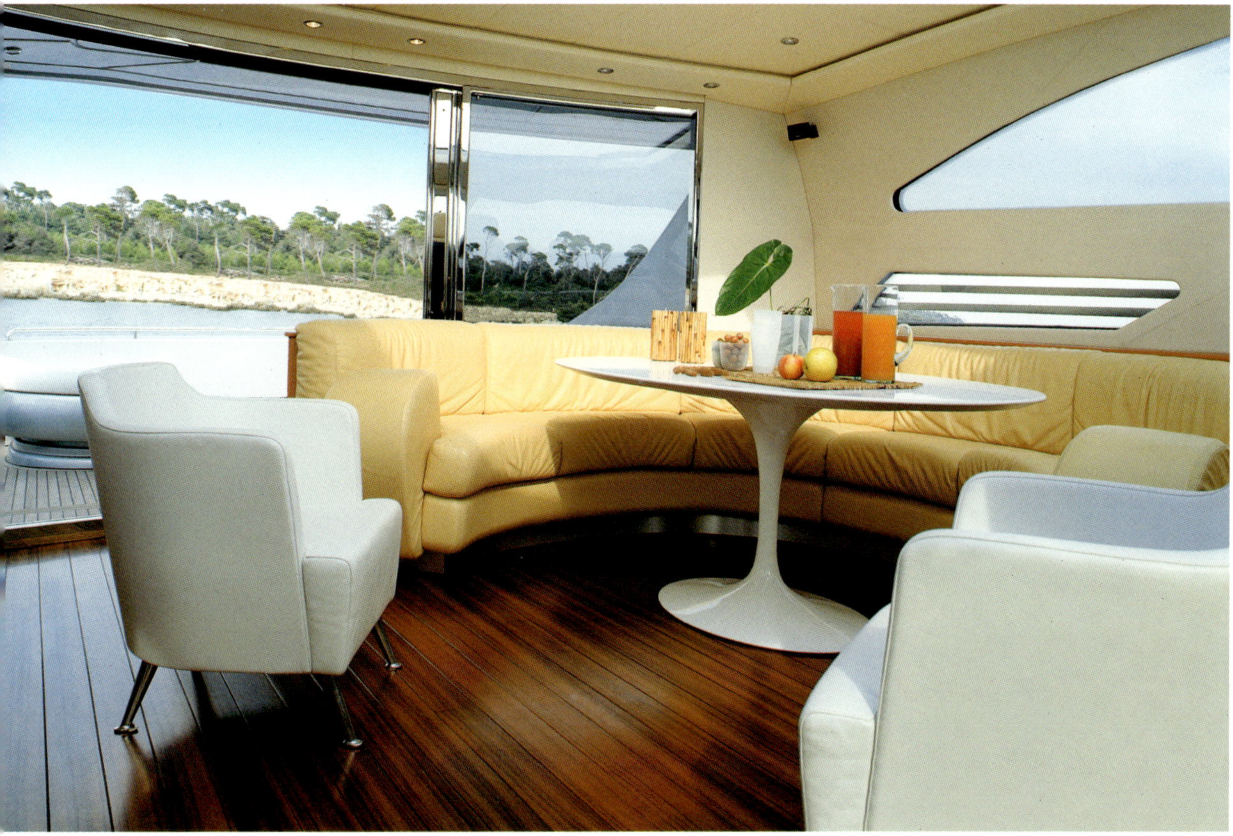

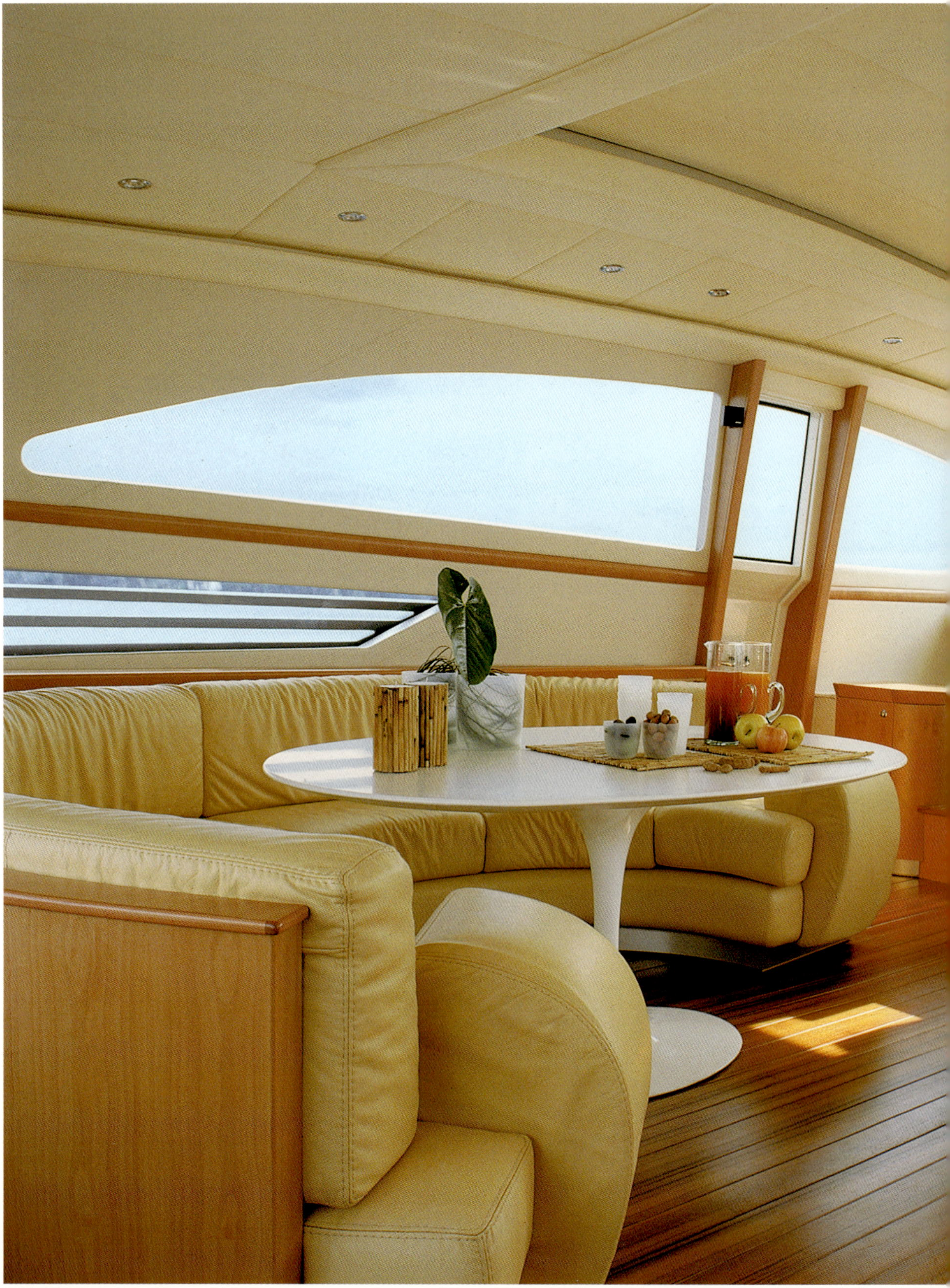

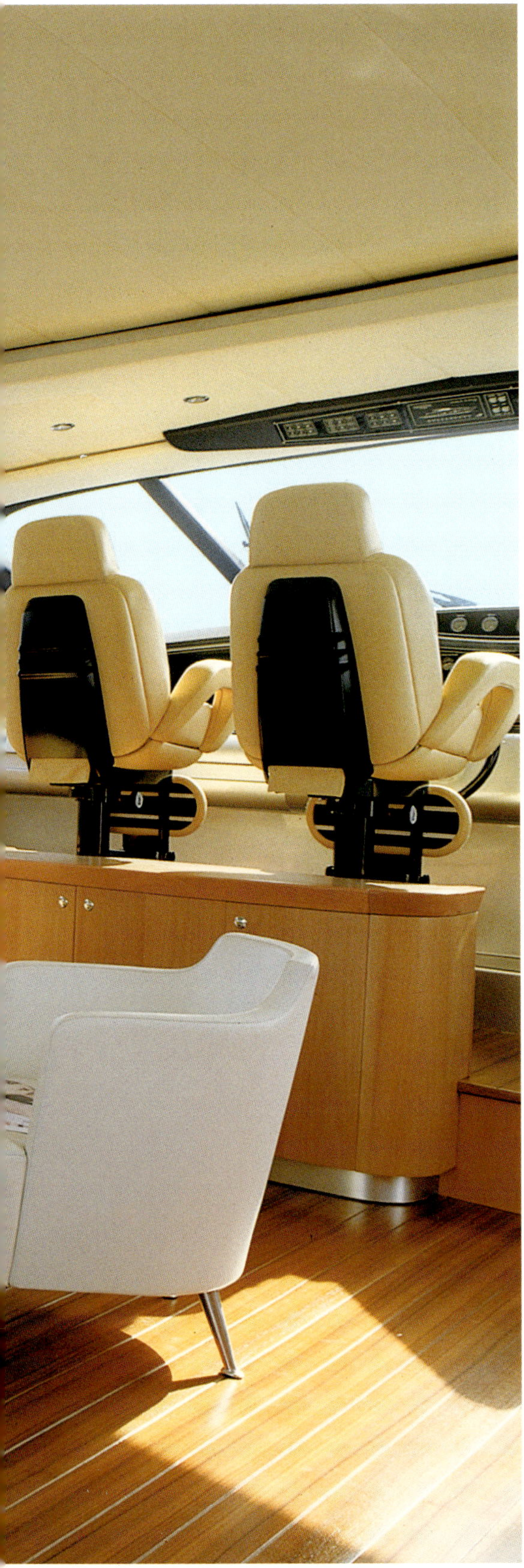

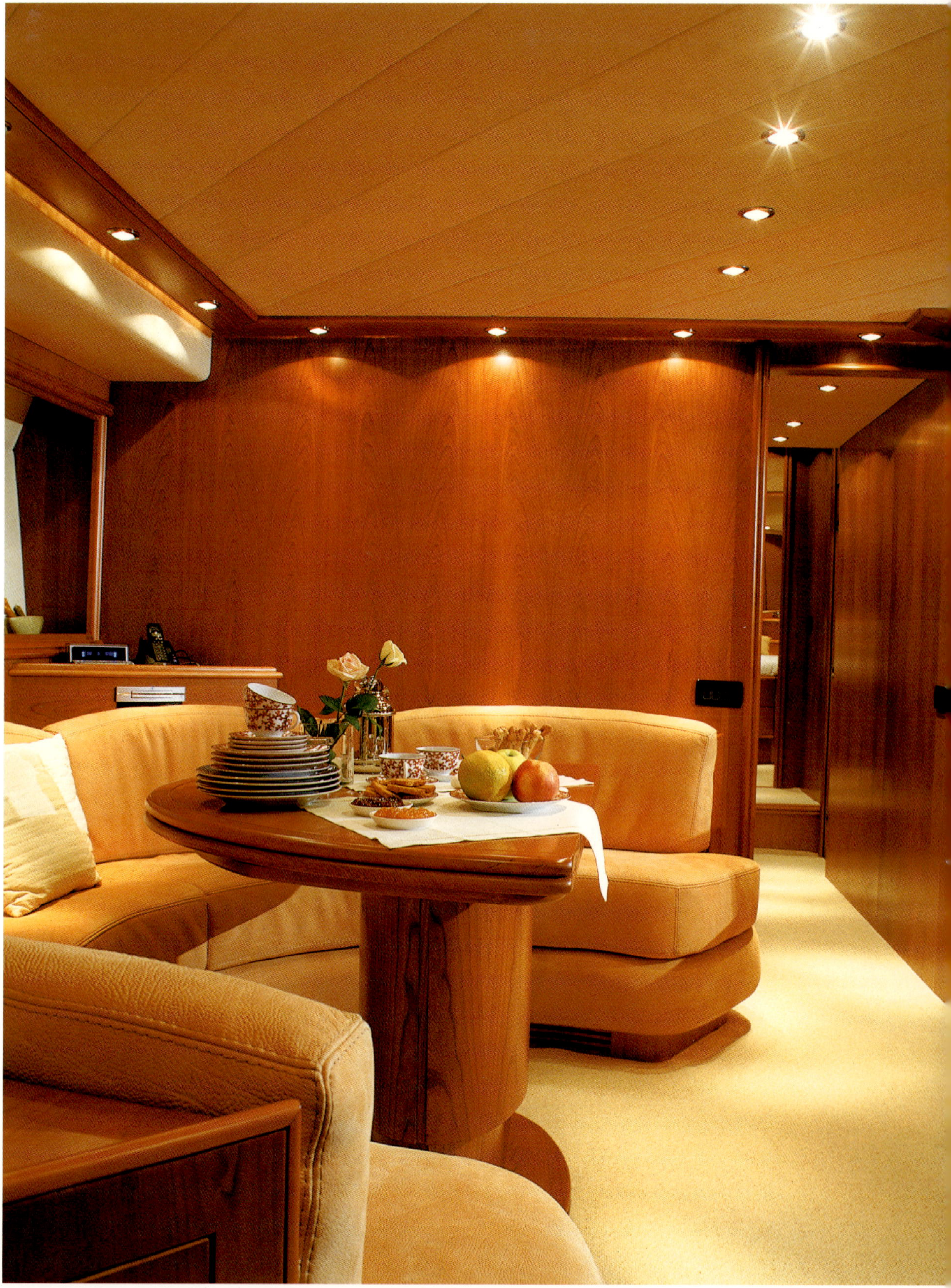

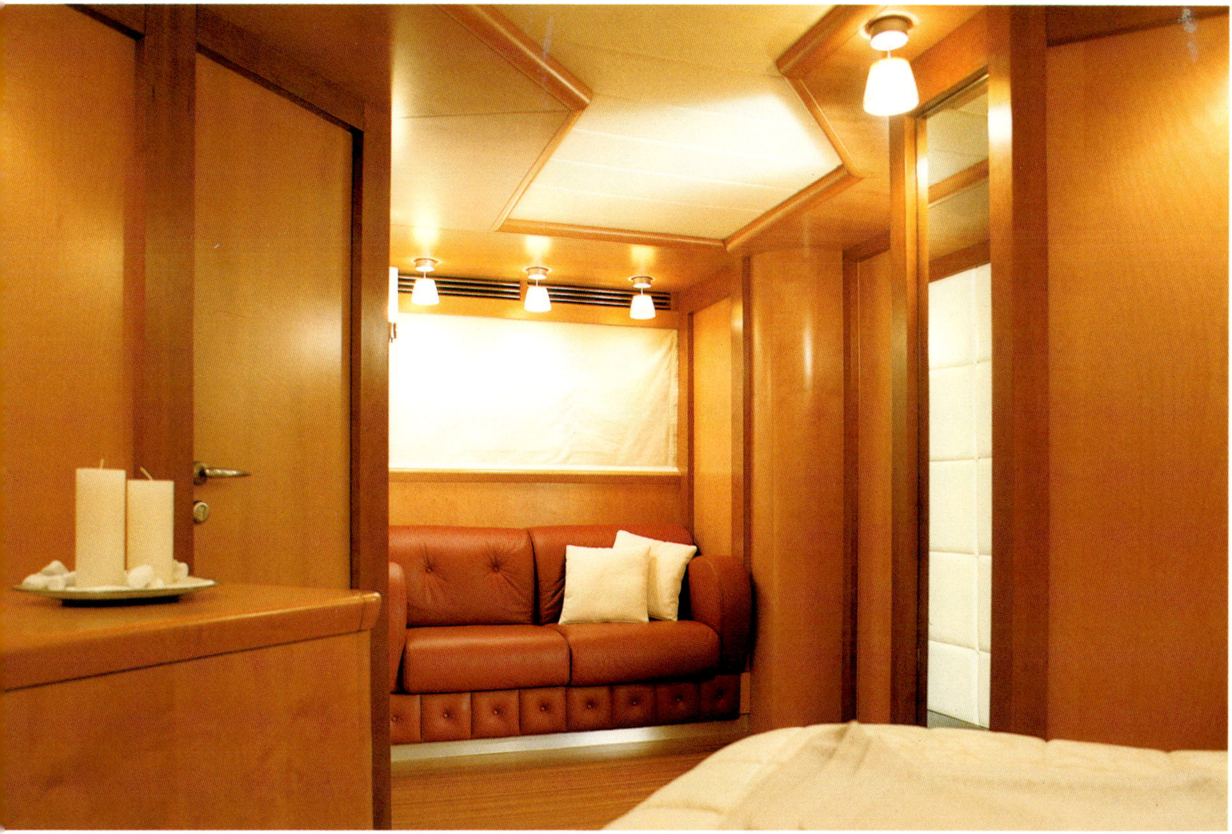

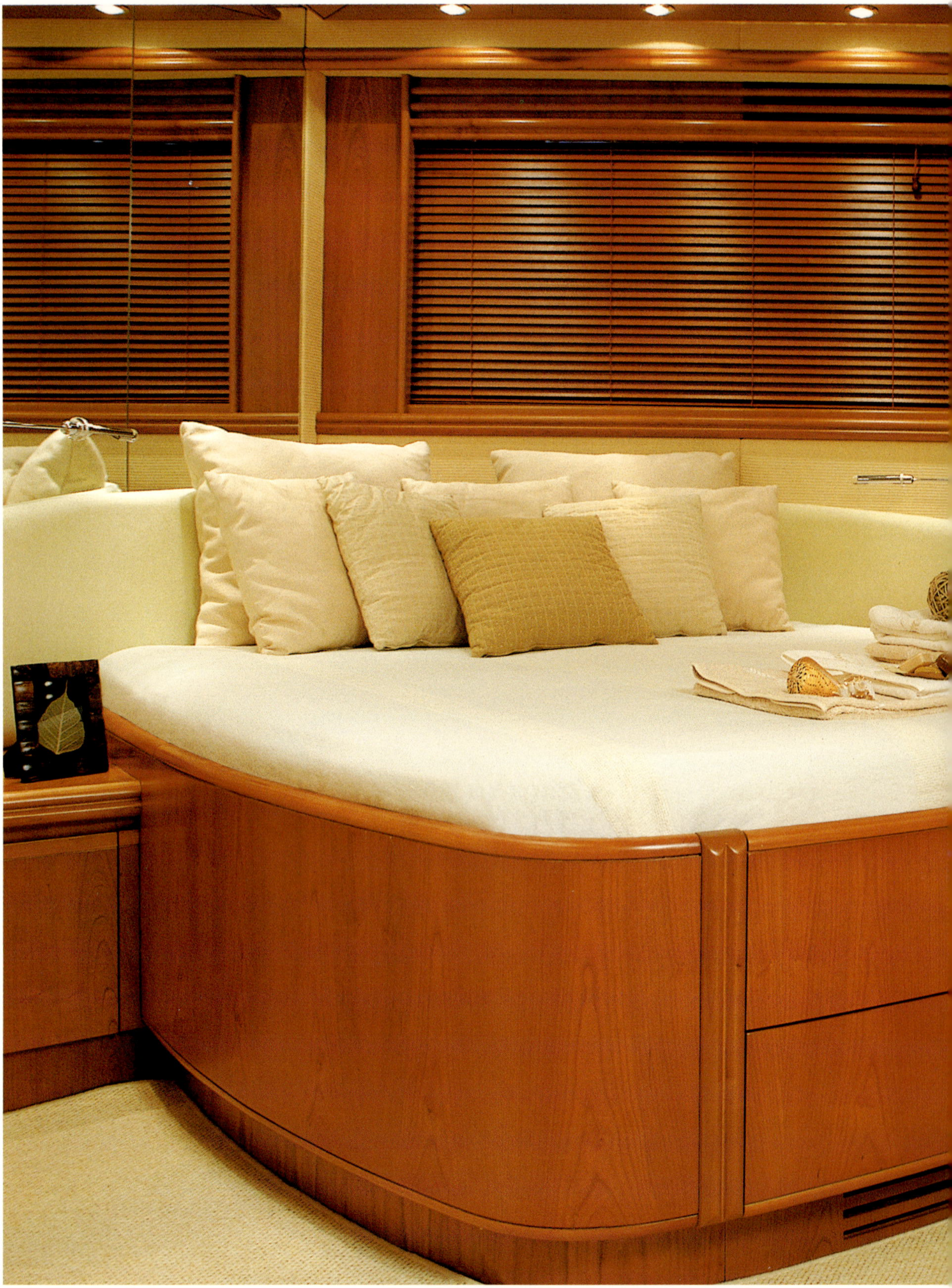

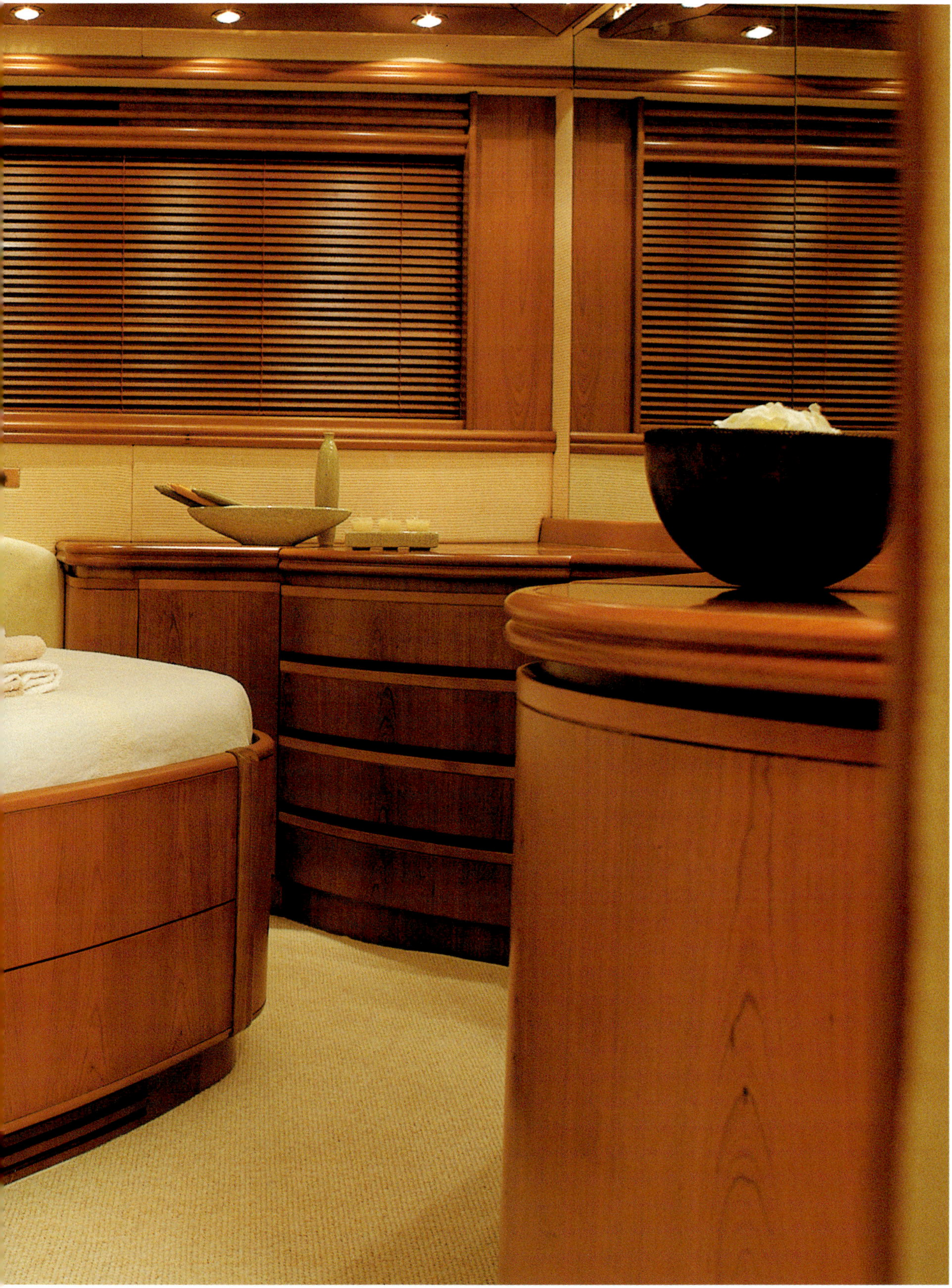

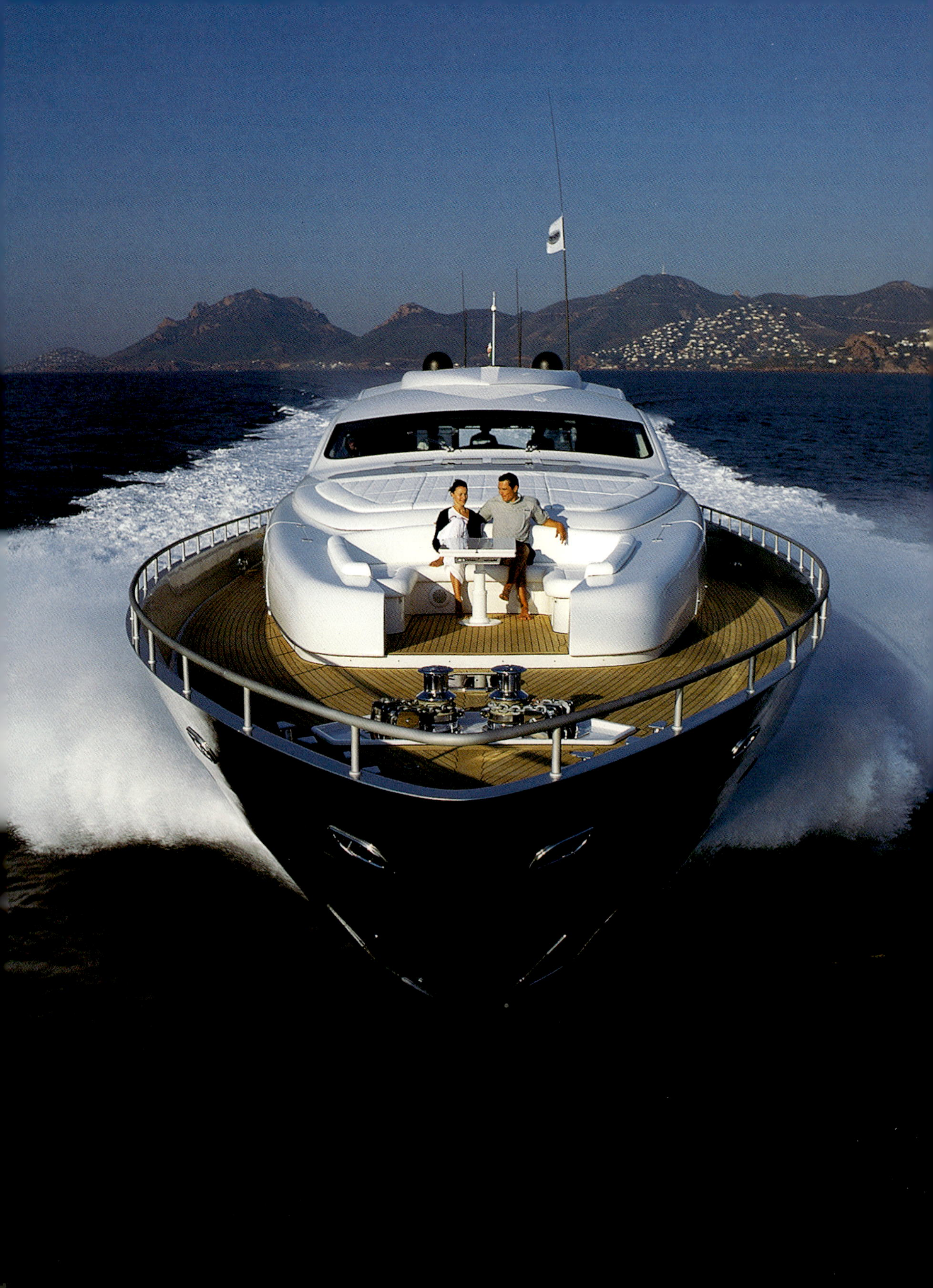

FULVIO DE SIMONI
PERSHING 115 | 2005
Pershing

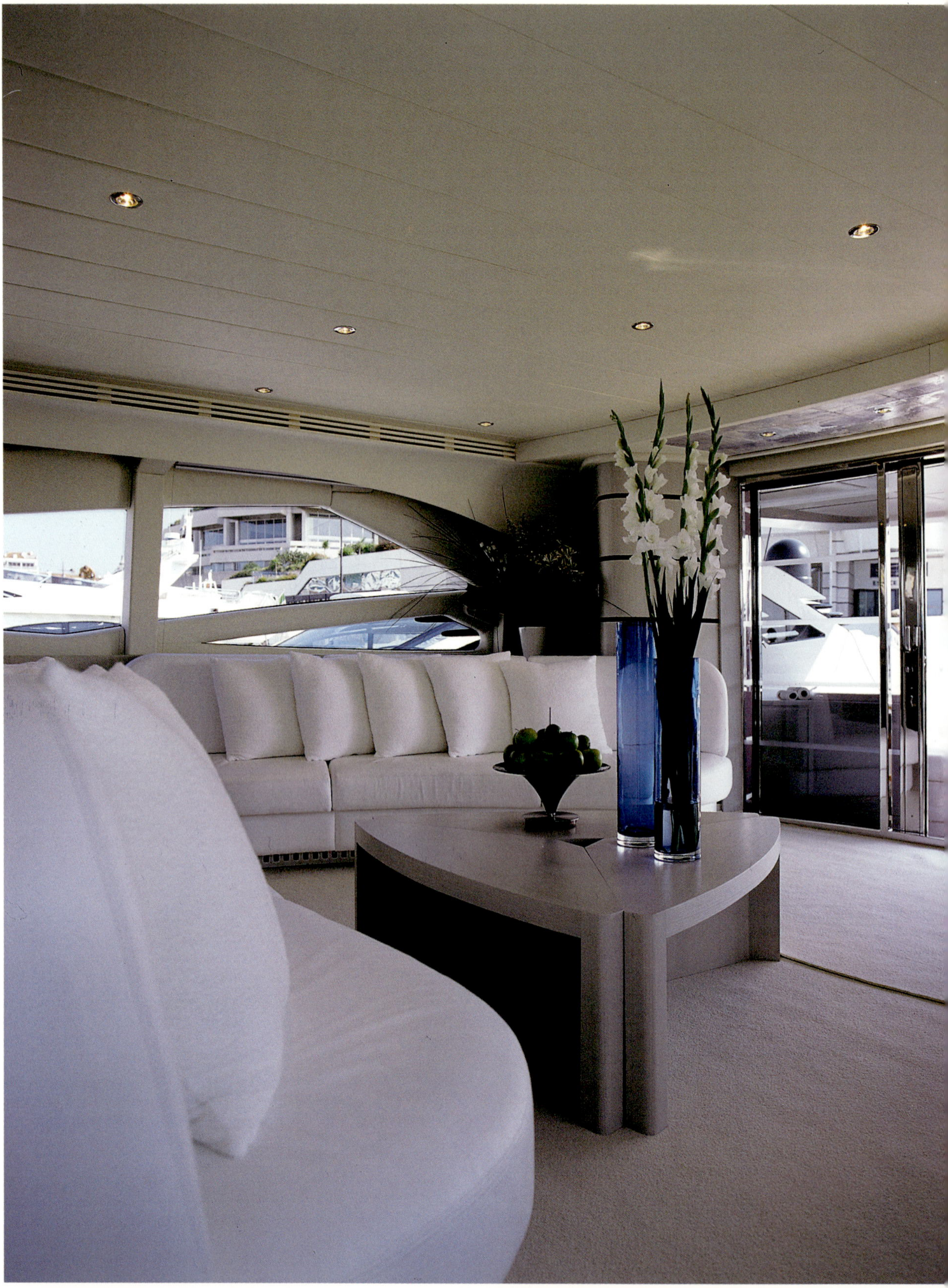

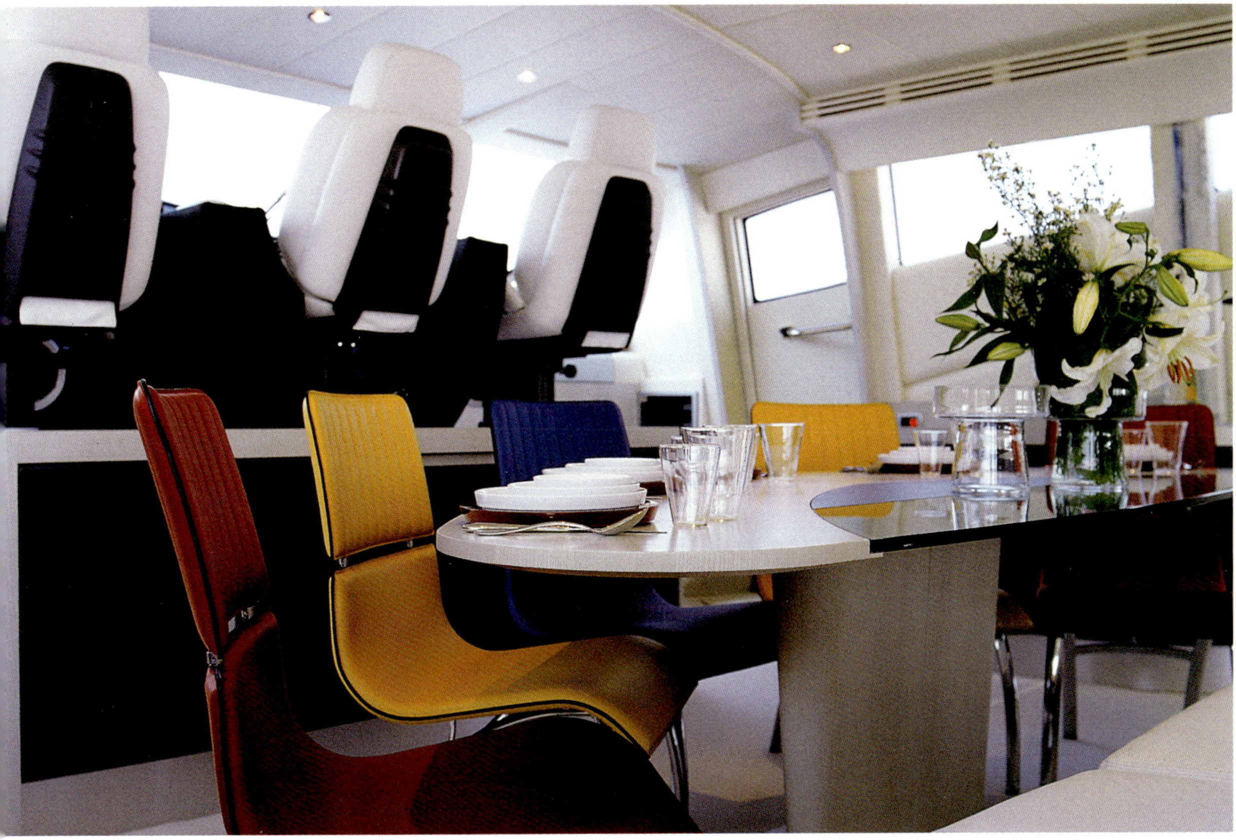

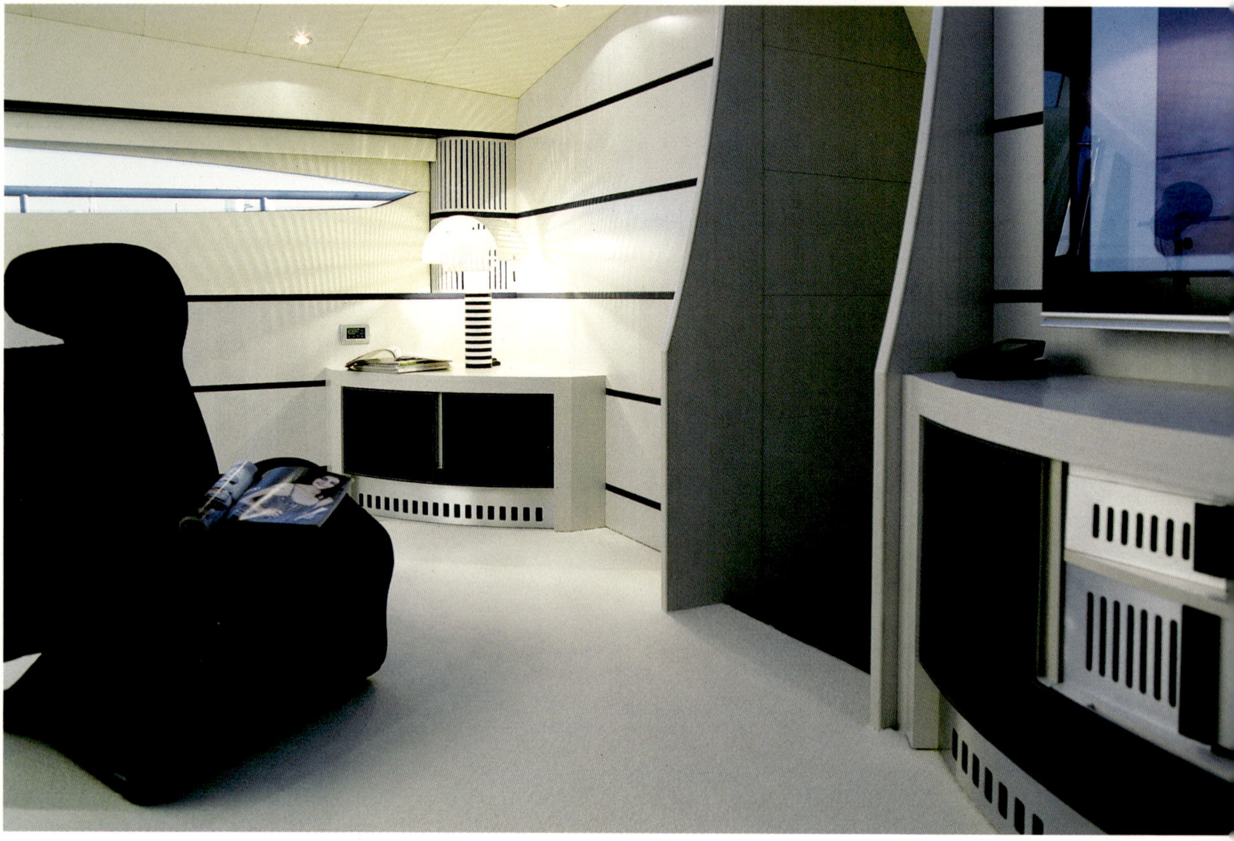

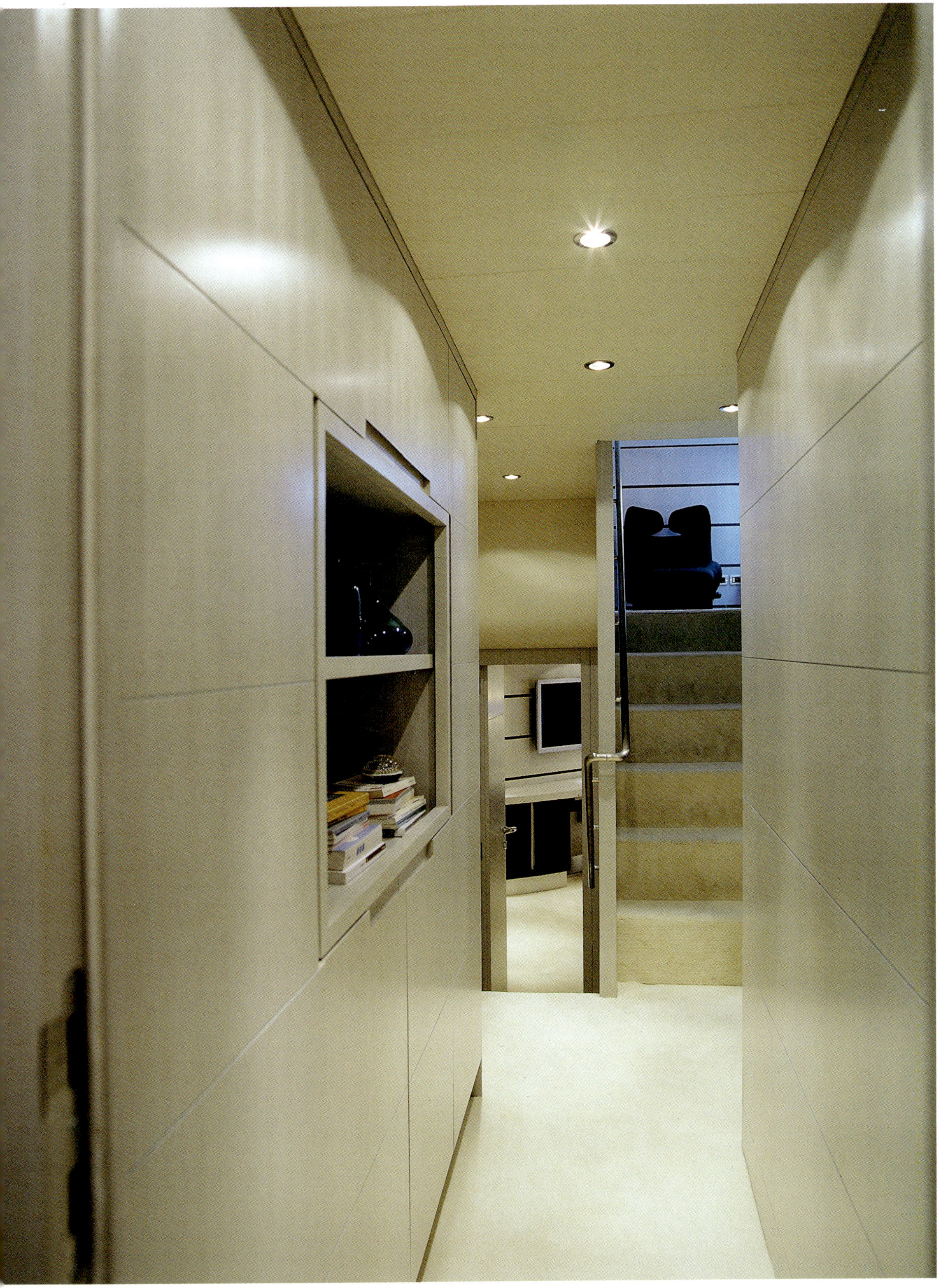

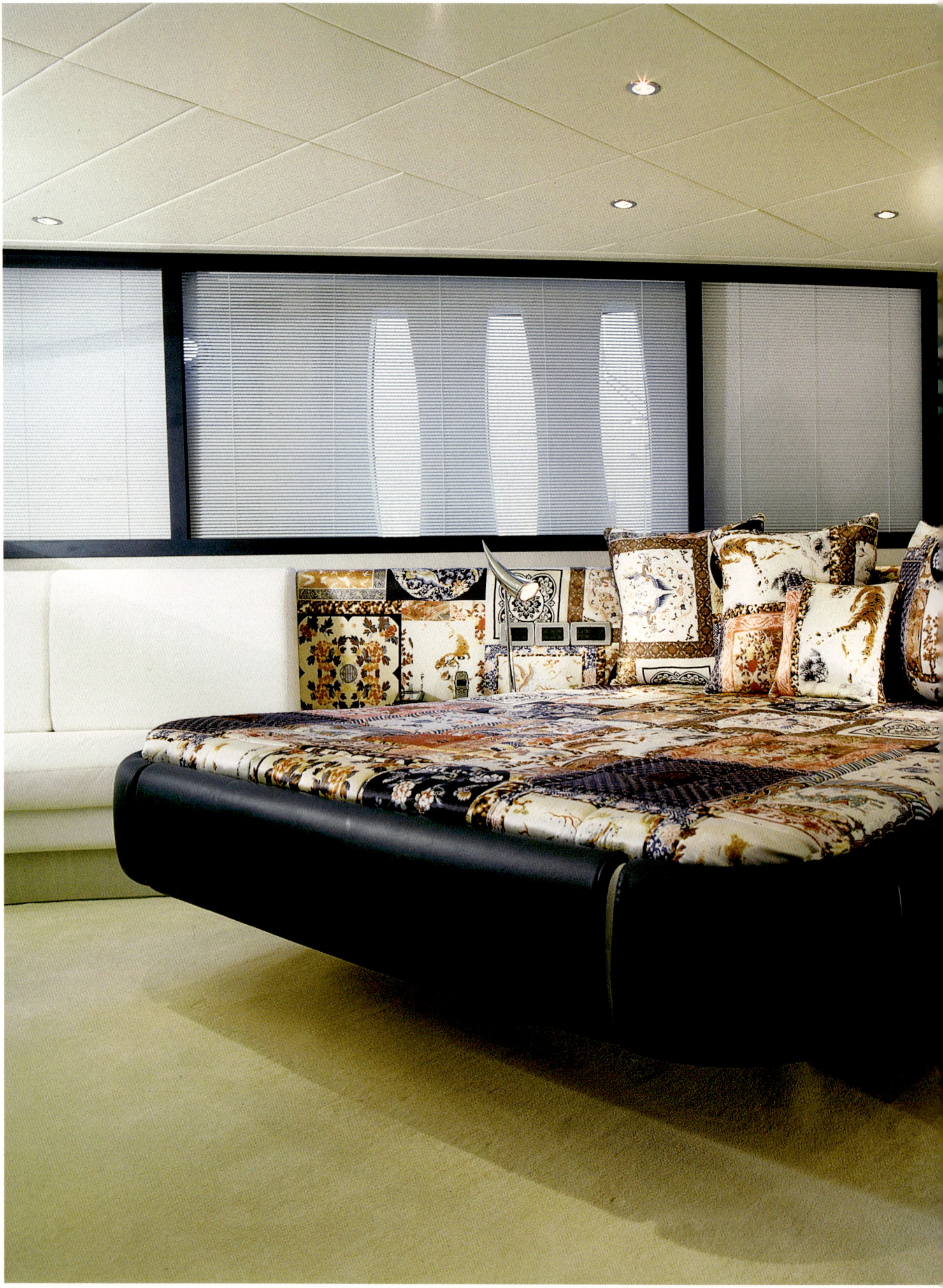

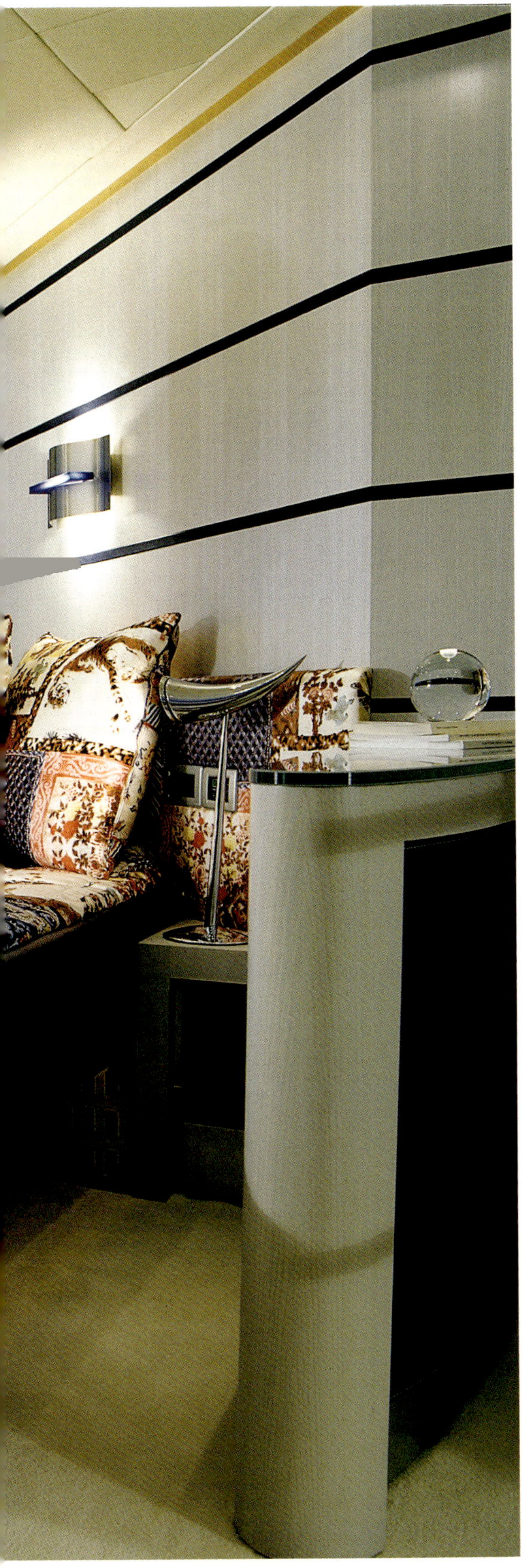

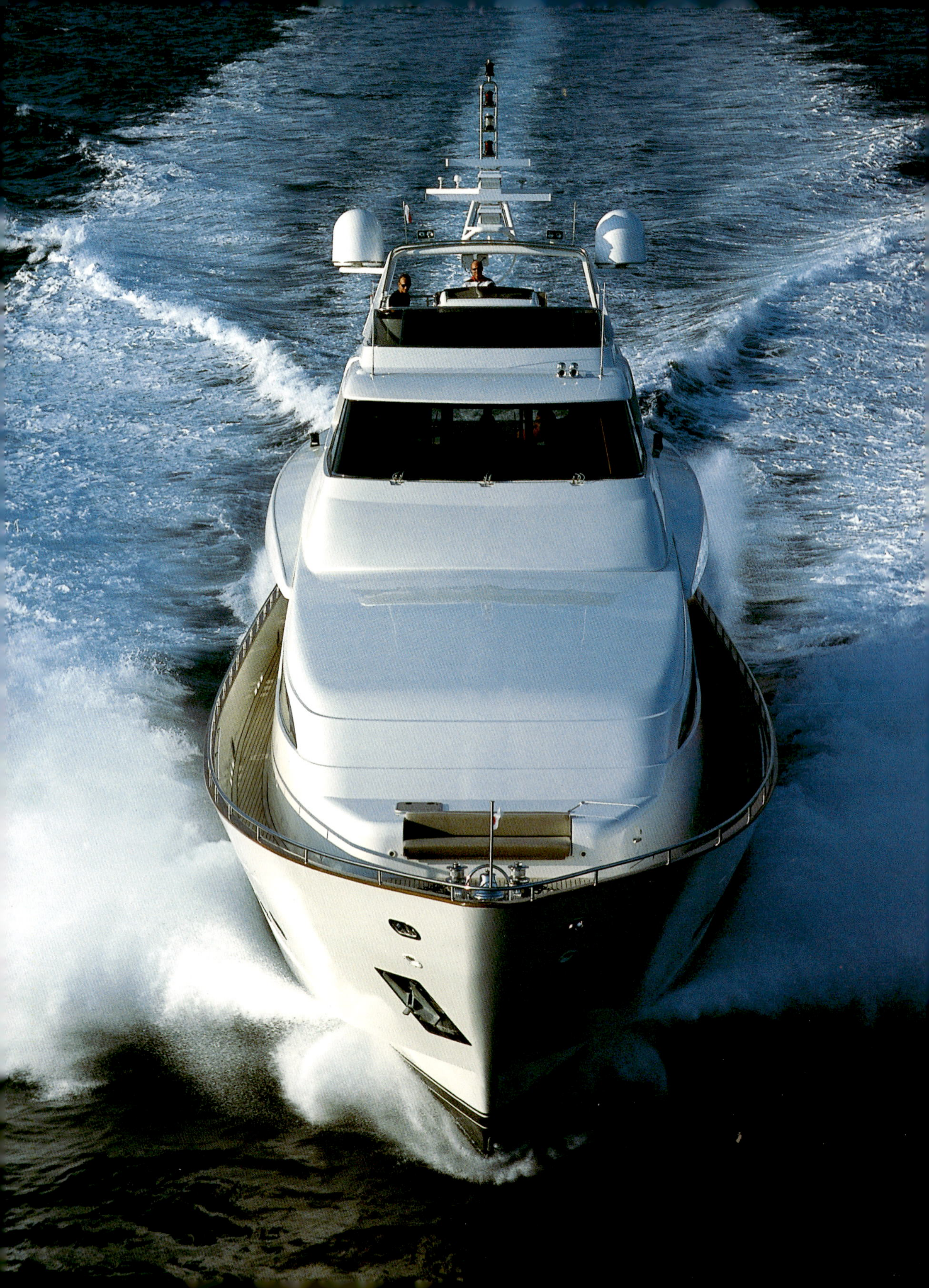

GUY COUACH
3600 | 2002
Guy Couach

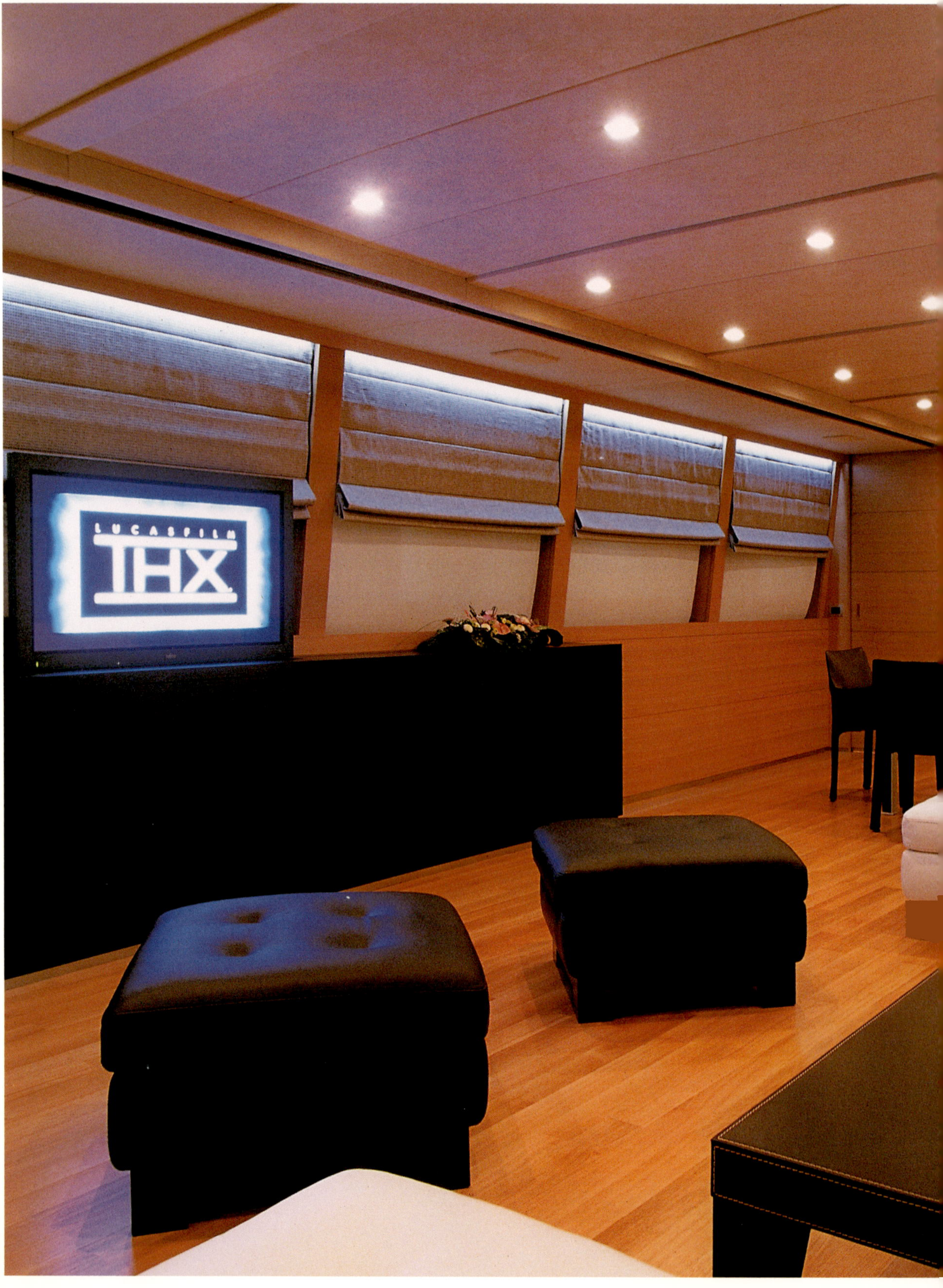
LUCASFILM
THX

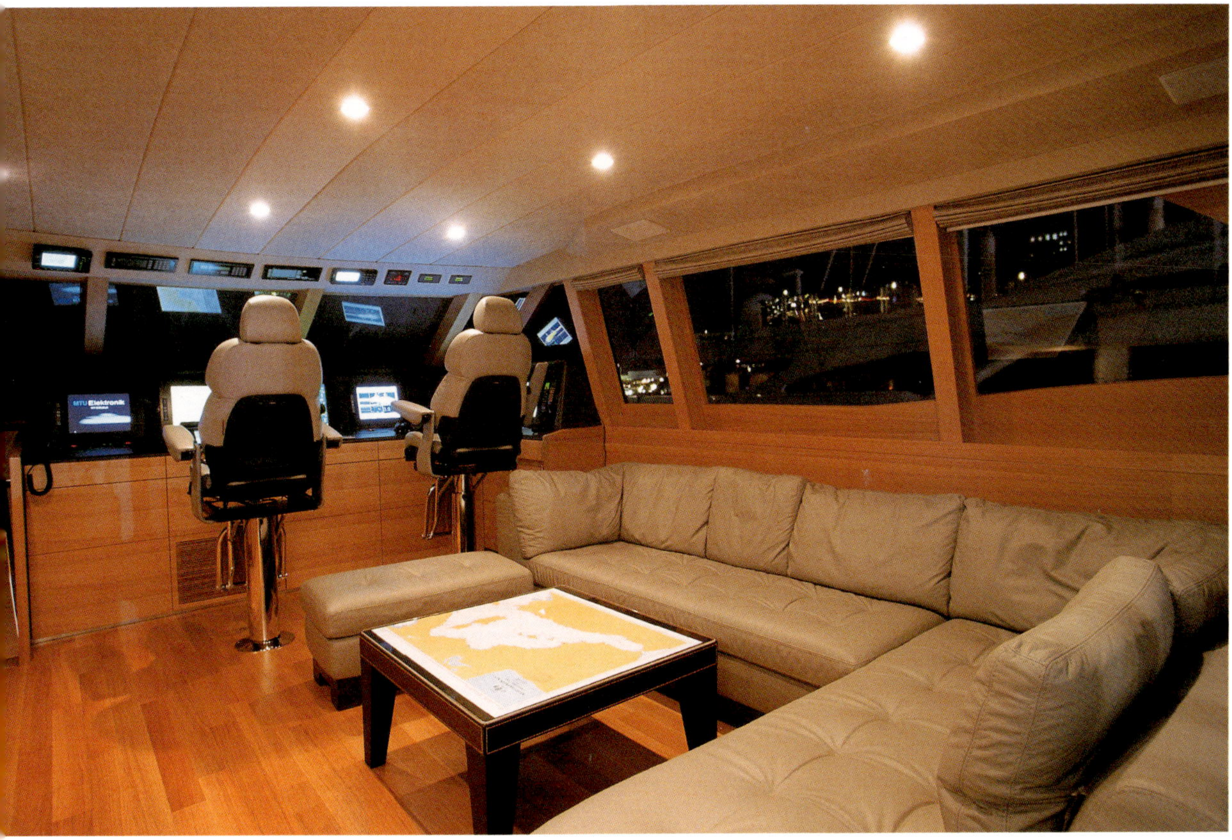

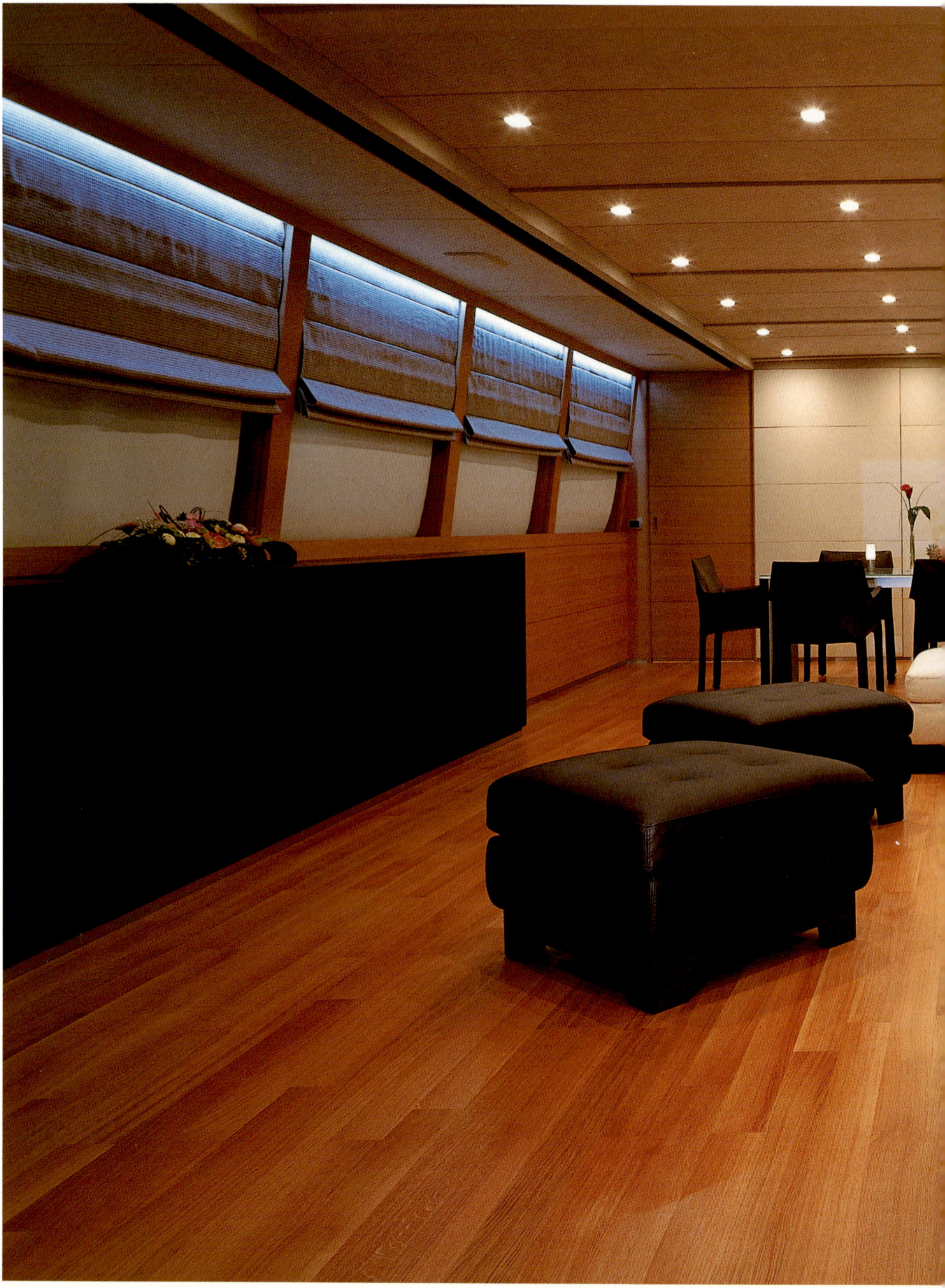

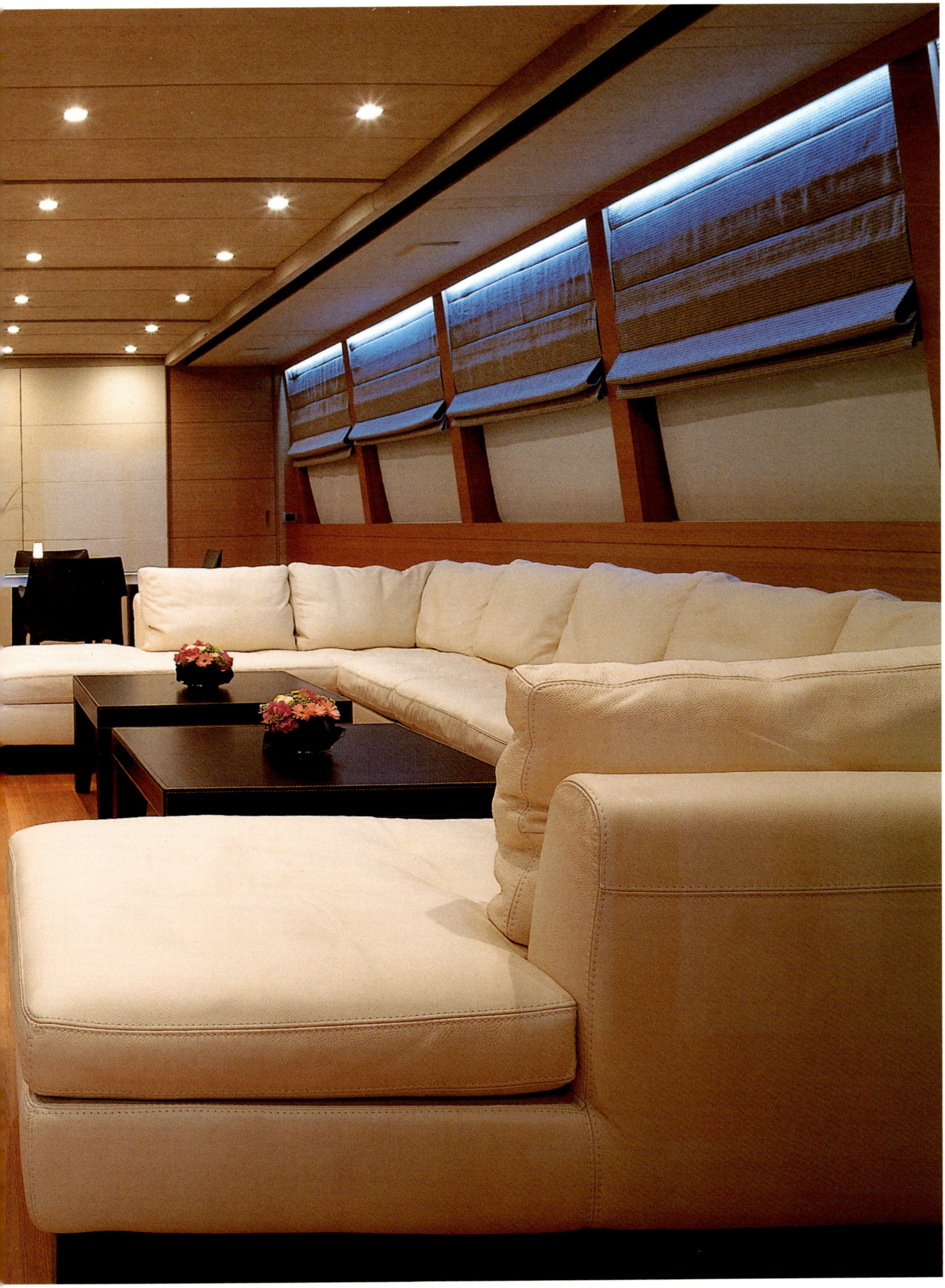

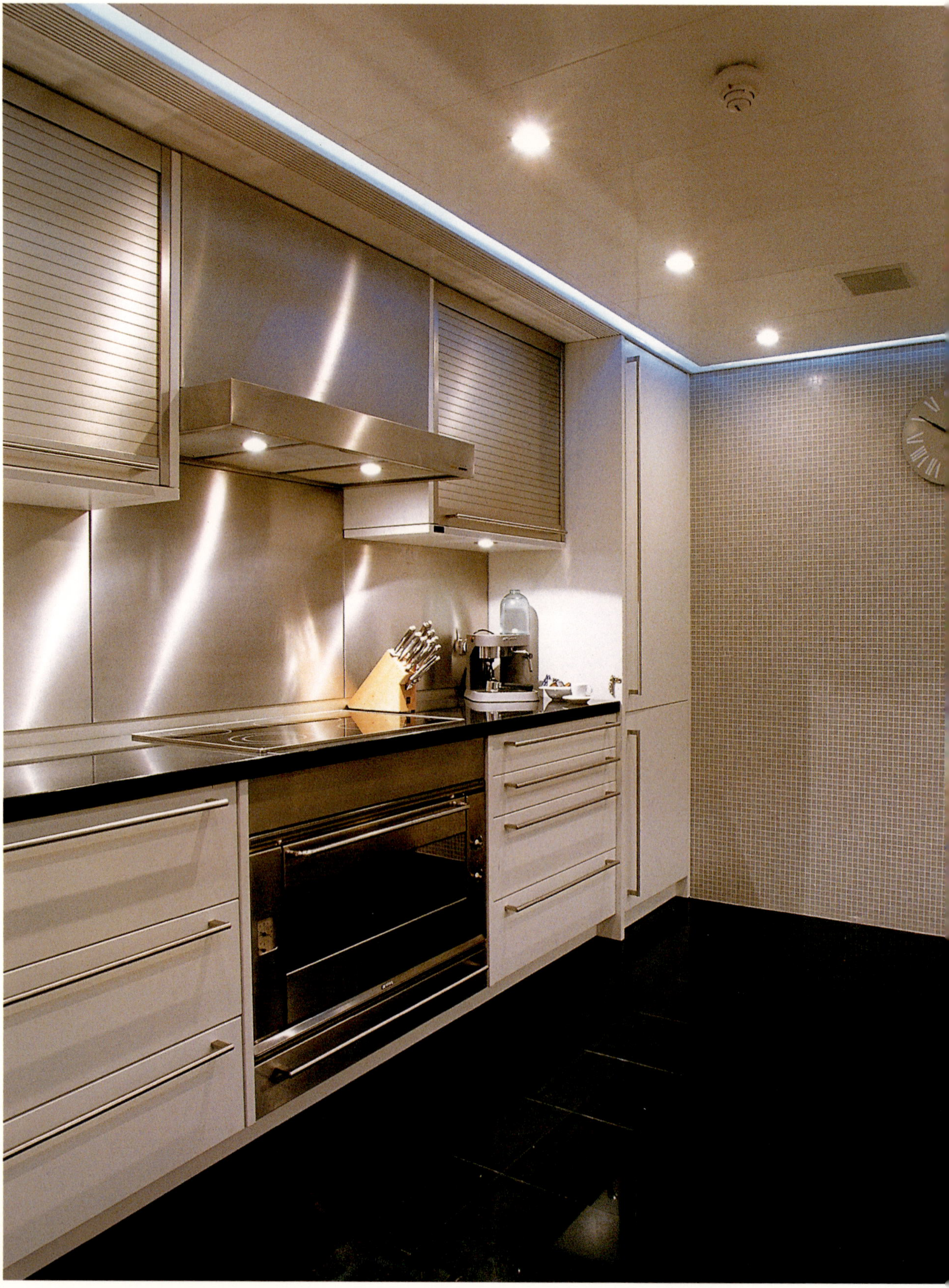

147

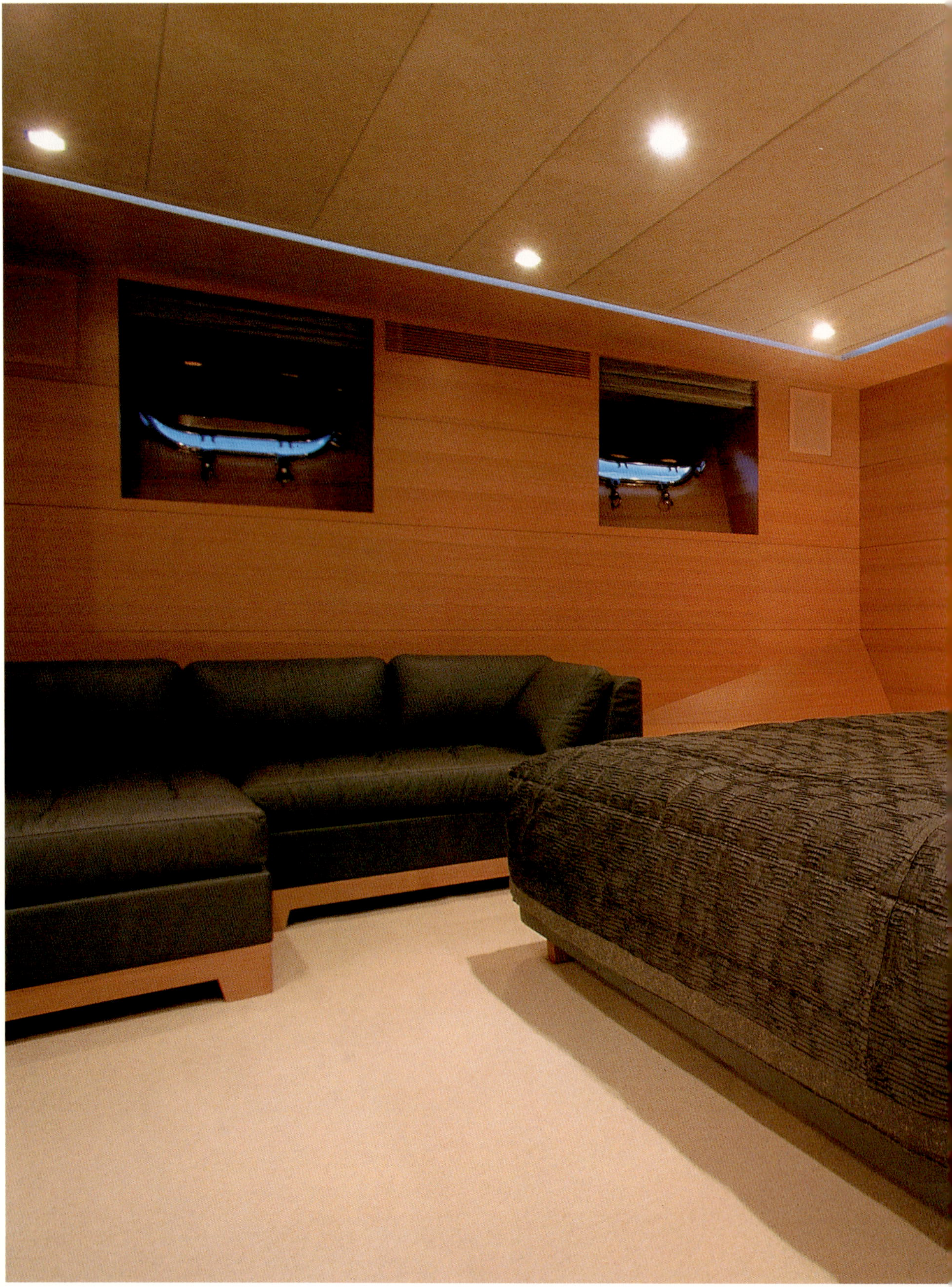

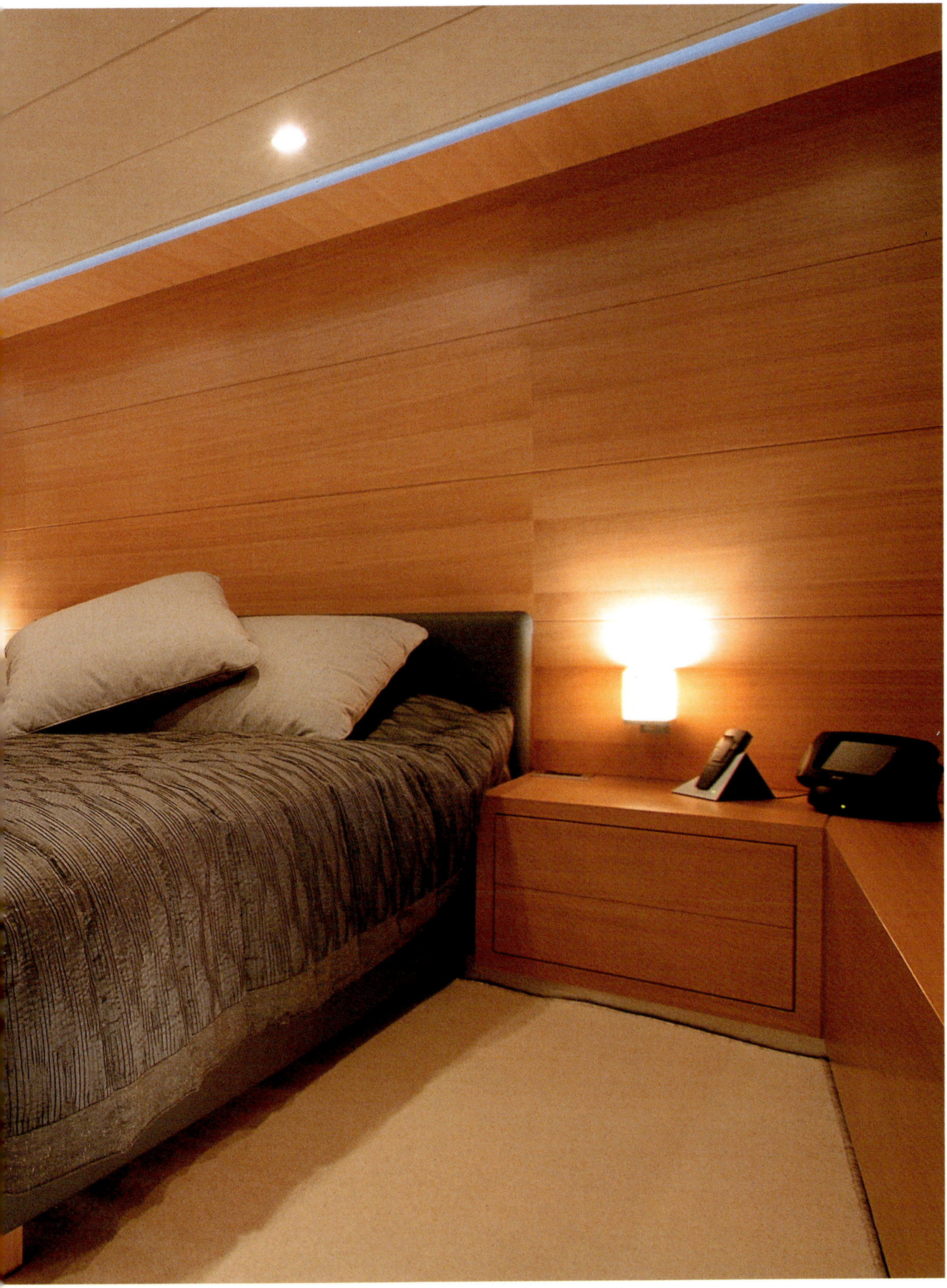

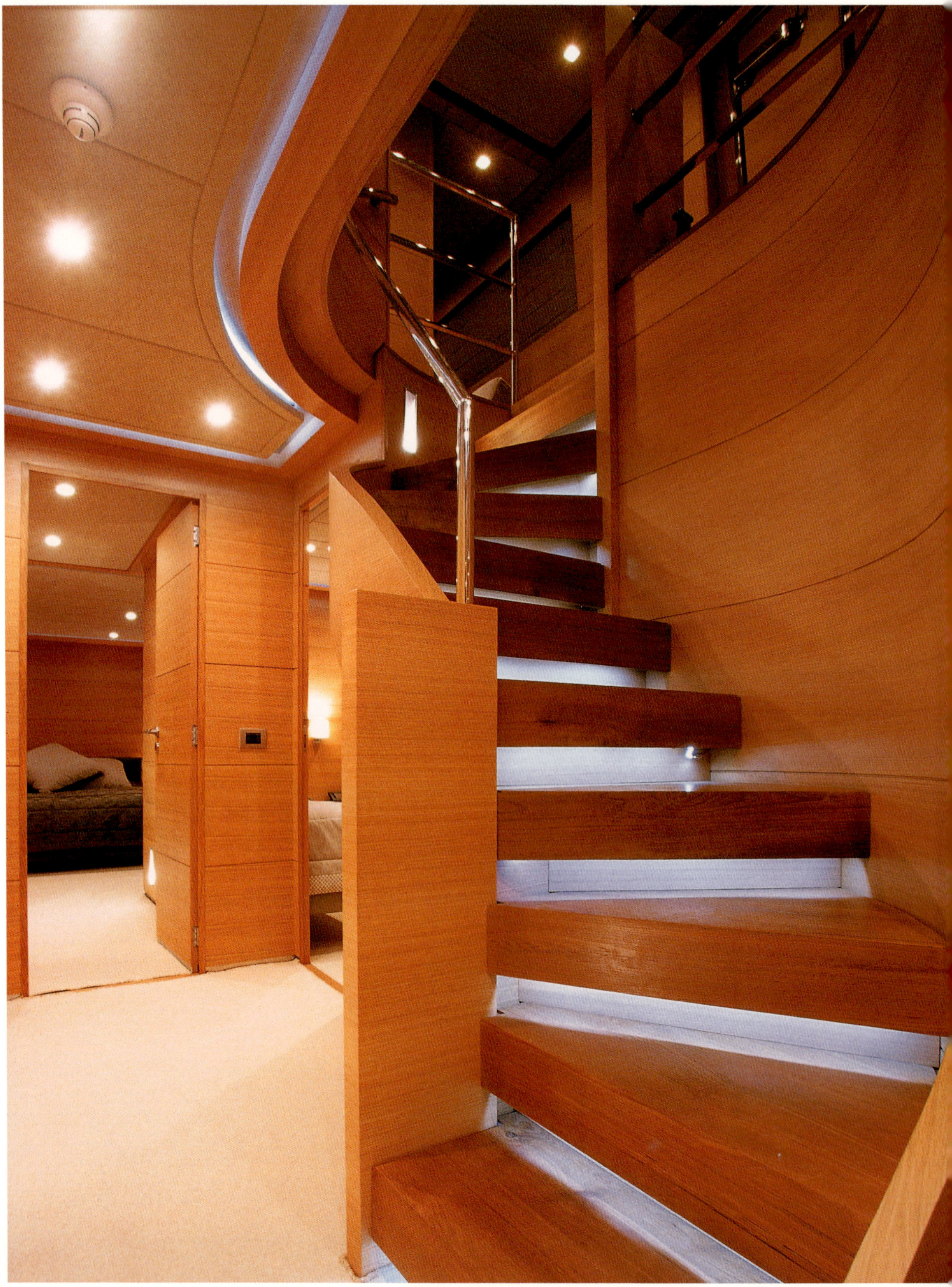

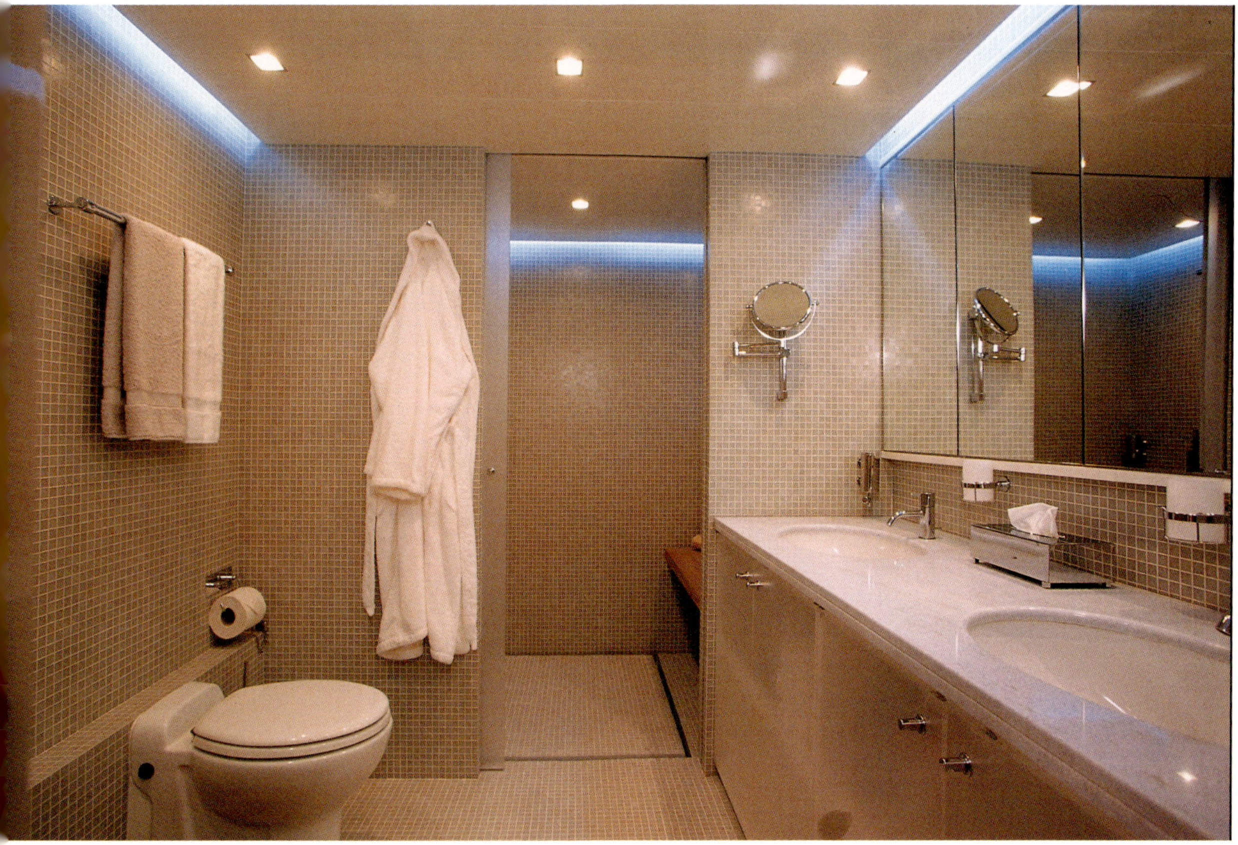

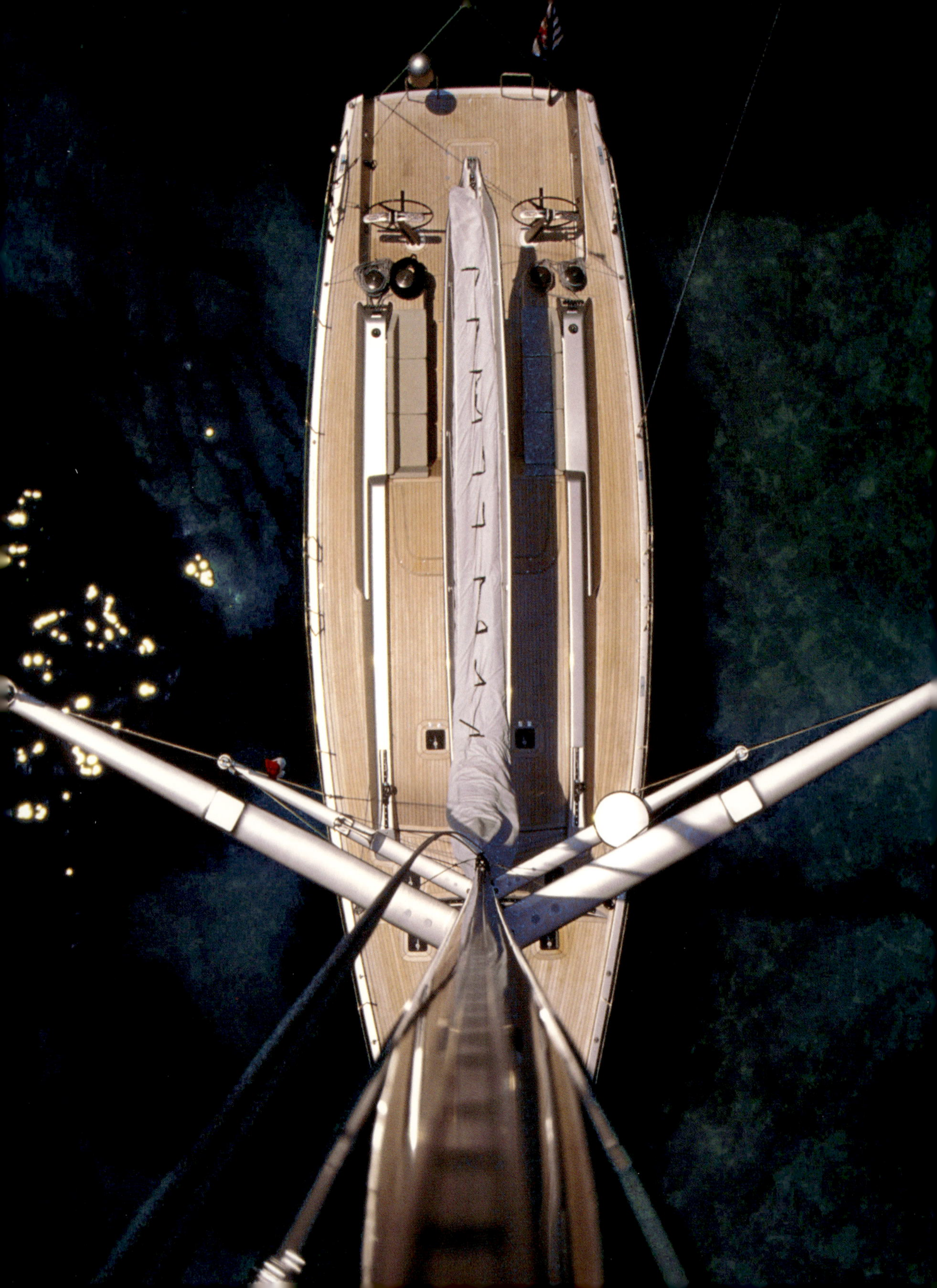

LAZZARINI PICKERING ARCHITETTI, FARR YACHT DESIGN, WALLY
DANGEROUS BUT FUN | 2004
Wally

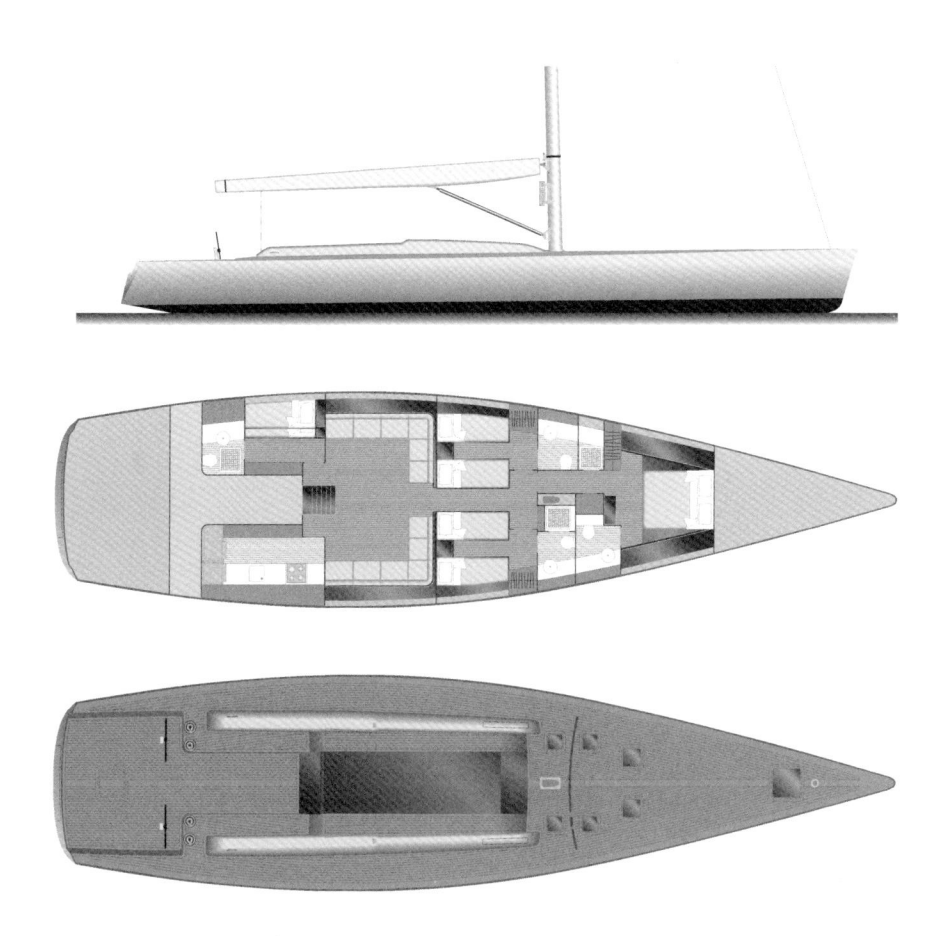

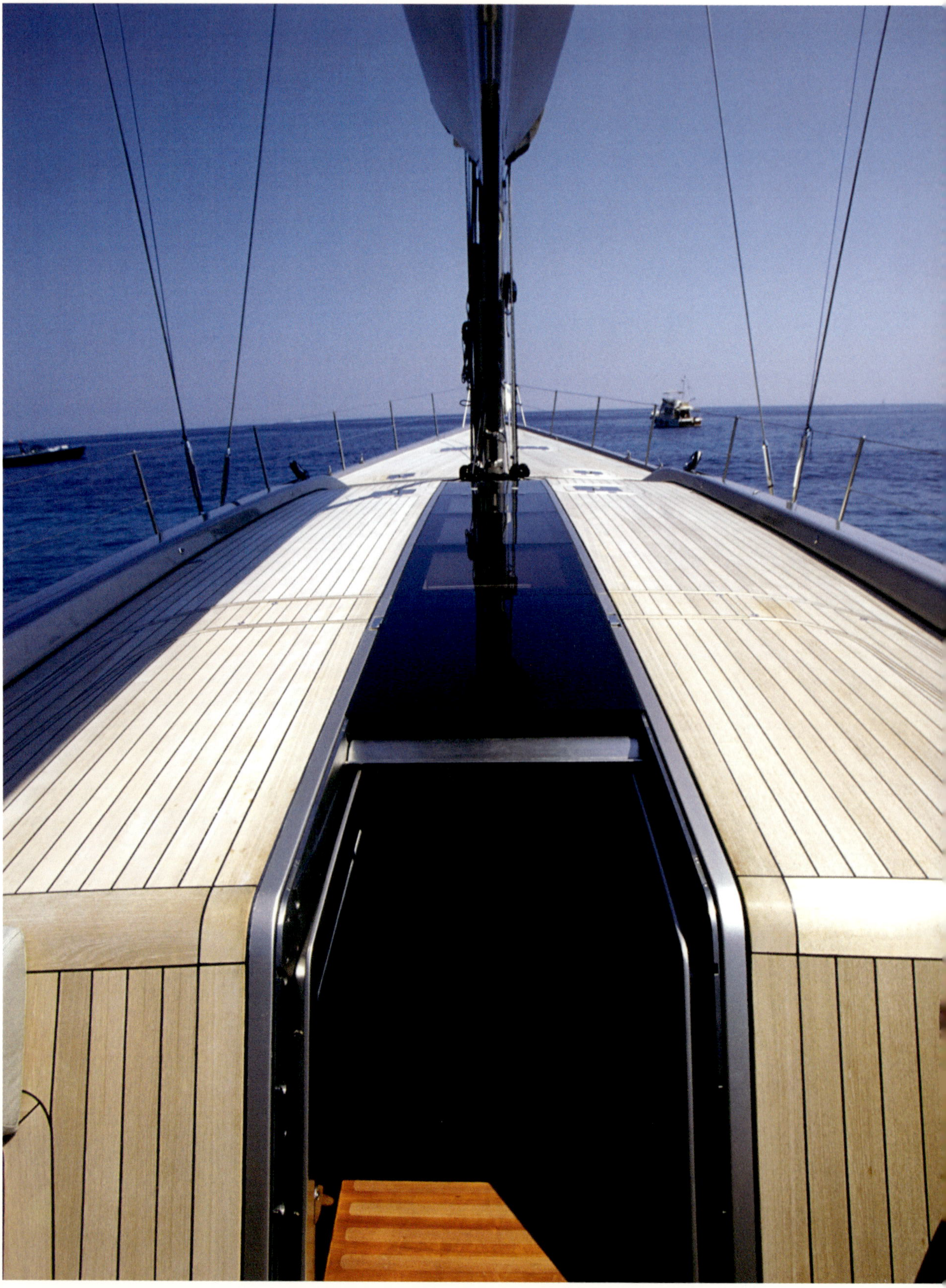

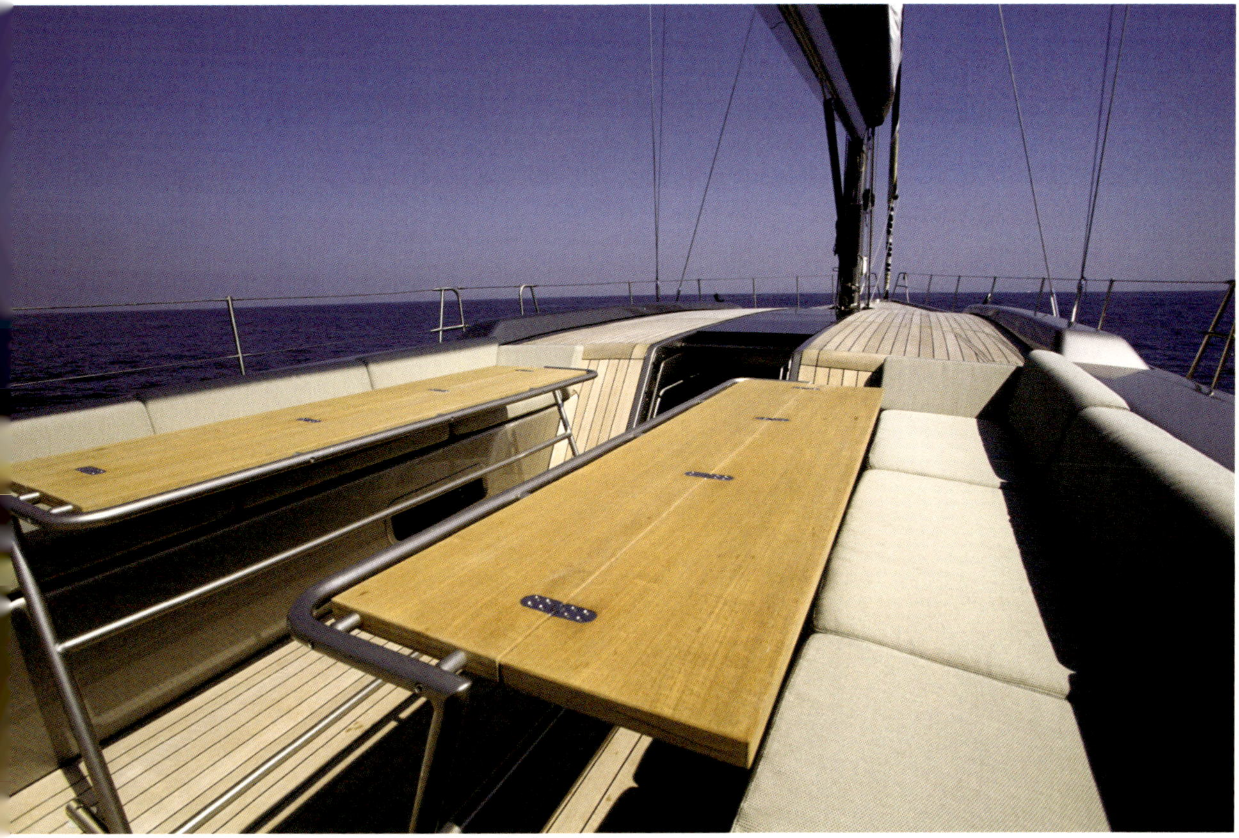

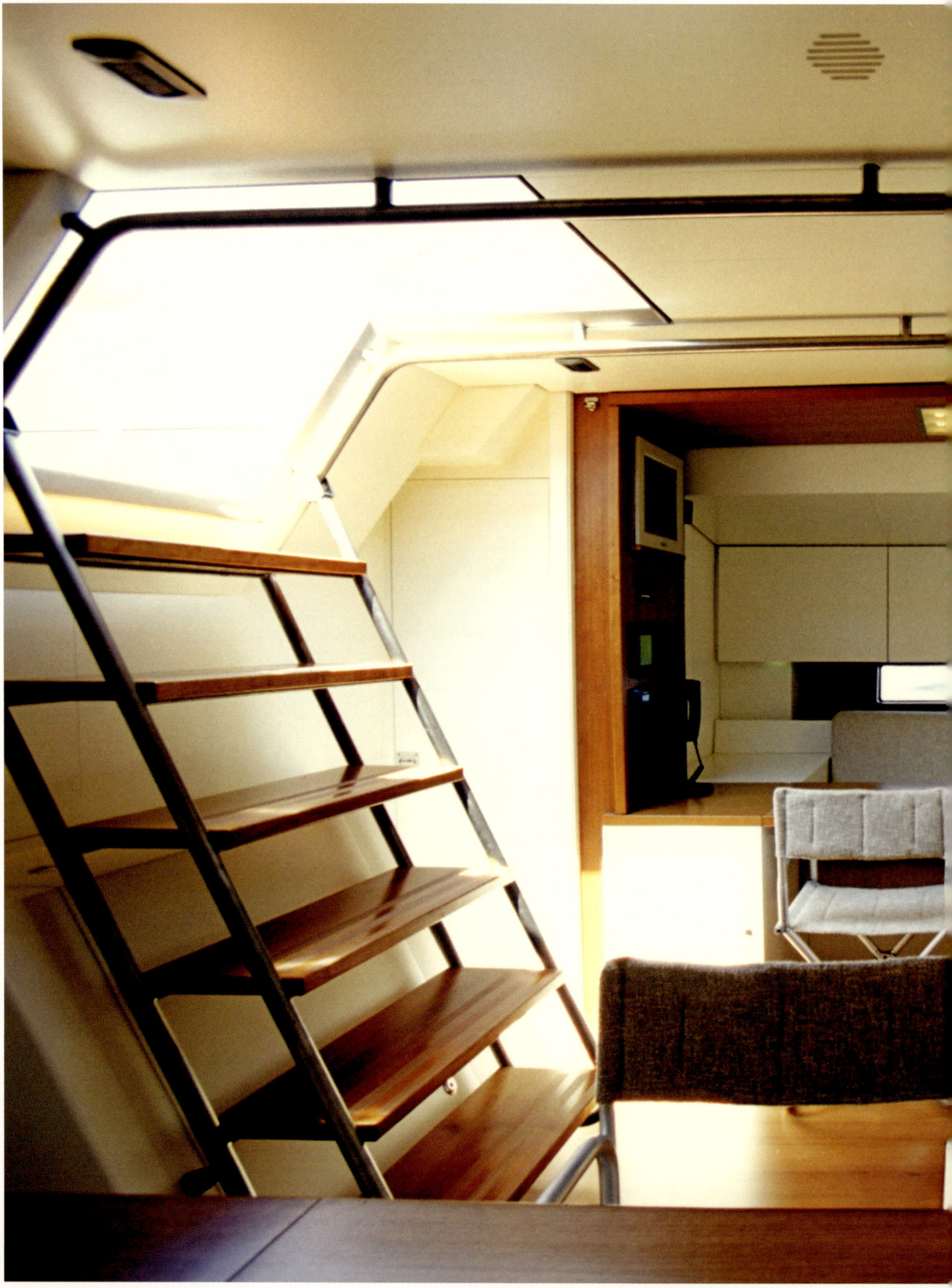

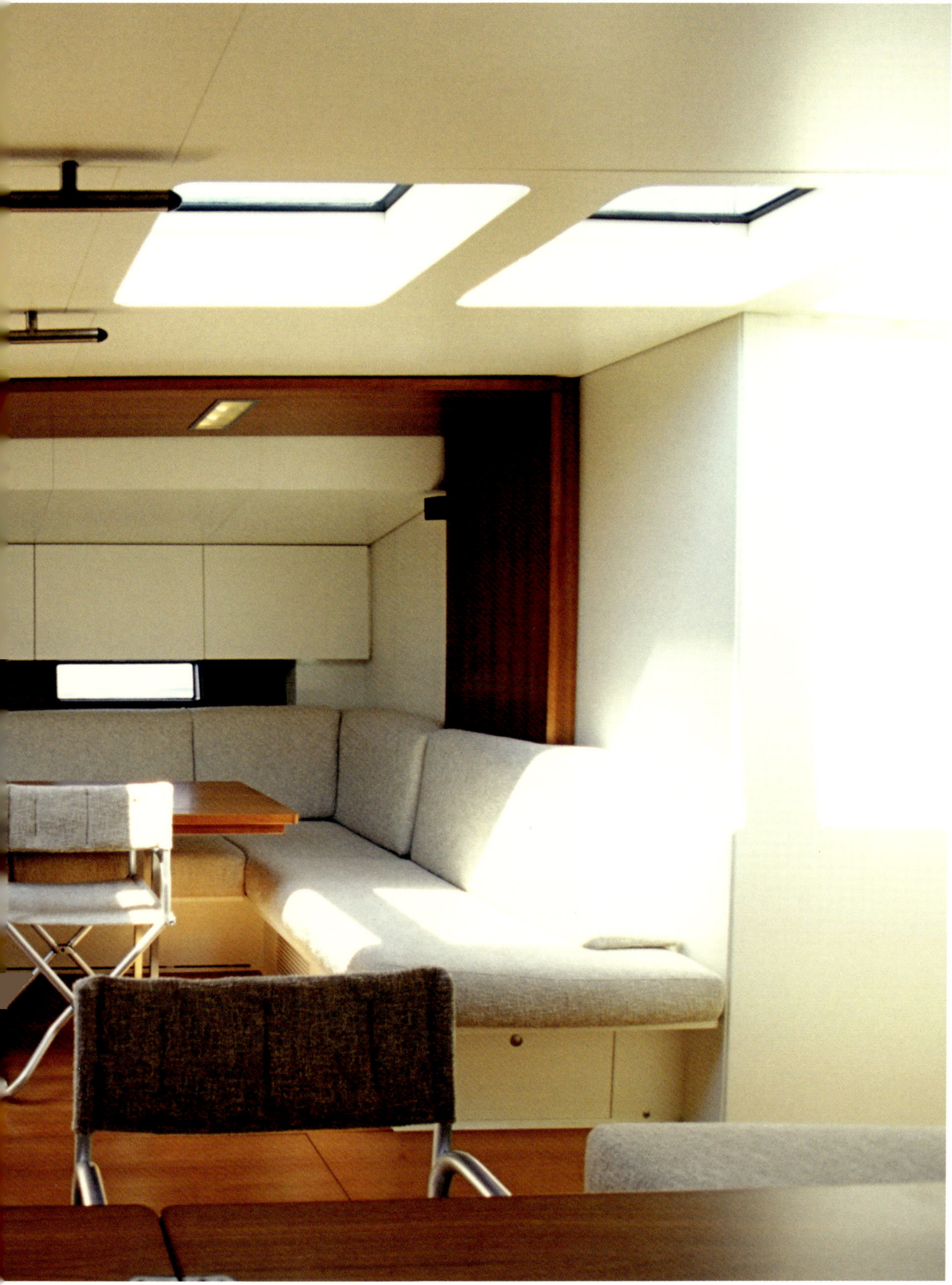

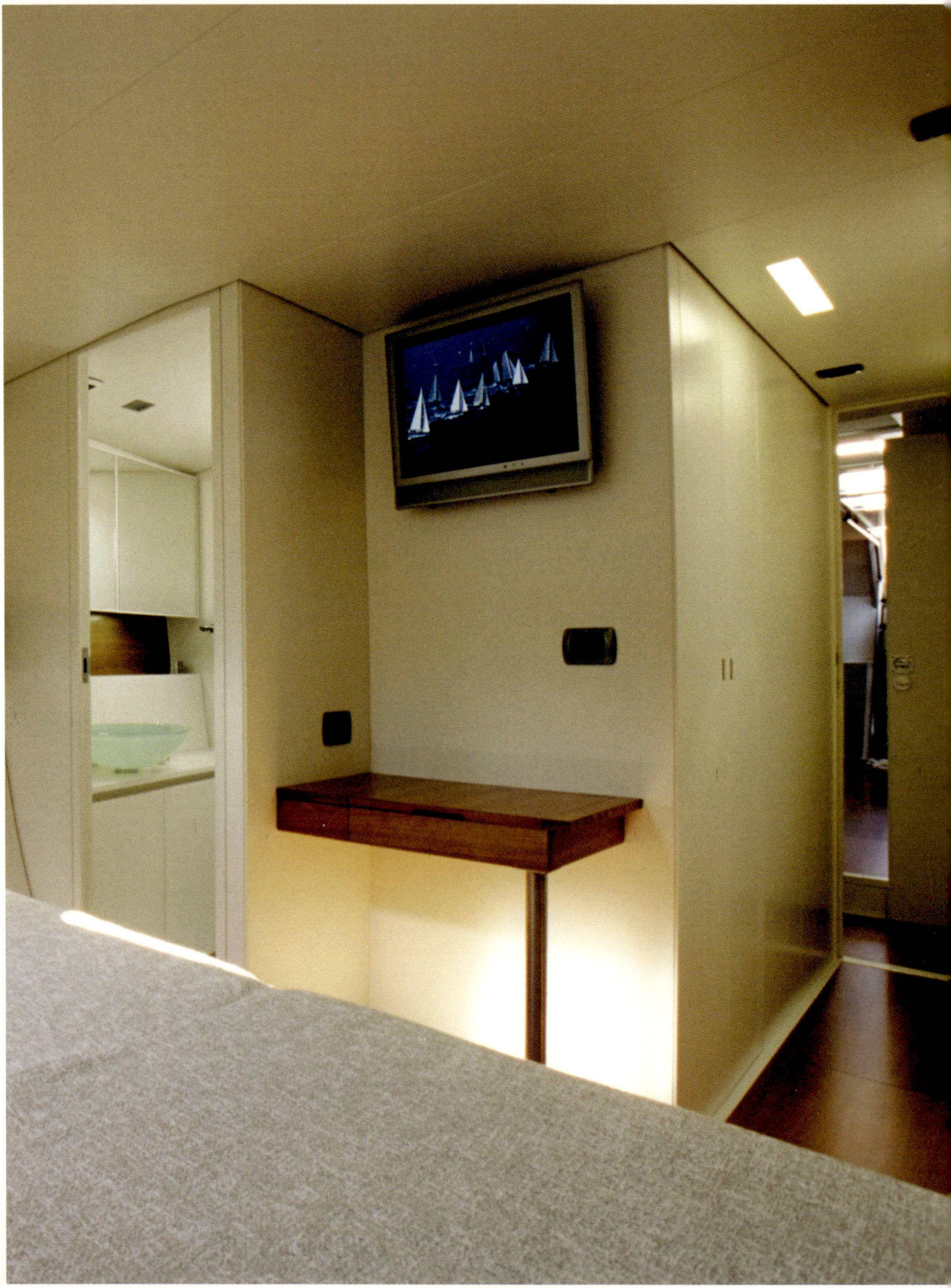

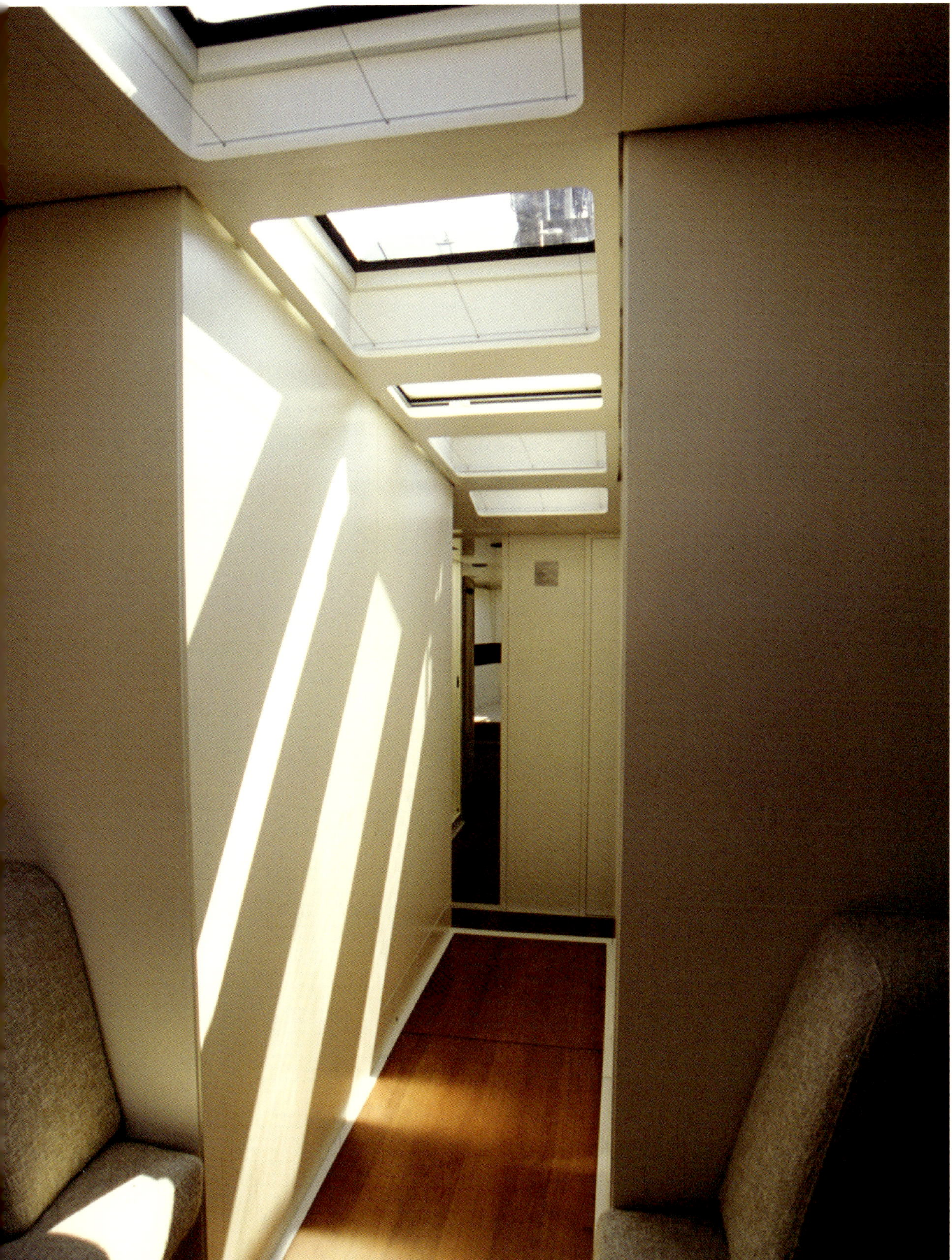

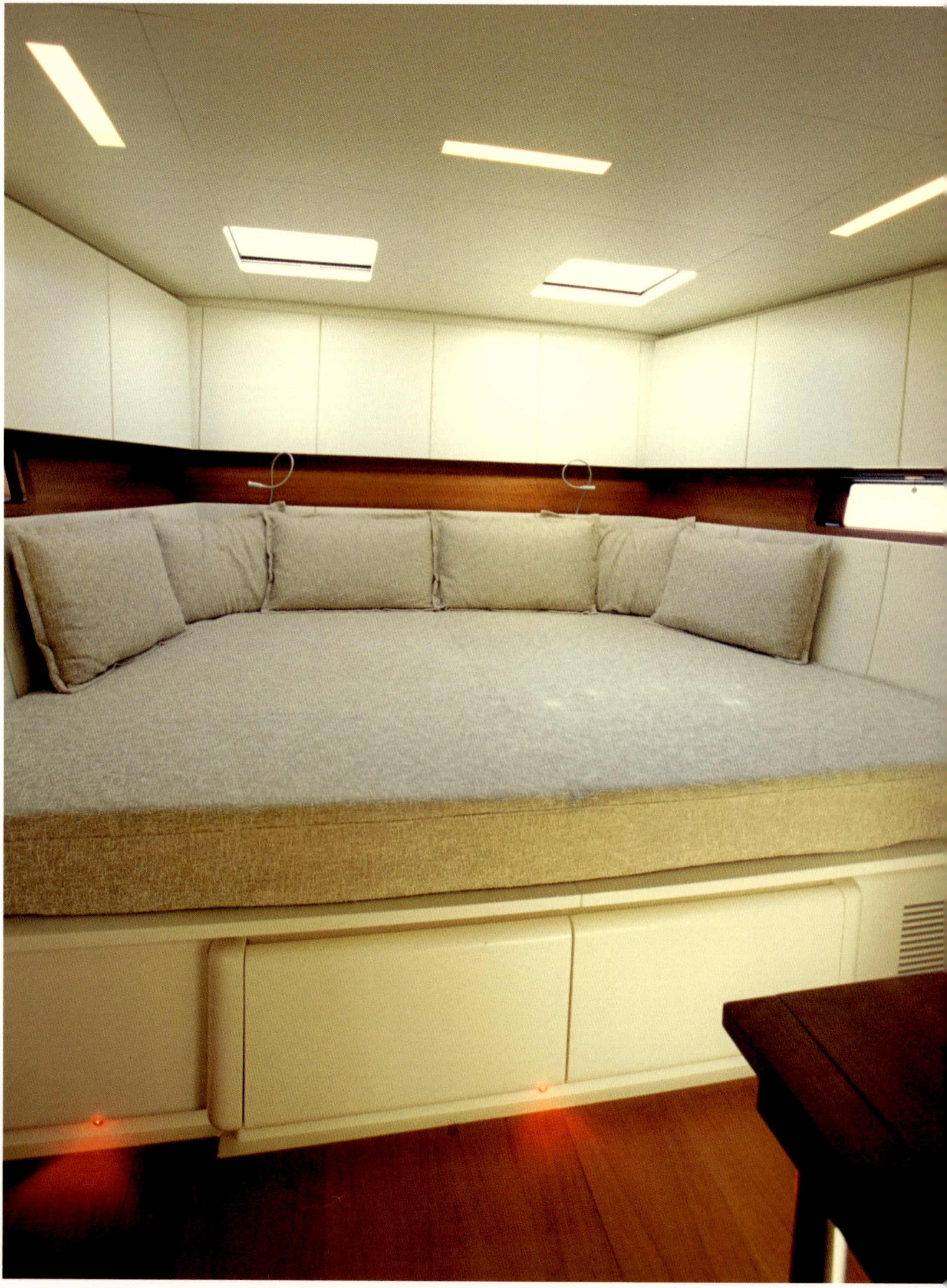

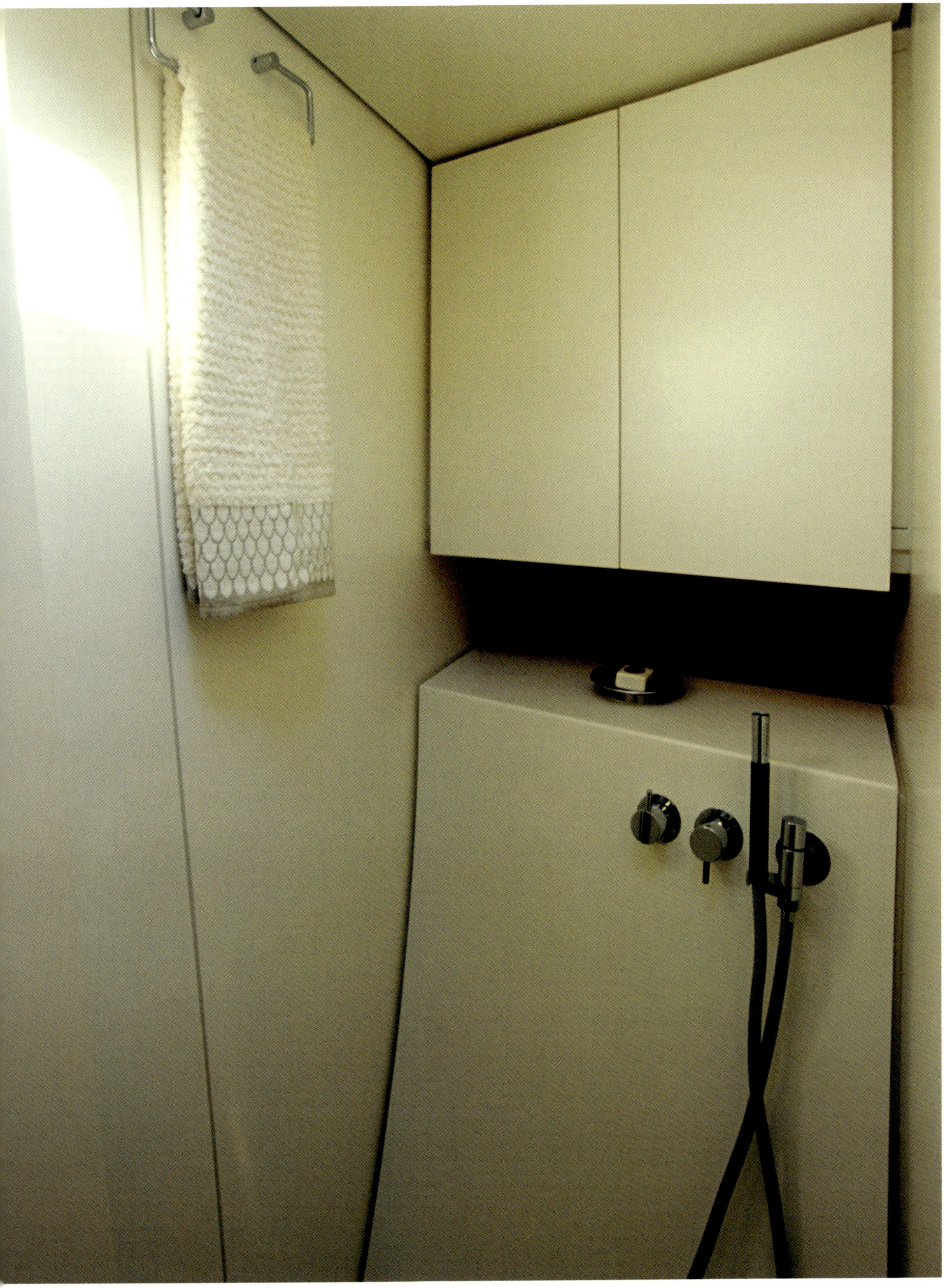

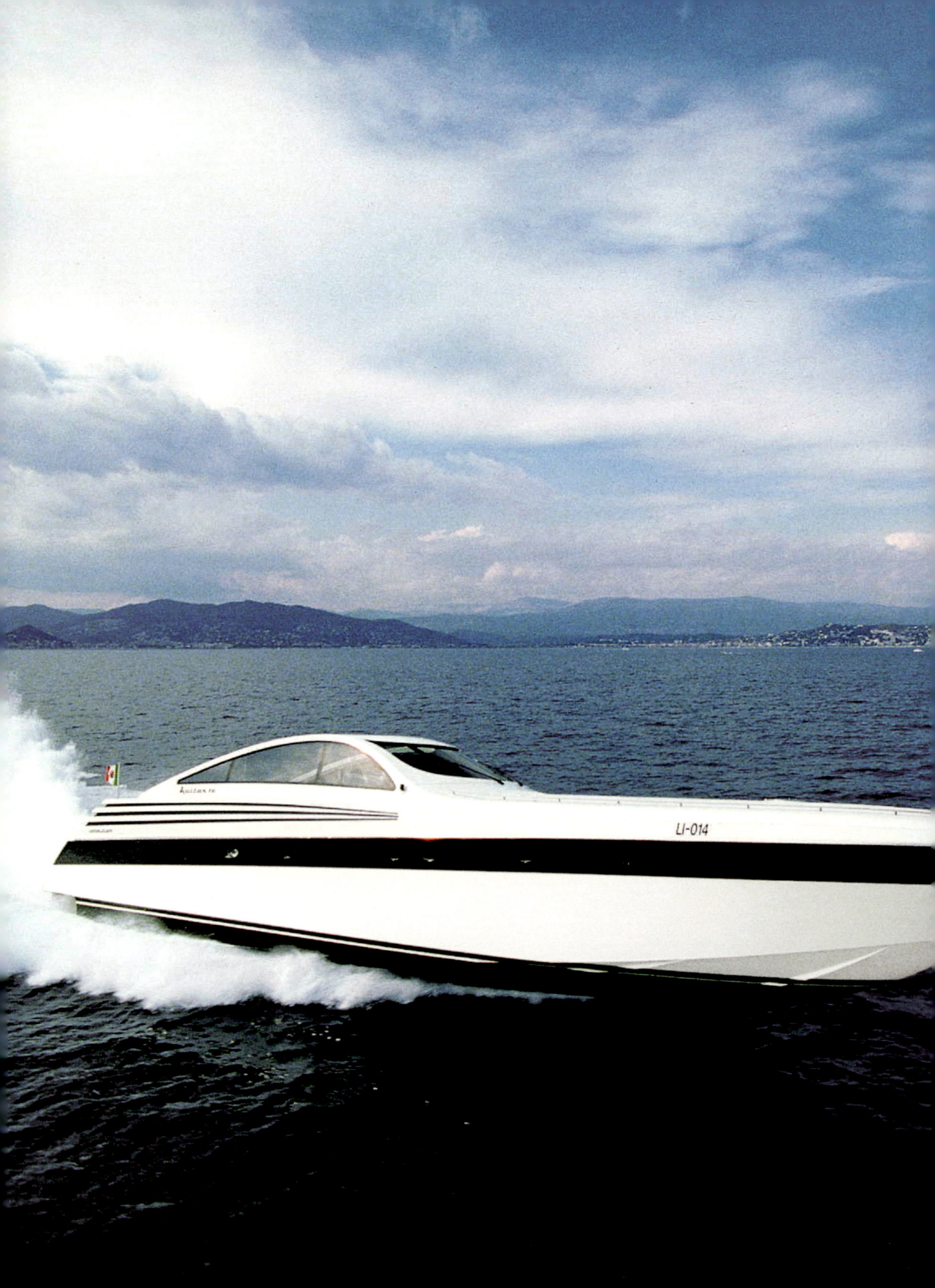
LI-014

LAZZARINI PICKERING ARCHITETTI
KAITOS 76 | 2003
Cantieri di Pisa

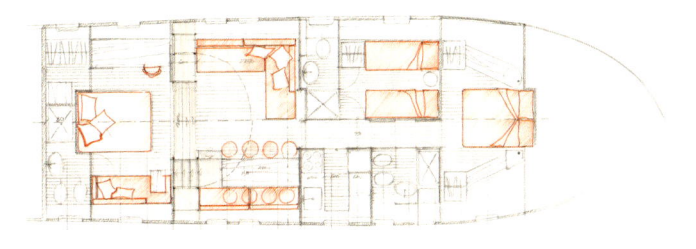

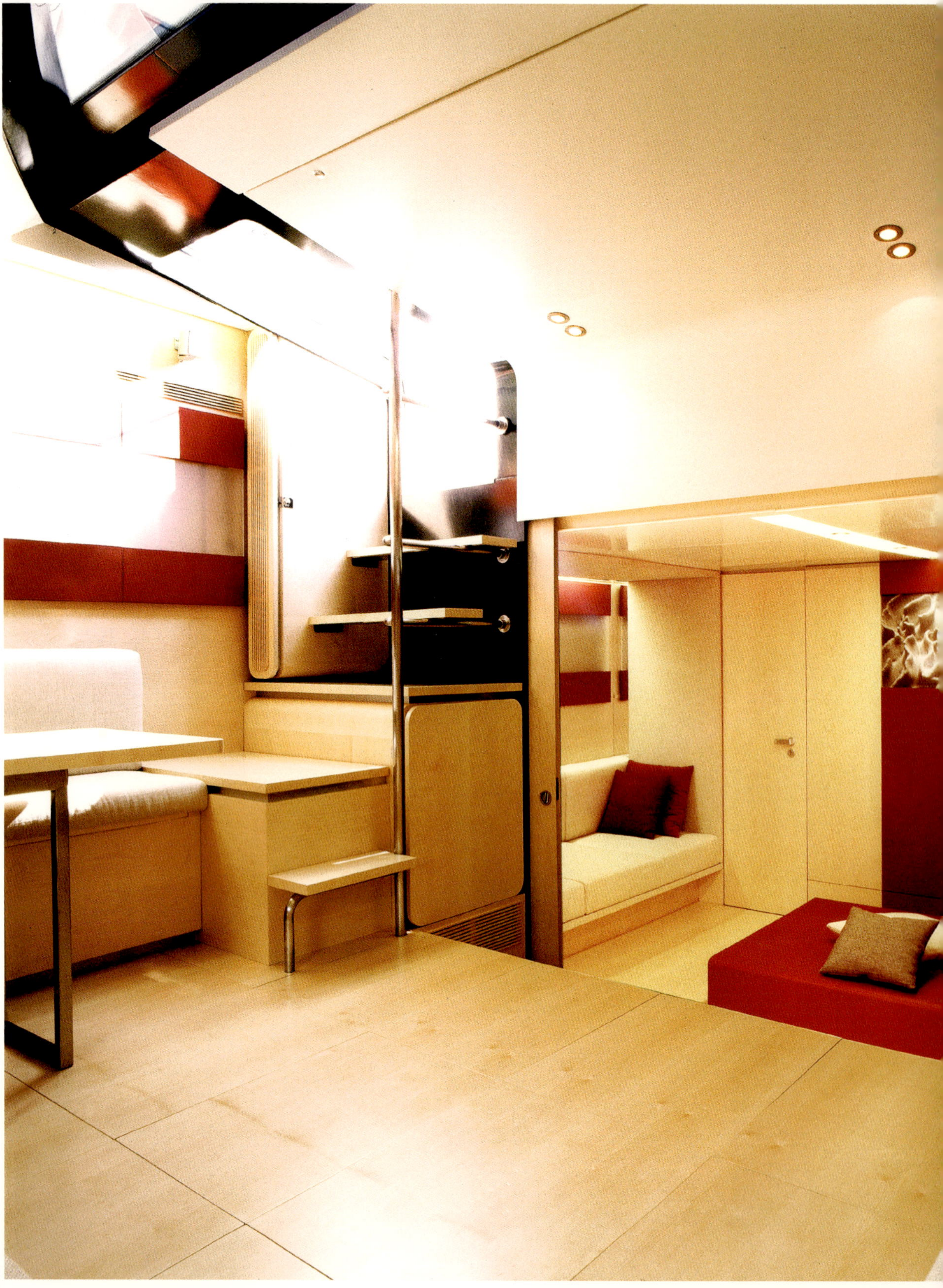

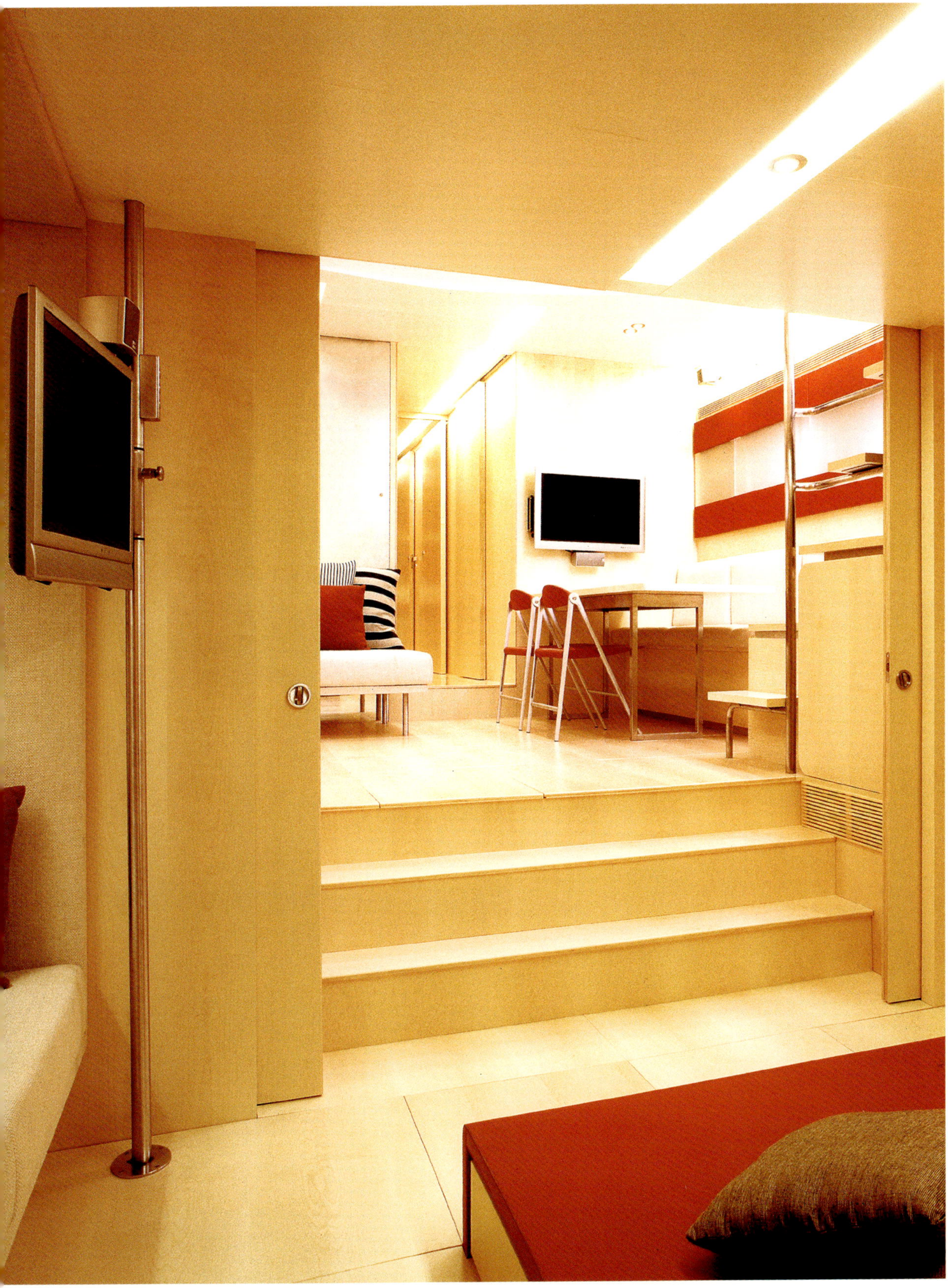

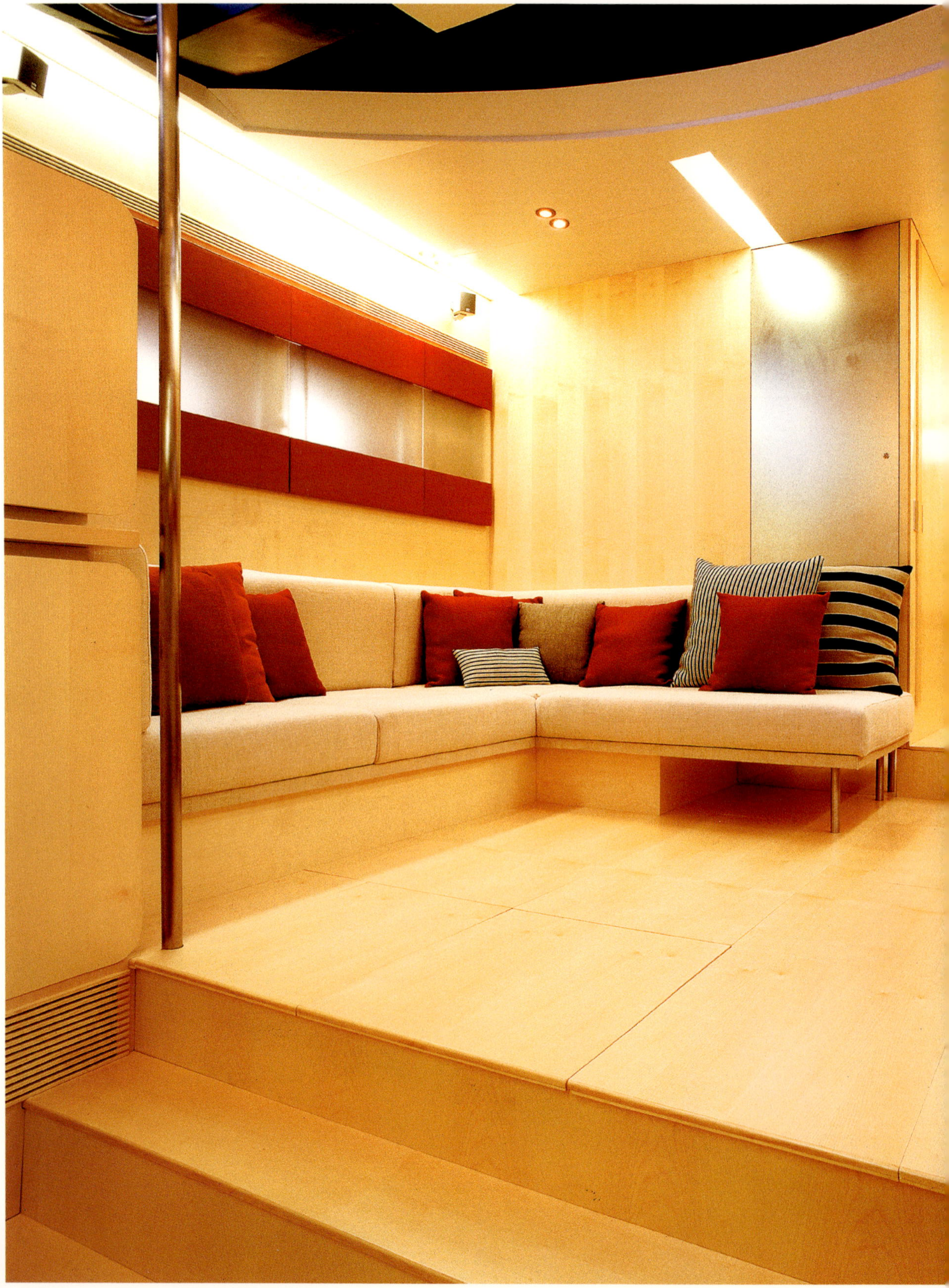

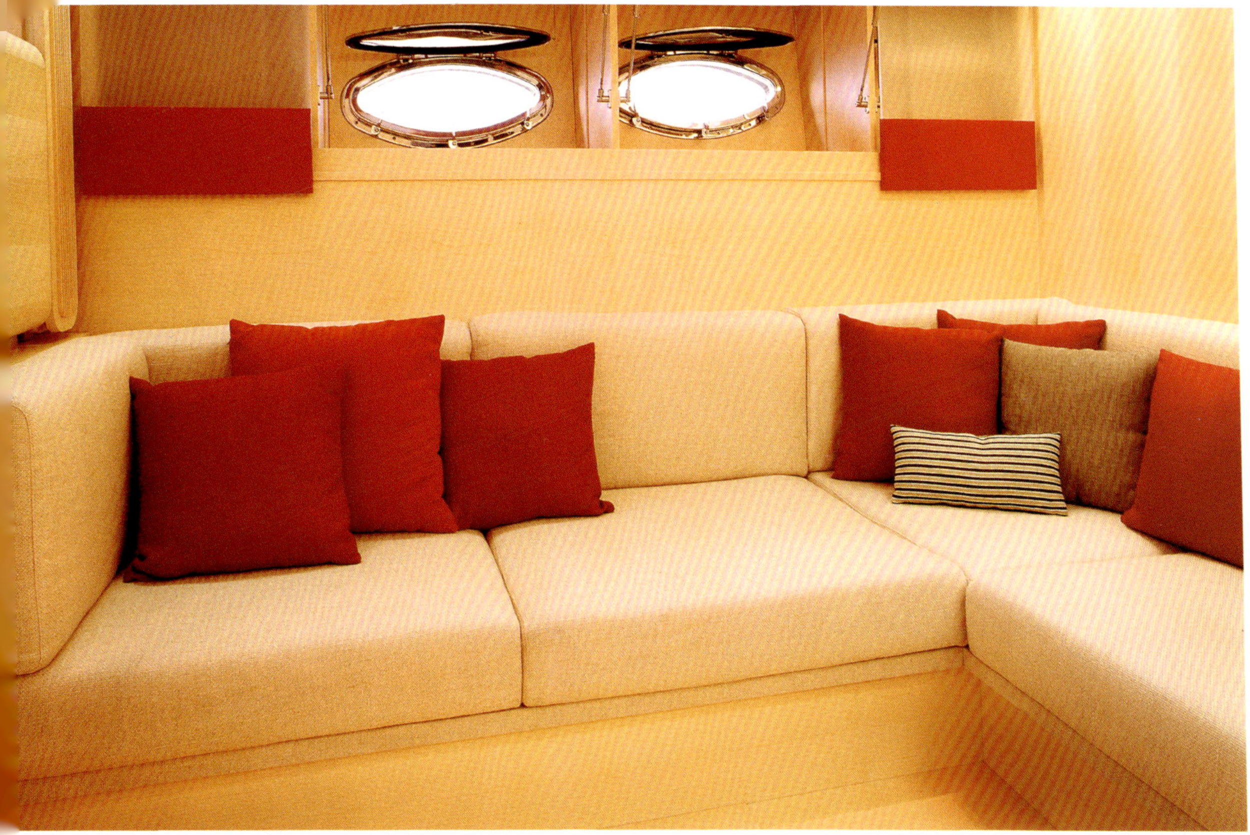

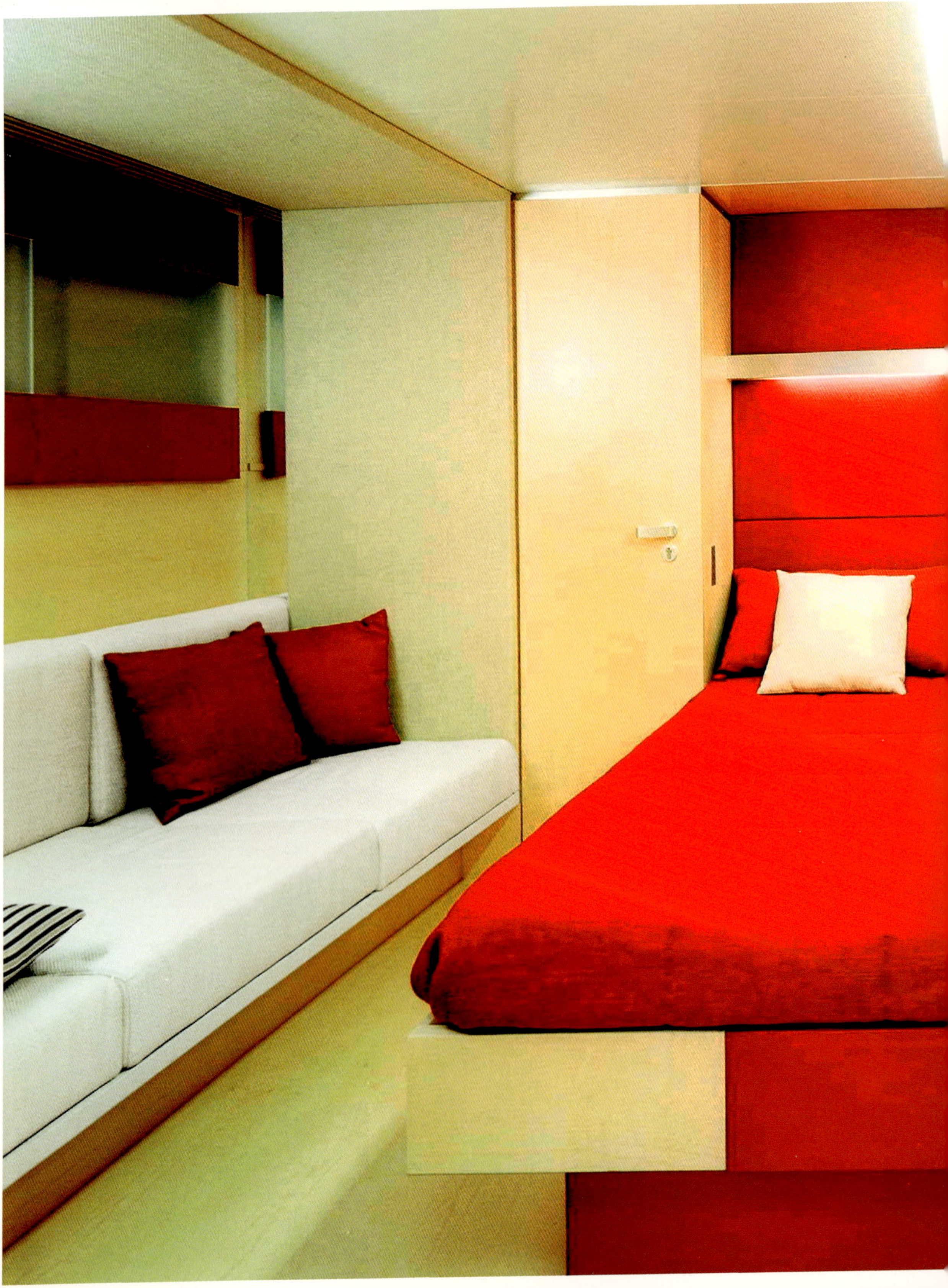

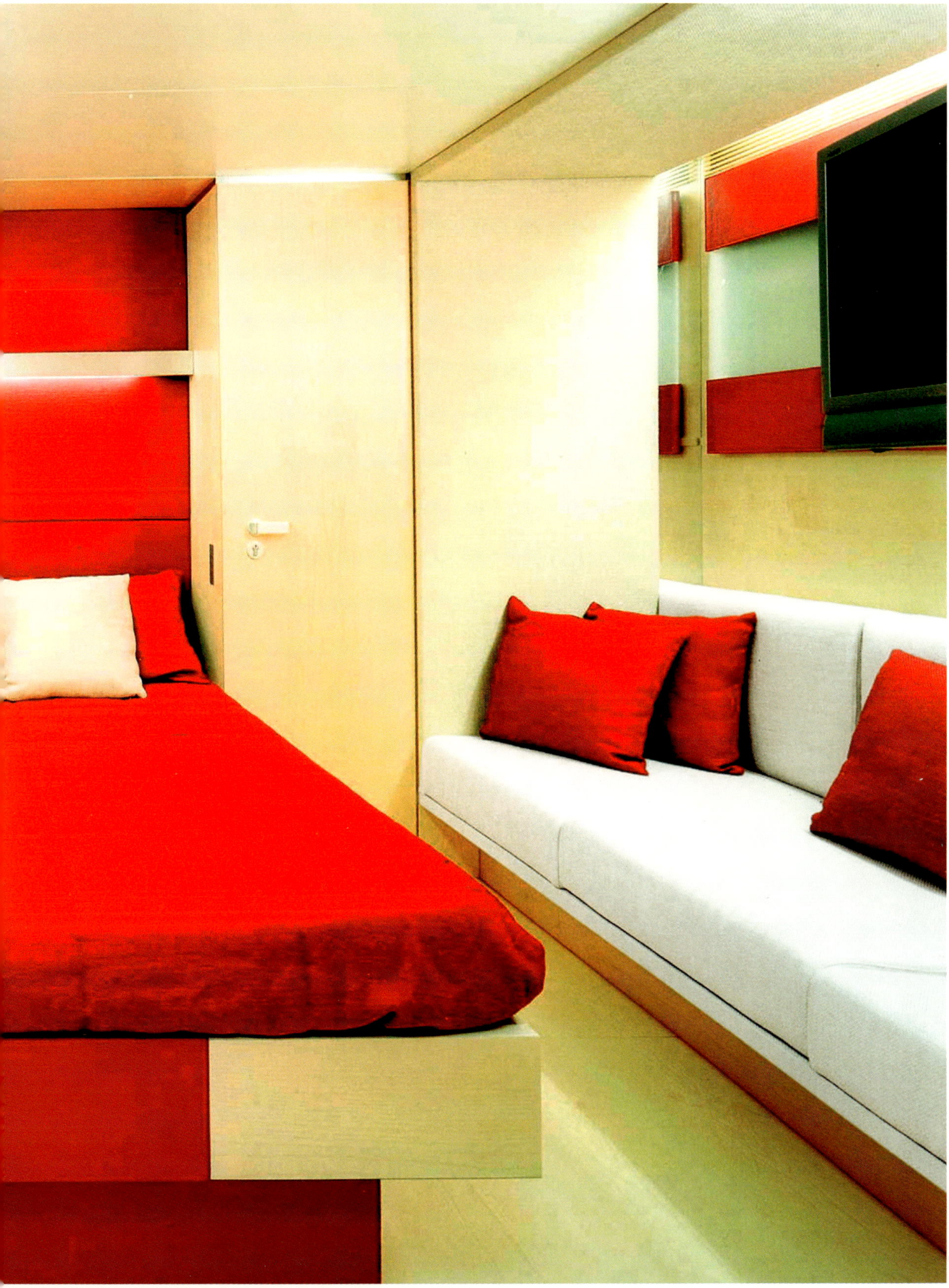

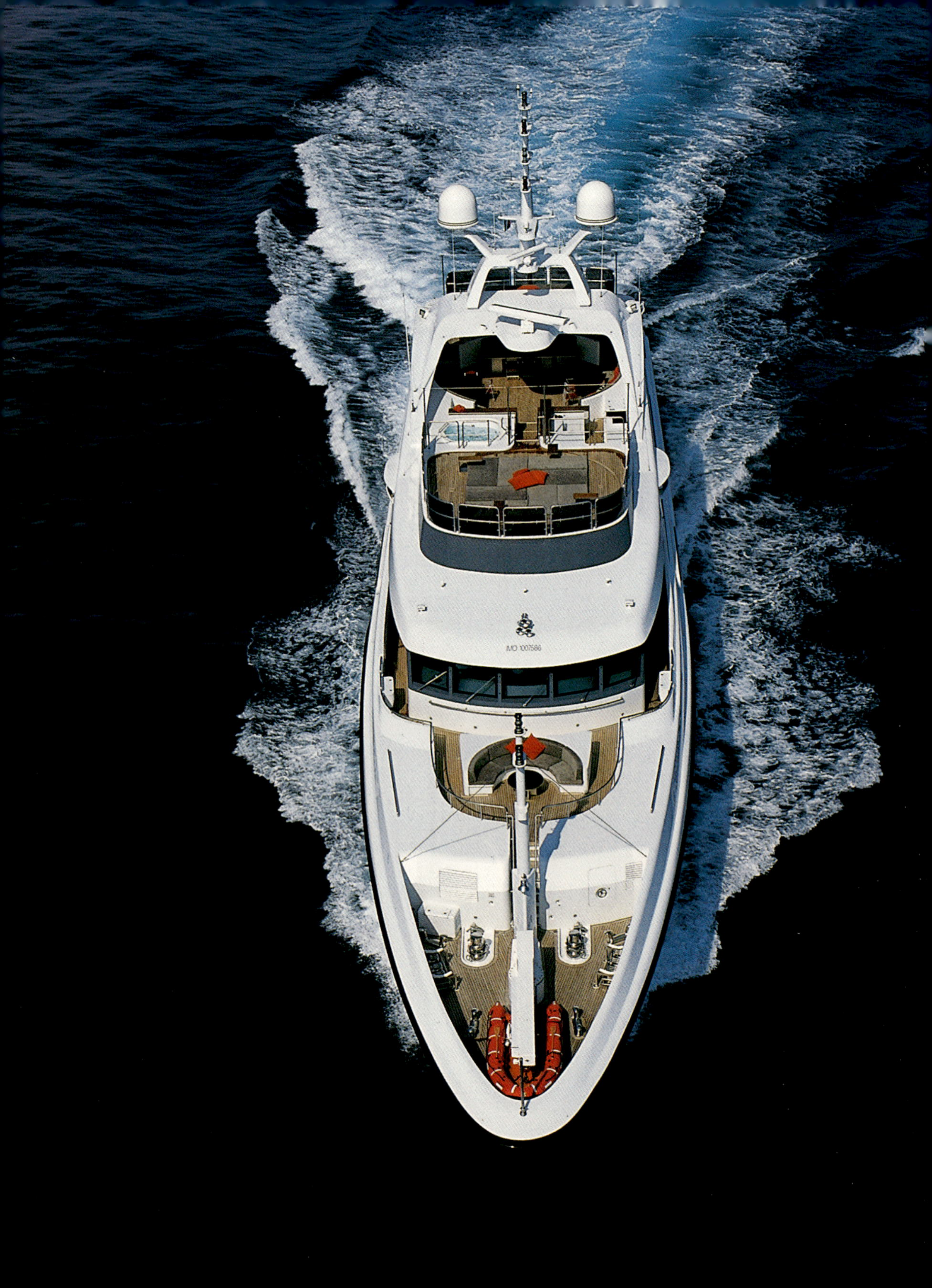
IMO 1007586

LAZZARINI PICKERING ARCHITETTI
SAI RAM | 2004
Benetti

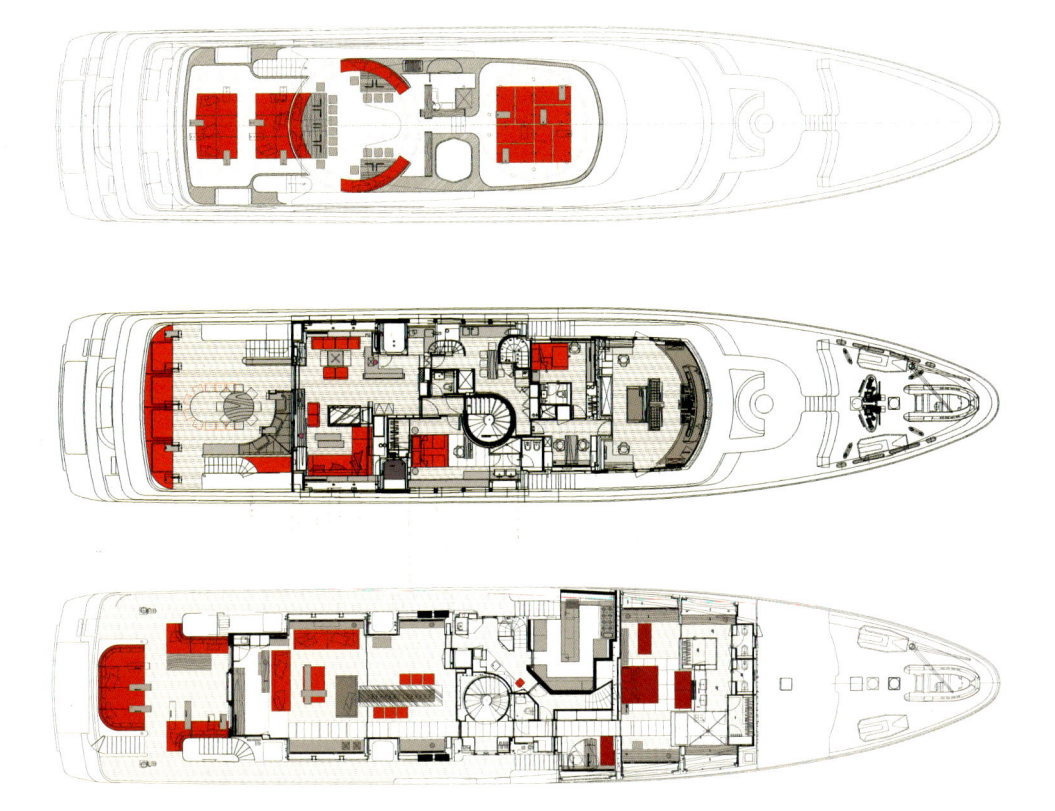

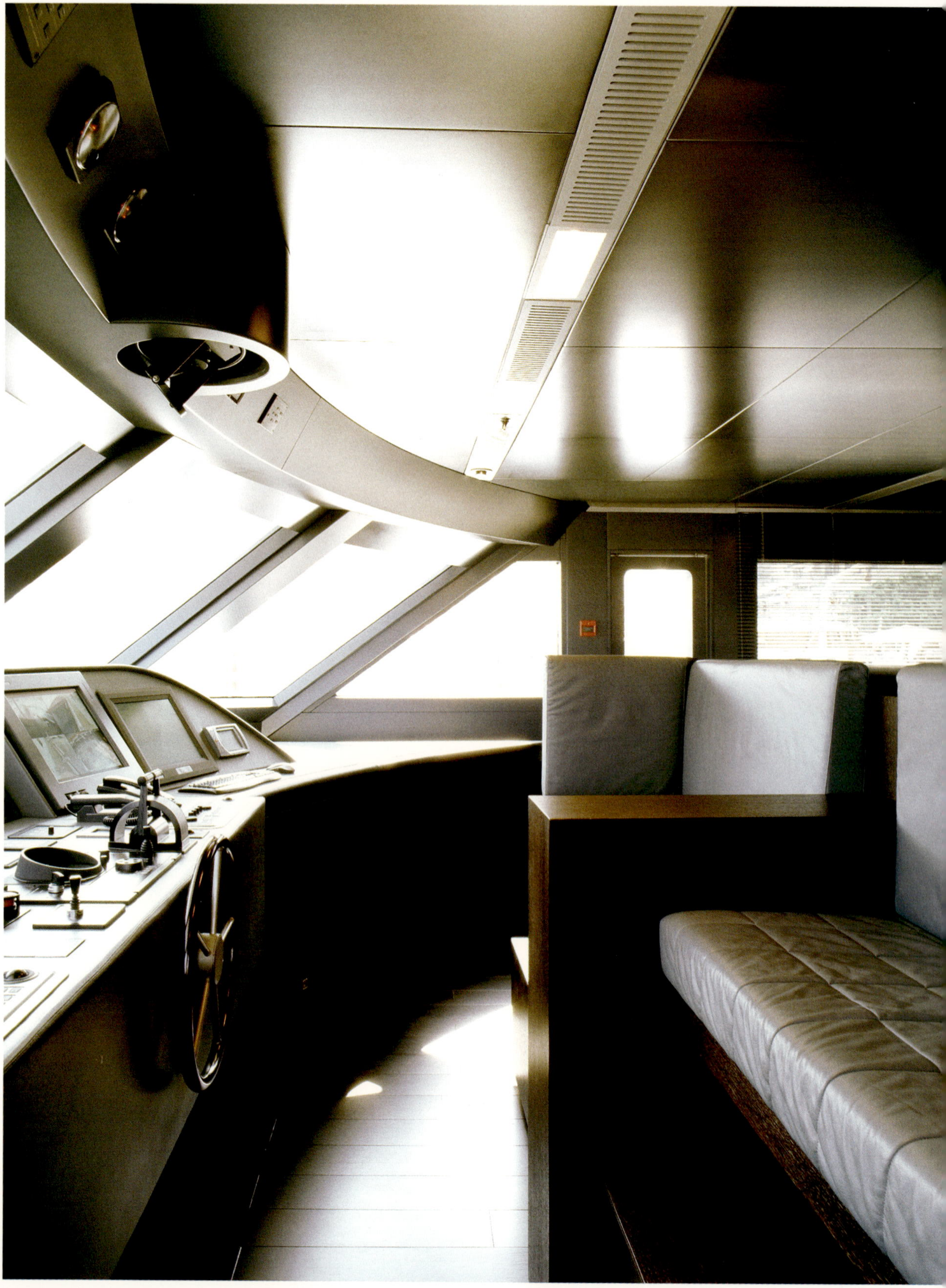

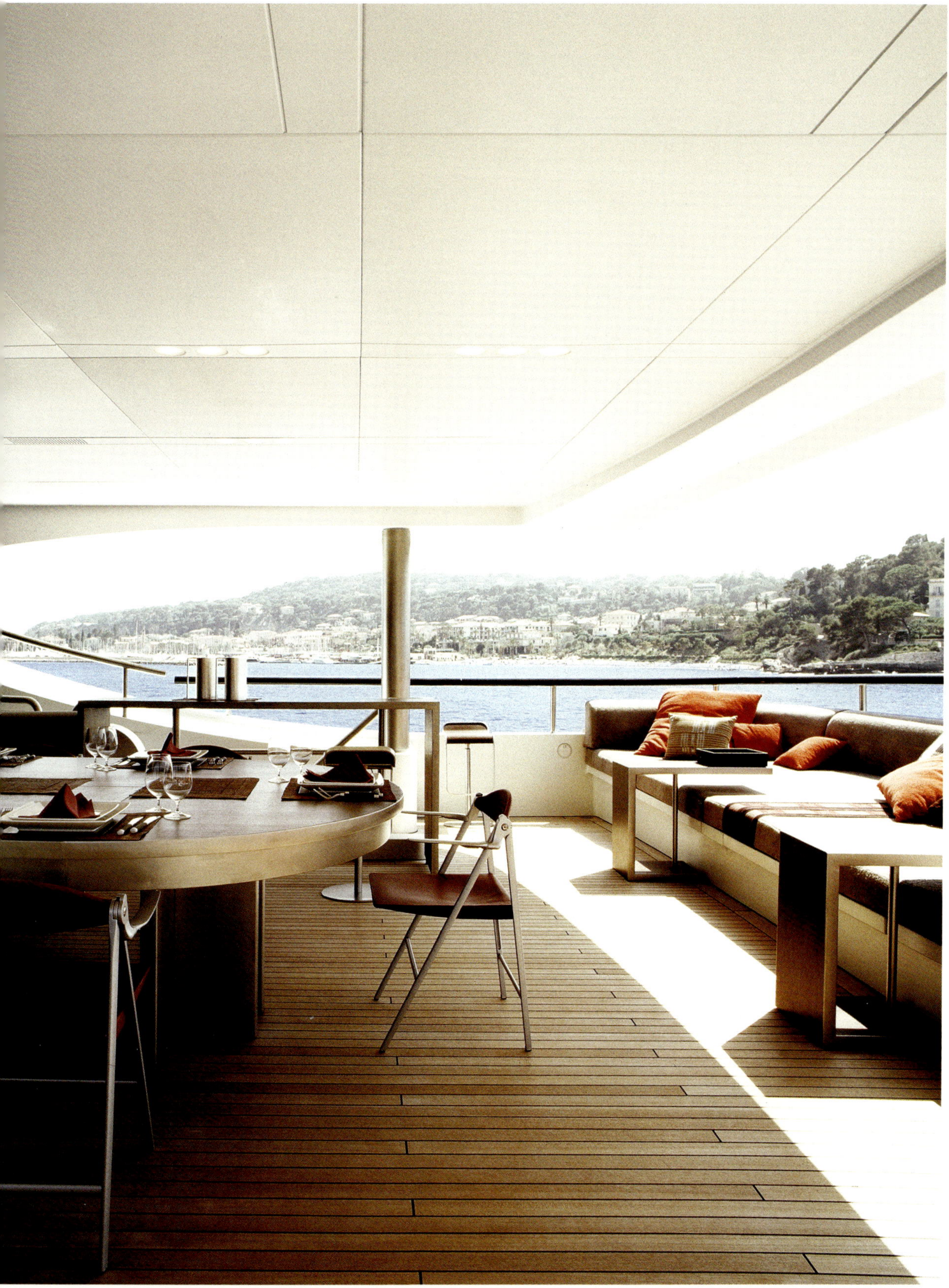

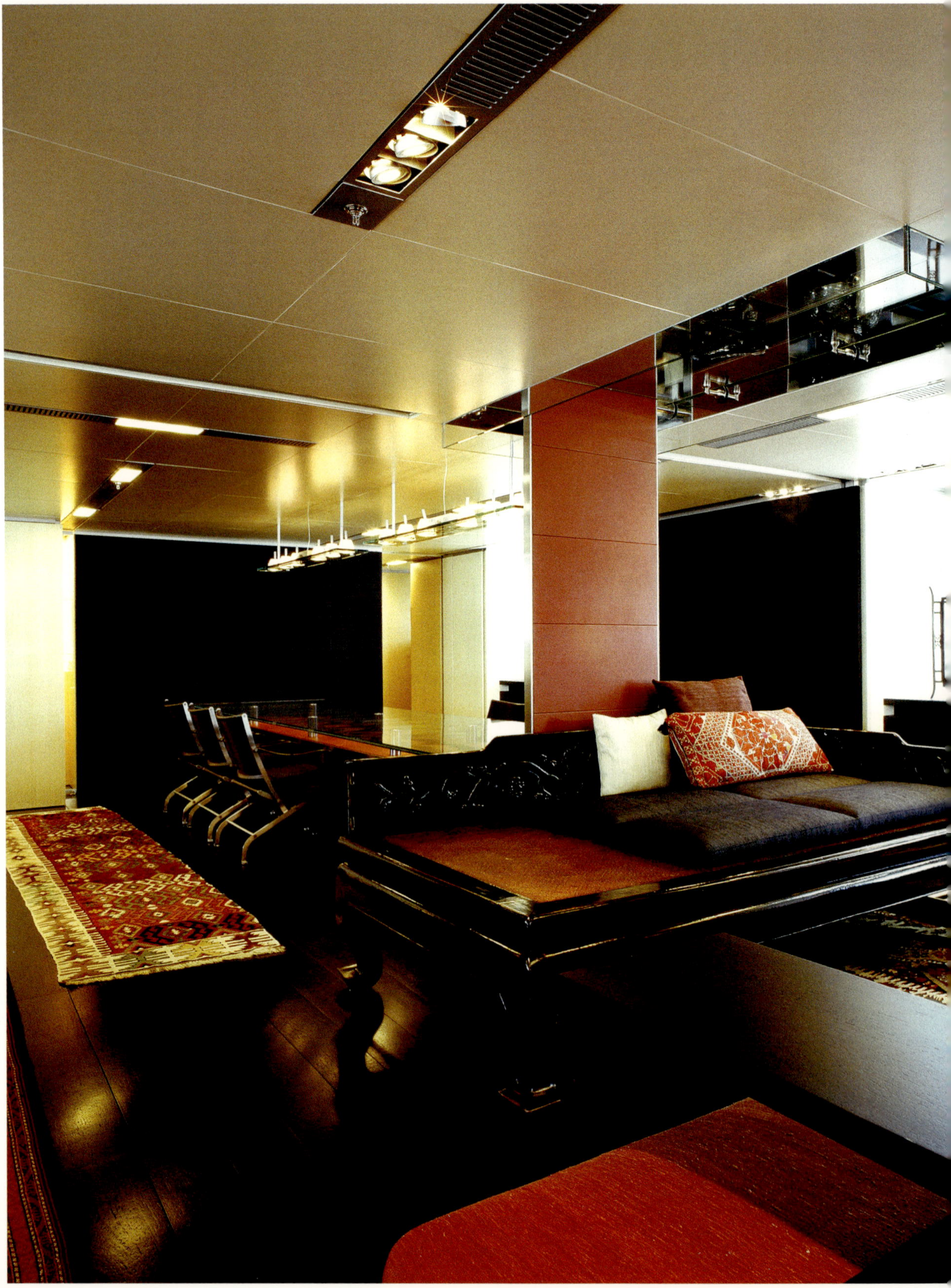

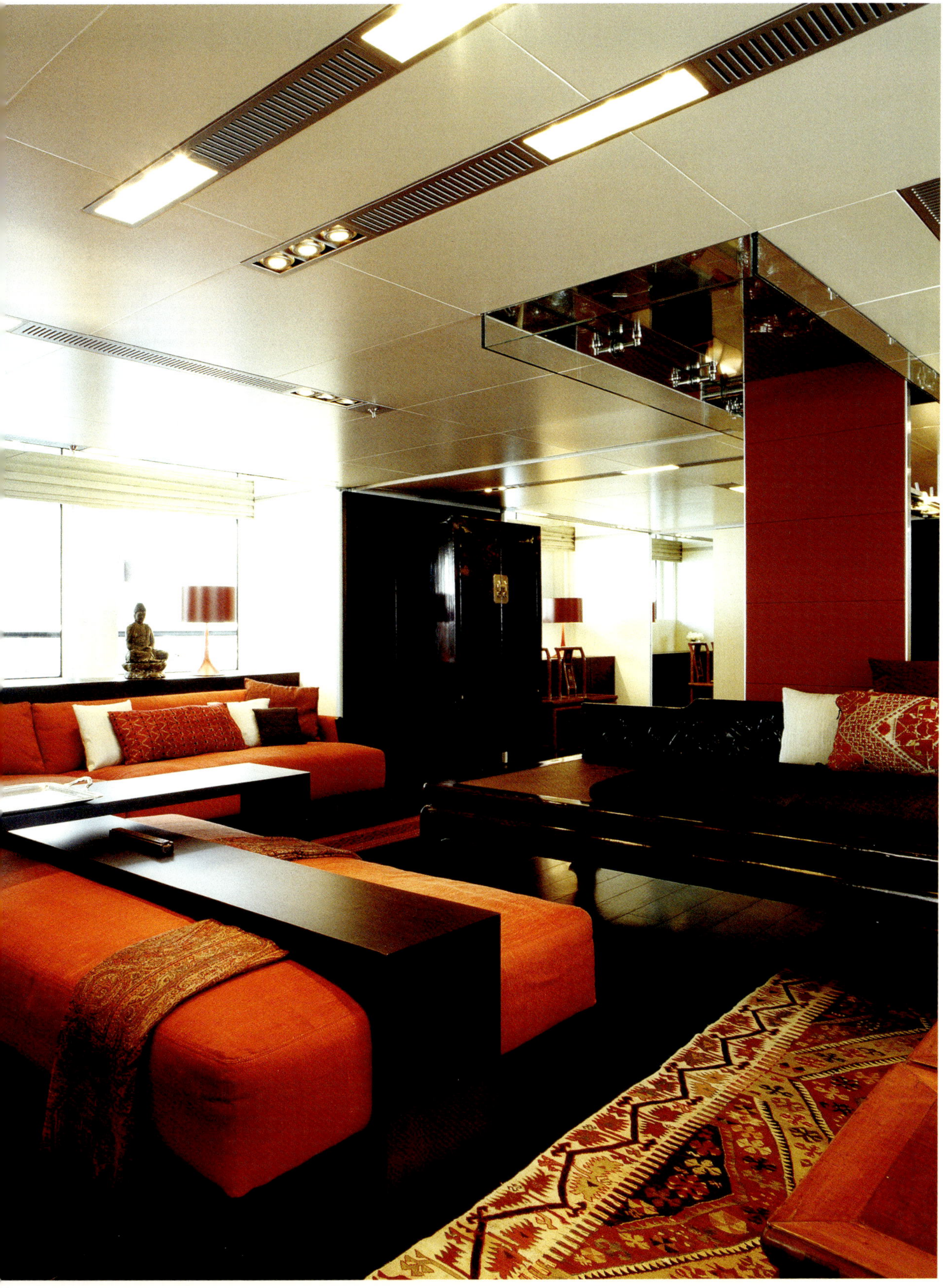

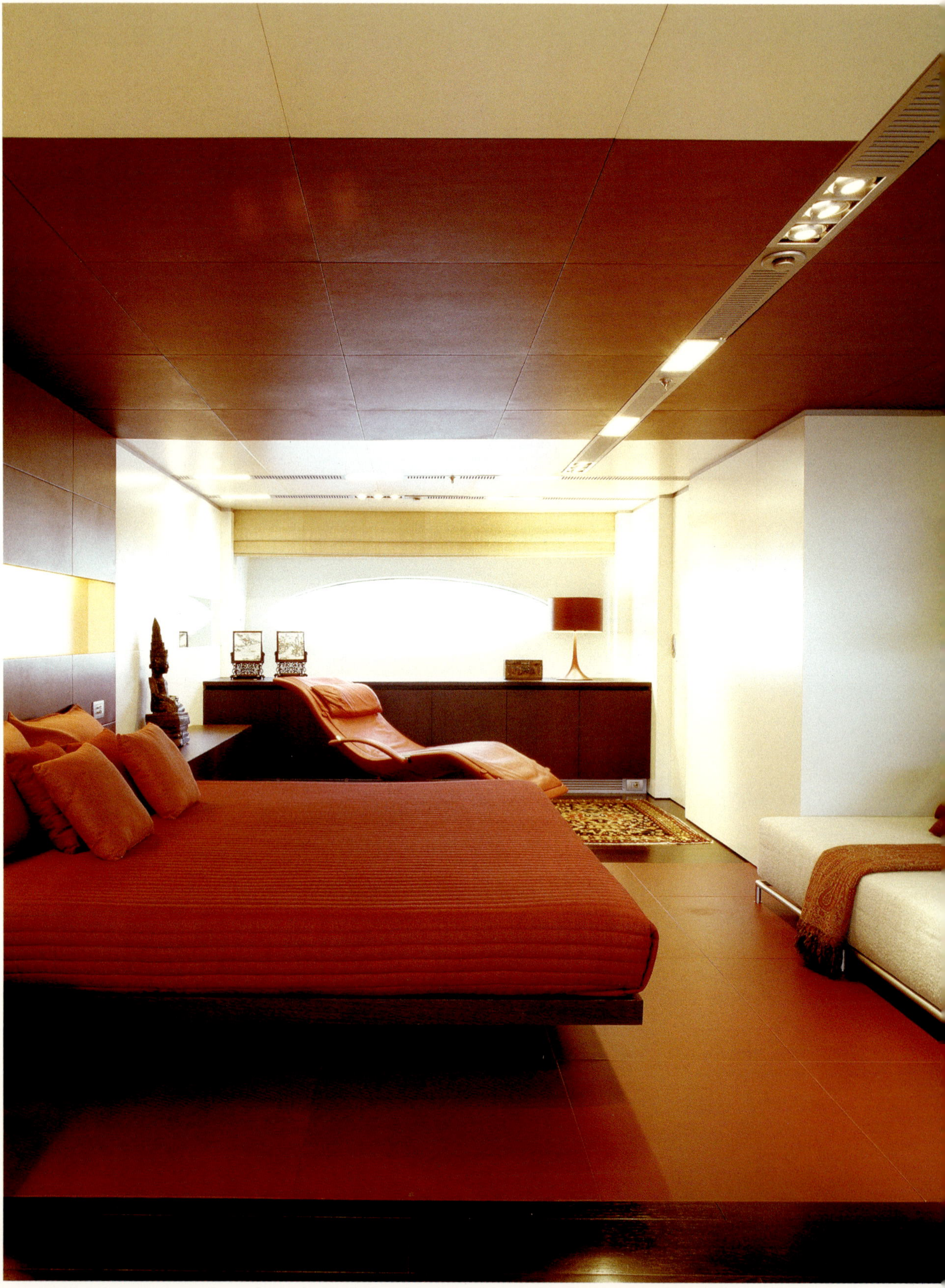

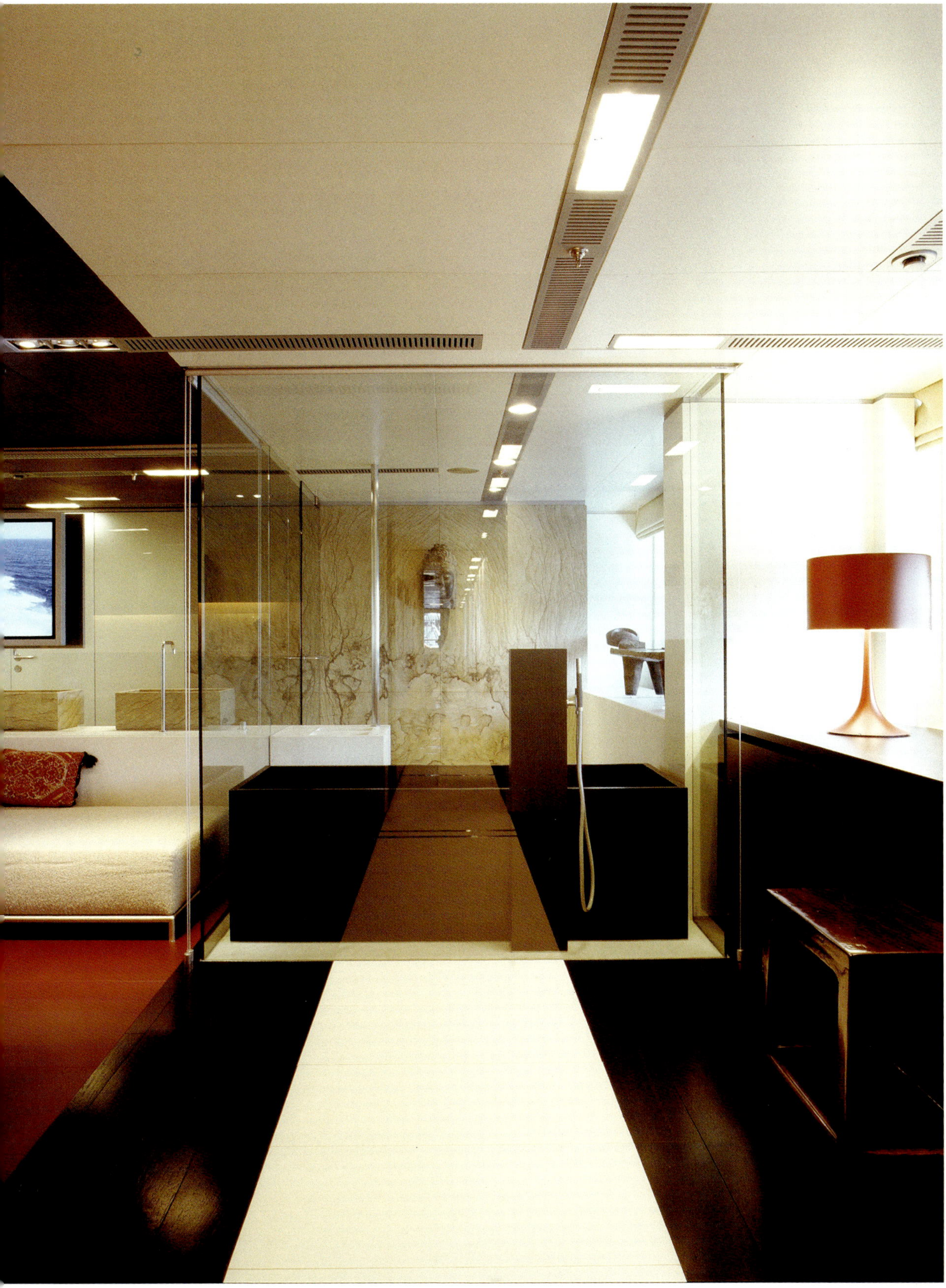

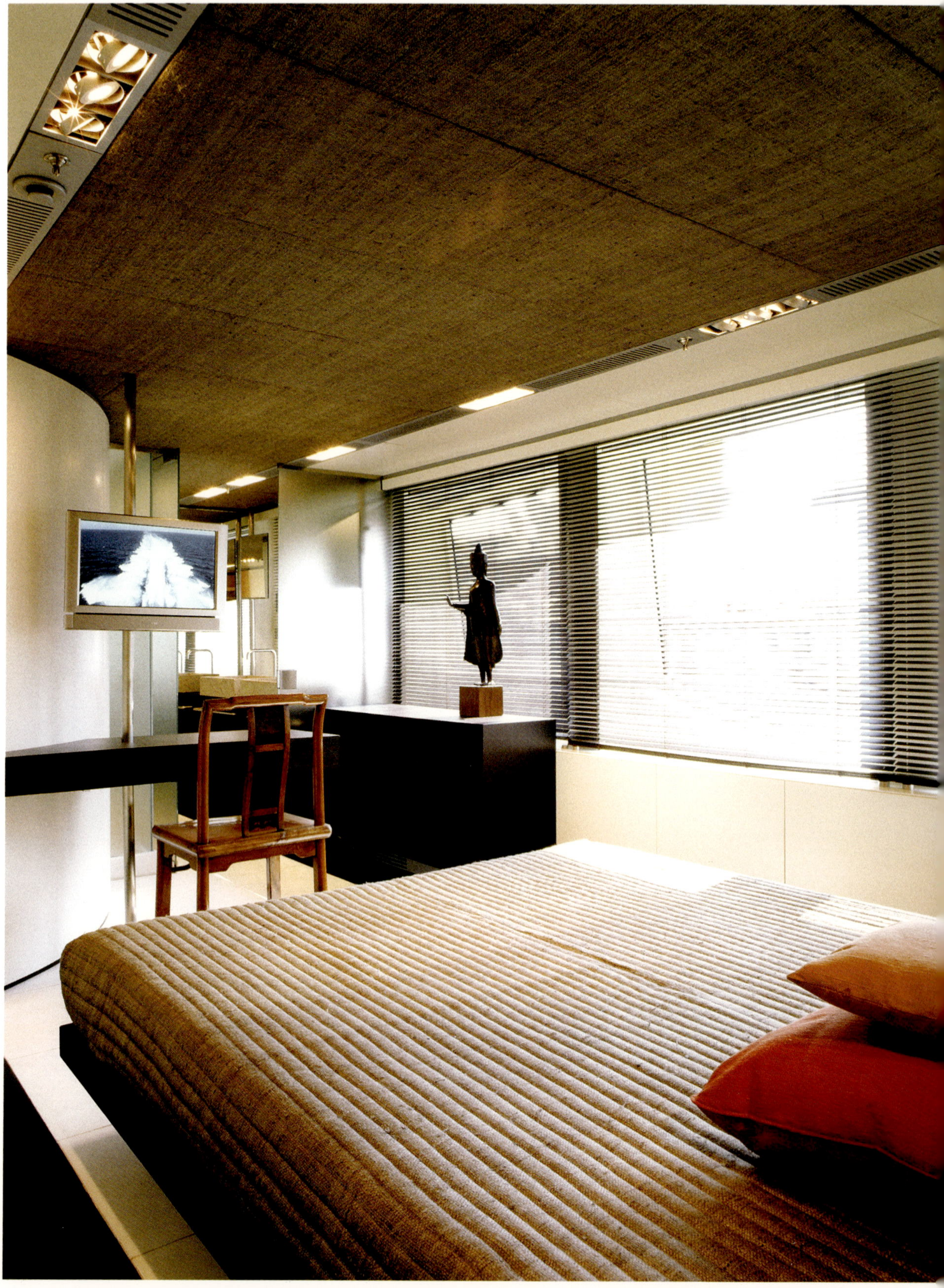

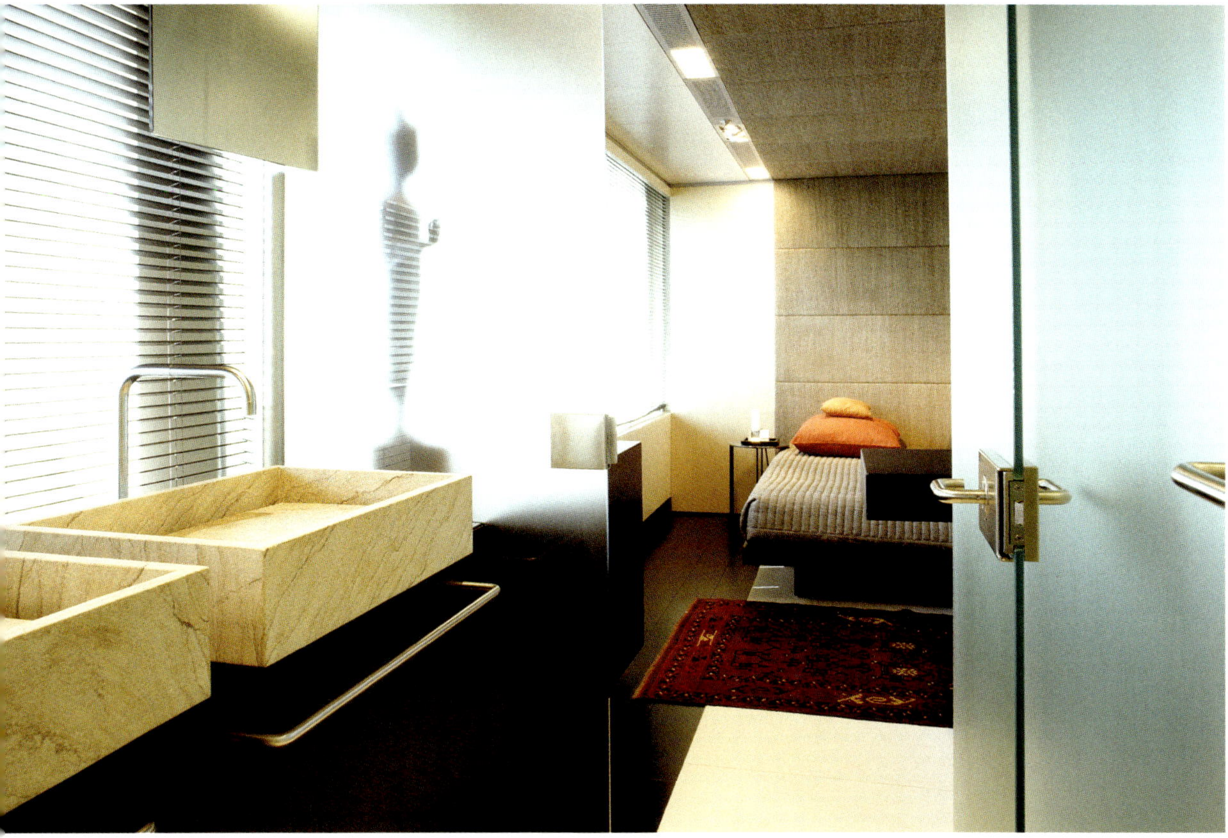

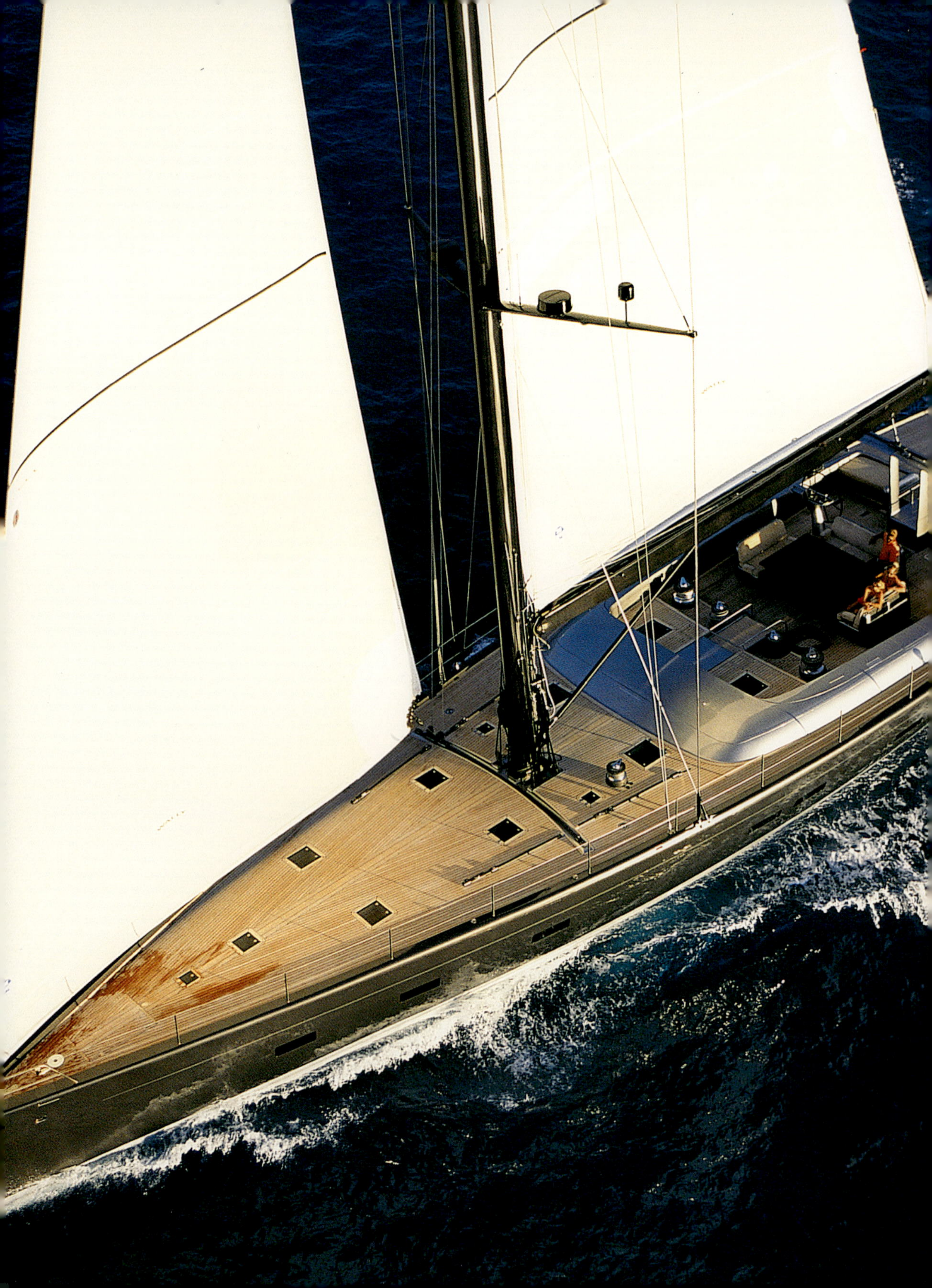

LAZZARINI PICKERING ARCHITETTI, LUCA BRENTA & CO
WALLY B | 1998
Pendenis Shipyard
Wally

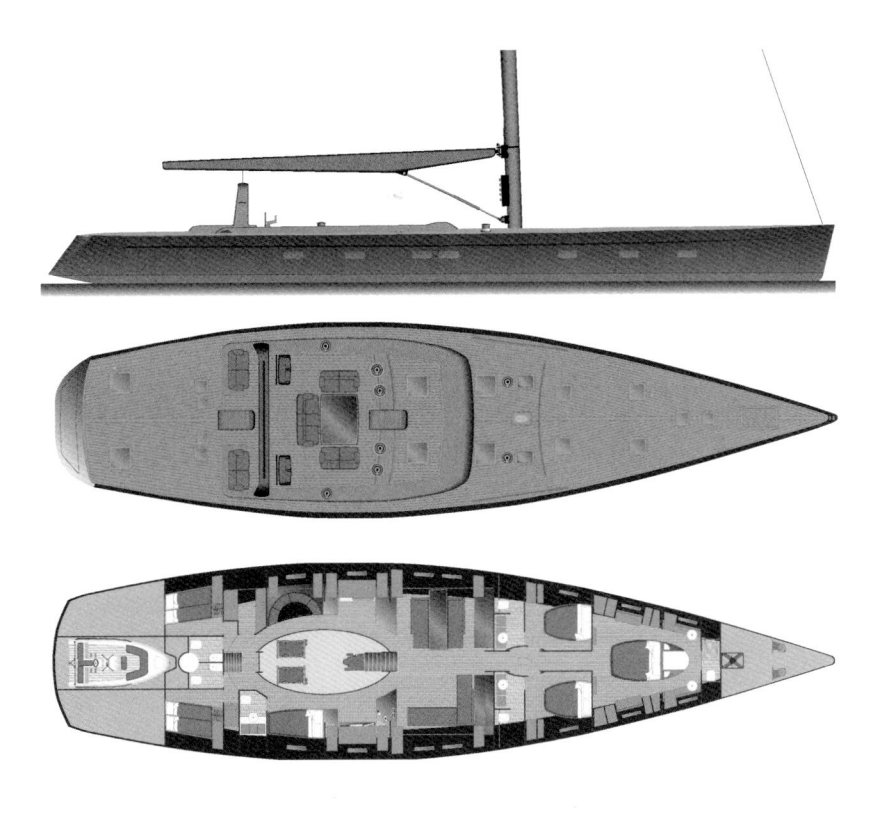

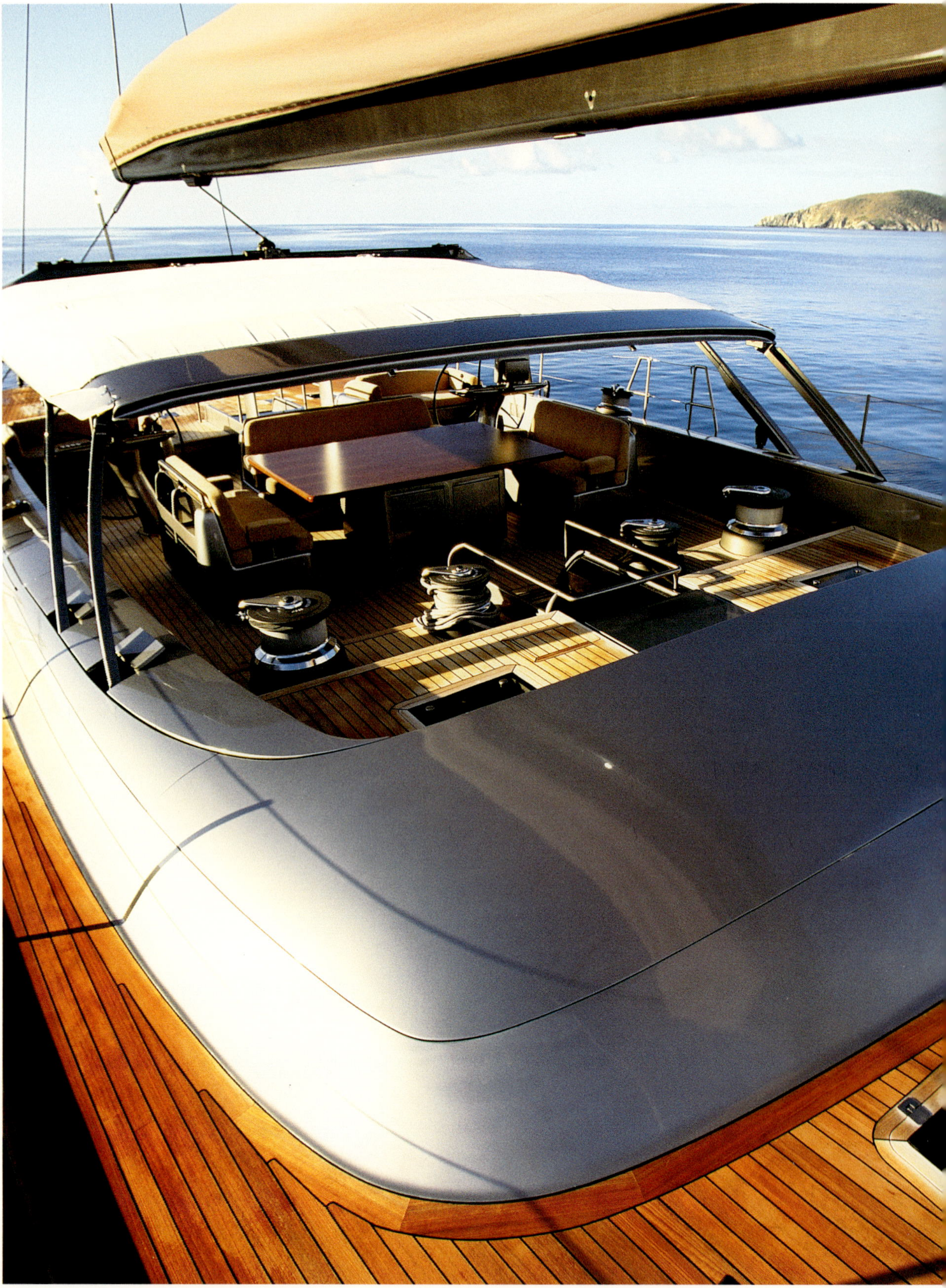

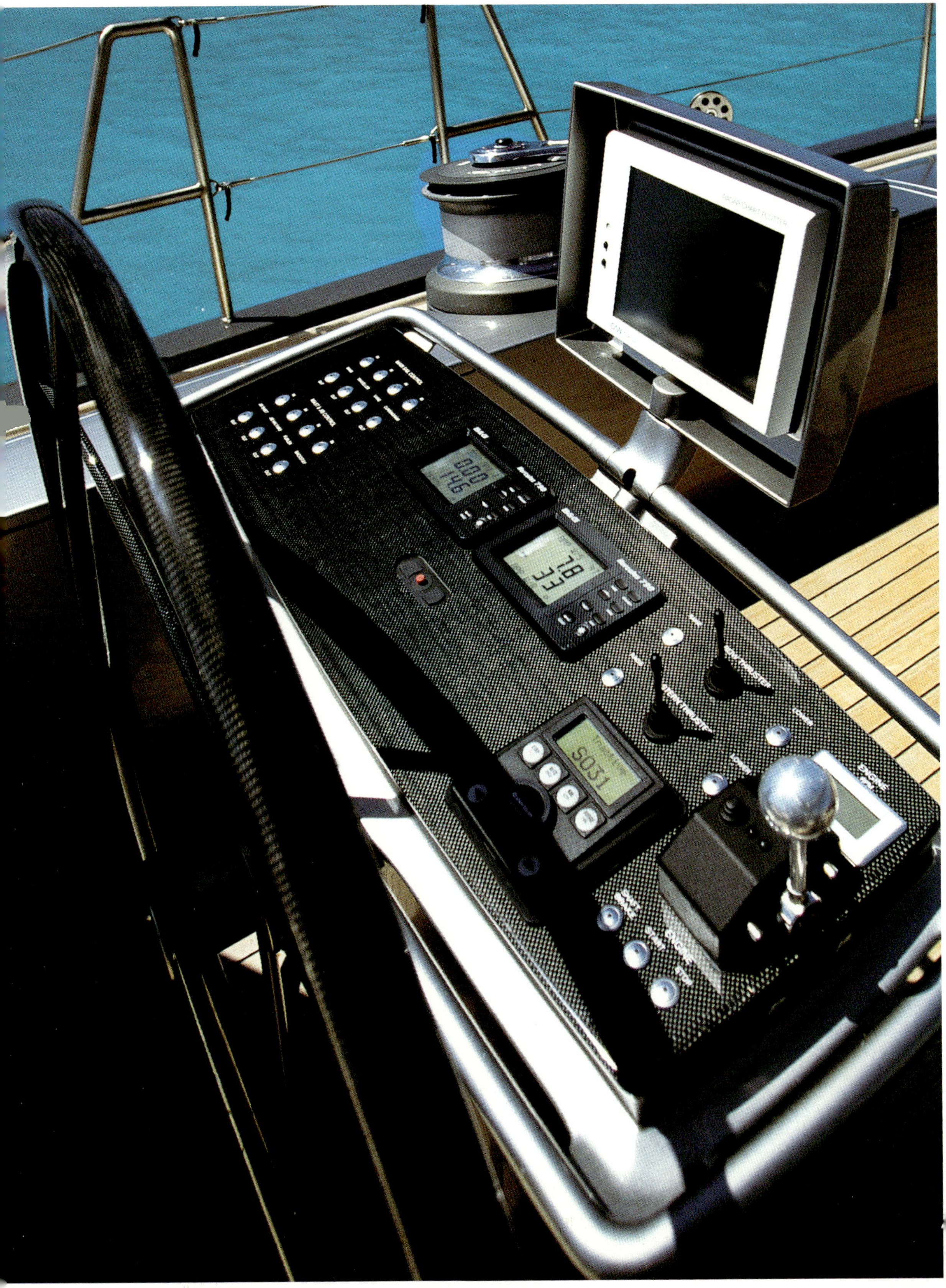
ENGINE

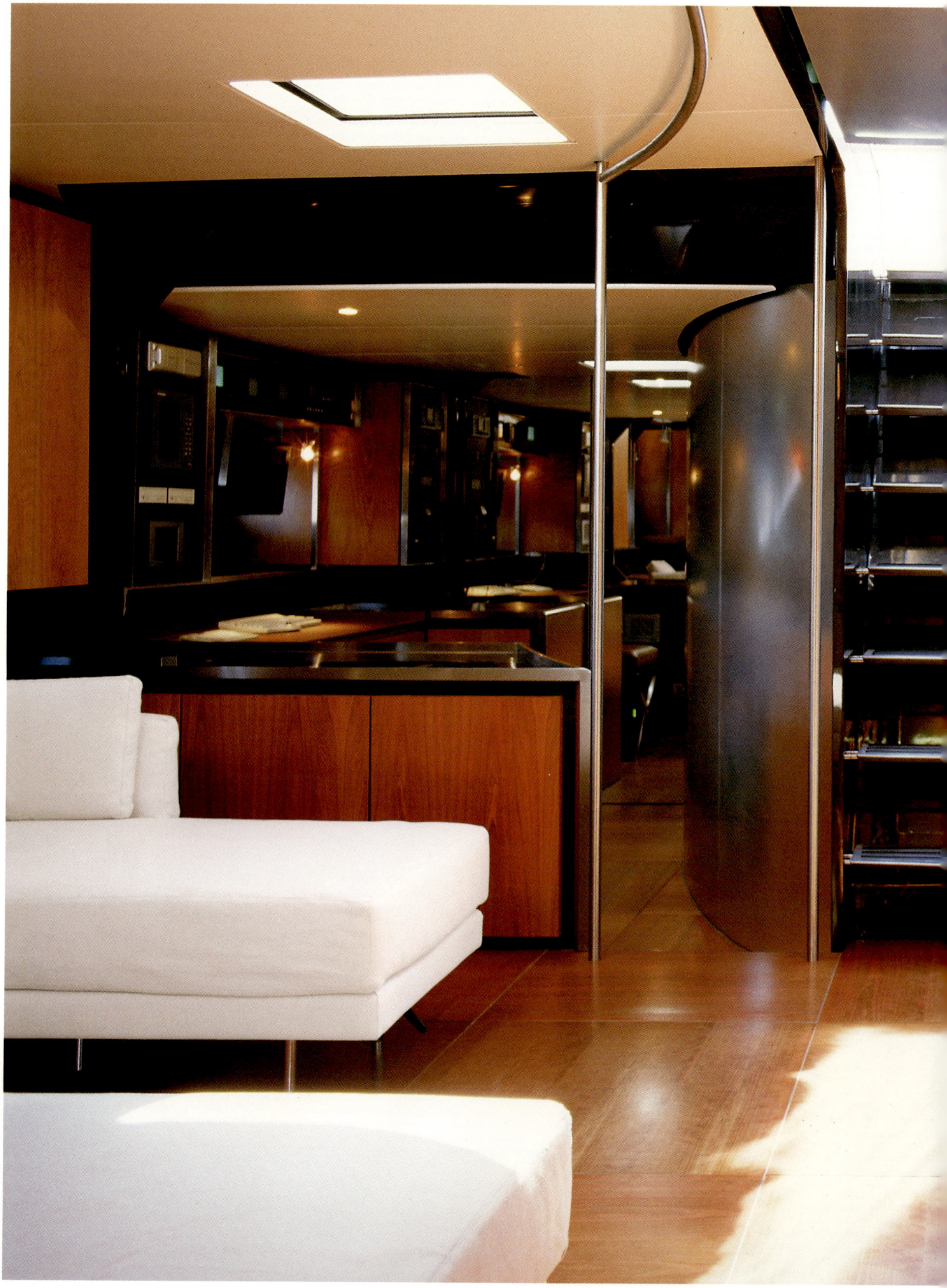

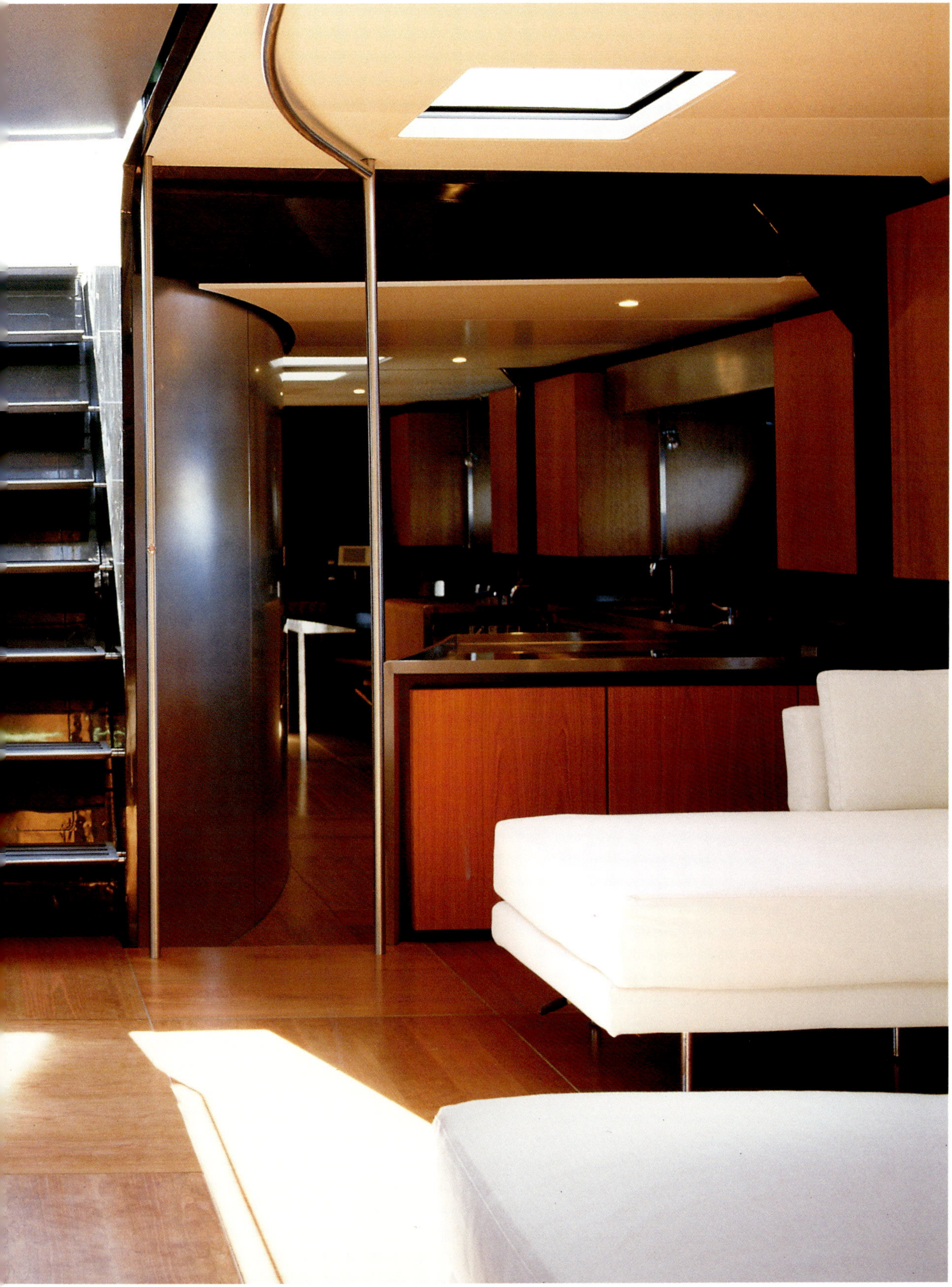

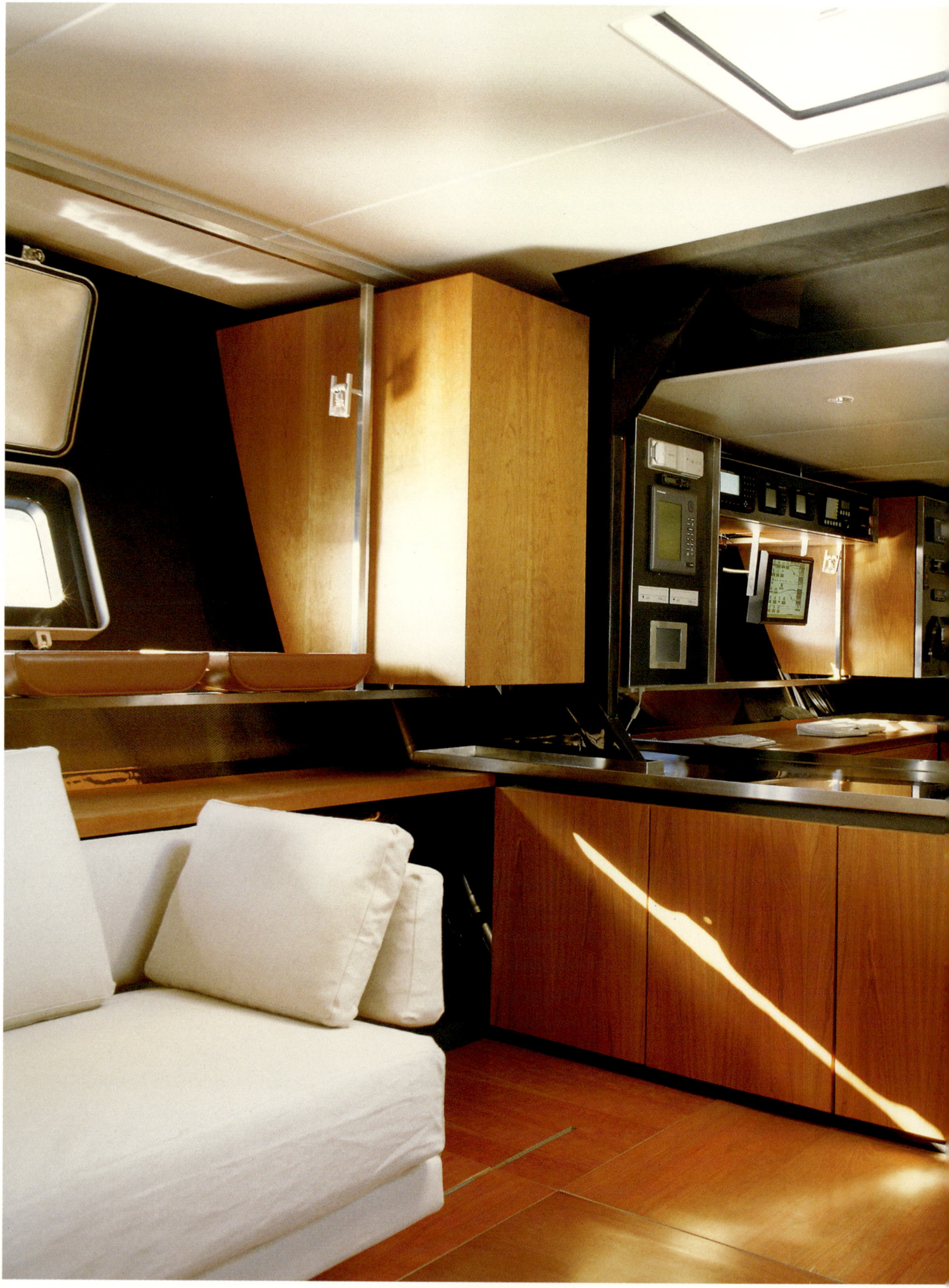

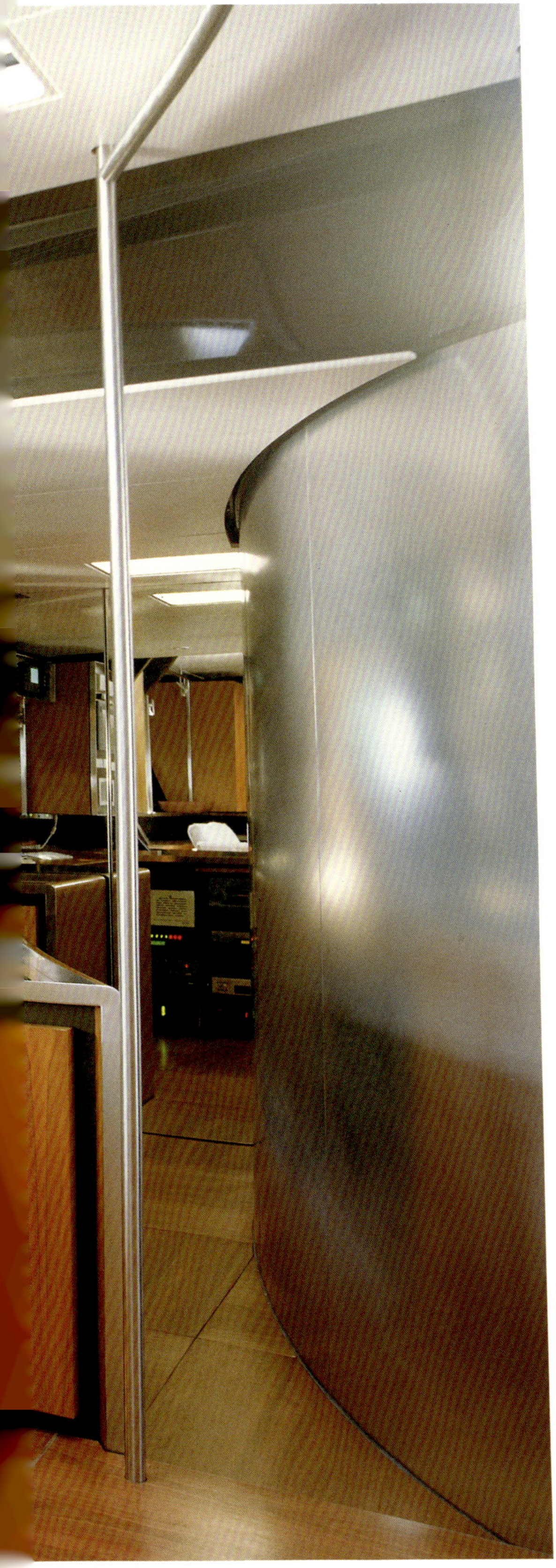

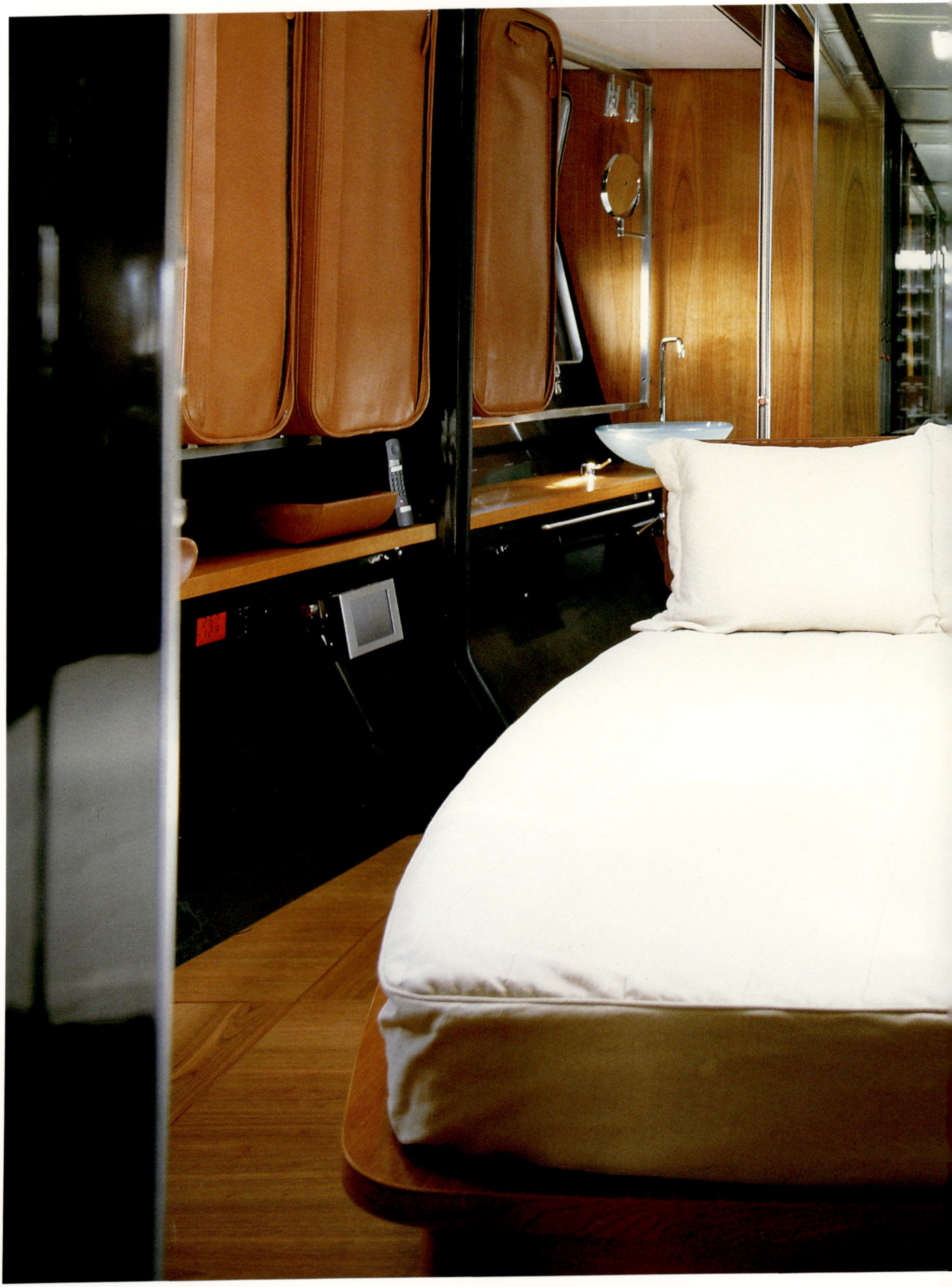

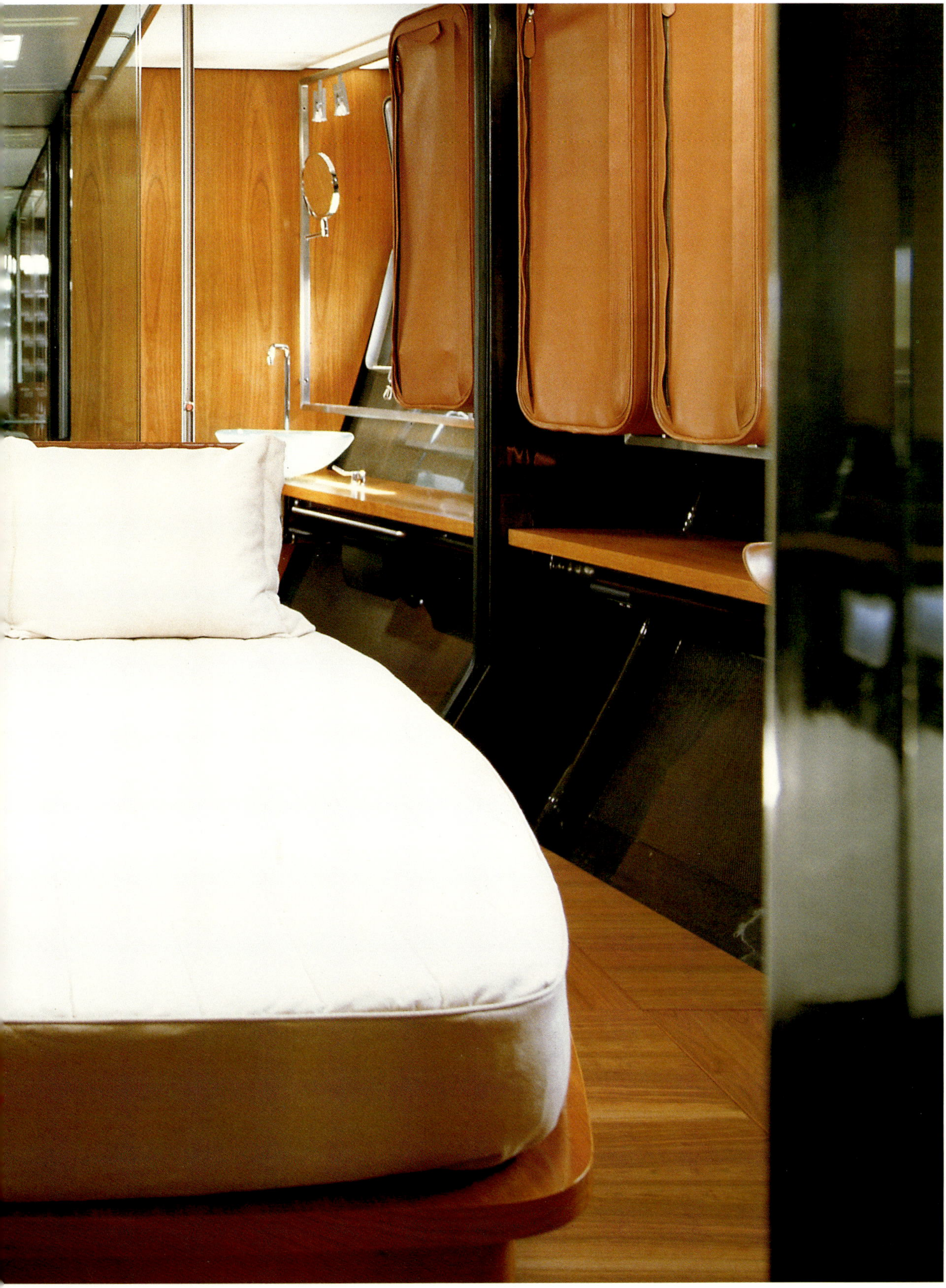

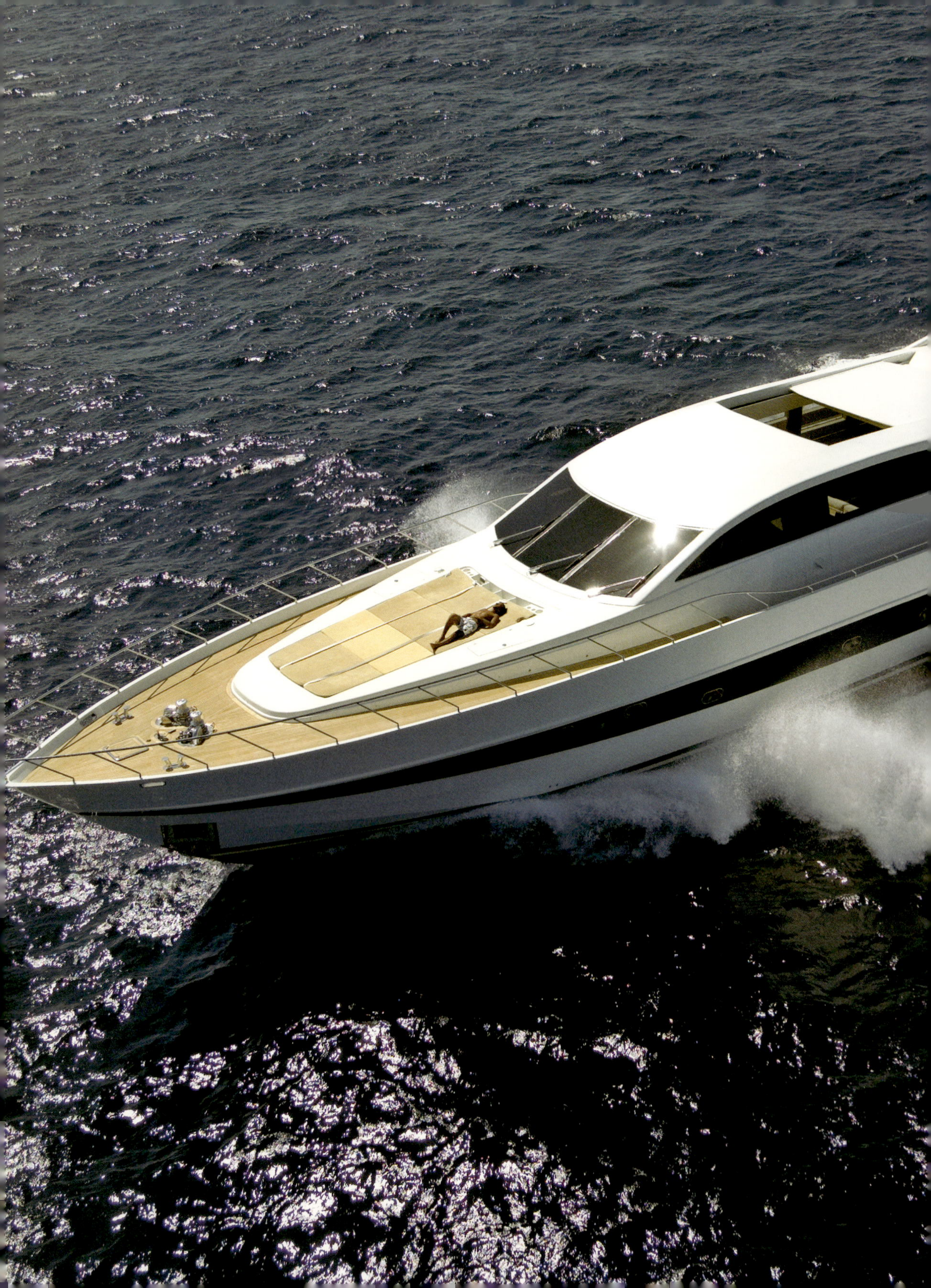

LUCA DINI
VELVET 35 | 2004
Tecnomar

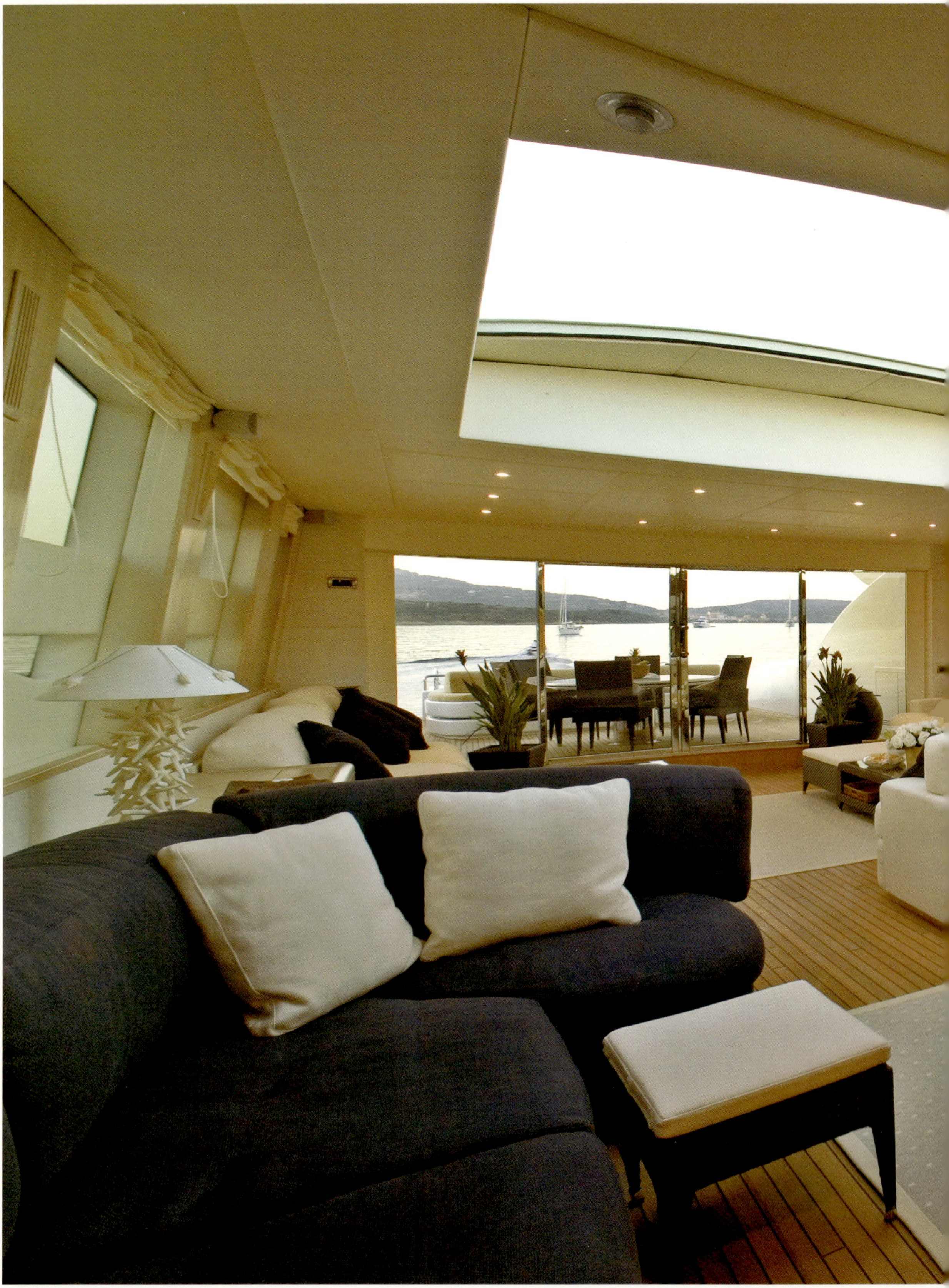

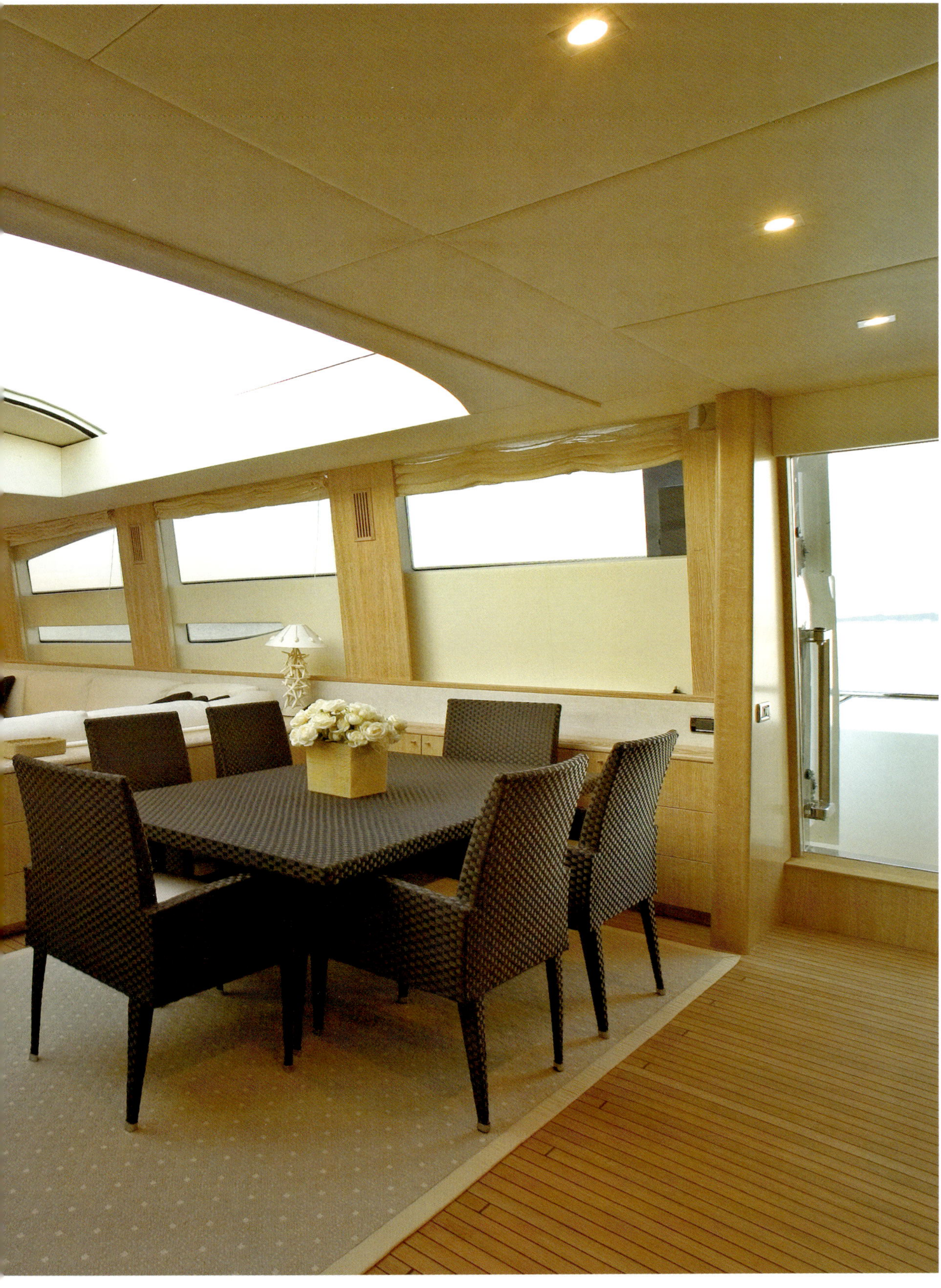

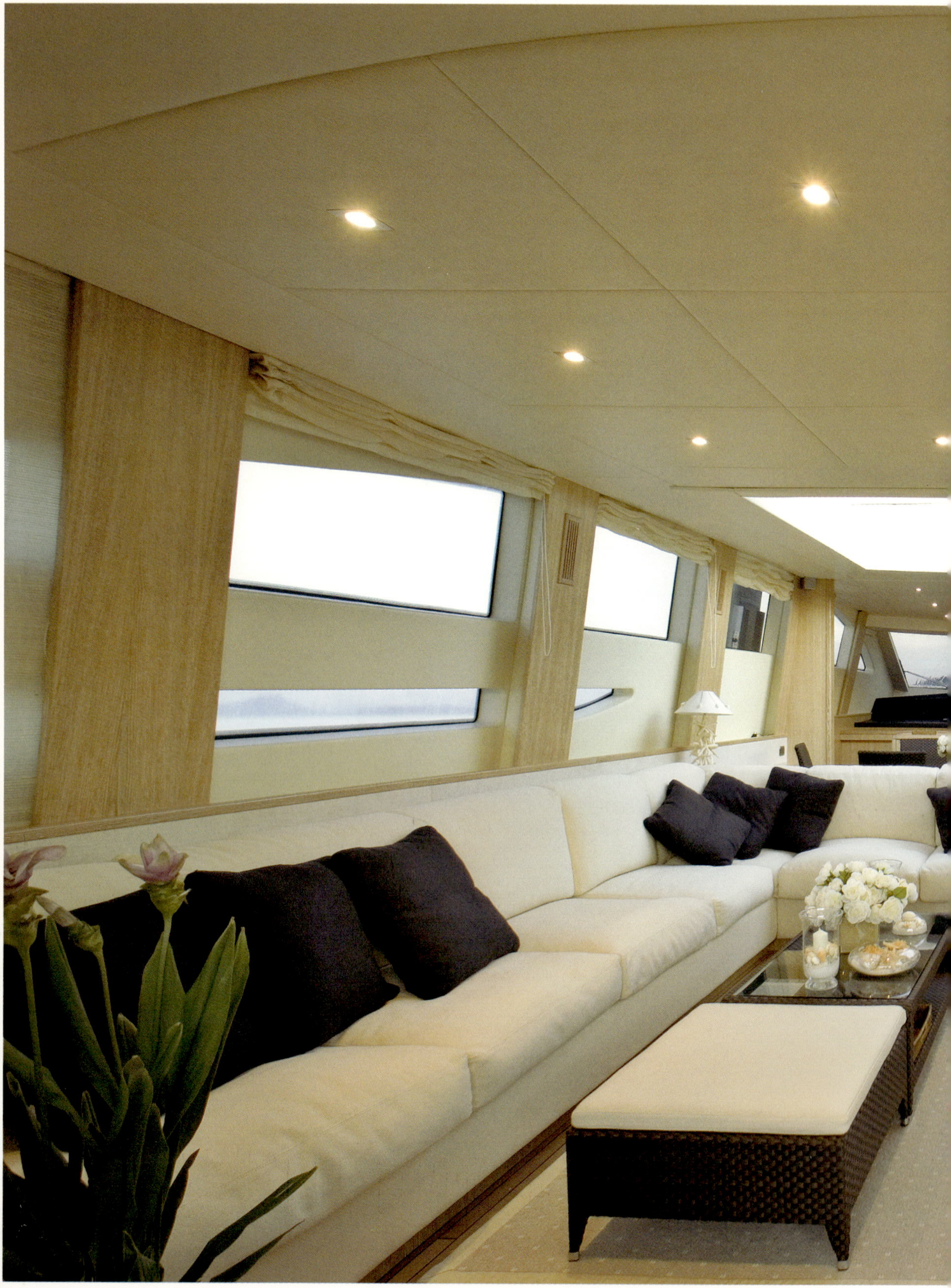

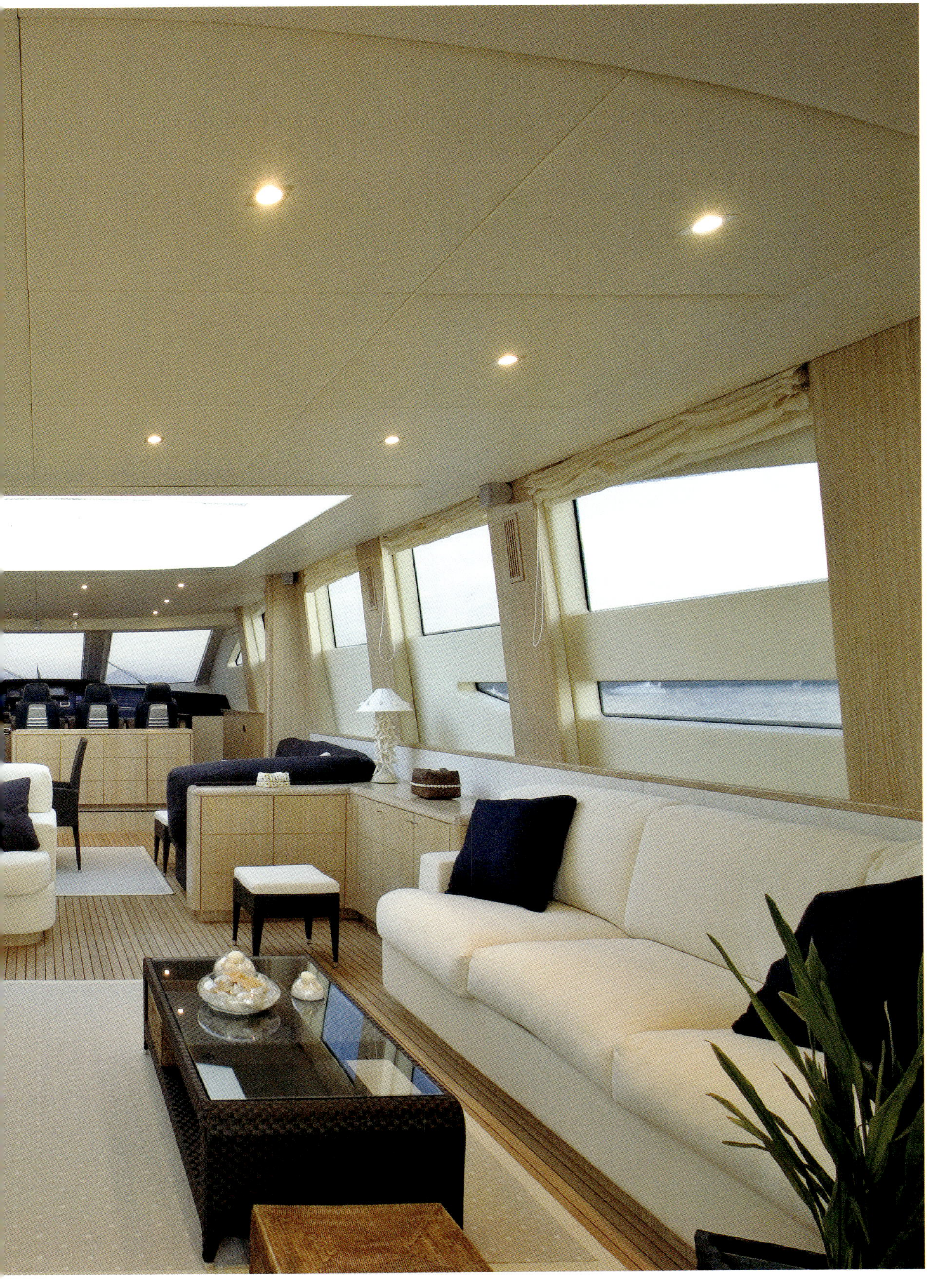

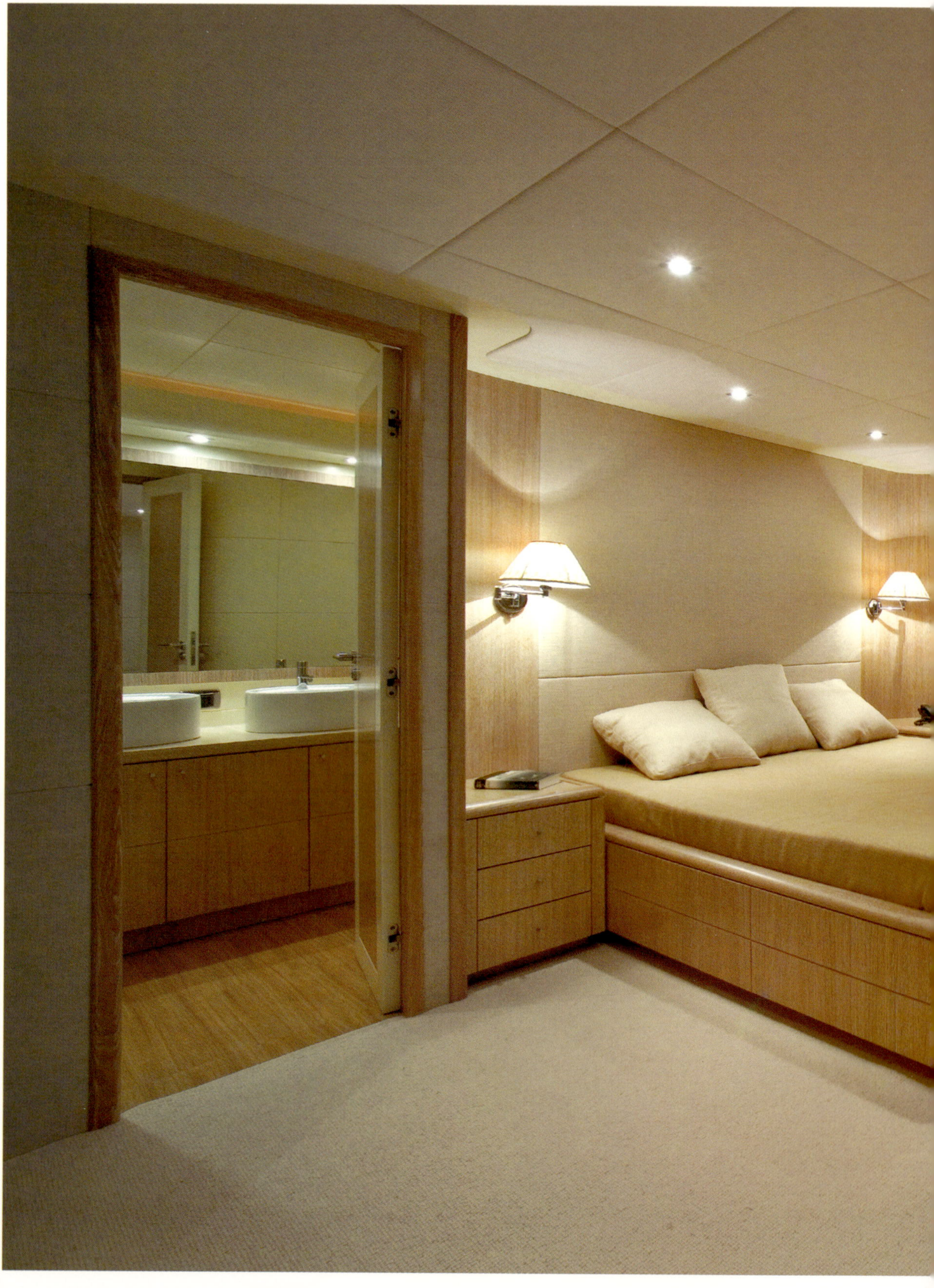

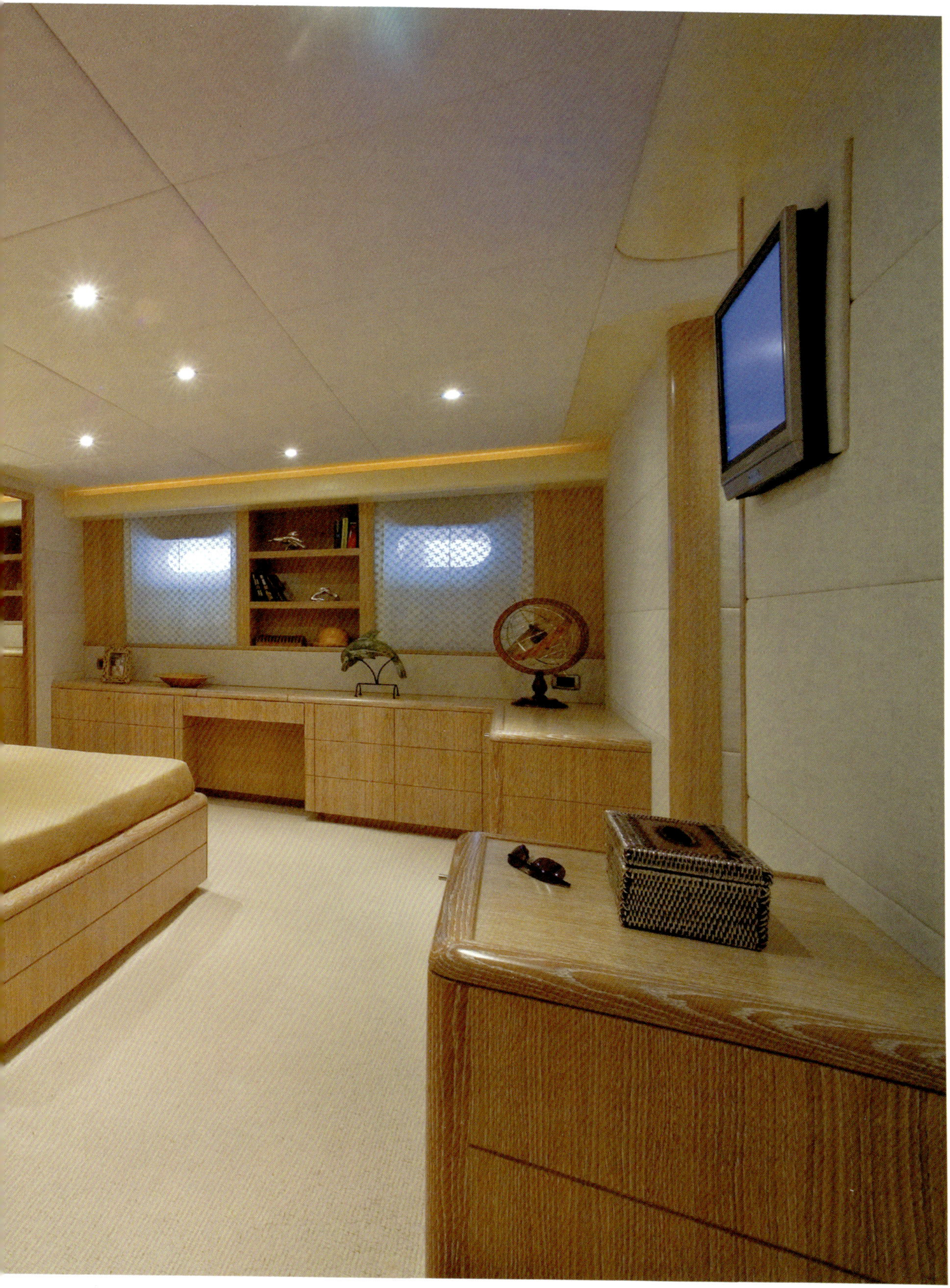

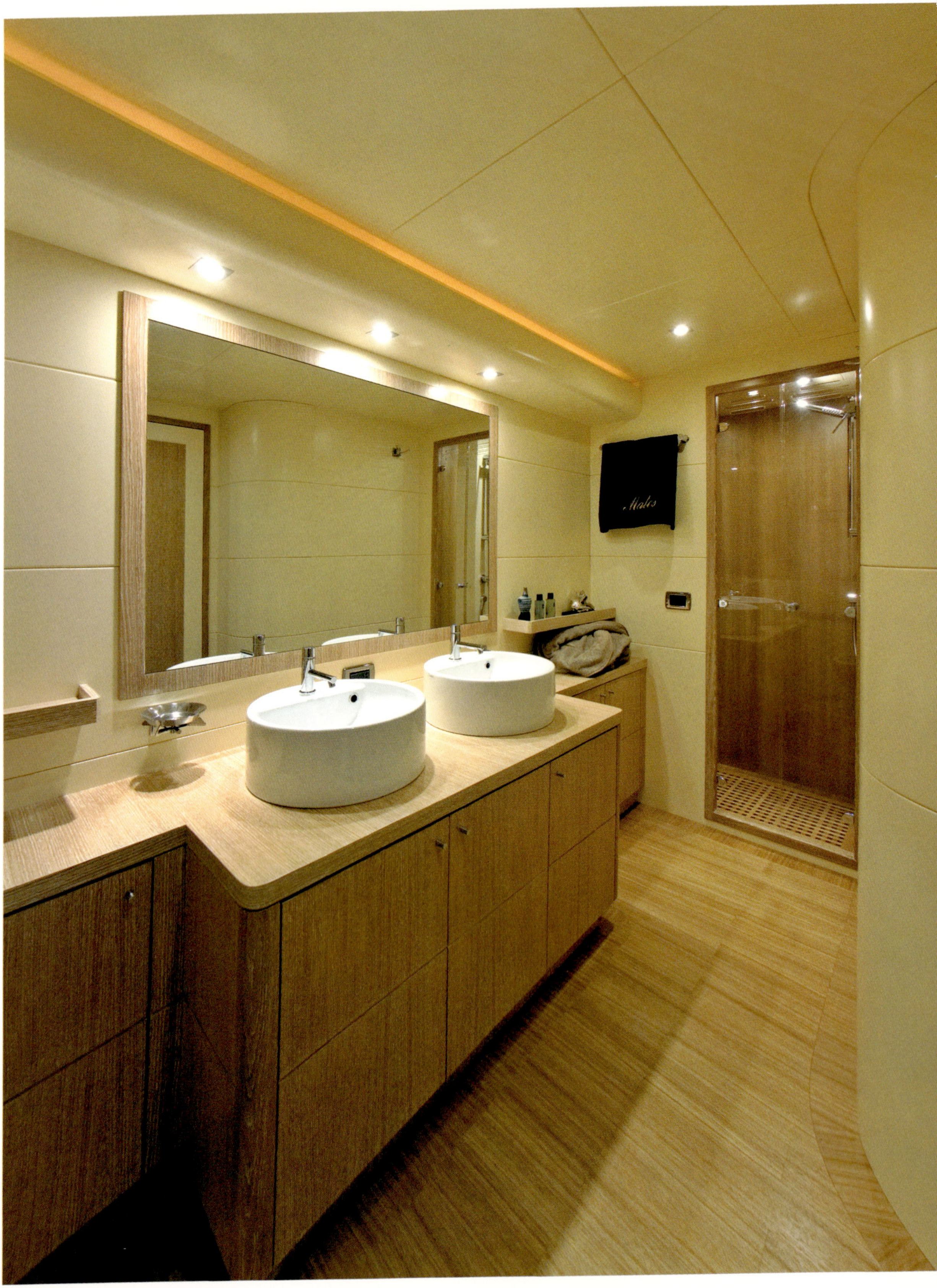

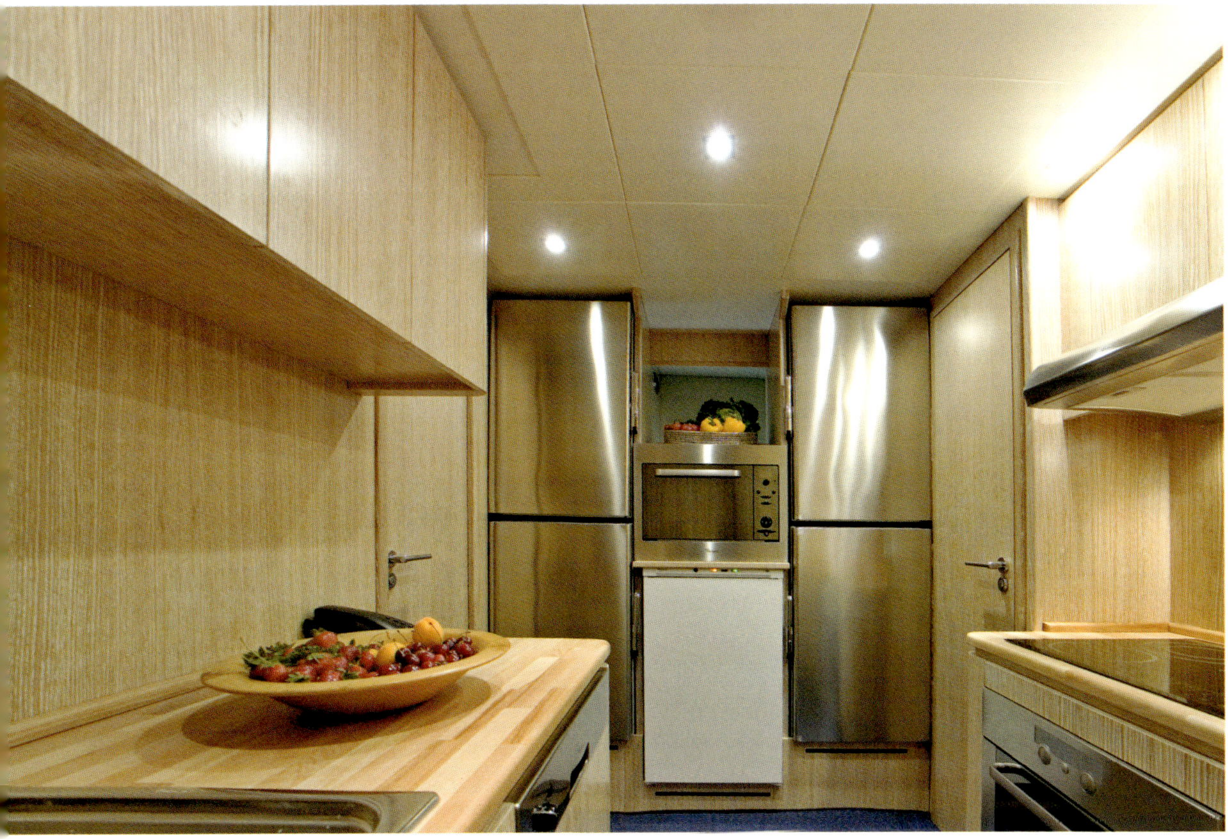

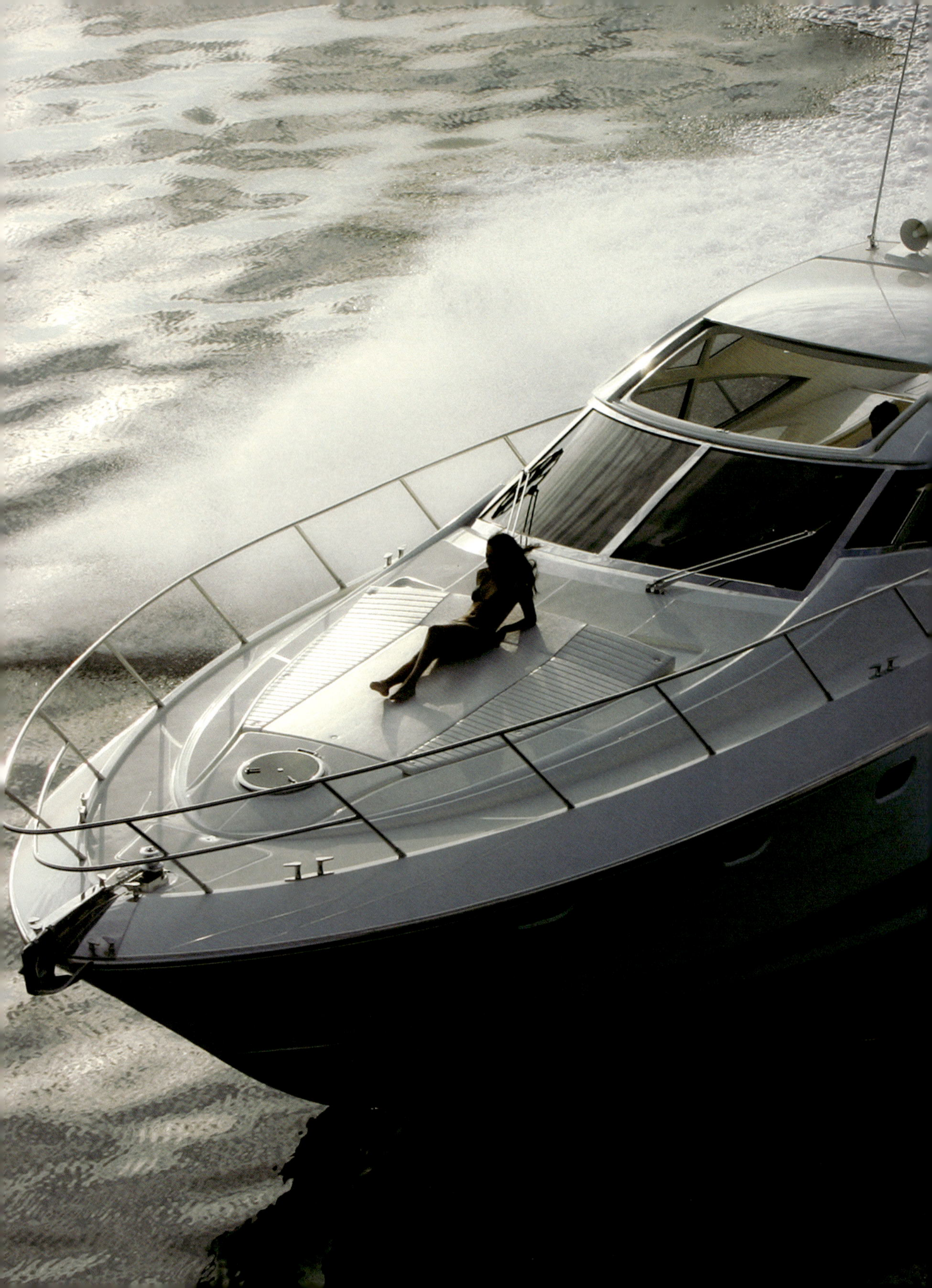

NUVOLARI LENARD NAVAL DESIGN
SARNICO 50 | 2004
Cantieri di Sarnico

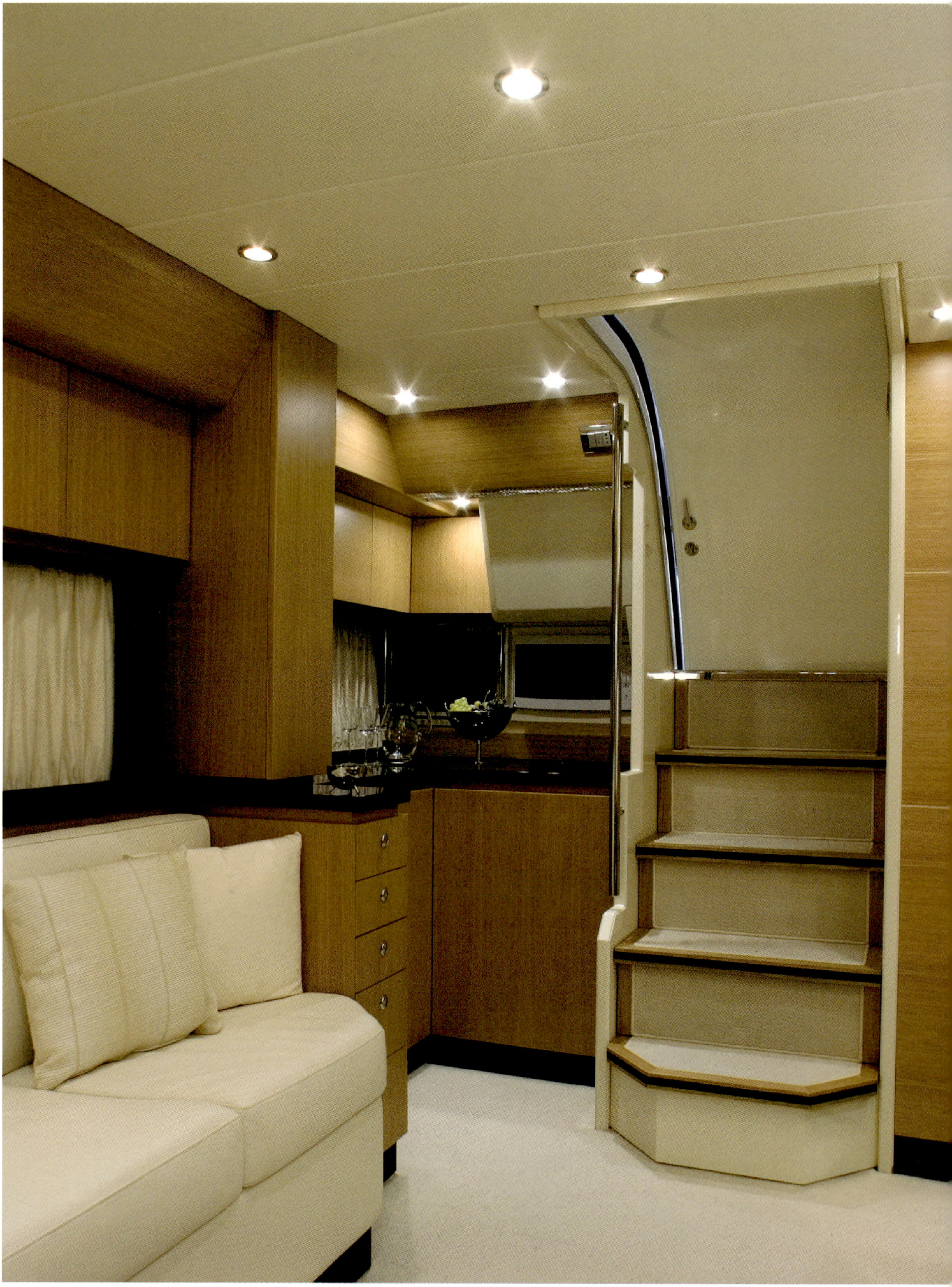

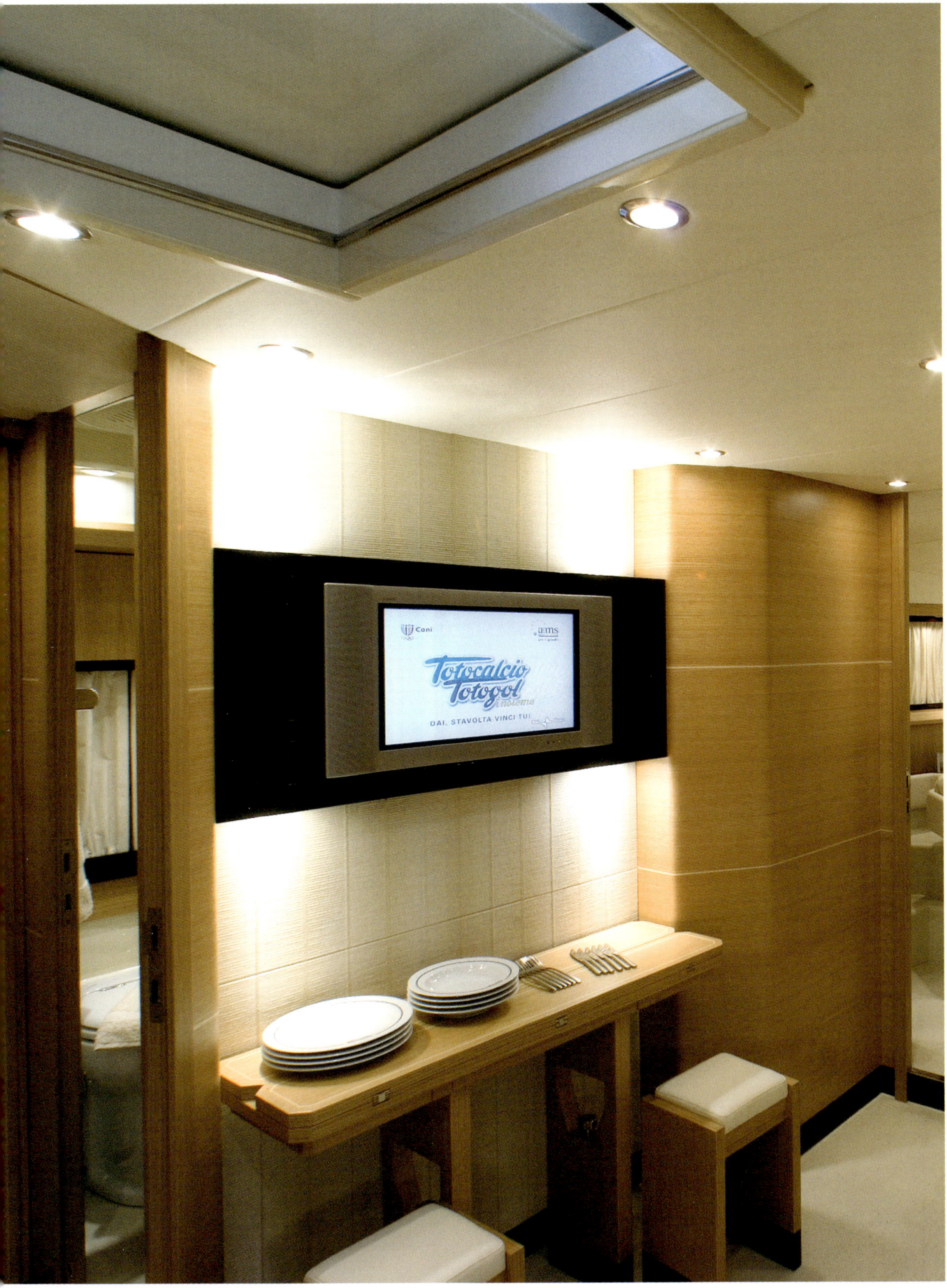
Coni
Totocalcio
Totogol
DAI, STAVOLTA VINCI TU!

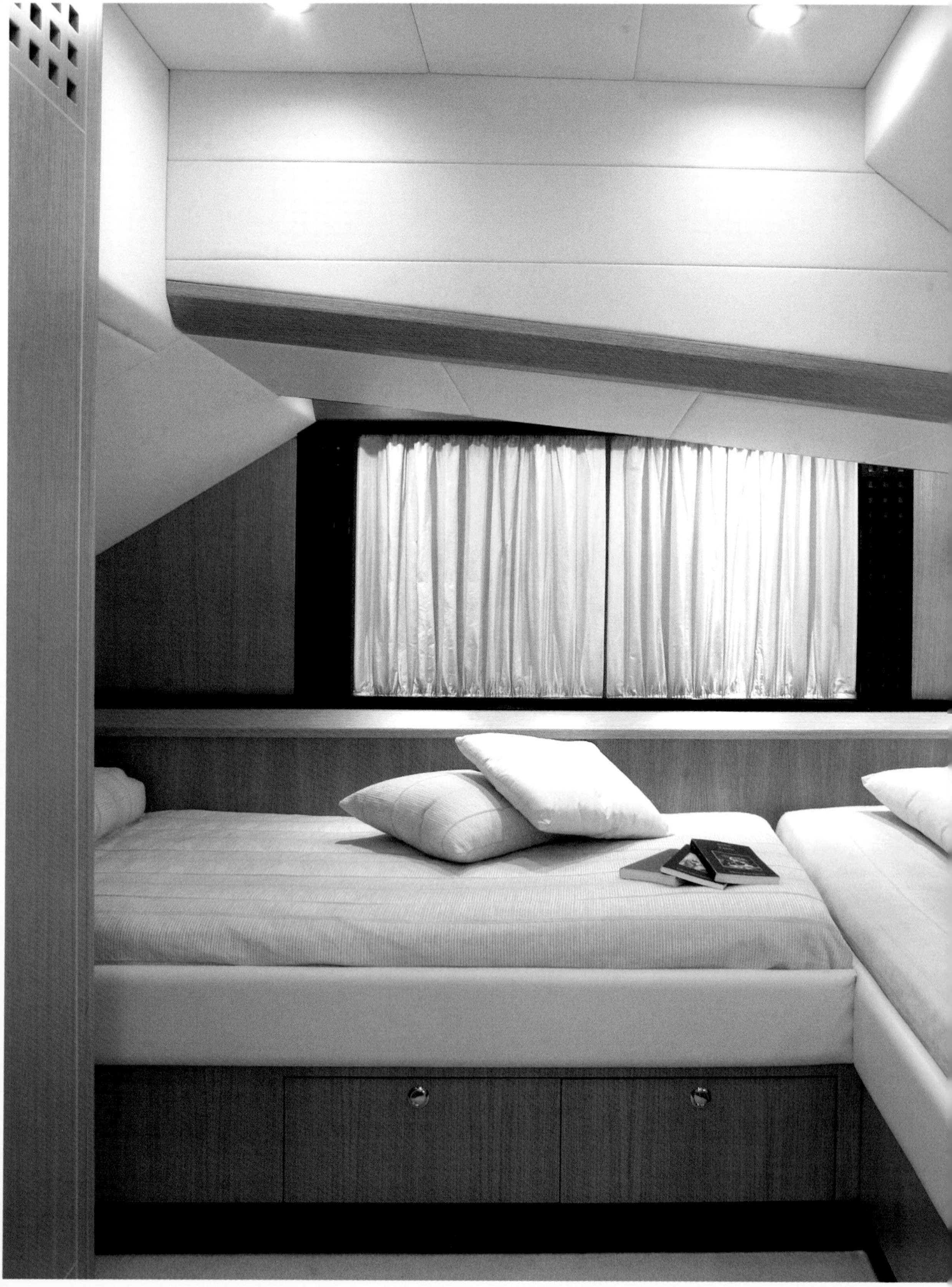

209

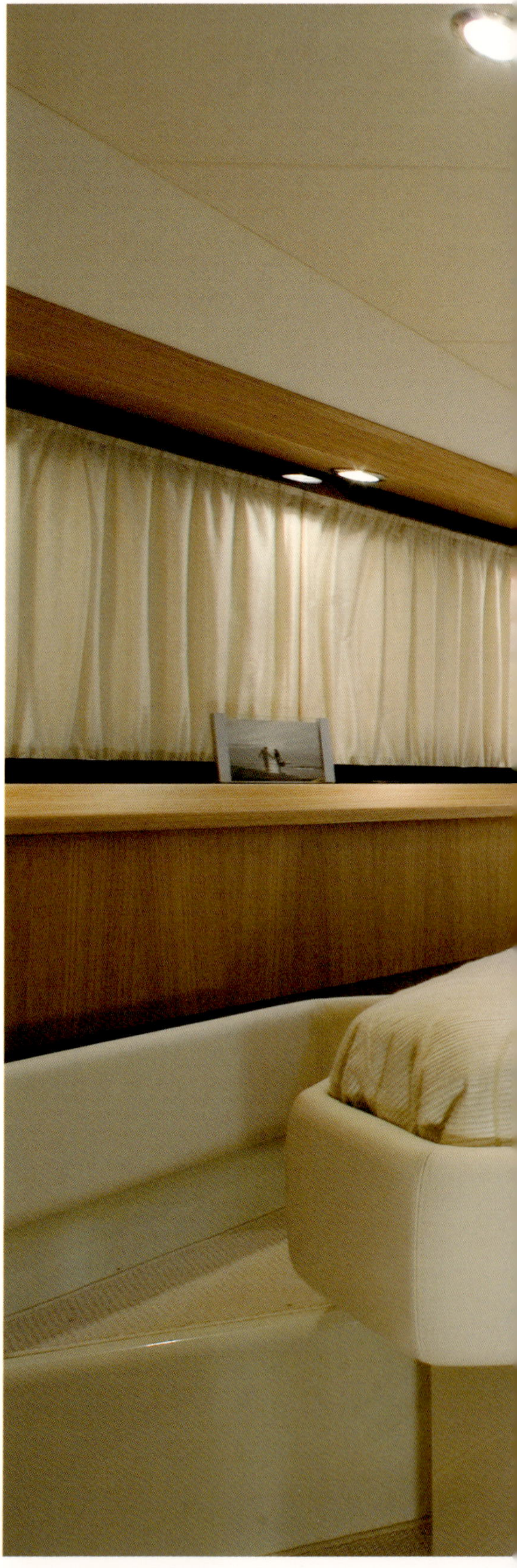

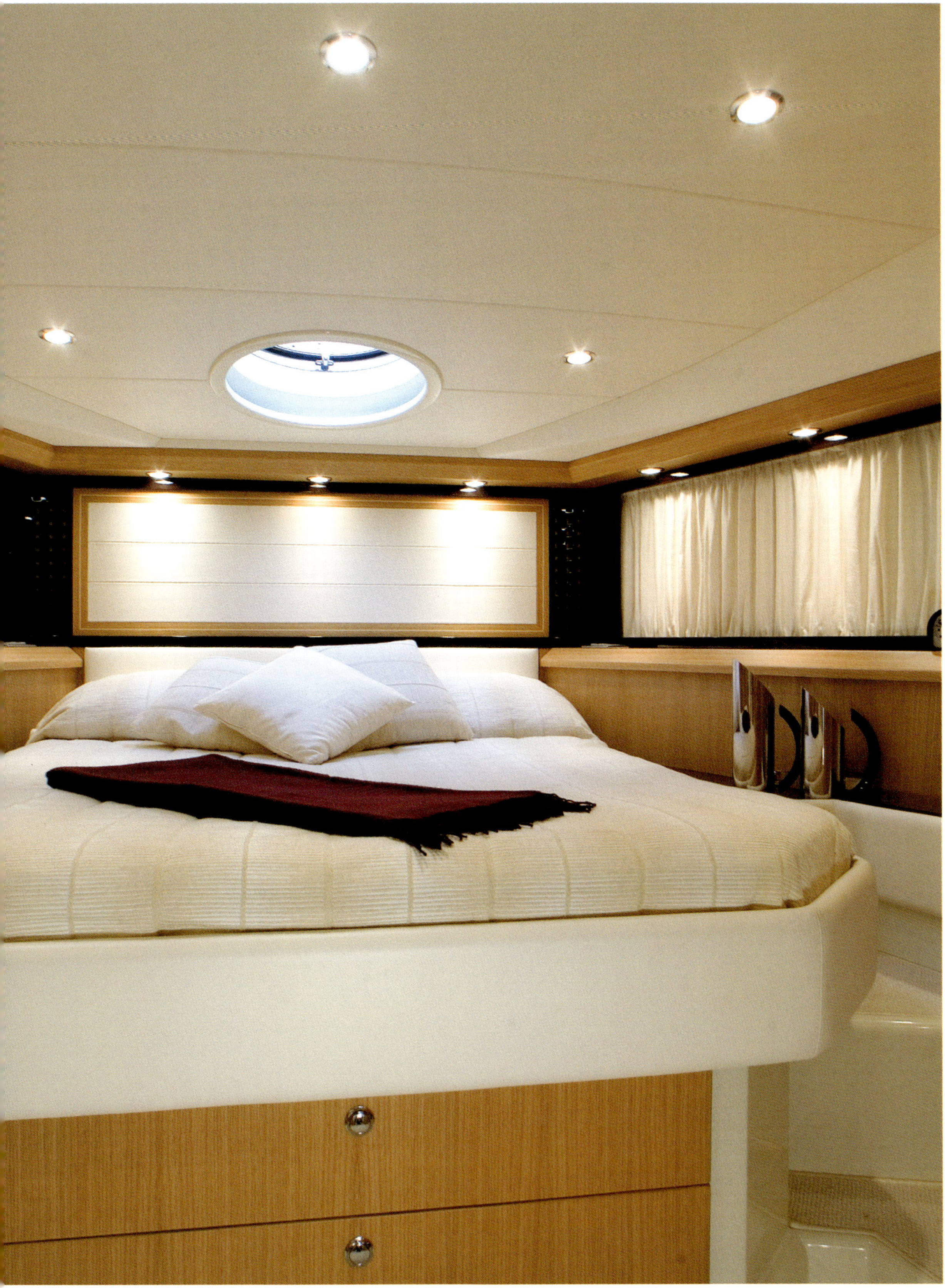

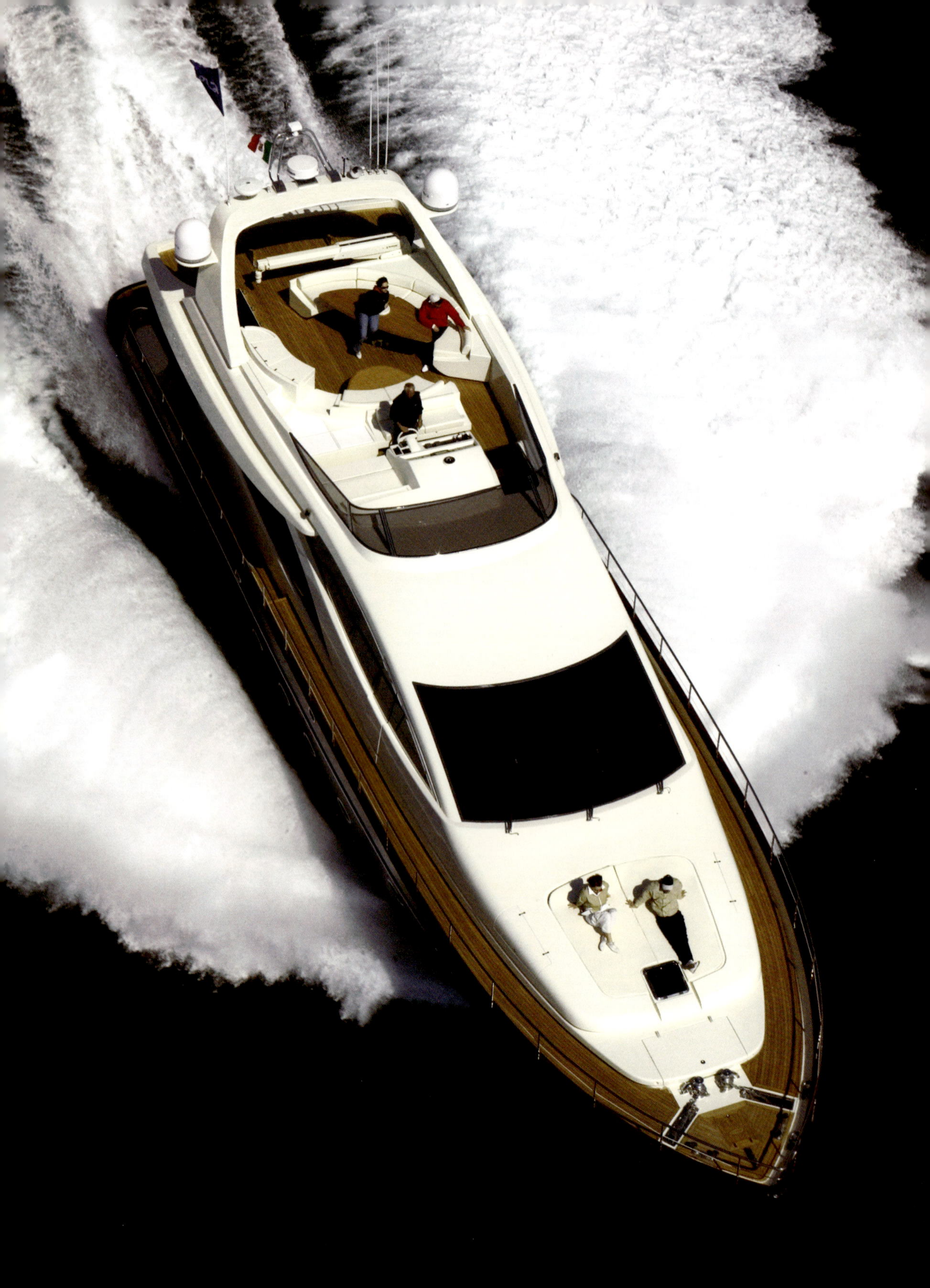

OFFICINA ITALIANA DESIGN
OPERA 85 | 2004
Riva SpA

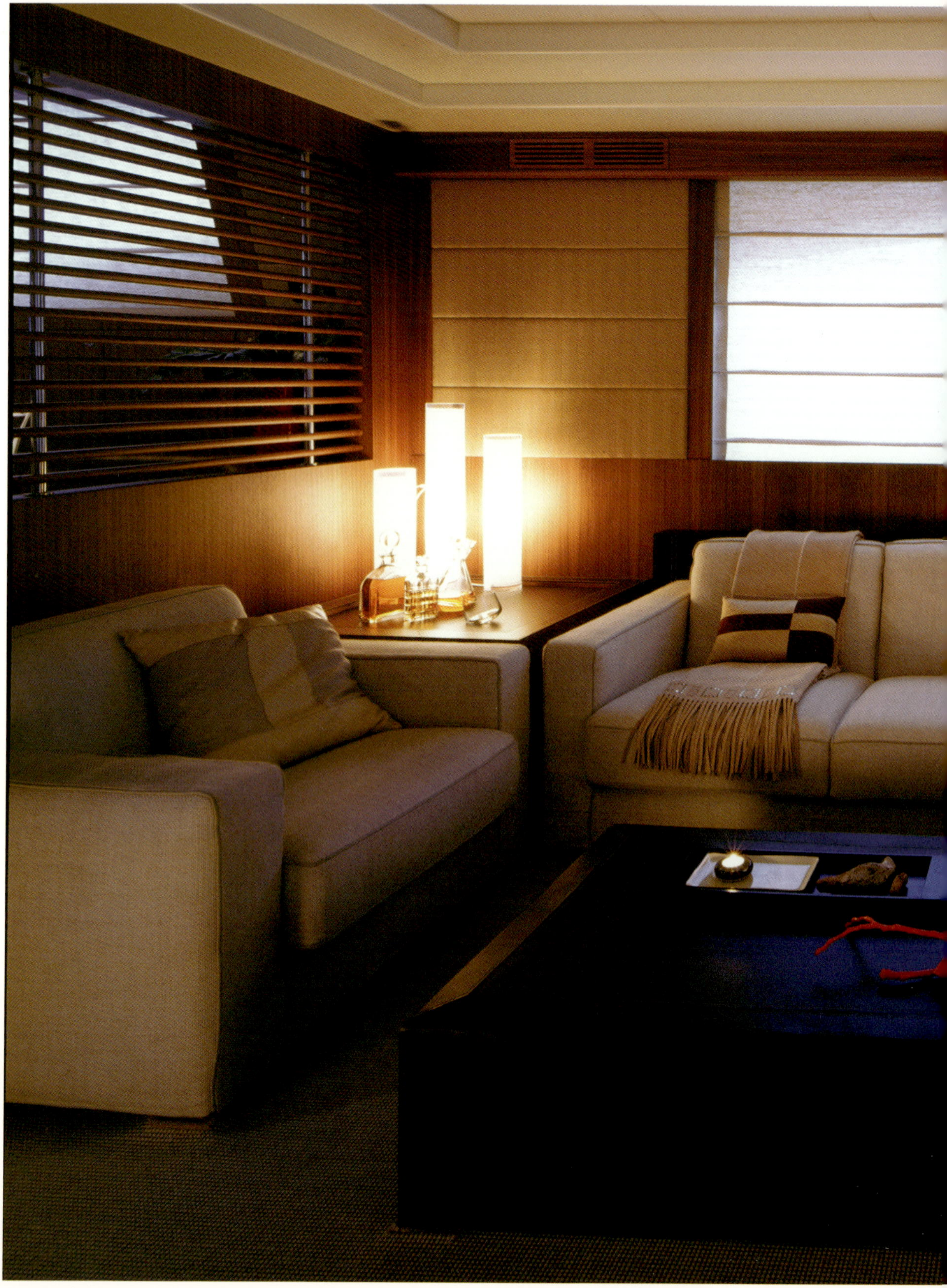

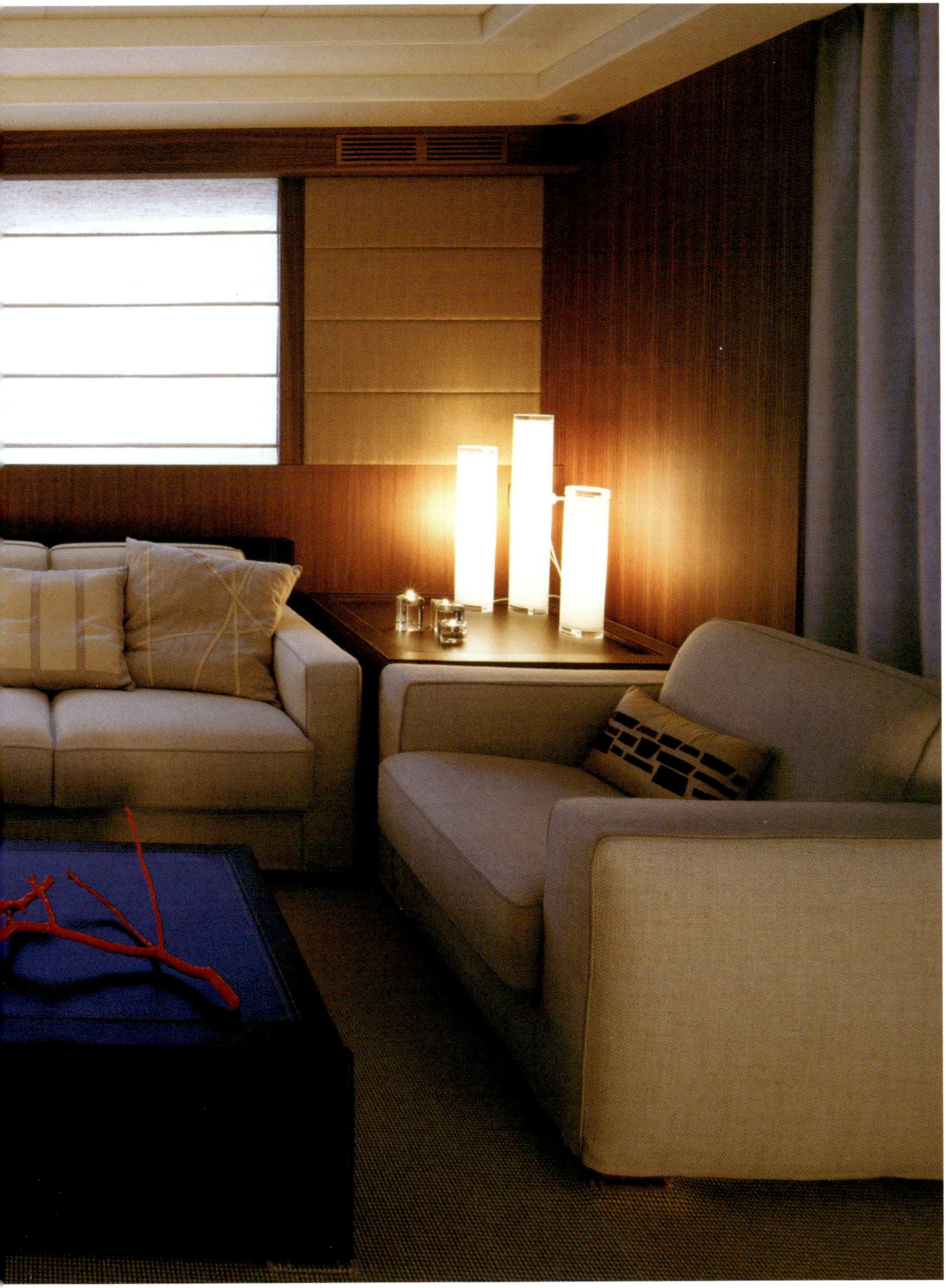

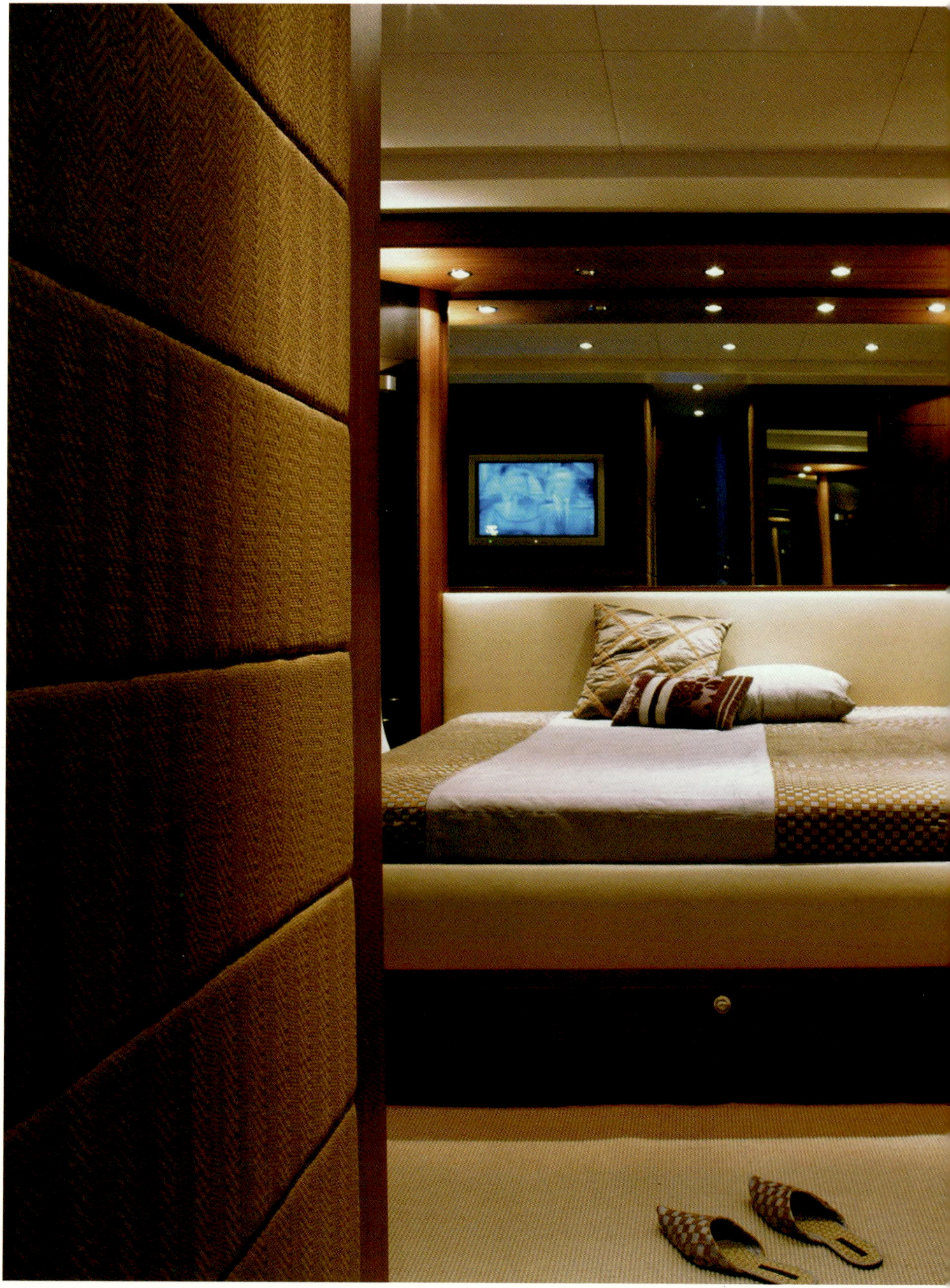

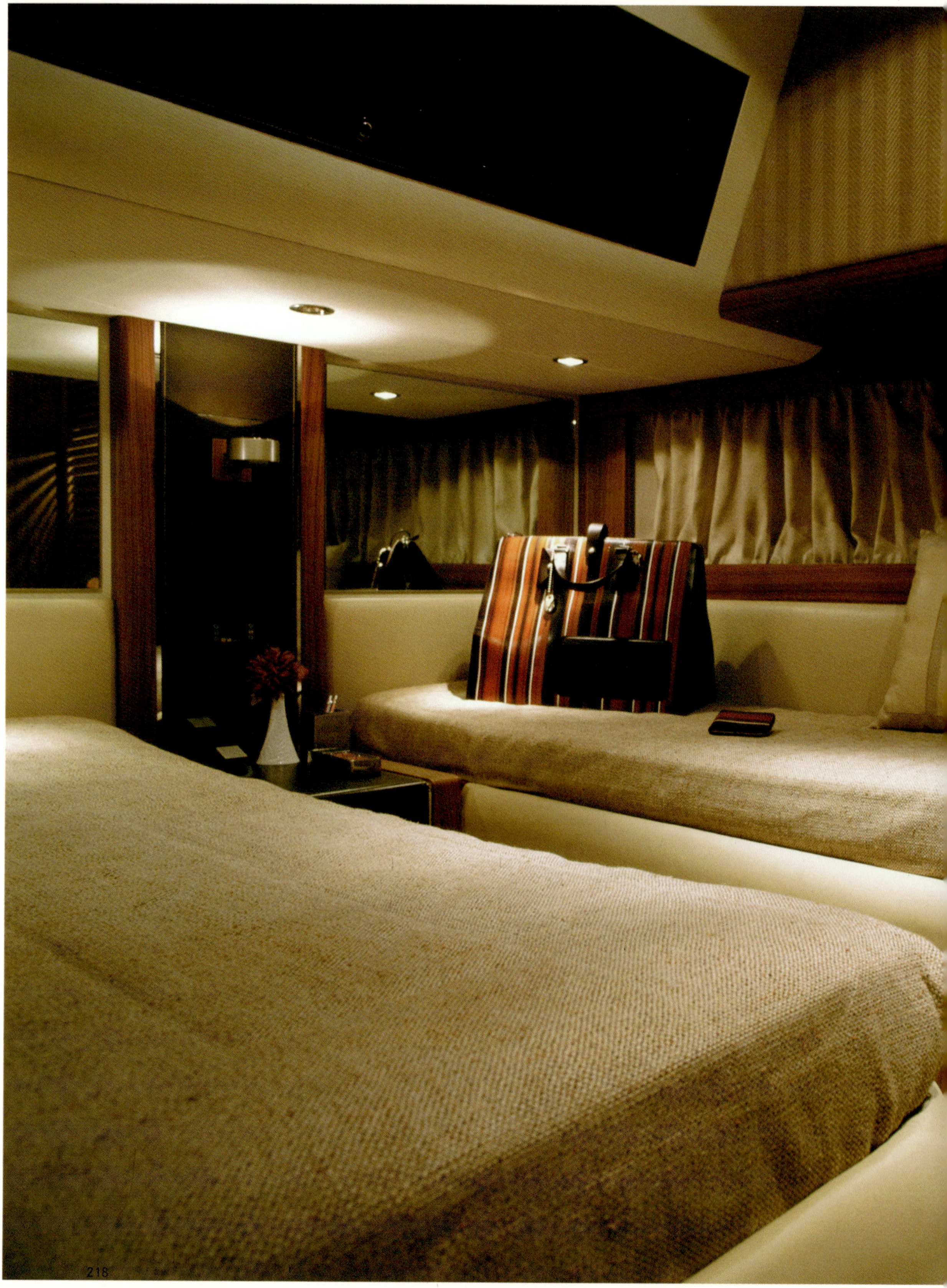

219

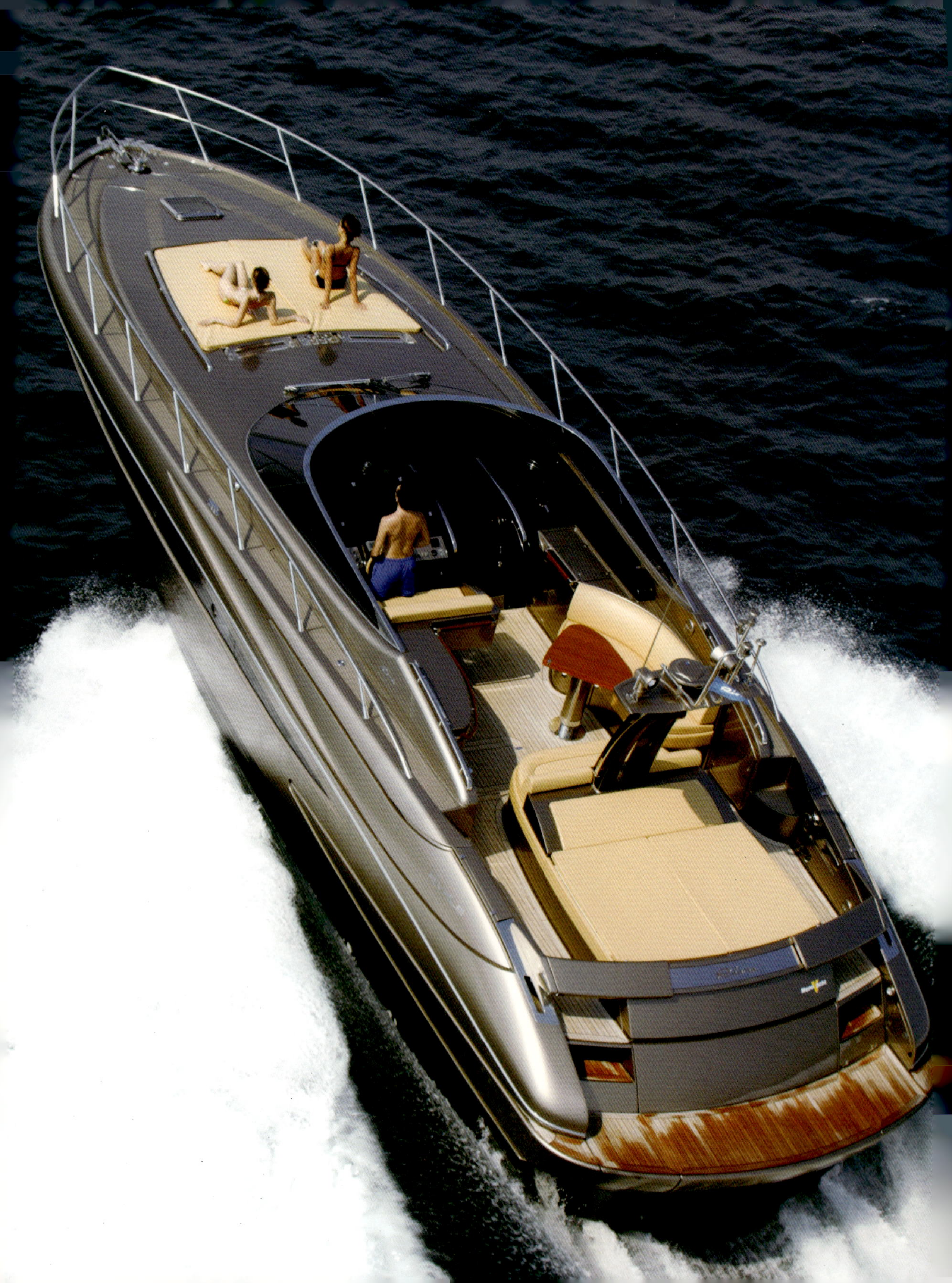

OFFICINA ITALIANA DESIGN
RIVALE | 2003
Riva SpA

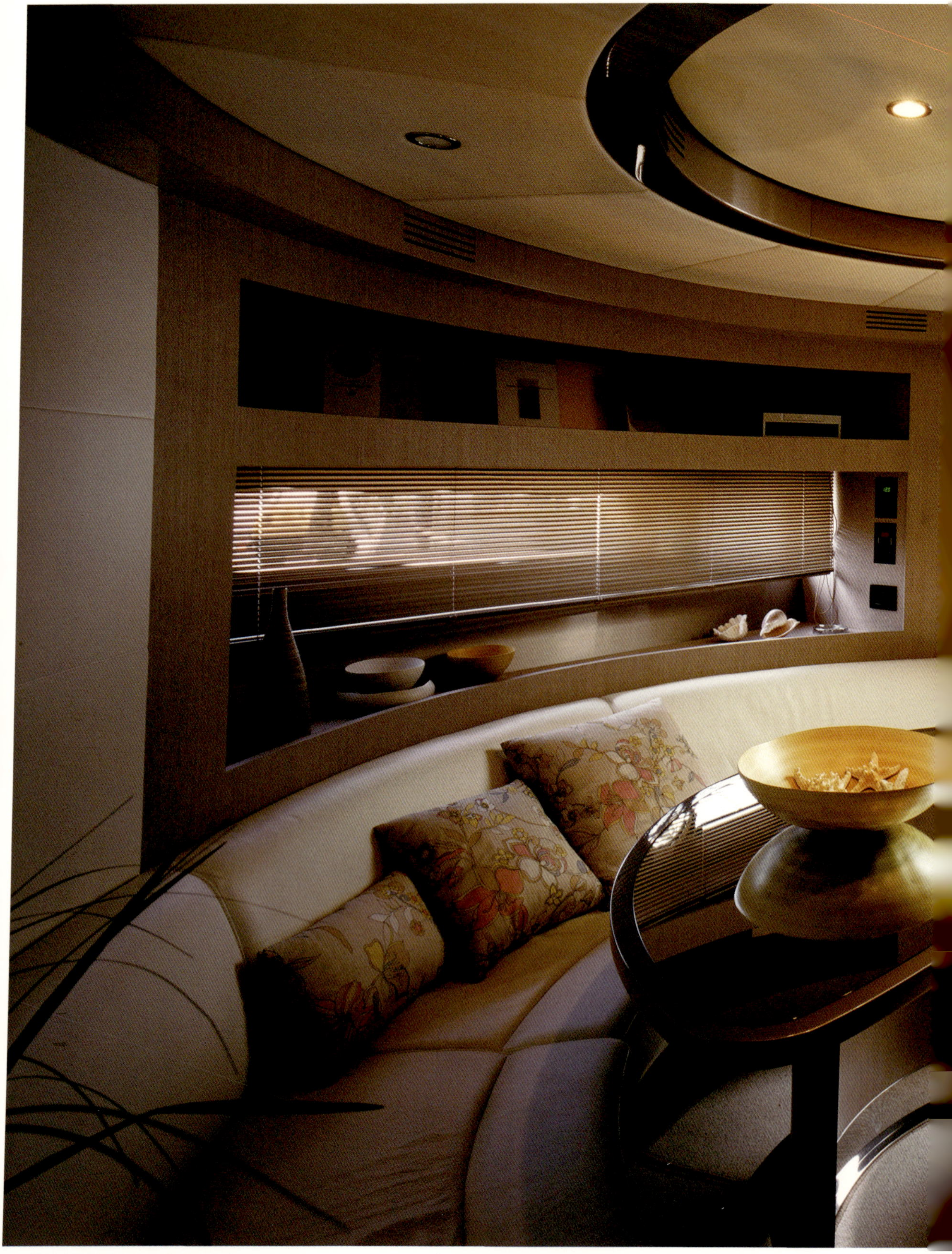

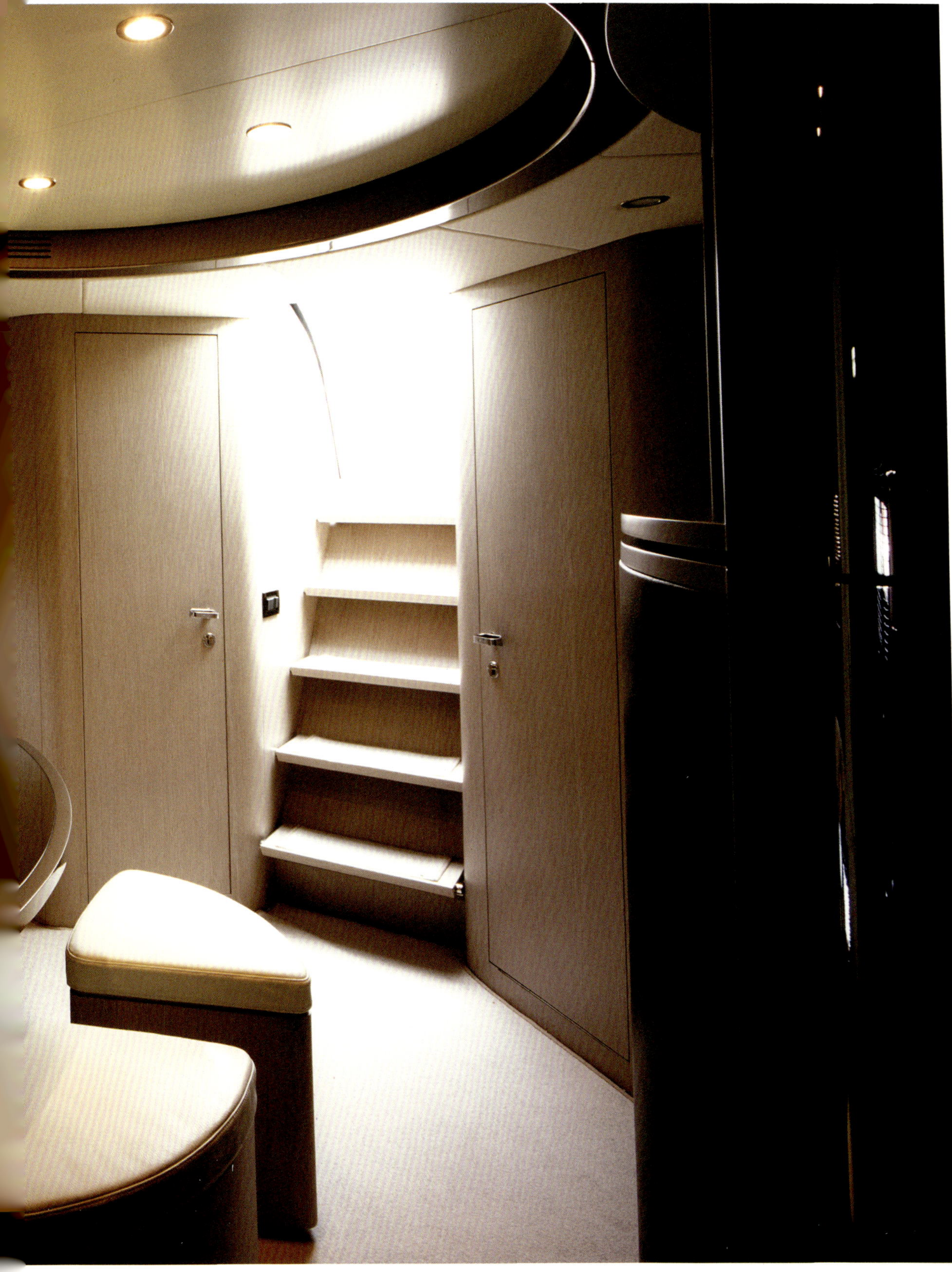

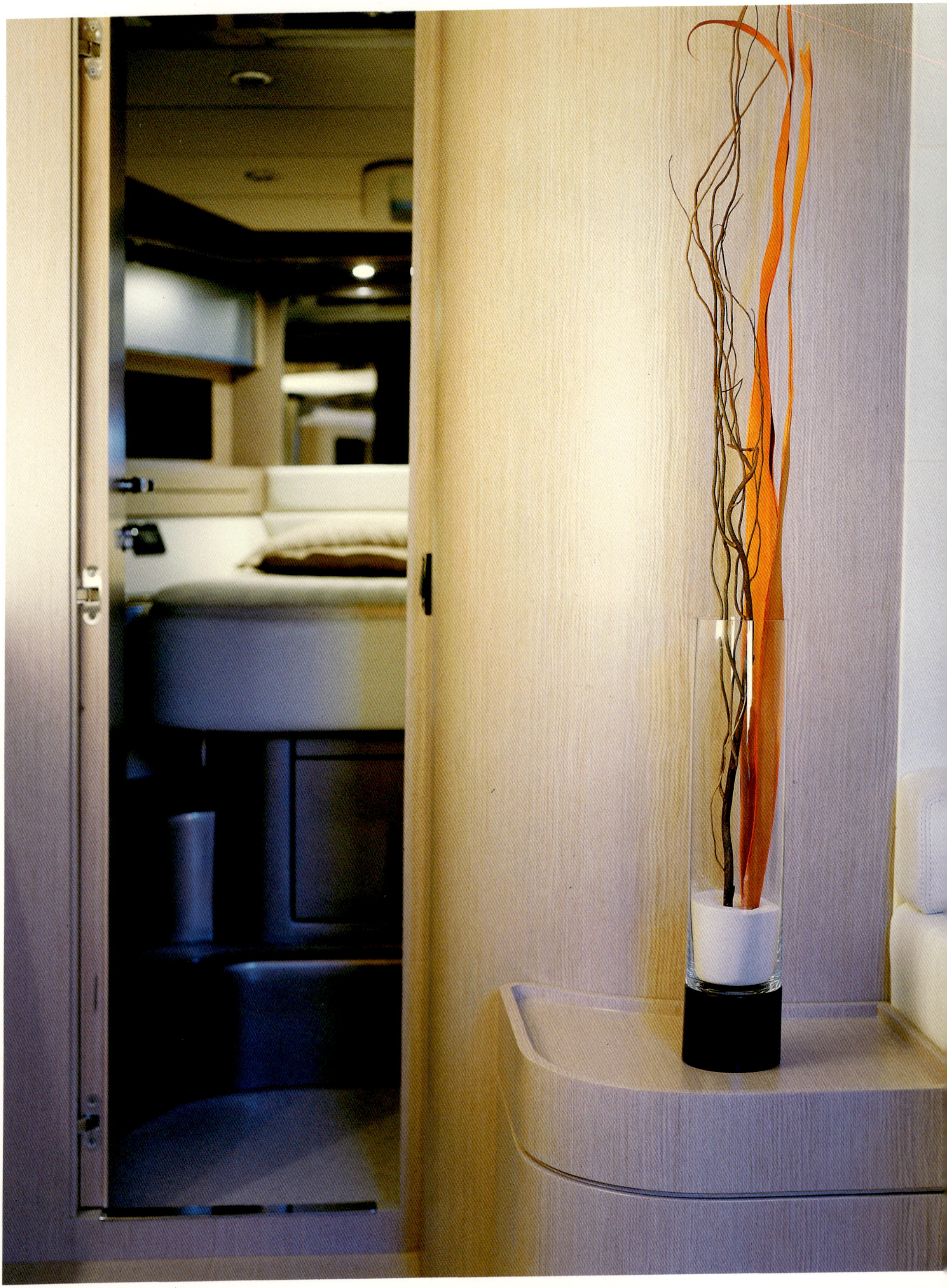

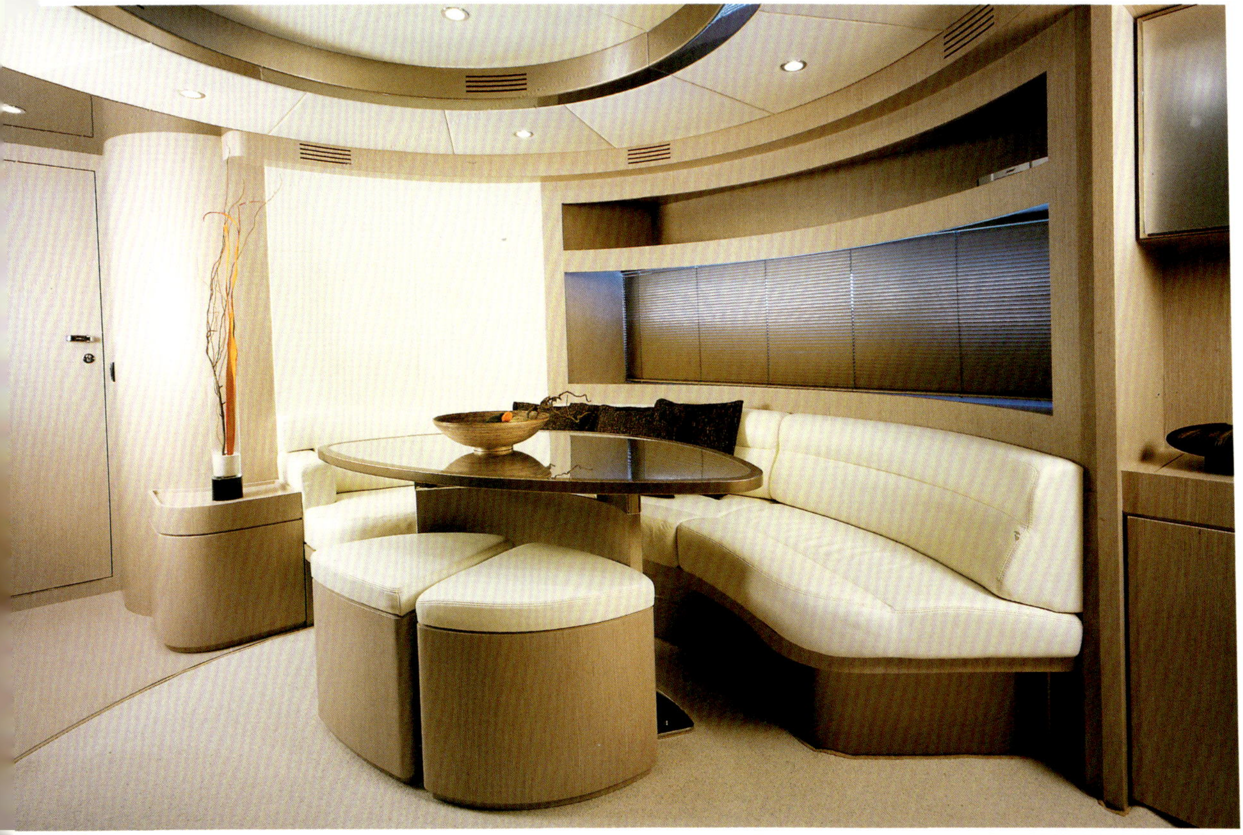

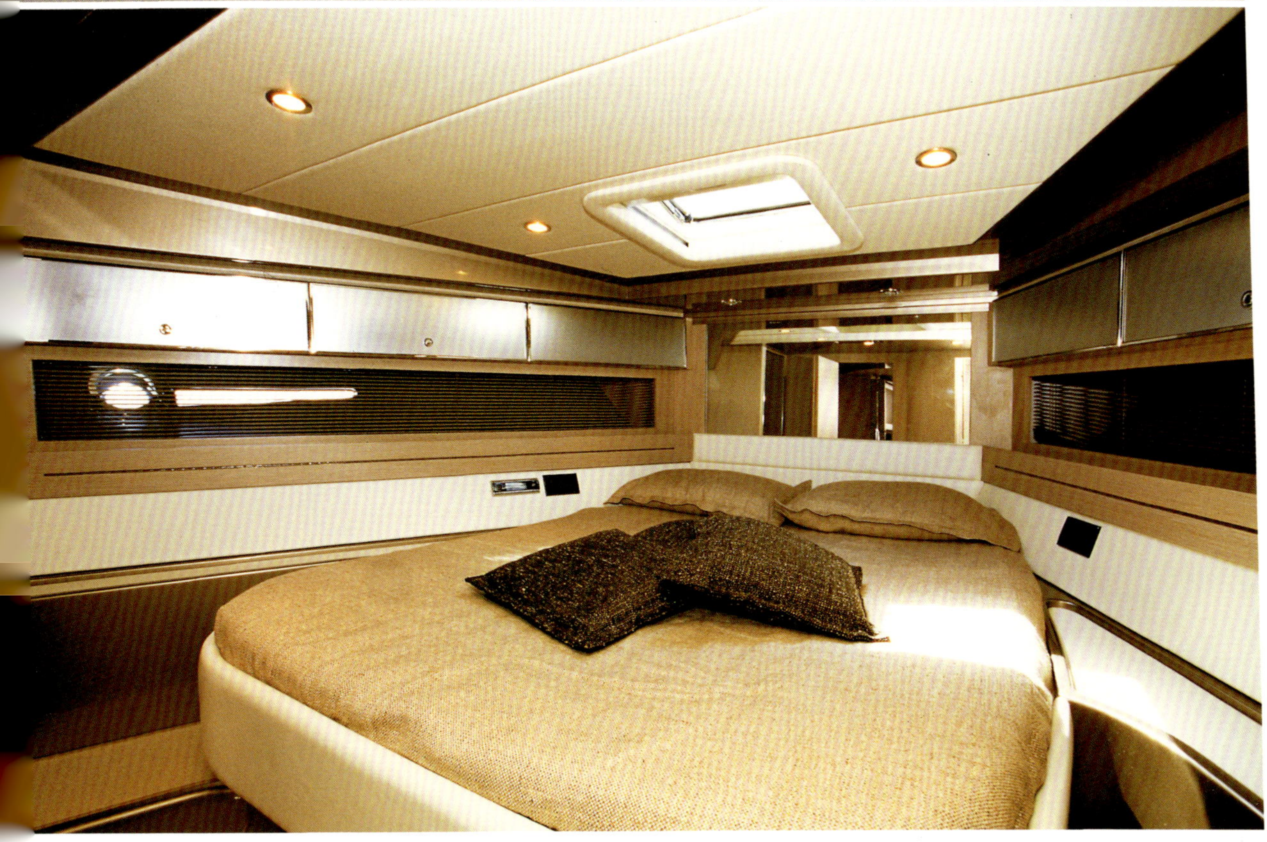

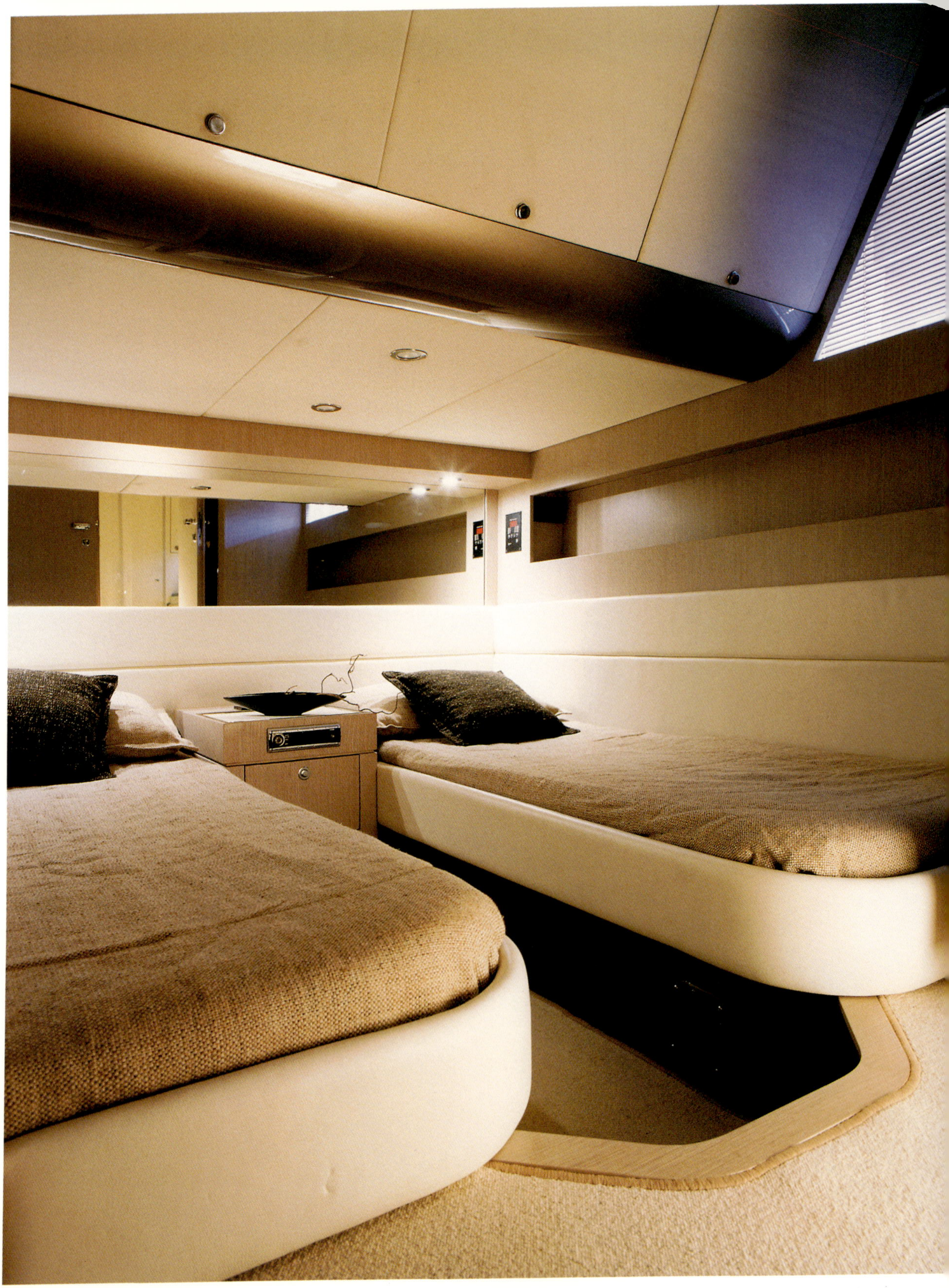

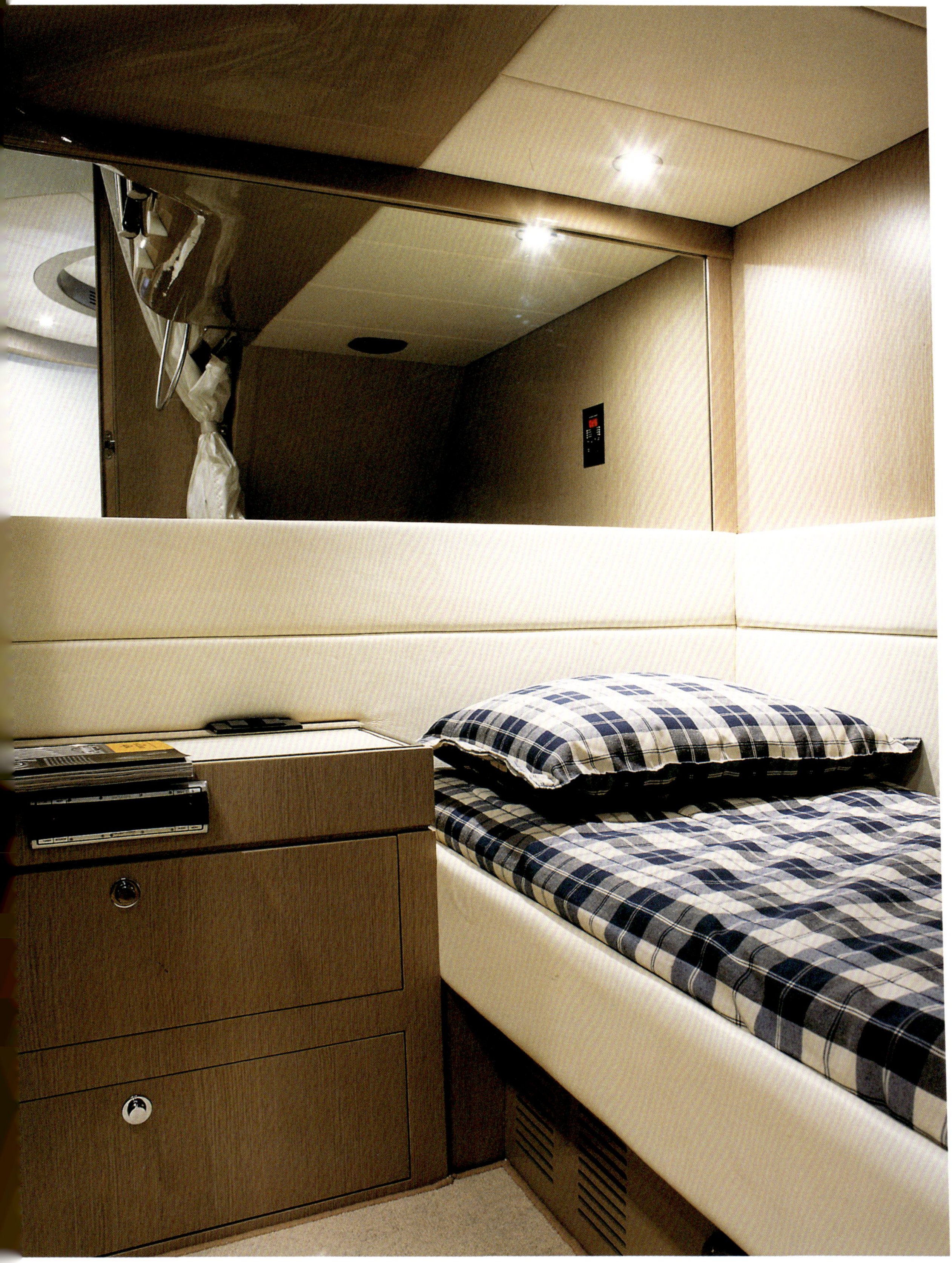

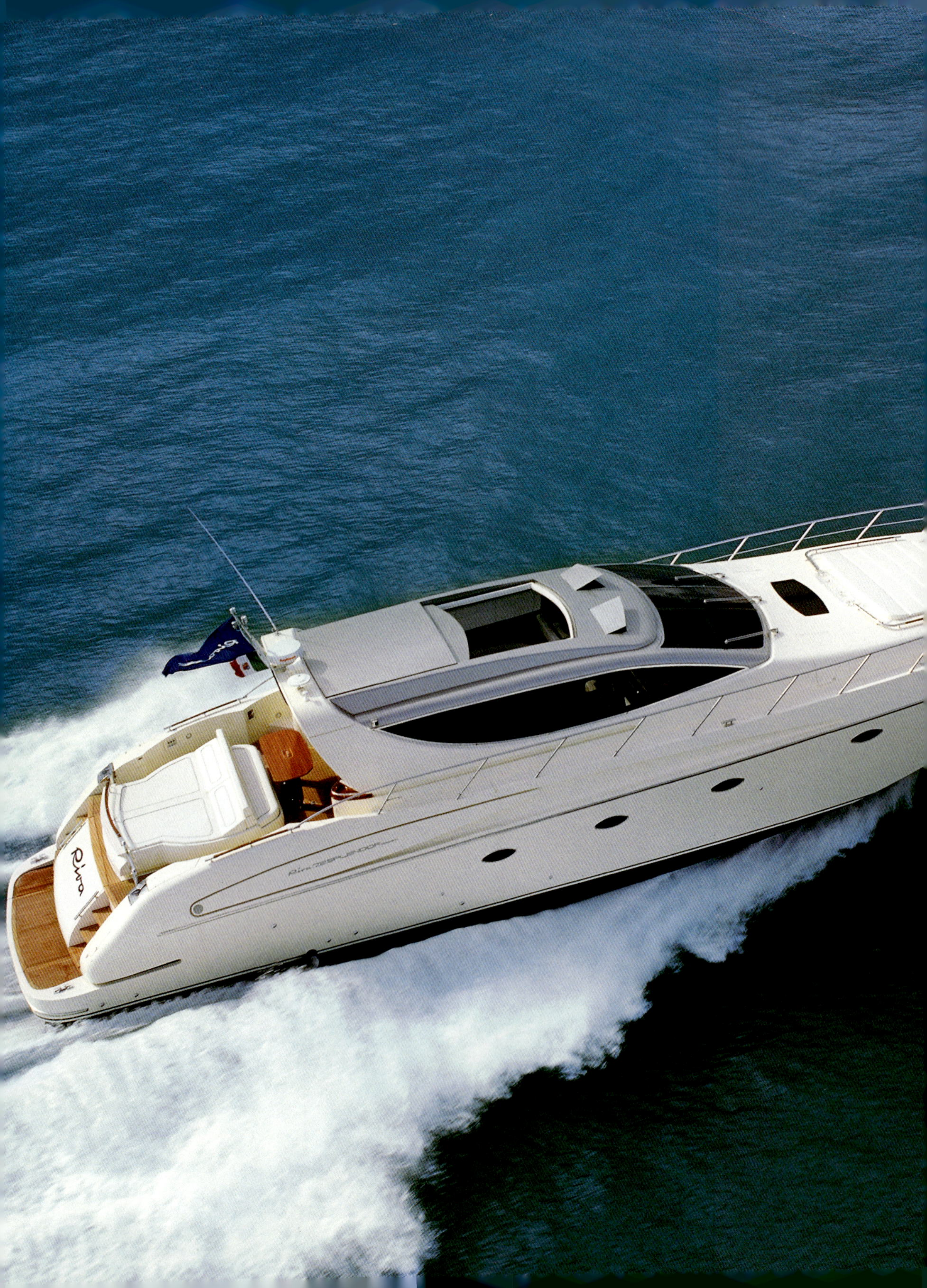
Riva

OFFICINA ITALIANA DESIGN
SPLENDIDA | 2000
Riva SpA

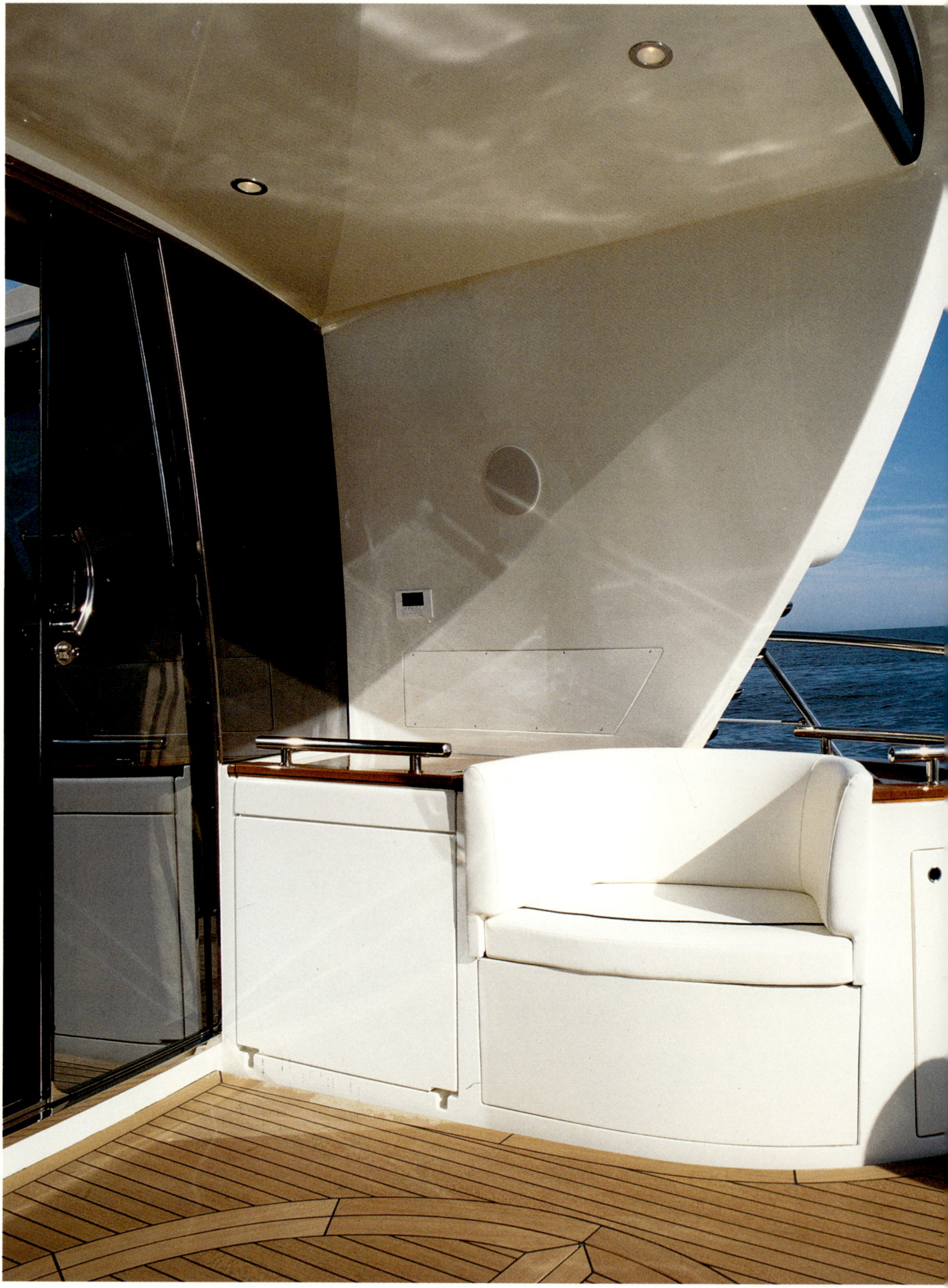

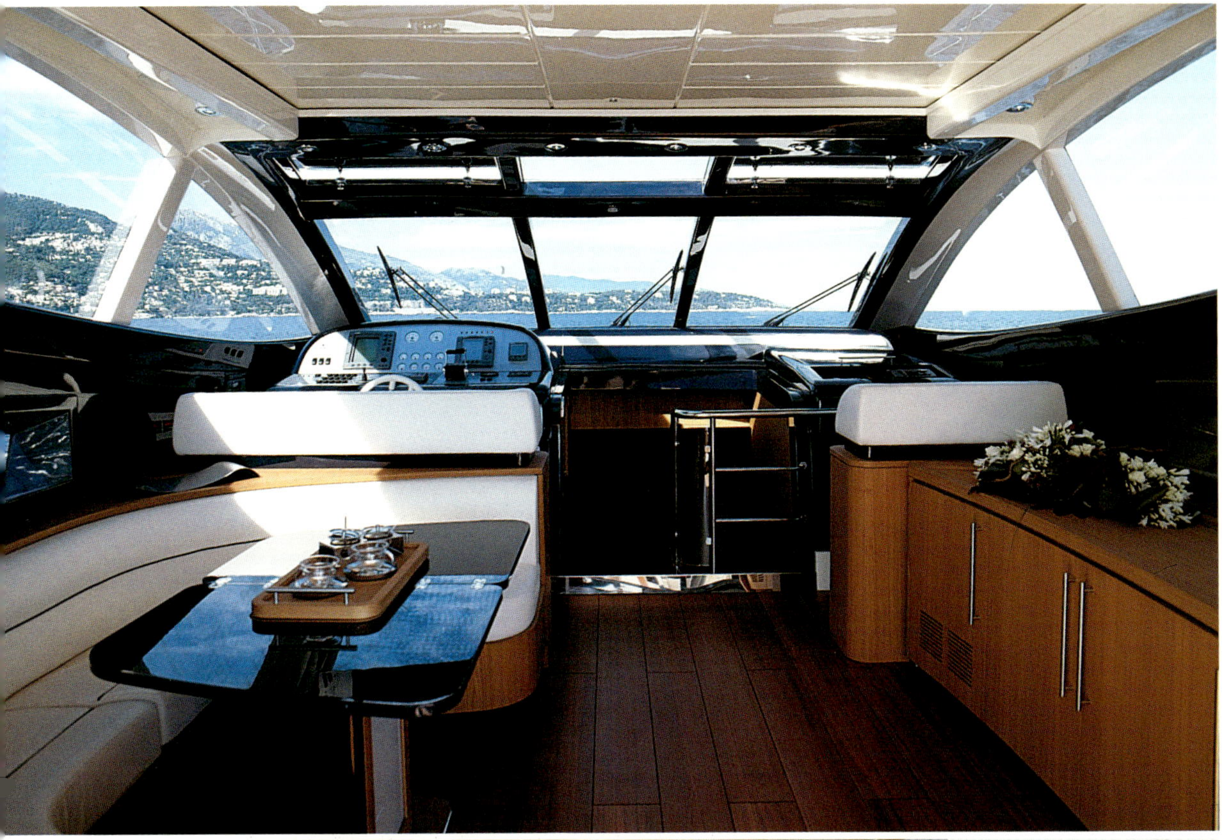

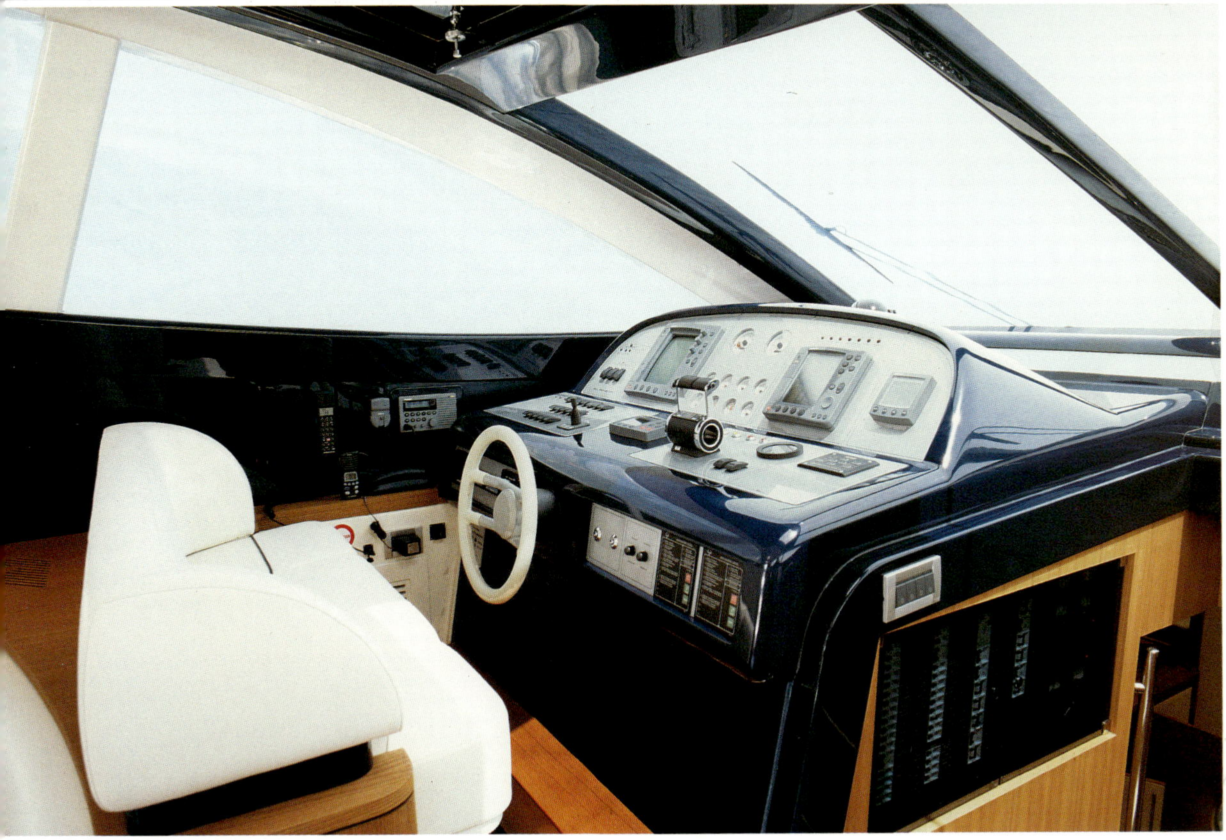

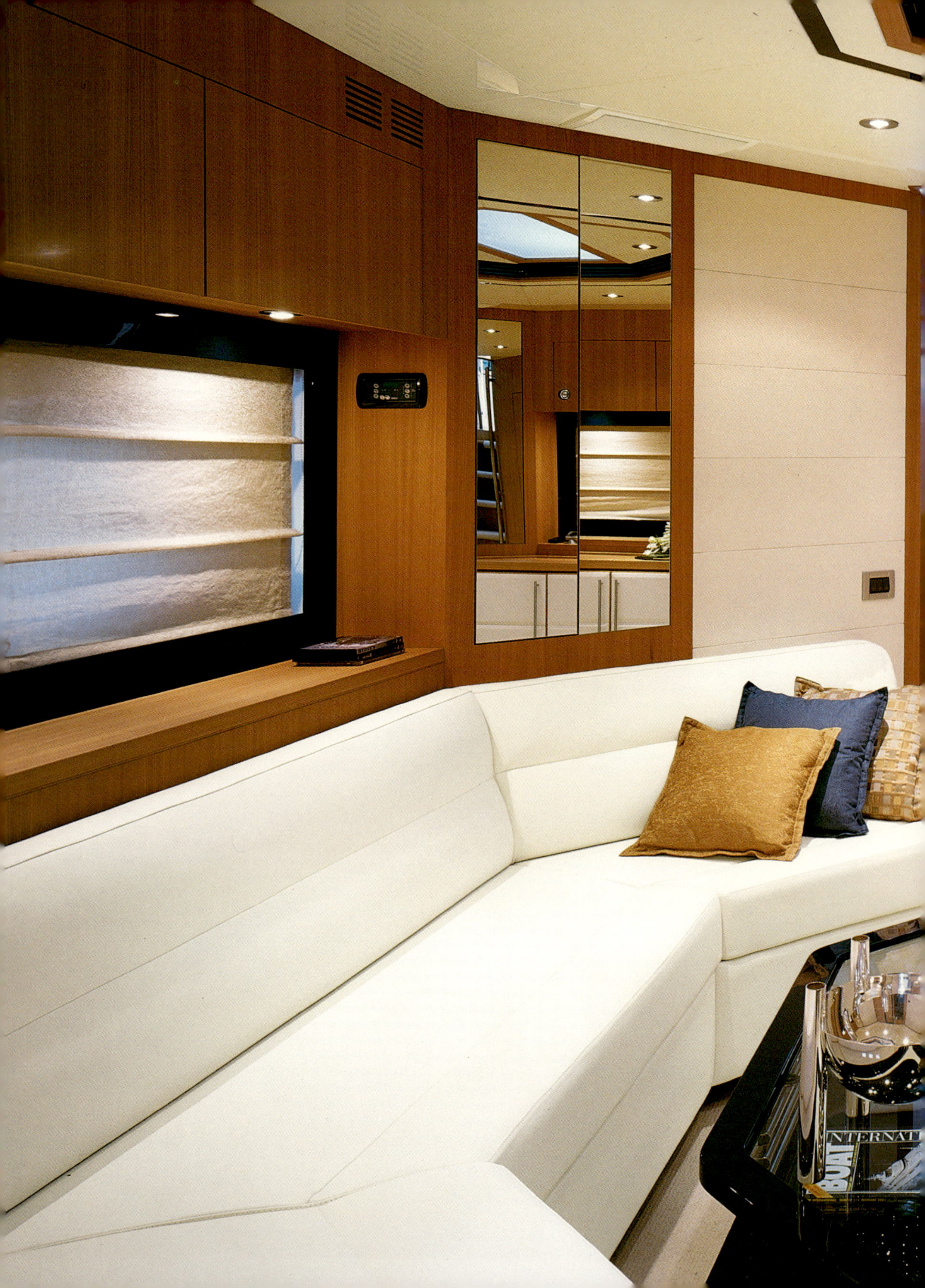

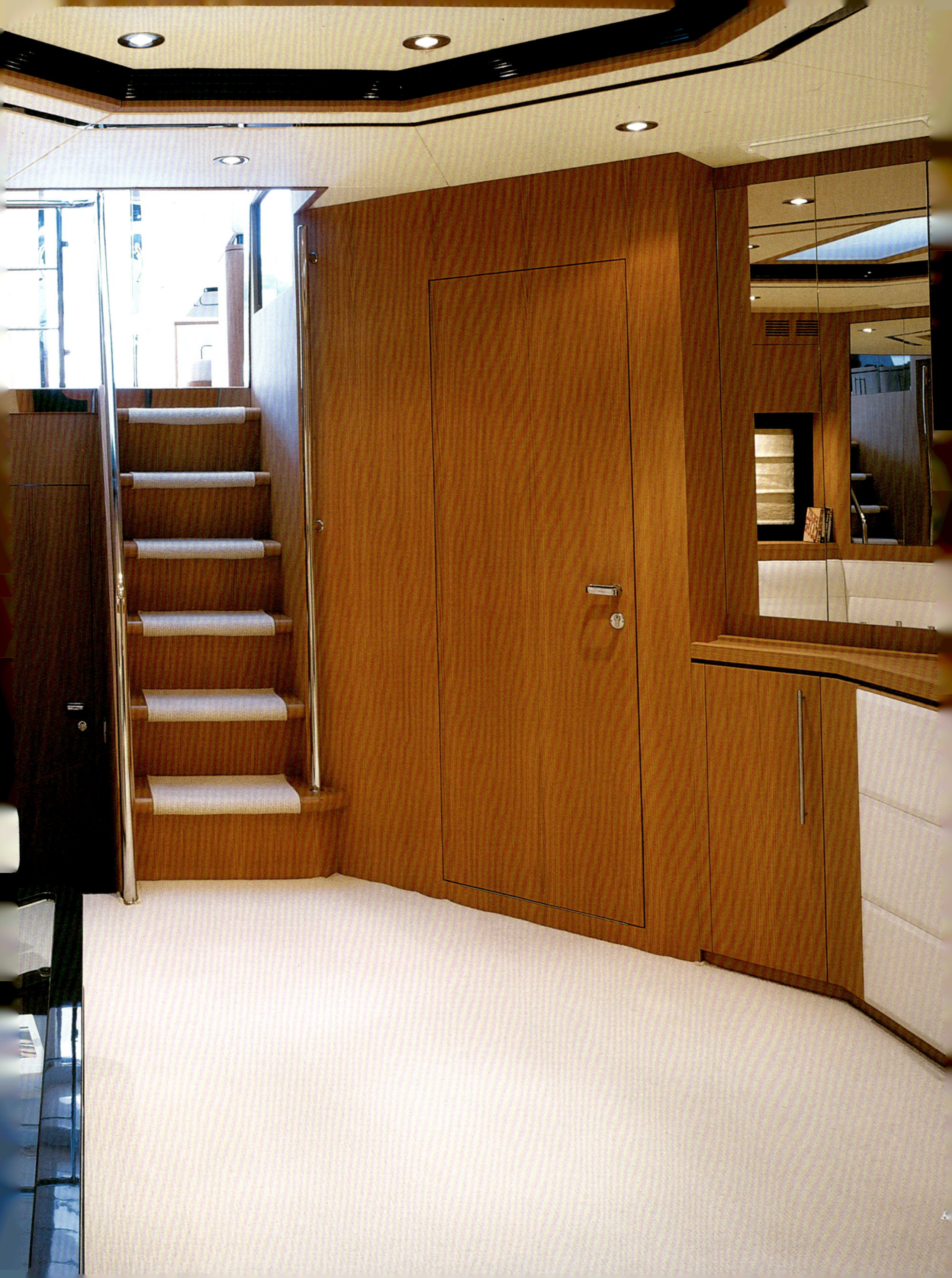

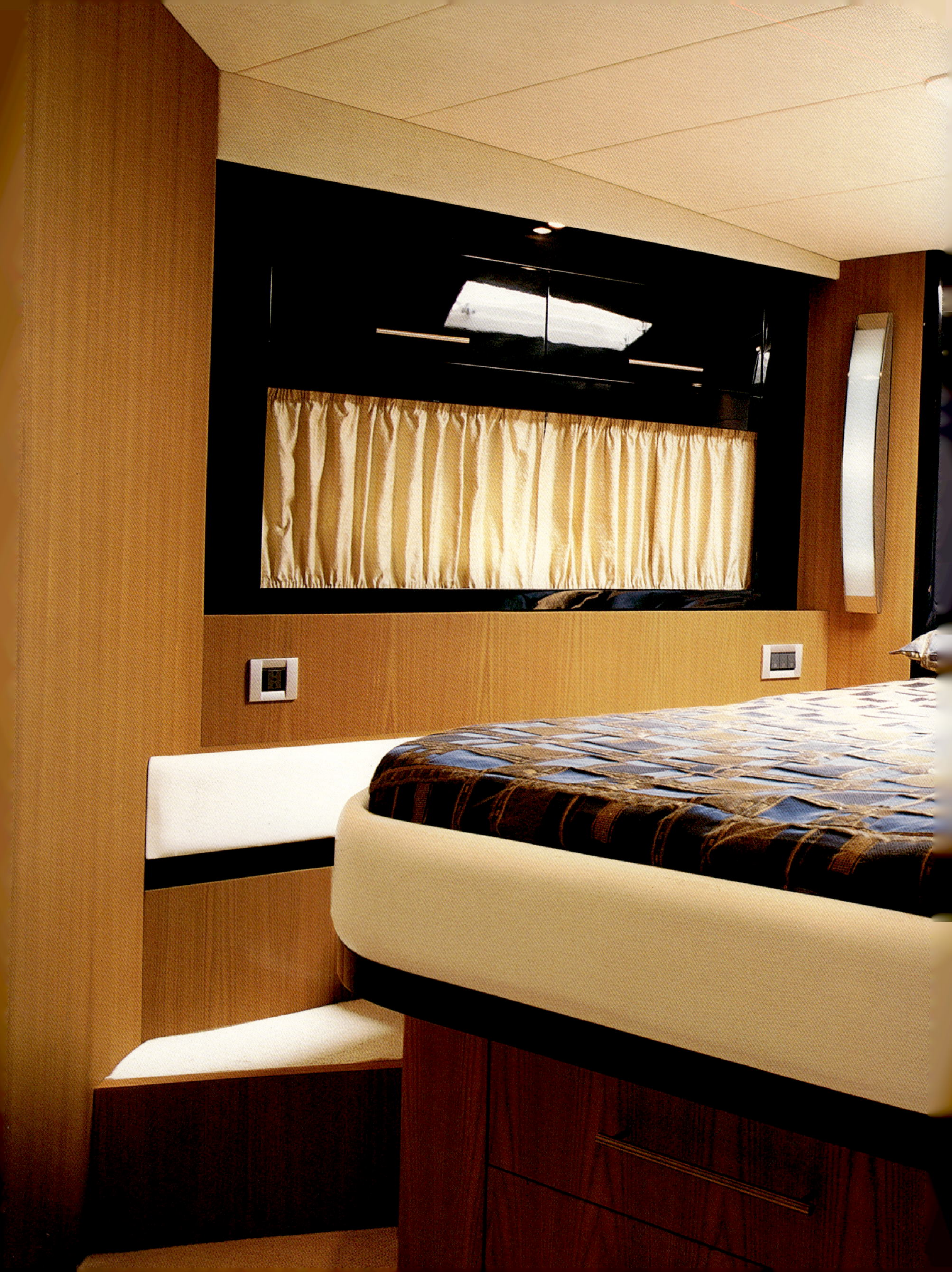

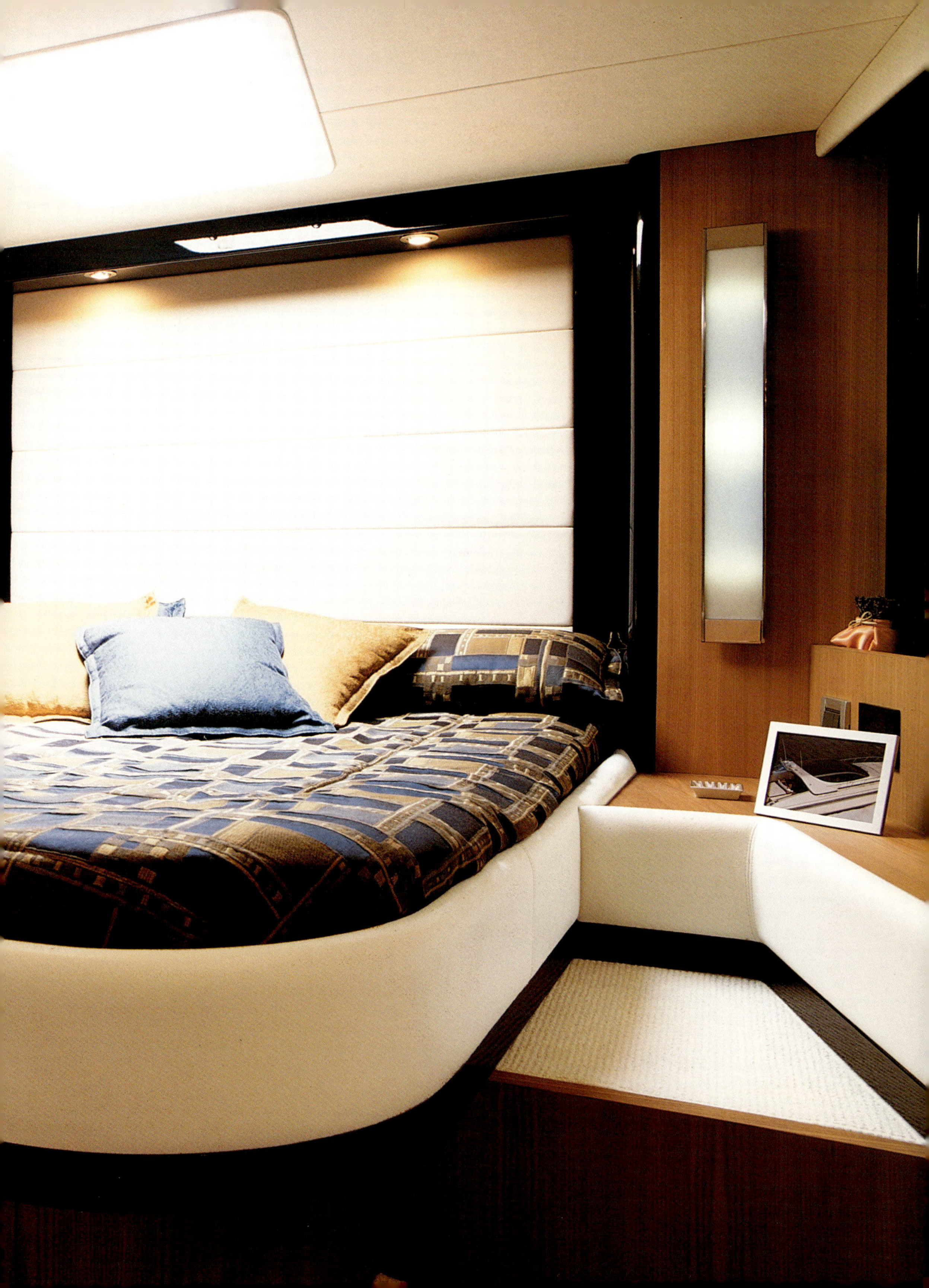

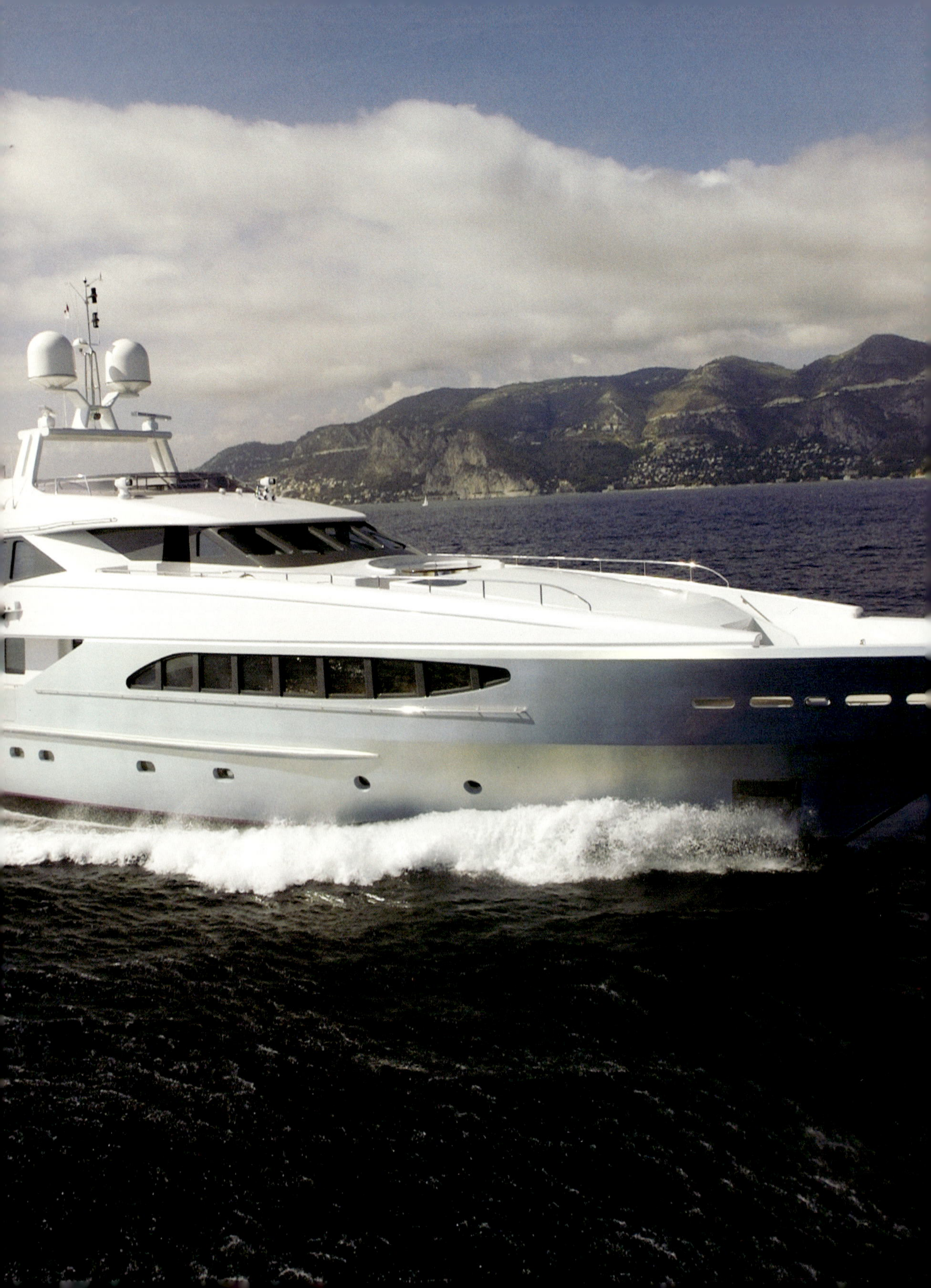

OMEGA ARCHITECTS
SWEET DOLL | 2003
Heesen Yachts

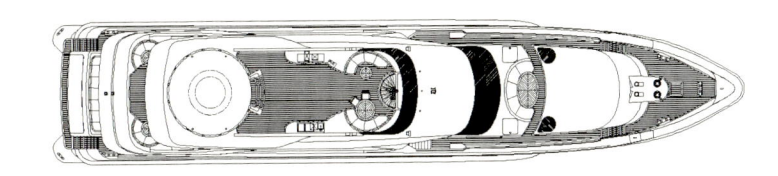

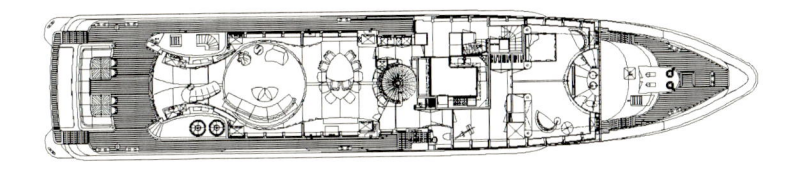

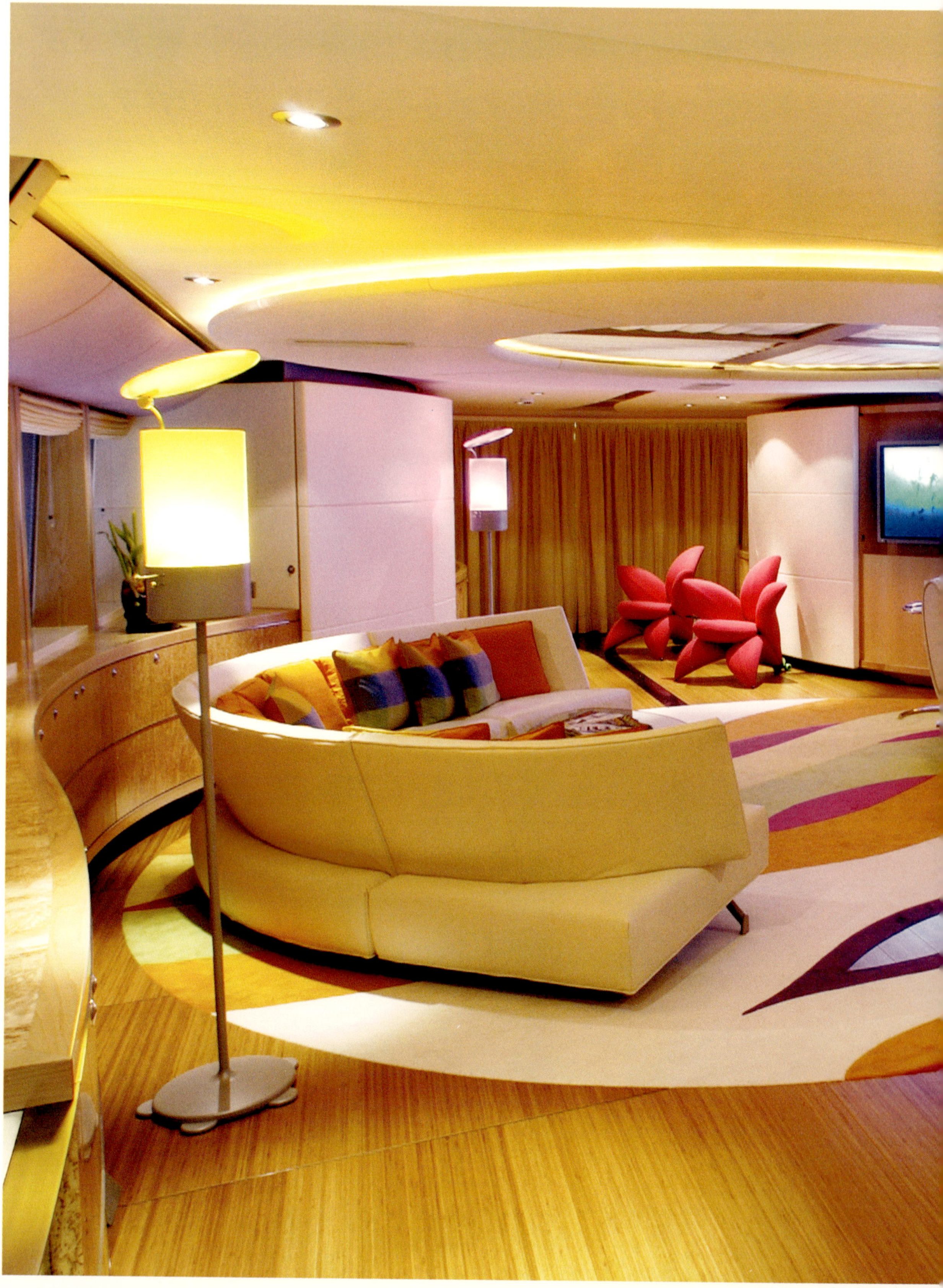

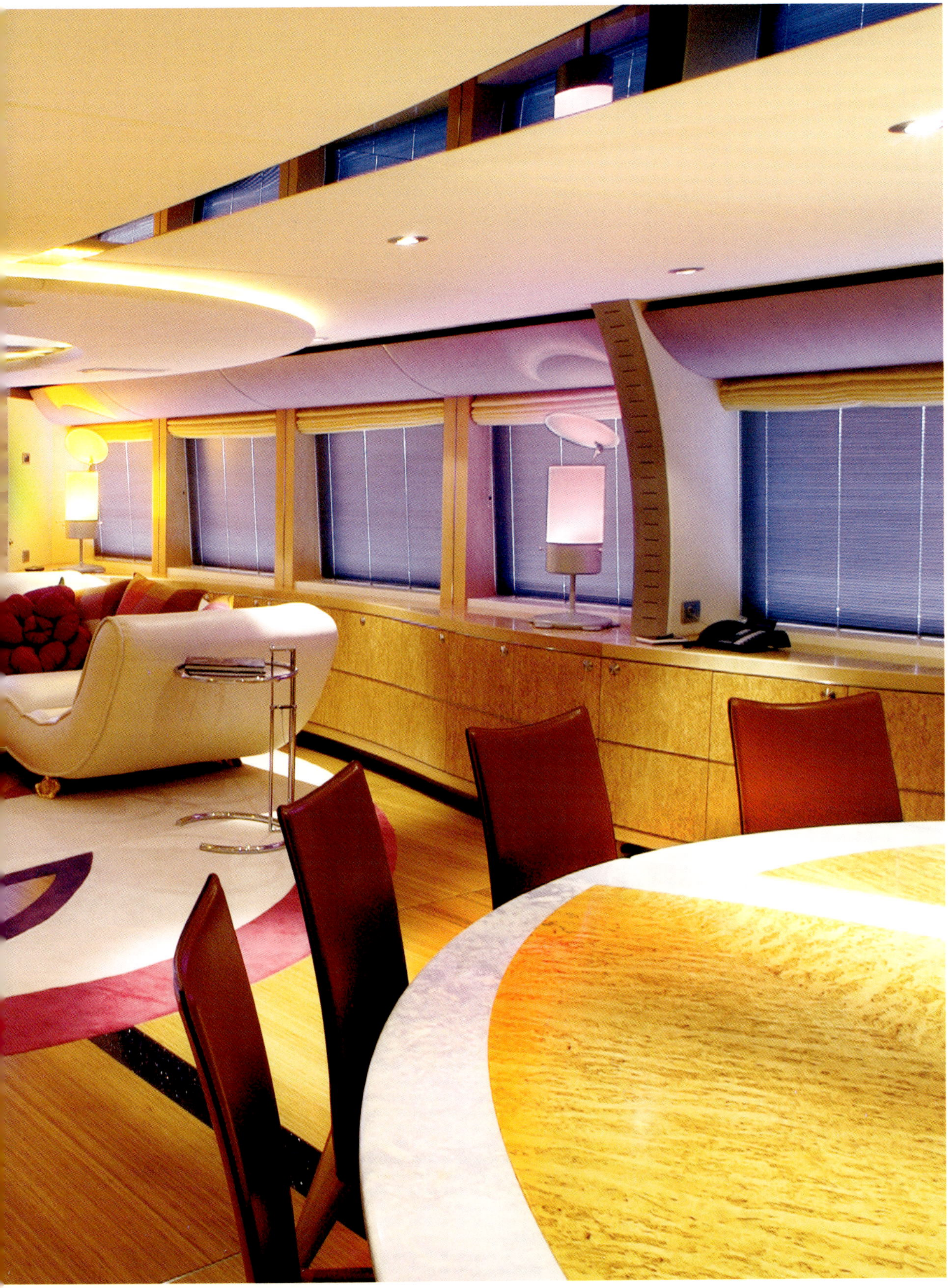

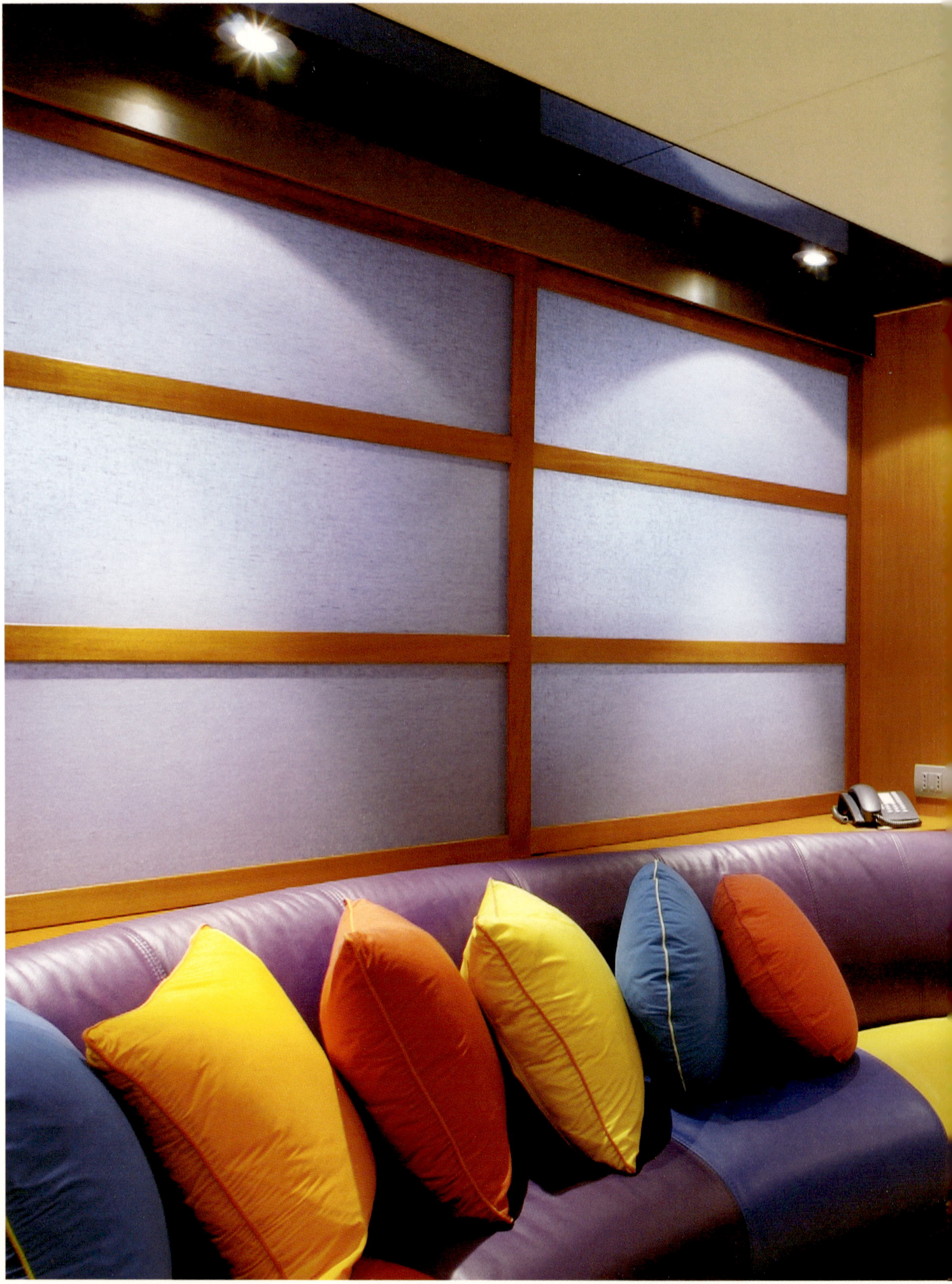

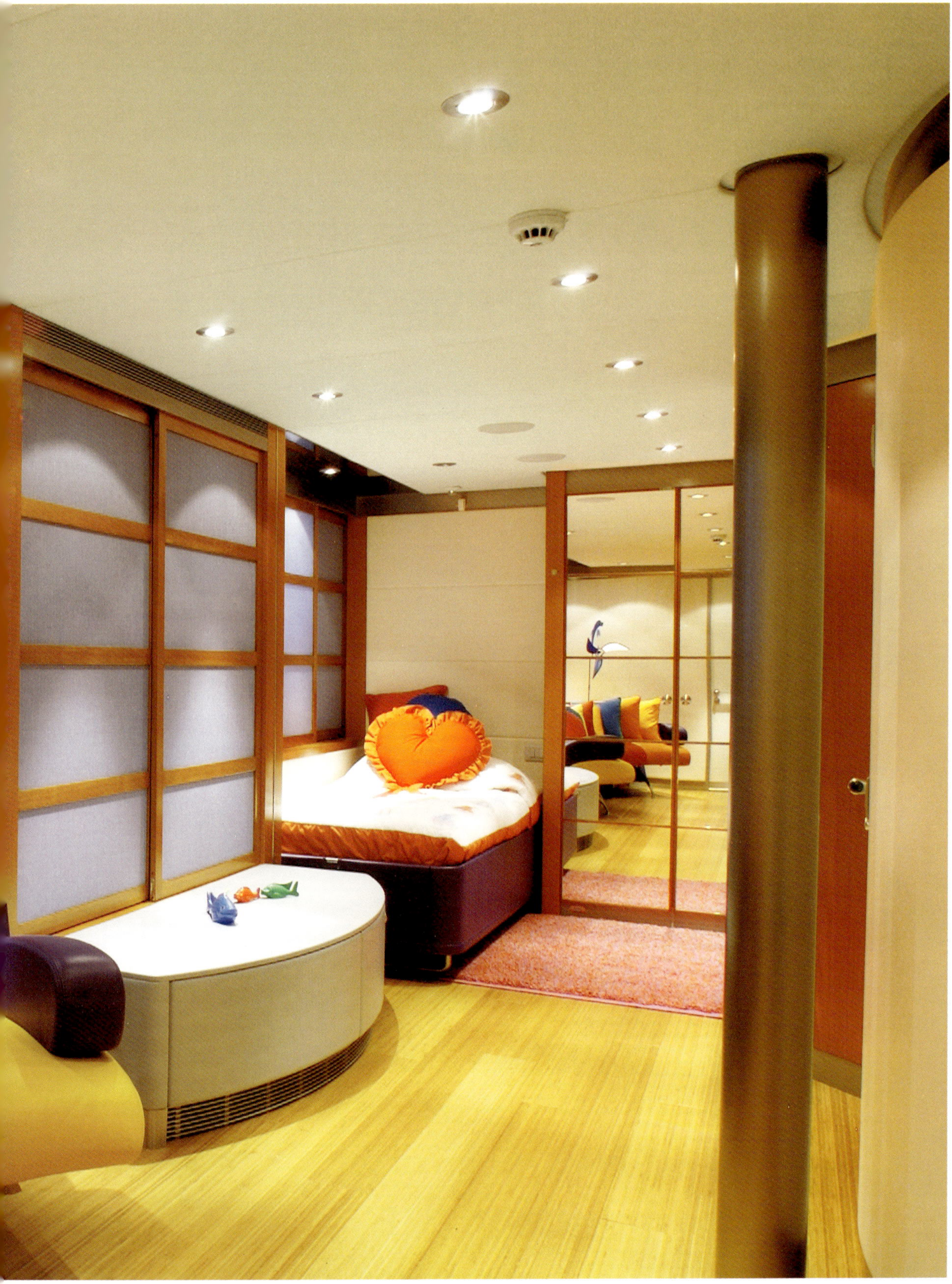

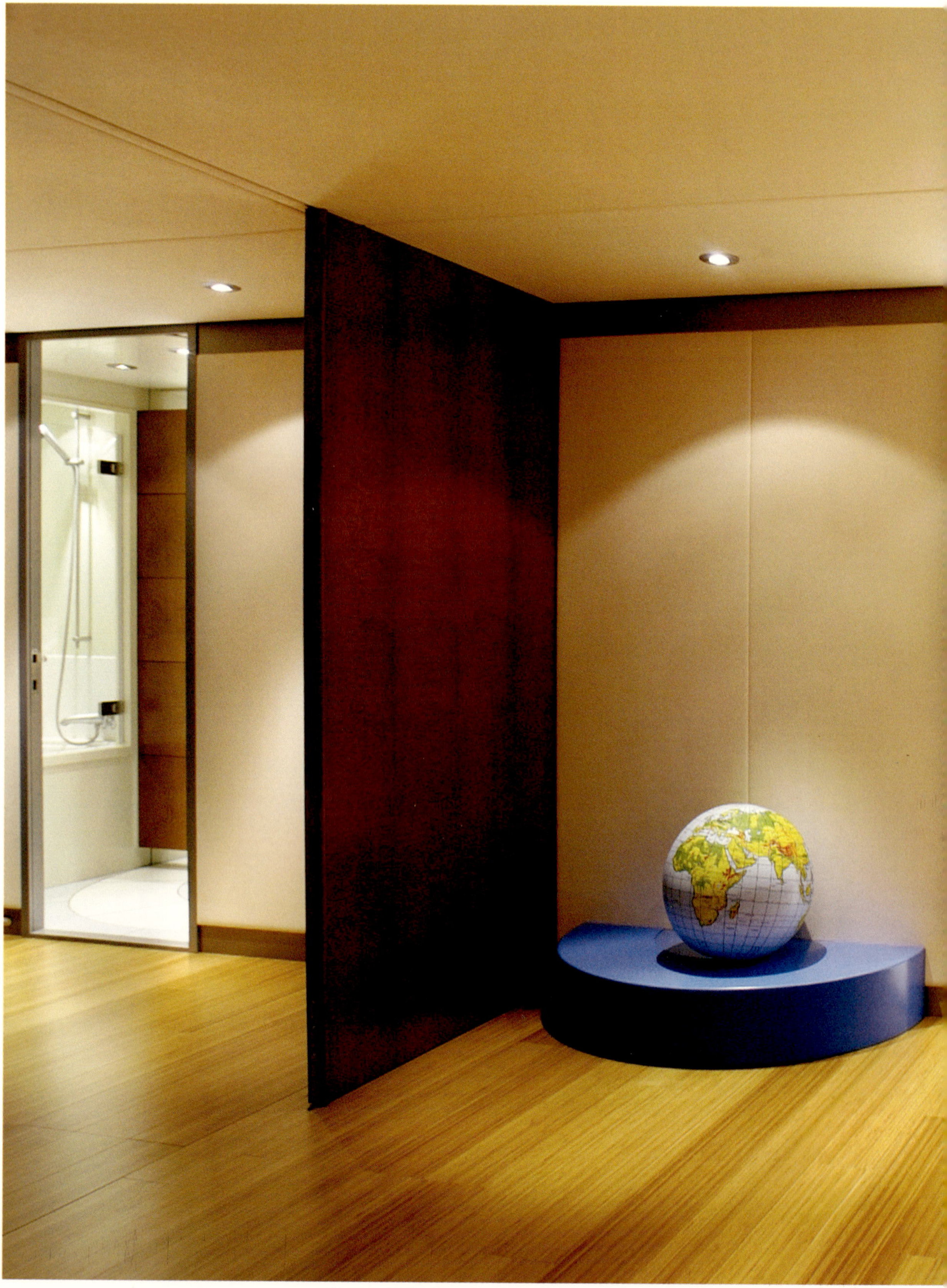

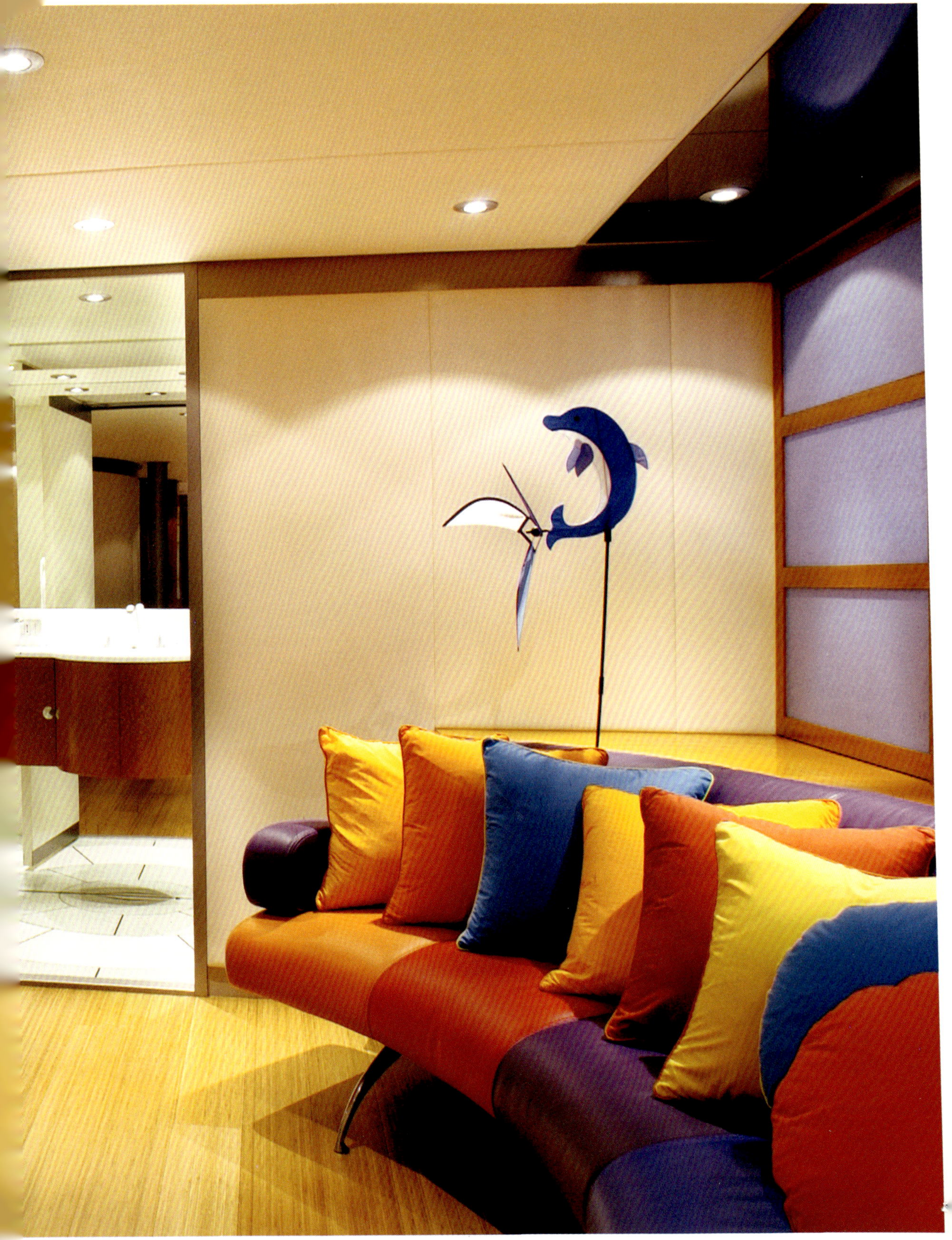

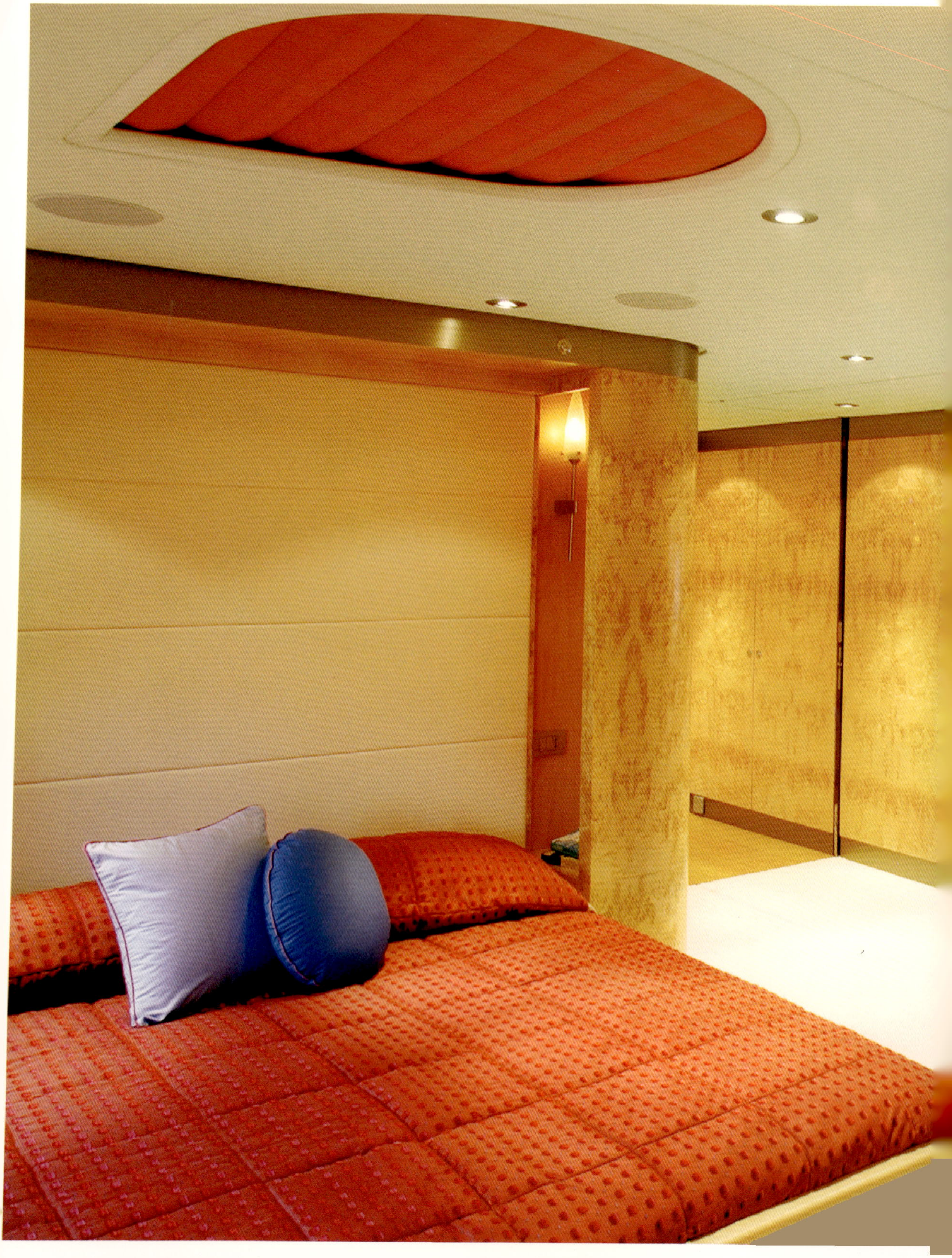

245

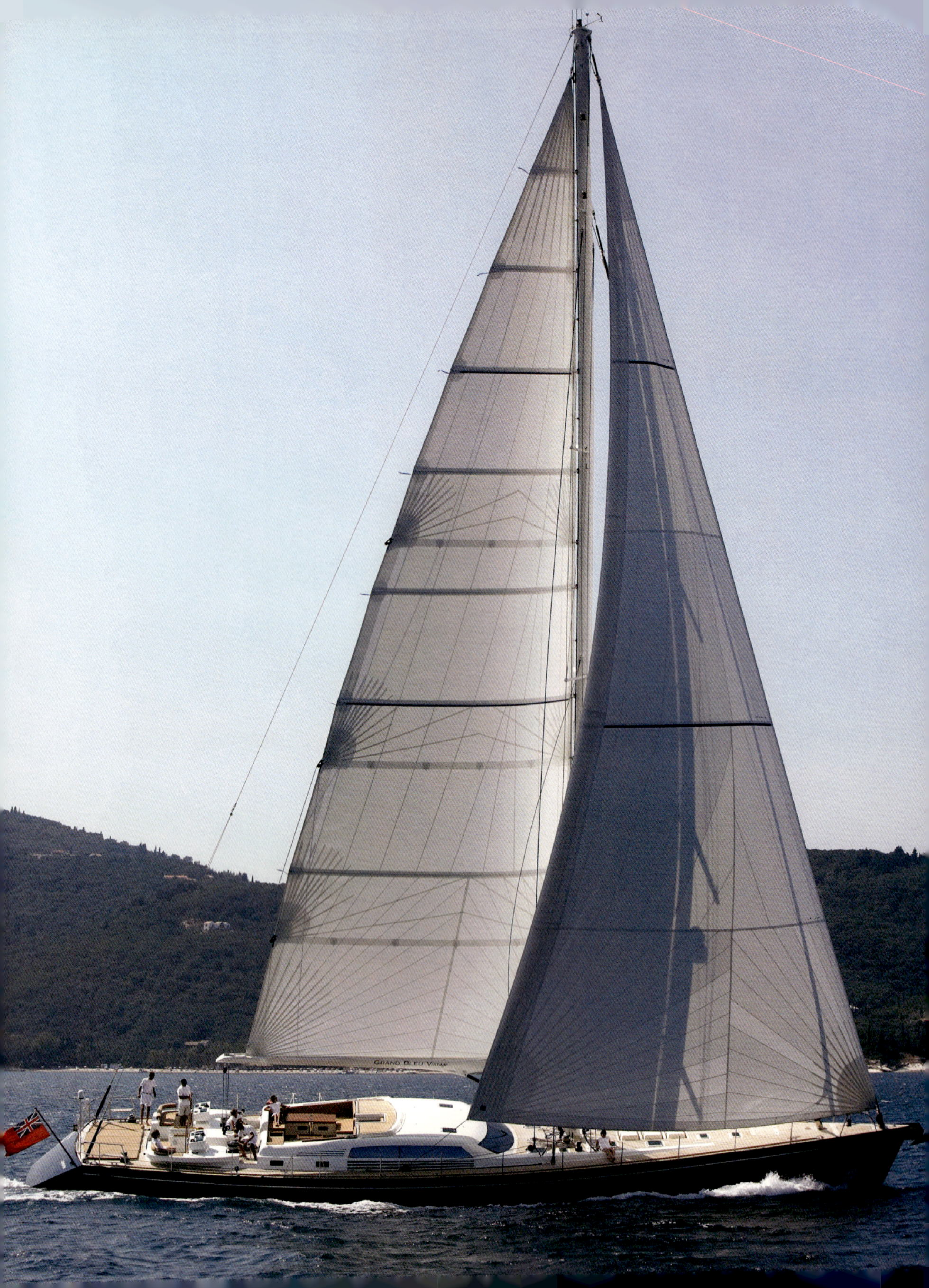
GRAND BLEU

PHILIPPE BRIAND
GRAND BLEU VINTAGE | 2003
CNB

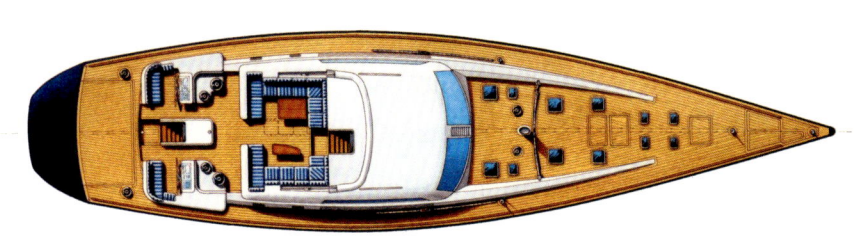

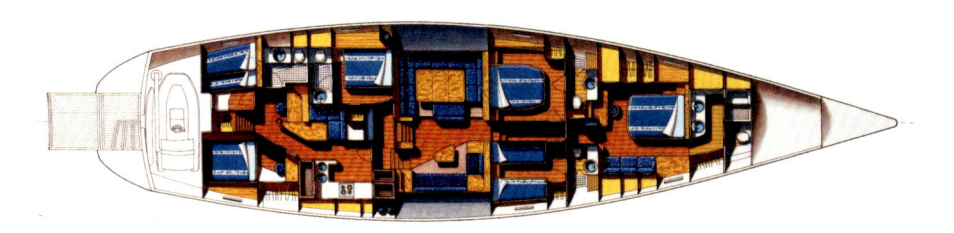

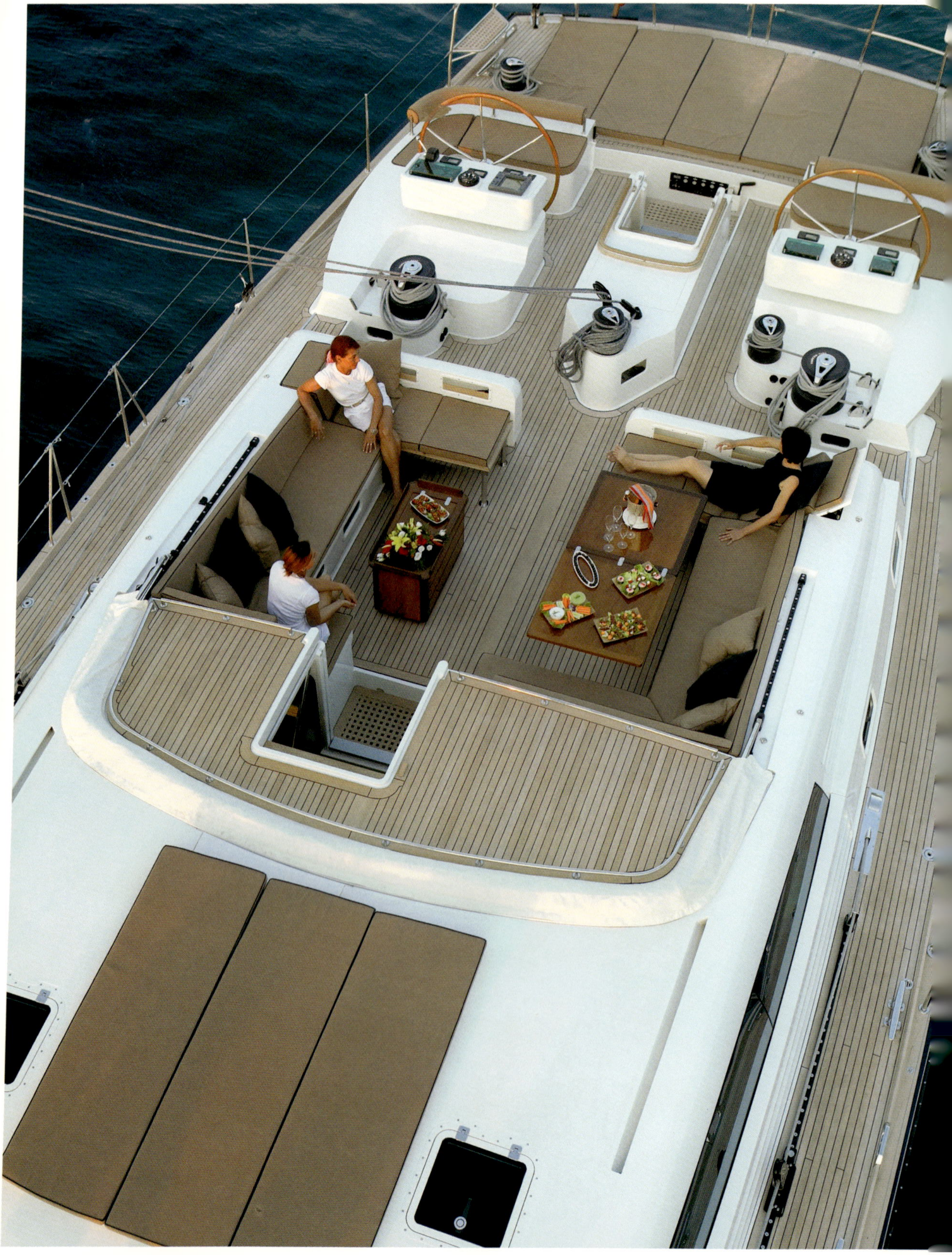

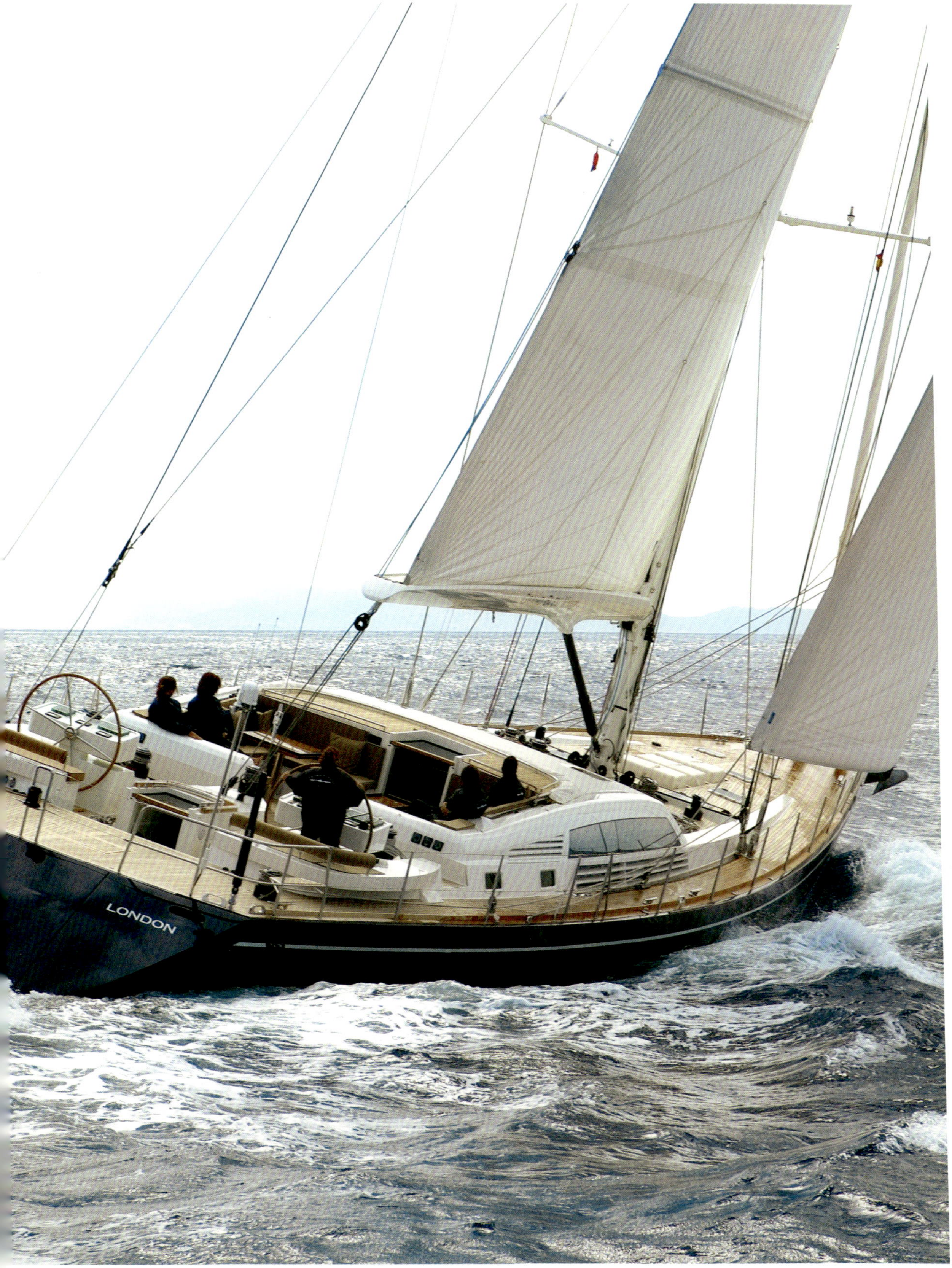
LONDON

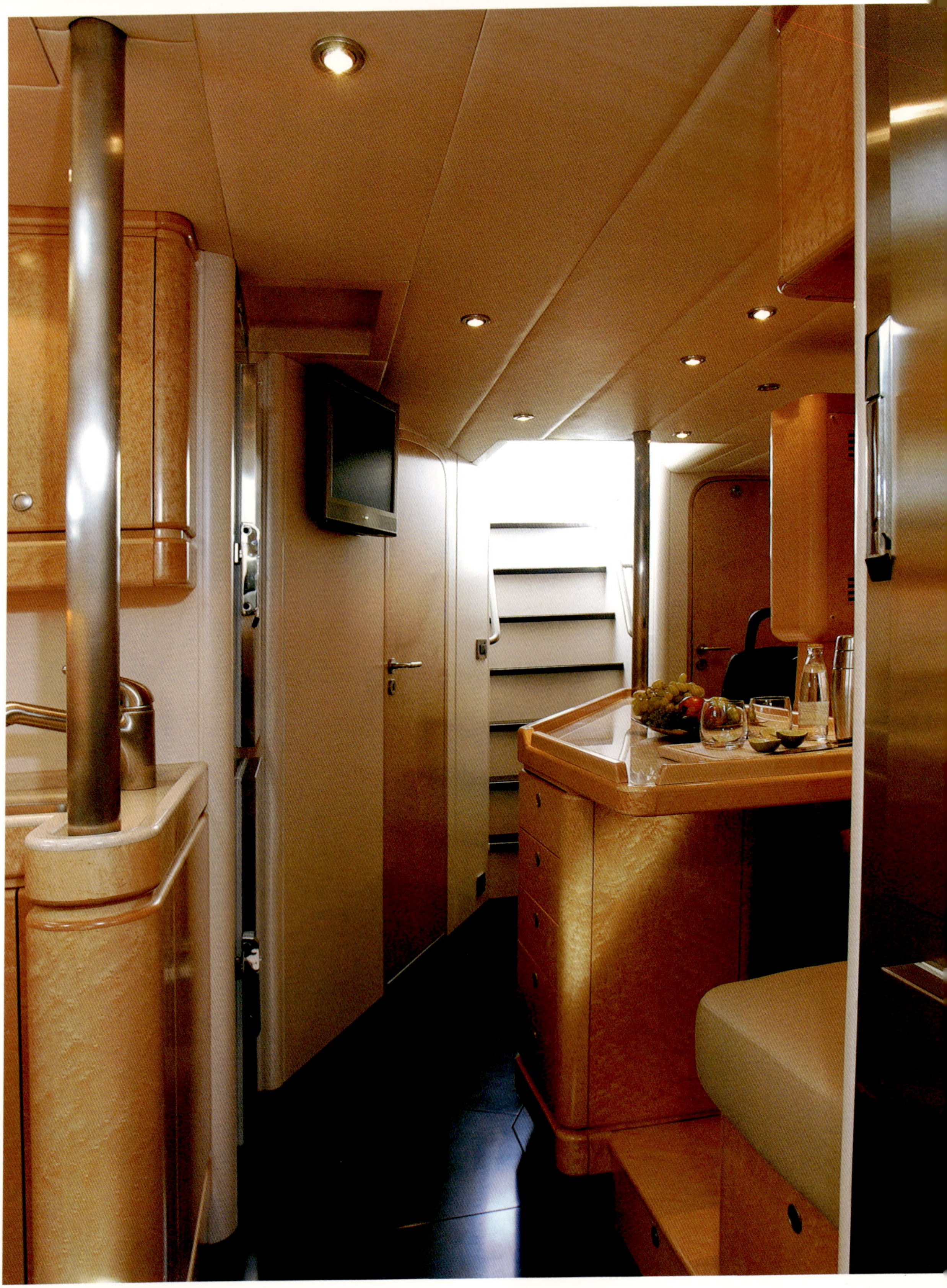

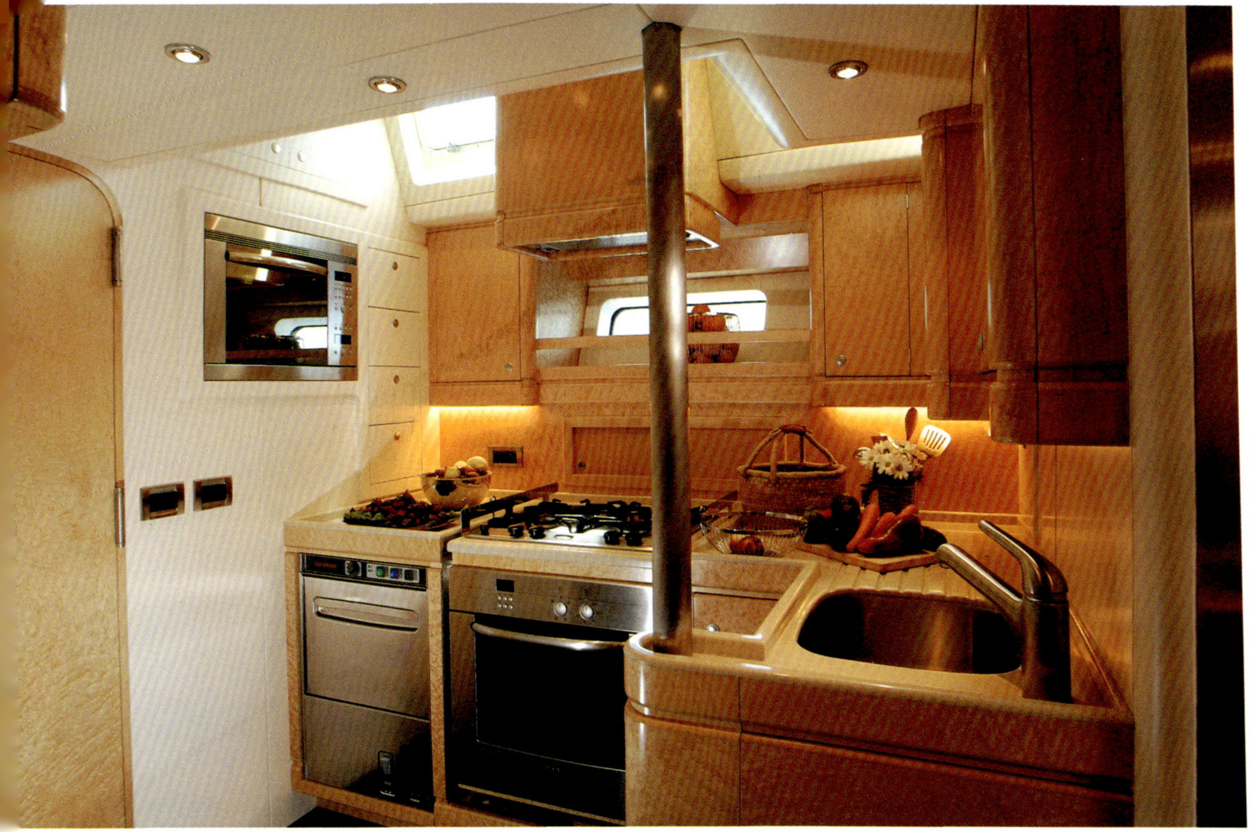

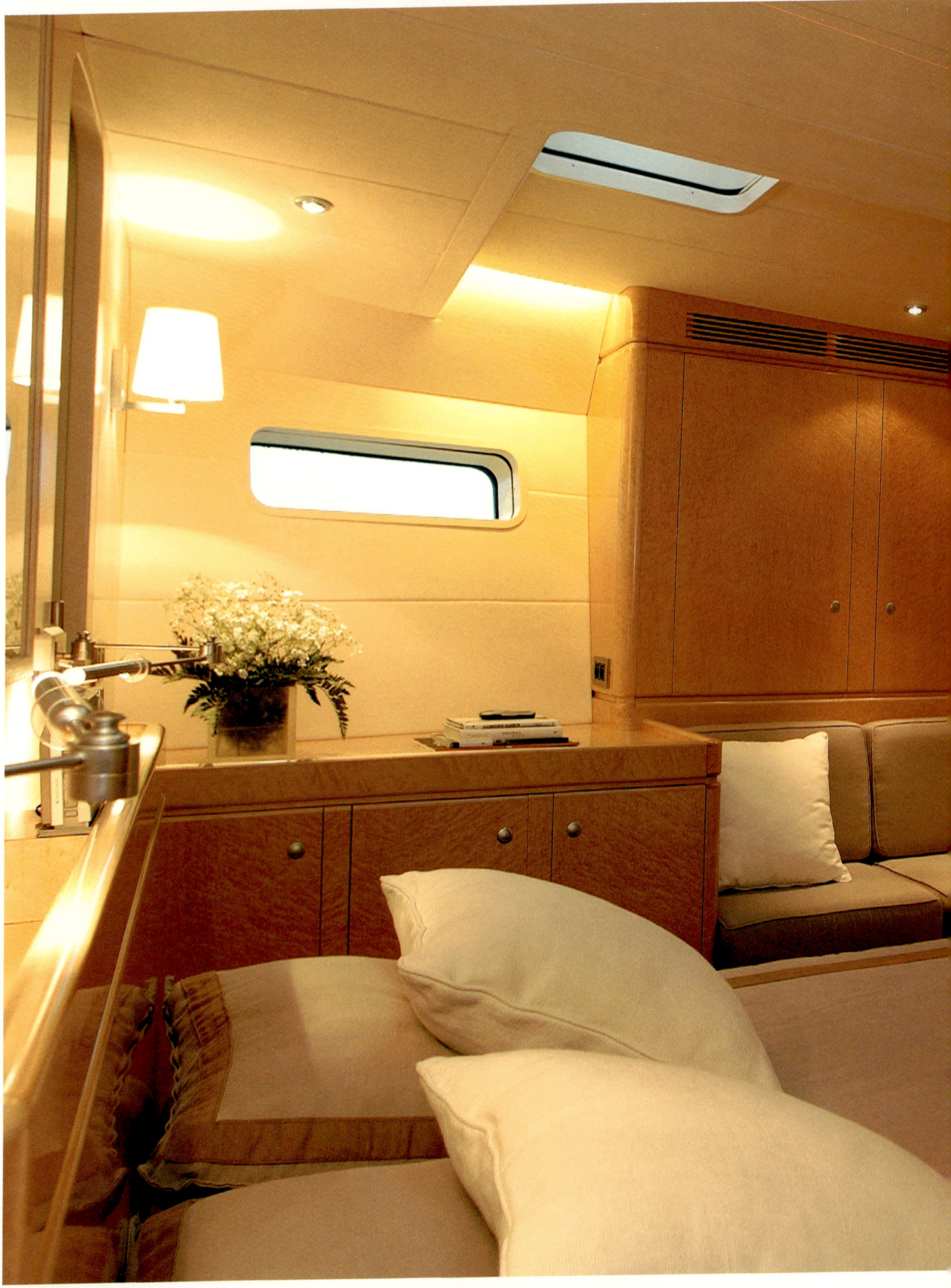

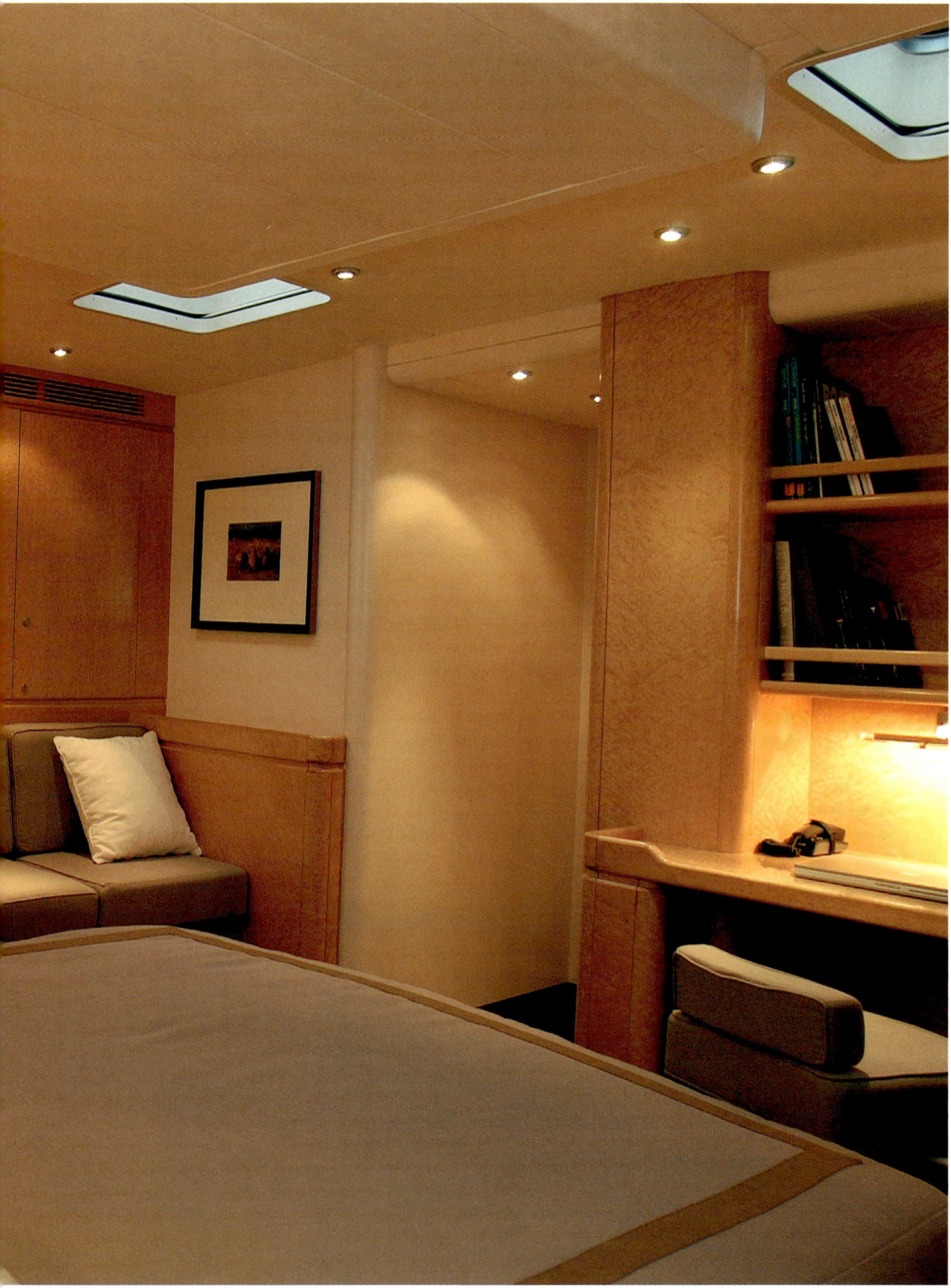

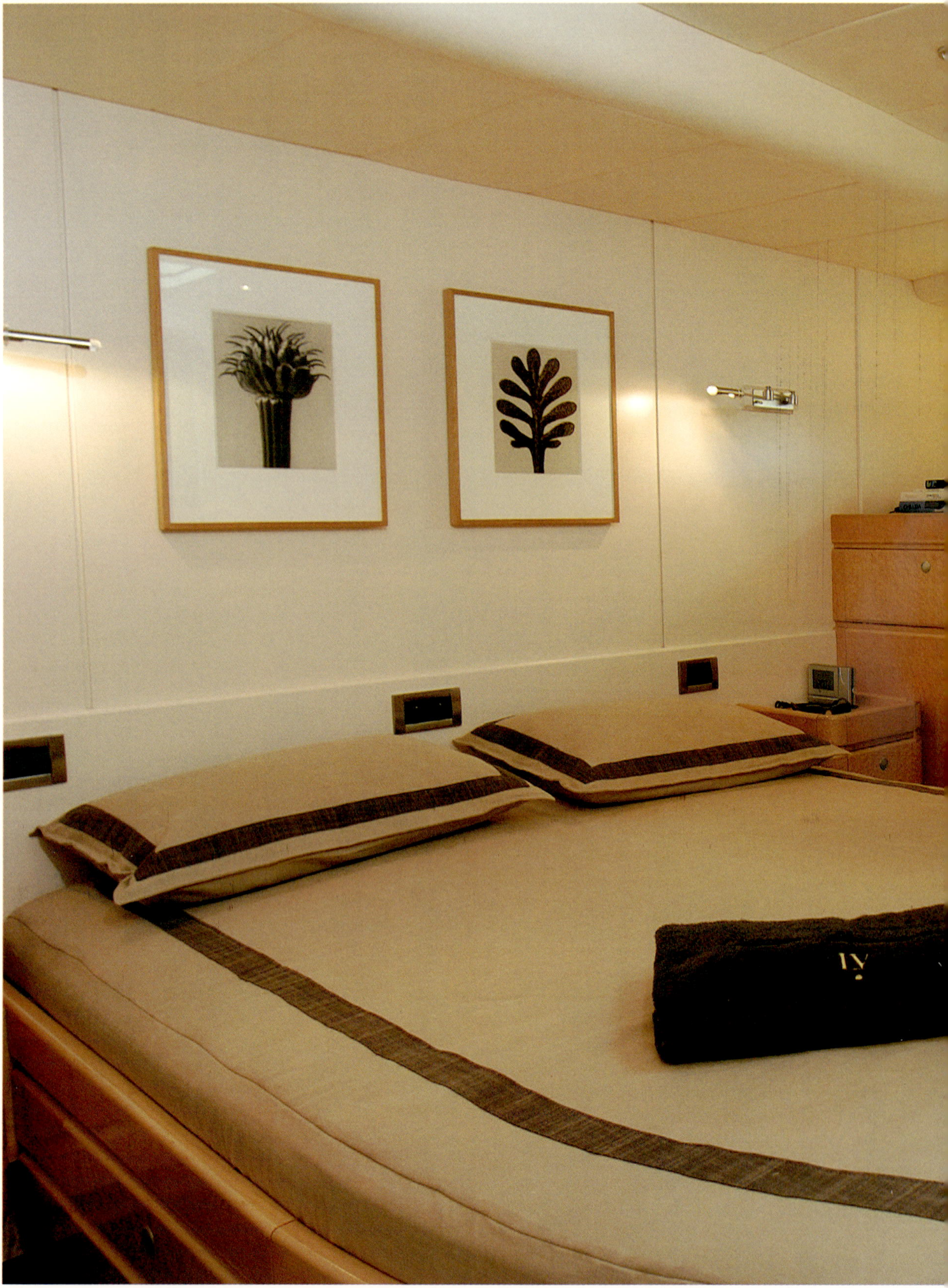

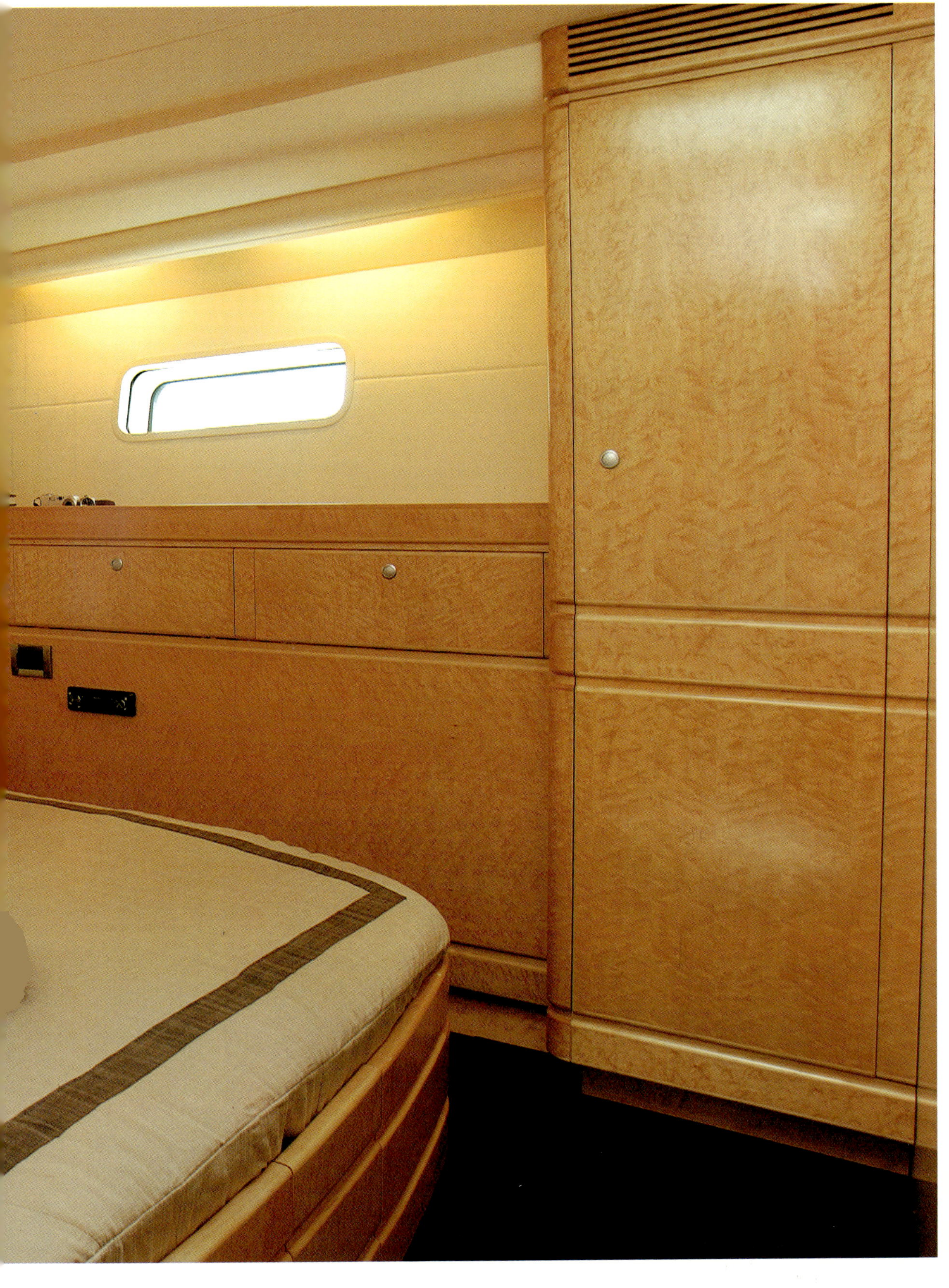

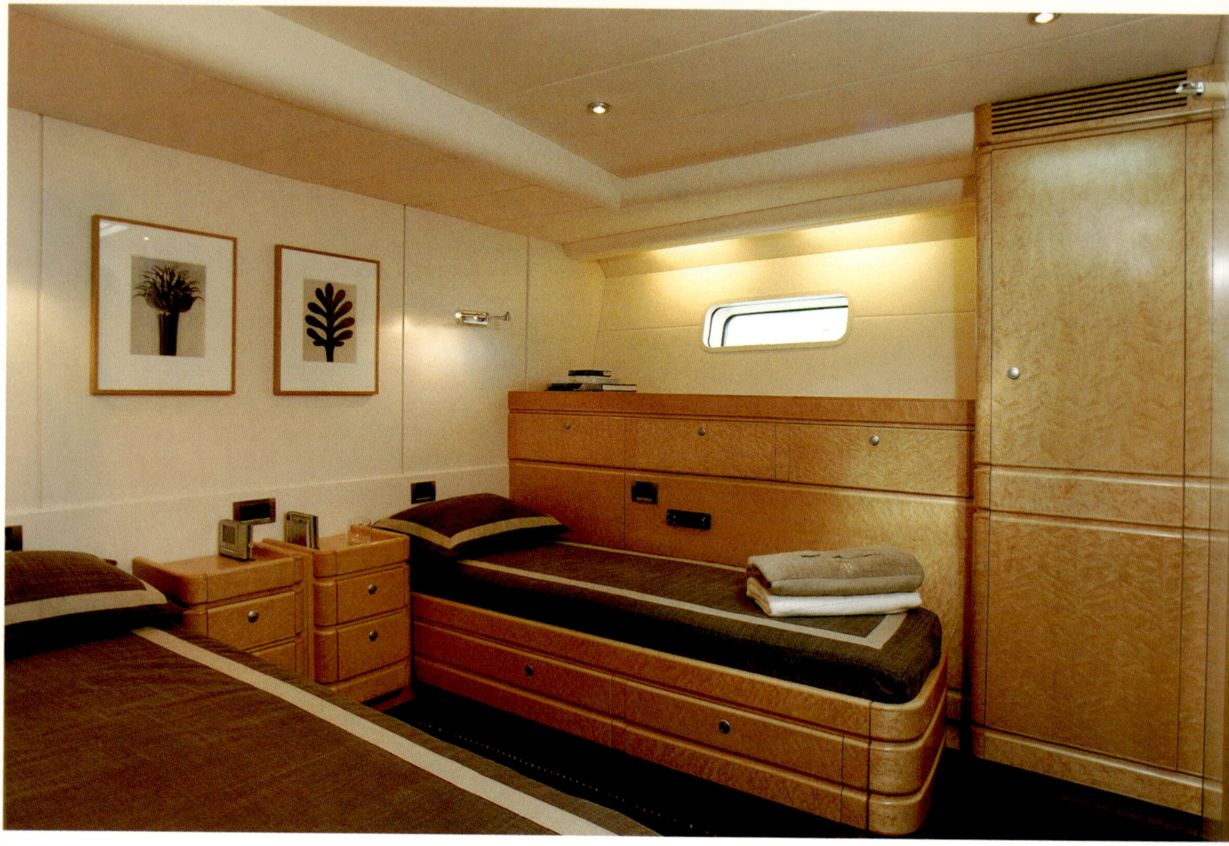

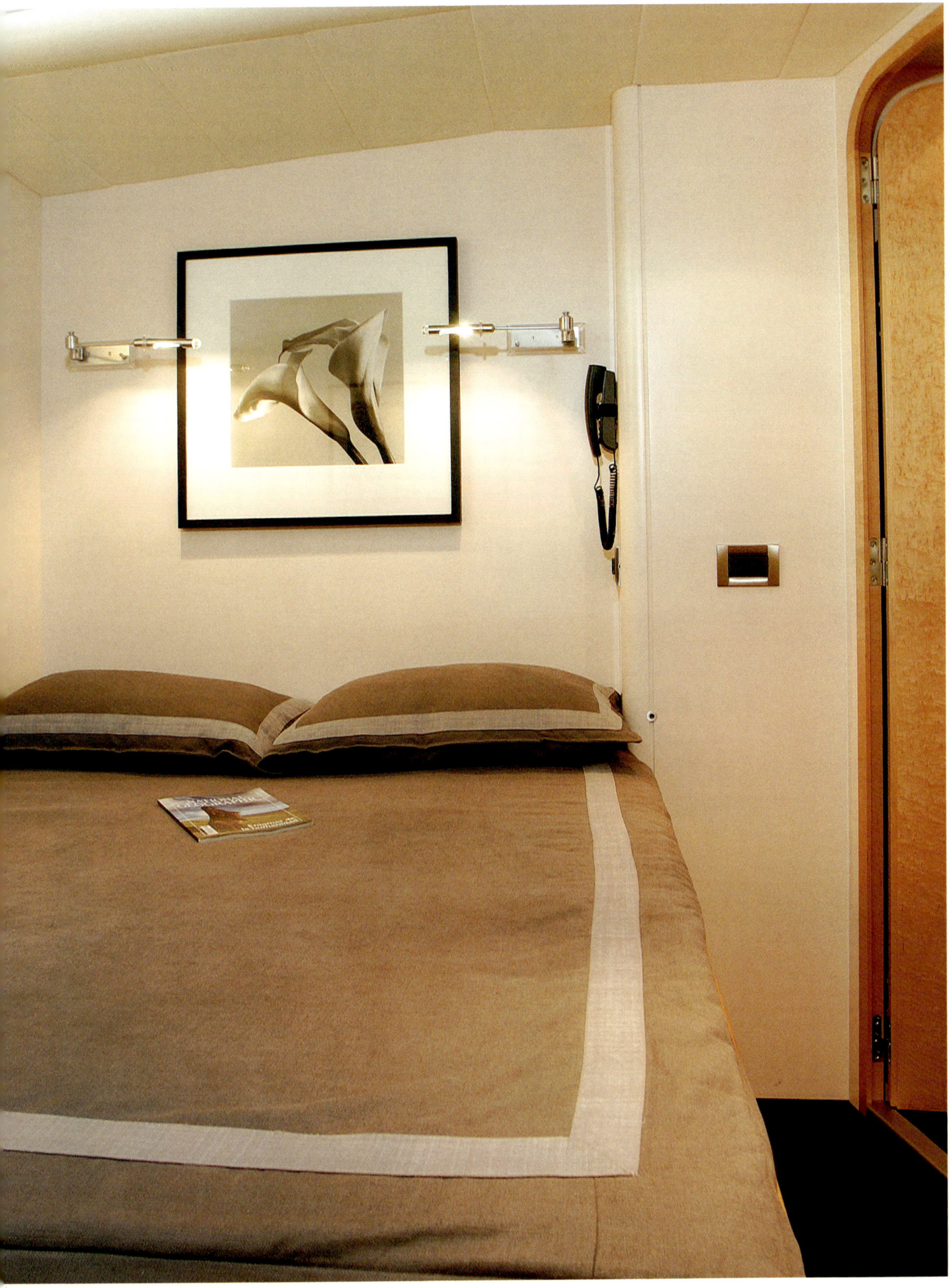

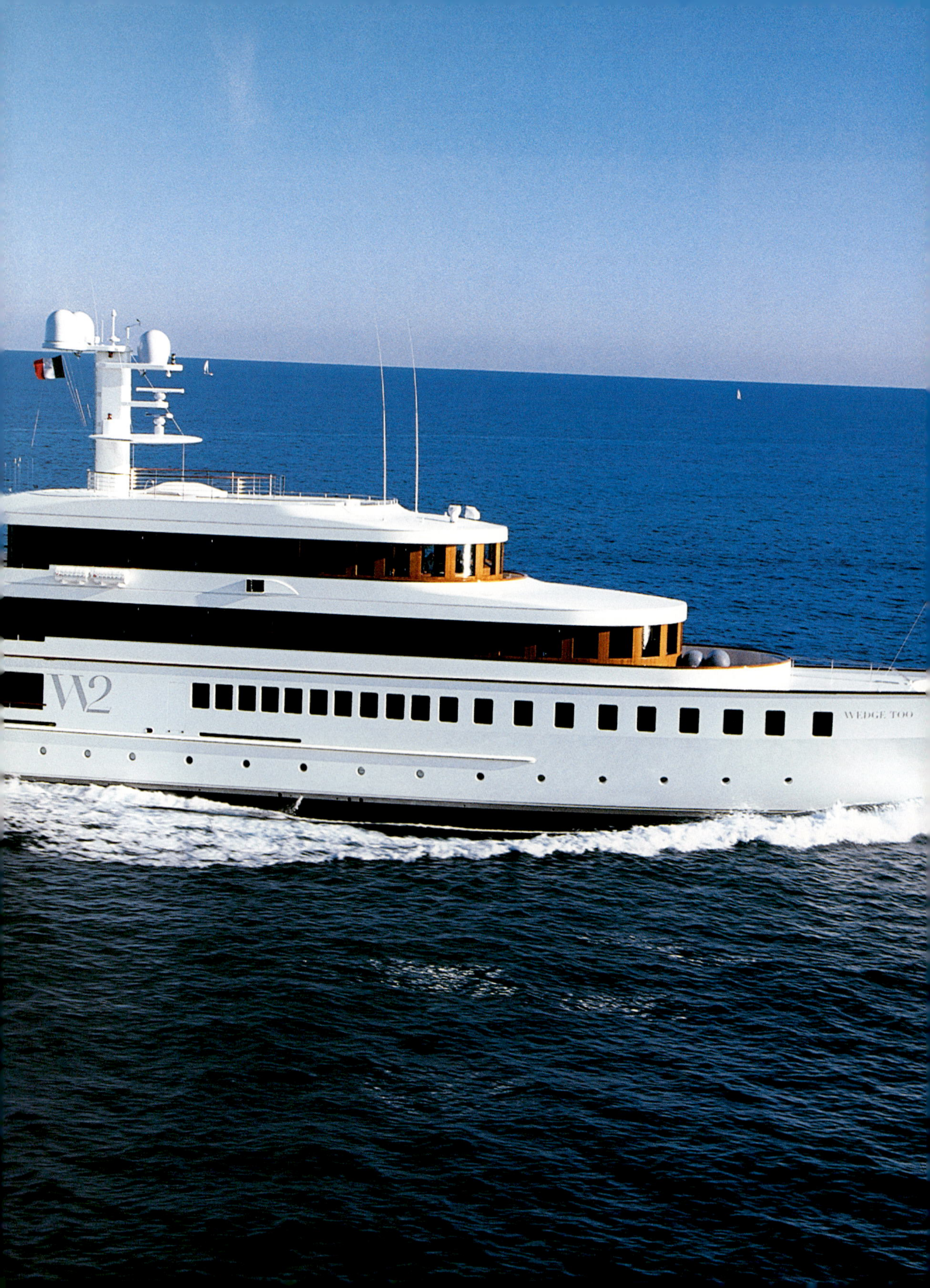
W2
WEDGE TOO

PHILIPPE STARCK, DEVOOGT NAVAL ARCHITECTS
WEDGE TOO | 2002
Feadship Holland B.V.

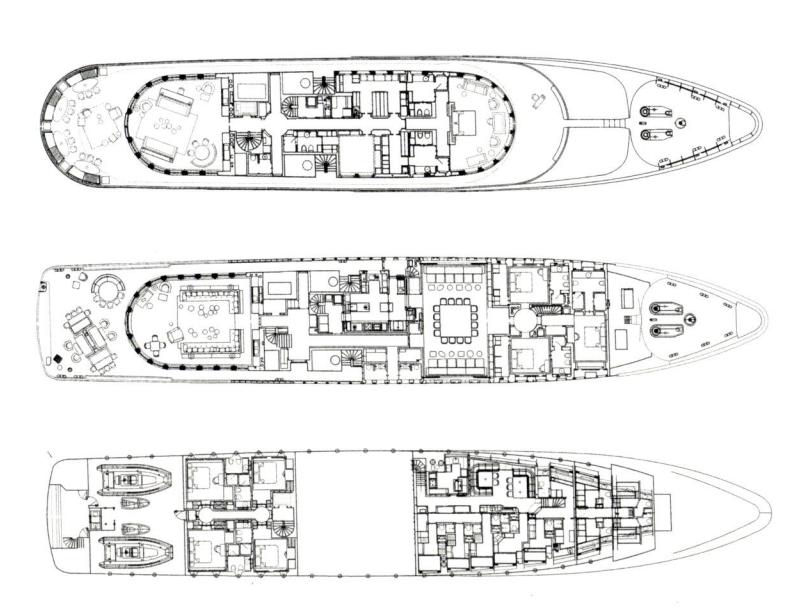

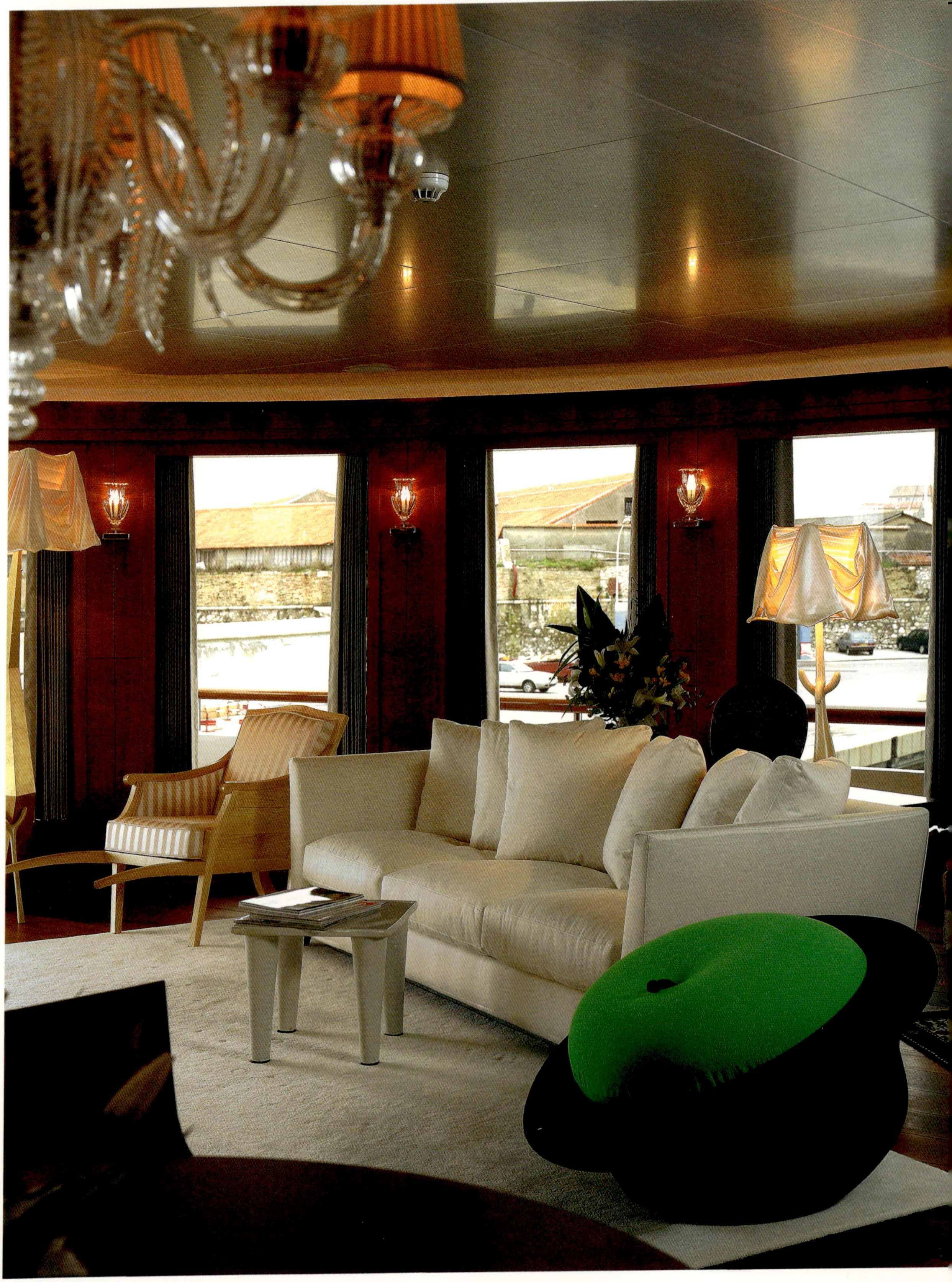

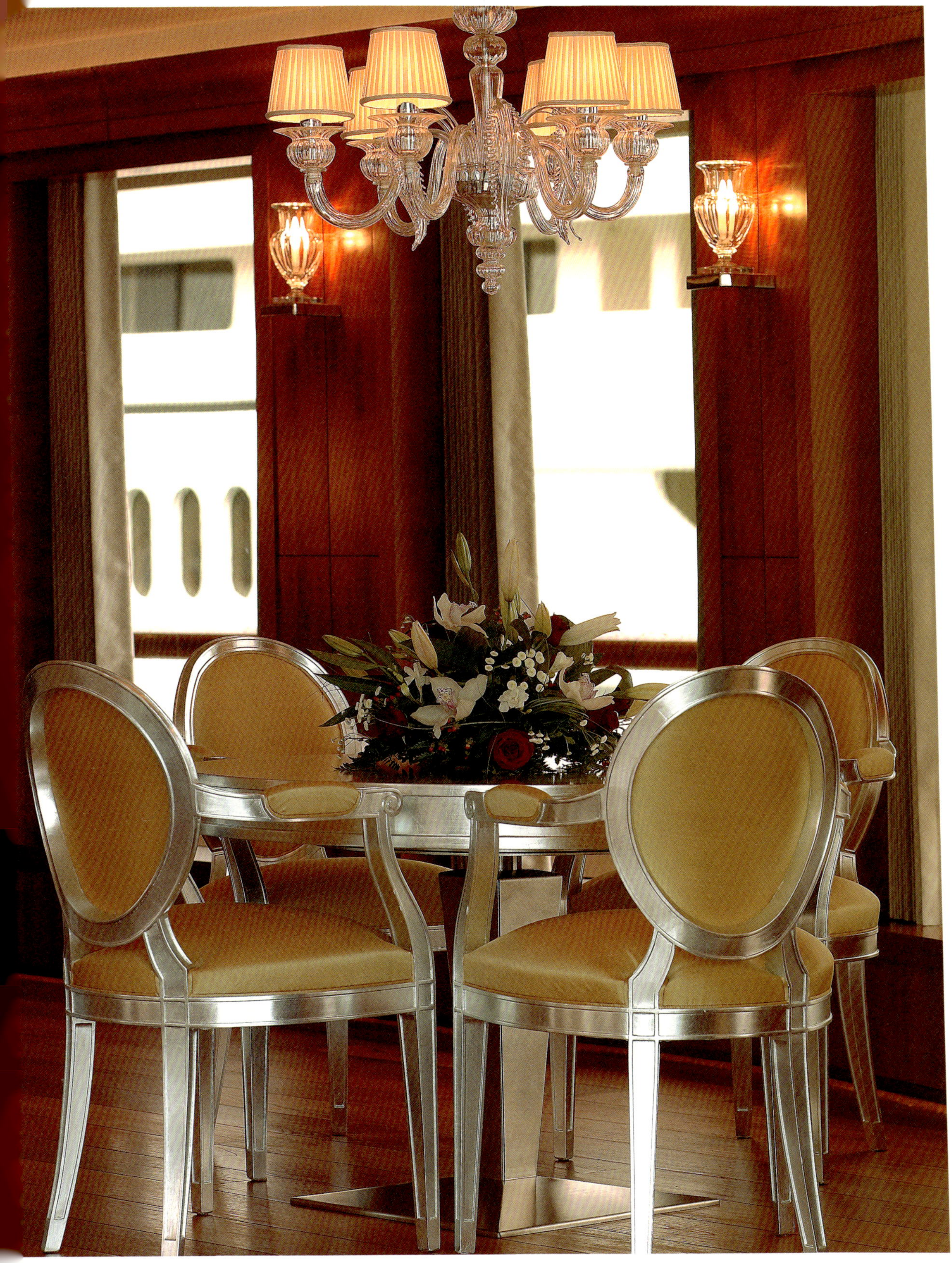

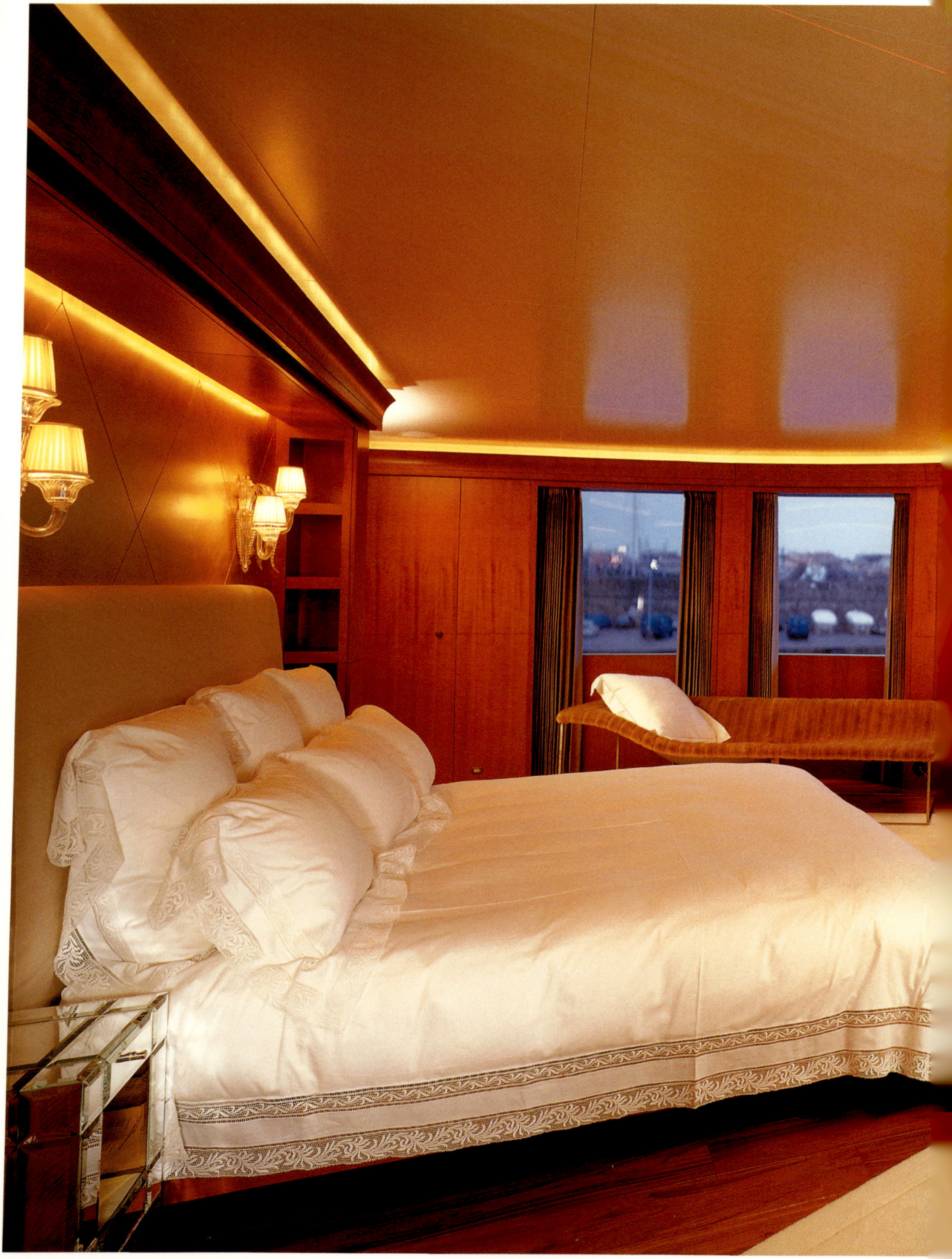

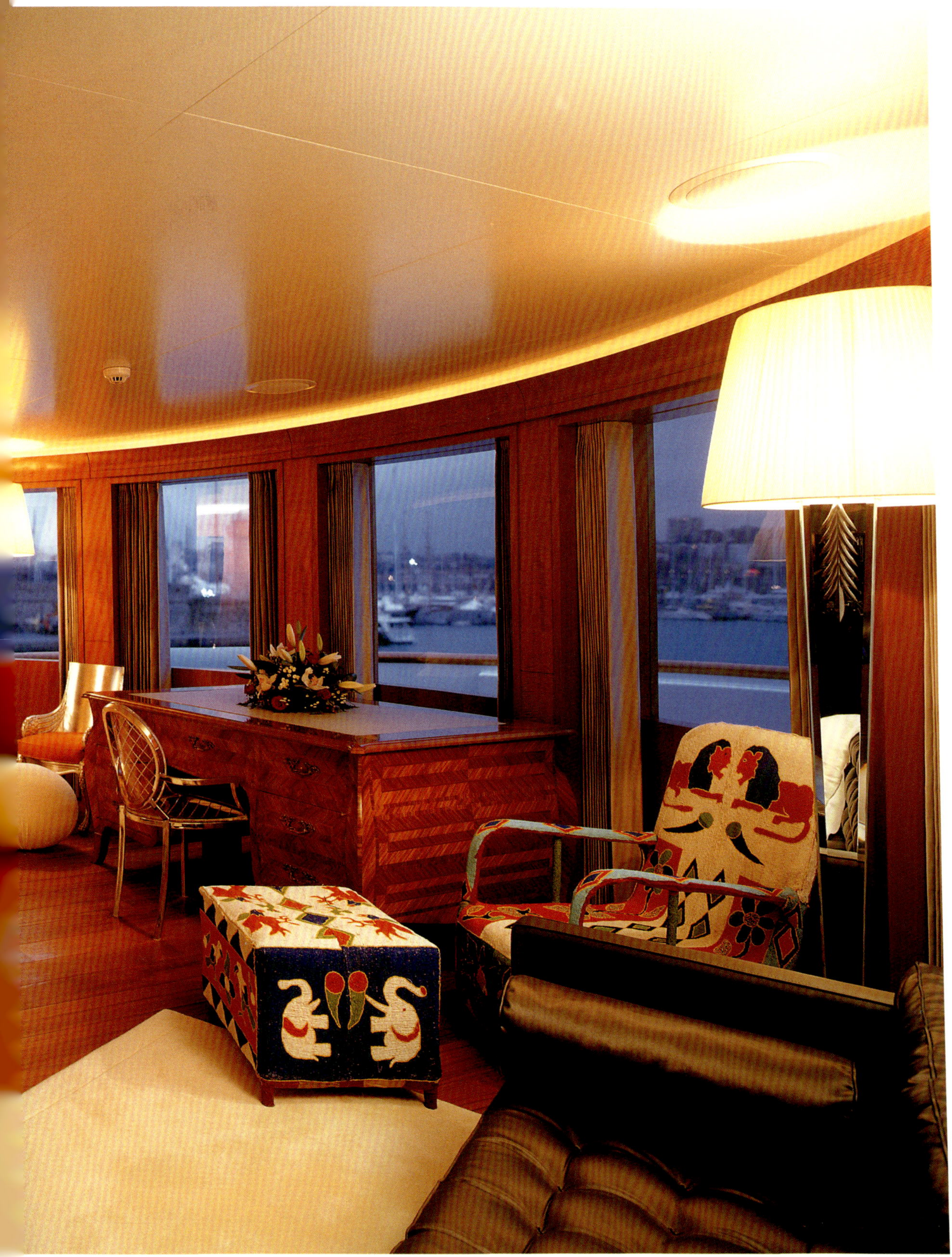

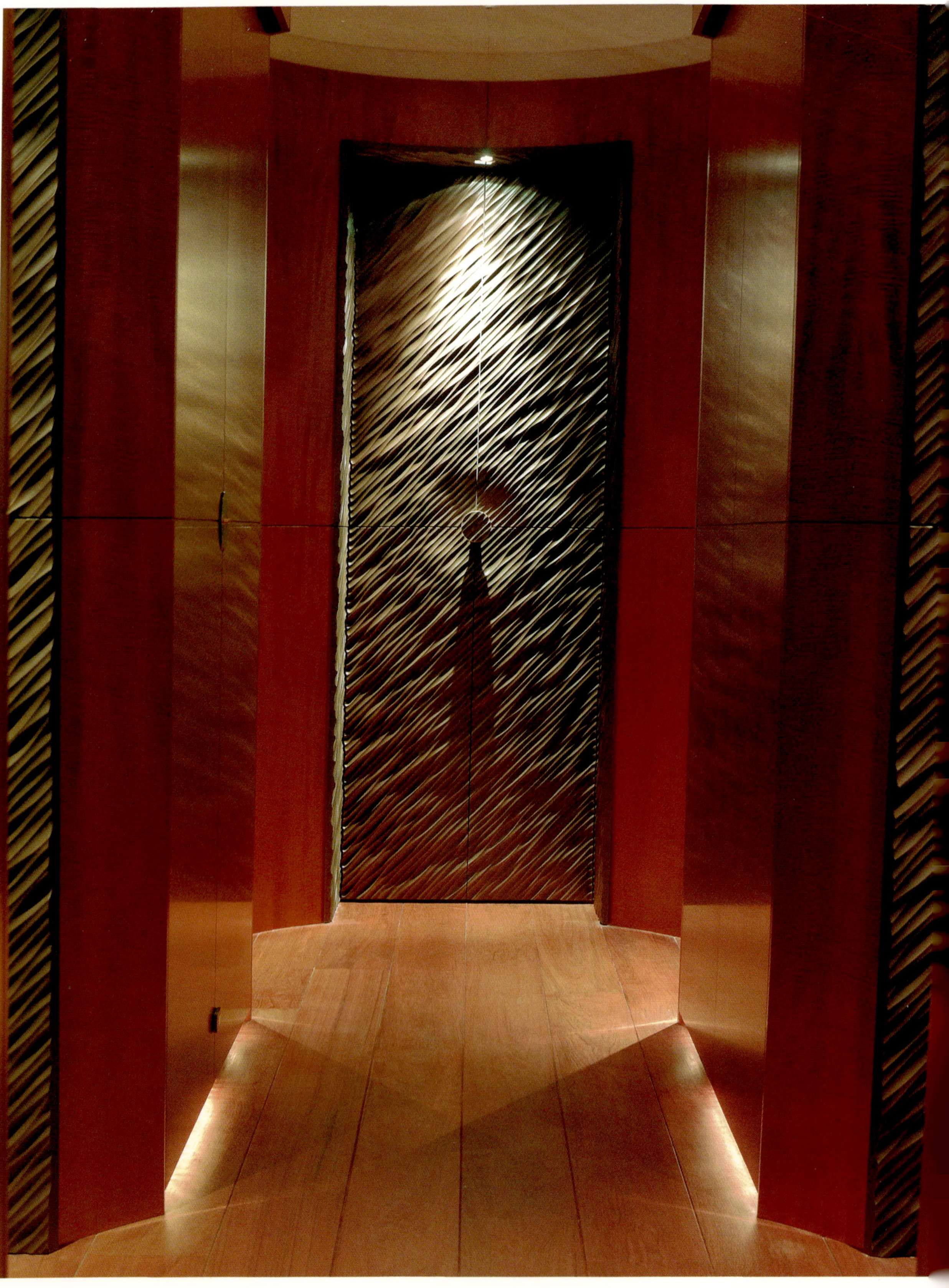

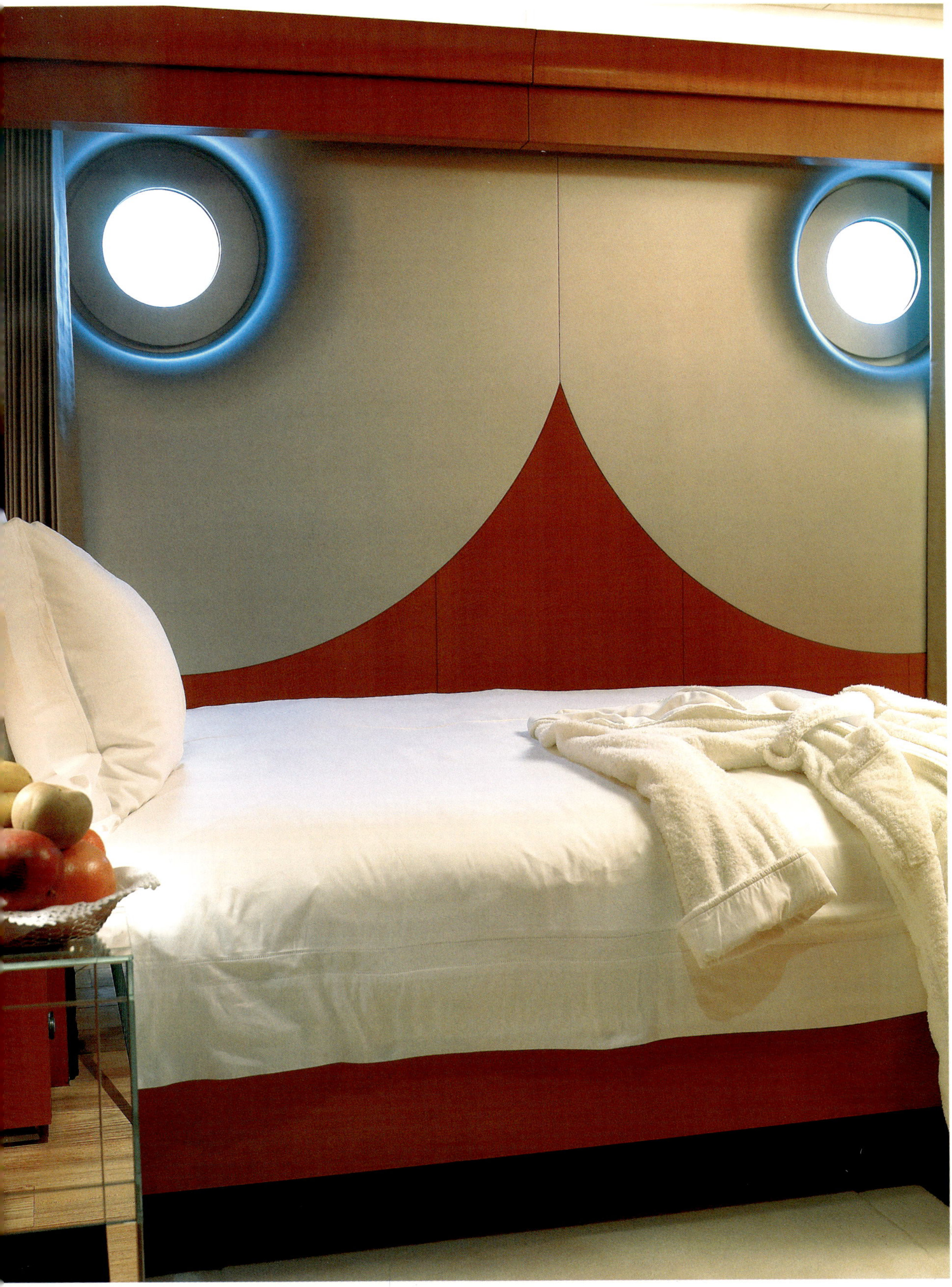

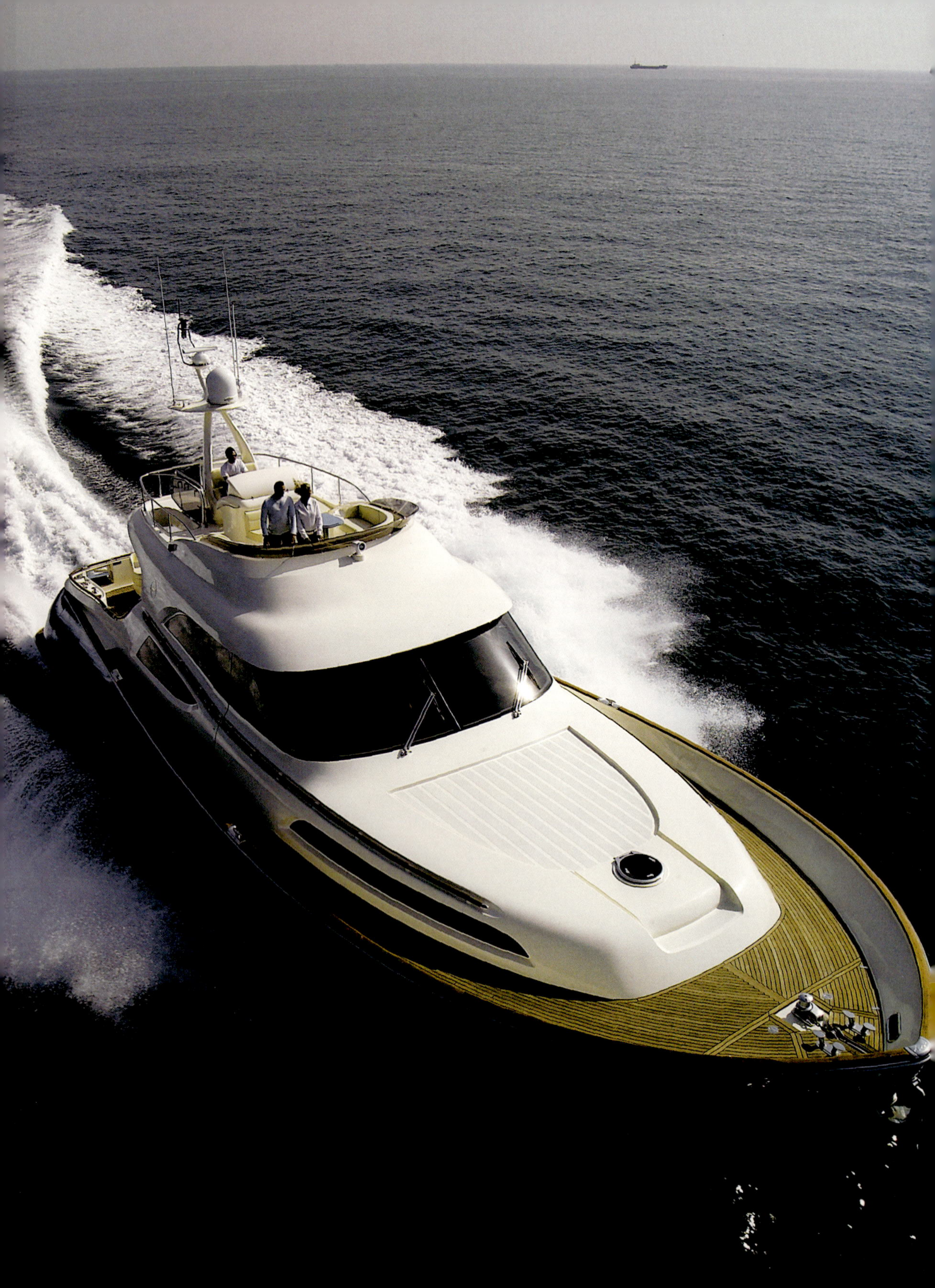

STUDIO VICTORY DESIGN
72 DOLPHIN | 2004
Mochi Craft

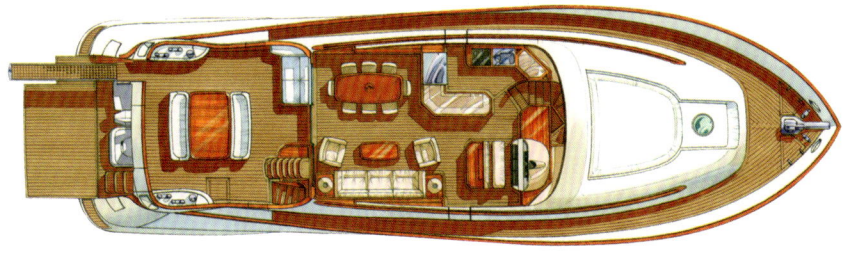

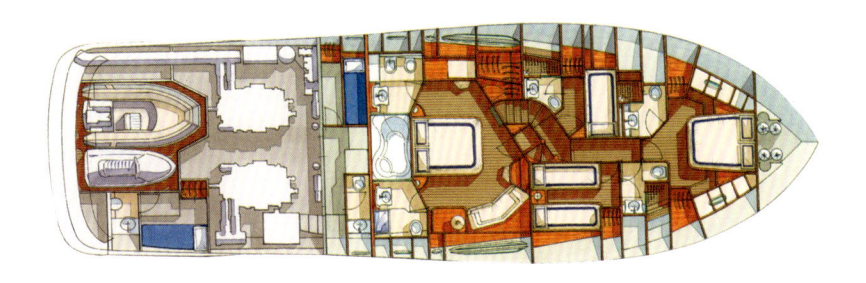

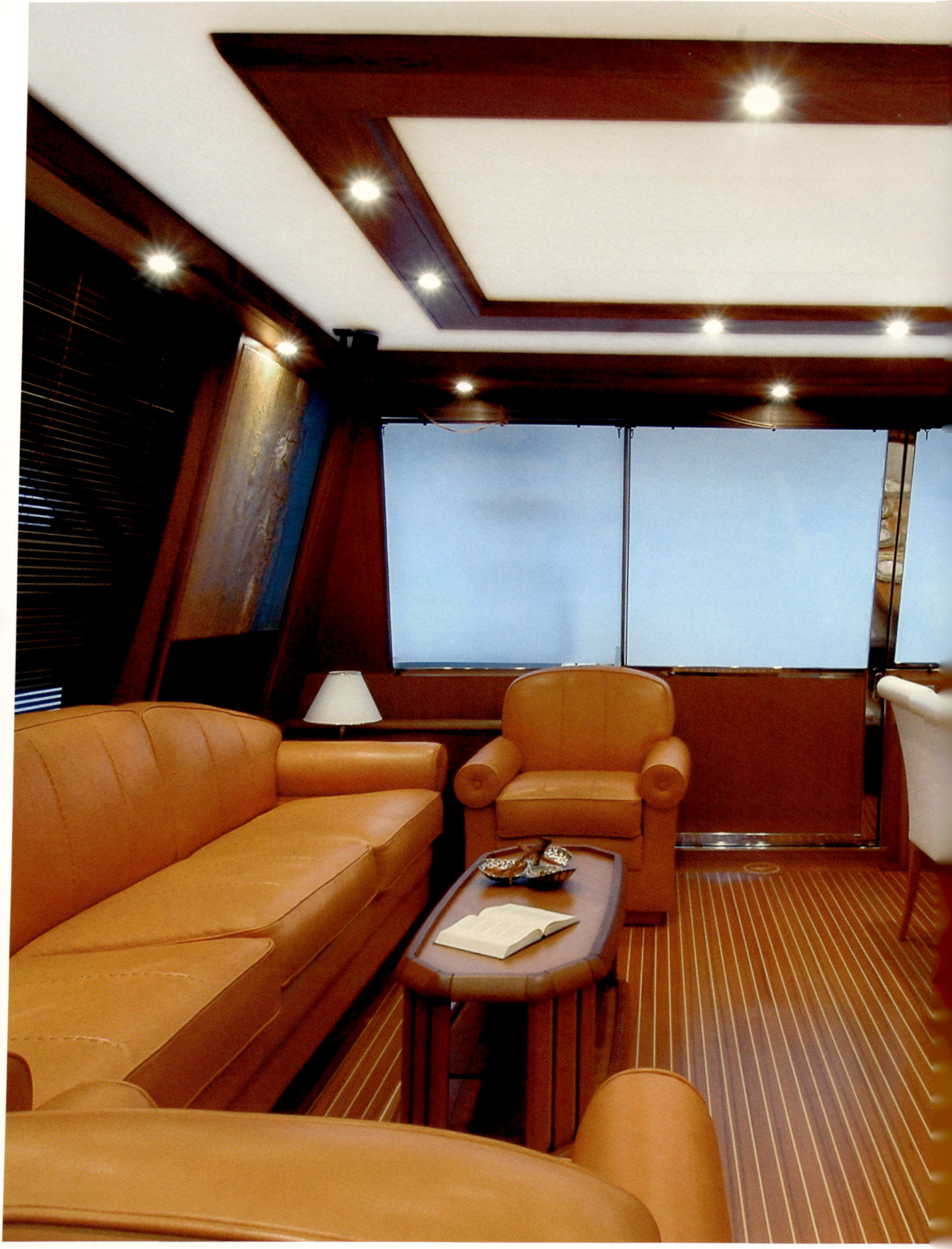

269

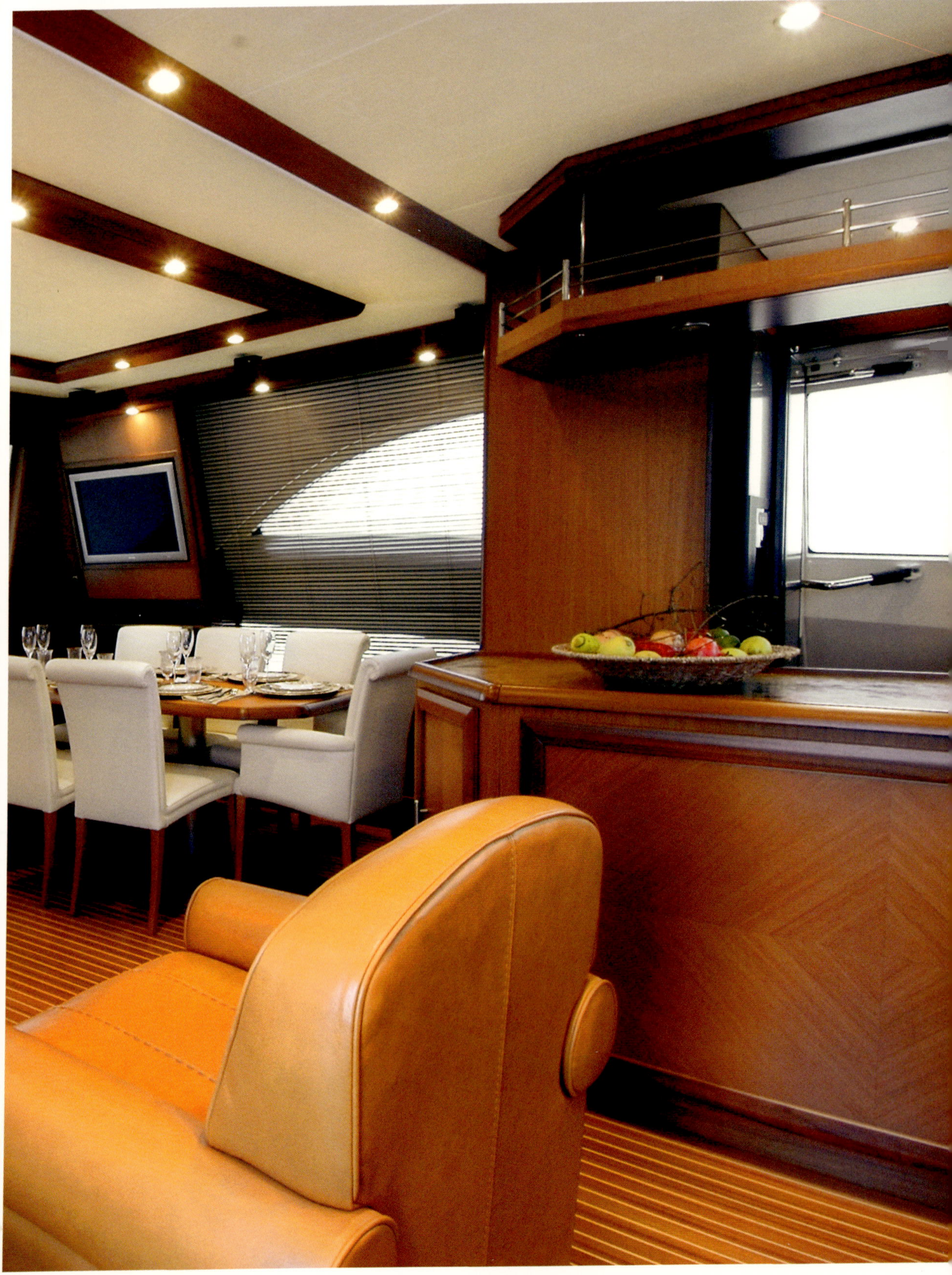

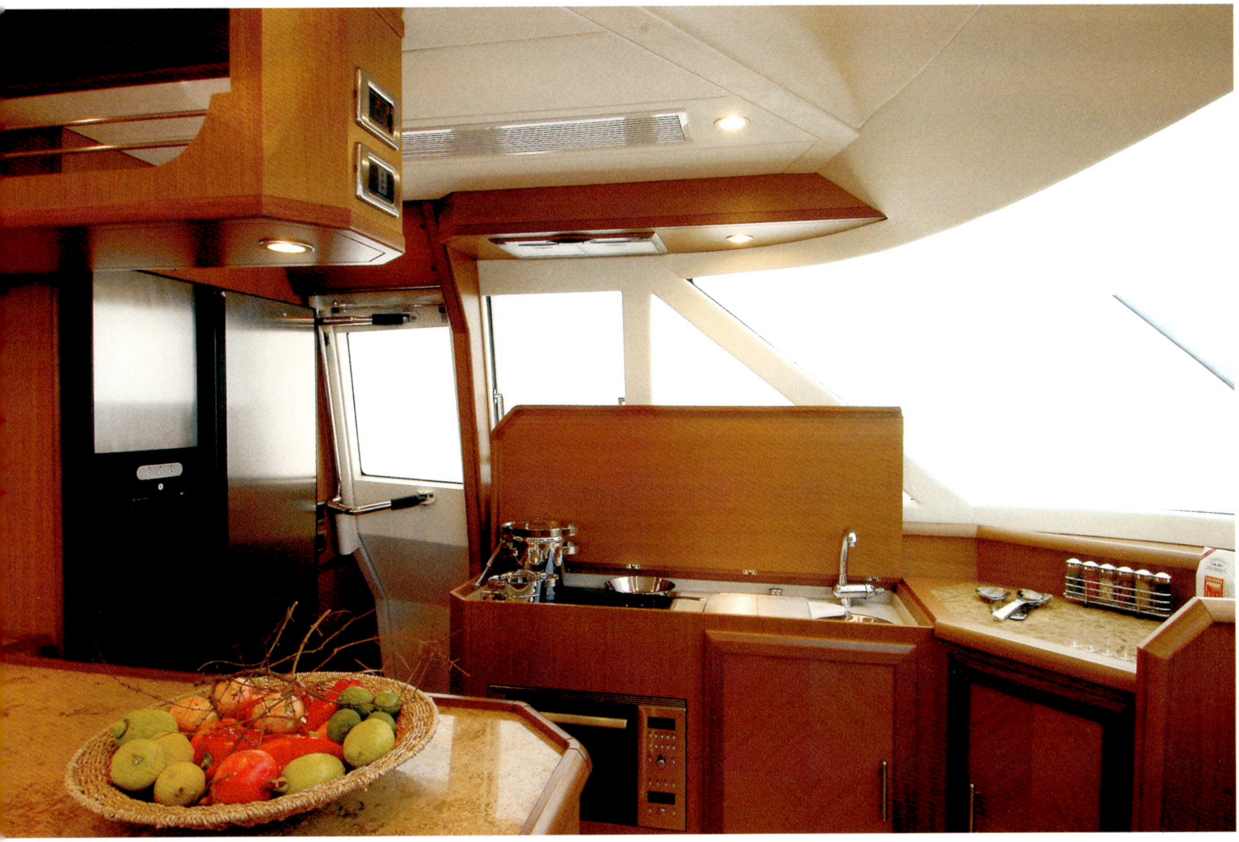

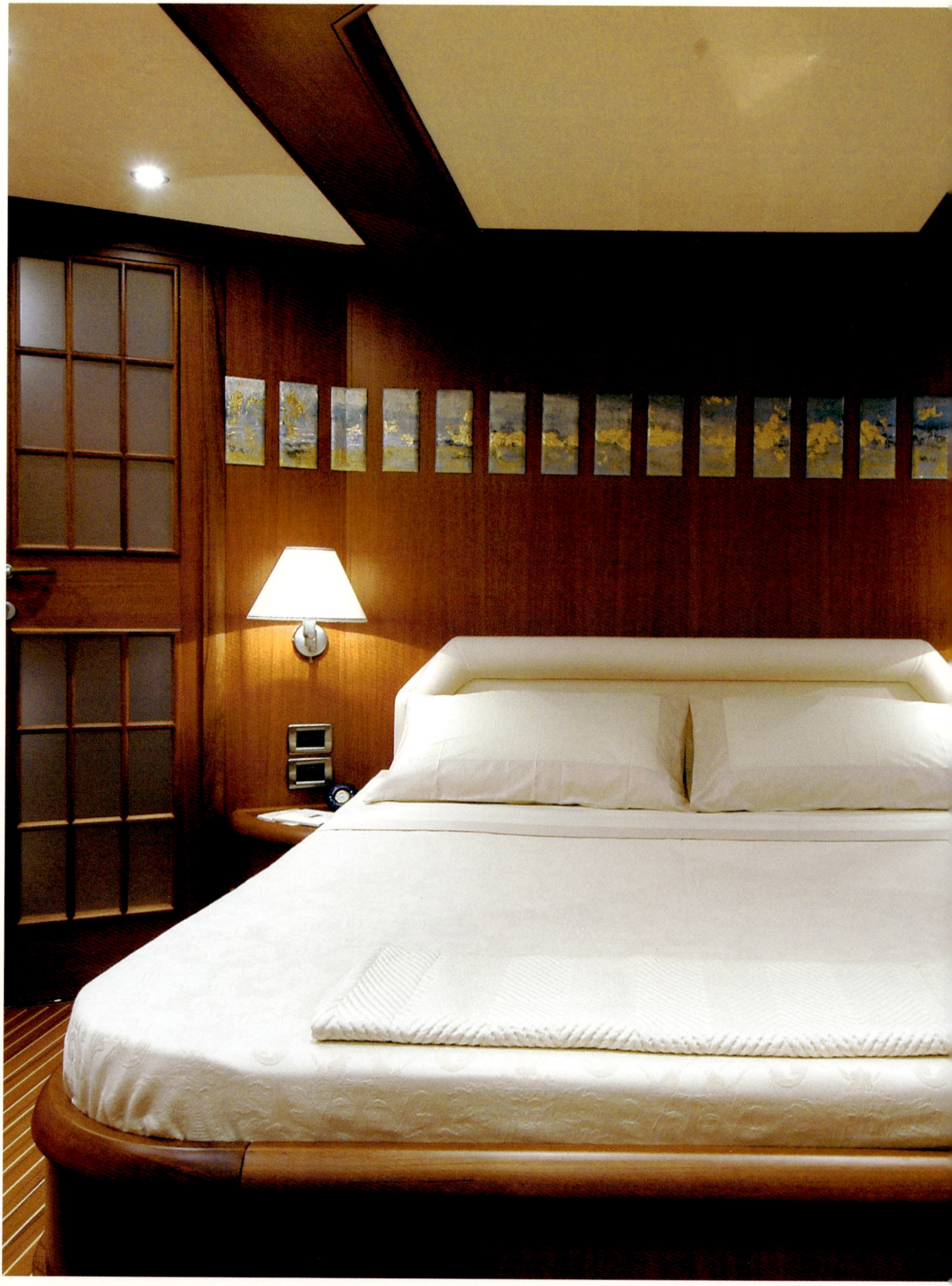

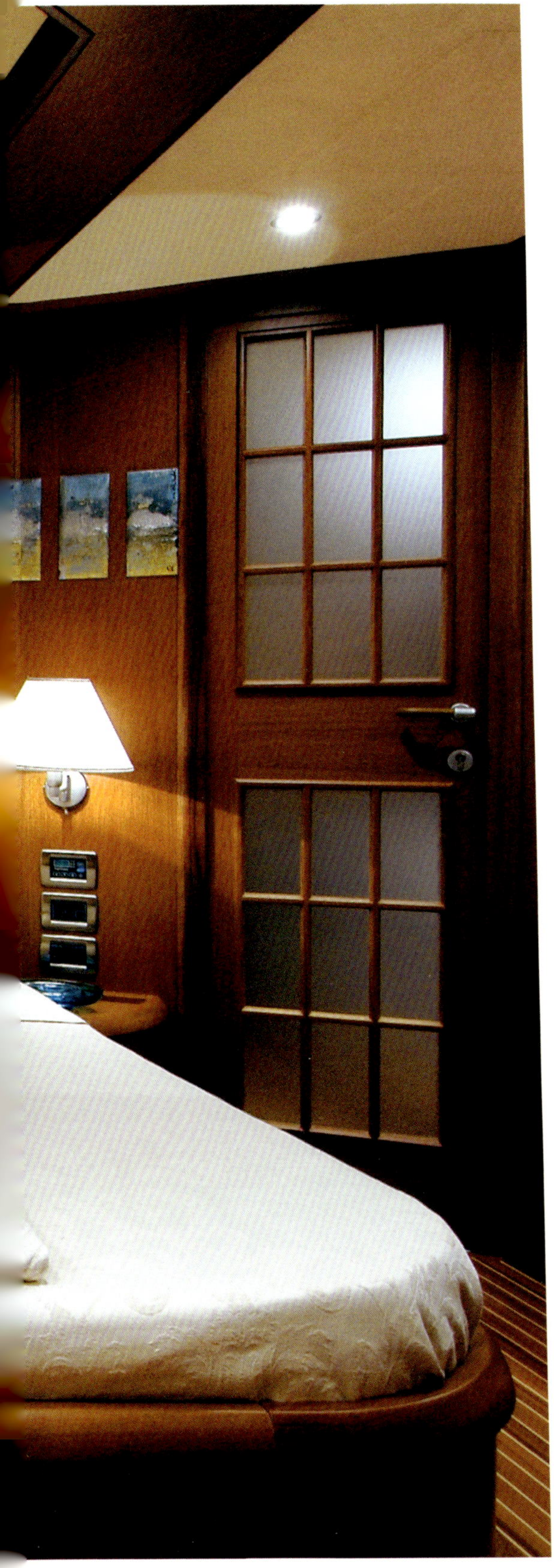

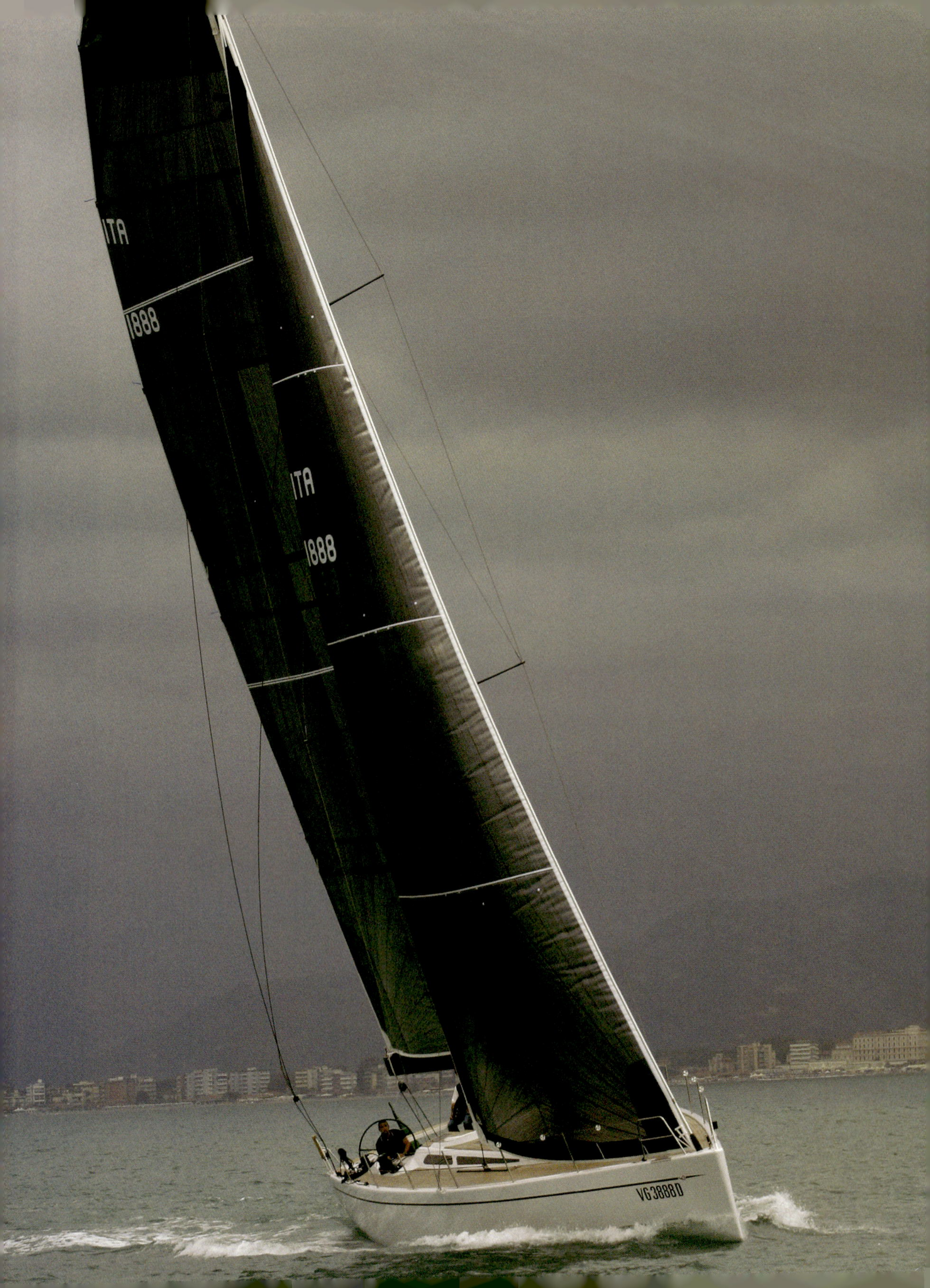
ITA
1888
ITA
1888
VG3888D

VISMARA YACHT DESIGN
MISTRESS | 2004
Marine Services srl

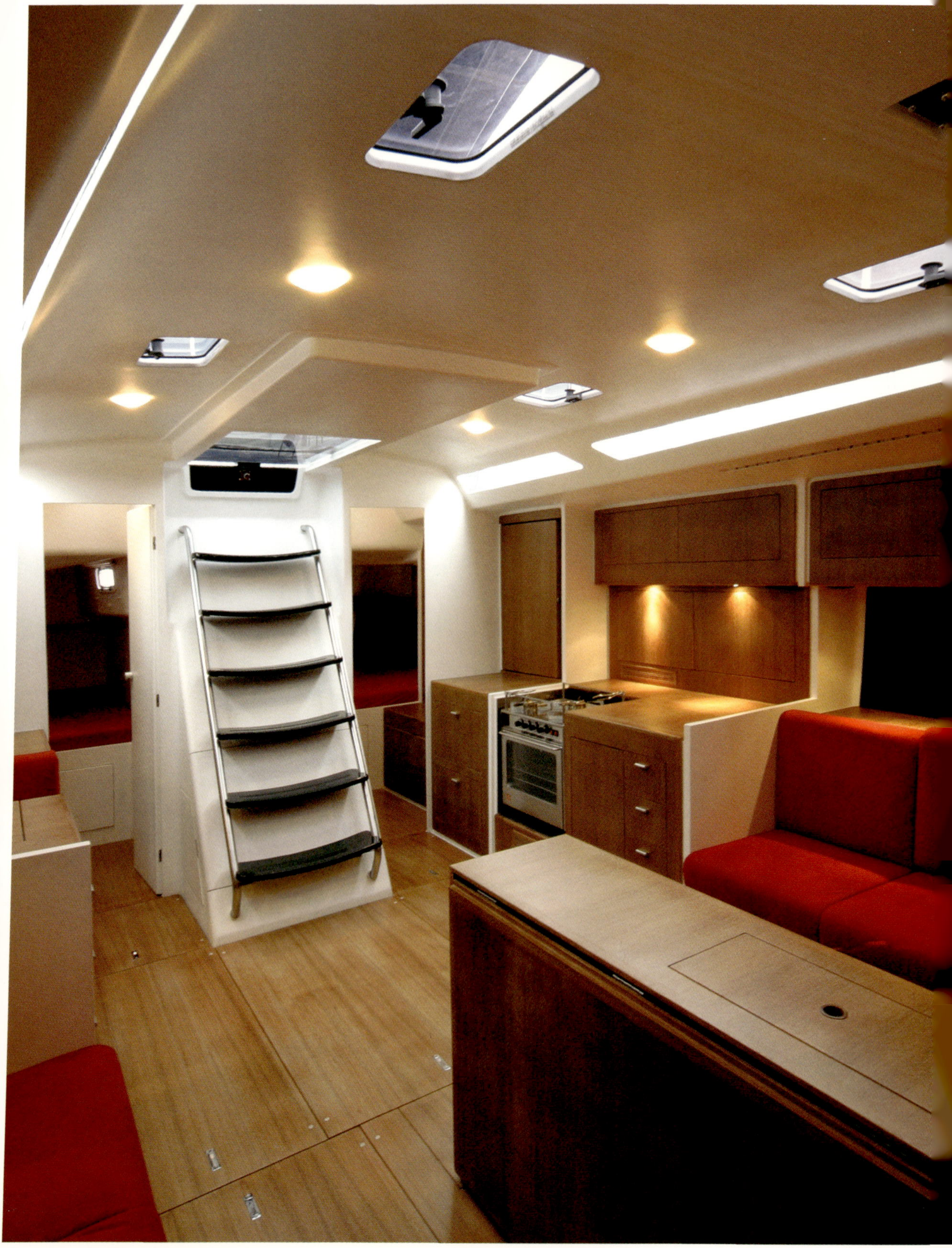

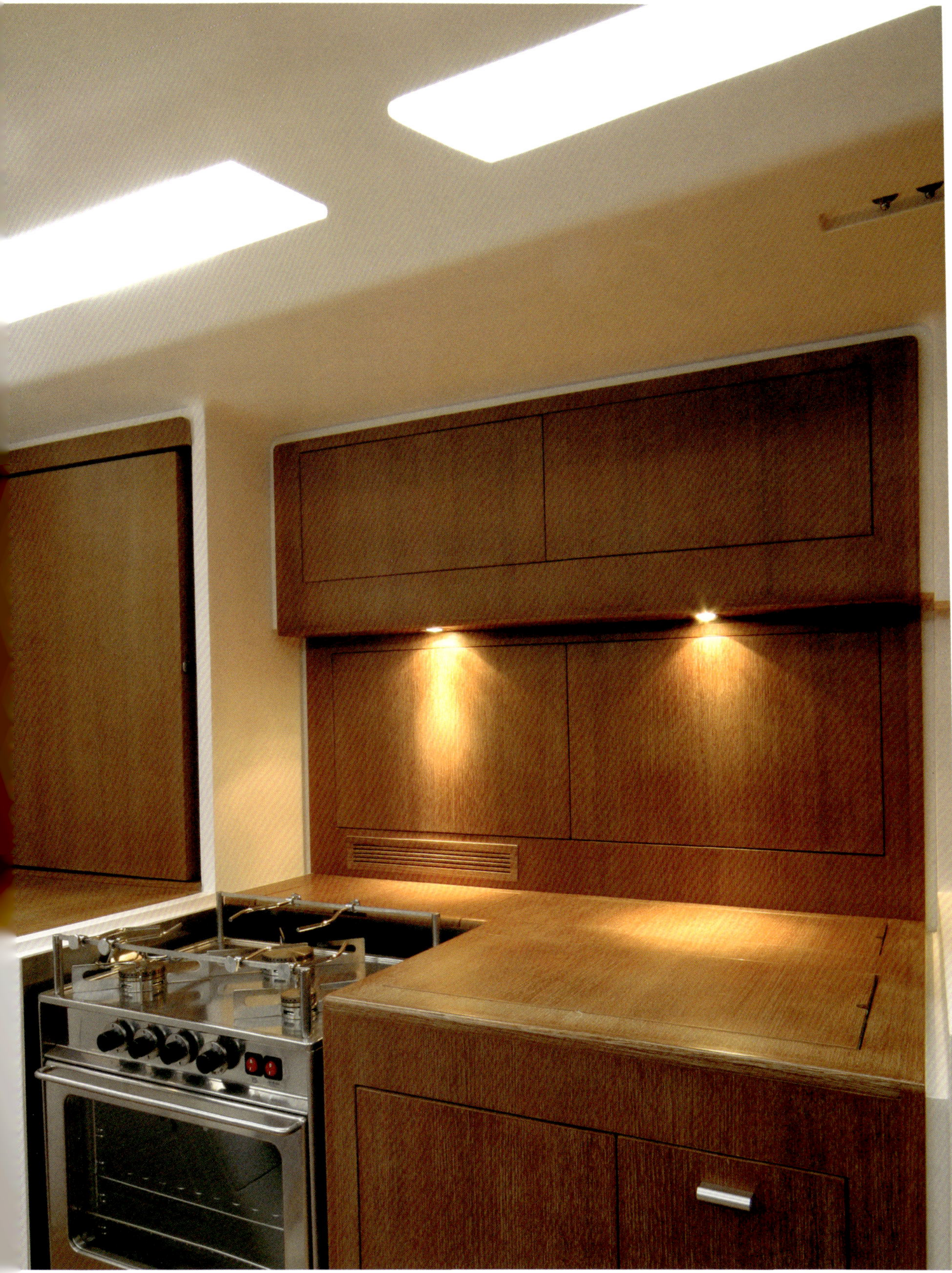

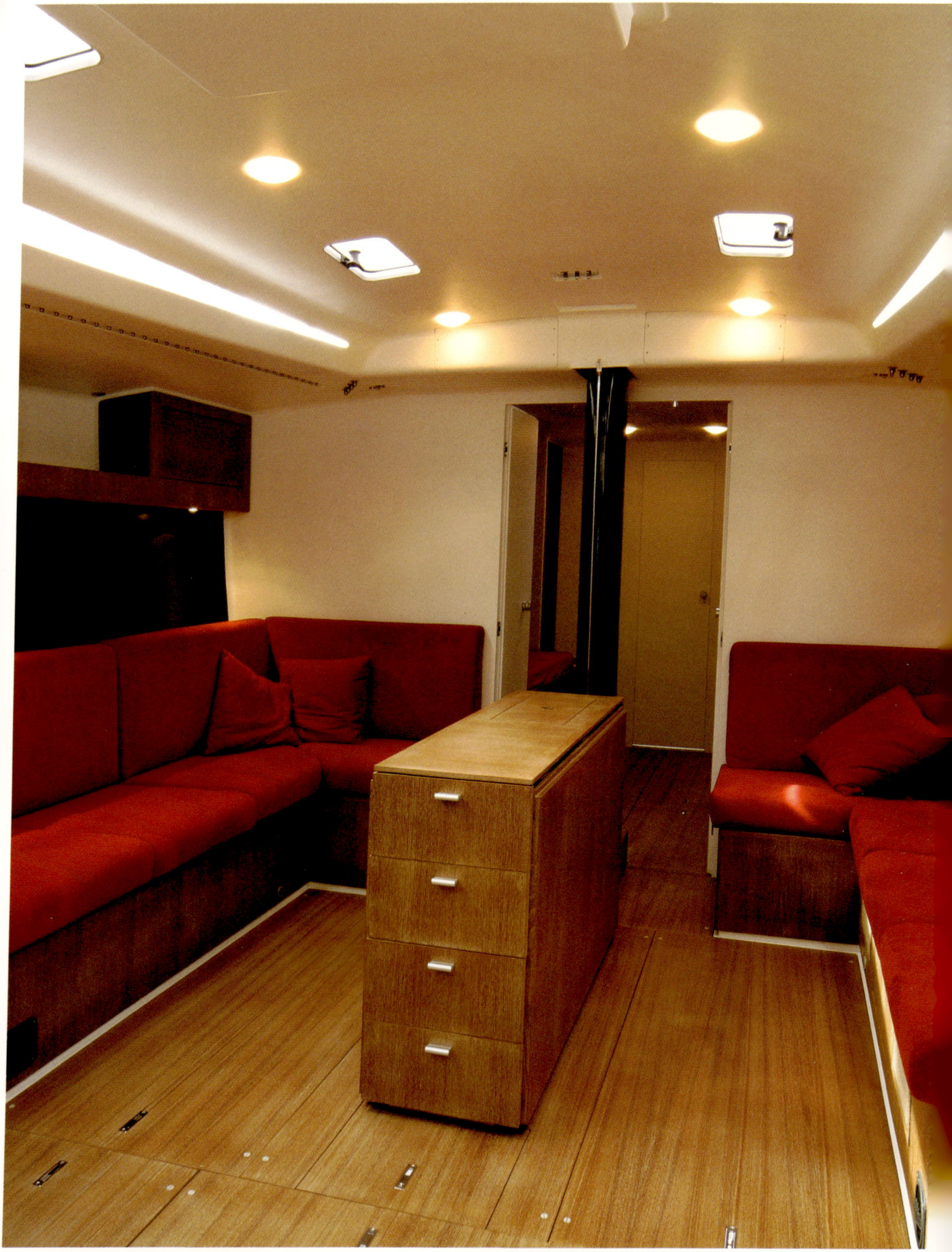

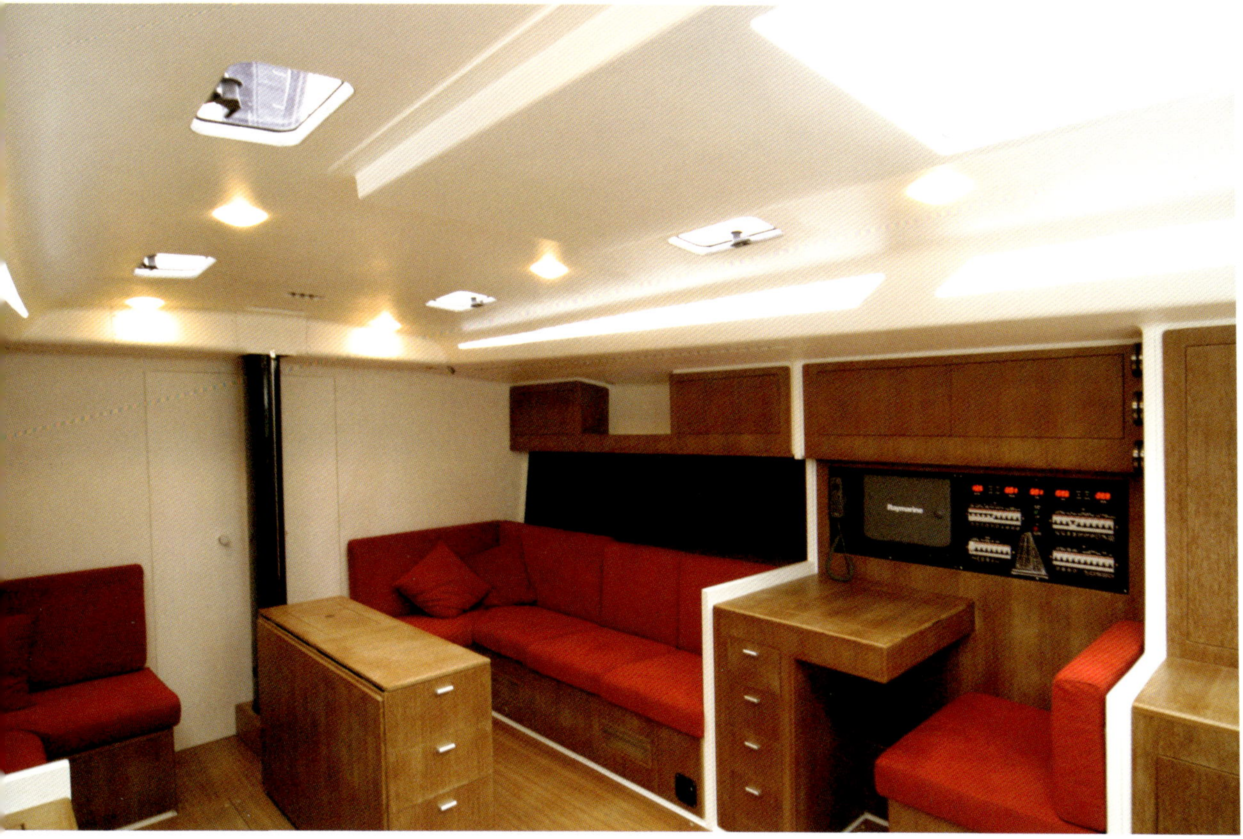

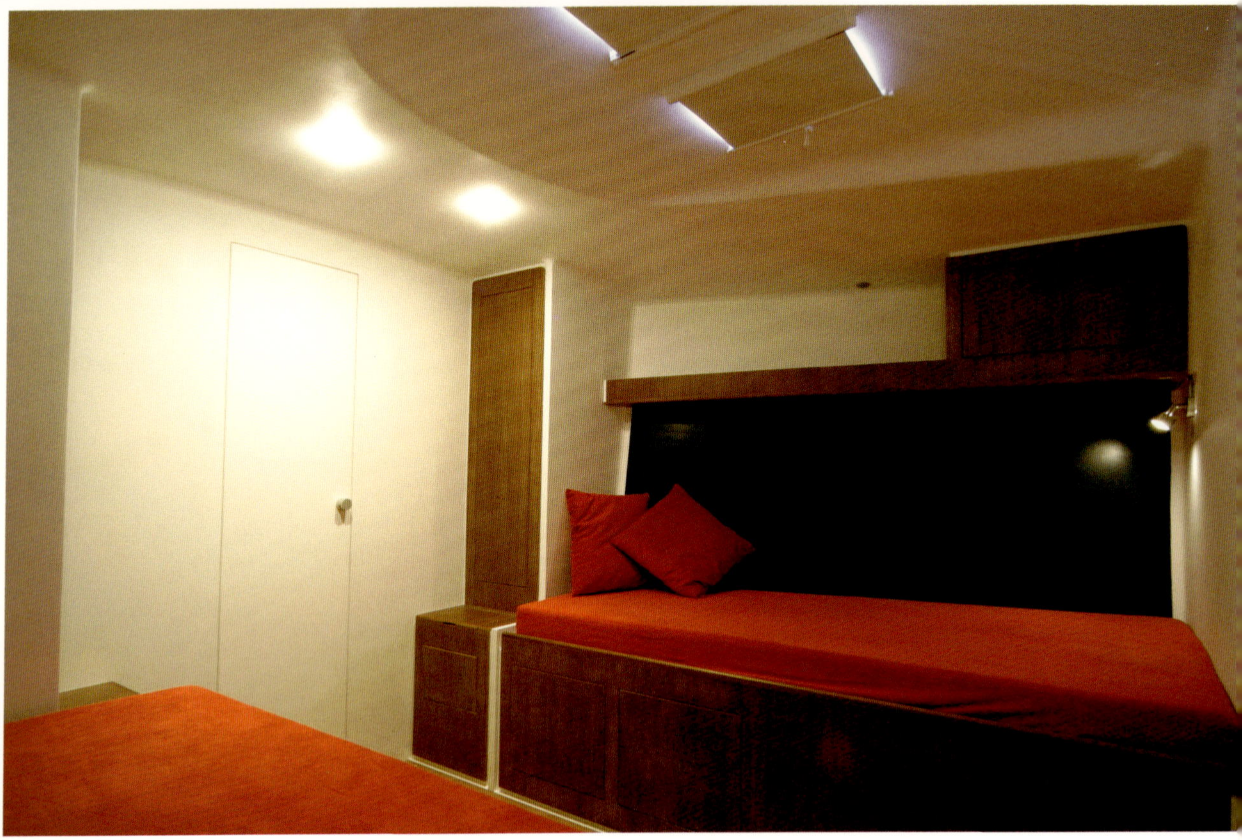

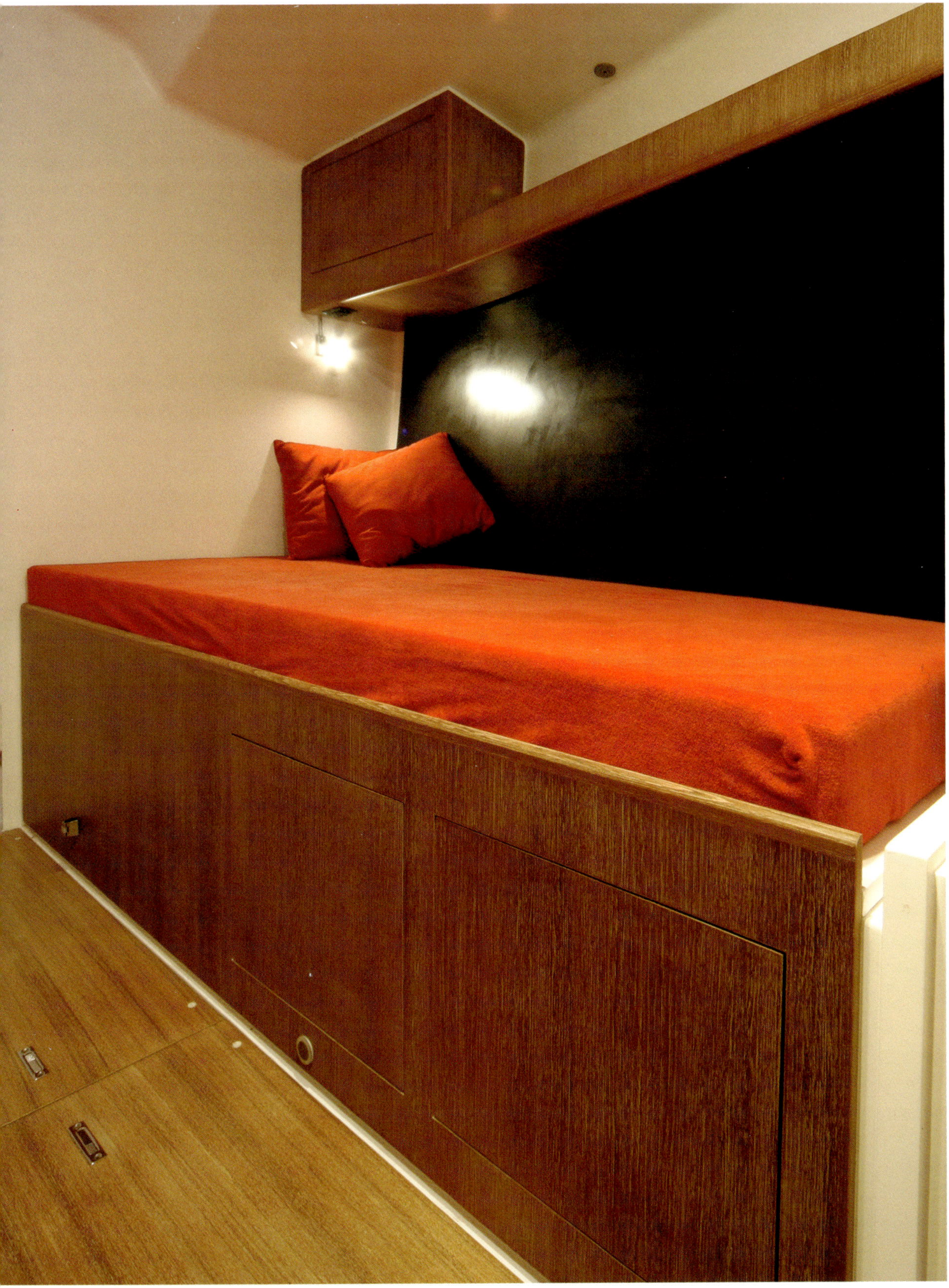

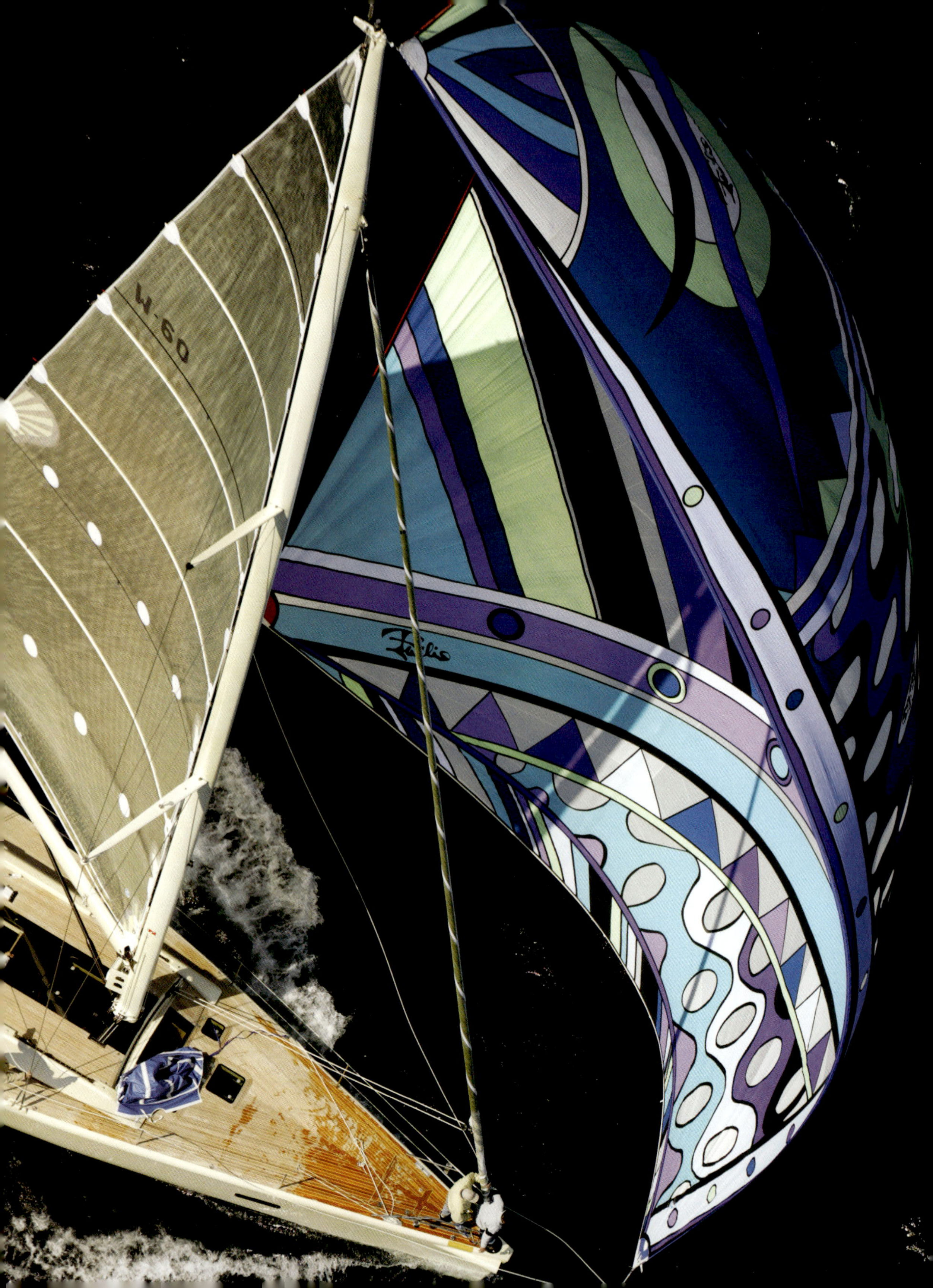
W-60

WALLY, FARR YACHT DESIGN
WALLYÑO | 2004
Carroll Marine
Wally

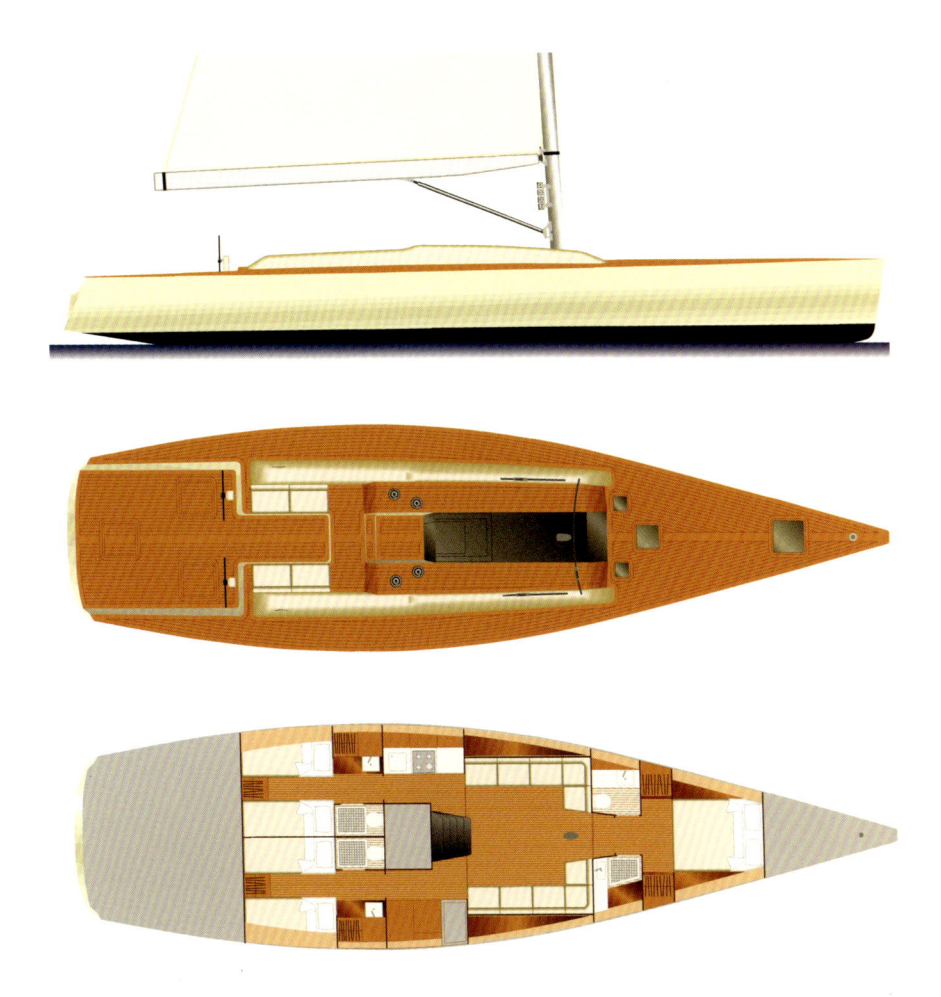

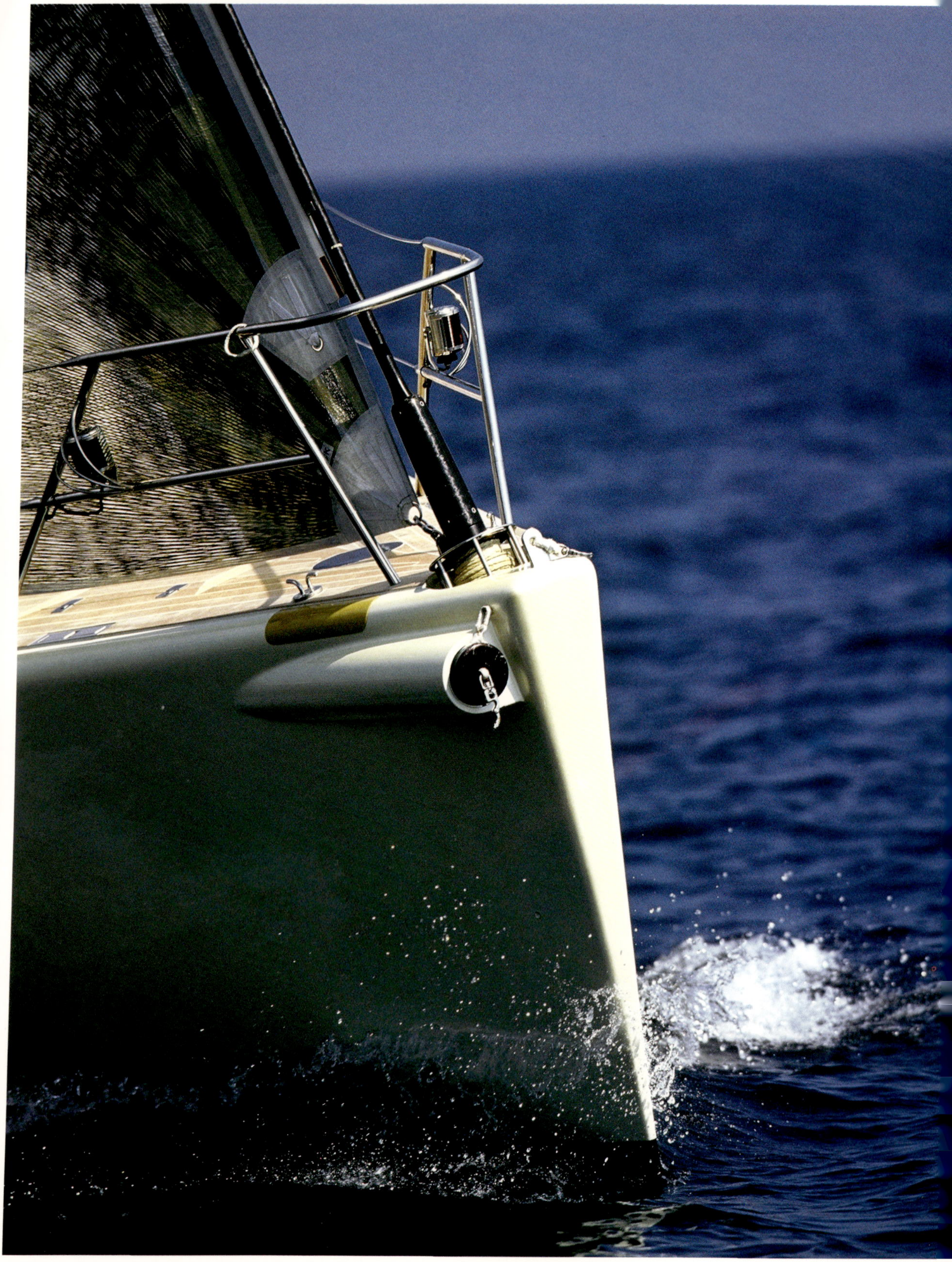

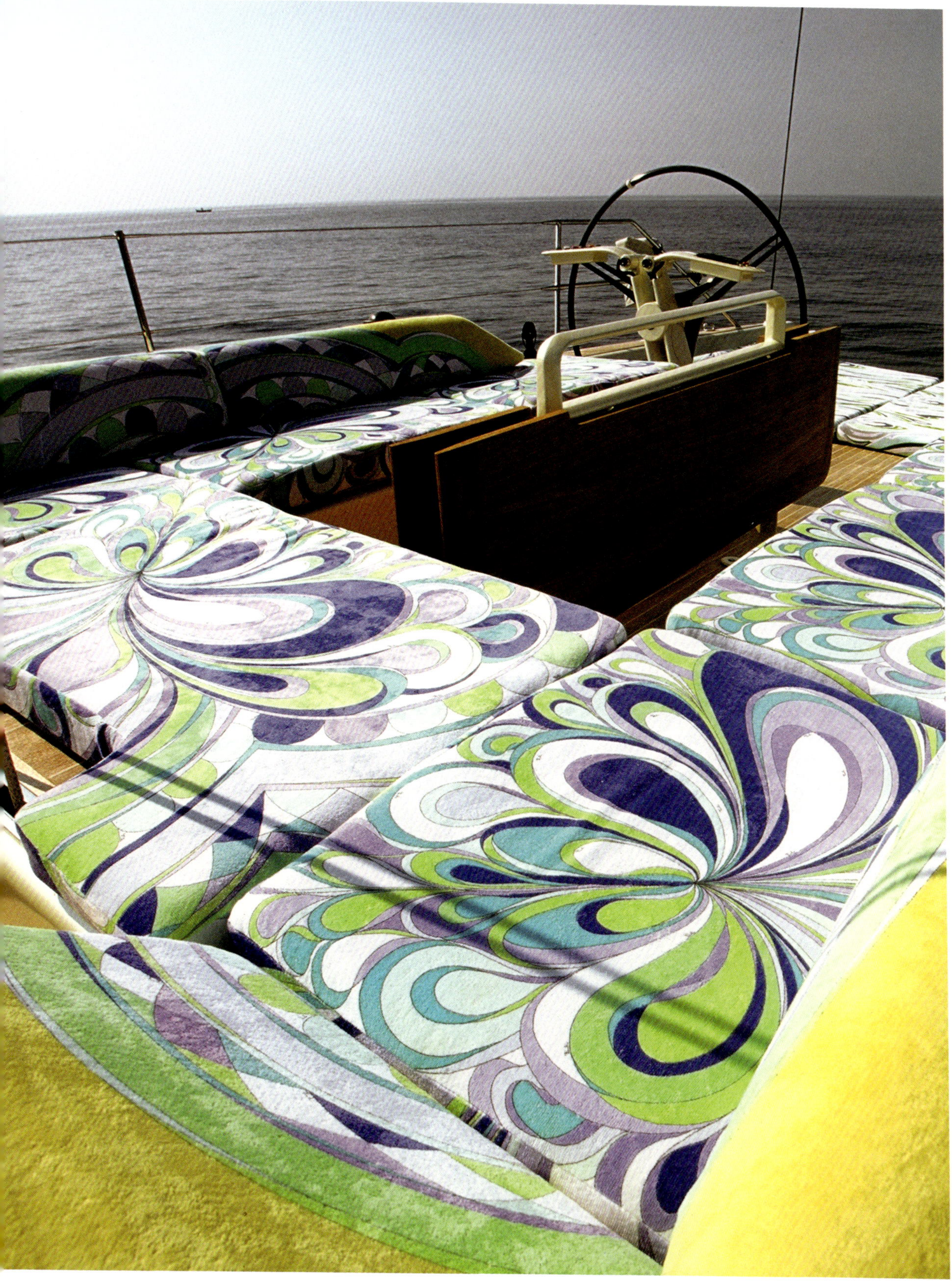

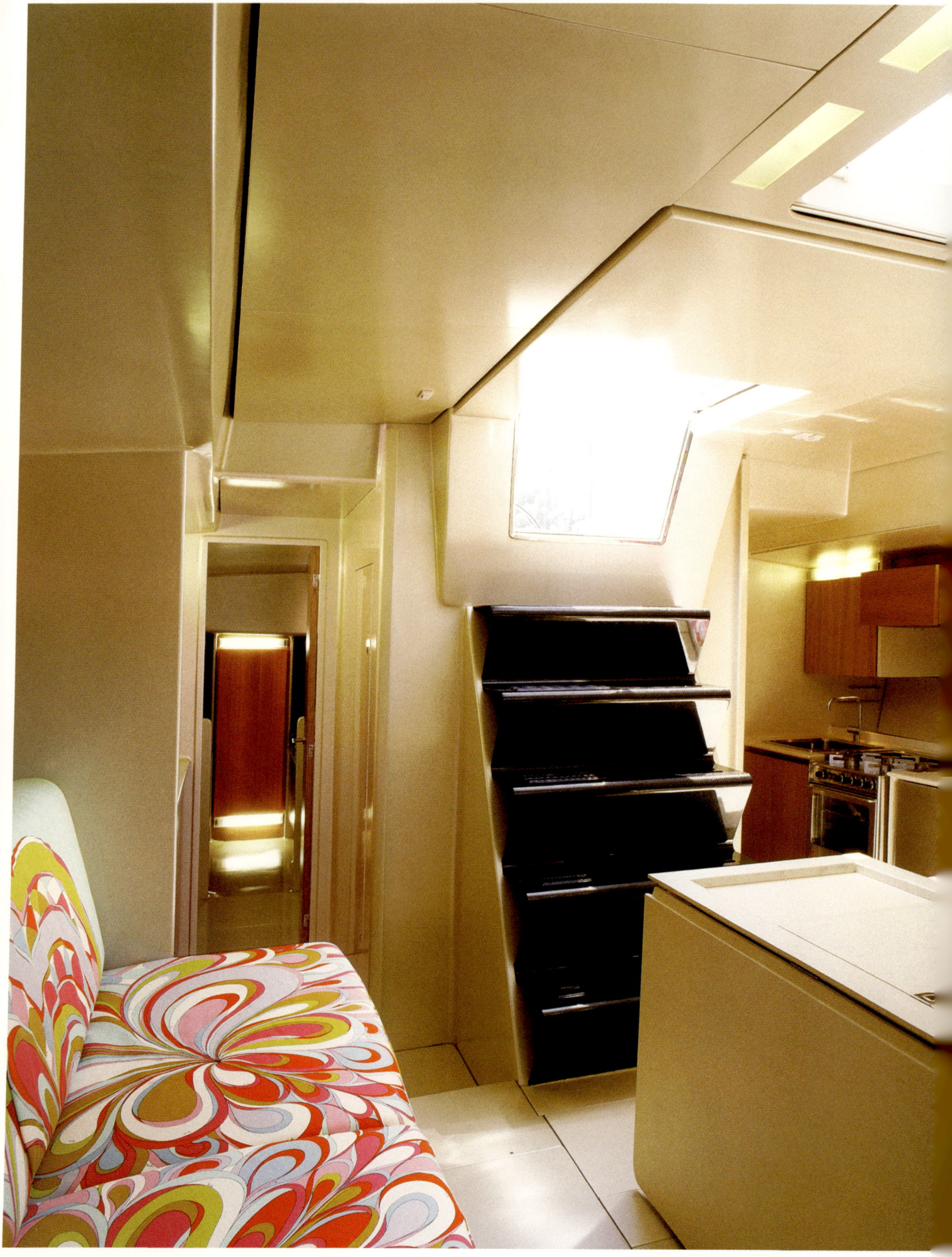

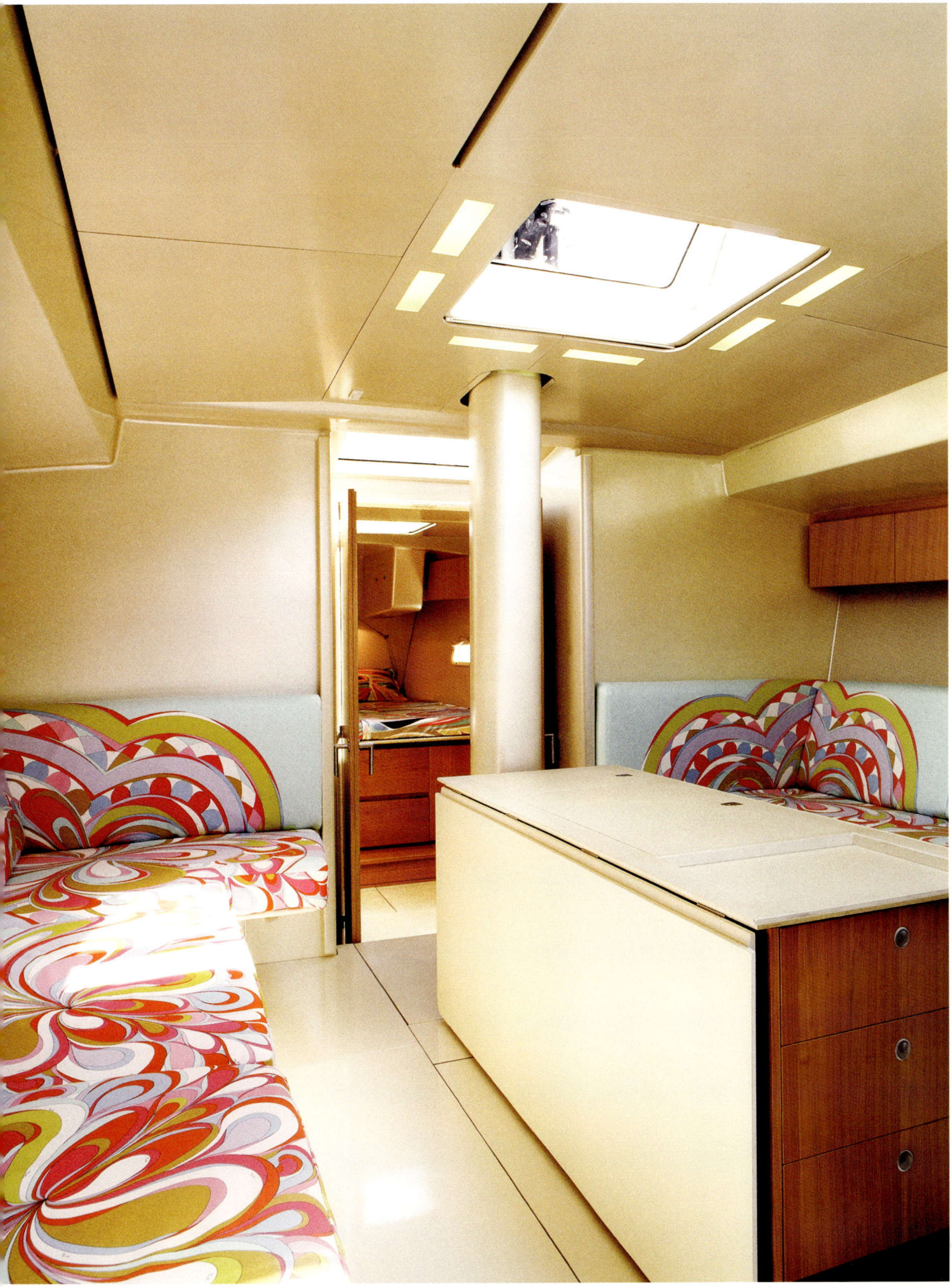

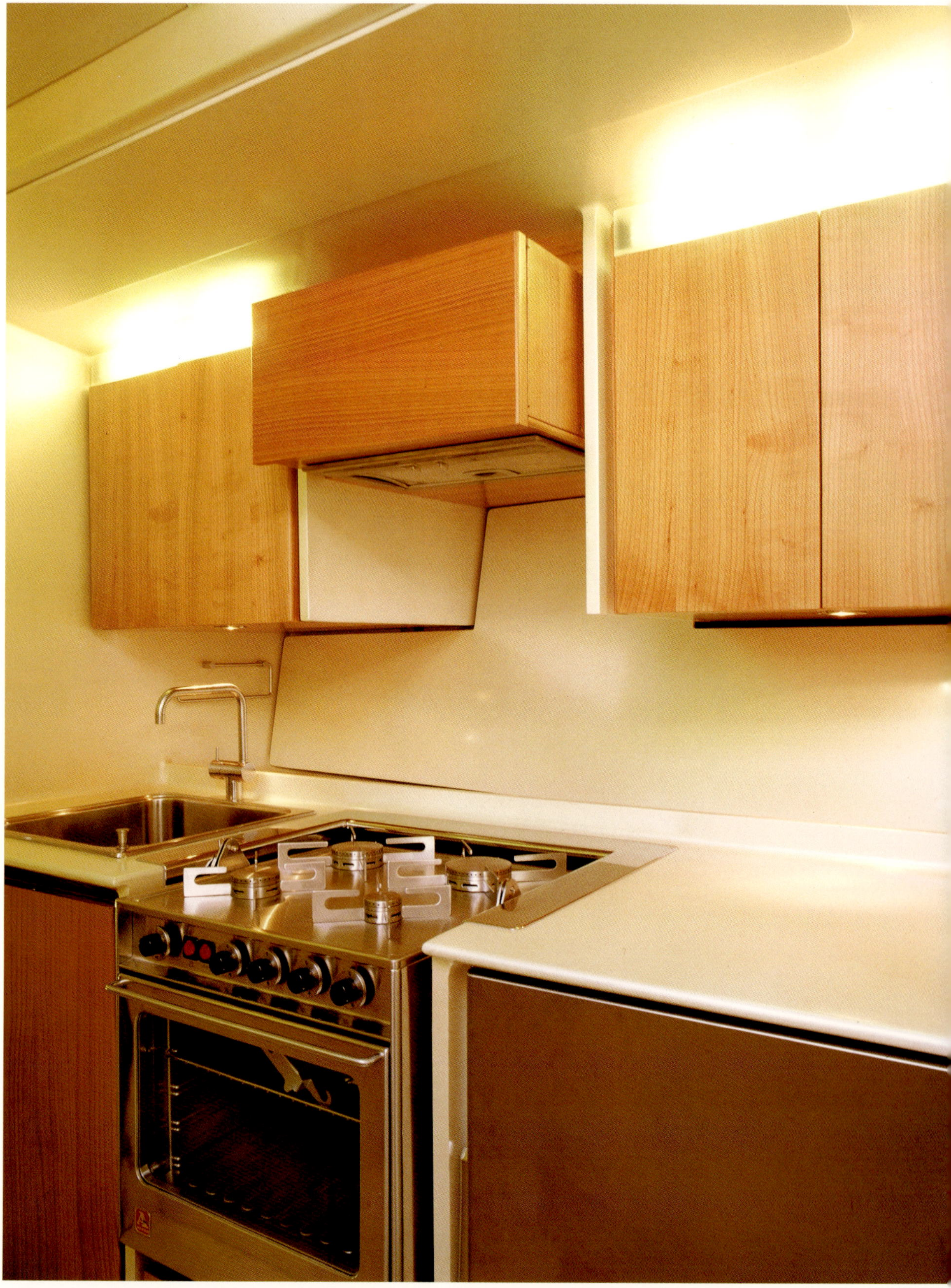

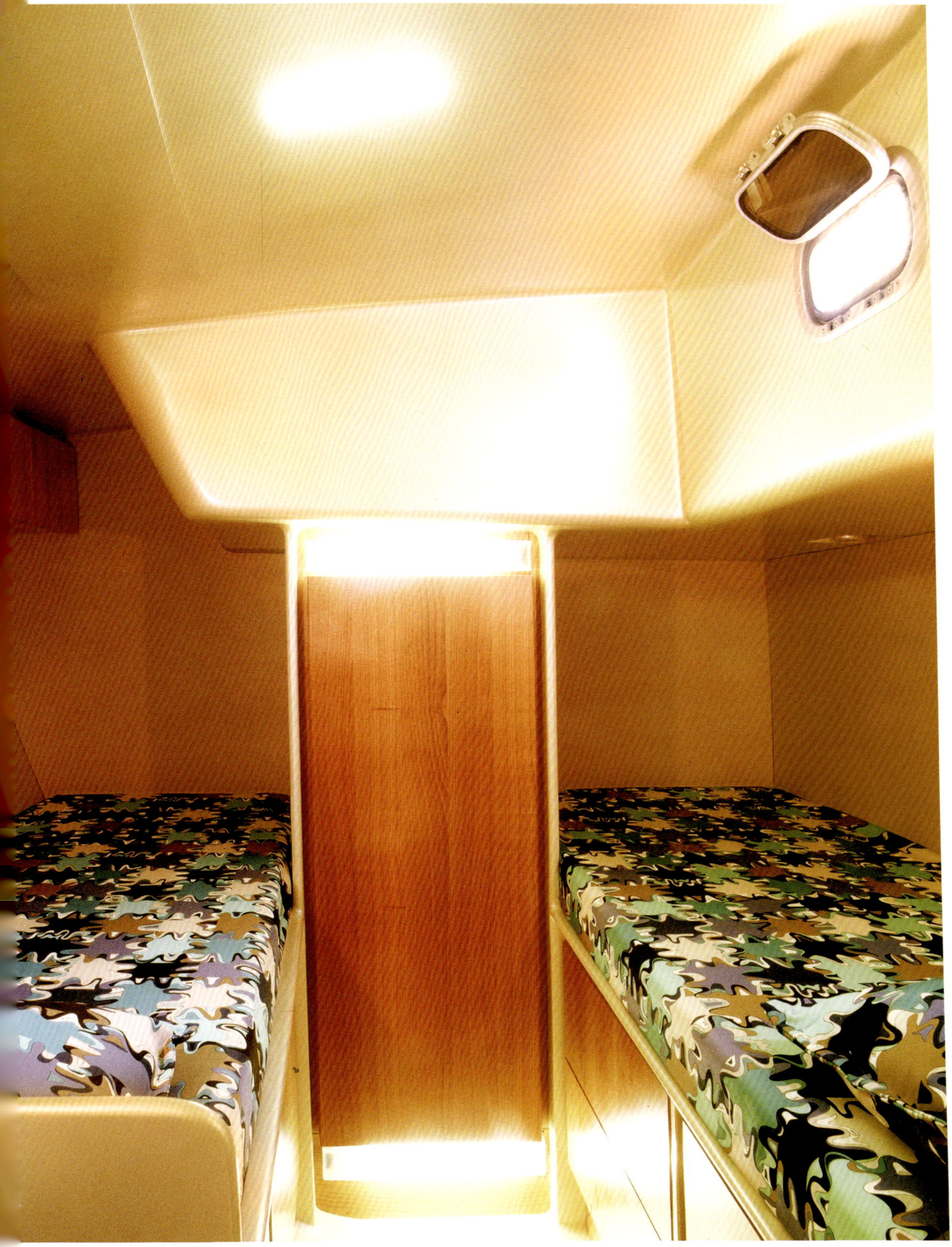

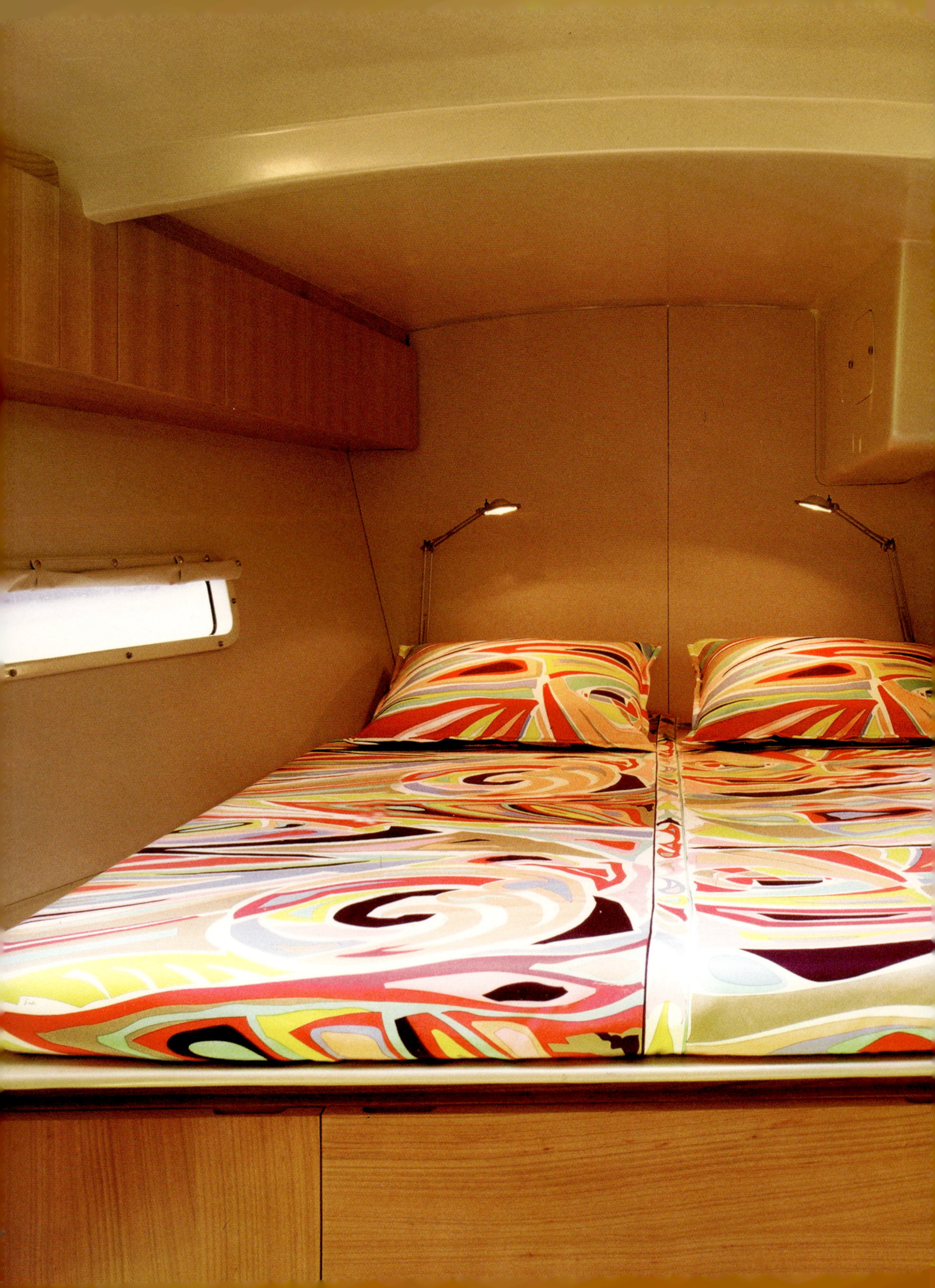

291

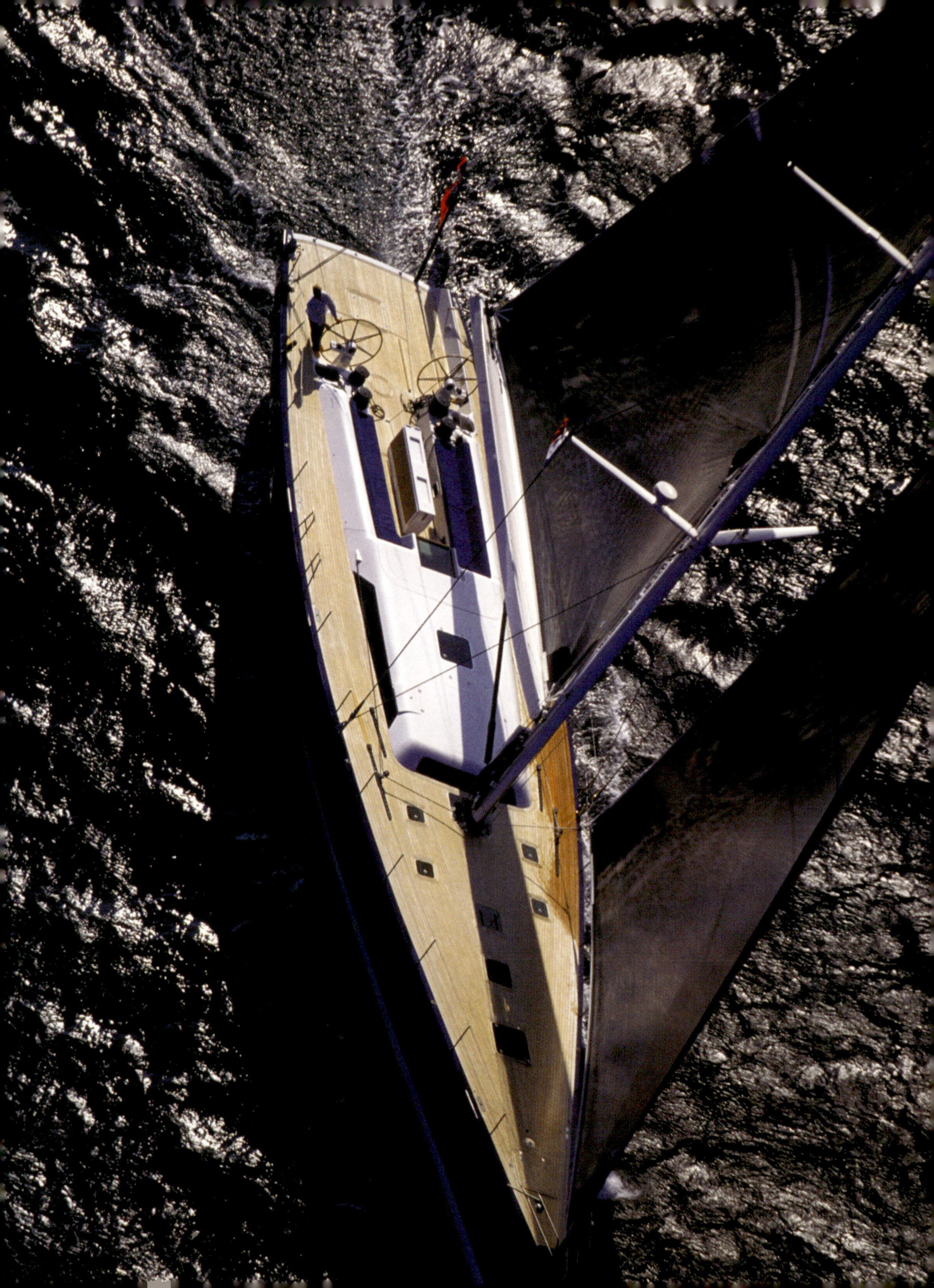

WALLY, GERMAN FRERS
MAGIC CARPET SQUARED | 2002
Wally

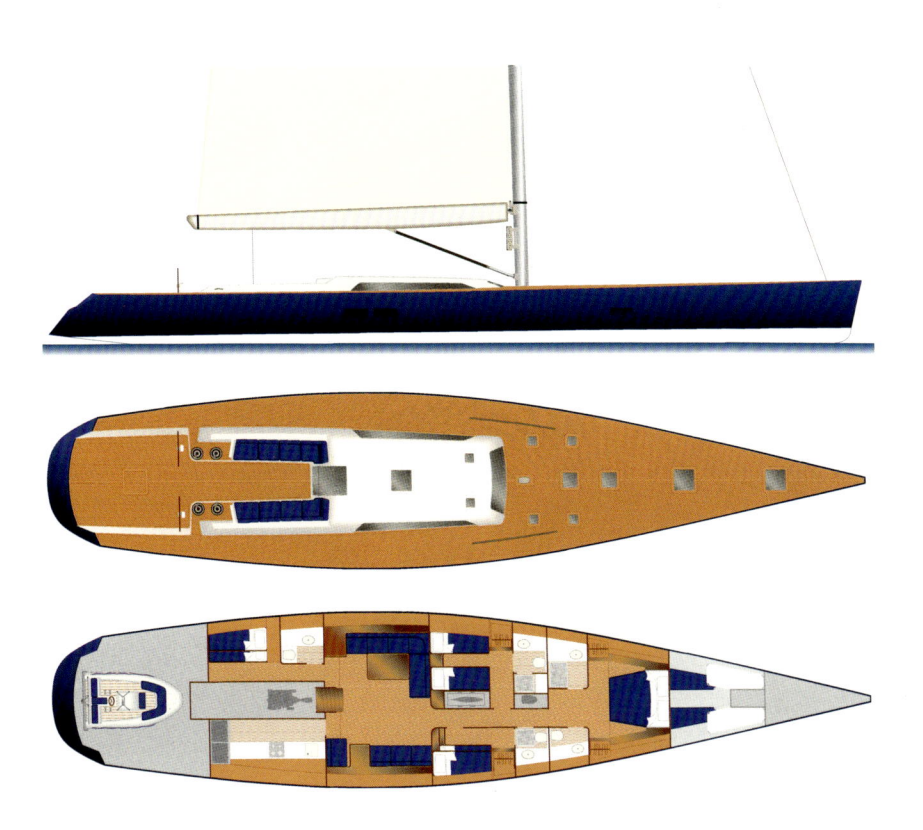

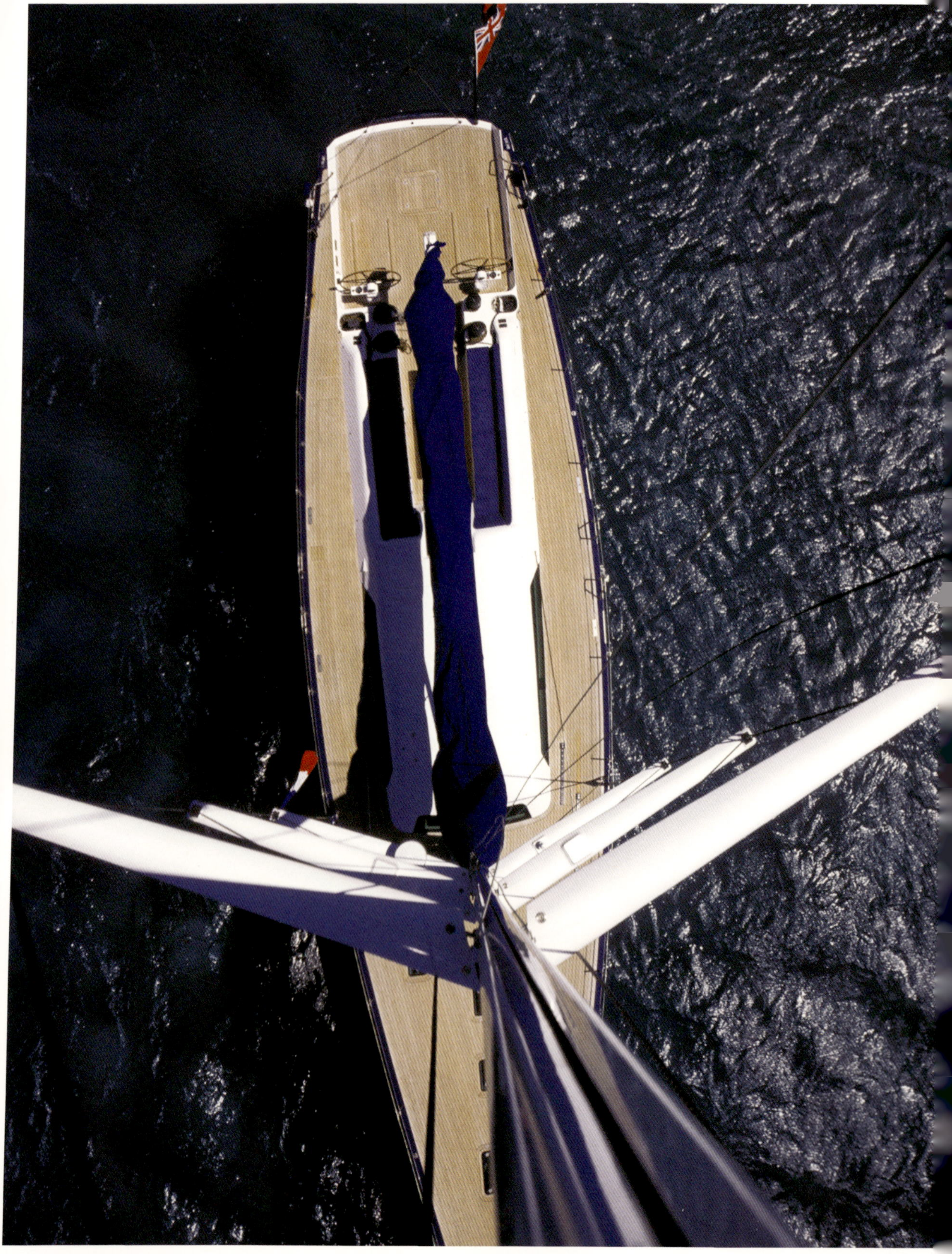

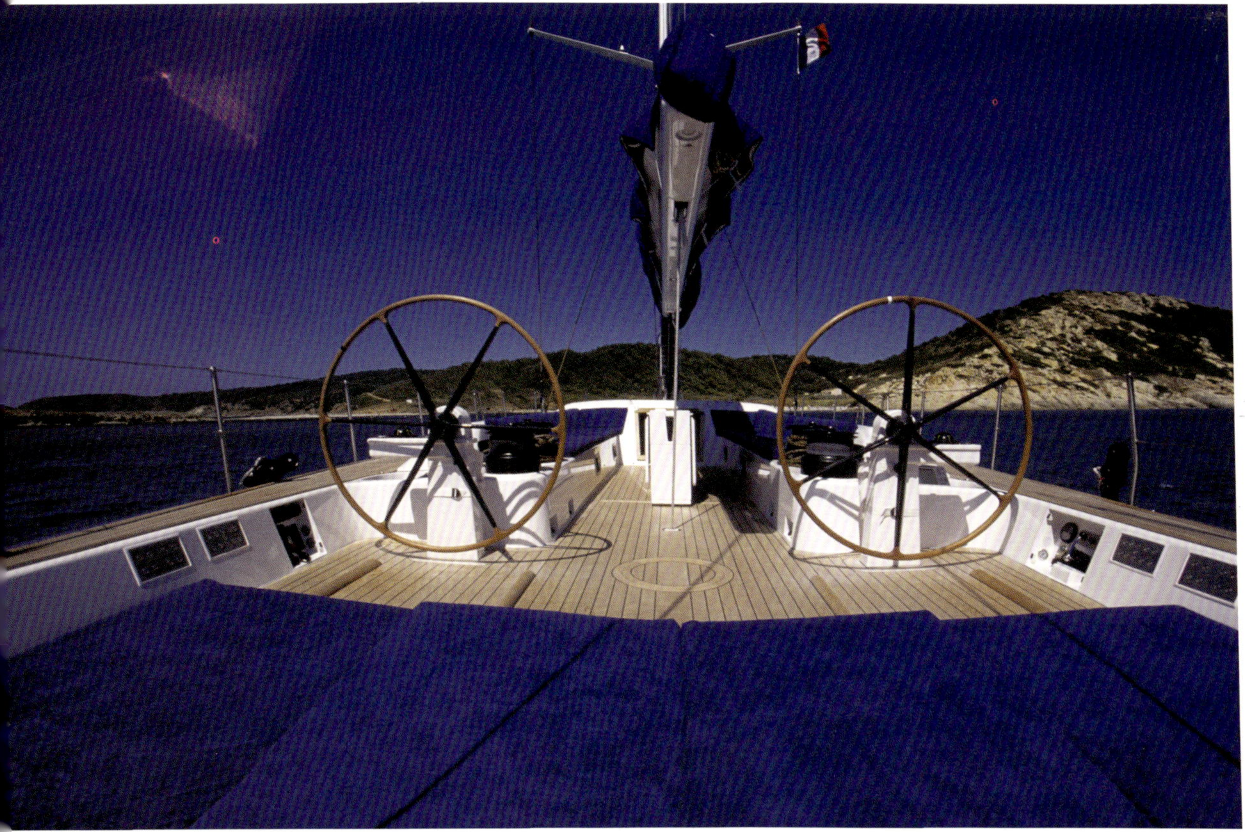

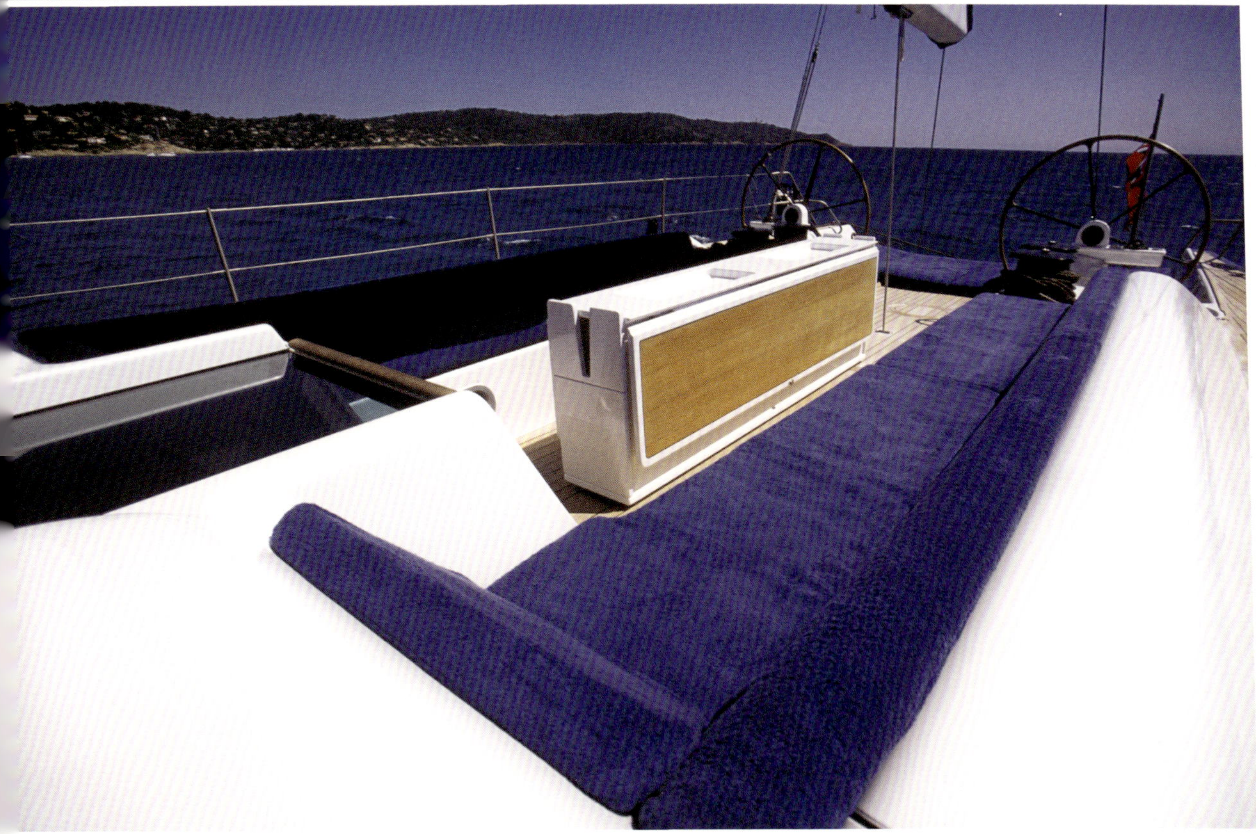

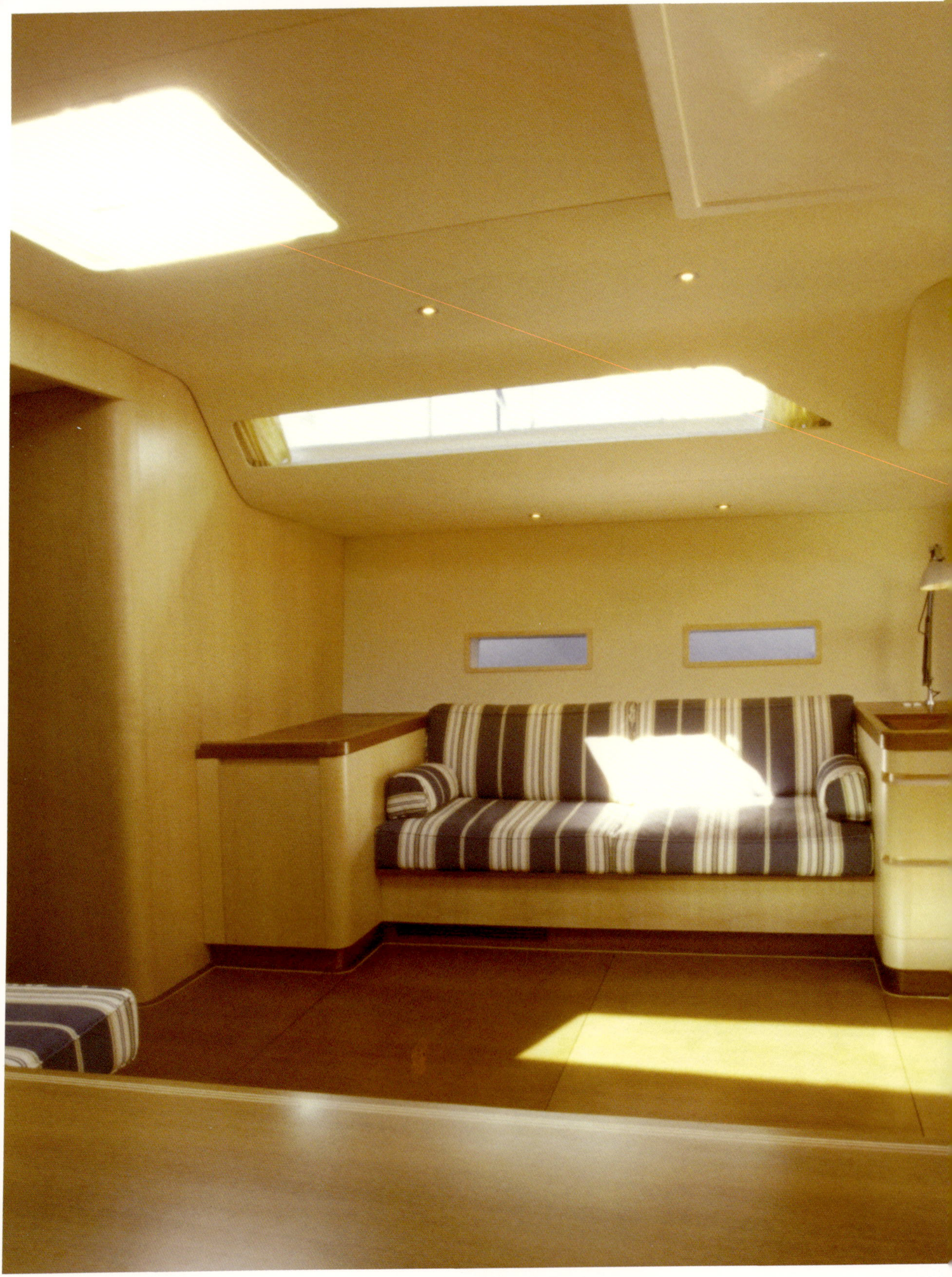

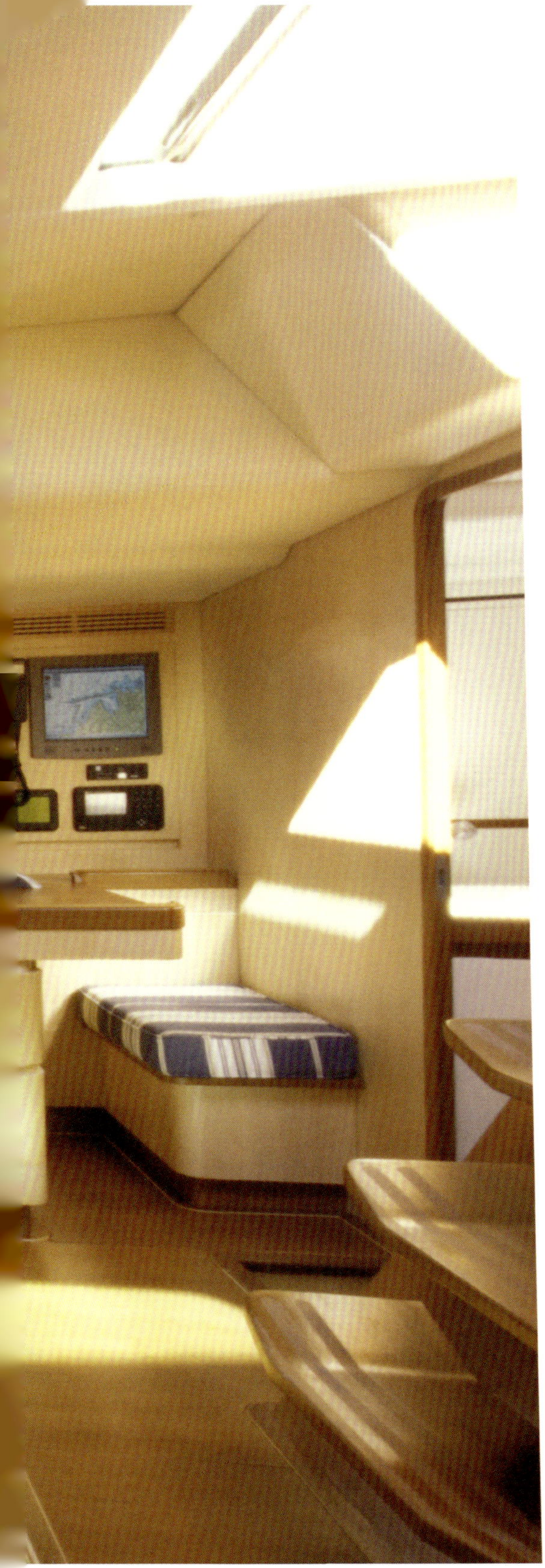

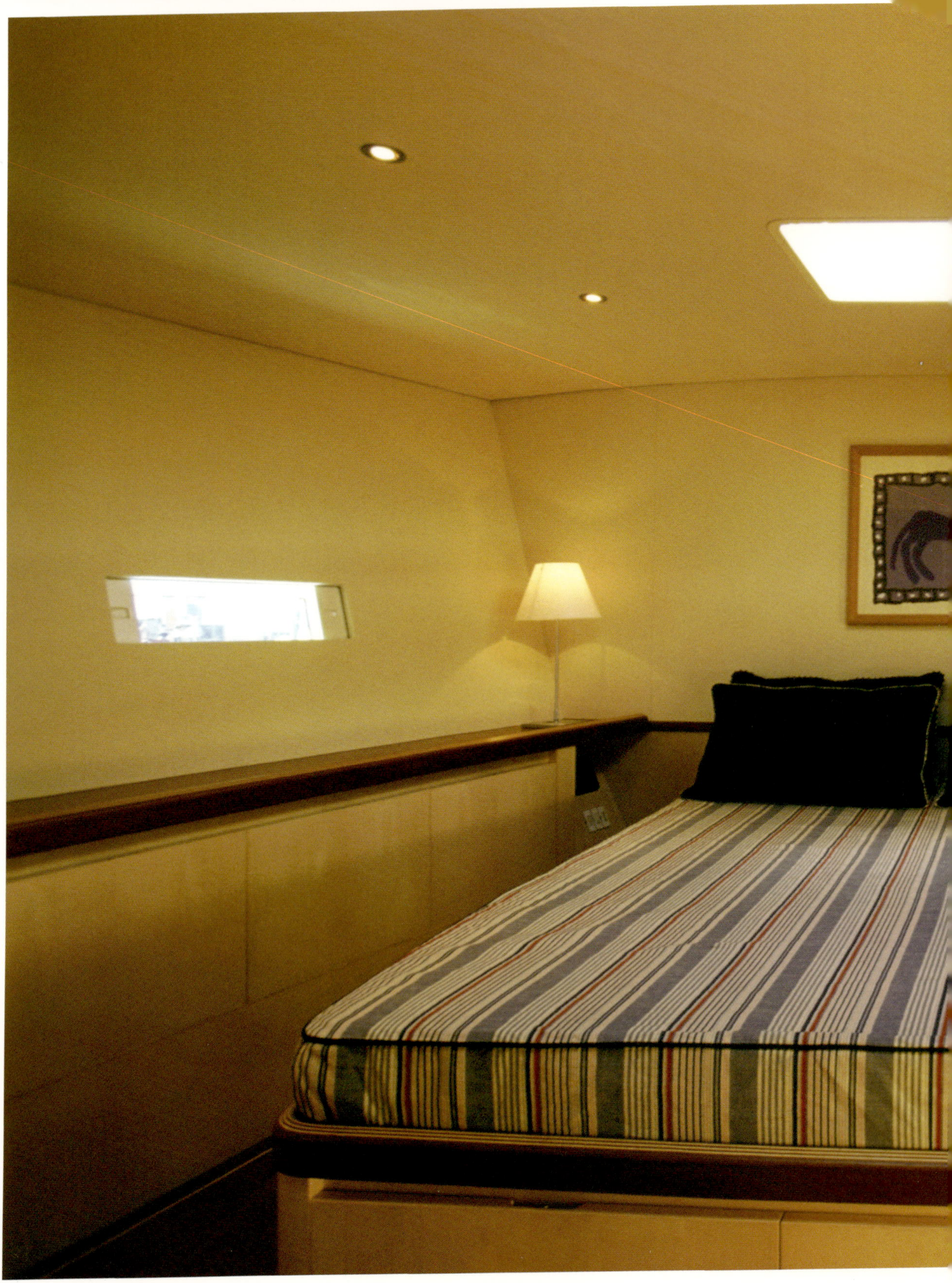

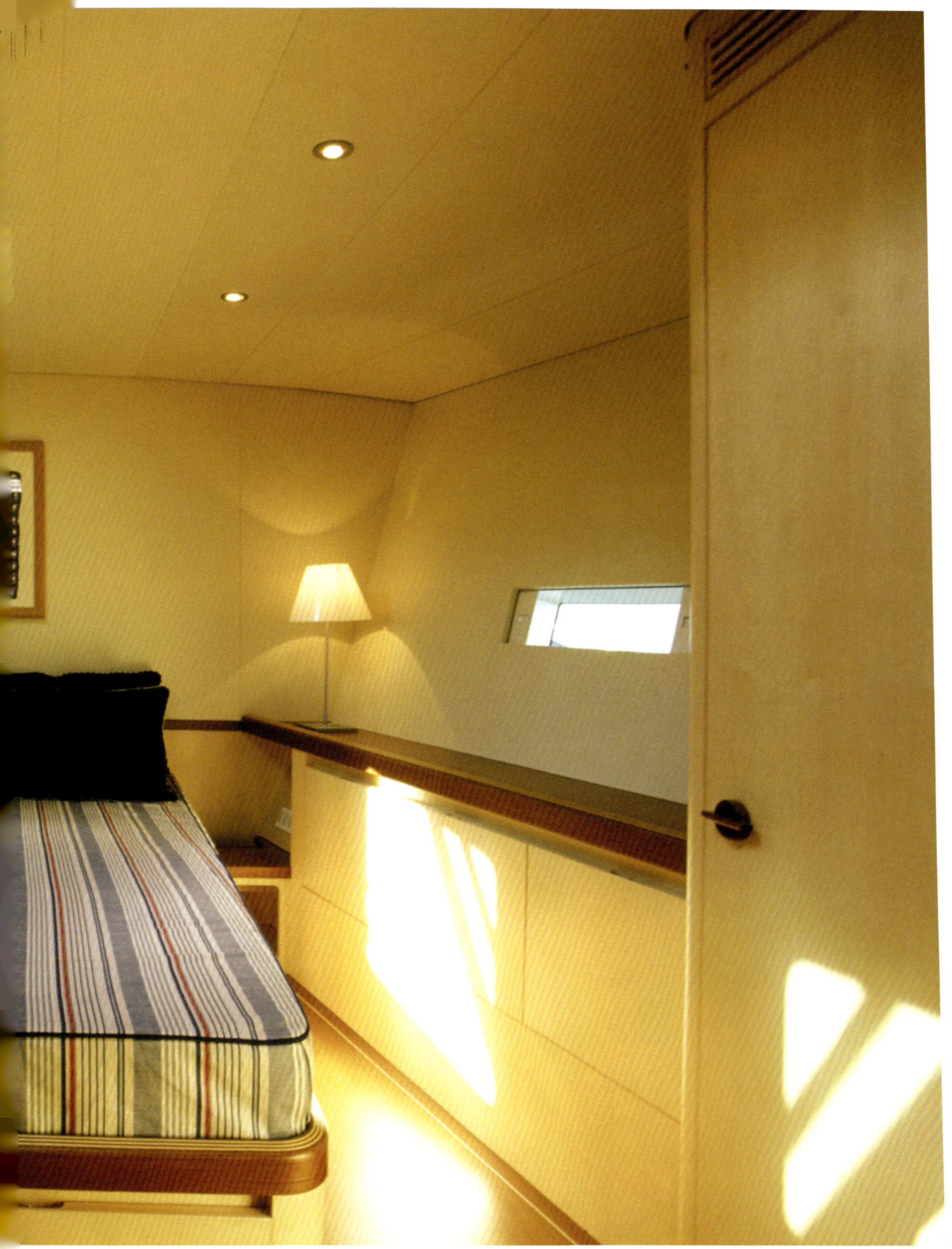

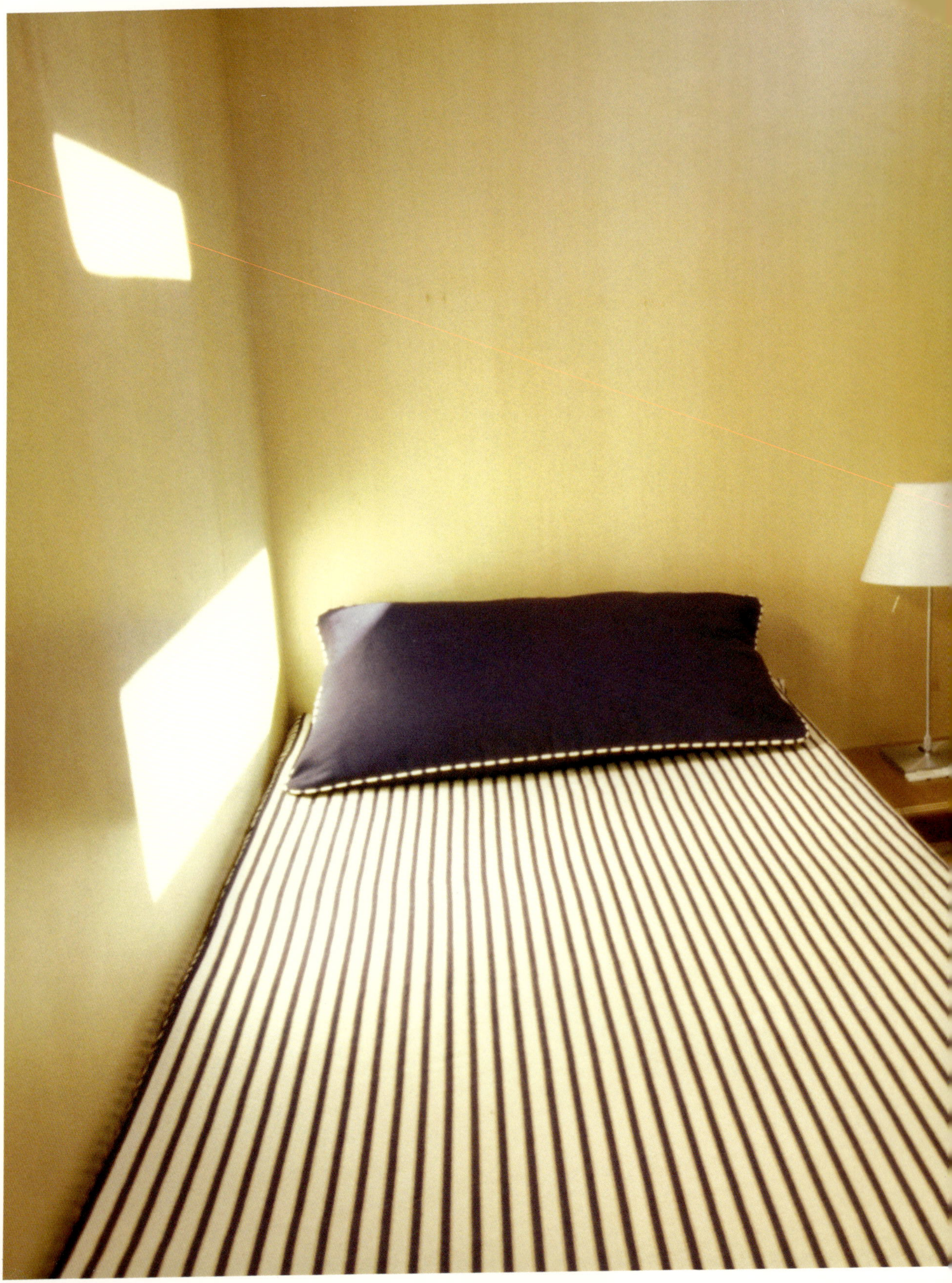

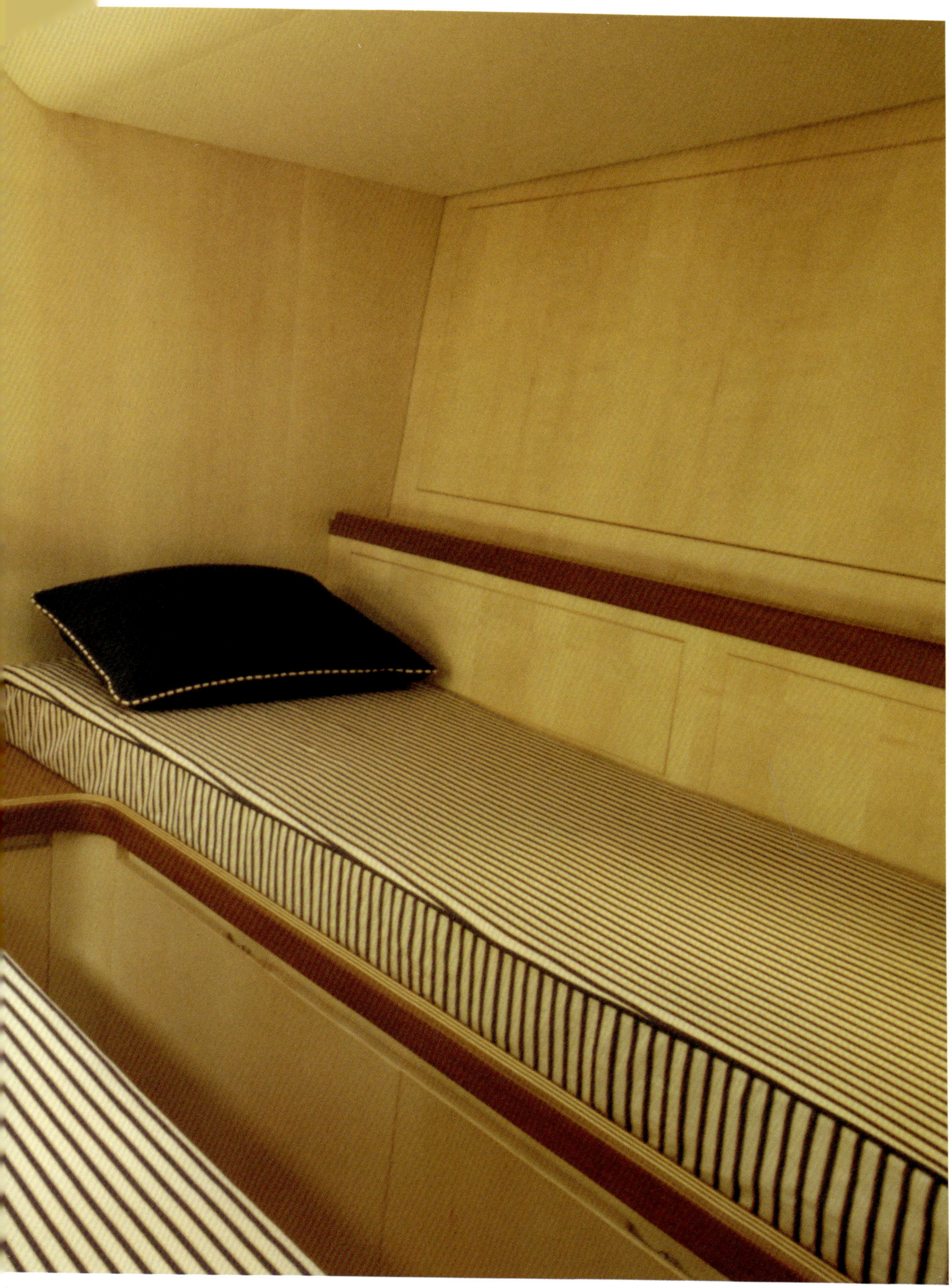

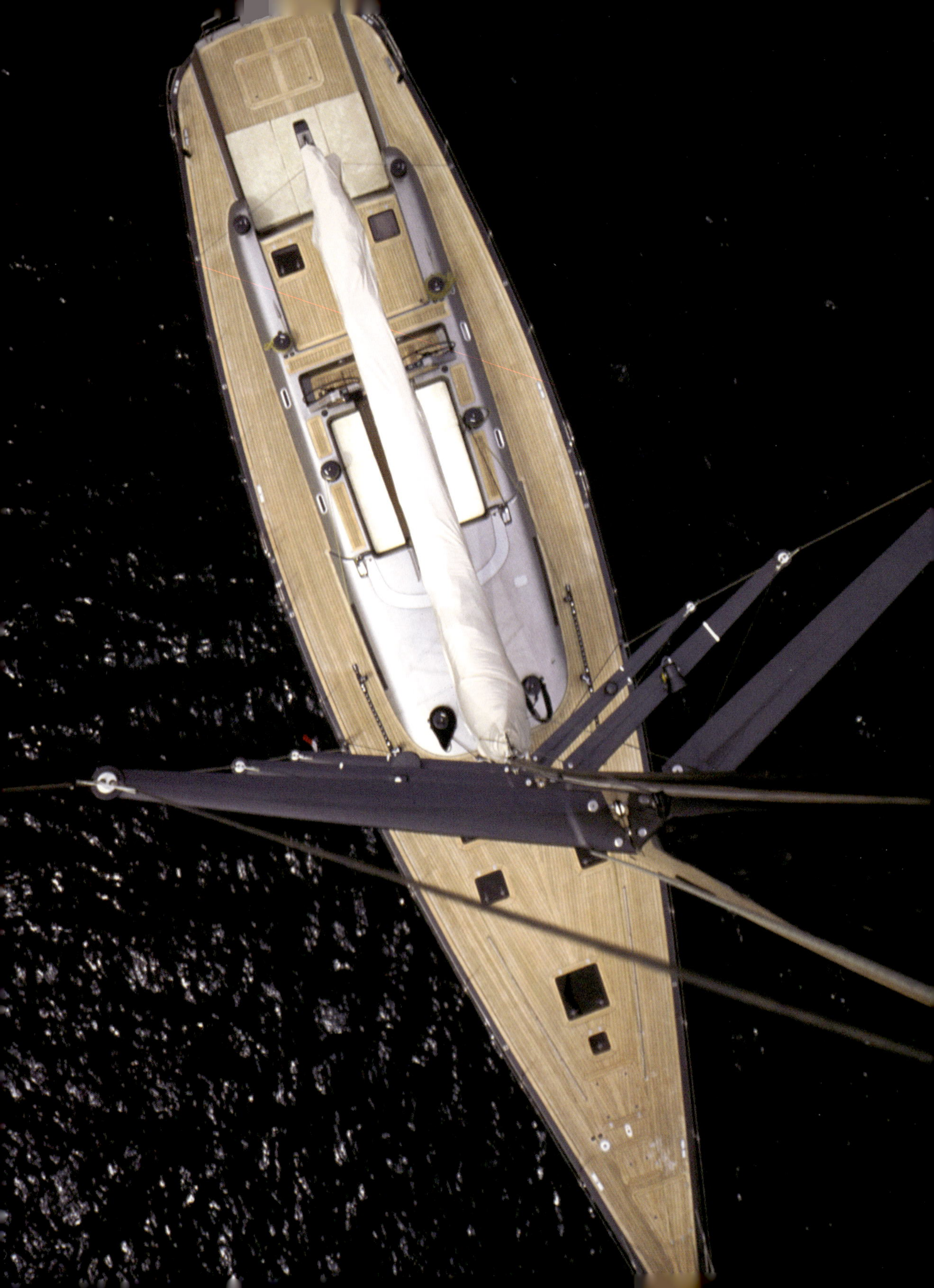

WALLY, GERMAN FRERS
Y3K | 2003
Wally

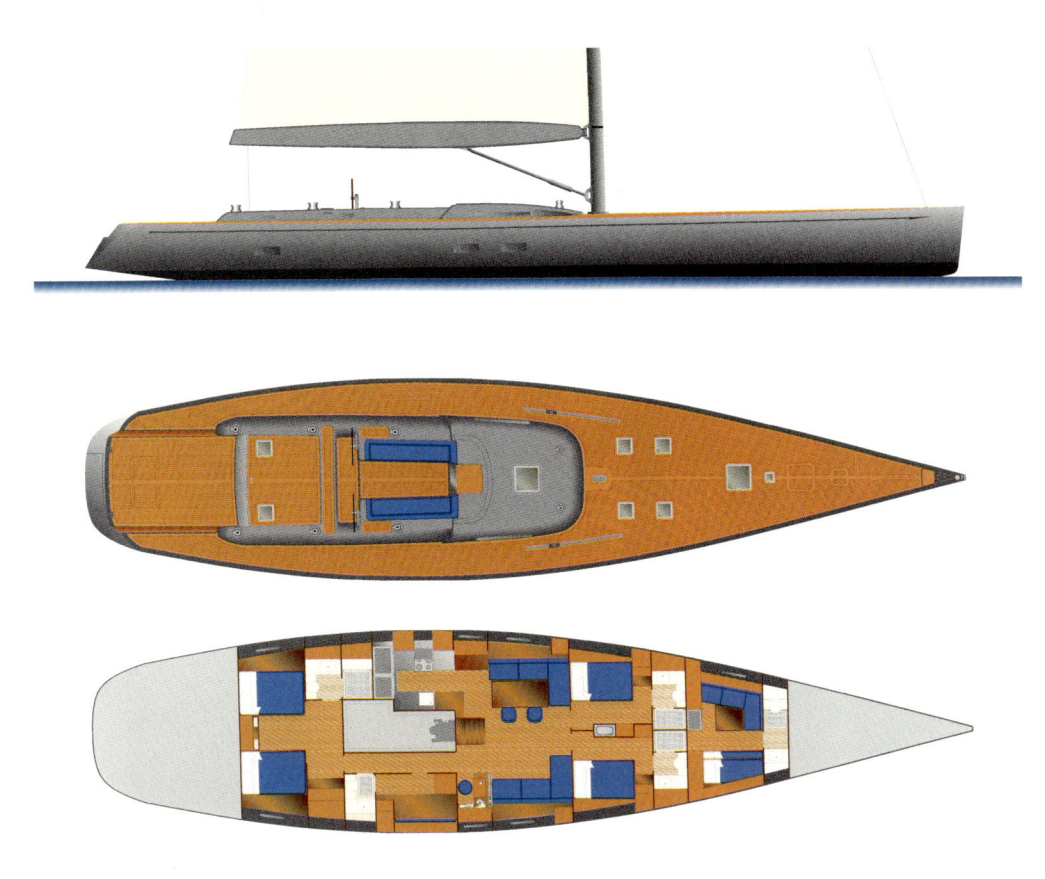

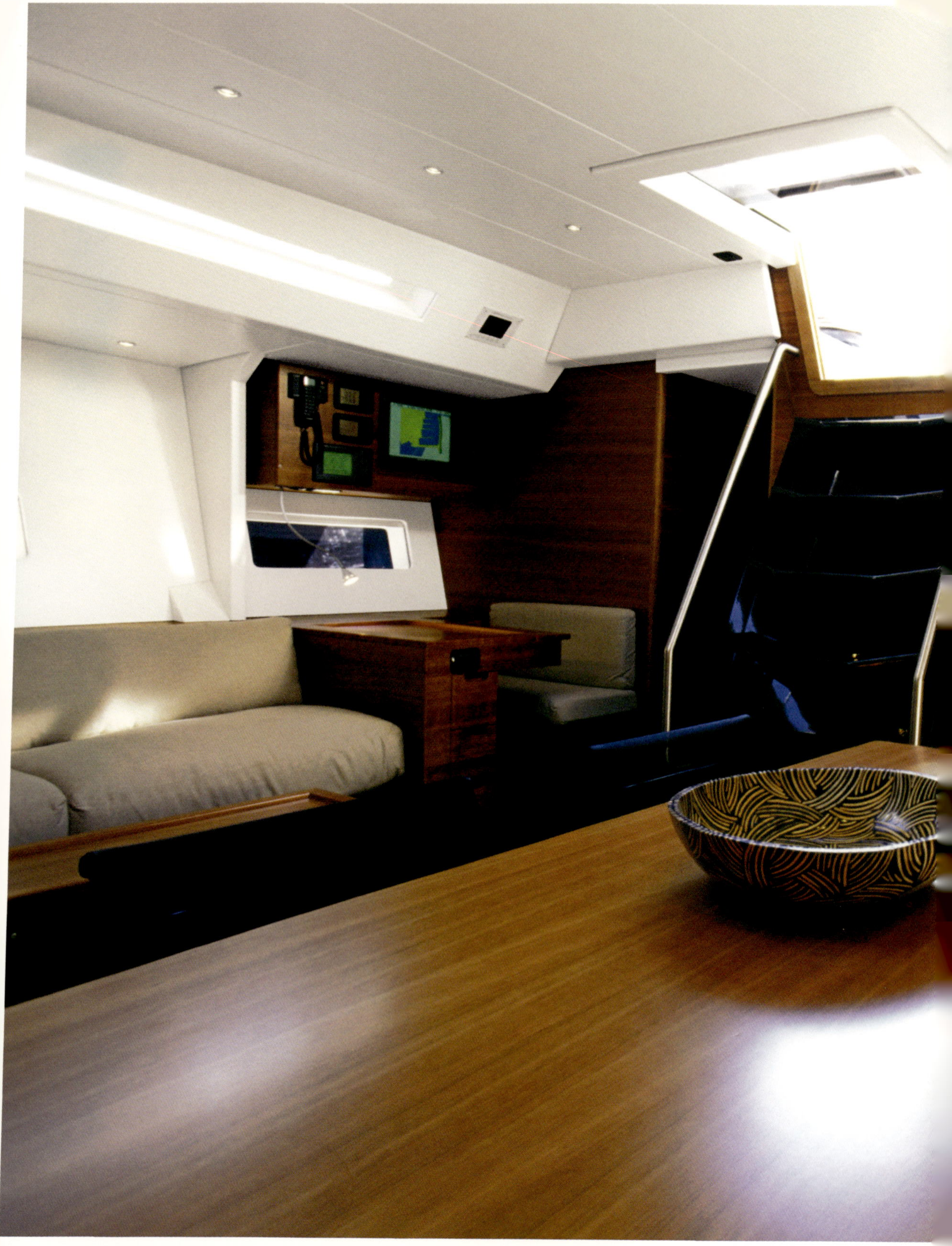

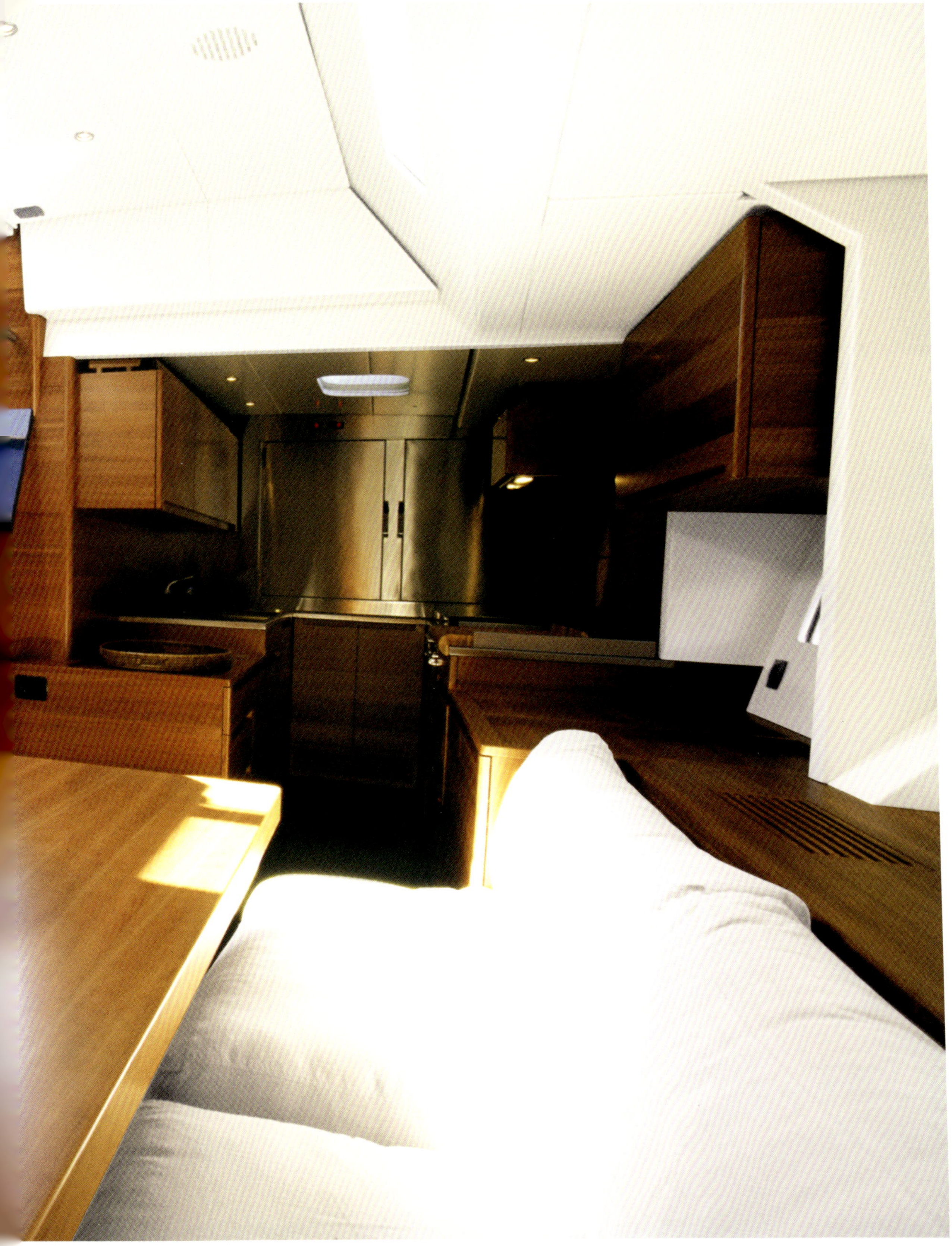

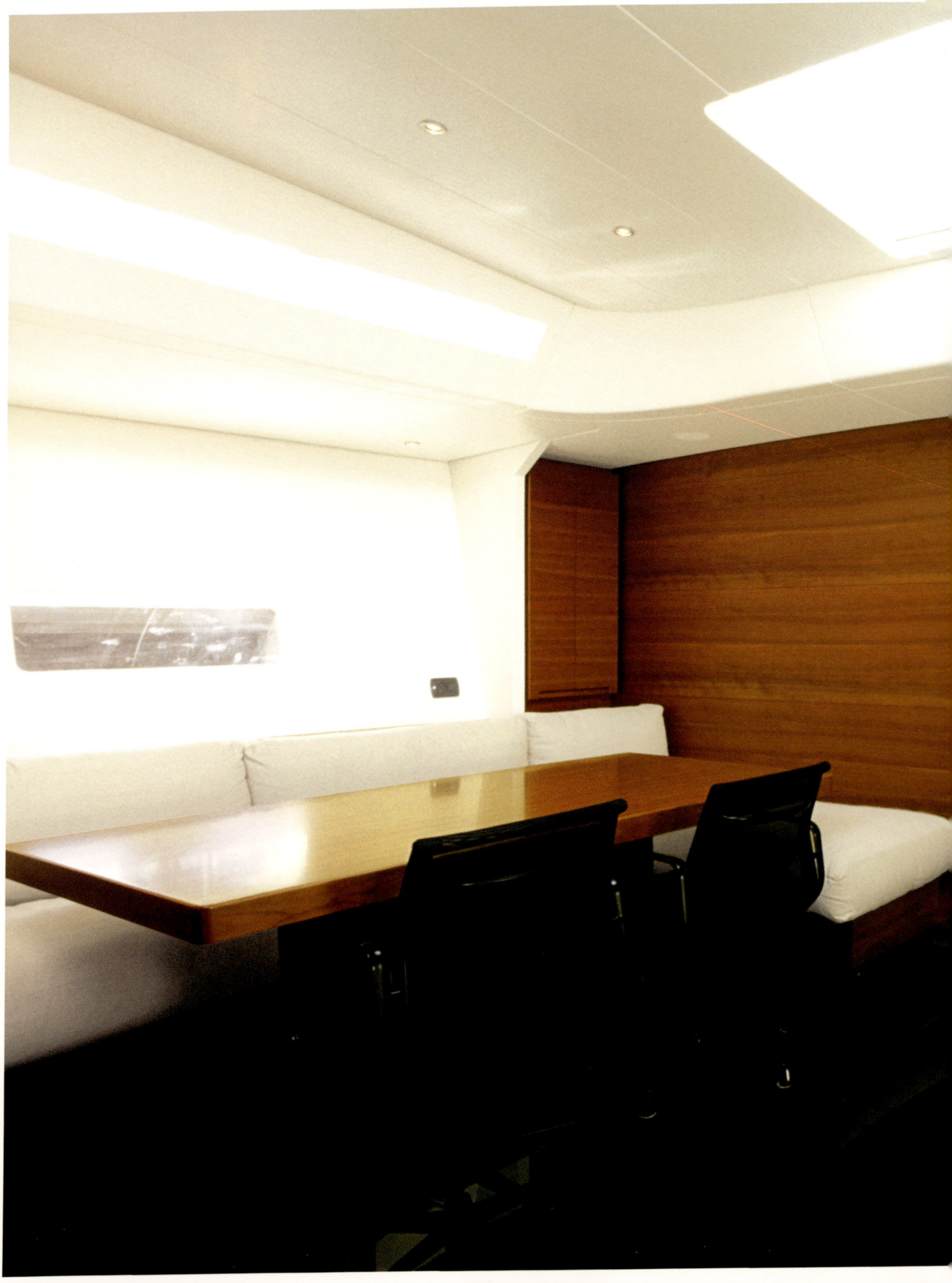

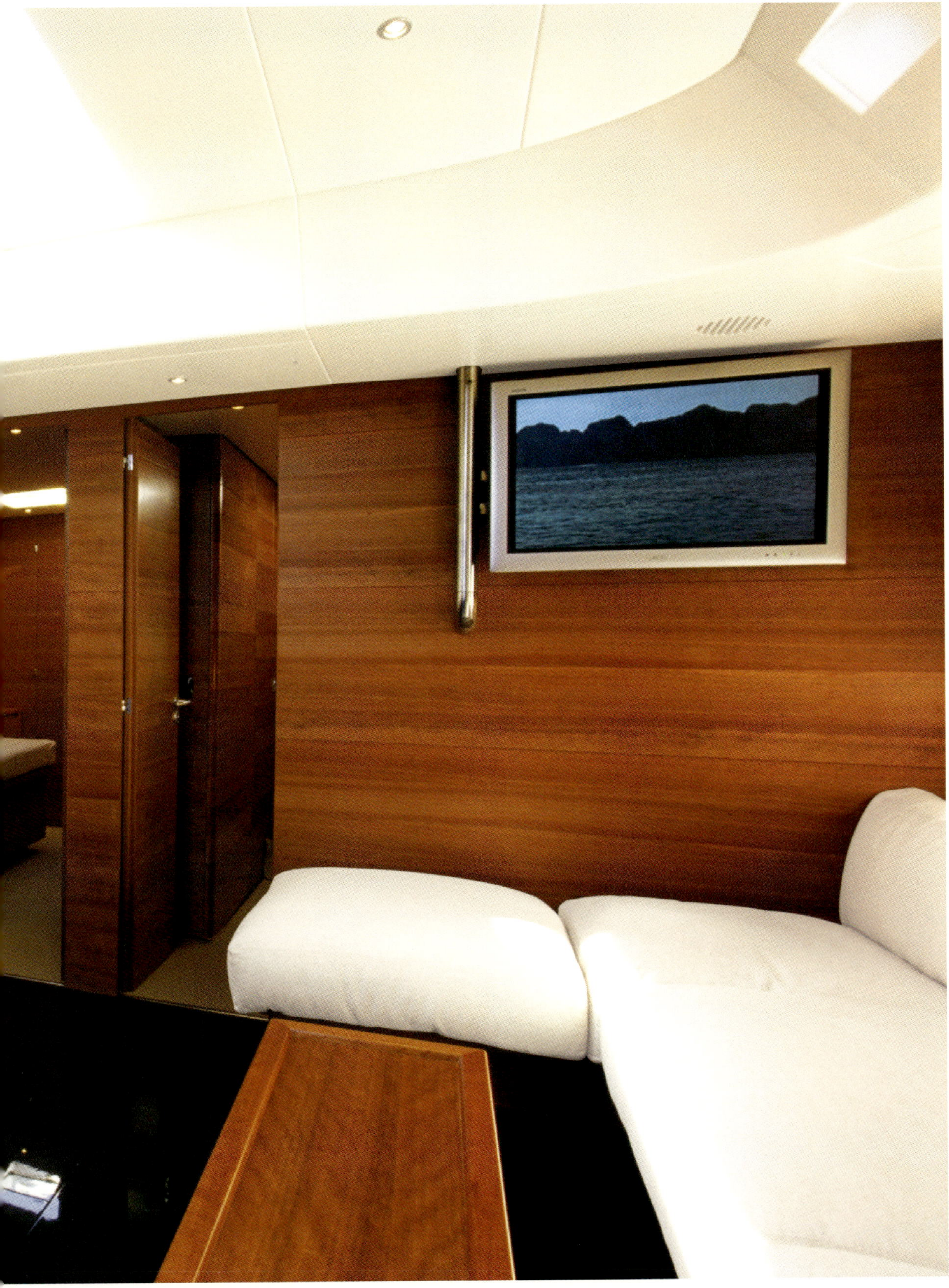

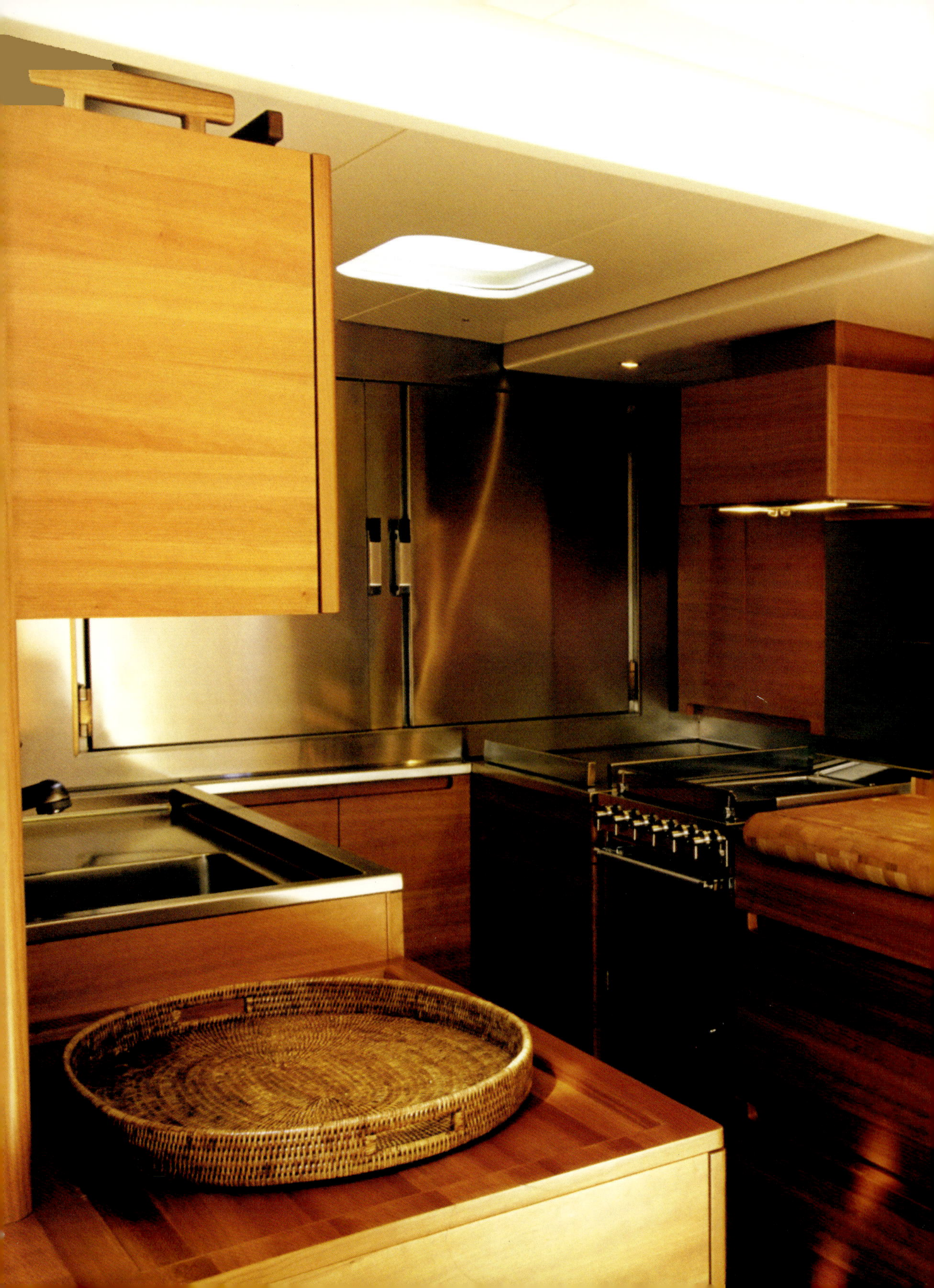

309

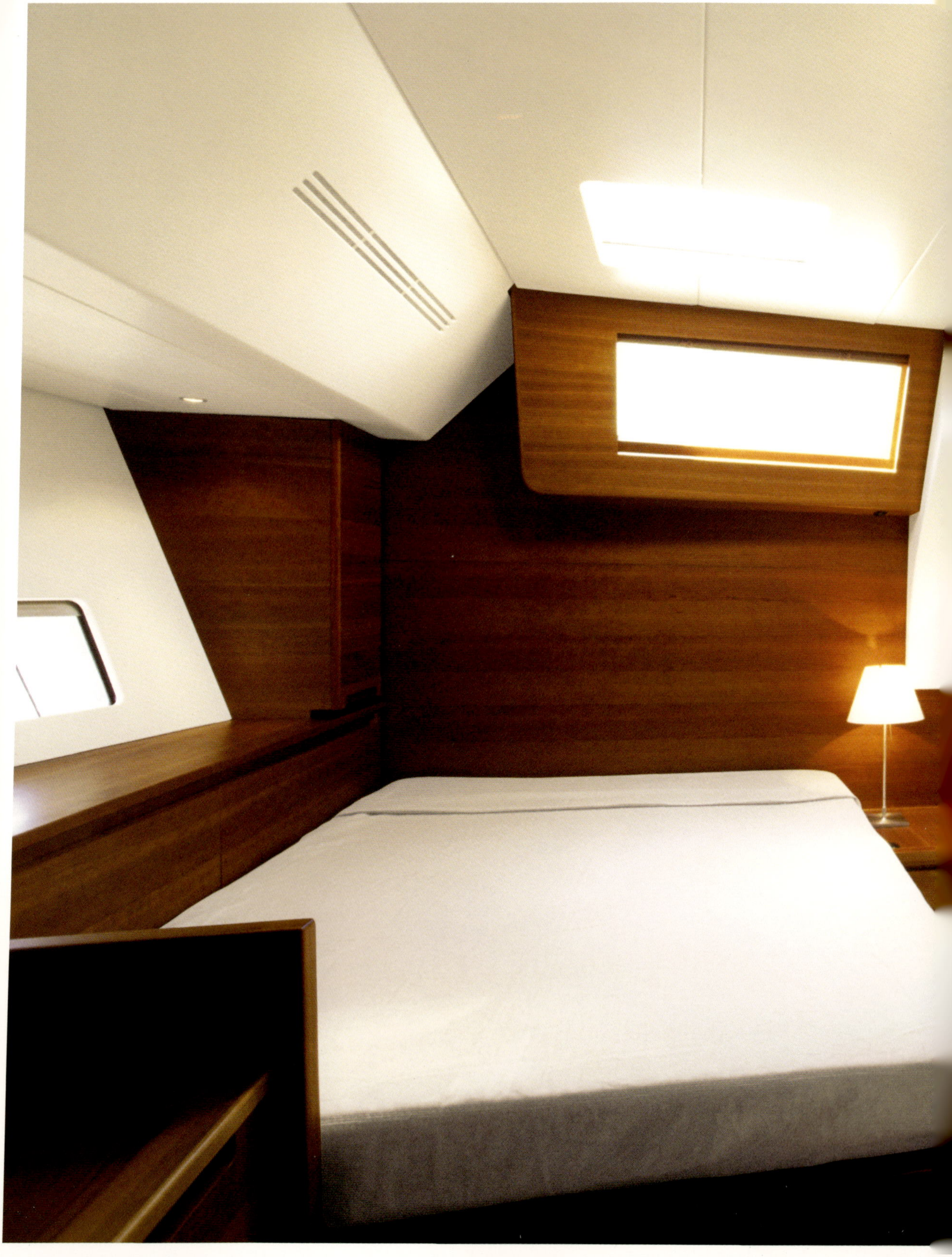

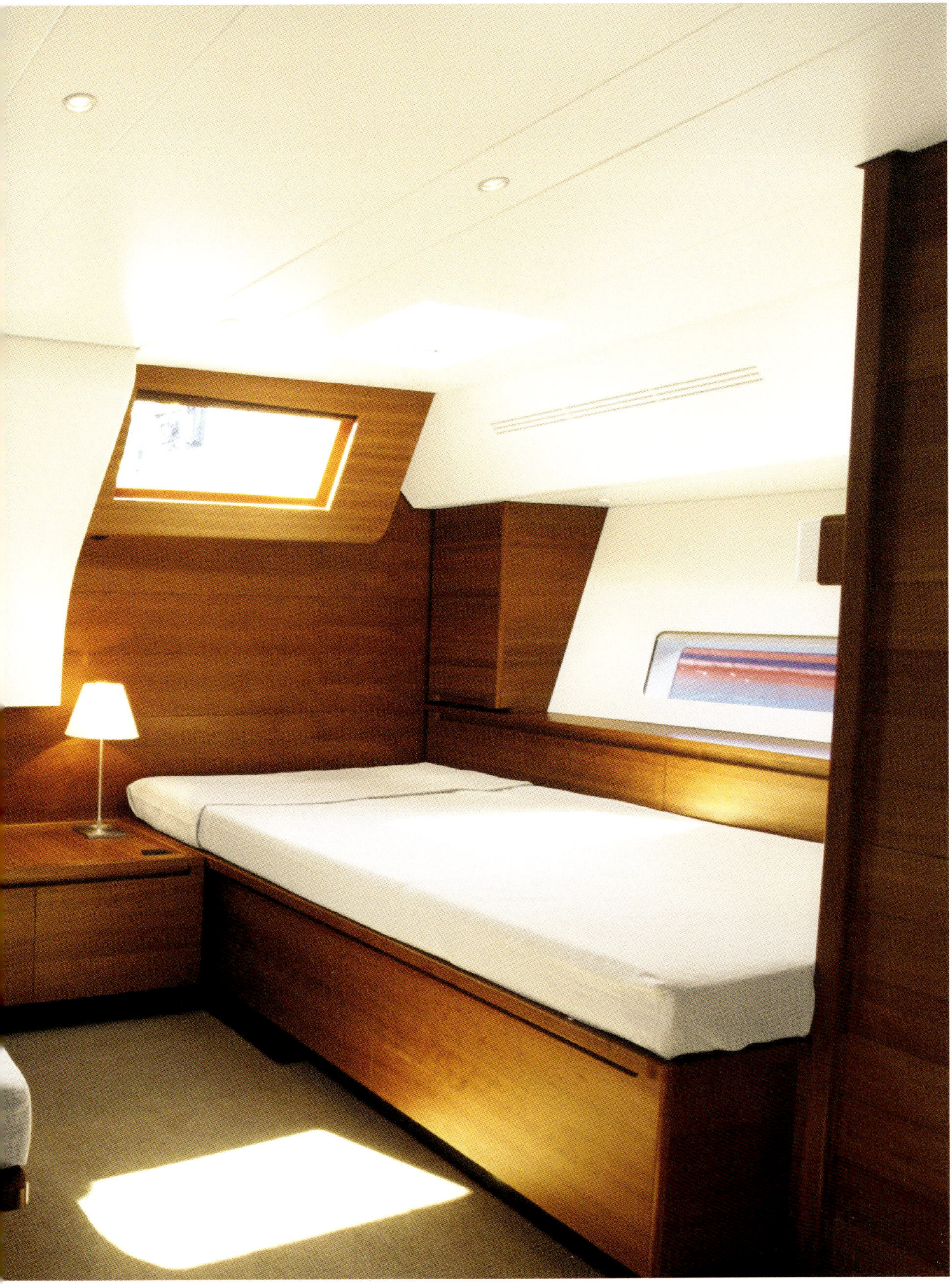

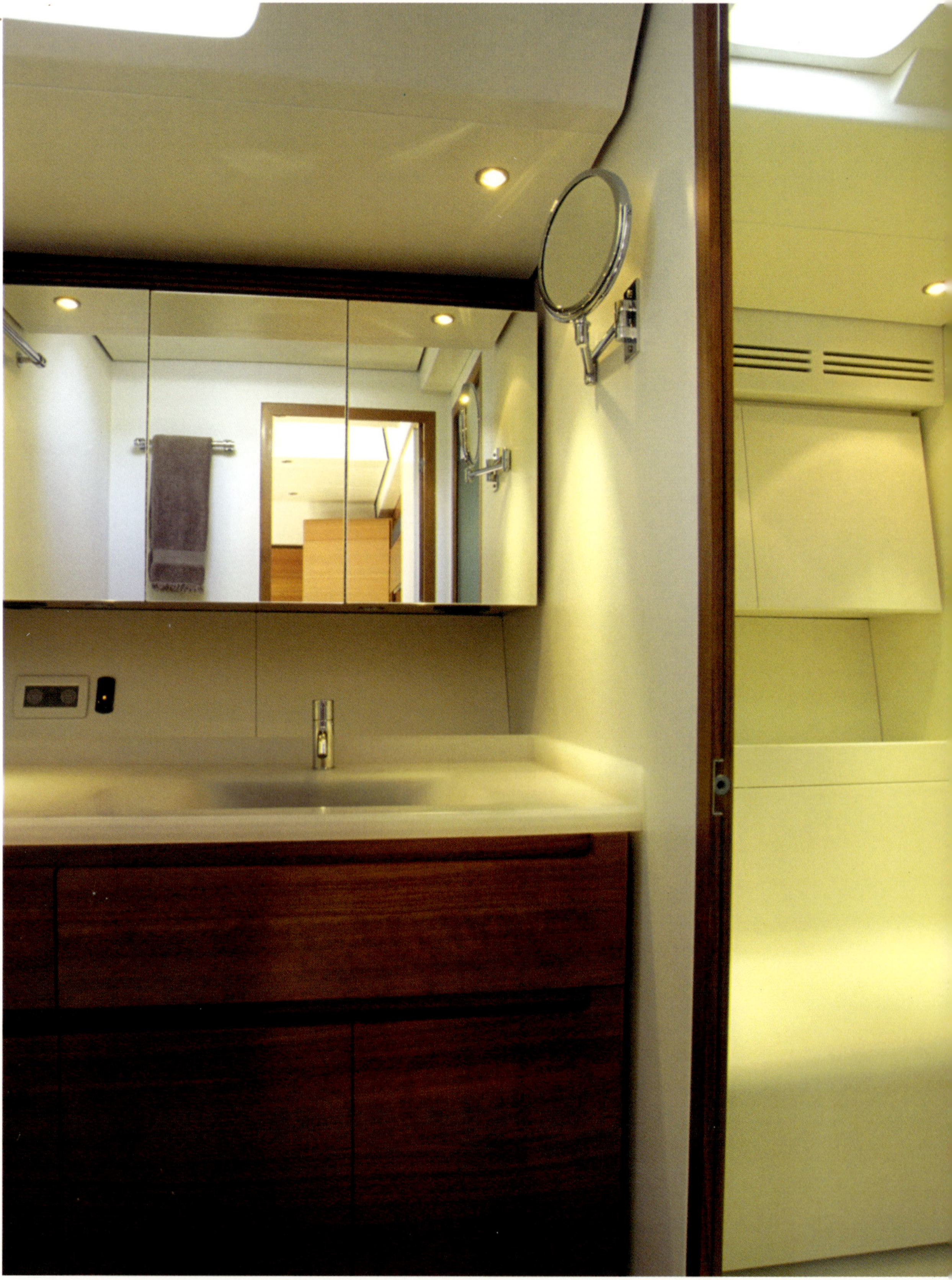

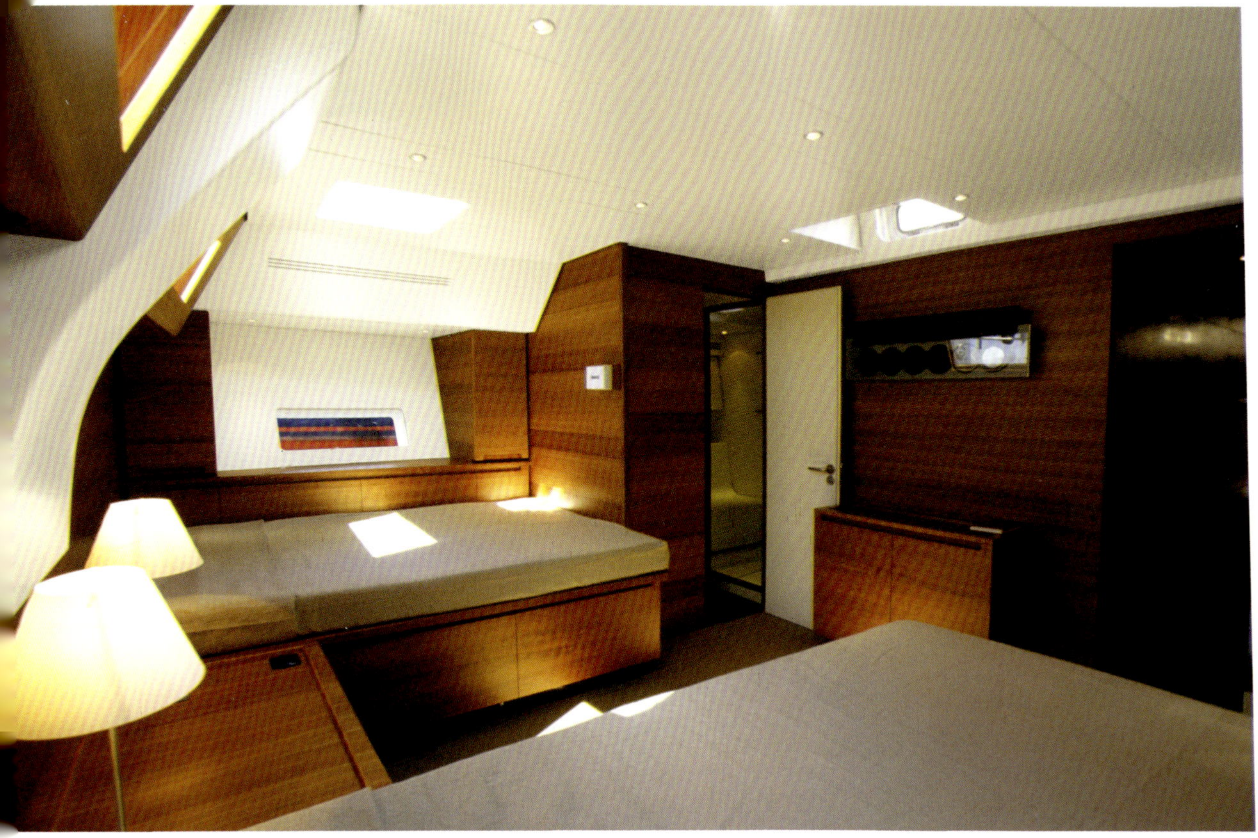

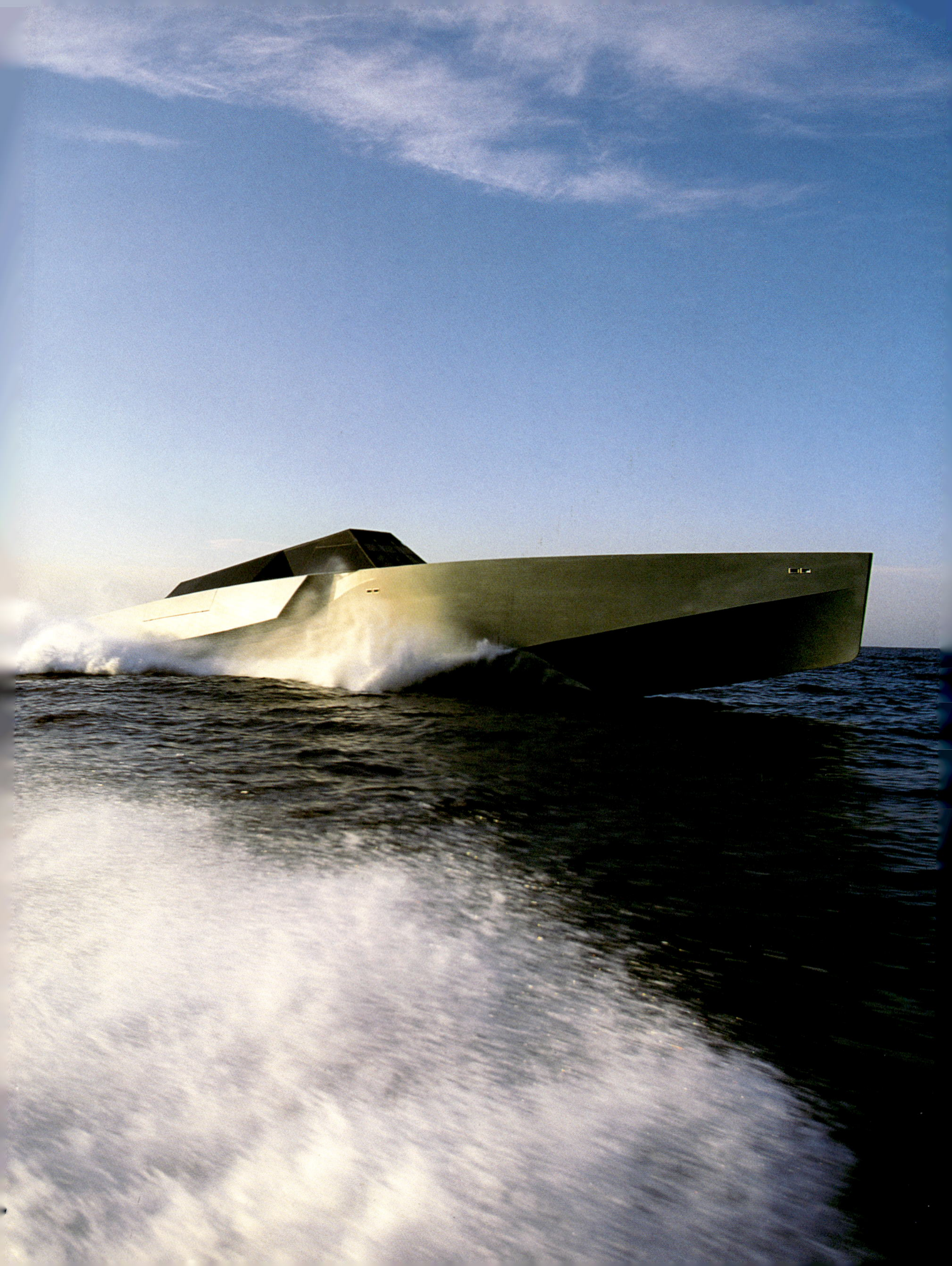

WALLY, LAZZARINI PICKERING ARCHITETTI, INTERMARINE
WALLYPOWER | 2002
Rodriquez Intermarine
Wally

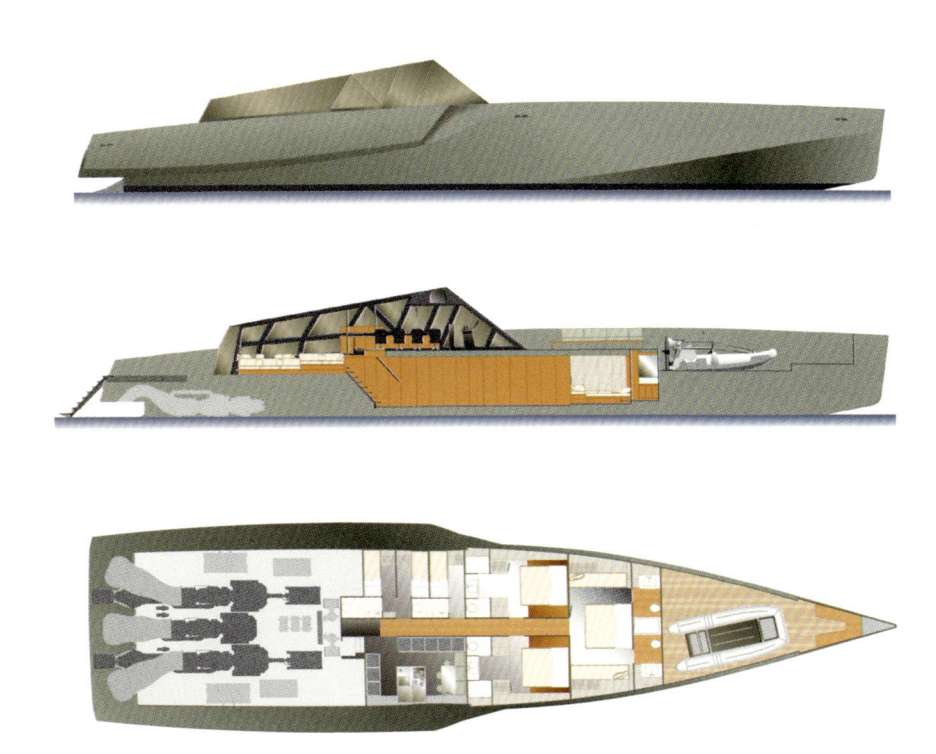

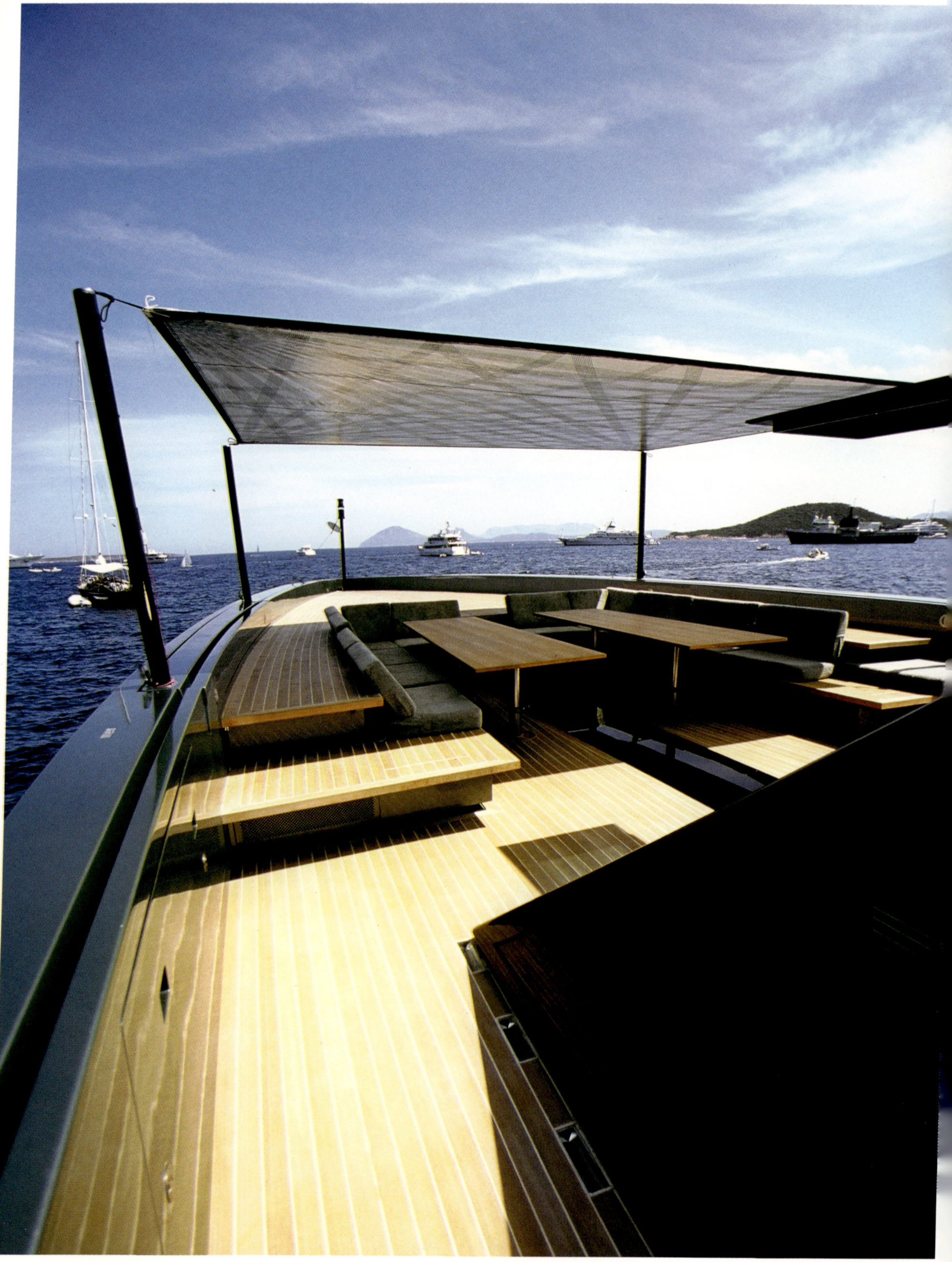

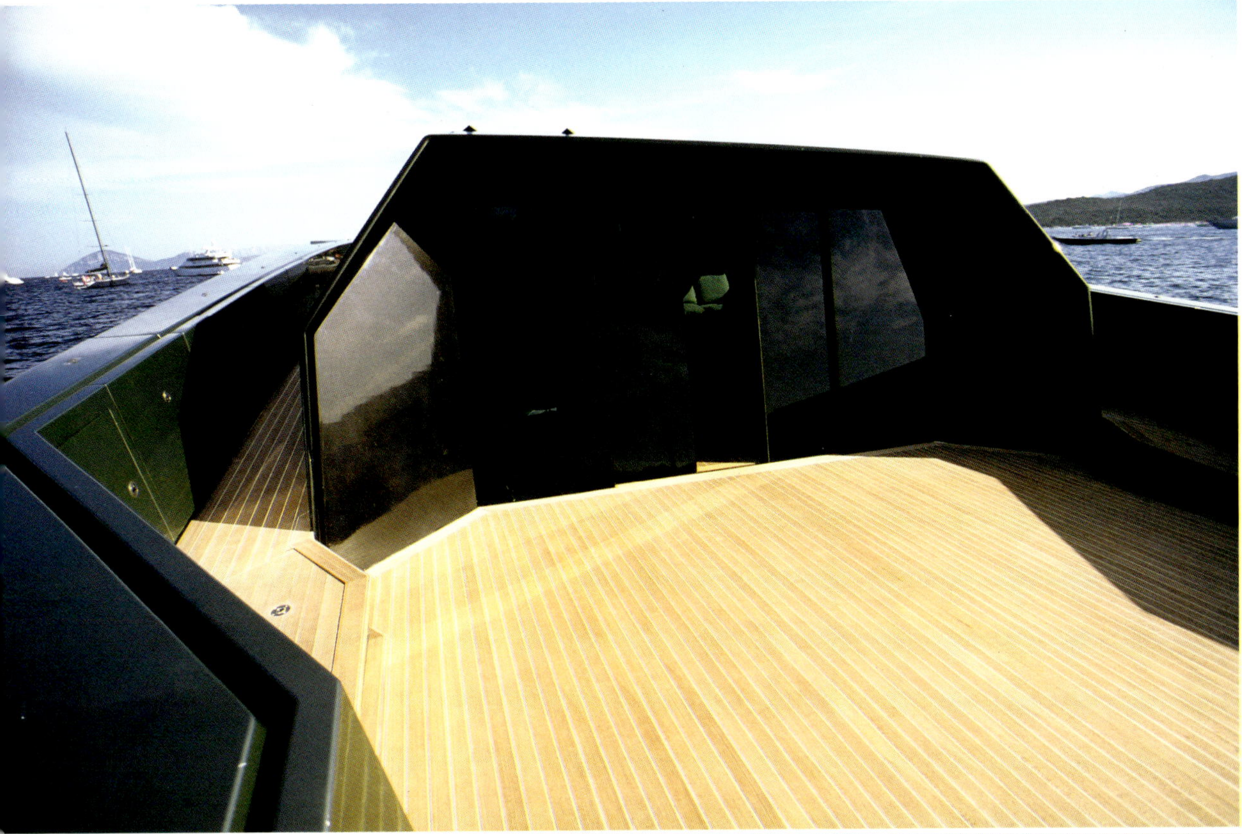

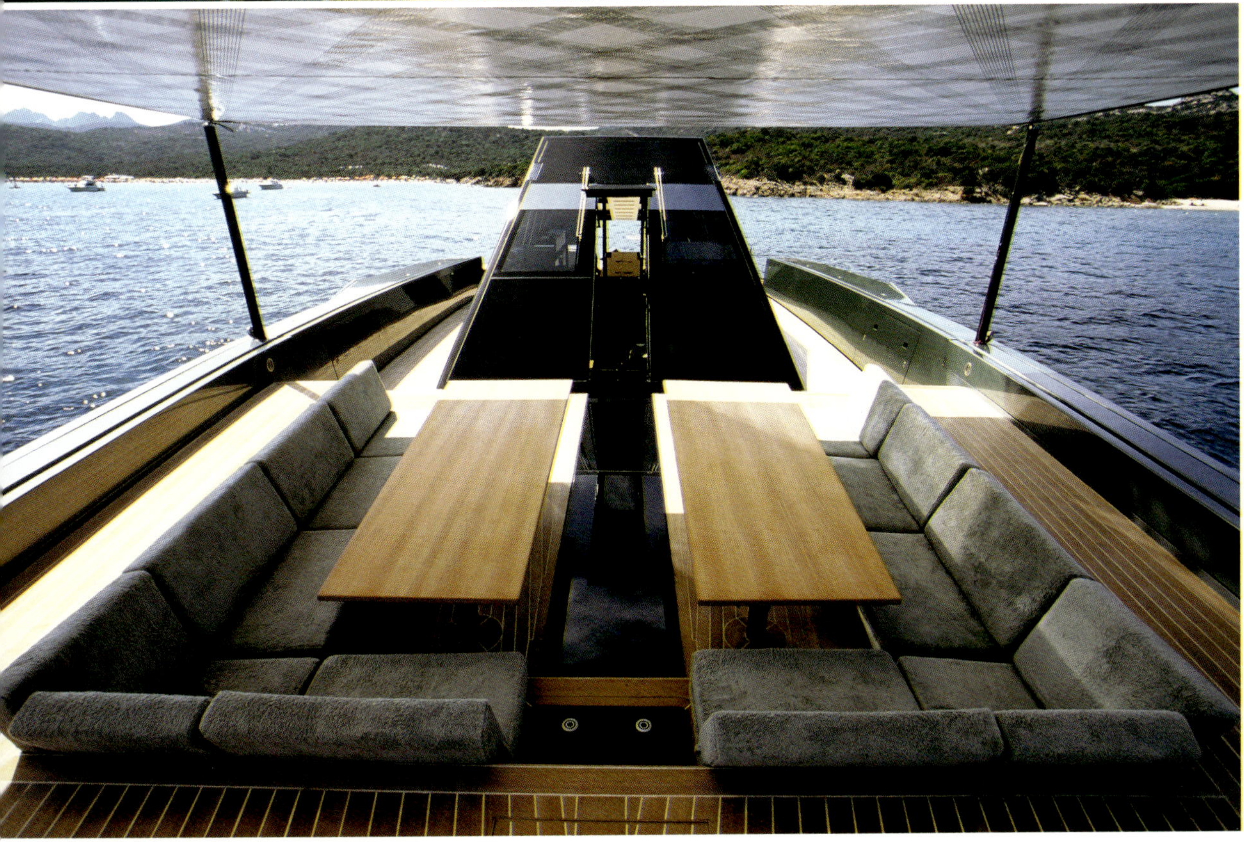

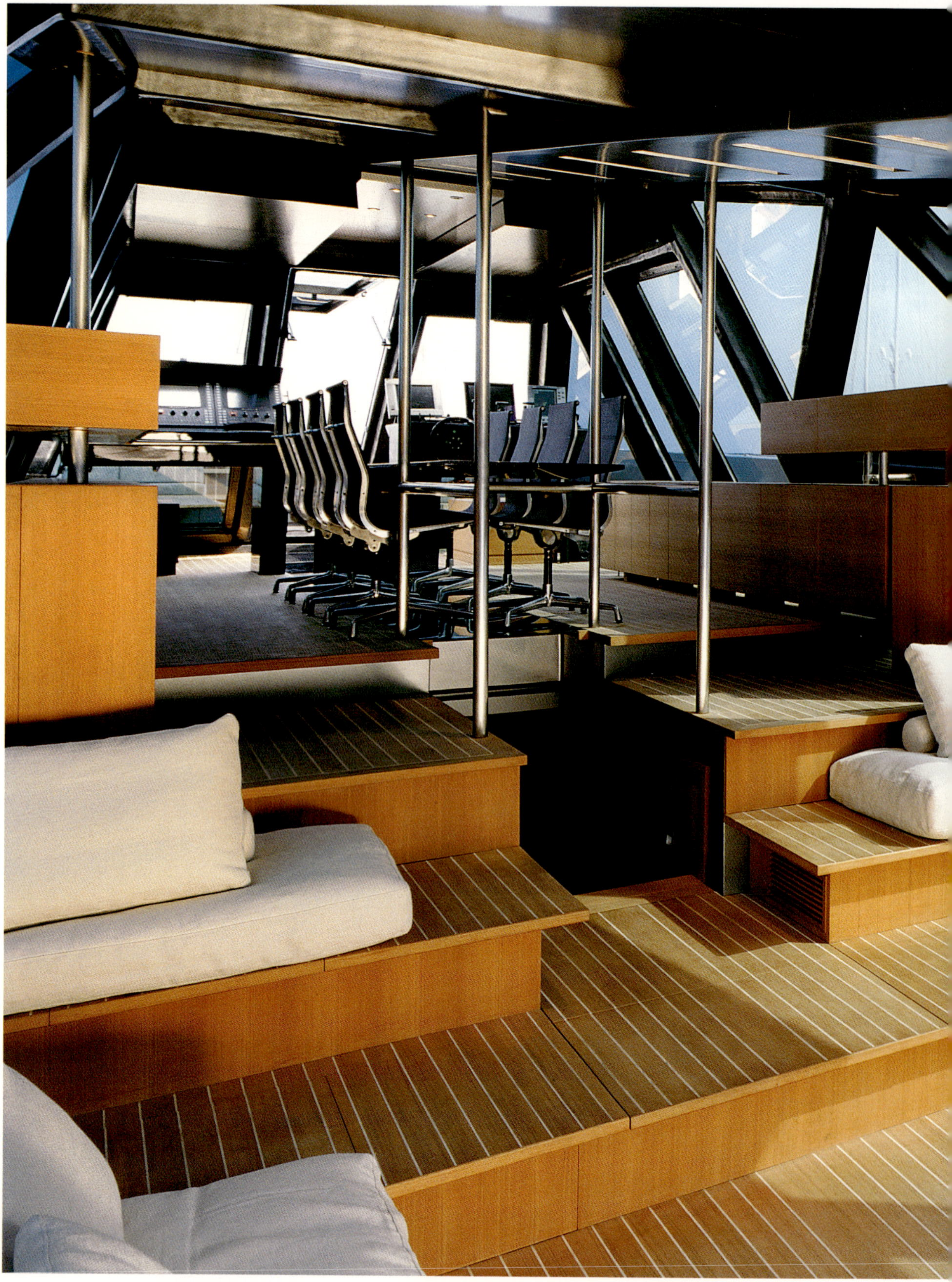

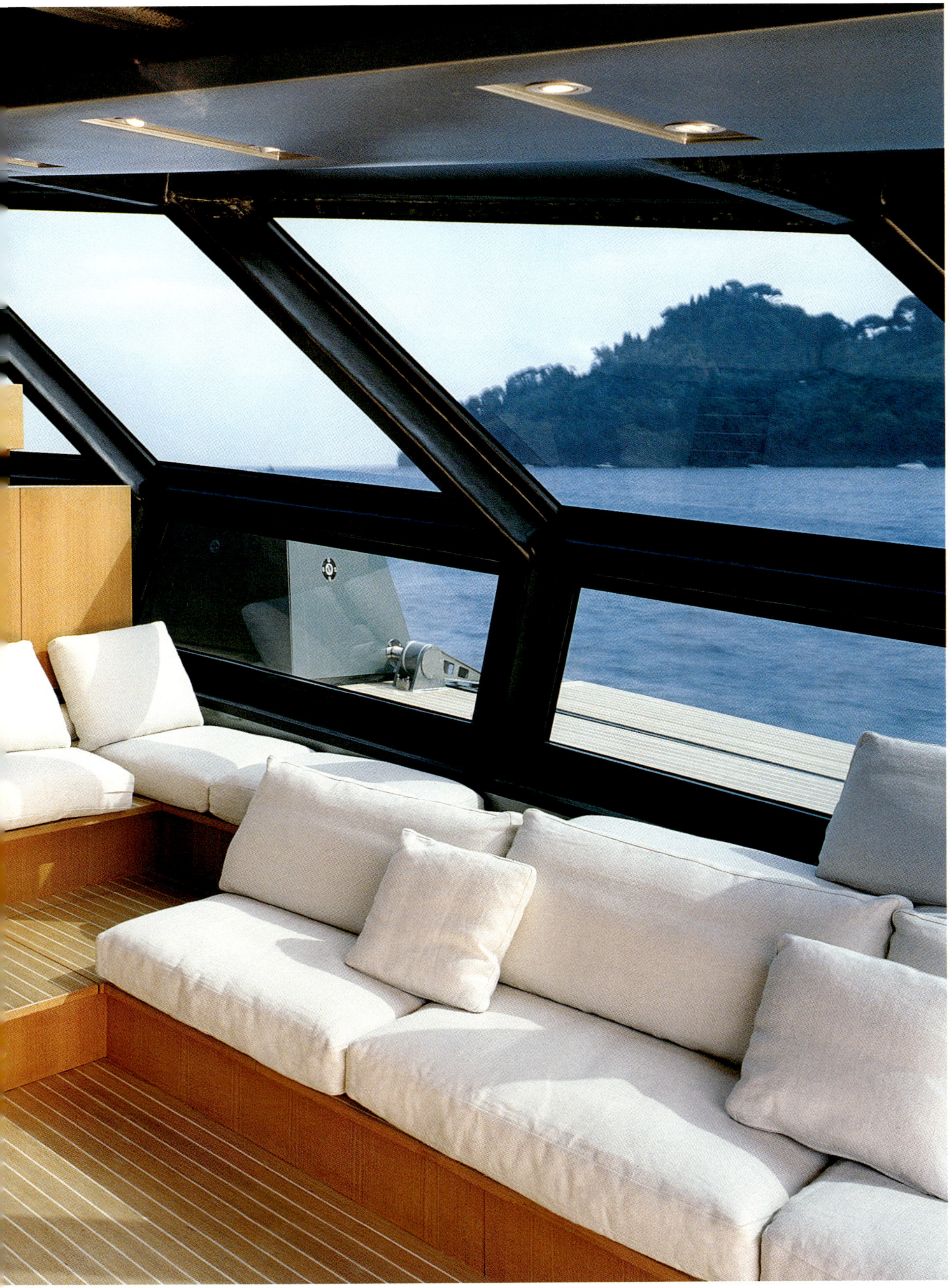

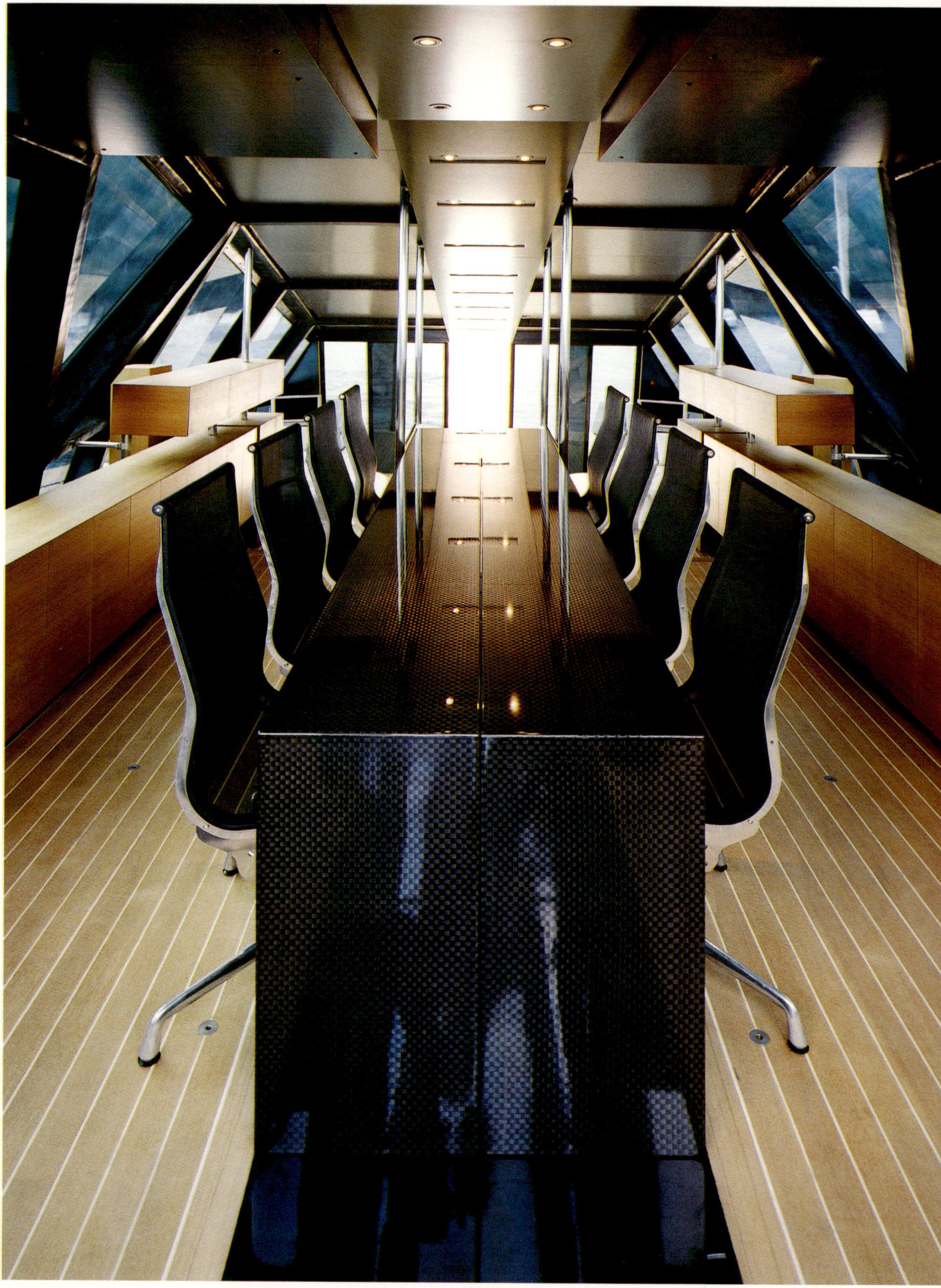

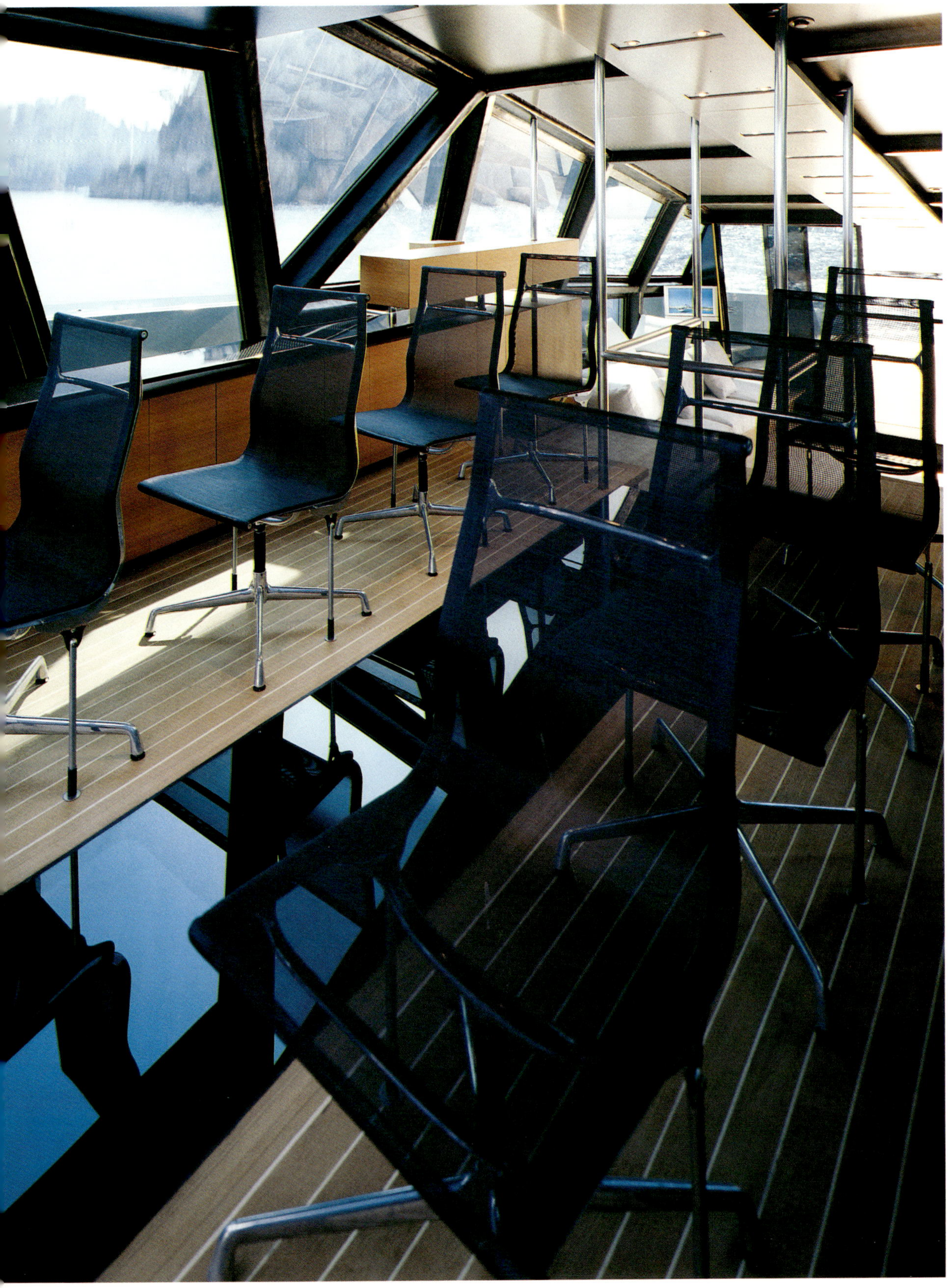

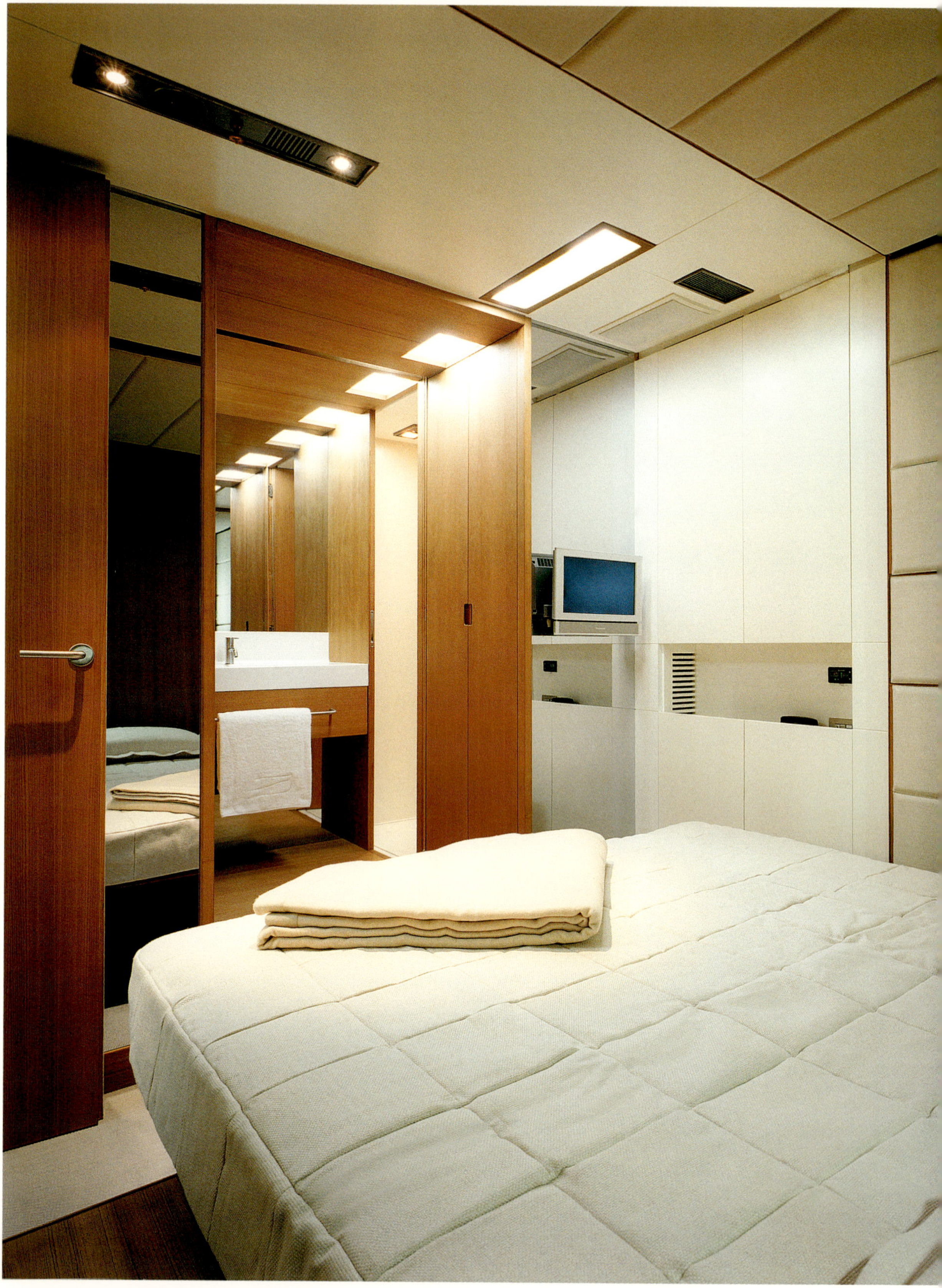

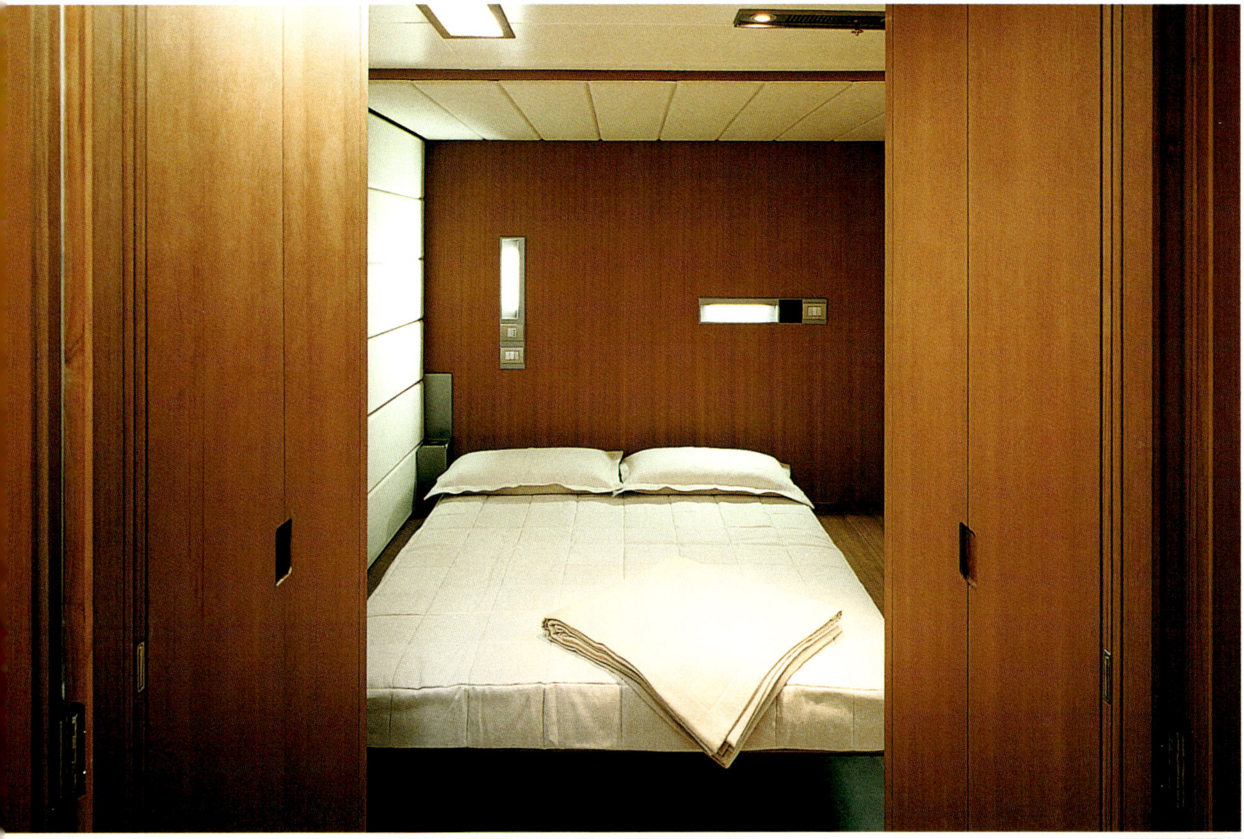

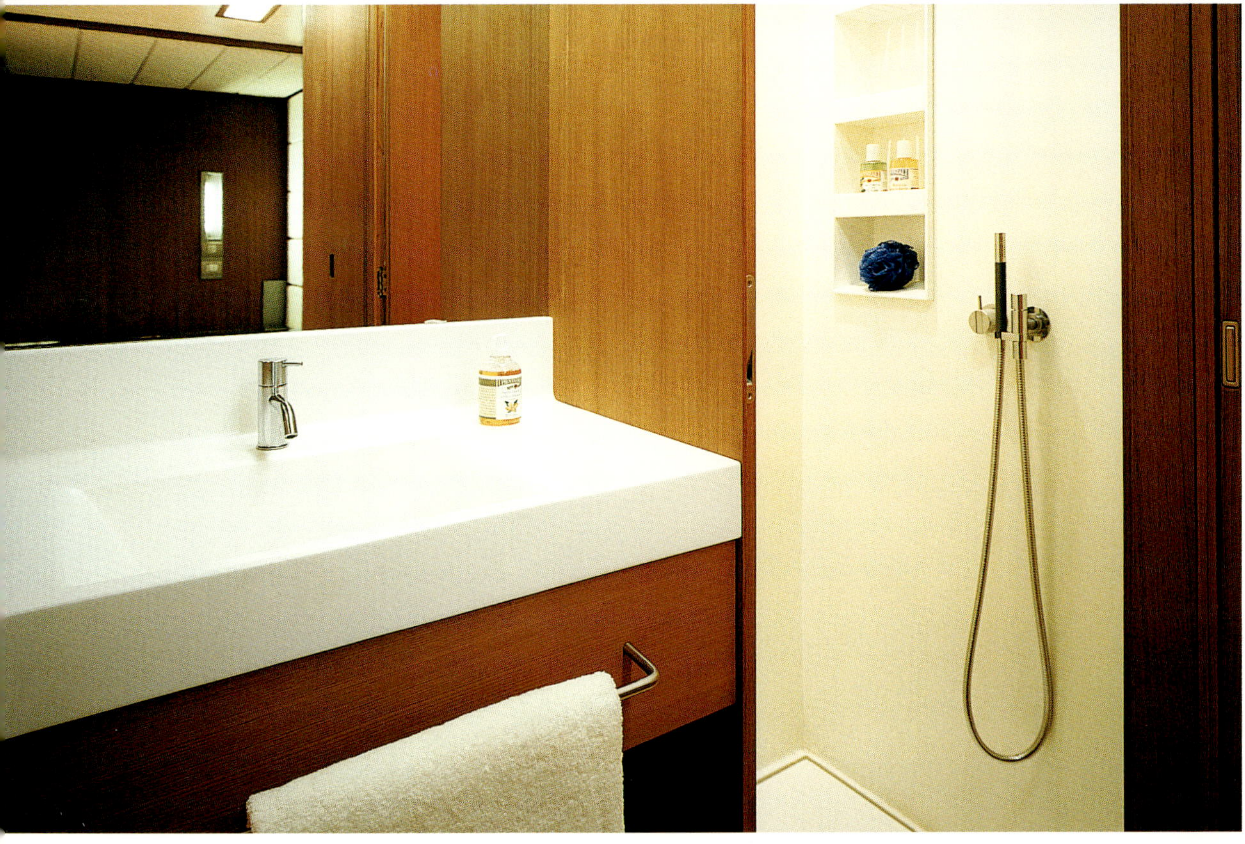

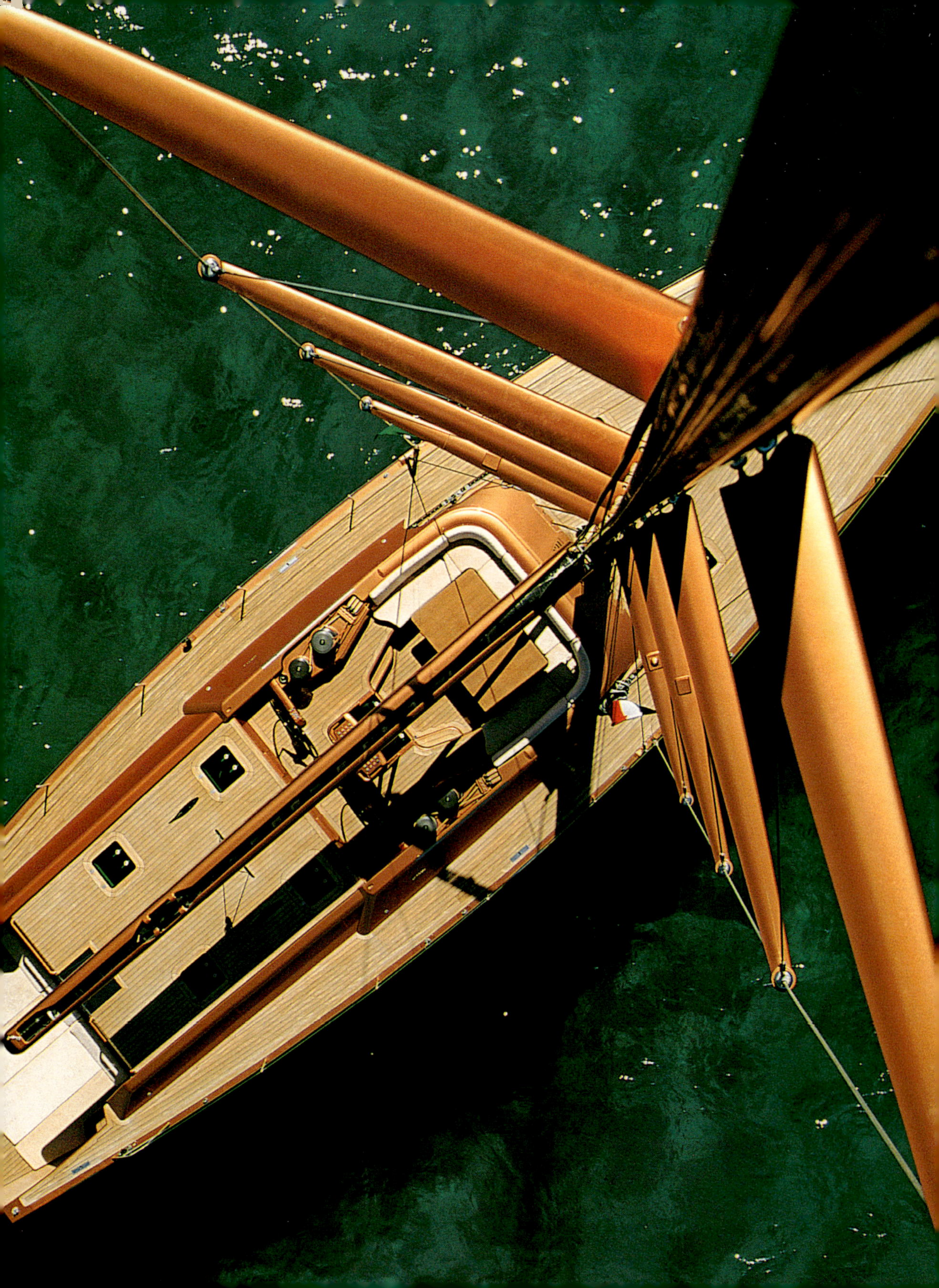

WALLY, SERENA ANIBALDI, GERMAN FRERS
WY 88.2 TIKETITOO | 2001
CNB
Wally

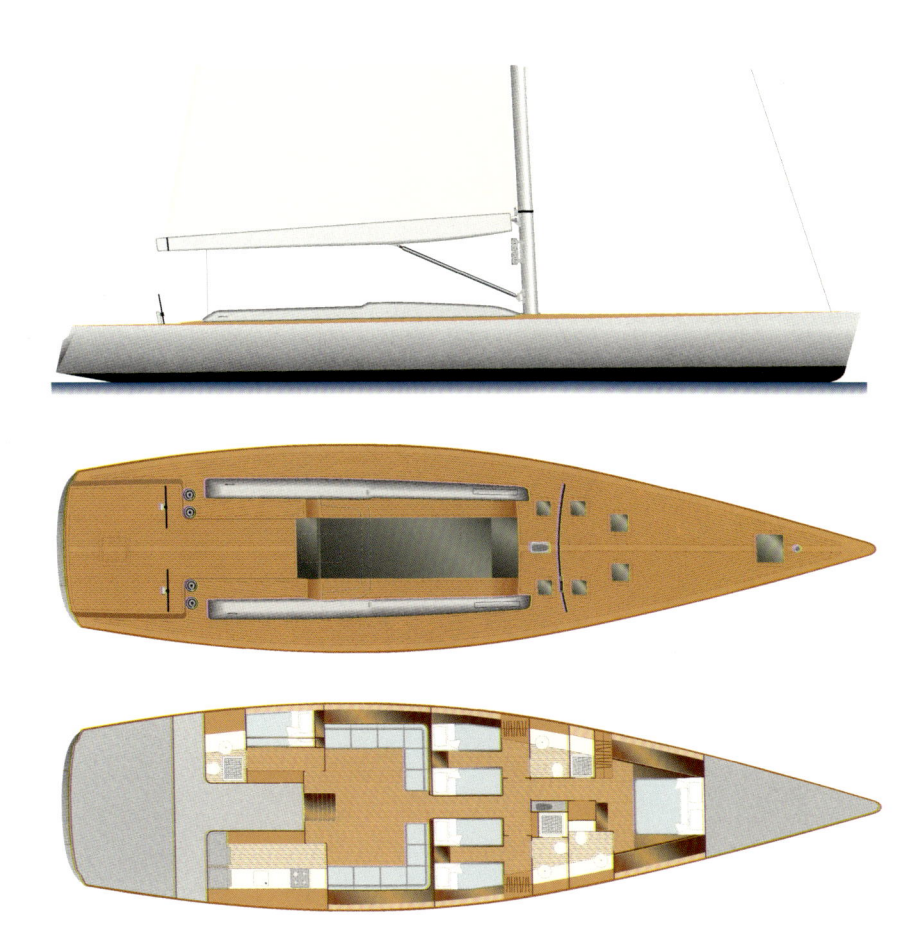

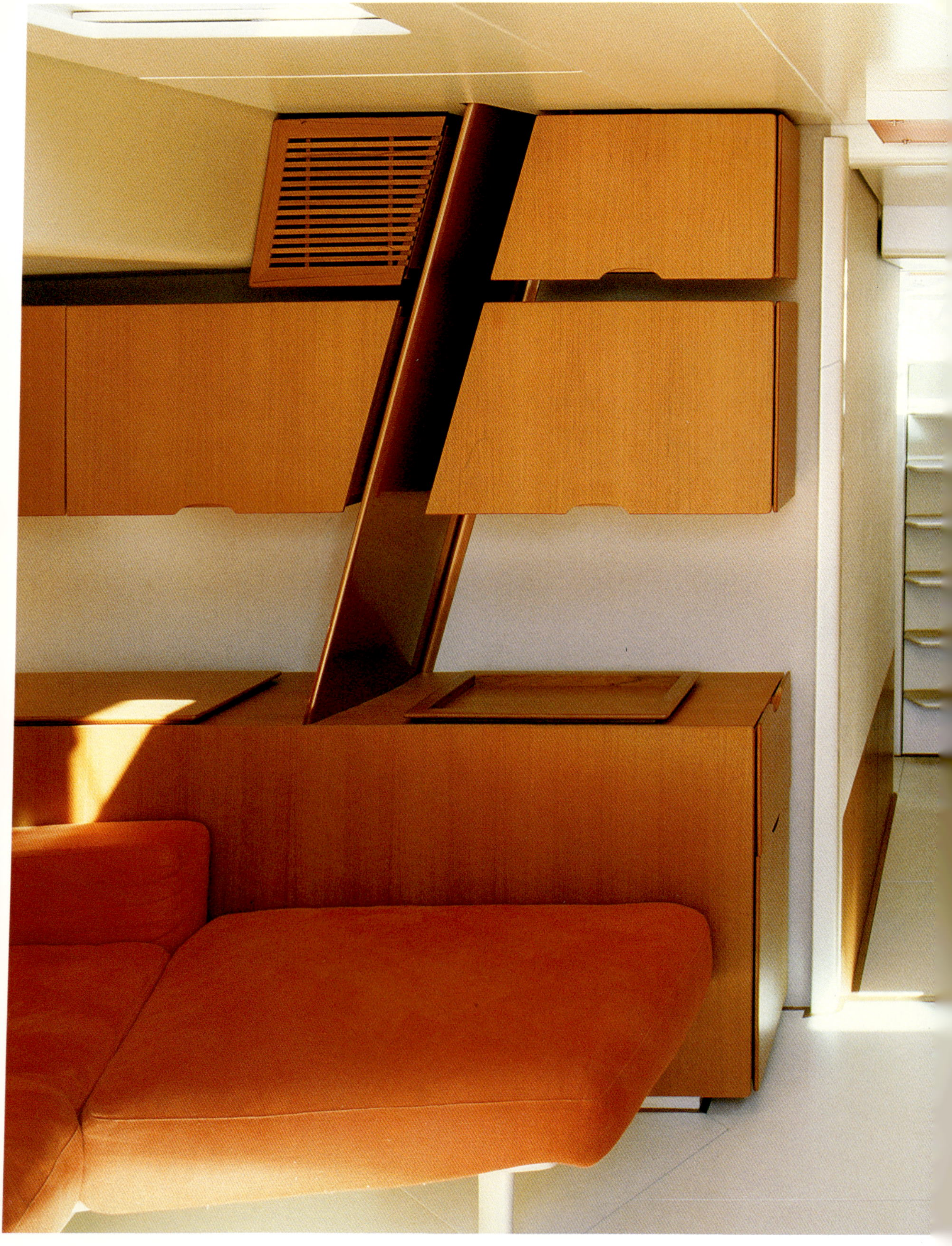

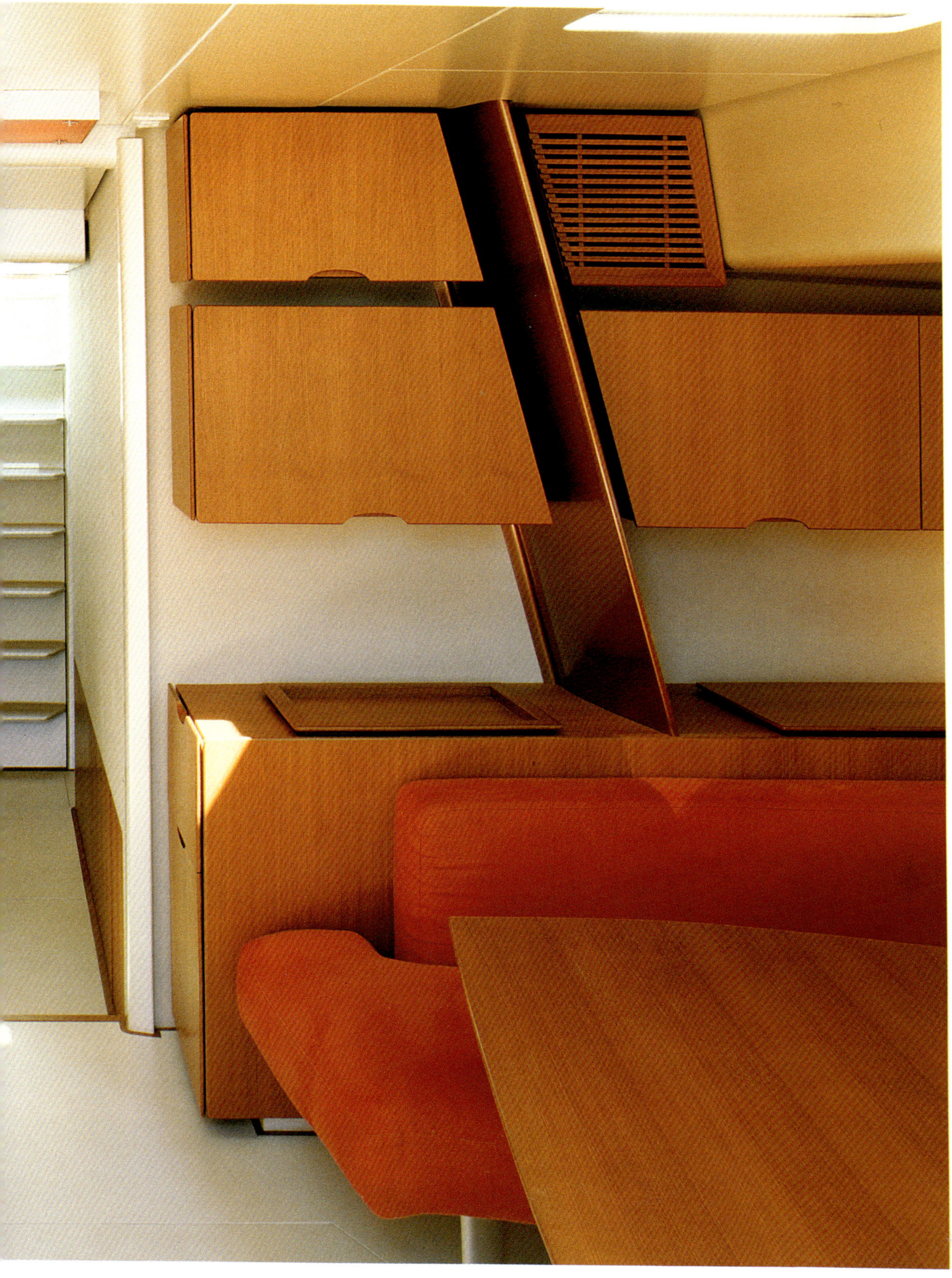

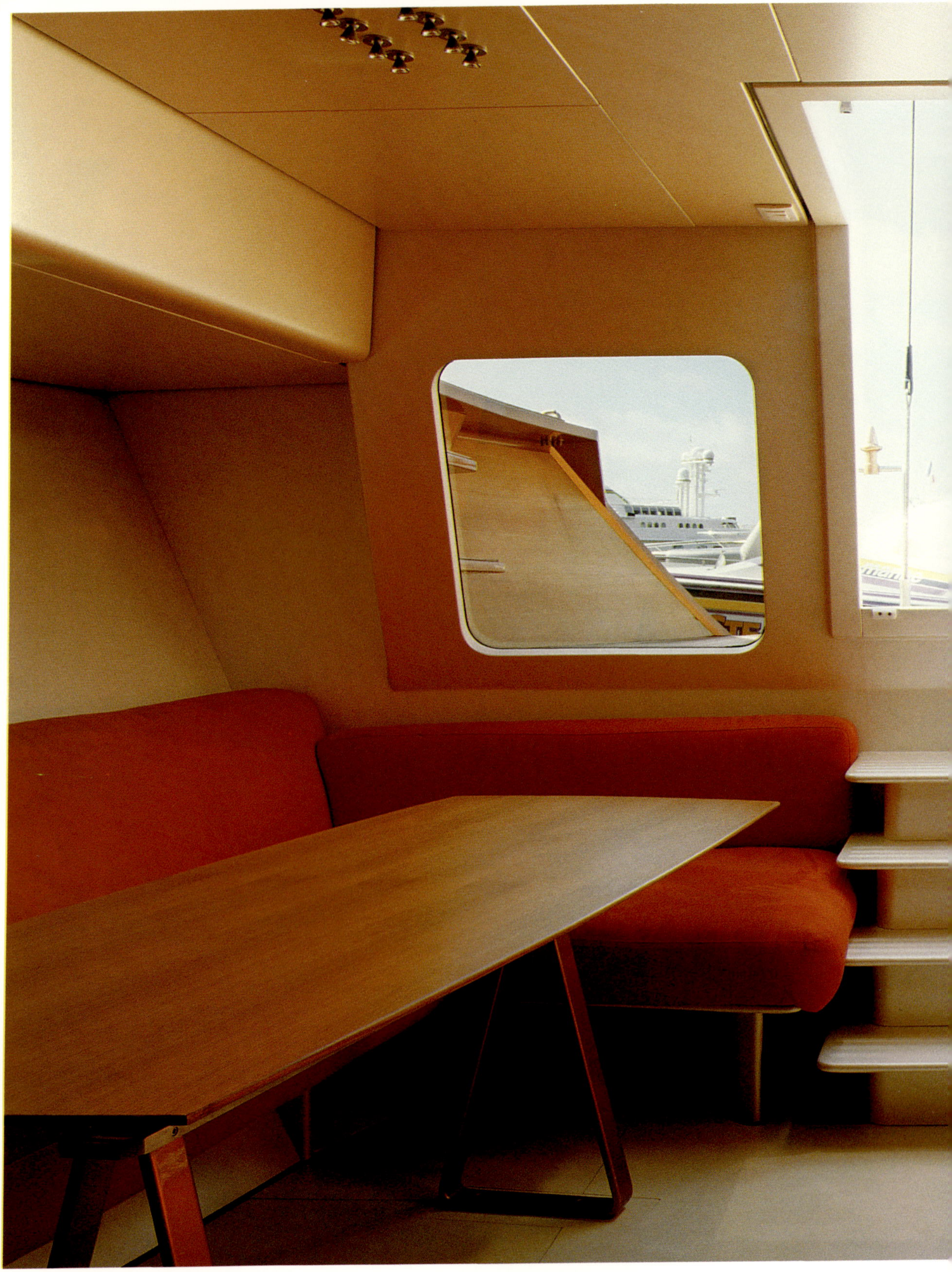

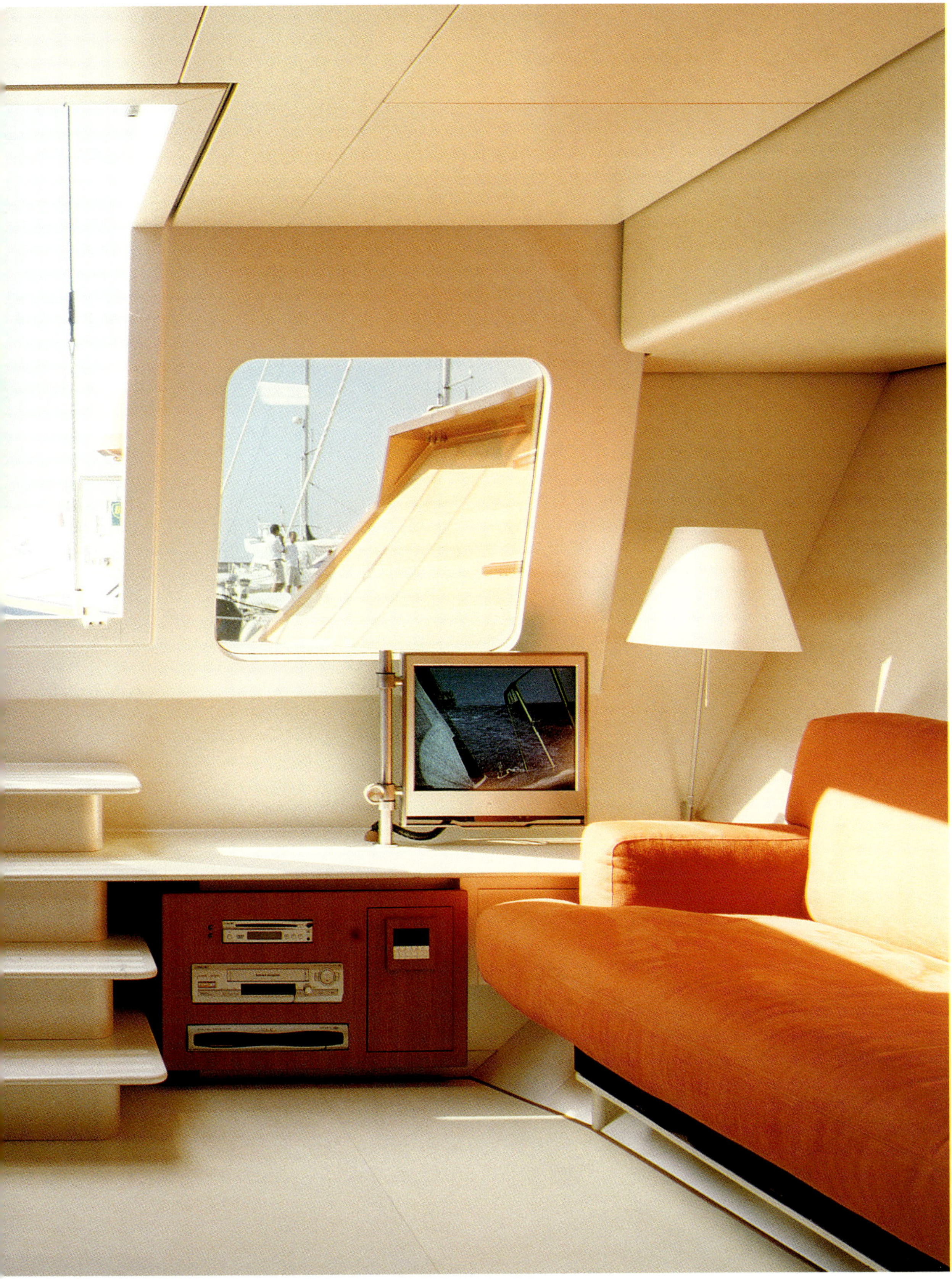

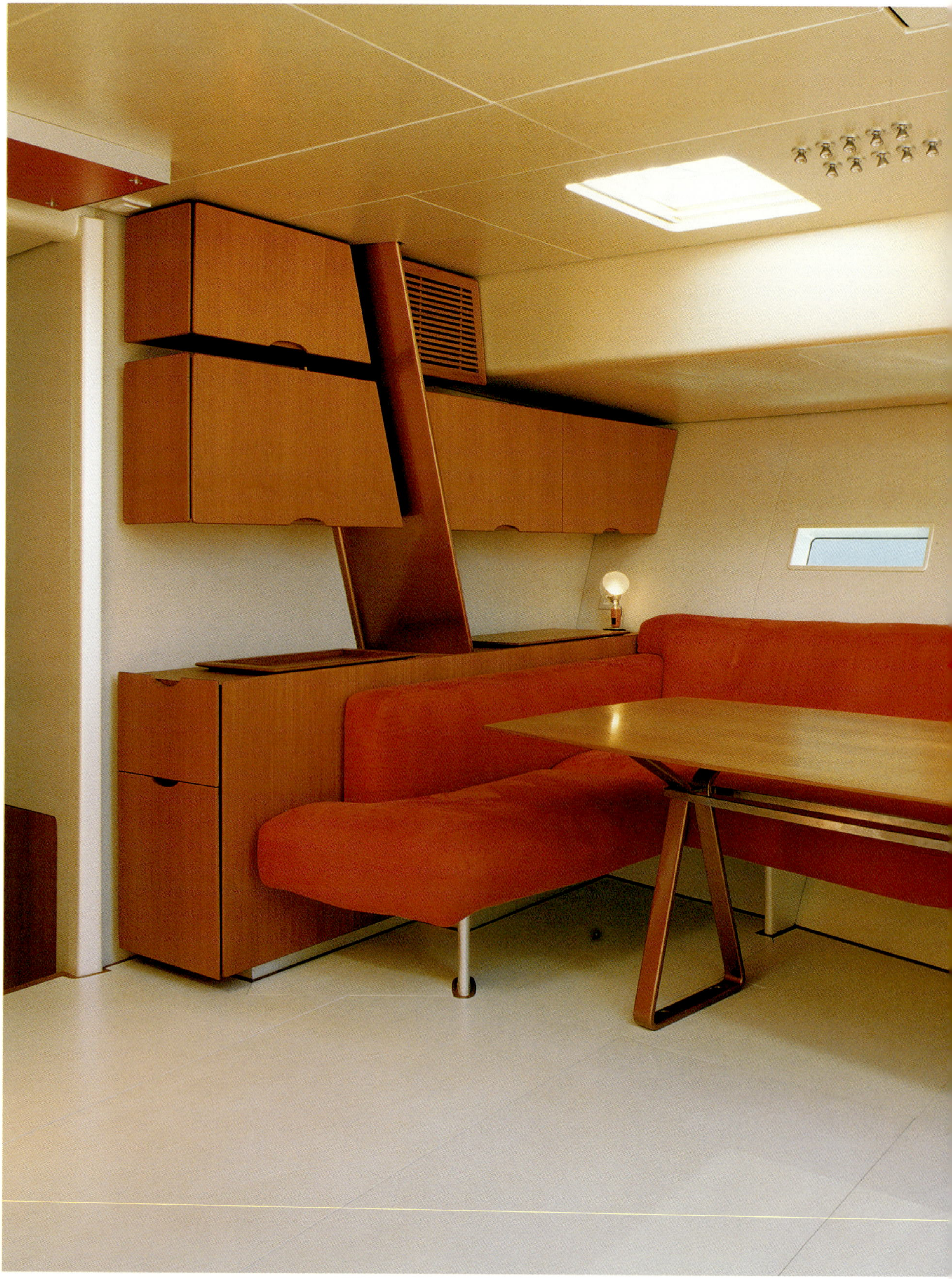

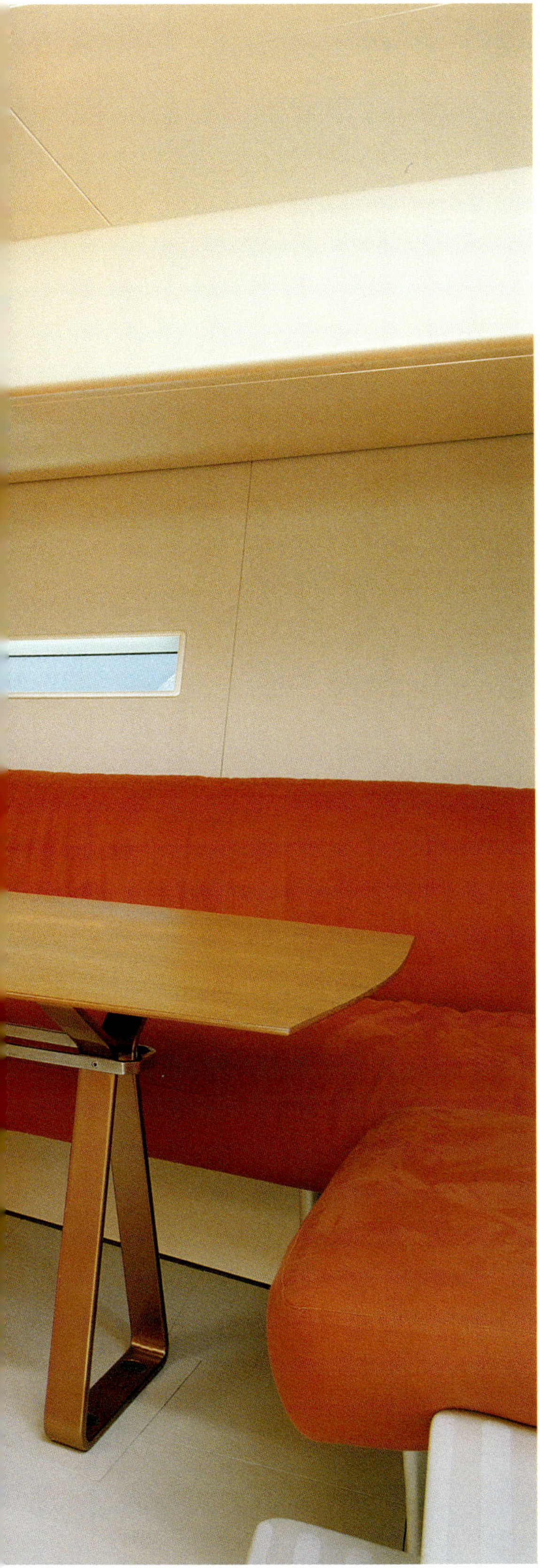

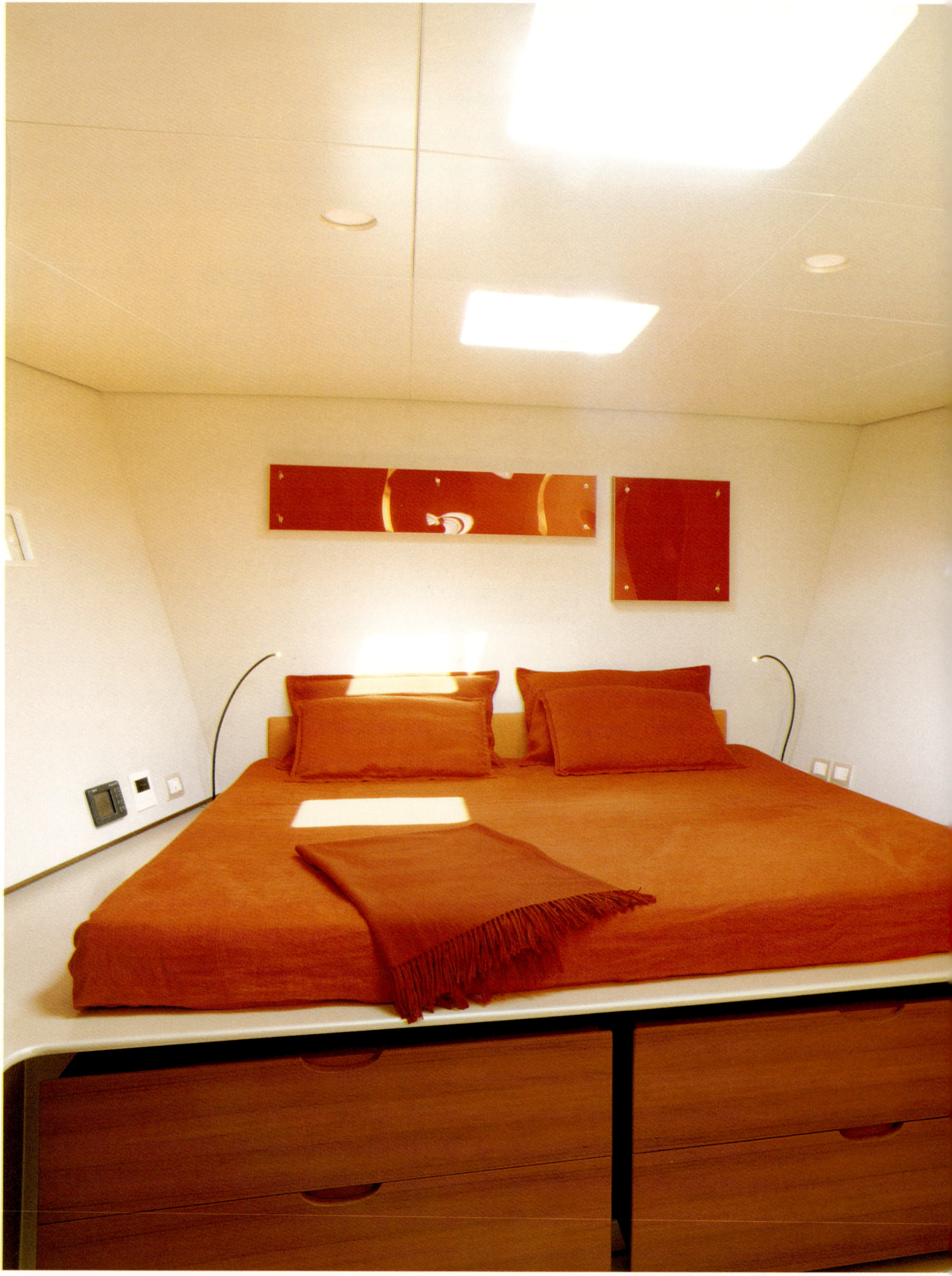

333

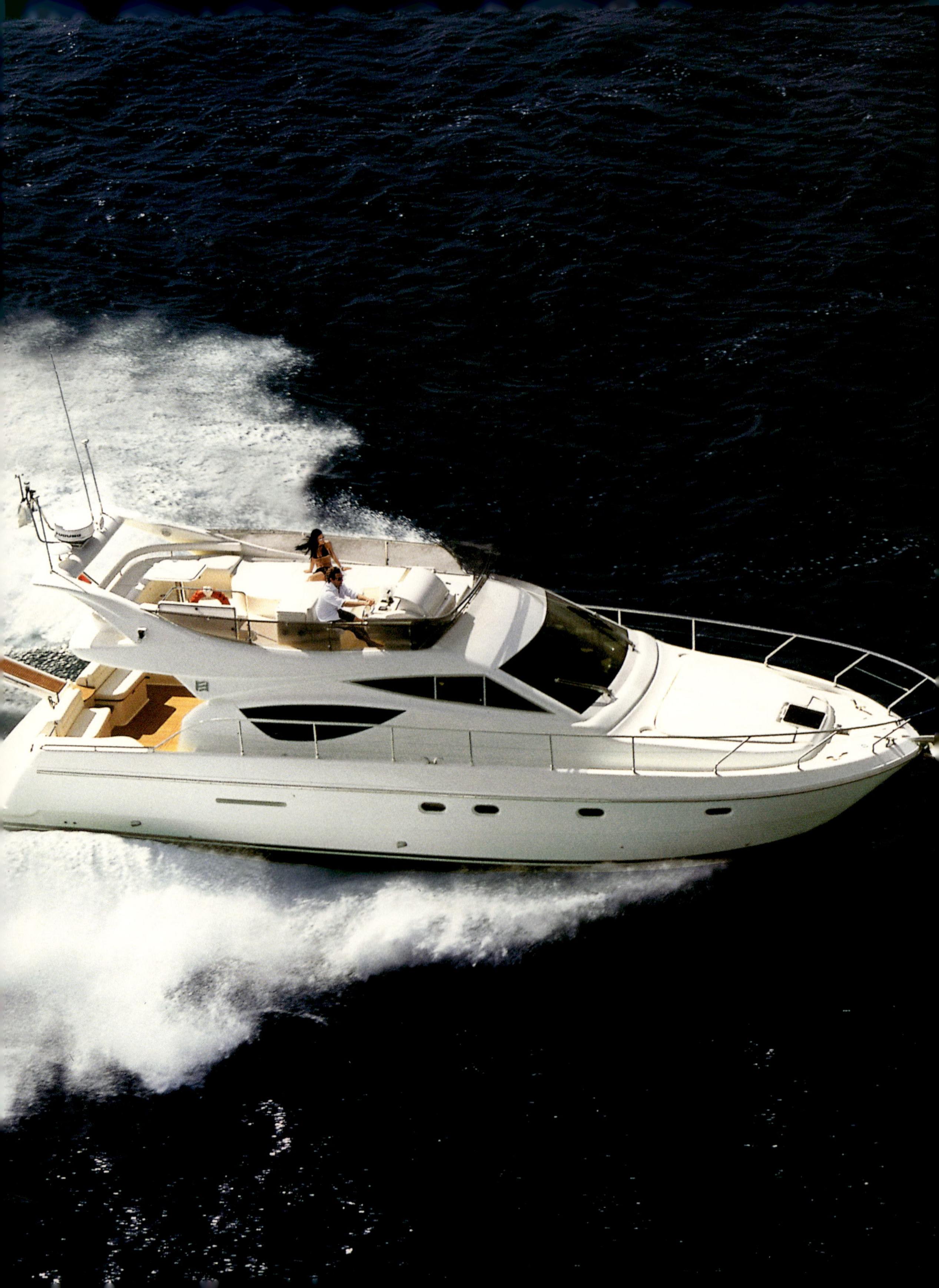

ZUCCON INTERNATIONAL PROJECT STUDIO
FERRETTI 460 | 2005
Ferretti Yachts

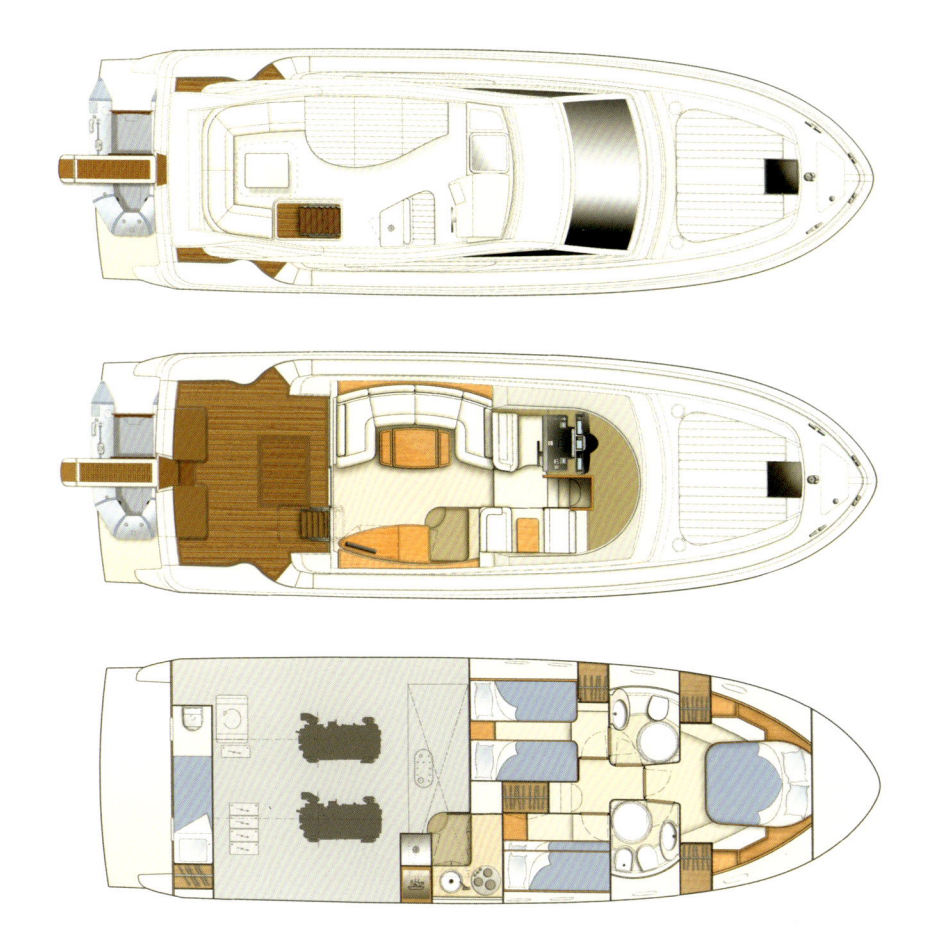

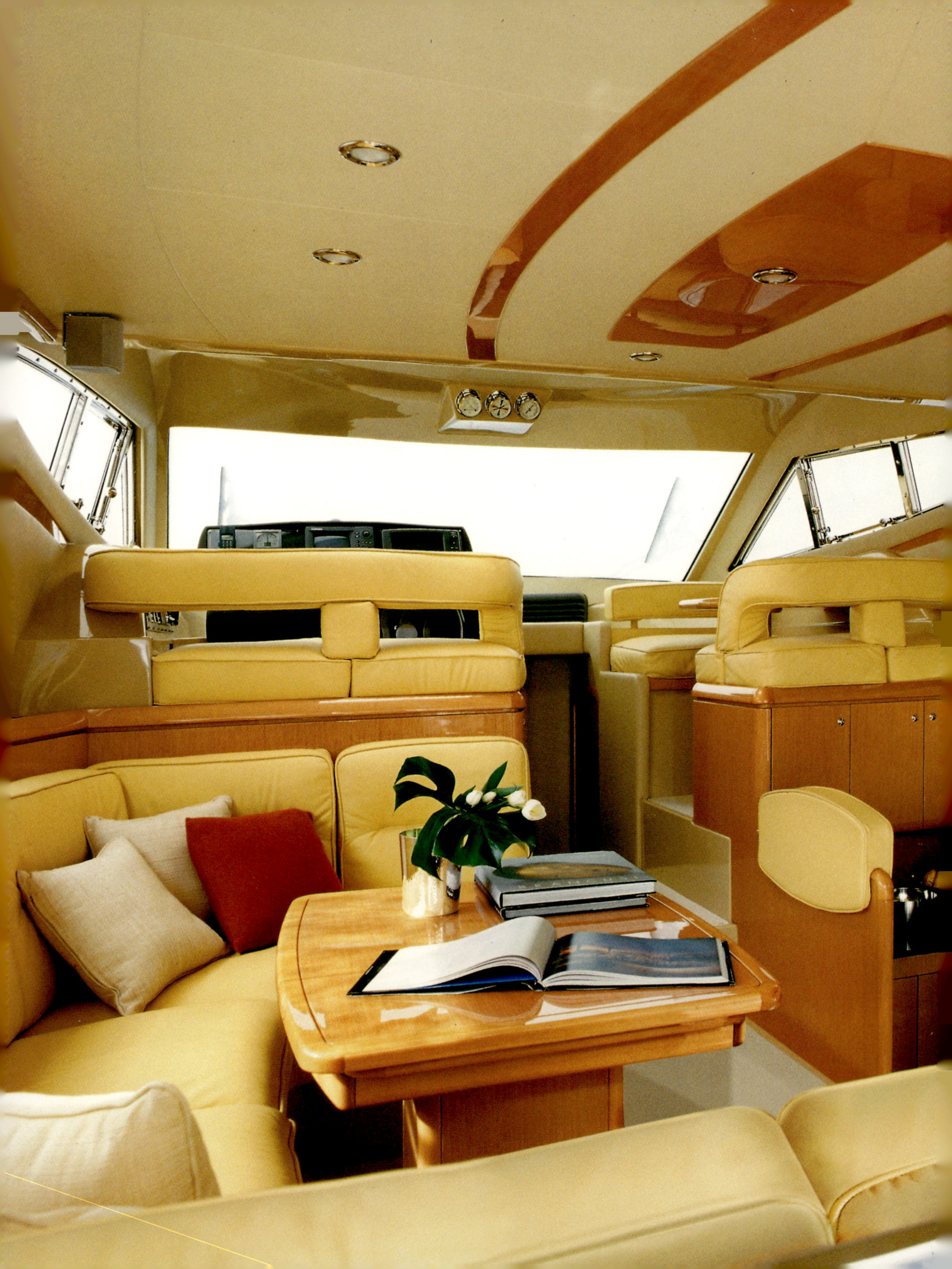

337

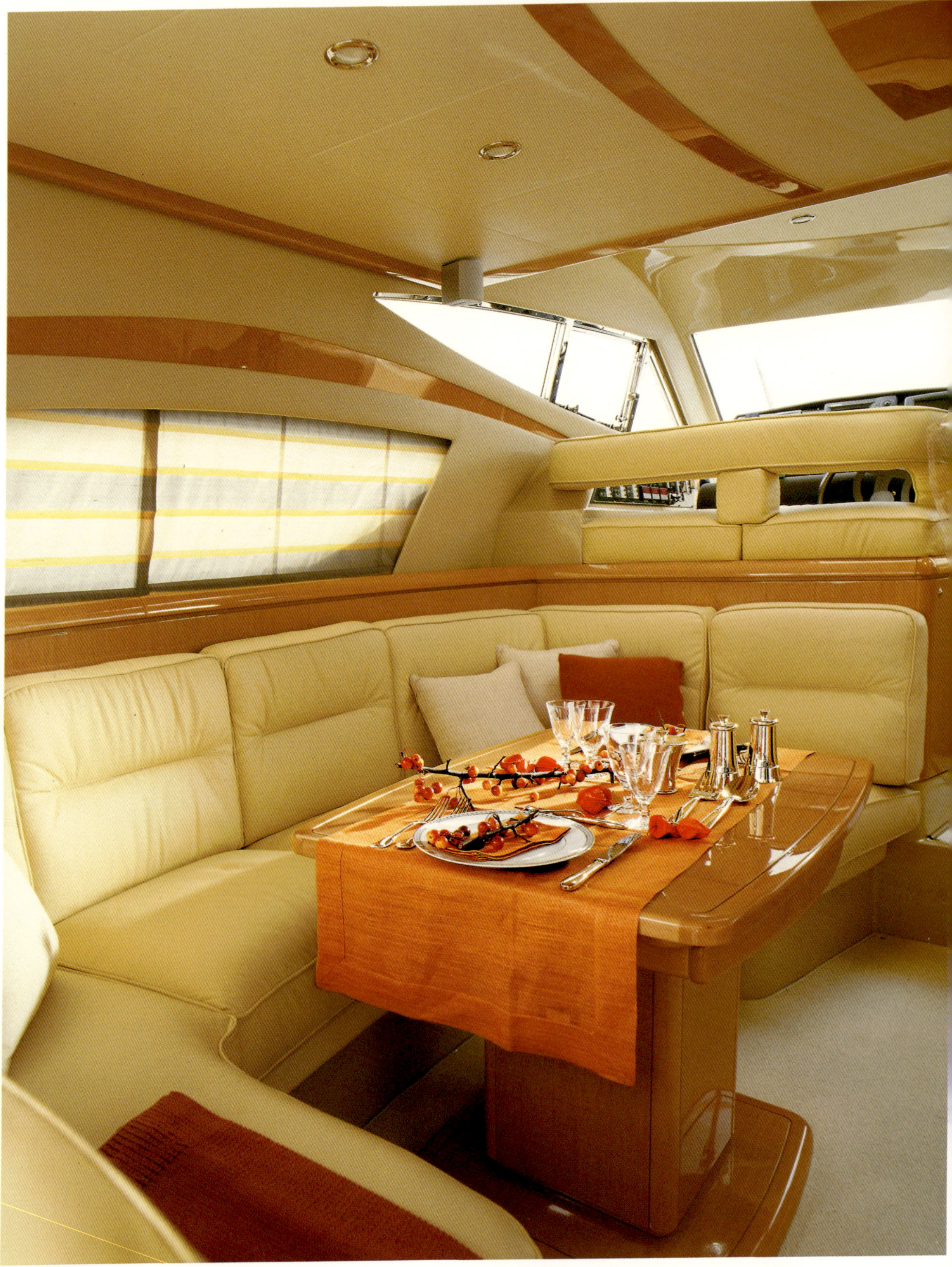

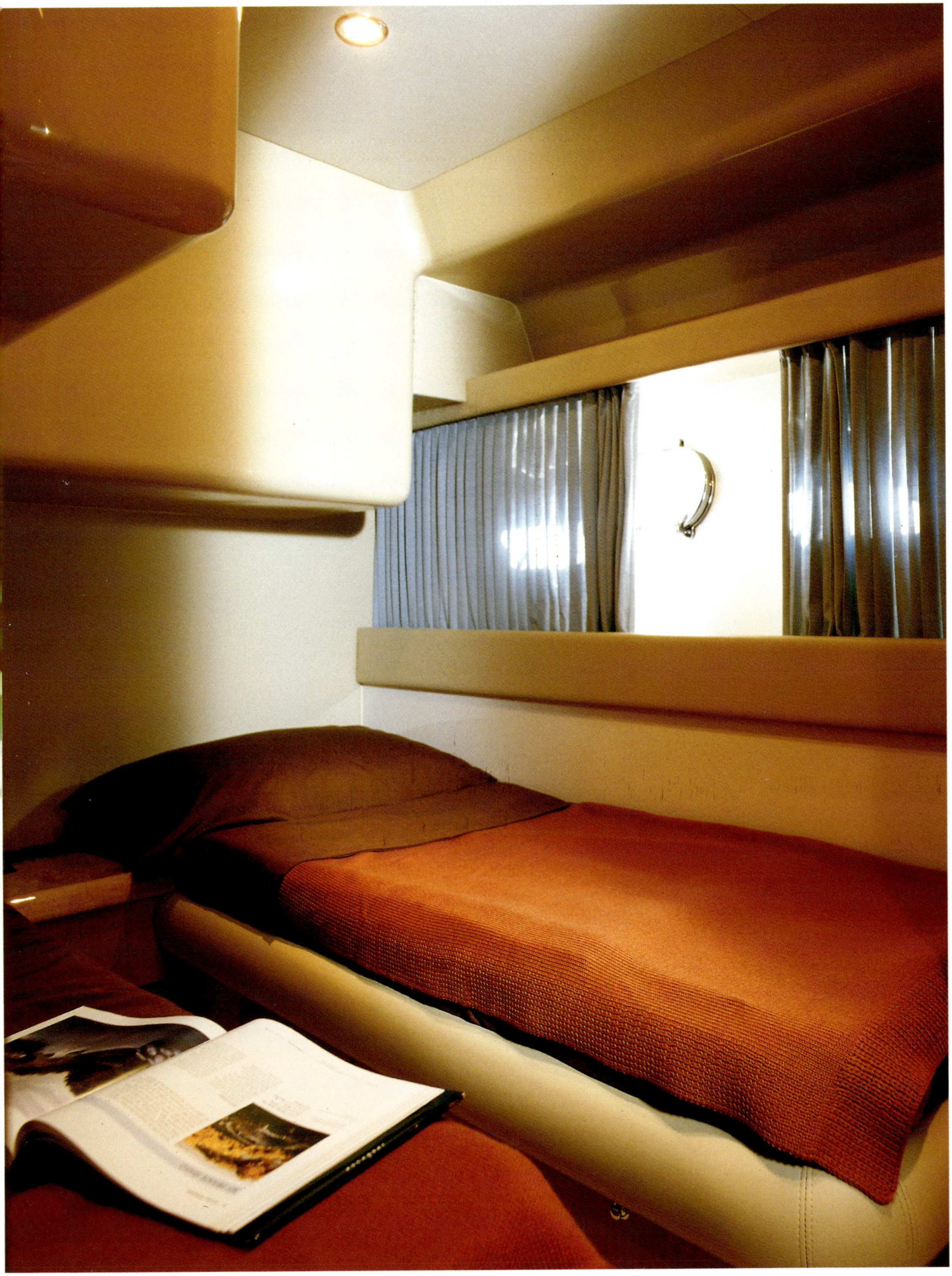

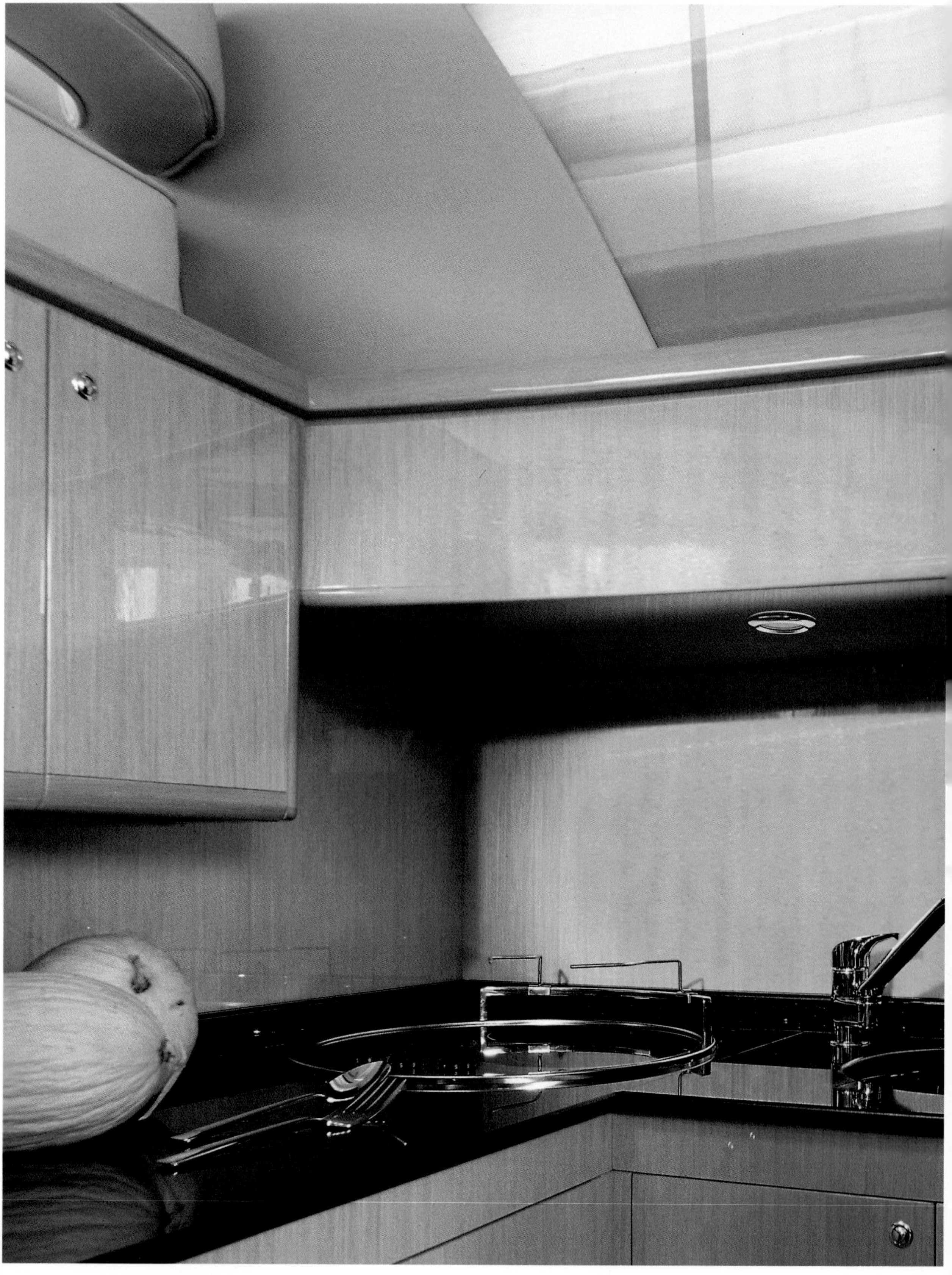

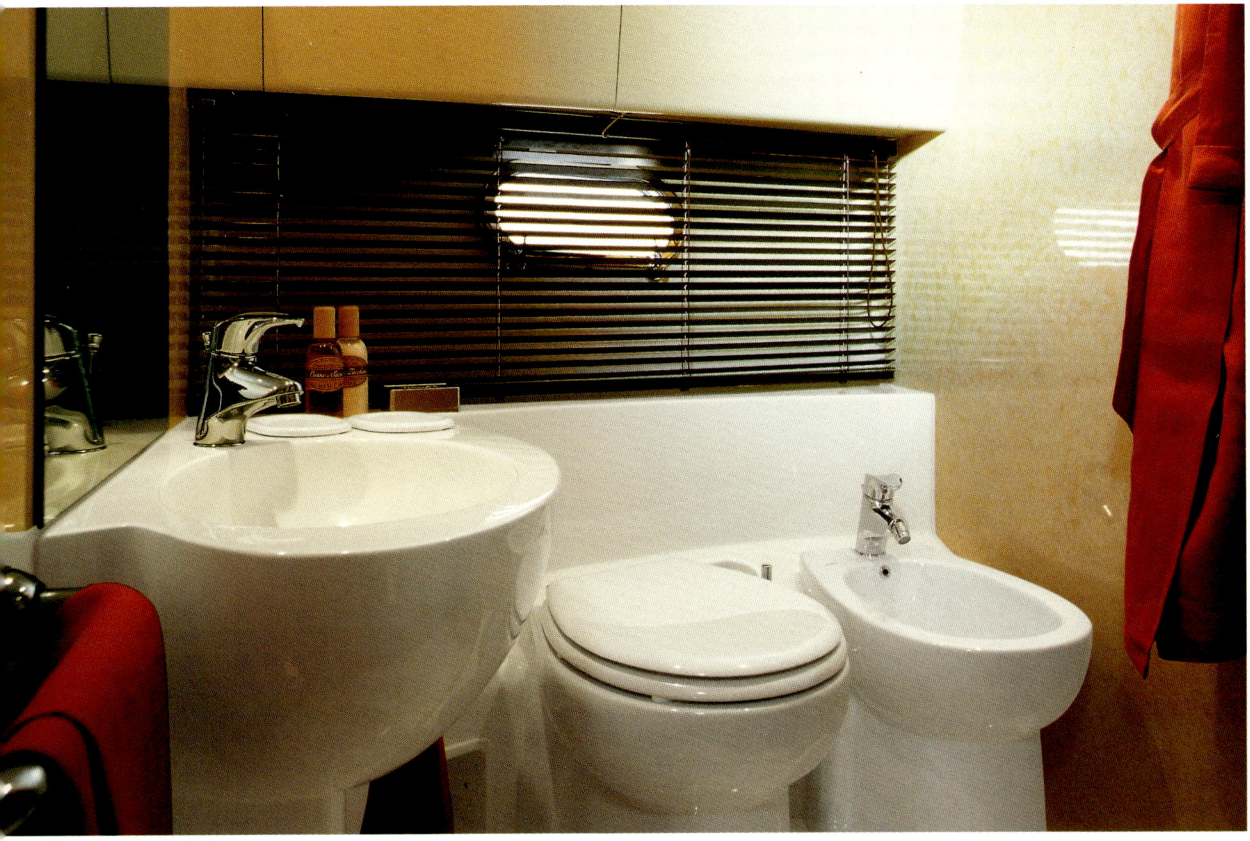

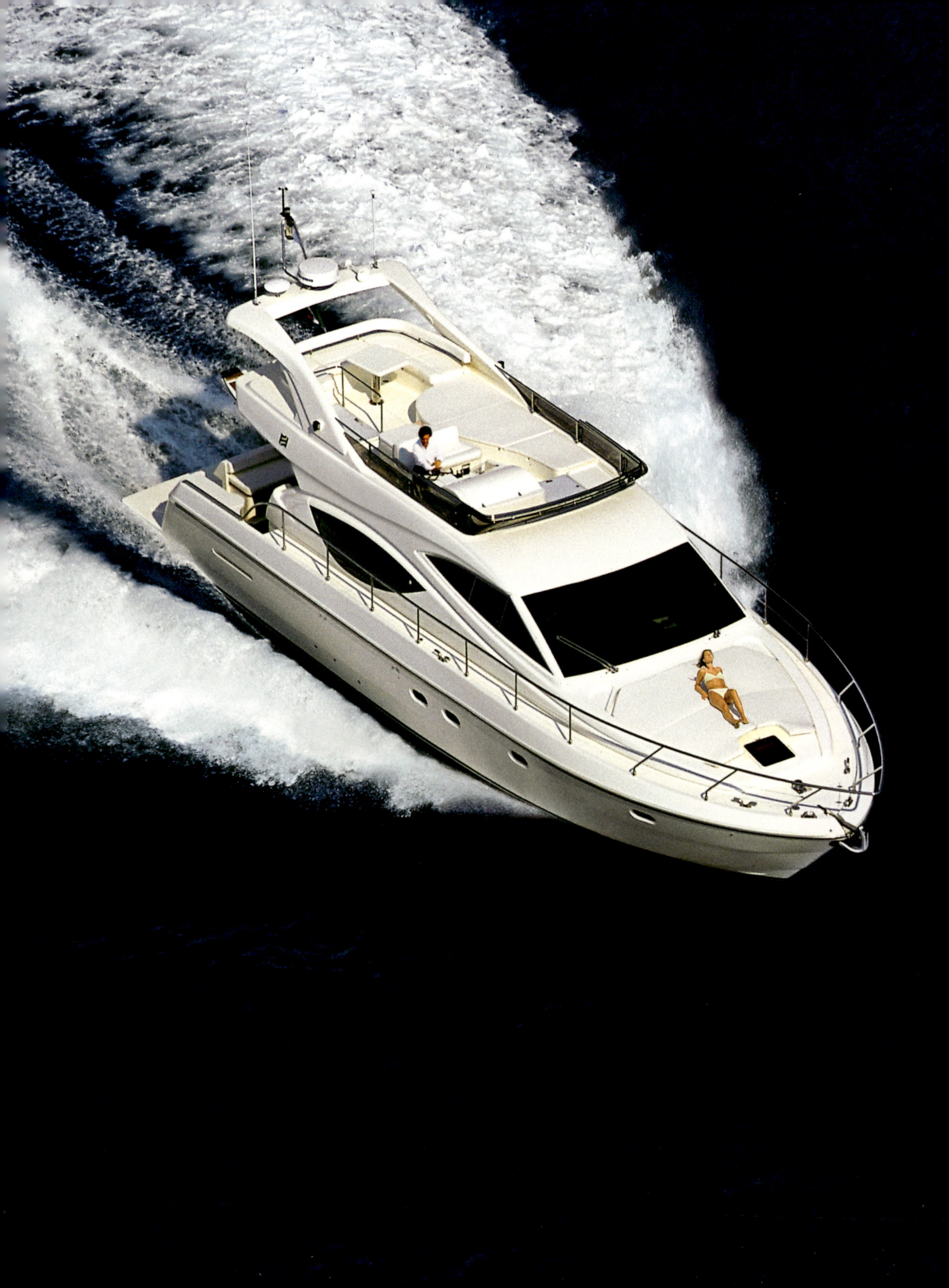

ZUCCON INTERNATIONAL PROJECT STUDIO
FERRETTI 500 | 2004
Ferretti Yachts

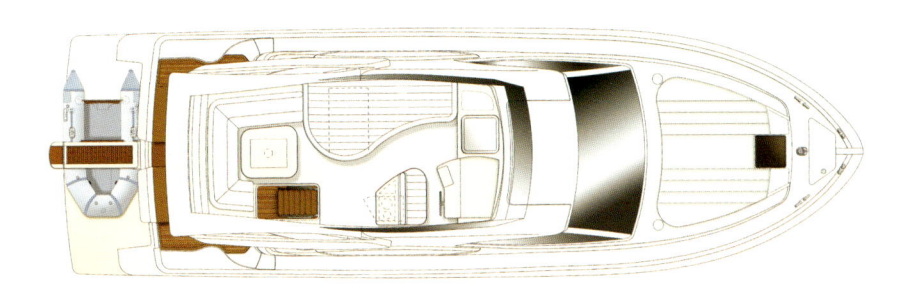

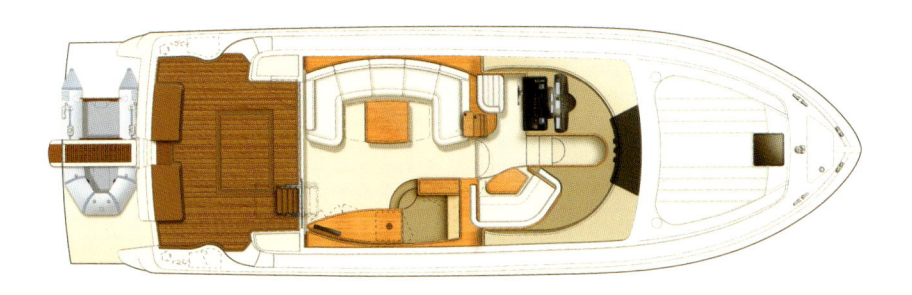

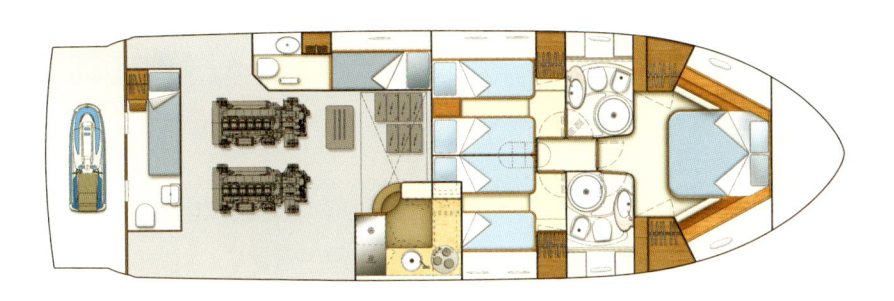

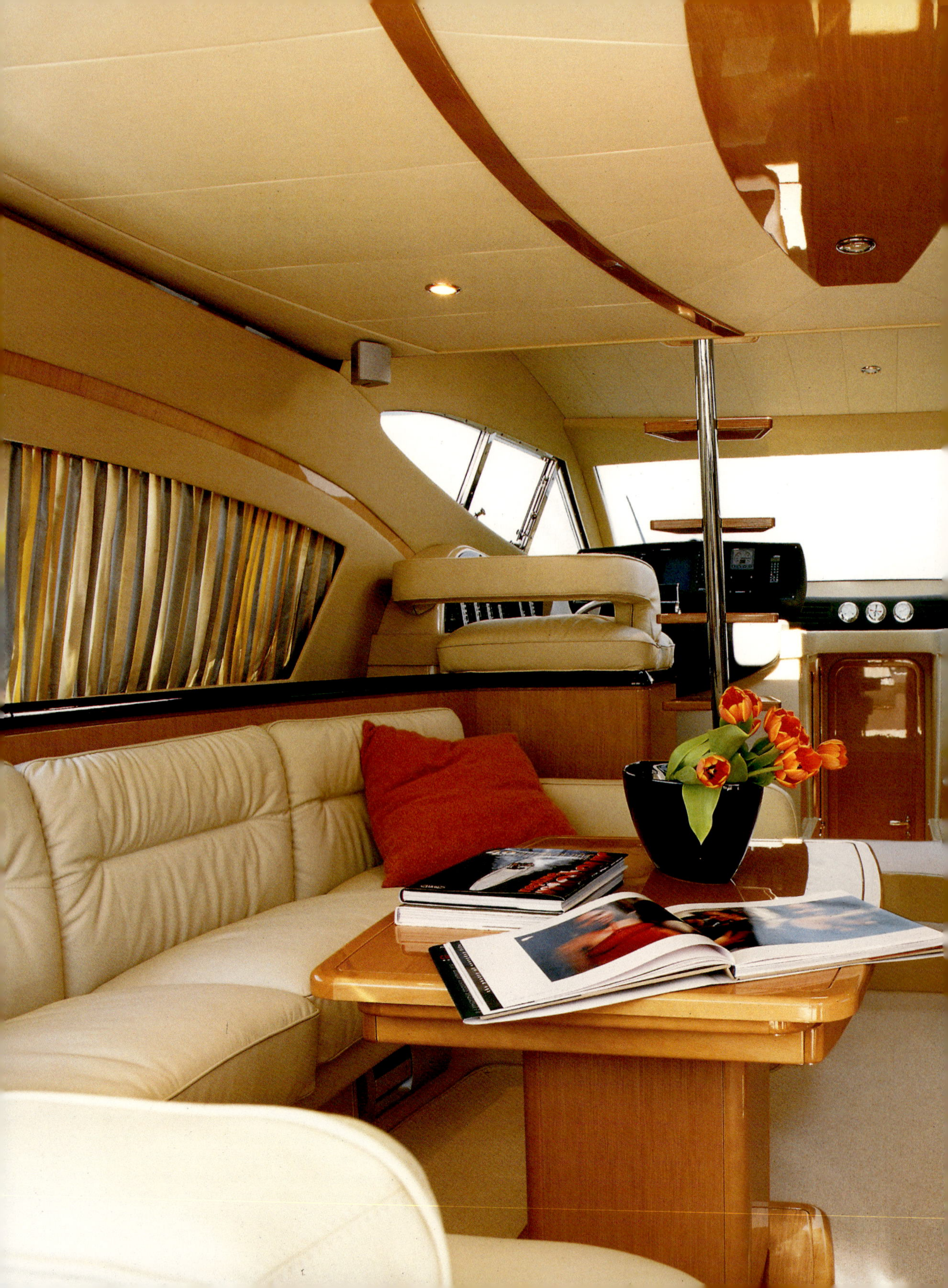

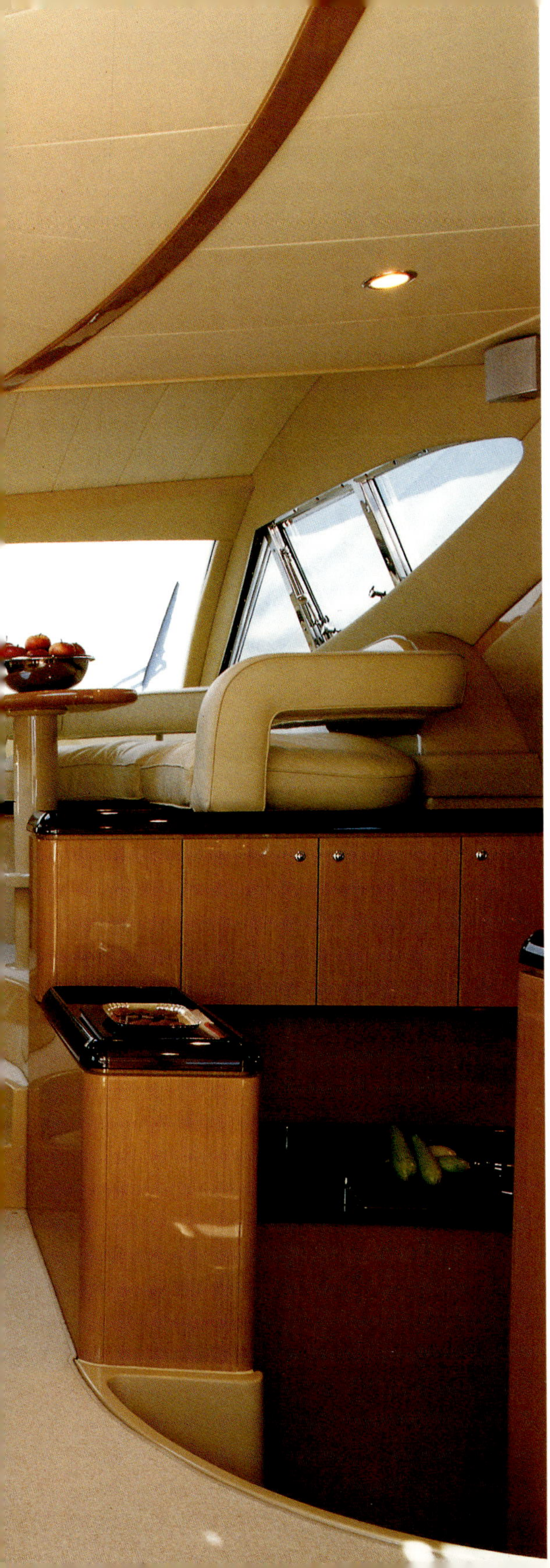

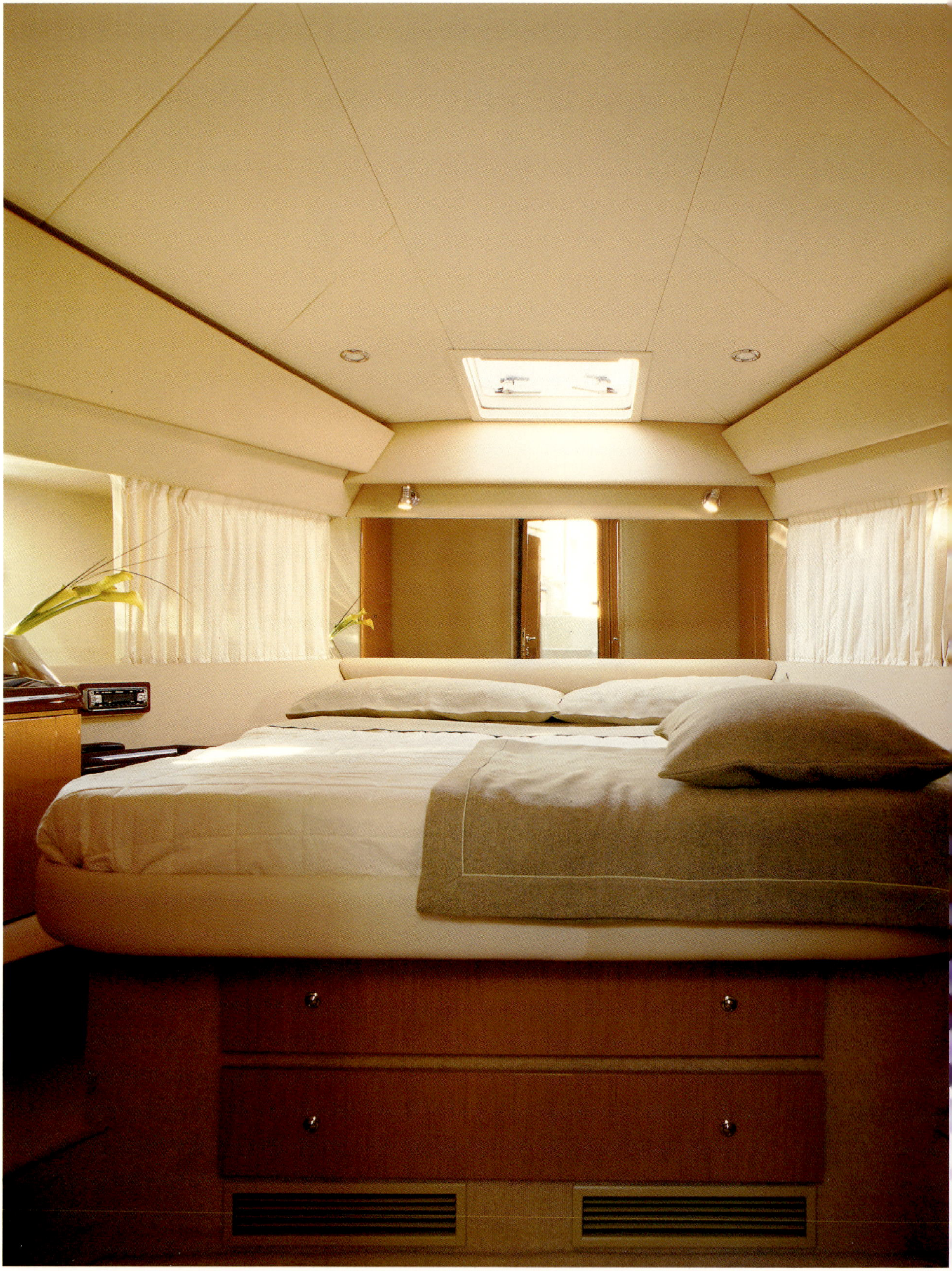

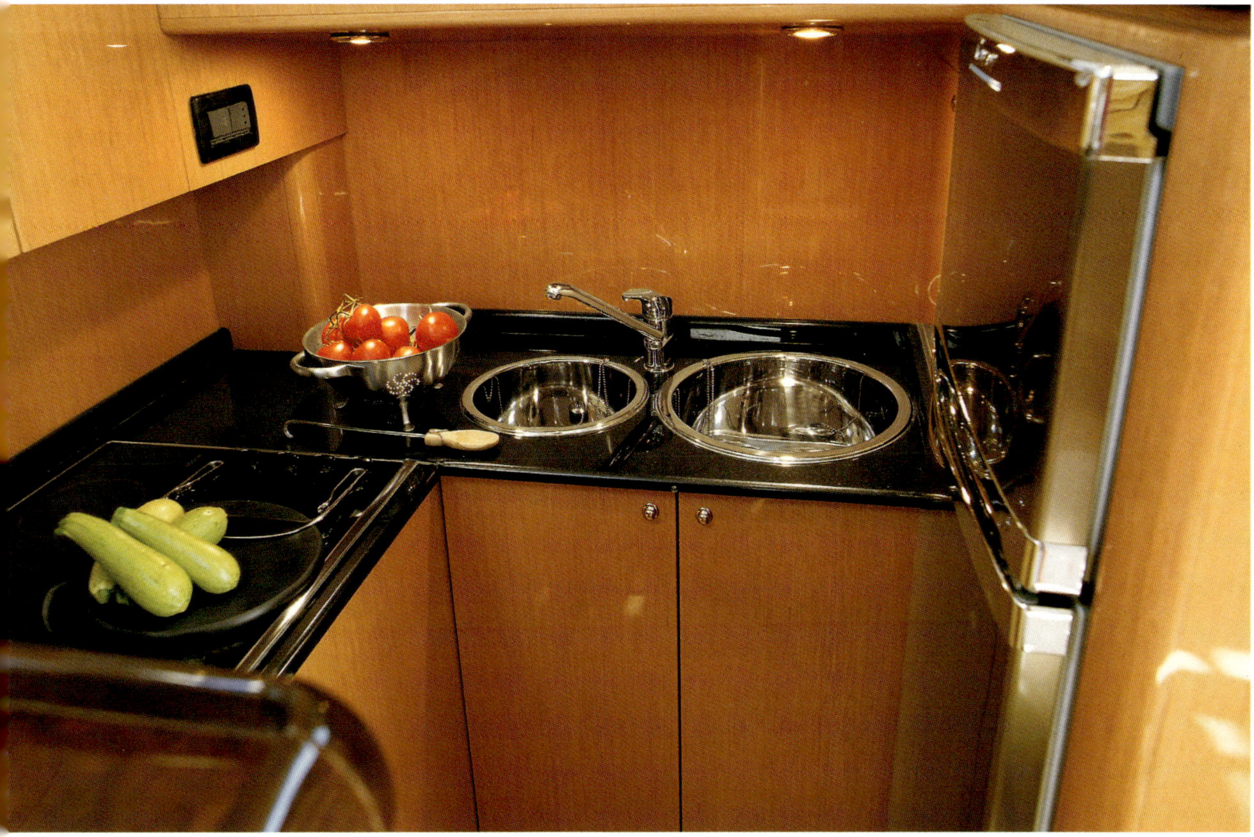

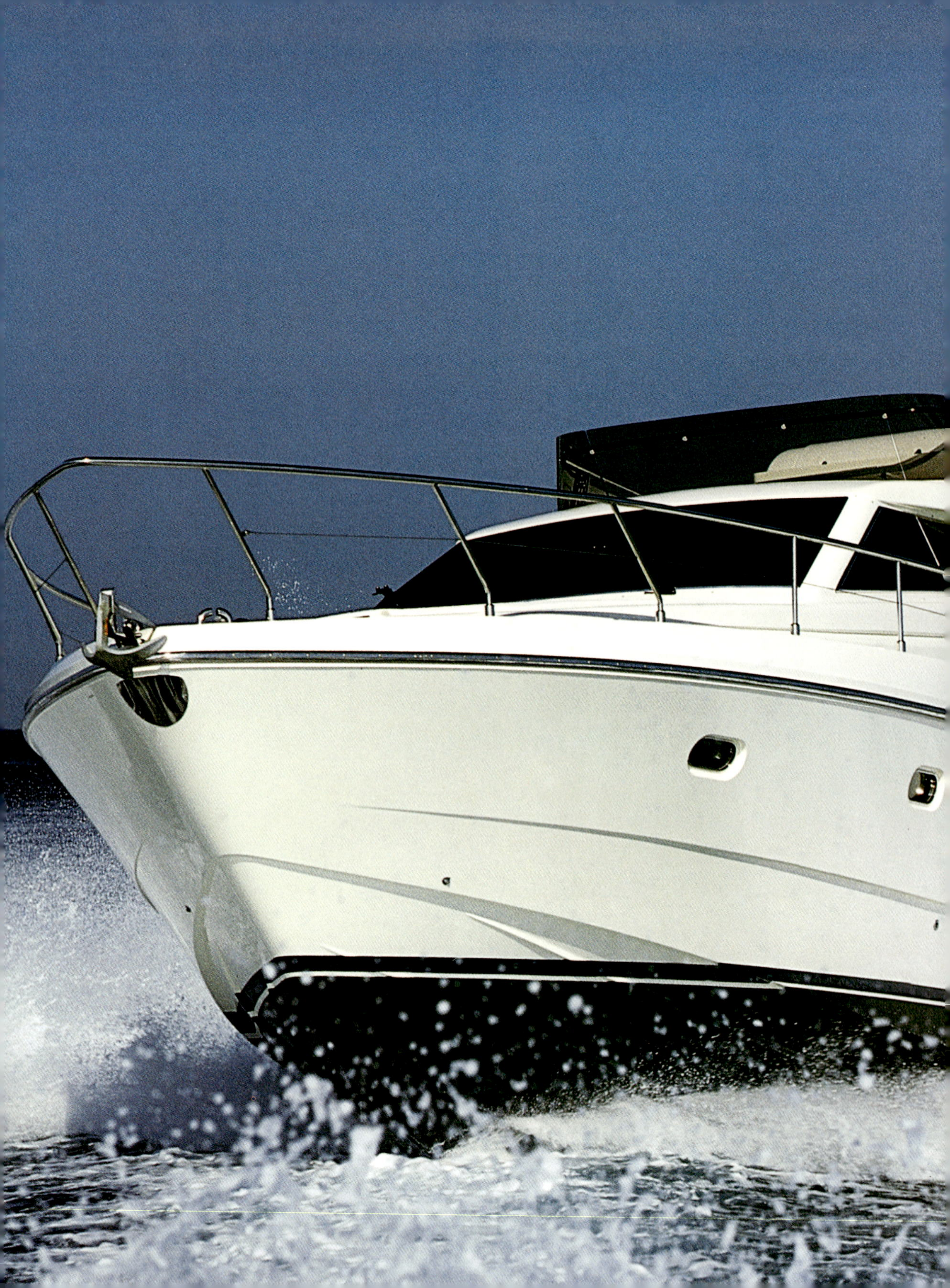

ZUCCON INTERNATIONAL PROJECT STUDIO
FERRETTI 530 | 1997
Ferretti Yachts

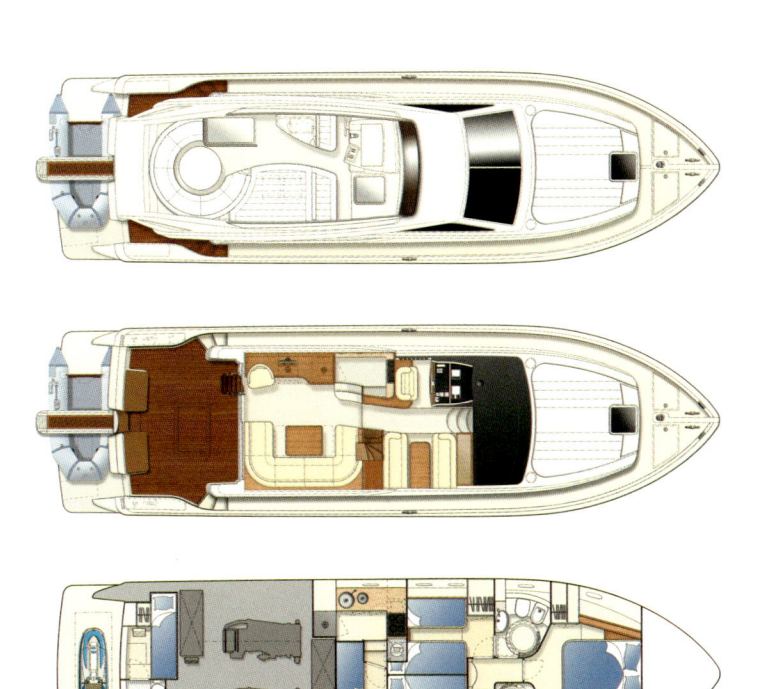

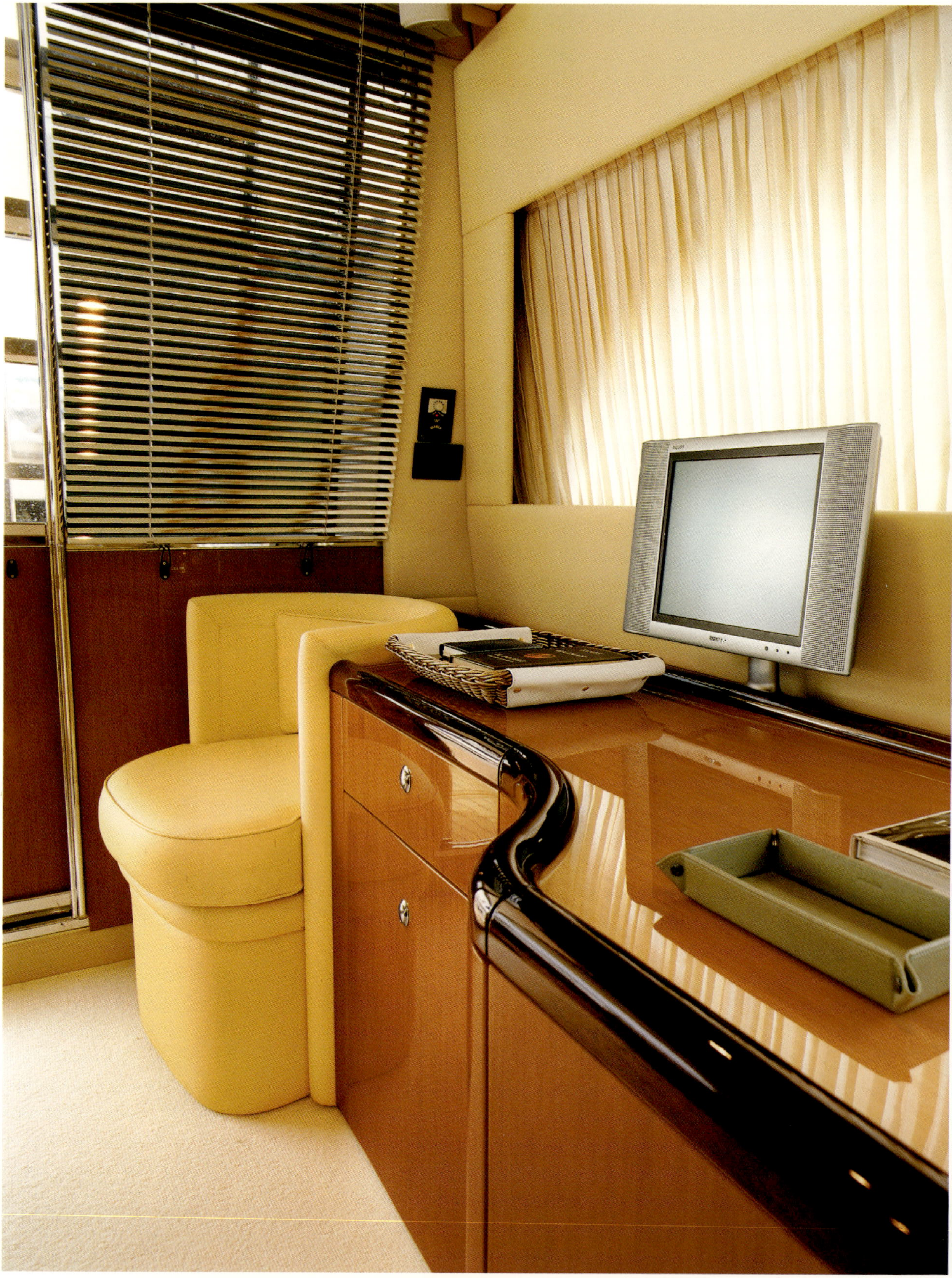

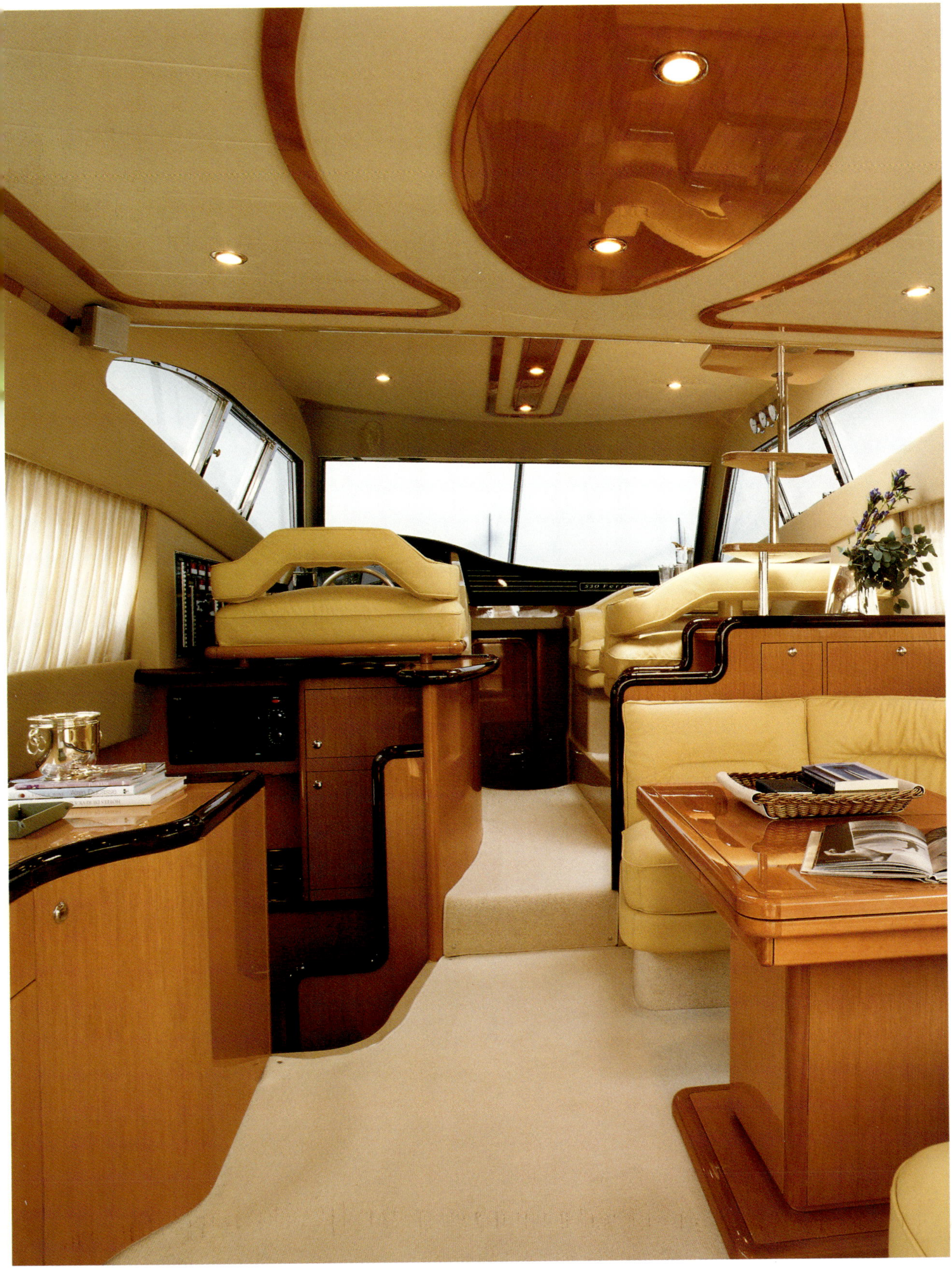

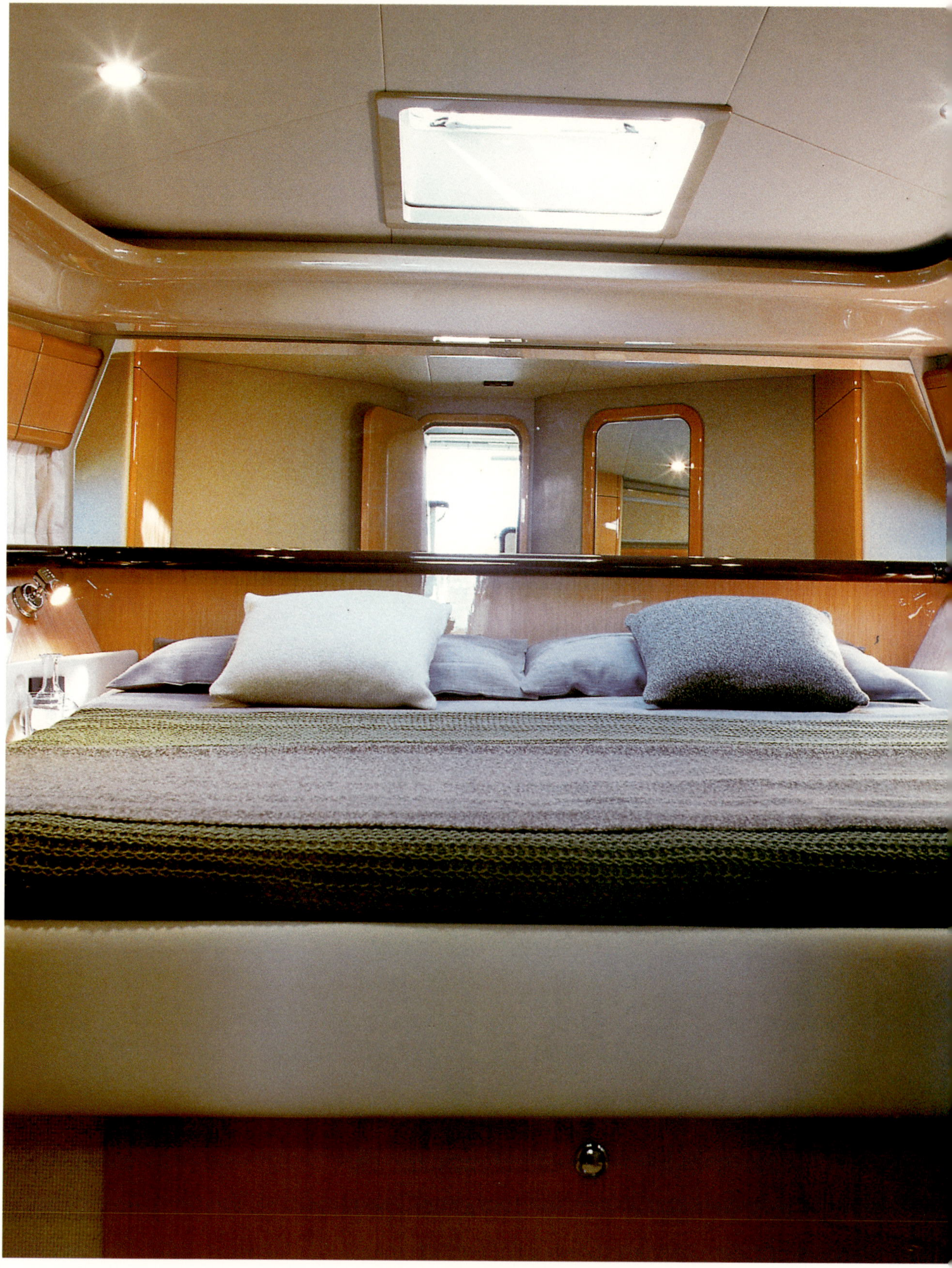

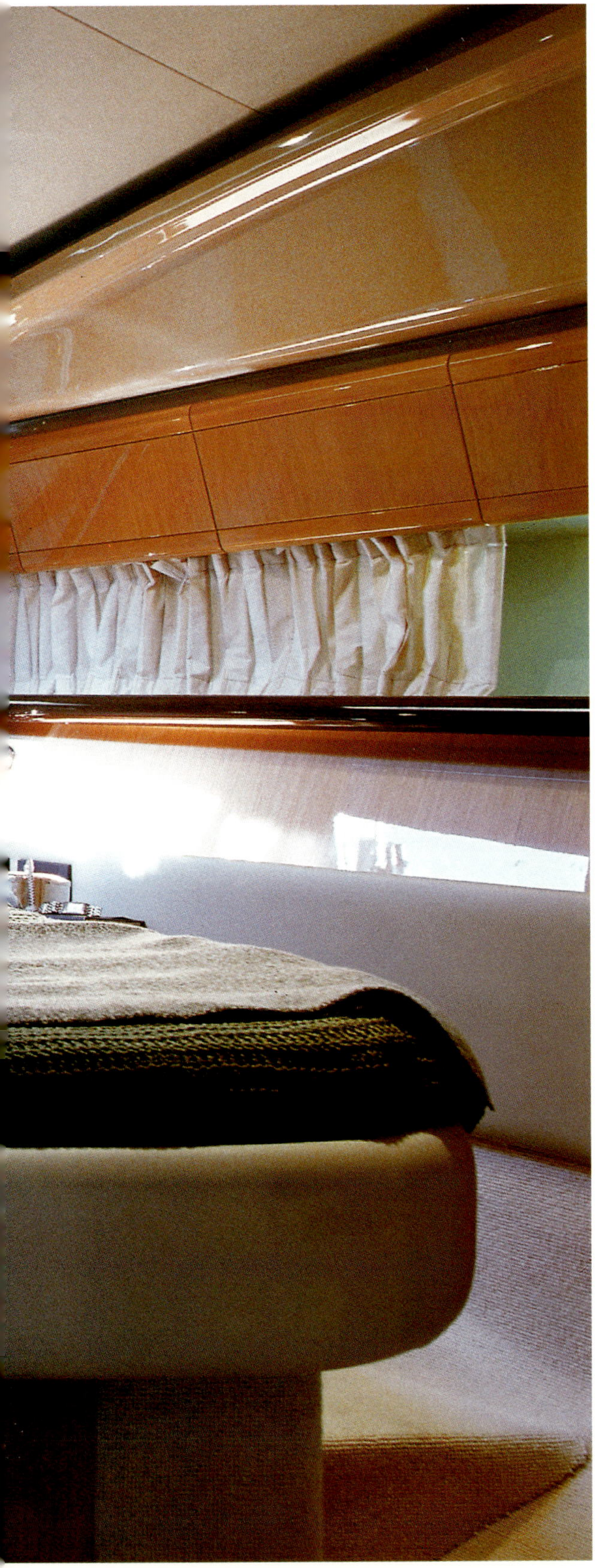

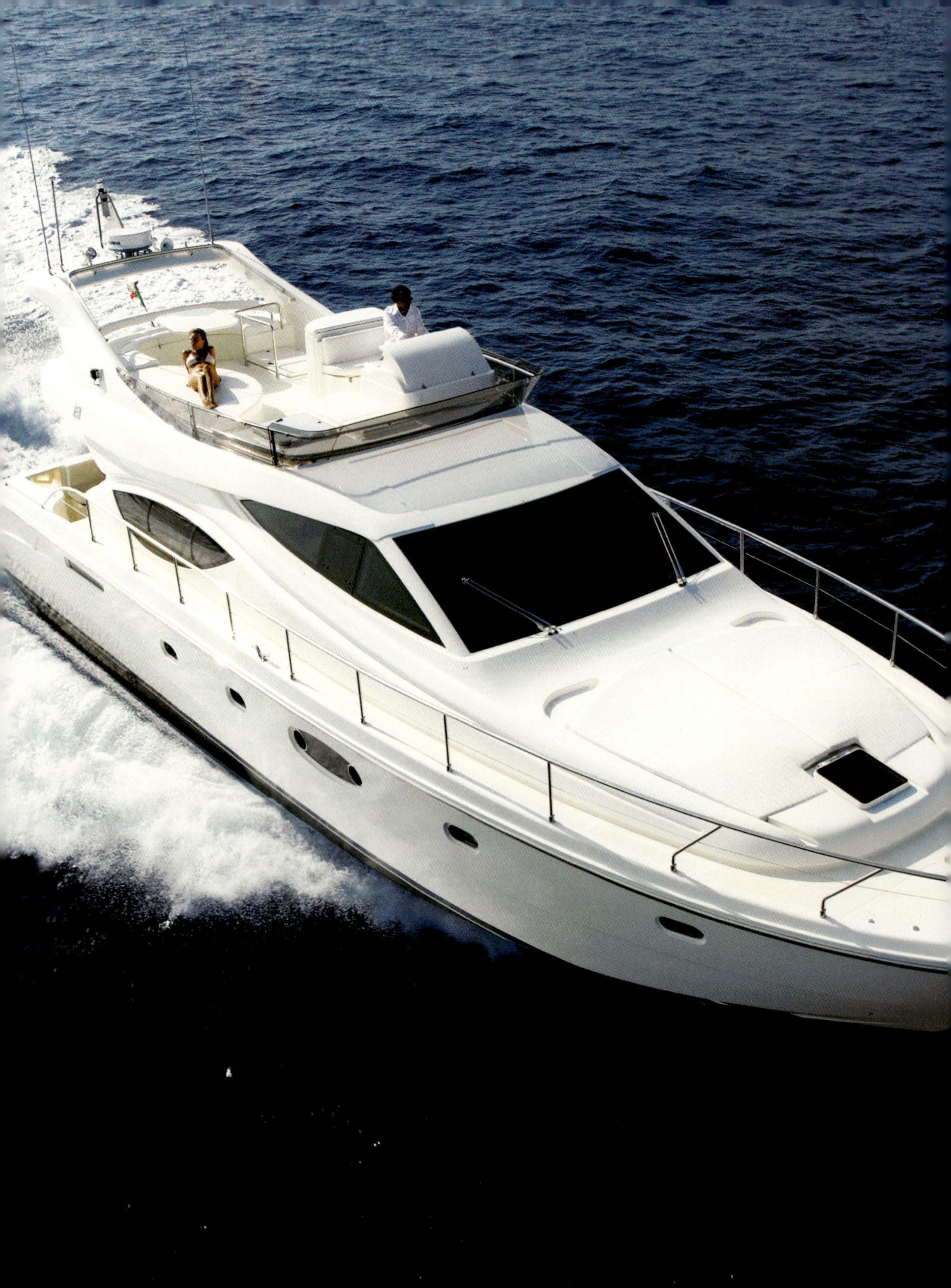

ZUCCON INTERNATIONAL PROJECT STUDIO
FERRETTI 550 | 2005
Ferretti Yachts

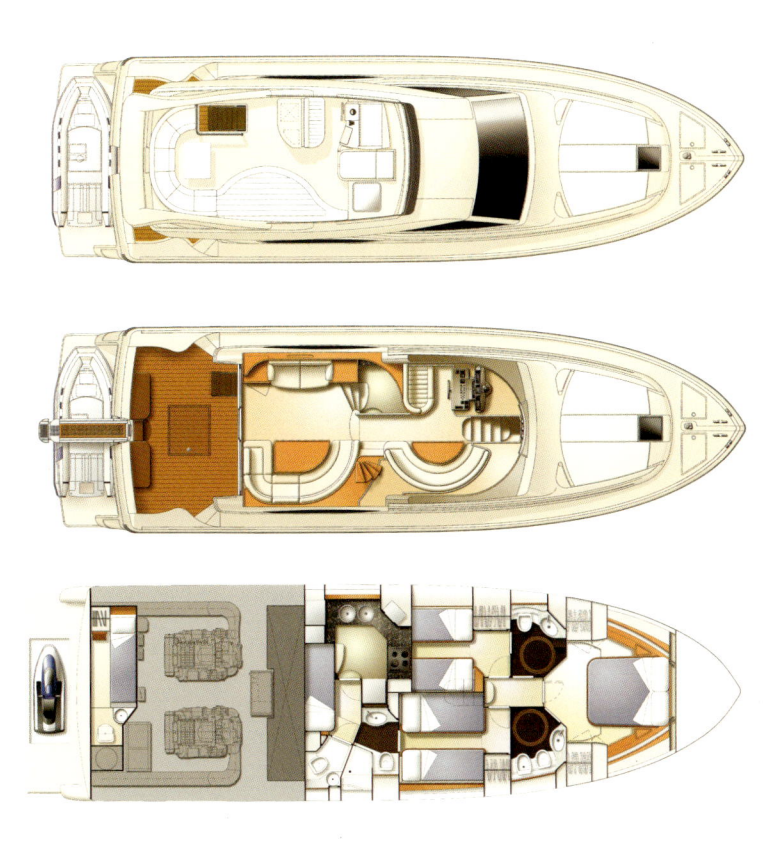

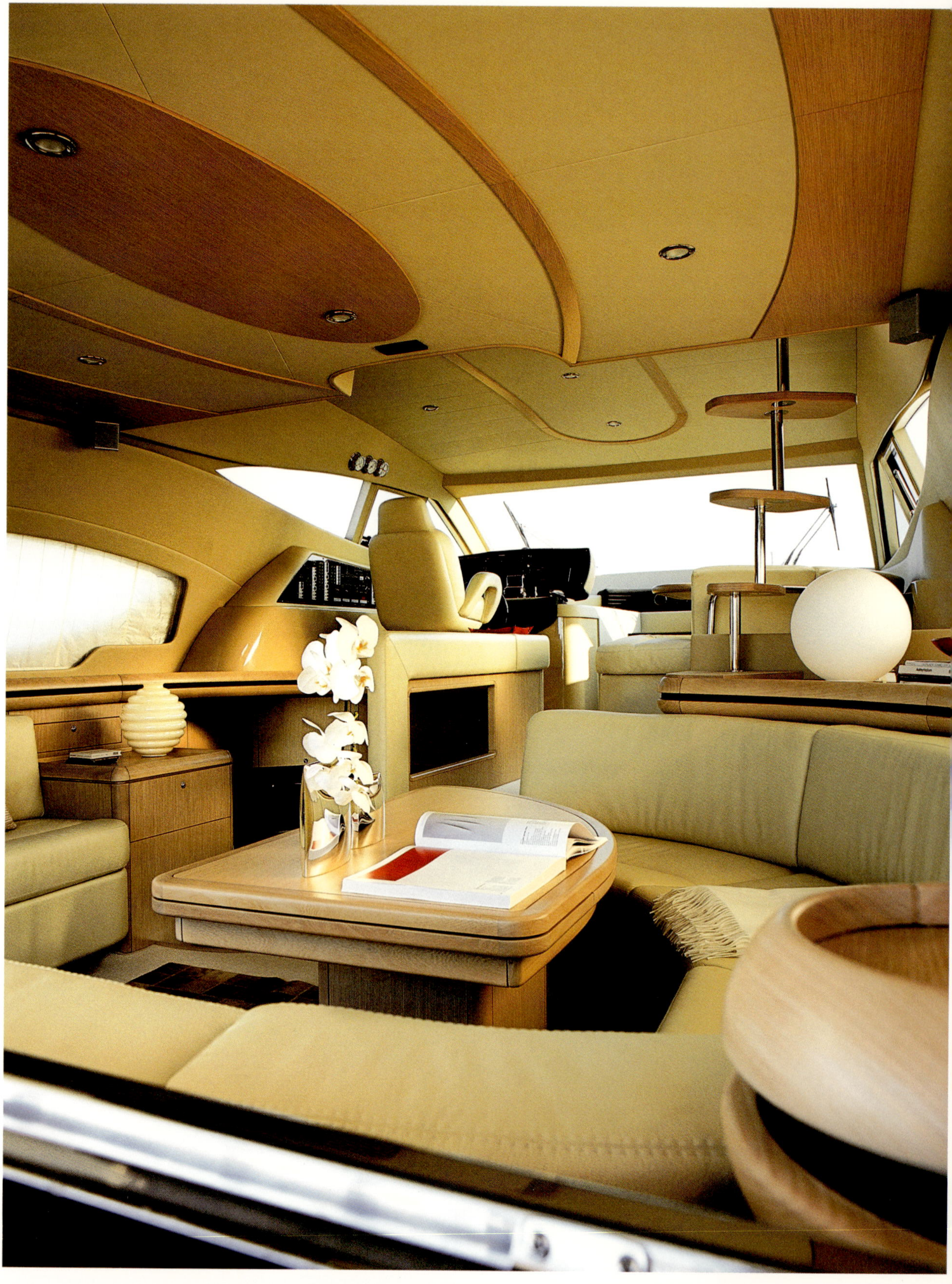

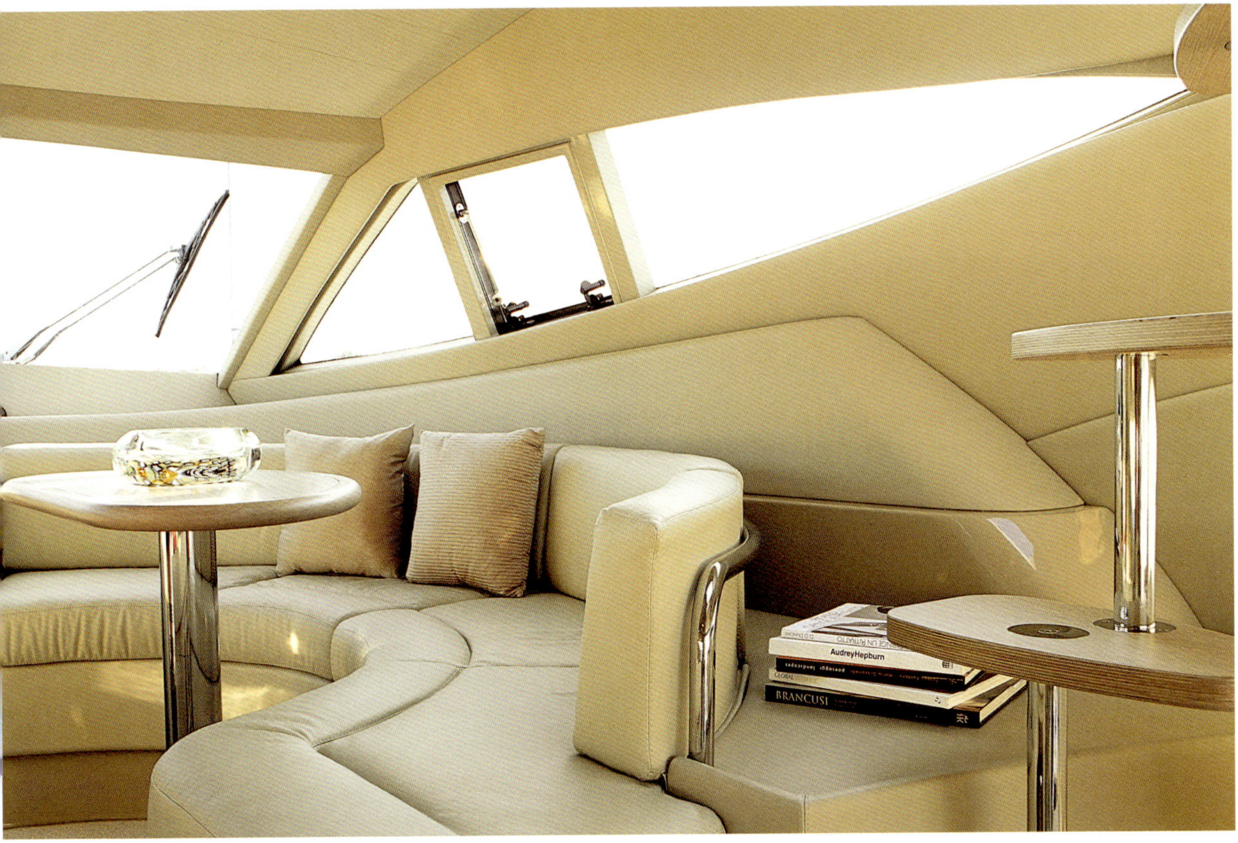
AudreyHepburn
BRANCUSI

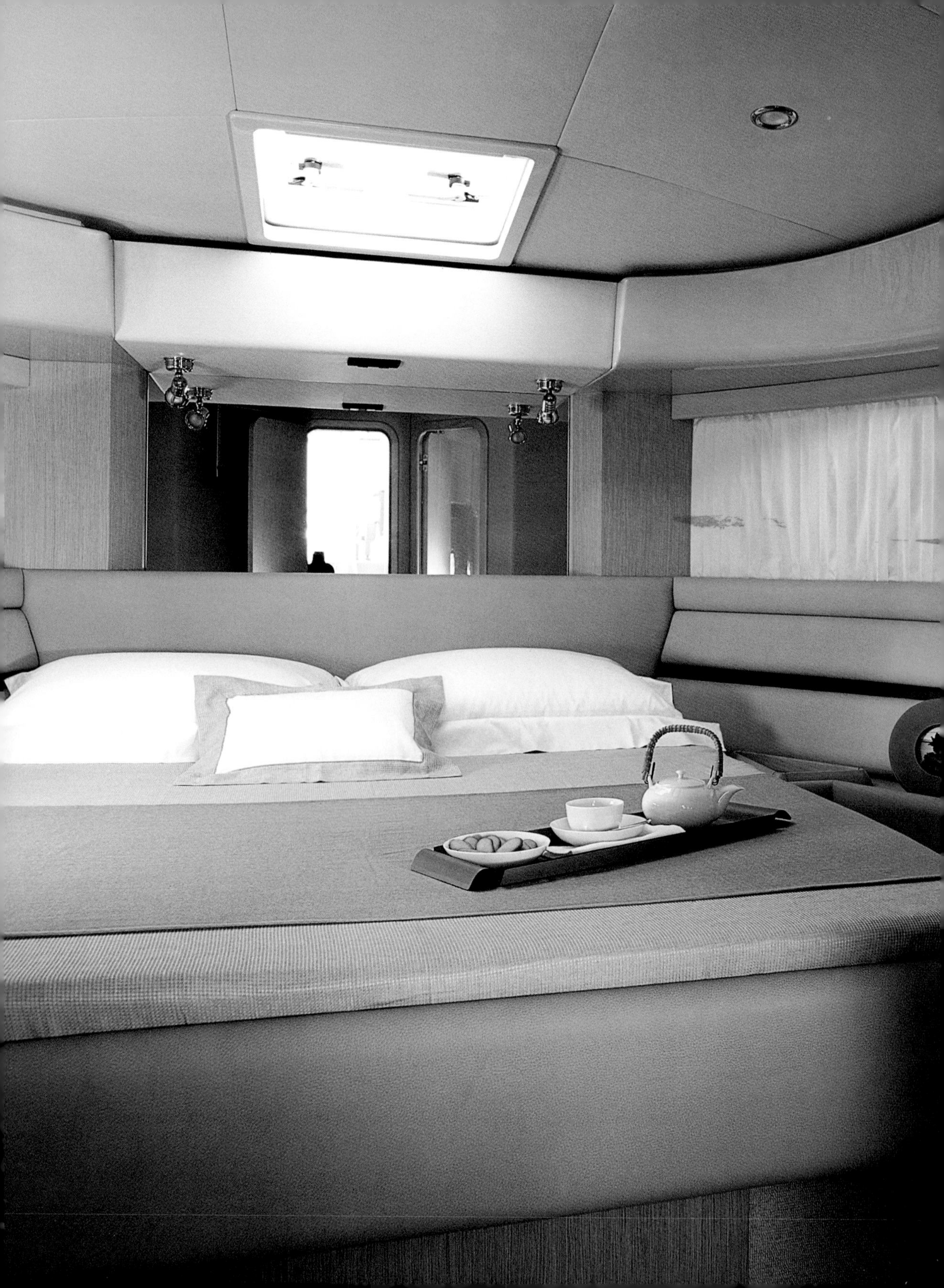

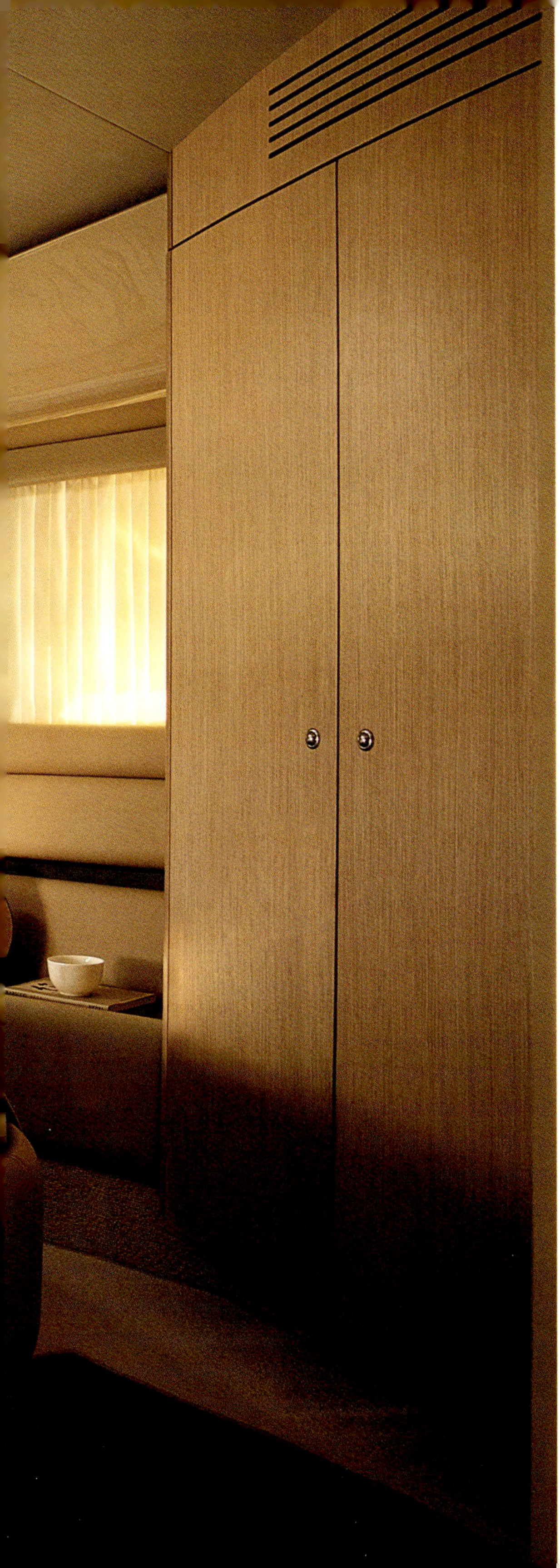

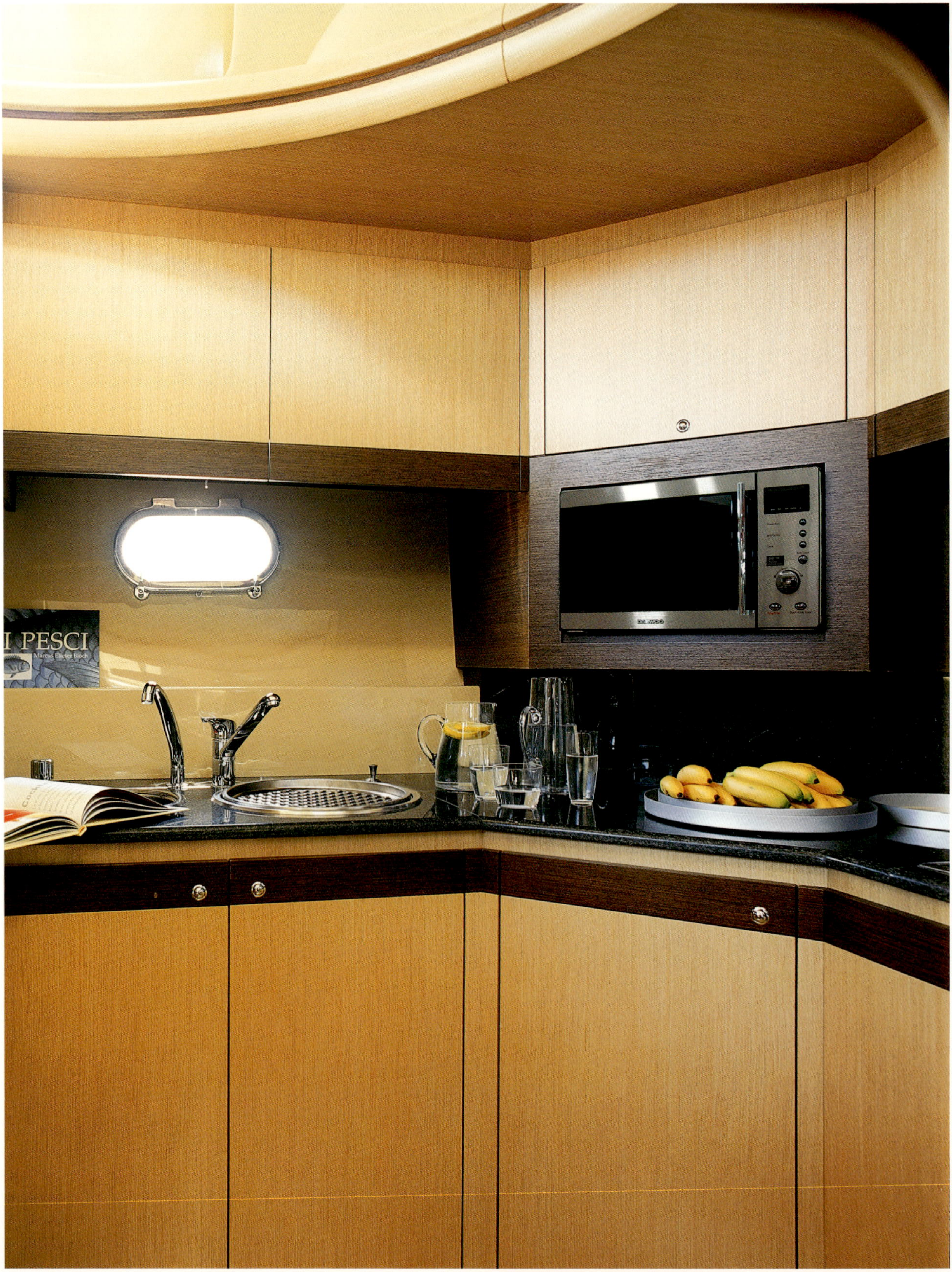
I PESCI
Marcus Elieser Bloch

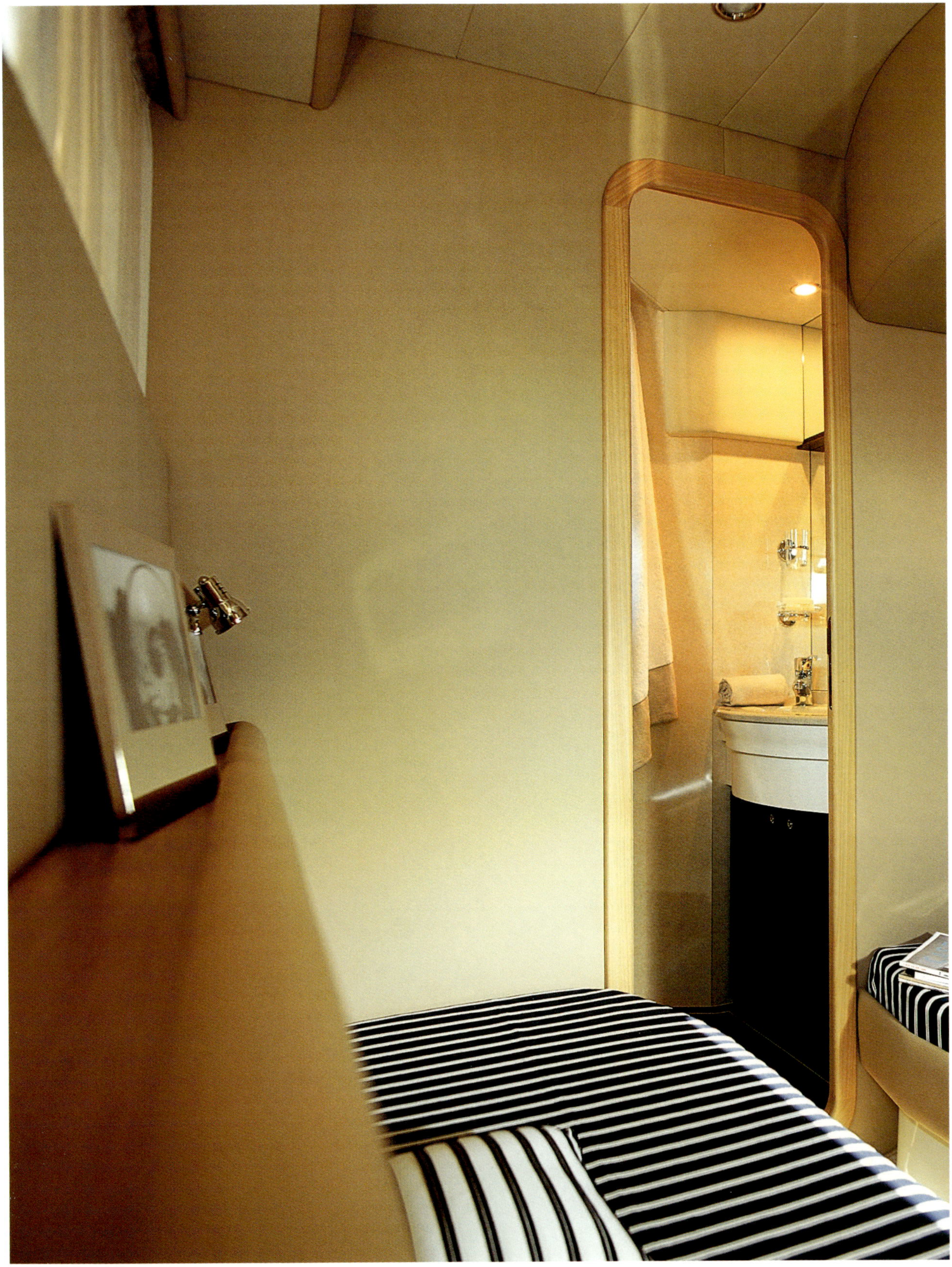

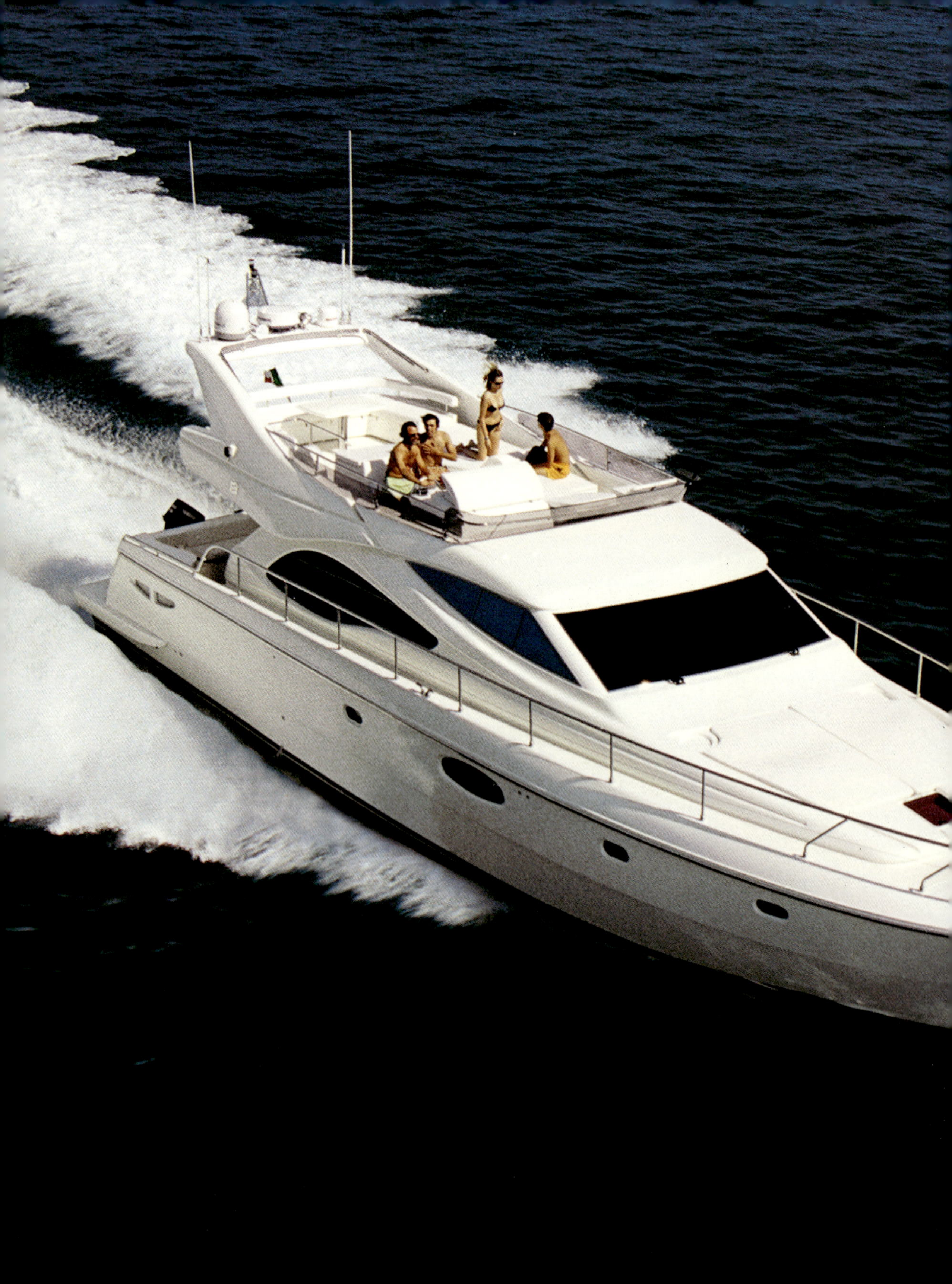

ZUCCON INTERNATIONAL PROJECT STUDIO
FERRETTI 590 | 2002
Ferretti Yachts

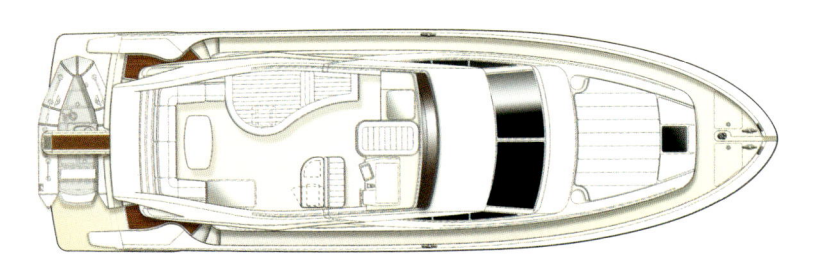

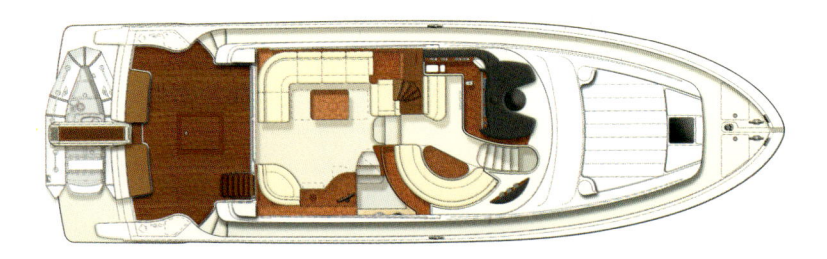

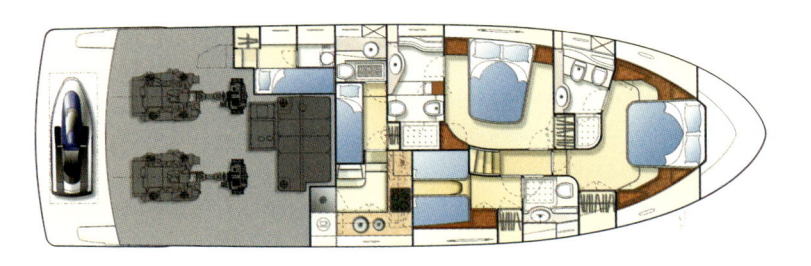

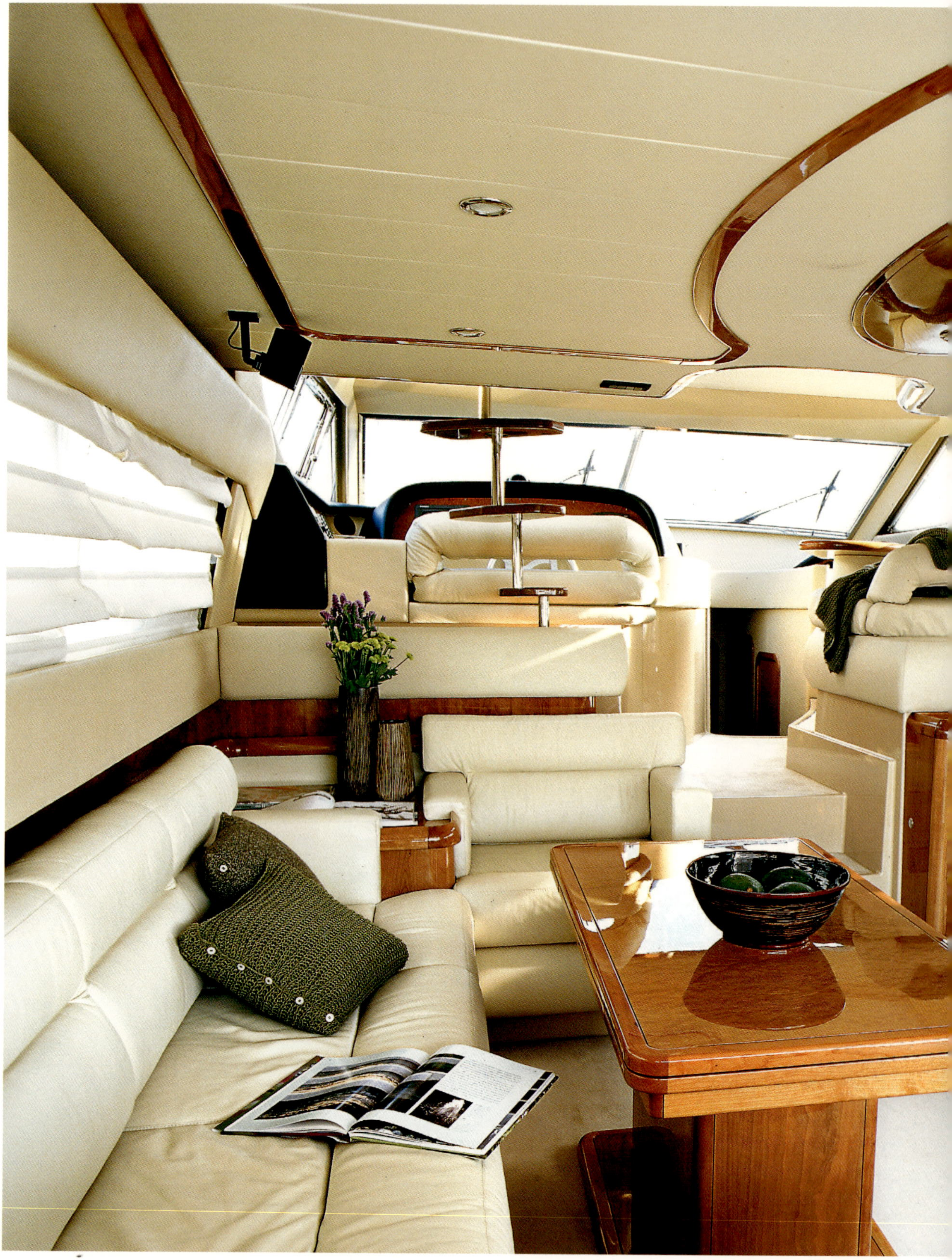

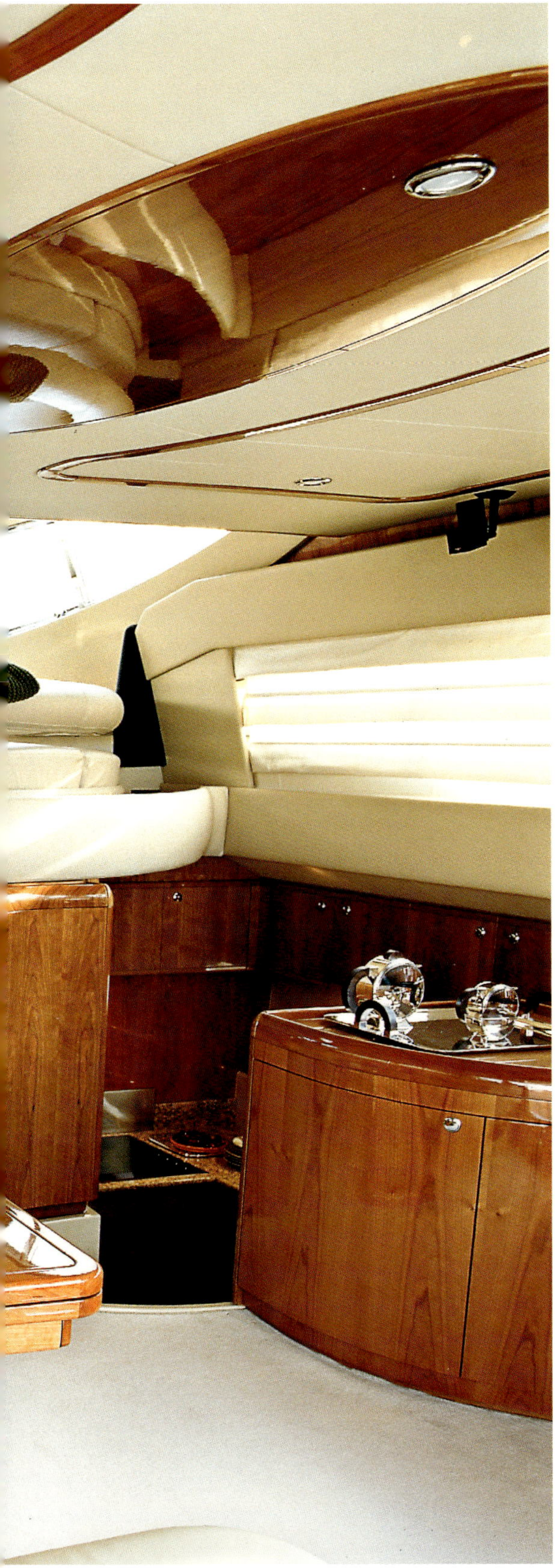

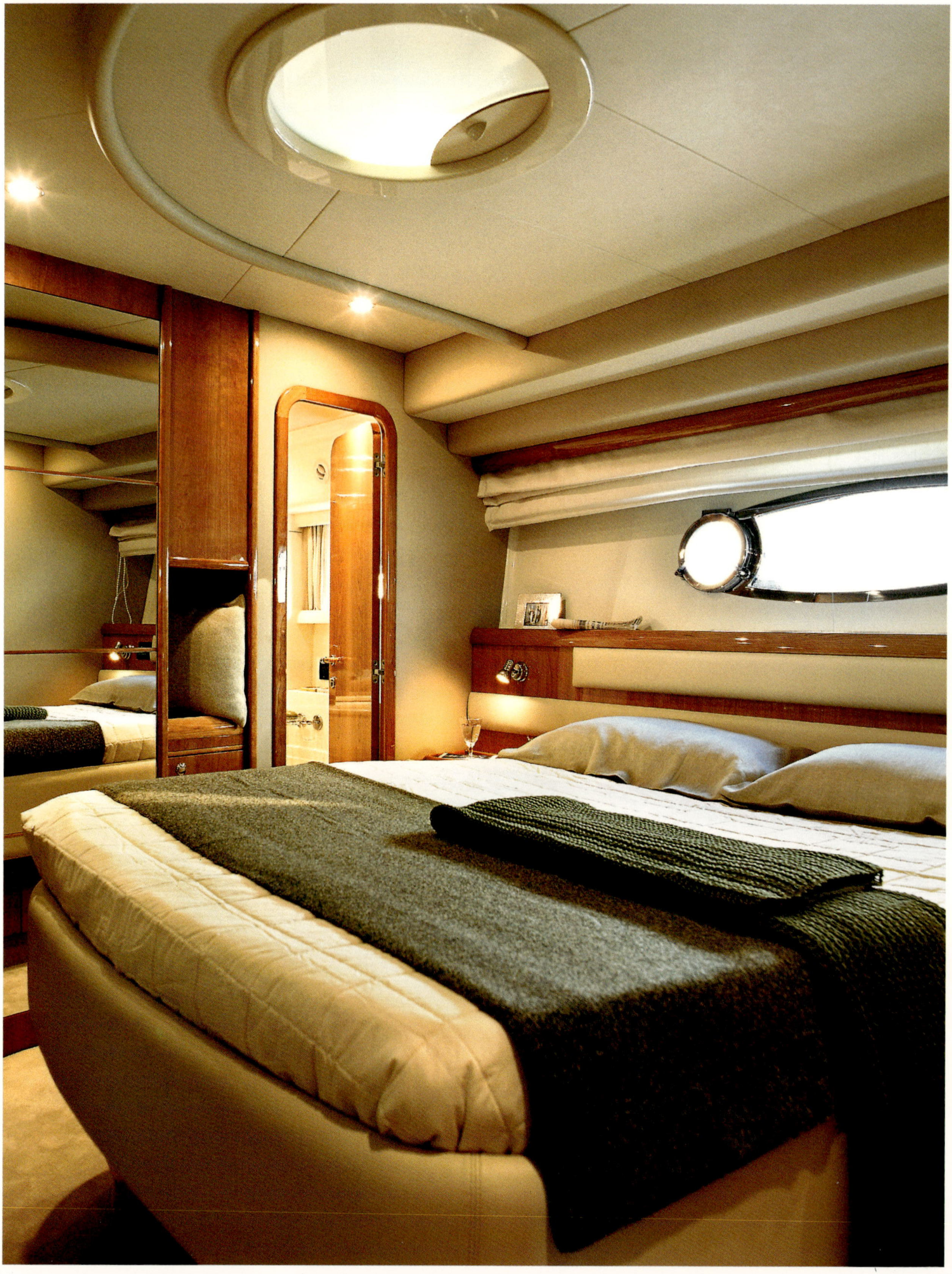

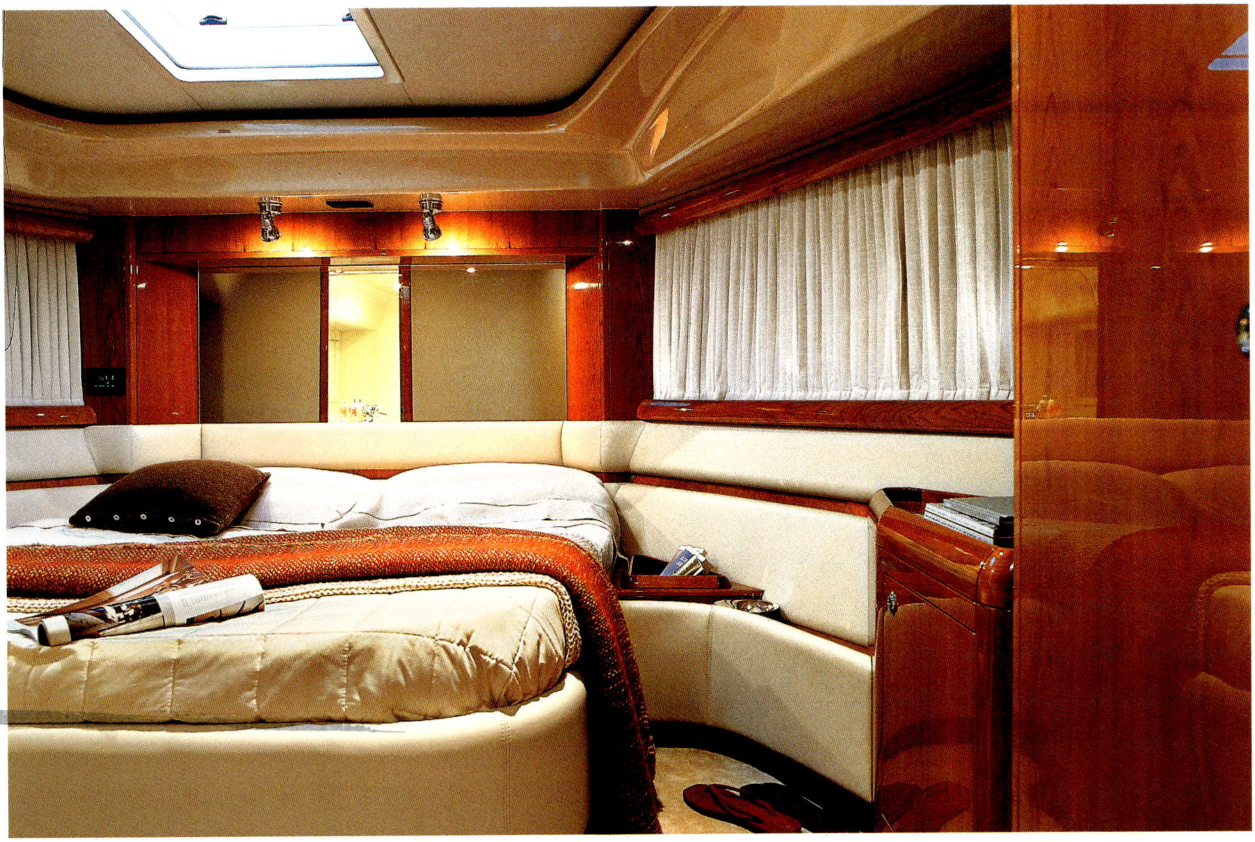

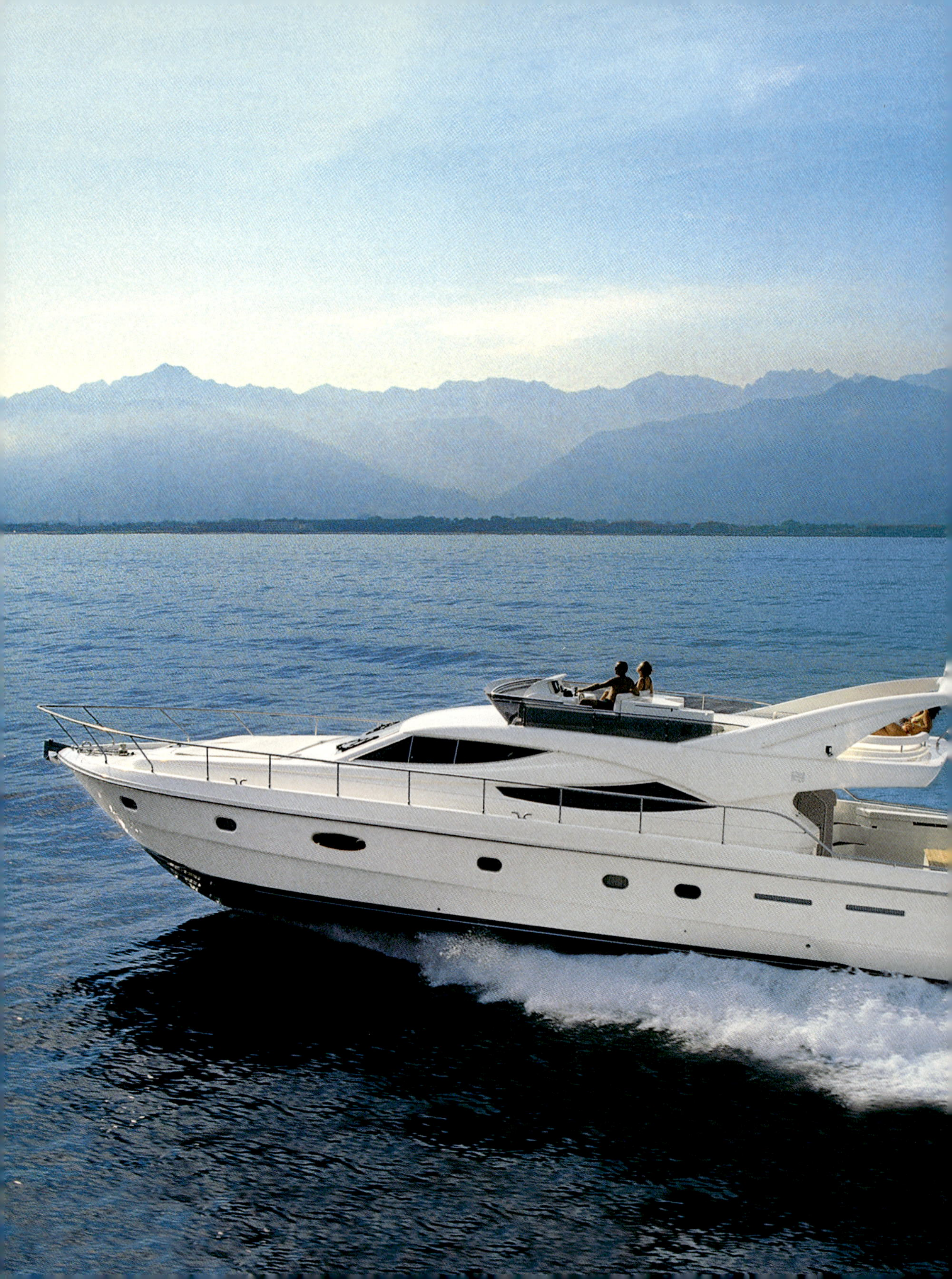

ZUCCON INTERNATIONAL PROJECT STUDIO
FERRETTI 620 | 2000
Ferretti Yachts

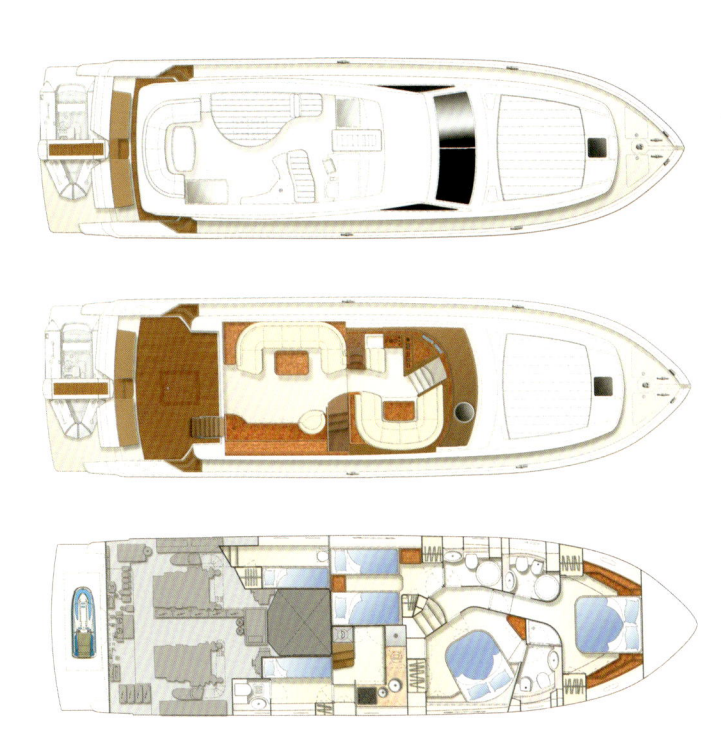

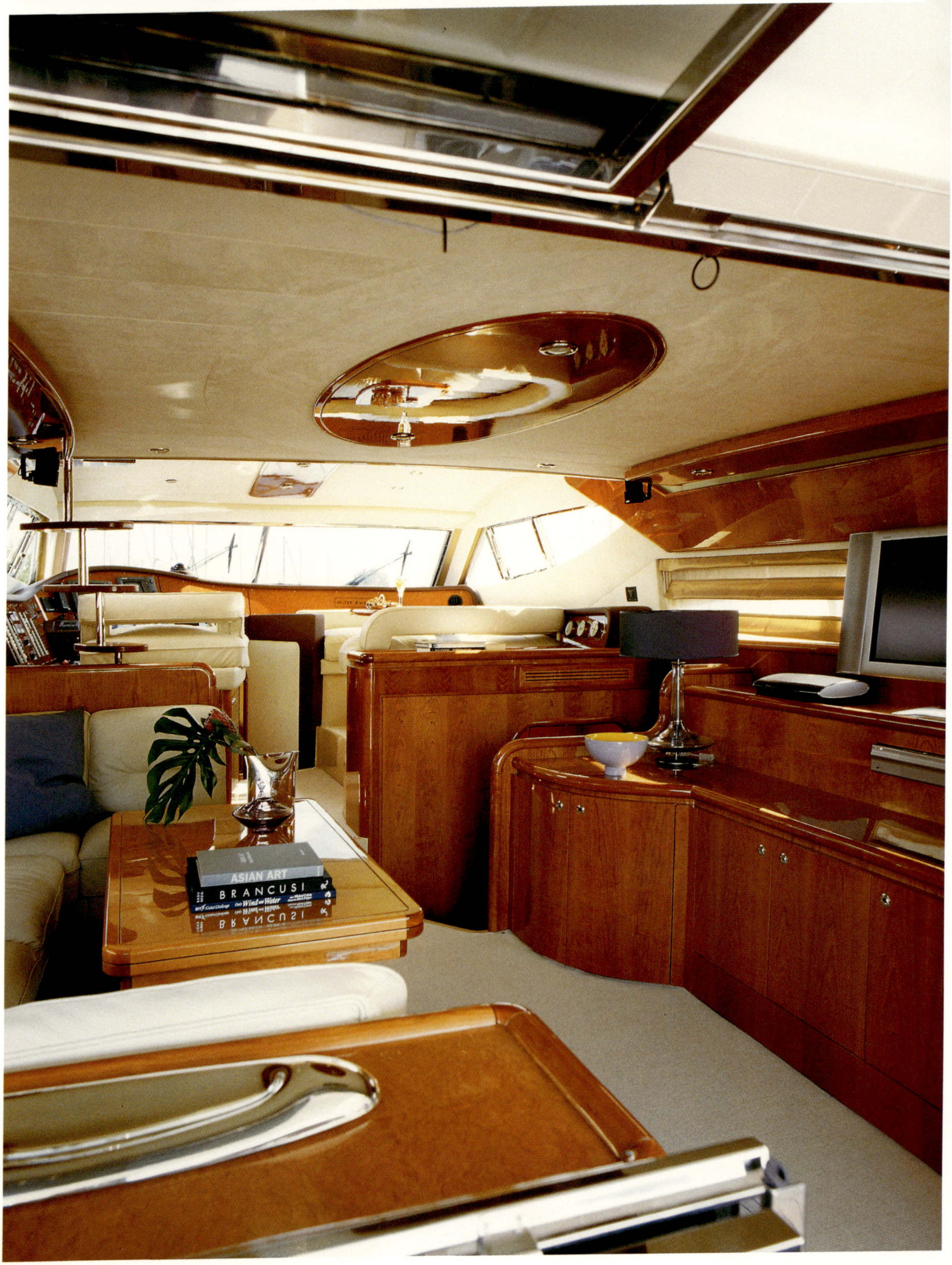
ASIAN ART
BRANCUSI

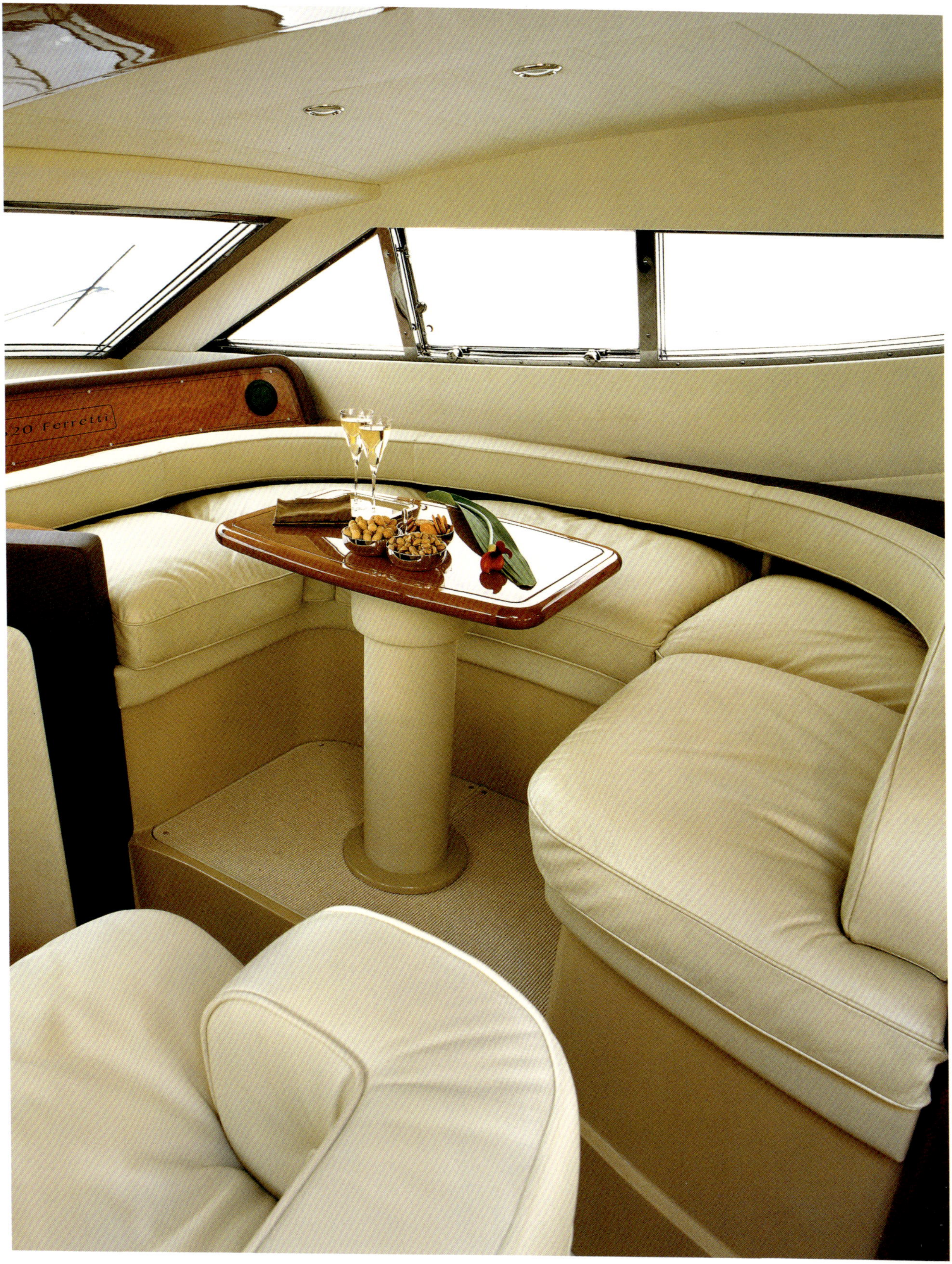
Ferretti

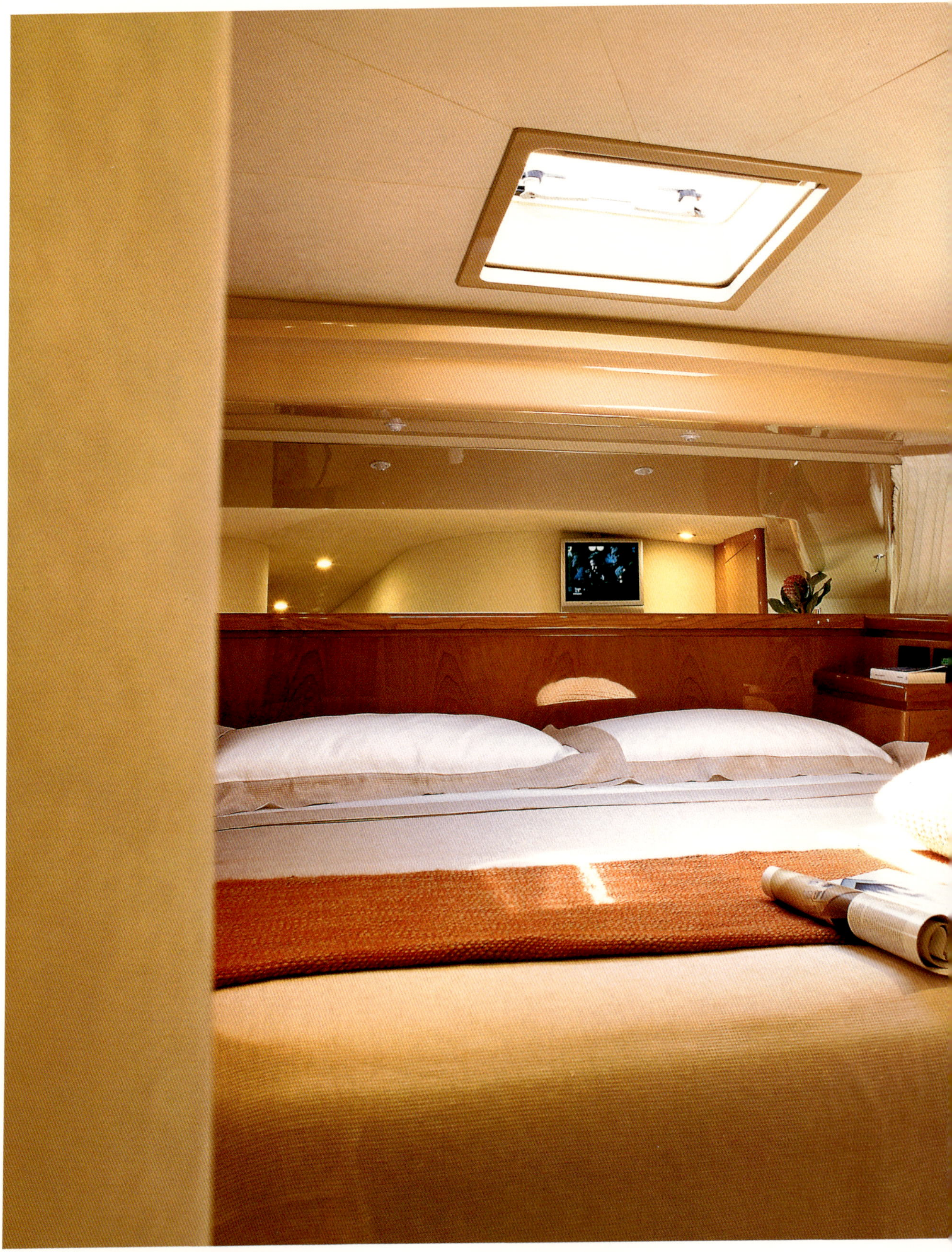

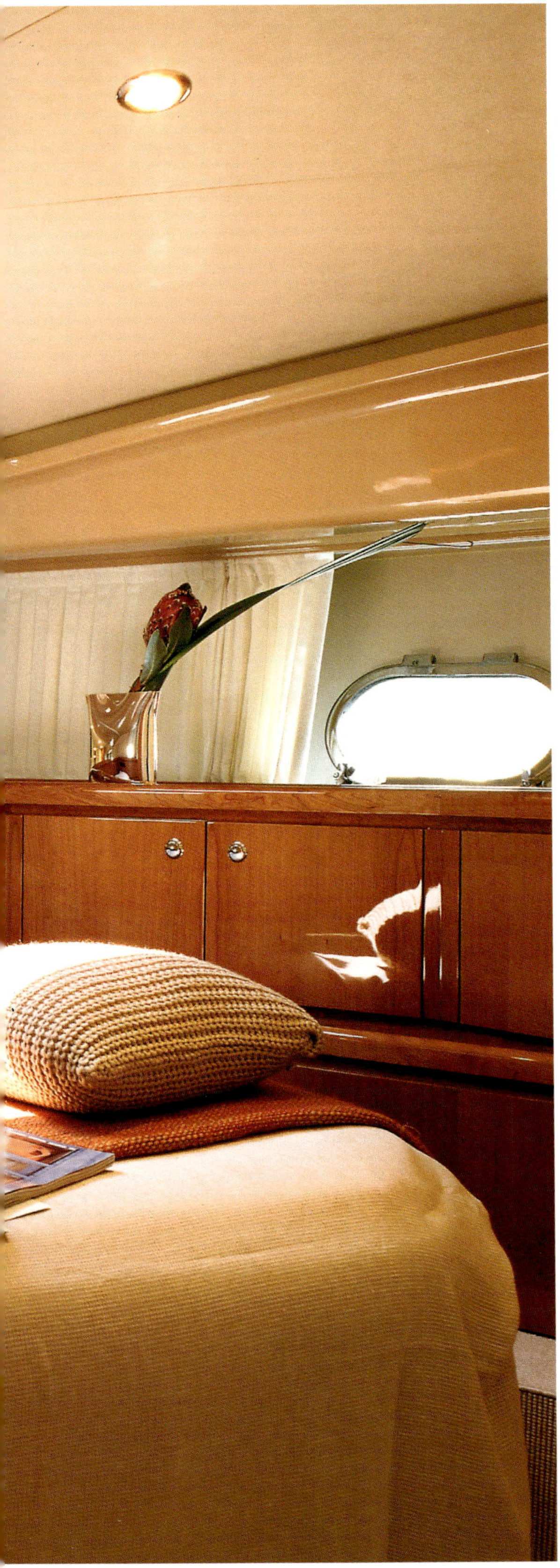

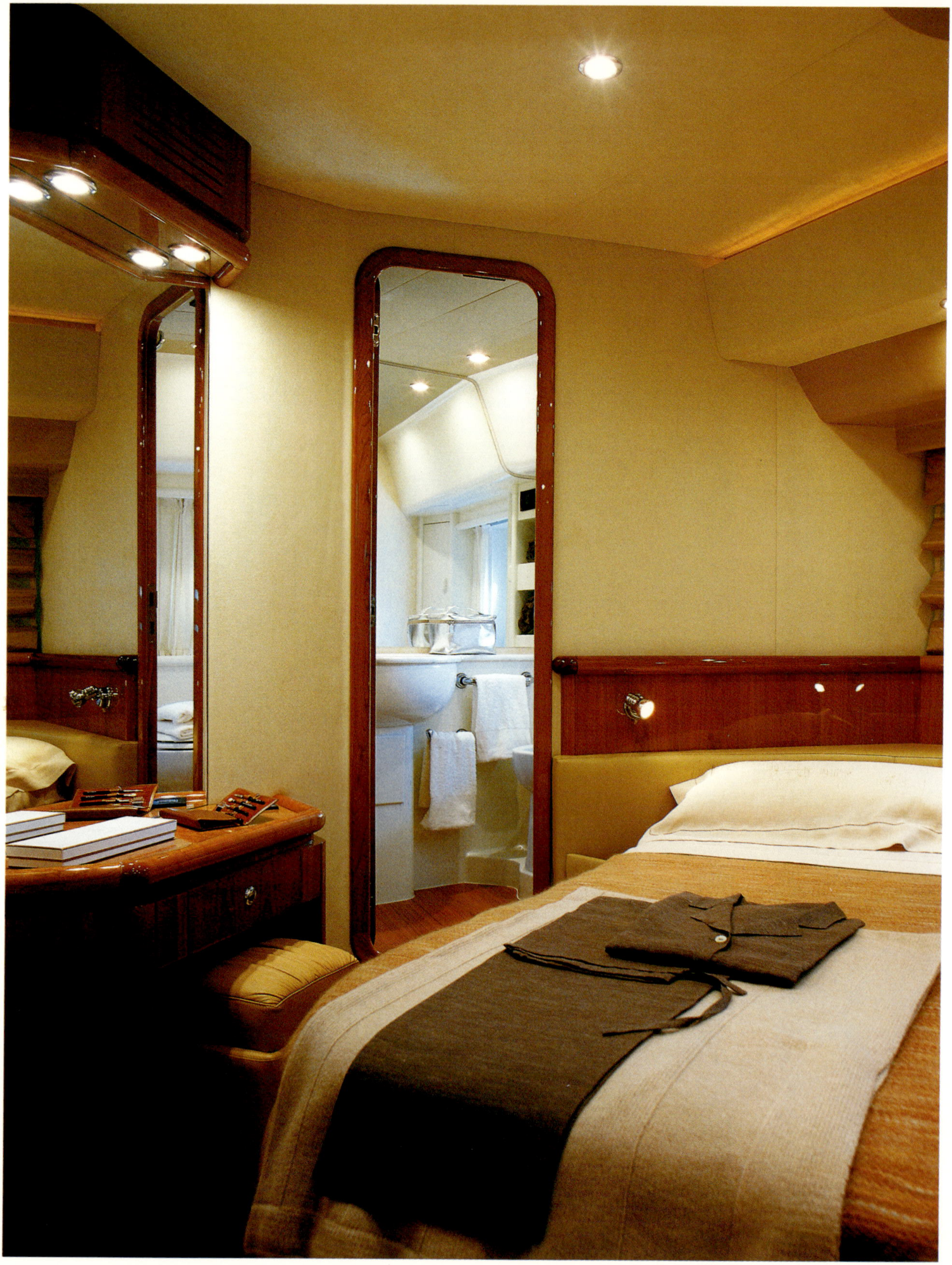

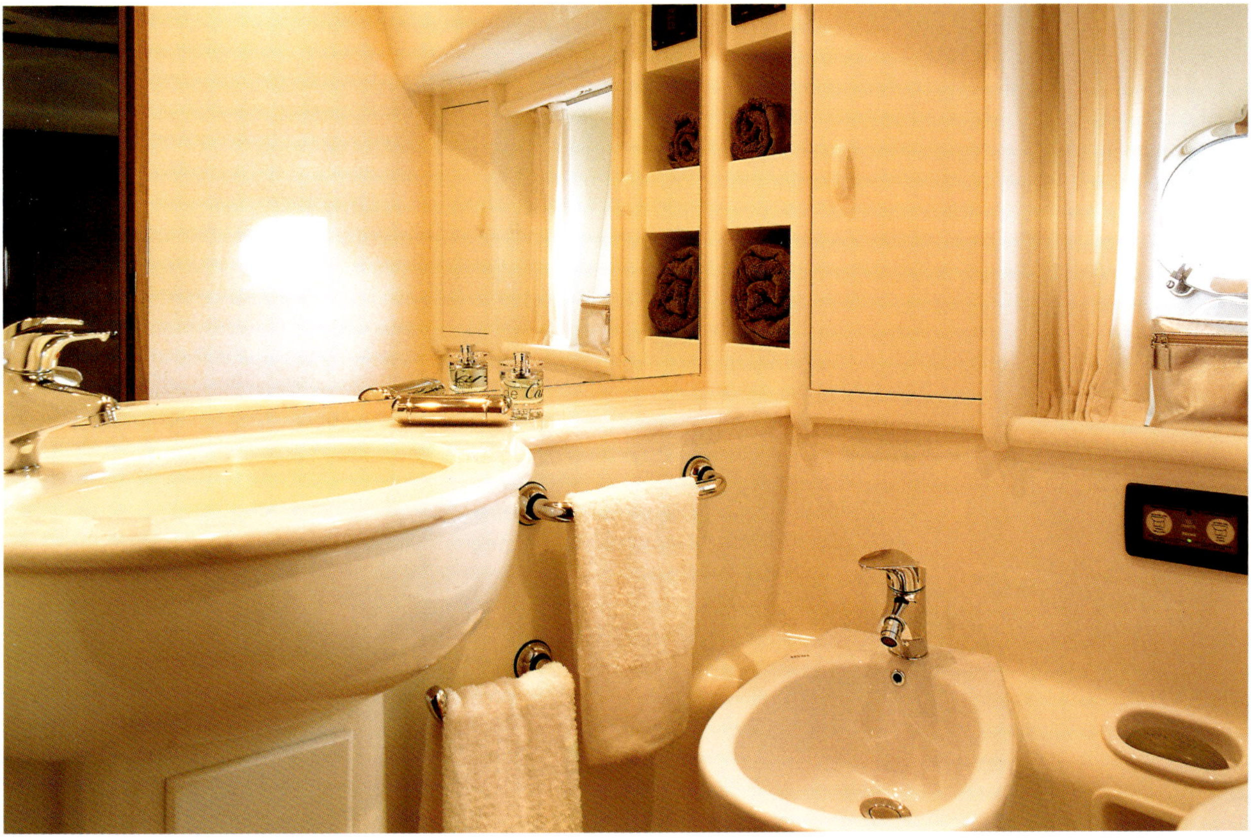

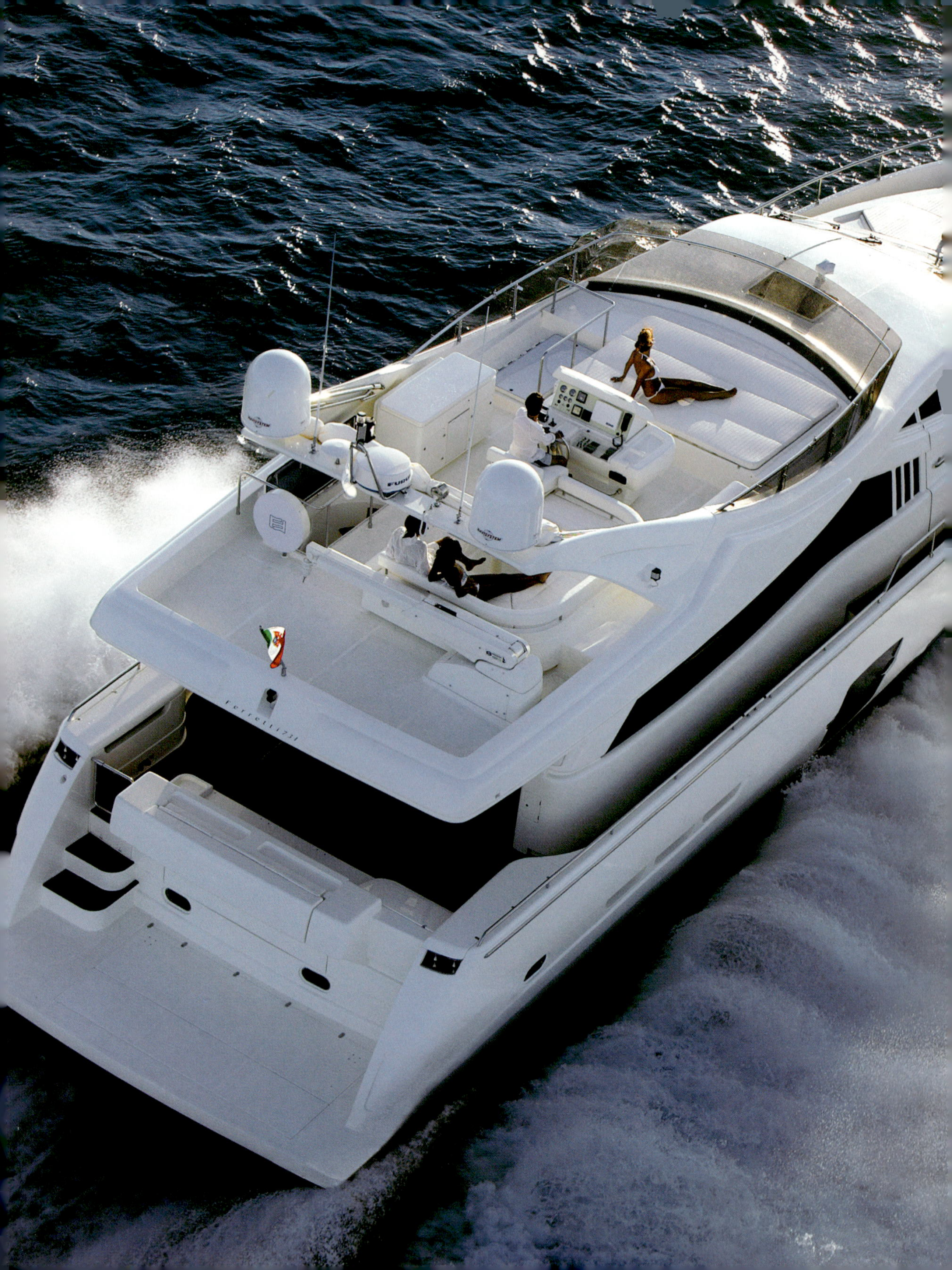

ZUCCON INTERNATIONAL PROJECT STUDIO
FERRETTI 731 | 2005
Ferretti Yachts

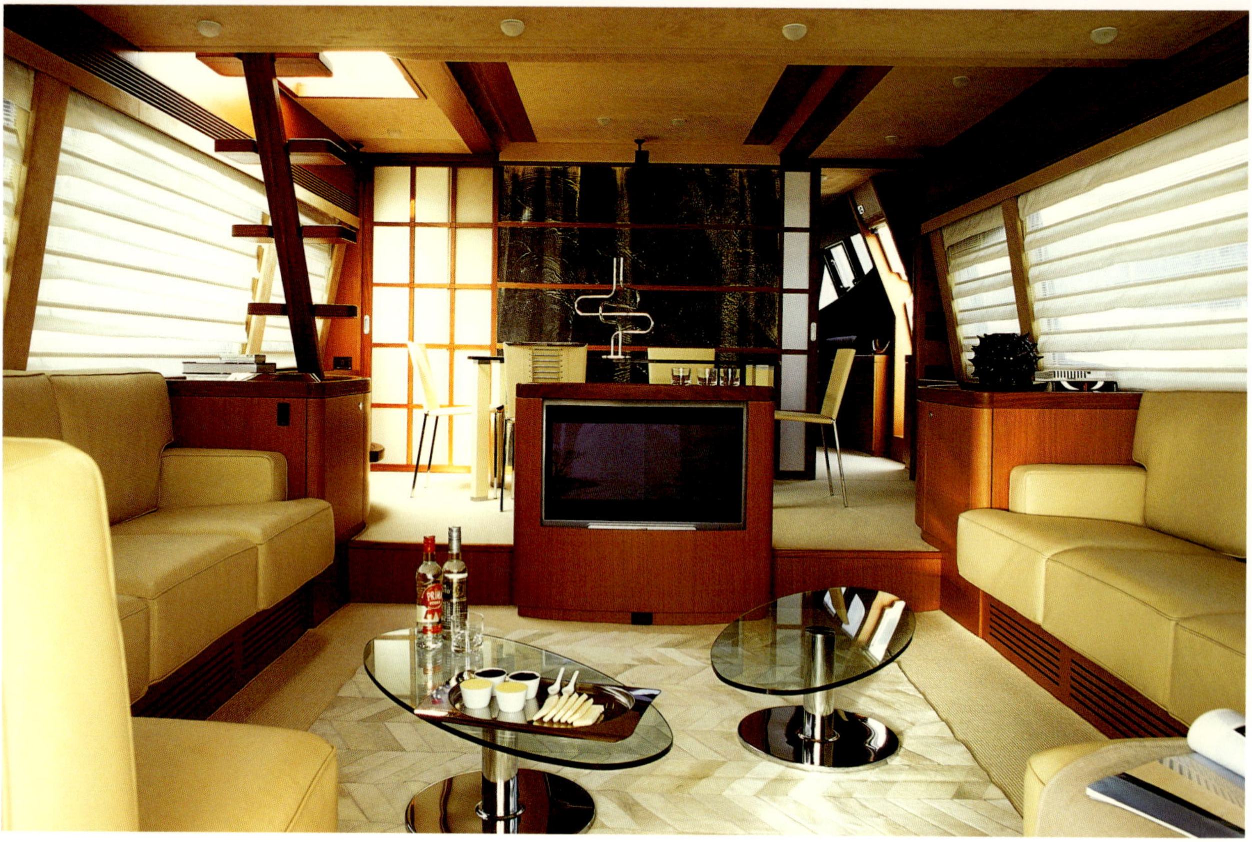

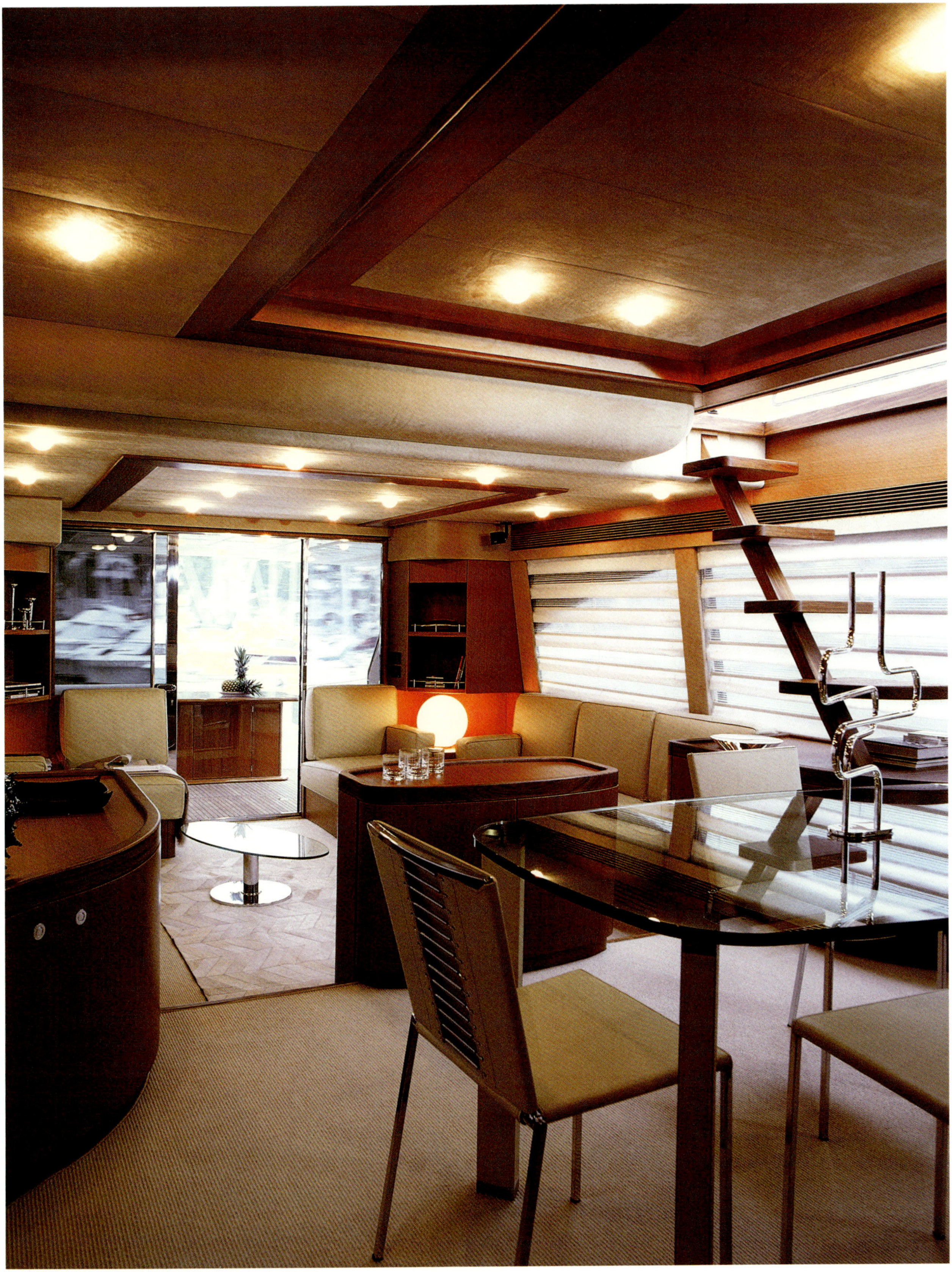

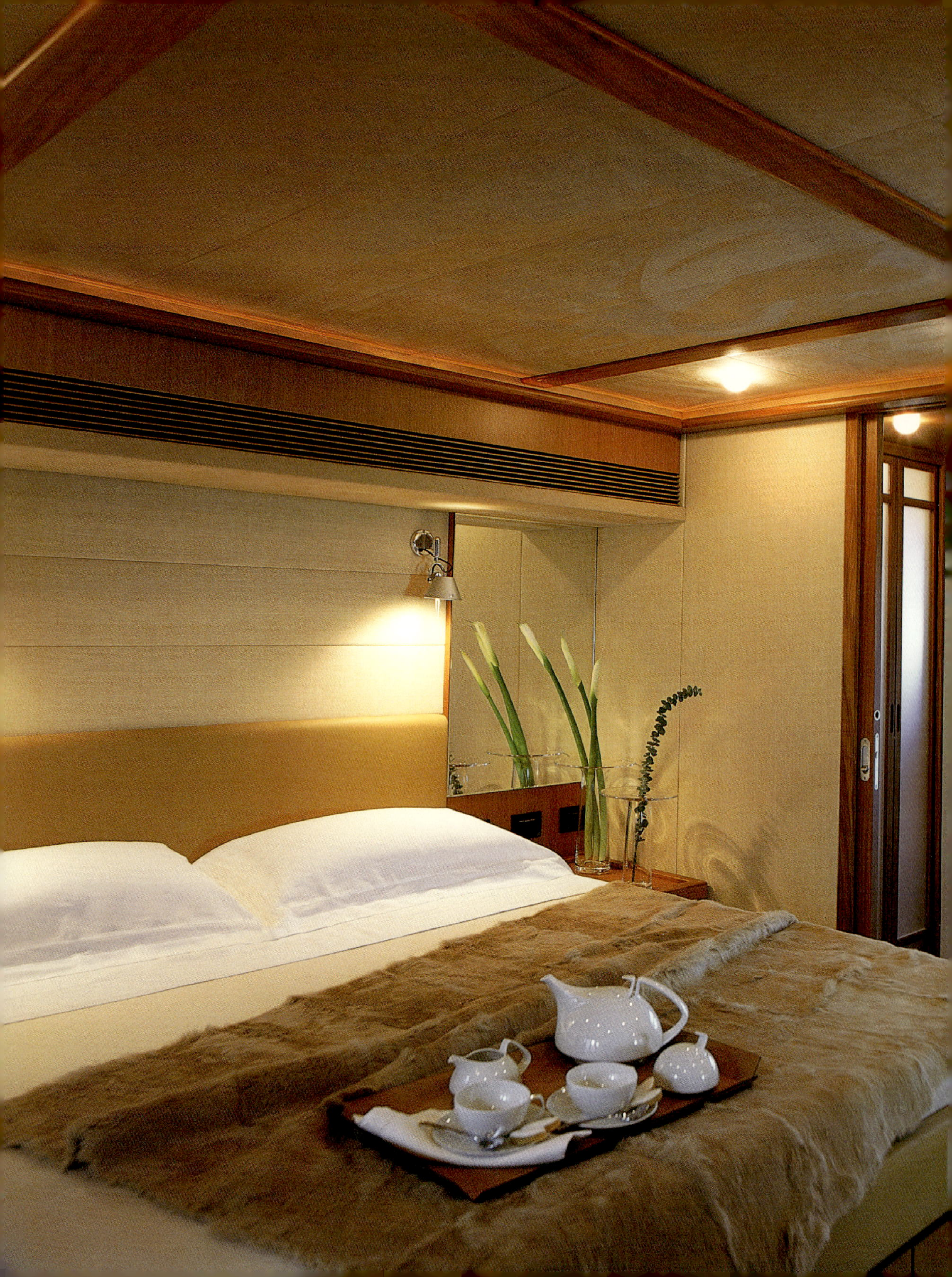

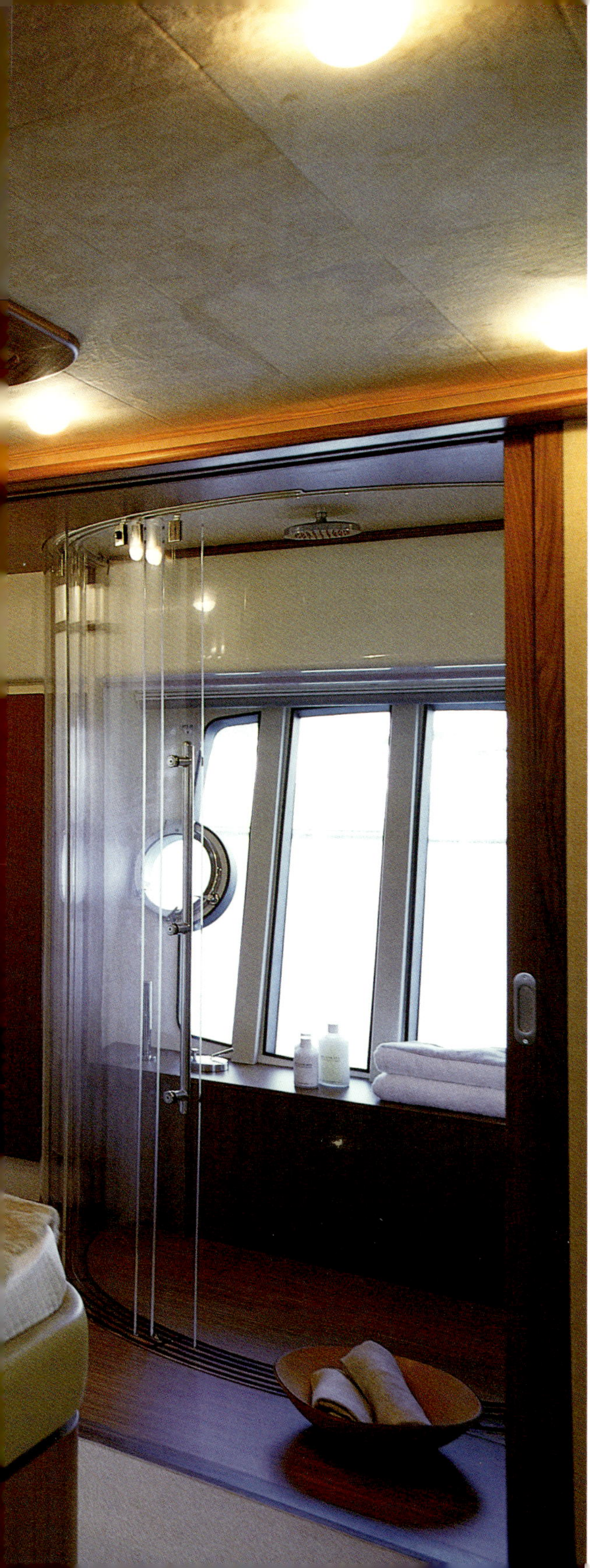

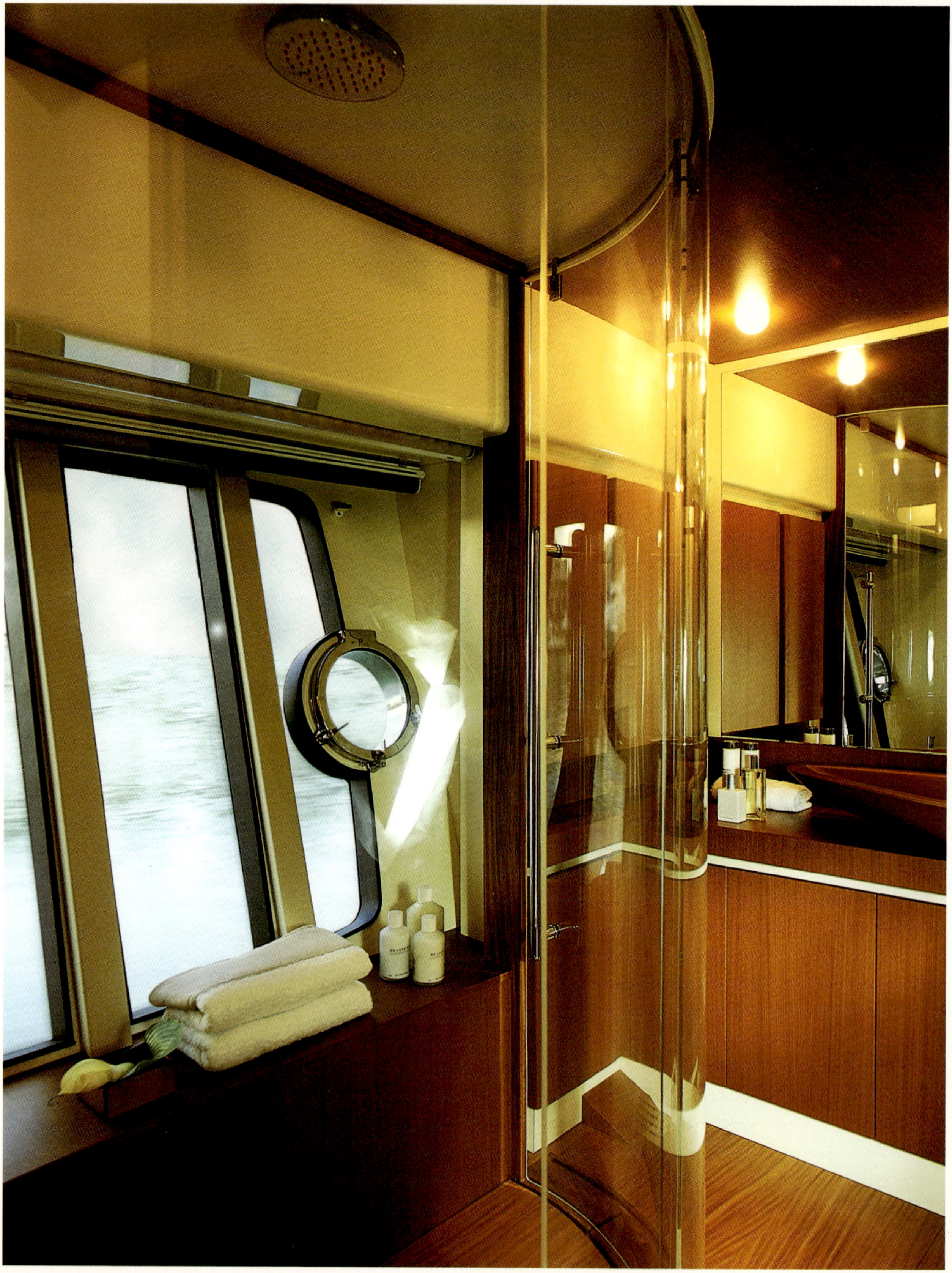

383

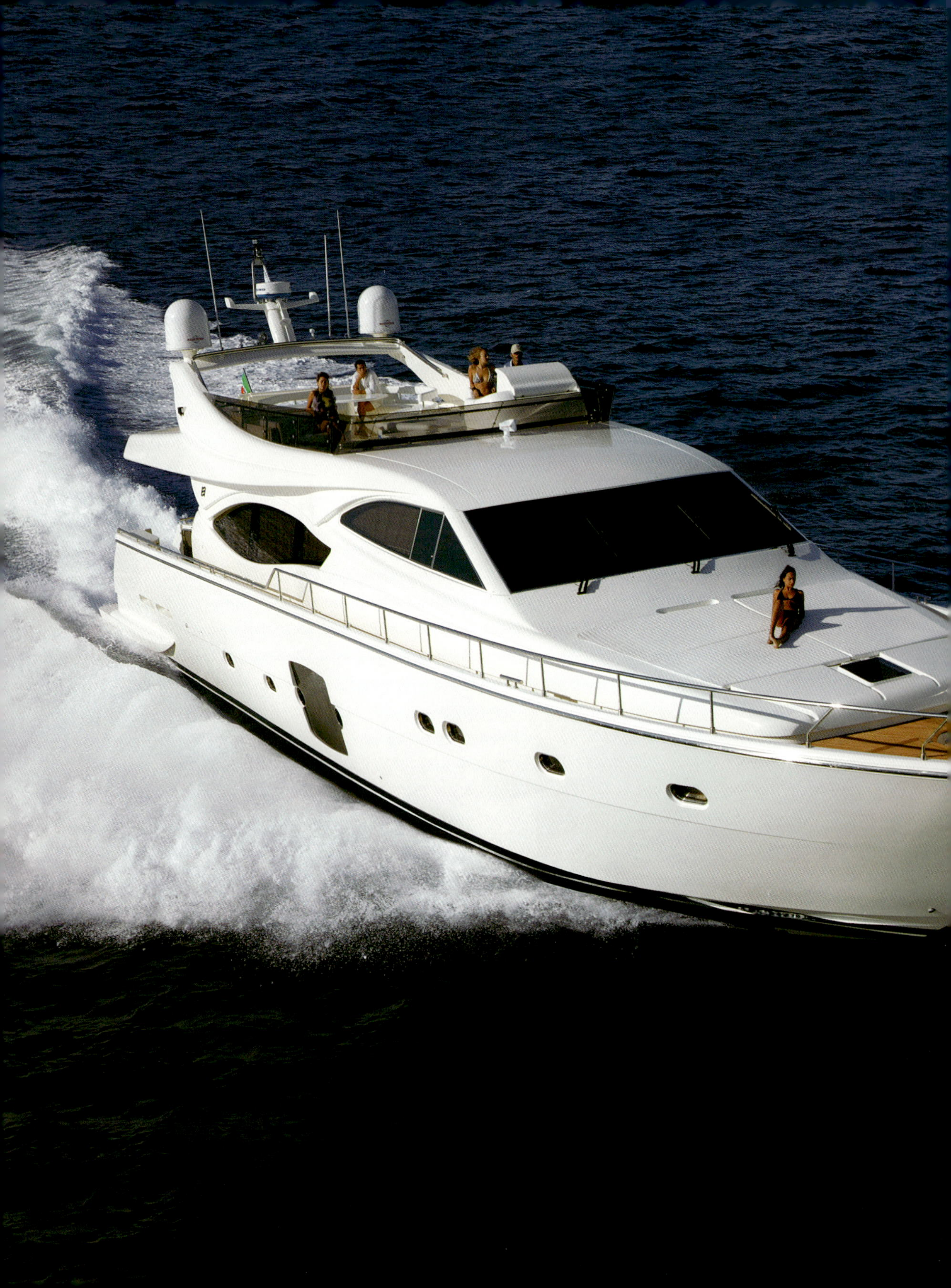

ZUCCON INTERNATIONAL PROJECT STUDIO
FERRETTI 761 | 2005
Ferretti Yachts

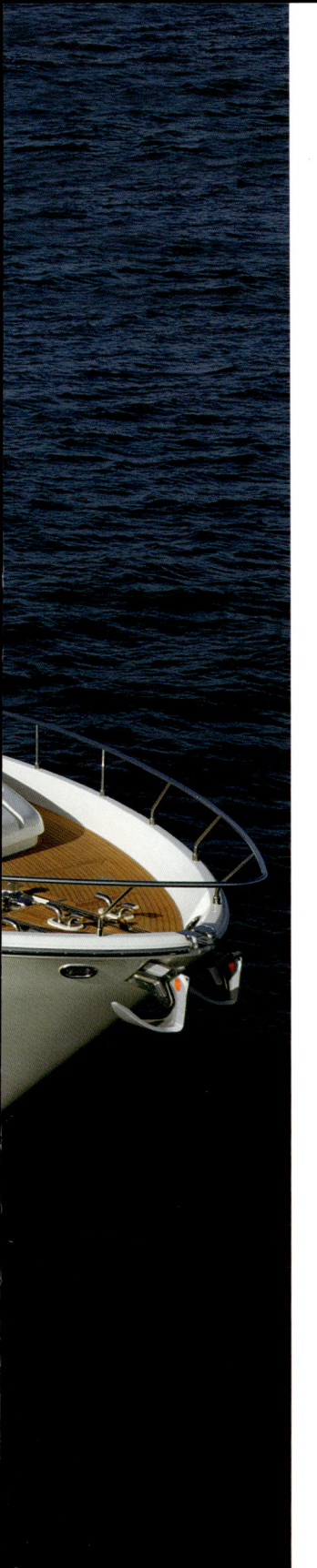

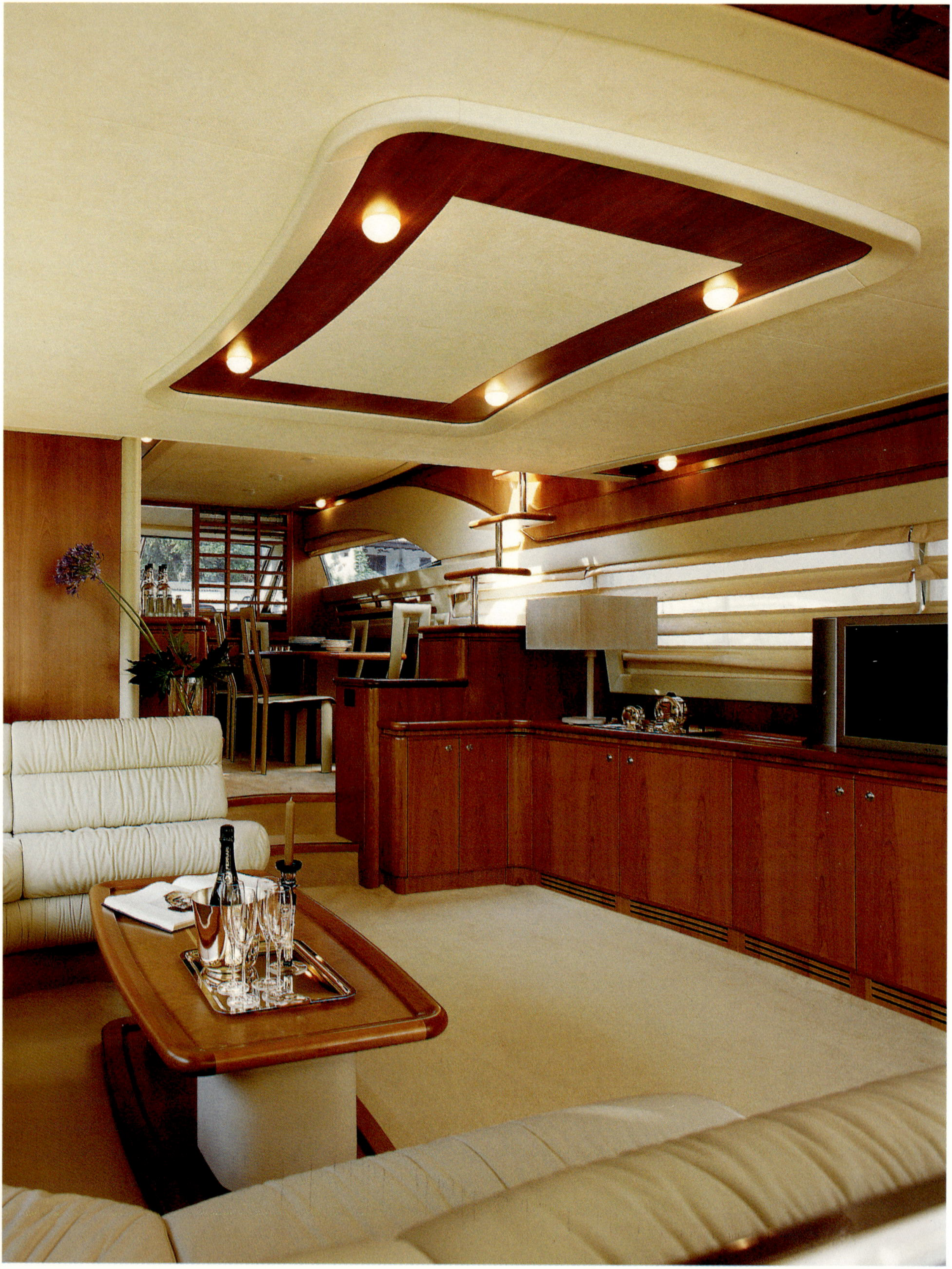

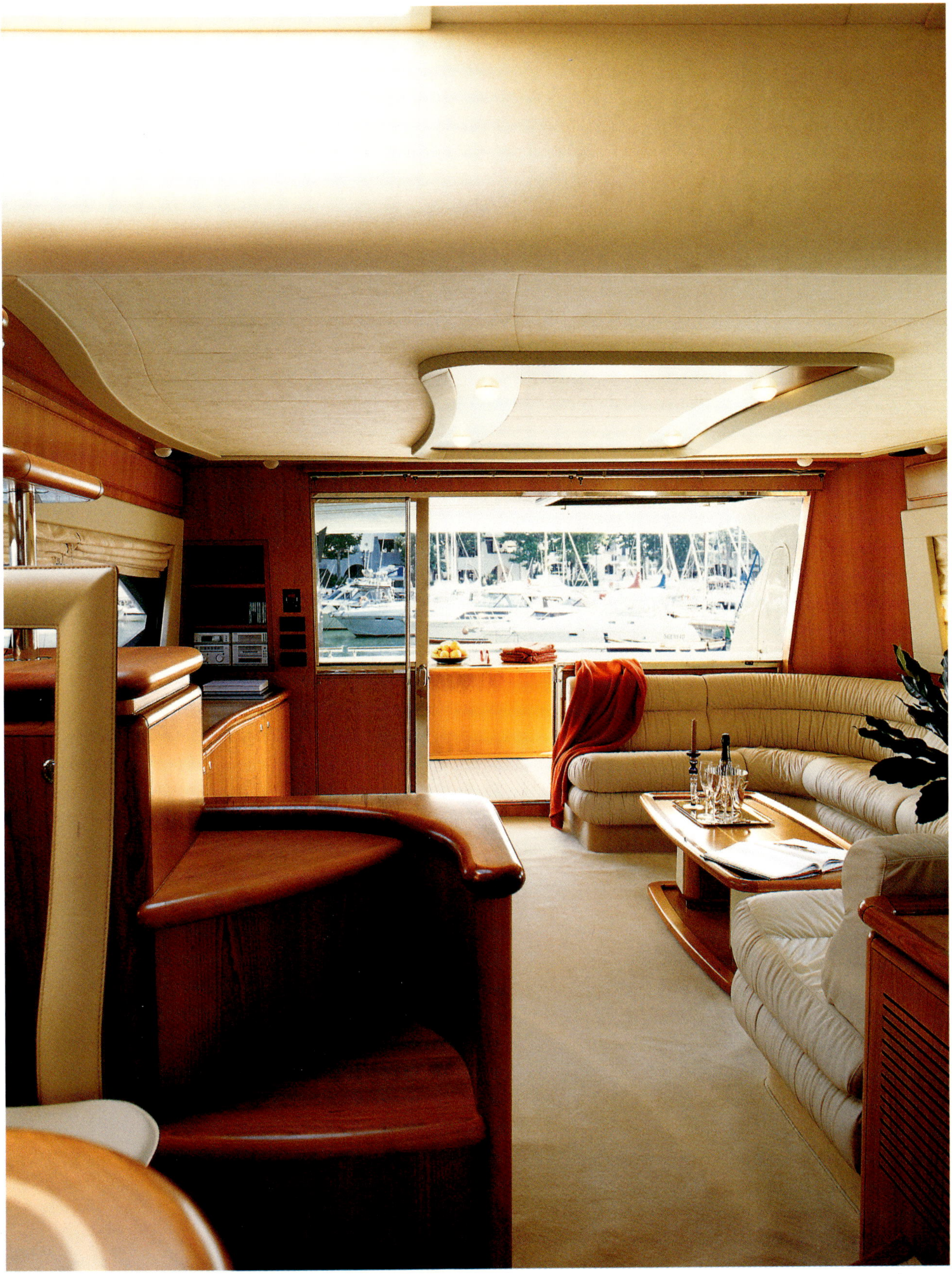

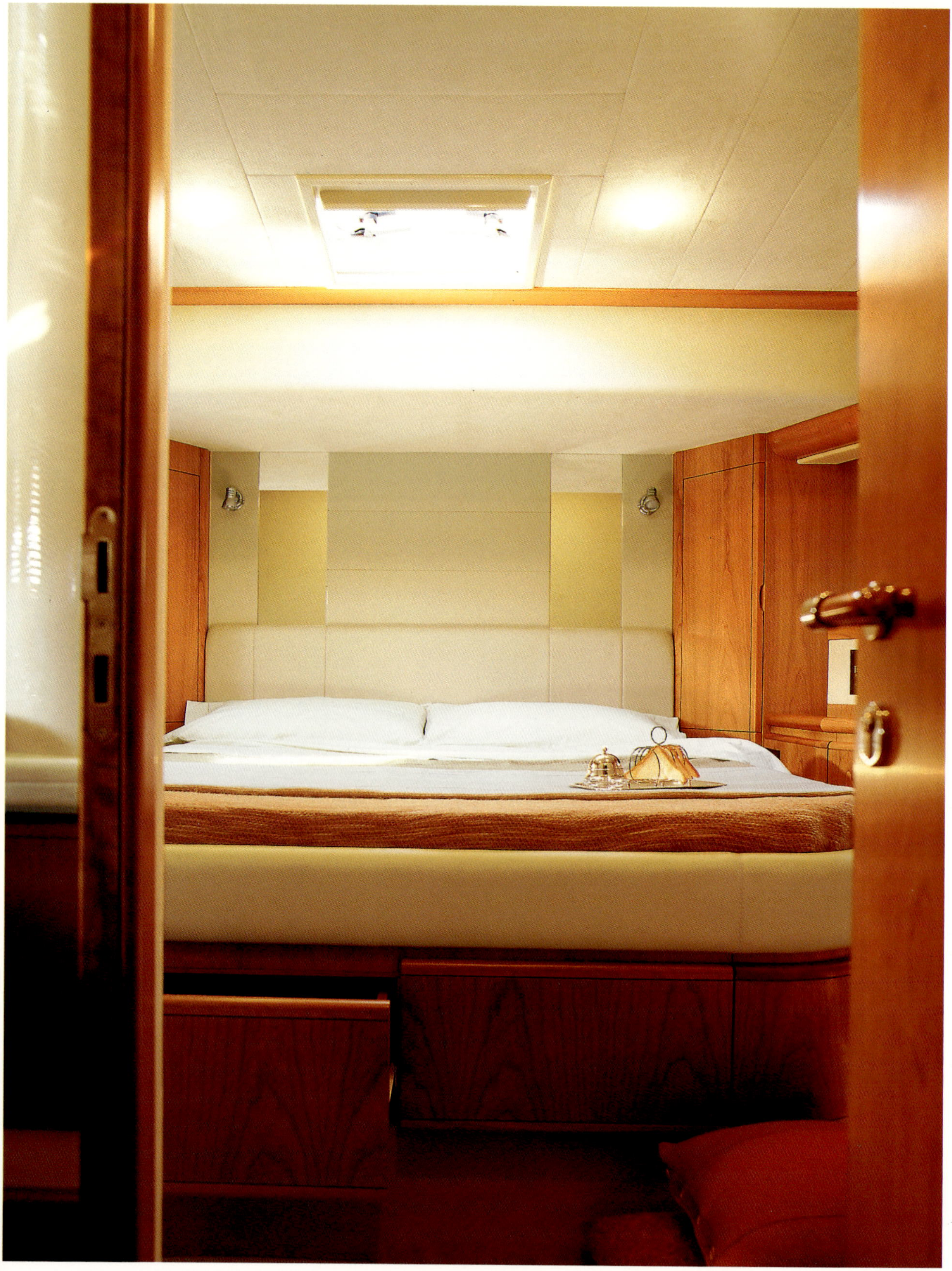

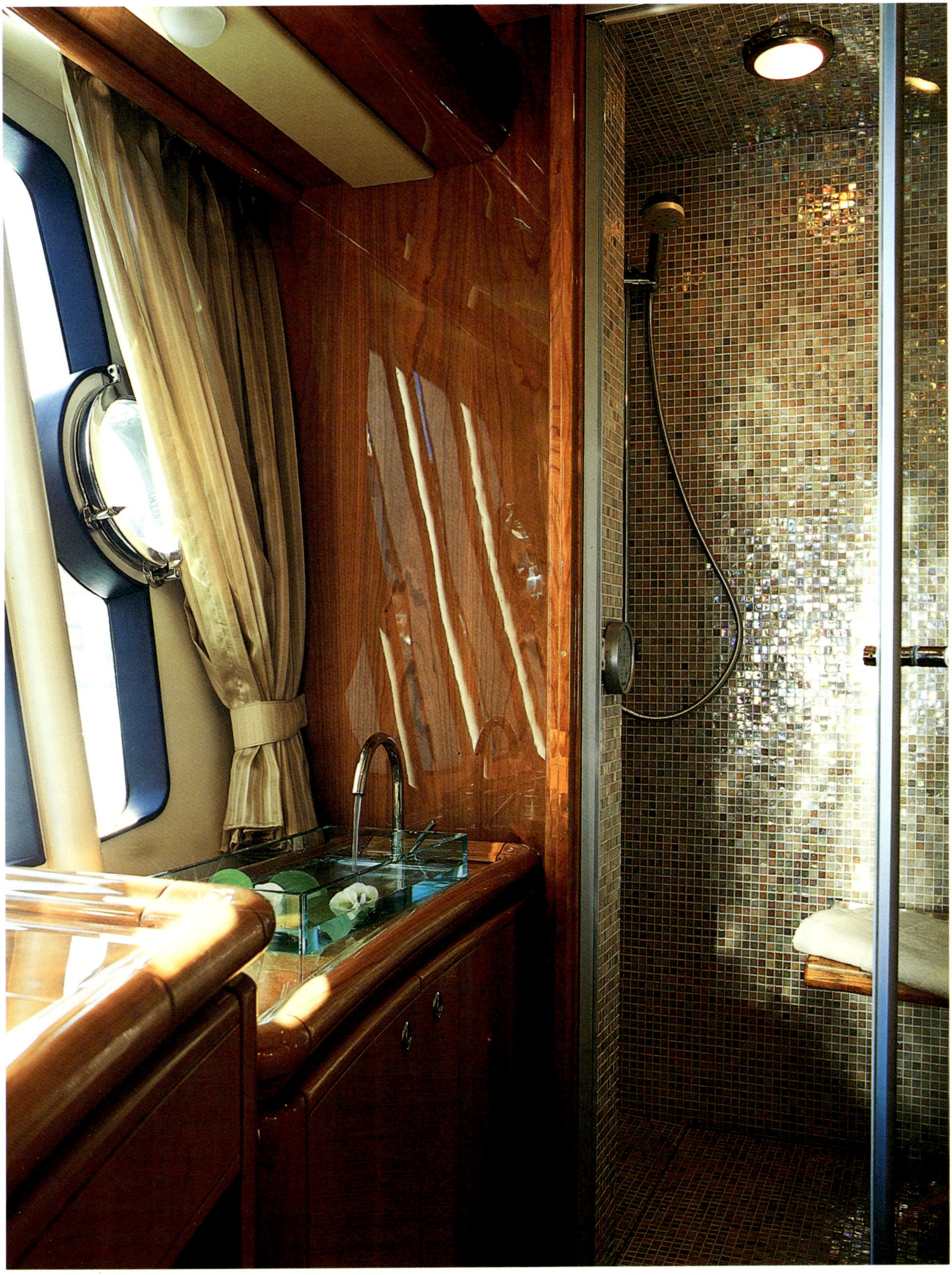

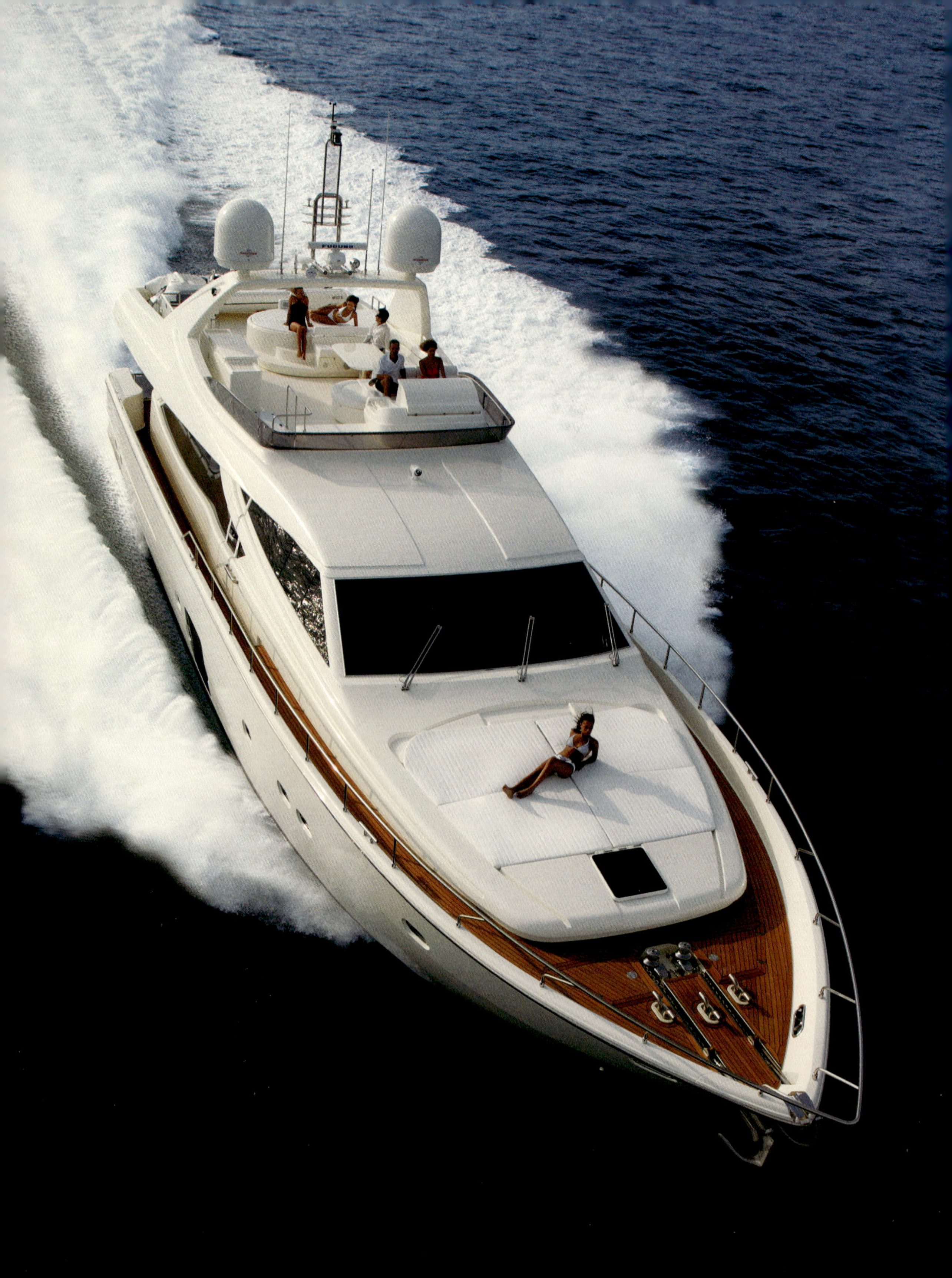

ZUCCON INTERNATIONAL PROJECT STUDIO
FERRETTI 830 | 2005
Ferretti Yachts

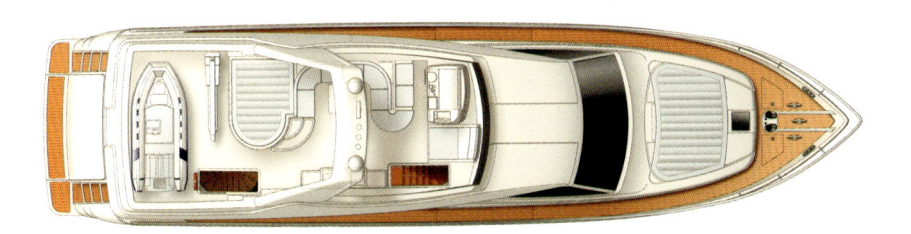

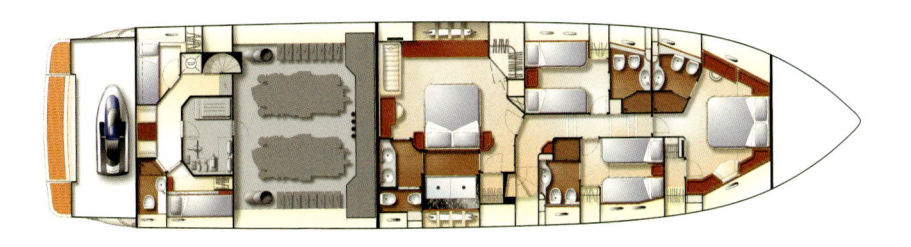

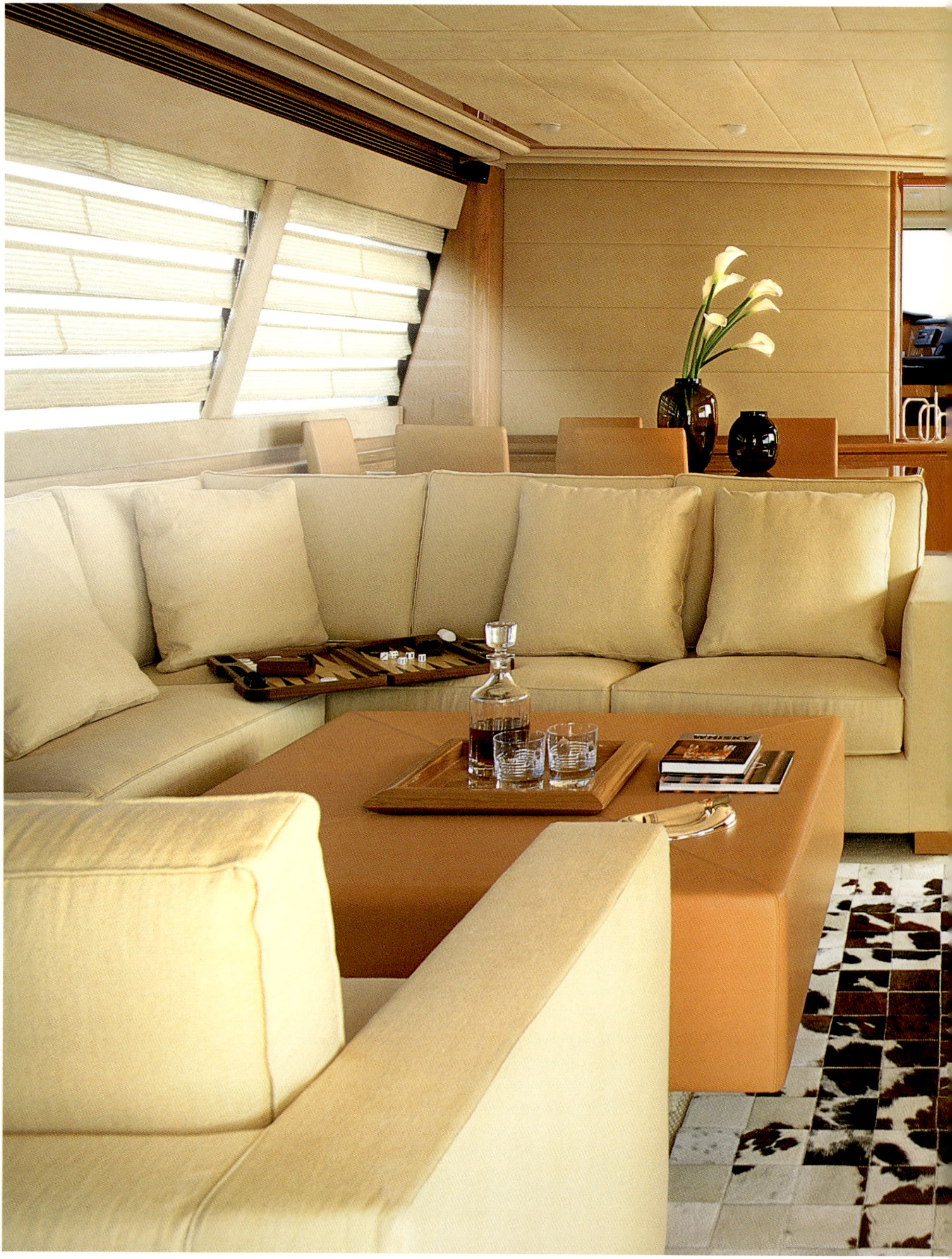
WHISKY

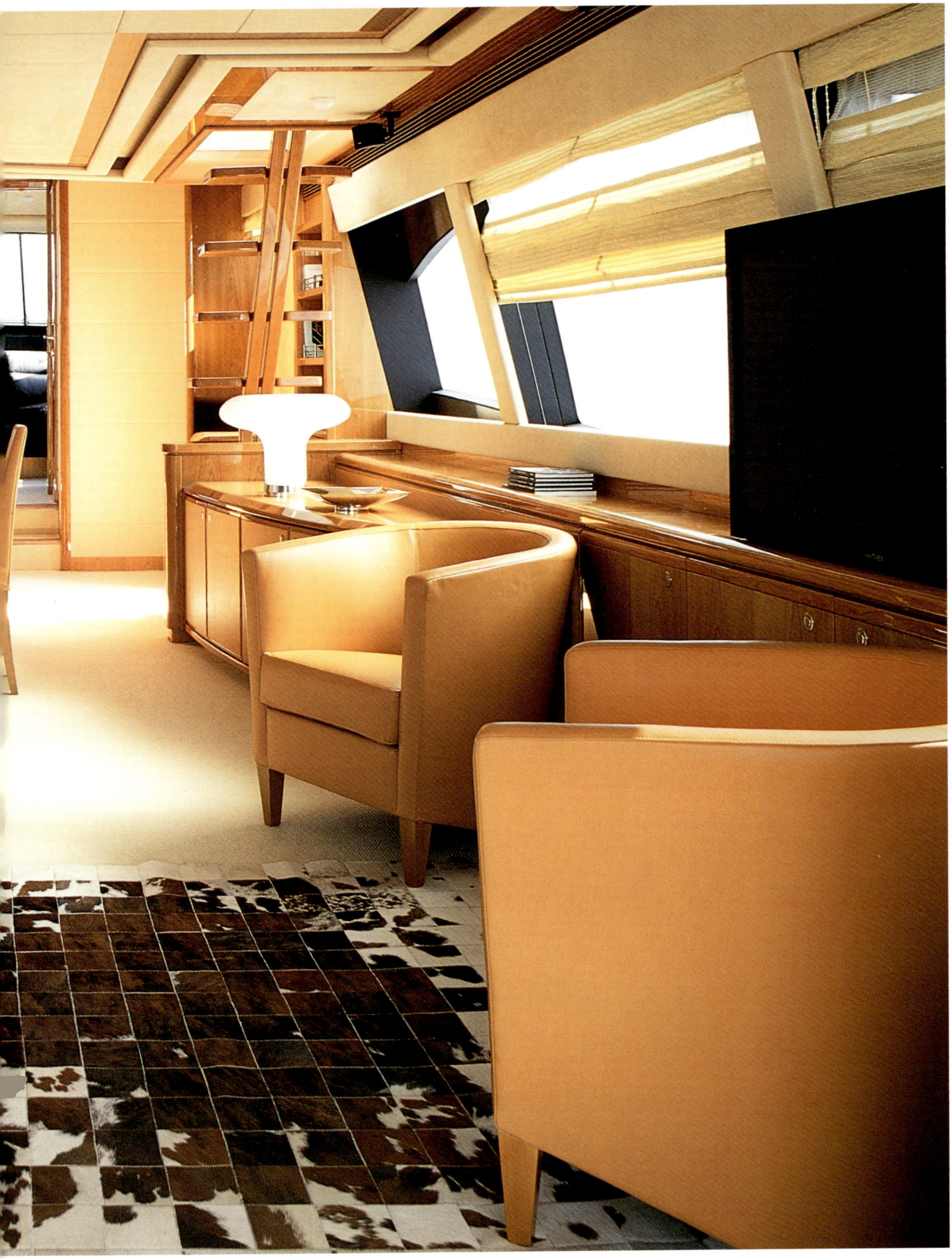

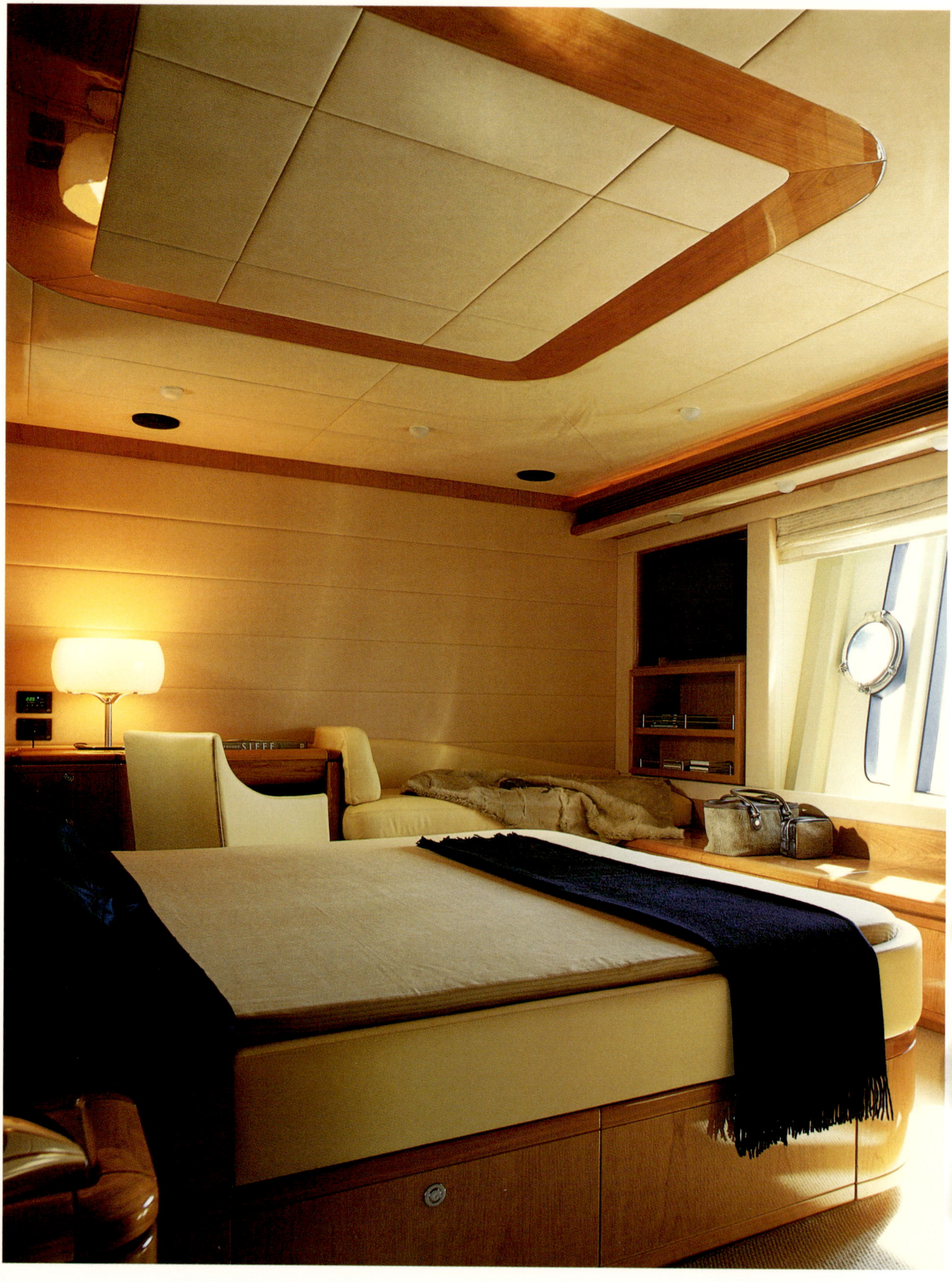
SIEFF

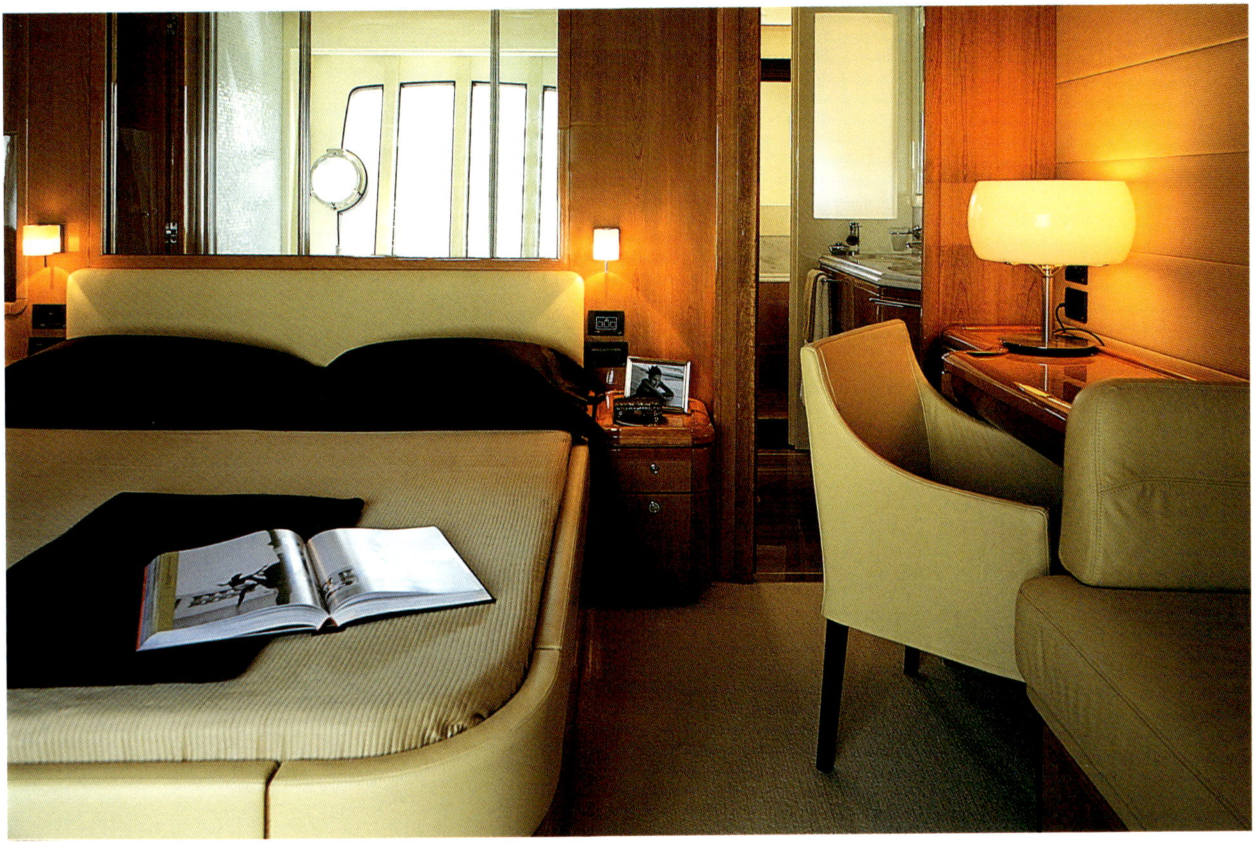

Azimut Yachts
Via M. L. King 9/11, 10051 Avigliana, Turin, Italy
P +39 011 93 161
F +39 011 93 67 270
erenna@azimutyachts.net
www.azimutyachts.net
Leonardo 98
© Azimut Yachts

Benetti
Via M. Coppino 104, 55049 Viareggio, Lucca, Italy
P +39 0584 3821
F +39 0584 39 62 32
info@benettiyachts.it
www.benettiyachts.it
Sai Ram
© Thierry Ameller, Matteo Piazza

Canados Group
Via dell'Idroscalo 182, 00121 Rome, Italy
P +39 06 56 33 97 32
F +39 06 56 33 99 69
canadosgroup@canadosgroup.com
www.canadosgroup.com
Canados 86
© Andrea Panegrossi, Jerome Kelagopian, Paolo Cipollina

Cantieri di Pisa
Via Aurelia Sud Km 334, 56121 Pisa, Italy
P +39 050 22 05 51
F +39 050 50 07 99
info@cantieridipisa.it
www.cantieridipisa.it
Kaitos 76
Unica
© Sandro Braida

Cantieri di Sarnico
Viale Degli Abruzzi 25, 25031 Capriolo, Brescia, Italy
P +39 030 74 61 165
F +39 030 74 61 704
info@cantieridisarnico.it
www.cantieridisarnico.it
Sarnico 50
© Carlo Borlenghi, Gianfranco Capodilupo

CNB
162, Quai de Brazza, 33100 Bordeaux, France
P +33 557 80 85 50
F +33 557 80 58 51
cnb@cnb.fr
www.cnb.fr
Grand Bleu Vintage
Only Now
© Andre Simon, Nicolas Claris

Craig Loomes Design Group Limited
P. O. Box 147–027, Ponsonby Auckland, New Zealand
P +64 9360 9799
F +64 9360 9795
designer@cld.co.nz
www.cld.co.nz
Sampitres
© Chris Lewis

Egg and Dart Design Corporation
Lindwurmstraße 44, 80337 Munich, Germany
P +49 89 76 73 65 0
F +49 89 76 73 65 25
studio@egganddart.com
www.egganddart.com
Baron 102 Ocean of Love
© Christian René Schulz

Feadship Holland B.V.
Zijlweg 148c, 2000 GE Haarlem, The Netherlands
P +31 23 524 70 00
F +31 23 524 86 39
info@feadship.nl
www.feadship.nl
Wedge Too
© Visions

FerrettiYachts
Via Ansaldo 9/B, 47100 Forlì, Italy
P +39 0543 47 44 11
F +39 0543 78 24 10
info@ferretti-yachts.com
www.ferretti-yachts.com
Ferretti 460
Ferretti 500
Ferretti 530
Ferretti 550
Ferretti 590
Ferretti 620
Ferretti 731
Ferretti 761
Ferretti 830
© Ferretti Yachts

Guy Couach
Rue de l'Yser, 33470 Gujan-Mestras, France
P +33 556 22 35 50
F +33 556 66 08 20
couach@couach.com
www.couach.com
Guy Couach 3600
© EDIM@GE

Heesen Yachts
Rijnstraat 2, 5347 KL OSS, The Netherlands
P +31 412 66 5544
F +31 412 66 5566
info@heesenyachts.nl
www.heesenyachts.nl
Sweet Doll
© Heesen Yachts

Marine Services srl
Via Paolo Savi 381, 55049 Viareggio, Lucca, Italy
P +39 0584 38 82 29
F +39 0584 38 79 49
info@marineservices.it
www.marineservices.it
Mistress
© Daniele Oberrauch

Mochi Craft
Via Ansaldo 5/7, 47100 Forlí, Italy
P +39 0543 78 78 08
F +39 0270 05 75 54
info@mochicraft-yacht.com
www.mochicraft-yacht.com
72 Dolphin
© Antonio Bignami, Luca Massari

Pershing
Via J. J. Pershing 1/3, 61037 Mondolfo, Pesaro-Urbino, Italy
P +39 0721 95 62 111
F +39 0721 95 57 84
info@pershing-yacht.com
www.pershing.it
Pershing 50
Pershing 62
Pershing 76
Pershing 88
Pershing 115
© Antonio Bignami, Gianluca Simoni, Jerome Kelagopian

Riva S.p.A.
Via Predore 30, 24067 Sarnico, Bergamo, Italy
P +39 035 91 02 02
F +39 035 91 10 59
info@riva-yacht.com
www.riva-yacht.com
Opera 85, © Carlo Borlenghi, Luca Massari
Rivale, © Anthony Holder, Luca Massari
Splendida, © Carlo Borlenghi, Luca Massari

Royal Huisman Shipyard
Flevoweg 1, 8325 PA Vollenhove, Holland
P +31 527 24 31 31
F +31 527 24 38 00
yachts@royalhuisman.com
www.royalhuisman.com
Unfurled
© Royal Huisman Shipyard

Sea Independences SL
Club de Mar, 07015 Palma de Mallorca, Spain
P +34 971 40 44 12
F +34 971 40 23 27
brokerage@sea-independence.com
www.sea-independence.com
Phoenix
© Ken Hayden

Tecnomar
Via Virgilio 220, 55049 Viareggio, Lucca, Italy
P +39 0584 39 29 01
F +39 0584 39 29 02
infotec@tecnomar.com
www.tecnomar.com
Velvet 35
© Angelo Giampiccolo

Vitters Shipyard
Stouweweg 33, 8064 PD Zwartsluis, The Netherlands
P +31 38 386 7145
F +31 38 386 8433
info@vitters.com
www.vitters.com
Gimlä
© Albert Brunsting, André Minkema

Wally
8, Av. des Ligures, MC98000 Monte Carlo, Monaco
P +377 93 10 00 93
F +377 93 10 00 94
sales@wally.com
www.wally.com
Dangerous But Fun, © Gilles Martin-Raget
Dark Shadow, © Gilles Martin-Raget, Matteo Piazza
Magic Carpet Squared, © Gilles Martin-Raget
Wally B, © Matteo Piazza, Neil Rabinowitz
Wallyño, © Carlo Borlenghi, Gilles Martin-Raget, Matteo Piazza
Wallypower, © Gilles Martin-Raget
WY 88.2 Tiketitoo, © Gilles Martin-Raget
Y3K, © Gilles Martin-Raget

copyright © 2005 daab
cologne london new york

published and distributed worldwide by
daab gmbh
friesenstr. 50
d-50935 köln

p +49-221-94 10 740
f +49-221-94 10 741

mail@daab-online.de
www.daab-online.de

publisher ralf daab
rdaab@daab-online.de

art director feyyaz
mail@feyyaz.com

editorial project by loft publications
copyright © 2005 loft publications

editor and text Anja Llorella

layout Cris Tarradas Dulcet
english translation Scott Klaeger
french translation Marion Westerhoff
italian translation Sara Tonelli
spanish translation Almudena Sasiain
copy editing Alessandro Orsi

printed in spain
Anman Gràfiques del Vallès, Spain
www.anman.com

isbn 3-937718-06-5
d.l.: B-14.669-05

all rights reserved.
no part of this publication may be reproduced in any manner.